Greek Islands

David Willett
Brigitte Barta
Rosemary Hall
Paul Hellander
Jeanne Oliver

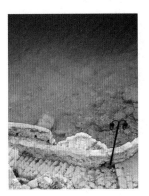

LONELY PLANET PUBLICATIONS
Melbourne • Oakland • London • Paris

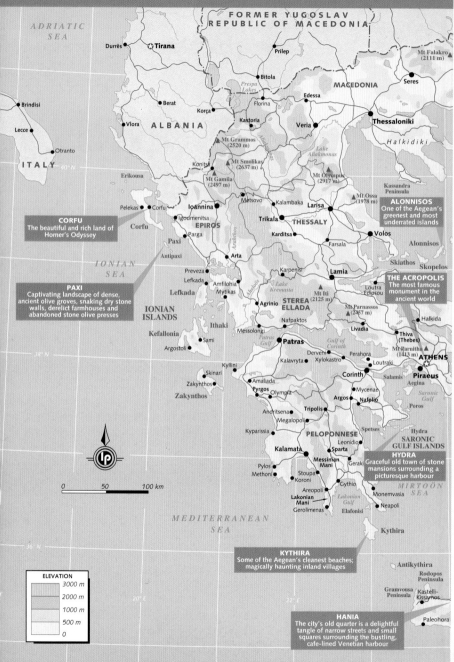

ADRIATIC
SEA

FORMER YUGOSLAV
REPUBLIC OF MACEDONIA

Mt Falakro
(2111 m)

Durrës
★ Tirana
Prilep

Bitola
Seres

Berat
Edessa
MACEDONIA

Brindisi
Florina
Veria
Thessaloniki

Lecce
Vlora
Korça
Kastoria
Halkidiki

Otranto
ALBANIA
Lake
Atsikonanos

ITALY
40° N
Konitsa
Mt Grammos
(2520 m)
Kassandra
Peninsula

Erikousa
Mt Smolikas
(2637 m)
Mt Olympus
(2917 m)
Mt Ossa
(1978 m)

Mt Gamila
(2497 m)
Metsovo
Kalambaka
Larisa
ALONNISOS
One of the Aegean's
greenest and most
underrated islands

Pelekas
Corfu
Ioannina
Kalambaka
THESSALY
Volos
Alonnisos

CORFU
The beautiful and rich land of
Homer's Odyssey
Corfu
Igoumenitsa
EPIROS
Trikala
Larisa
Skiathos
Skopelos

Paxi
Parga
Karditsa
Farsala

Antipaxi
Arta
Karpenisi
Lamia
THE ACROPOLIS
The most famous
monument in the
ancient world

IONIAN
SEA
Preveza
Lefkada
Loutra
Edipsou
Halkida

PAXI
Captivating landscape of dense,
ancient olive groves, snaking dry stone
walls, derelict farmhouses and
abandoned stone olive presses
Amfilohia
Mytikas
Lake
Kremasta
Mt Iti
(2125 m)
Mt Parnassos
(2457 m)

Lefkada
Agrinio
STEREA
ELLADA
Livadia

Nafpaktos
Thiva
(Thebes)
Mt Parnitha
(1413 m)
ATHENS

IONIAN
ISLANDS
Ithaki
Messolongi
Patras
Gulf of
Corinth
Piraeus

Kefallonia
Sami
Patras
Patras
Gulf
Derveni
Perahora
Loutraki
Aegina

Argostoli
Kyllini
Kalavryta
Xylokastro
Corinth
Salamis
Saronic
Gulf

Skinari
Amaliada
Olympia
Mycenae
Nafplio
Poros

Zakynthos
Pyrgos
Argos
Nafplio

Zakynthos
Andritsena
Tripolis
Spetses
Hydra

Megalopoli
PELOPONNESE
Leonidio
SARONIC
GULF ISLANDS

Kyparissia
Kalamata
Sparta
Geraki
HYDRA
Graceful old town of stone
mansions surrounding a
picturesque harbour

Pylos
Messinian
Mani
Gythio

Methoni
Stoupa
Koroni
Gythio
Monemvasia
MIRTOÖN
SEA

Areopoli
Lakonian
Mani
Gerolimenas
Lakonian
Gulf
Elafonisi
Neapoli

MEDITERRANEAN
SEA
Kythira

KYTHIRA
Some of the Aegean's cleanest beaches;
magically haunting inland villages
Antikythira

Rodopos
Peninsula

Gramvousa
Peninsula
Kastelli-
Kissamos

HANIA
The city's old quarter is a delightful
tangle of narrow streets and small
squares surrounding the bustling,
cafe-lined Venetian harbour
Paleohora

0   50   100 km

ELEVATION
3000 m
2000 m
1000 m
500 m
0

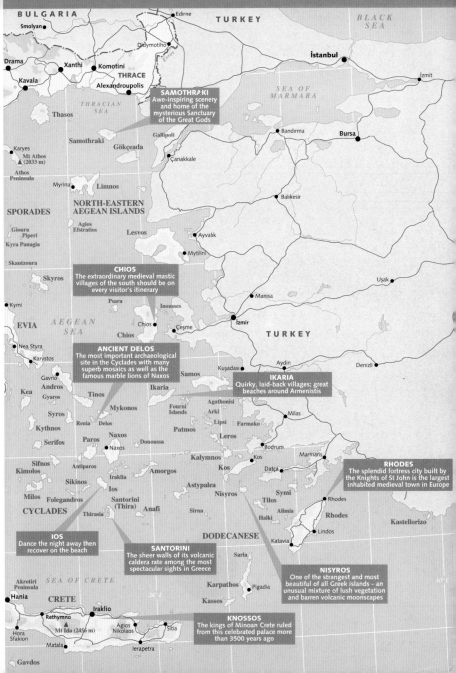

BULGARIA

Smolyan

Edirne

TURKEY

BLACK SEA

Drama

Didymotiho

İstanbul

İzmit

Kavala

Xanthi

Komotini

THRACE

Alexandroupolis

THRACIAN SEA

SEA OF MARMARA

Bandırma

Bursa

Thasos

SAMOTHRAKI
Awe-inspiring scenery
and home of the
mysterious Sanctuary
of the Great Gods

Samothraki

Gökçeada

Gallipoli

Çanakkale

Karyes
Mt Athos
△ (2033 m)

Athos
Peninsula

Myrina

Limnos

Balıkesir

SPORADES

NORTH-EASTERN
AEGEAN ISLANDS

Gioura
Piperi

Agios
Efstratios

Kyra Panagia

Lesvos

Ayvalık

Skantzoura

Mytilini

Skyros

Kymi

EVIA

AEGEAN
SEA

Psara

Inousses

CHIOS
The extraordinary medieval mastic
villages of the south should be on
every visitor's itinerary

Manisa

Uşak

Chios

Nea Styra

Chios

Çeşme

İzmir

TURKEY

Karystos

ANCIENT DELOS
The most important archaeological
site in the Cyclades with many
superb mosaics as well as the
famous marble lions of Naxos

Gavrio

Andros

Tinos

Ikaria

Samos

Kuşadası

Aydın

Denizli

Kea

Gyaros

Mykonos

IKARIA
Quirky, laid-back villages; great
beaches around Armenistis

Syros

Renia Delos

Agathonisi

Arki

Milas

Kythnos

Fourni
Islands

Lipsi

Farmako

Serifos

Paros

Naxos

Donoussa

Patmos

Leros

Sifnos

Antiparos

Amorgos

Kalymnos

Bodrum

Marmaris

Kimolos

Sikinos

Iraklia

Kos

Kos

Datça

RHODES
The splendid fortress city built by
the Knights of St John is the largest
inhabited medieval town in Europe

Milos

Ios

Santorini
(Thira)

Anafi

Astypalea

Nisyros

Symi

Tilos

Rhodes

Folegandros

CYCLADES

Thirasia

Sirna

Halki

Alimia

Rhodes

Kastellorizo

IOS
Dance the night away then
recover on the beach

SANTORINI
The sheer walls of its volcanic
caldera rate among the most
spectacular sights in Greece

DODECANESE

Katavia

Lindos

NISYROS
One of the strangest and most
beautiful of all Greek islands - an
unusual mixture of lush vegetation
and barren volcanic moonscapes

Saria

Akrotiri
Peninsula

SEA OF CRETE

Karpathos

Pigadia

Hania

CRETE

Rethymno

Iraklio

Agios
Nikolaos

KNOSSOS
The kings of Minoan Crete ruled
from this celebrated palace more
than 3500 years ago

Kassos

Hora
Sfakion

Mt Ida (2456 m)

Sitia

Matala

Ierapetra

Gavdos

Greek Islands
1st edition – February 2000

Published by
Lonely Planet Publications Pty Ltd A.C.N. 005 607 983
192 Burwood Rd, Hawthorn, Victoria 3122, Australia

Lonely Planet Offices
Australia PO Box 617, Hawthorn, Victoria 3122
USA 150 Linden St, Oakland, CA 94607
UK 10a Spring Place, London NW5 3BH
France 1 rue du Dahomey, 75011 Paris

Photographs
All of the images in this guide are available for licensing from
Lonely Planet Images.
email: lpi@lonelyplanet.com.au

Front cover photograph
View from the Knights of St John Castle on the island of Kastellorizo
in the Dodecanese (Tamsin Wilson)

ISBN 1 86450 109 X

text & maps © Lonely Planet 2000
photos © photographers as indicated 2000
climate charts for Lesvos and Rhodes compiled from information
supplied by Patrick J Tyson, © Patrick J Tyson, 1998

Printed by Colorcraft Ltd, Hong Kong

Contents – Text

DODECANESE 307

NORTH-EASTERN AEGEAN ISLANDS 379

IONIAN ISLANDS 439

EVIA & THE SPORADES 481

Contents – Maps

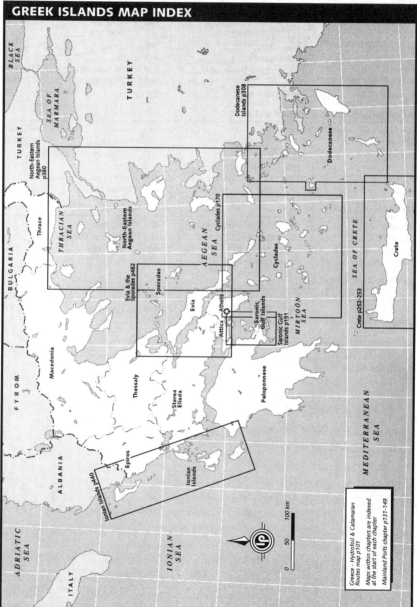

GREEK ISLANDS MAP INDEX

The Authors

David Willett

David is a freelance journalist based near Bellingen on the north coast of New South Wales, Australia. He grew up in Hampshire, England, and wound up in Australia in 1980 after stints working on newspapers in Iran (1975-78) and Bahrain. He spent two years working as a subeditor on the Melbourne *Sun* before trading a steady job for a warmer climate. Between jobs, David has travelled extensively in Europe, the Middle East and Asia.

He is also the author of Lonely Planet's *Greece* and *Tunisia* guides, and has contributed to various other guides, including *Africa, Australia, New South Wales, Indonesia, South-East Asia, Mediterranean Europe* and *Western Europe*.

Brigitte Barta

Brigitte was born in Wellington, New Zealand. At the age of six months her parents took her to live in Berlin, via Naples, and she first visited Greece when she was three. She grew up mostly in Melbourne, Australia, and later, while roaming Europe, lived for a year on the Greek island of Santorini, where she worked as a cocktail waitress, architectural draftsperson and everything in between. These days she resides in San Francisco and is a senior editor at Lonely Planet's Oakland office.

Rosemary Hall

Rosemary was born in Sunderland, England. She graduated in fine art, but fame and fortune as an artist eluded her, so she spent a few months bumming around Europe and India. After teaching in northern England, she decided to find something more exotic, finally landing a job in Iraq. When, after two years, the Iraqi government refused to renew her work permit, she settled in London, tried to make it again as a painter, did supply teaching, and then travelled in India, South-East Asia and Africa.

Rosemary researched Iraq for Lonely Planet's *West Asia on a shoestring* and wrote the 1st edition of *Greece*. She is the co-author of four walking guides to London.

Paul Hellander

Paul has never really stopped travelling since he was born in England to a Norwegian father and English mother. He graduated with a degree in Ancient, Byzantine and Modern Greek before arriving in Australia in 1977, via Greece and 30 other countries. He subsequently taught Modern Greek and trained interpreters and translators for 13 years before throwing it all away for a life as a travel writer. Paul wrote LP's *Greek phrasebook* before being assigned to *Greece* and *Eastern Europe* where he covers Albania, Bulgaria, the Former Yugoslav Republic of Macedonia and Yugoslavia. Paul has also updated *Singapore* and covered Singapore in the *Malaysia, Singapore & Brunei* and *South-East Asia* guides. He has also worked on *Israel & the Palestinian Territories*, *Jerusalem* and *Middle East*, *Greece*, and wrote the 1st edition of *Cyprus*.

He can usually be found in cyberspace at paul@planetmail.net. When not travelling, he resides in Adelaide, South Australia, where he enjoys cooking Asian food and growing hot chillies.

Jeanne Oliver

Born in New Jersey, USA, Jeanne spent her childhood mulling over the *New York Times* travel section and plotting her future voyages. She received a BA in English and then a law degree but her legal practice was interrupted by ever-more-frequent trips to Central and South America, Europe, the Middle East, Africa and Asia. She finally settled in France to work as a travel writer. Jeanne has contributed to Lonely Planet's *Greece*, *Mediterranean Europe* and *Eastern Europe* guides and wrote the 1st edition of *Croatia*. She can be found in cyberspace at j-oliver@worldnet.fr.

FROM THE AUTHORS

David Willett My thanks go first to my partner, Rowan, and our son, Tom, for holding the fort at home during another extended stay in Greece.

I had a great time in Greece, with a lot of help from friends old and new along the way. Five weeks in Athens flew by, aided and abetted by Maria Economou and Theodoros Nikolaidis from the Greek National Tourism Office; the mysterious Mr Poutsos; Paul and the long-lunch team – Dimitris, Angelos and Angeliki; Matt Barrett and family; Dimitris Agrafiotis; Ana Kamai; Vassilis and Lilika Nastos; and Yiannis and Katerina. Thanks also to the many travellers I met on the road, especially Peggy Ives, Janine, Daniel Marlin and Canadian Cathy.

Brigitte Barta Warm thanks to my old friends Sophia, Maria and Andreas Brakoulias and Kyria Giota Bakouli for their generous hospitality every time I visit Athens. Many thanks also to

Dimitrios Tsavdaridis for the *mezedes* tours, for the jokes and for the true stories, especially the one about the genie in the bottle at Akrotiri. One thousand thank yous go to the following lovely people: Francesco from Francesco's, and all at Acteon Travel (Ios); Despina Kitini and Stavros Panagopoulos at Naxos Tourist Information Centre, Dimitris Lianos, and Tassos at Vallindras (Naxos); Anna Dakoutros at Dakoutros Travel (Santorini); Giorgos and Rena from the Paros Rooms Association, Zacharias Roussos at Praxis Tours and Cathy Gavalas at Nissiotissa Tours (Paros); Flavio Focciolo at Sottovento Tourism Office (Folegandros); house-fixer Mihalis Venieris, and Ioannis Koundouris (Sikinos); master potter Antonis Kalogirou and master photographer Evangelos Pantazoglou (Sifnos); and Nikitas Simos at Villa Ostria (Koufonisia). Staff at the Sifnos municipal tourist office (Sifnos), Jeyzed Travel (Anafi), TeamWork (Syros), Andros Travel and Greek Sun Holidays (Andros), Sea & Sky (Mykonos) and Aegialis Tours (Amorgos) were also very helpful.

Finally, biggest, most special thanks to my man Rob for letting me go. If there's a next time, I hope you can come along.

Rosemary Hall I am grateful to Andrew Stoddart at the Hellenic Book Service in London for his assistance. I also wish to thank the staff of the Greek National Tourism Offices (EOT) and municipal tourist offices I visited in Greece, particularly in Karpenisi, Volos and Rhodes. A special thanks to Tolis in Athens for his hospitality; Nektaria (Arki) for the impromptu Greek lessons; Rena (Lipsi) for assistance and friendship, and for sending a boat to Arki for me when both the inter-island ferry and taxi boat broke down; Alexis from Pension Alexis for the enlightening and entertaining tour of Kos, and Marilena, Maria, Valia and Maro at the Kitsos Makris Folk Art Centre, and Virginia at Il Posto Di Caffe, for filling me in on the hot spots of Volos. Thanks also to Nikos from Hotel Romantzo on Nisyros, Wayne (Patmos), George and Sabine (Agathonisi), and David and Manos (Tilos) for advice and assistance. A big thank you as well to Effie Antonaras and her family on Rhodes for their hospitality, friendship and advice. Finally, thanks to David Willett for his supportive and humorous emails and thanks to all the staff involved with the production of the book.

Paul Hellander During what one person in Greece called the 'largest fly-drive program ever devised', I enlisted and was offered the assistance of many people. I would like to thank a few of them: my wife and photographic assistant Stella for travelling with me and supporting me; the British community of Hora, Alonnisos, for insights into expat life; Andreas & Konstantina Sarmonikas (Limnos) for showing us the good life; Dimitra Kaplanelli (Mytilini) for hospitality and practical assistance; Theo Kosmetos and

Melinda McRostie (Mythimna) for more insights and great food; George and Barbara Ballis (Vatera) for welcome hospitality; Demetres Dounas (Athens) for putting up with us yet again; Vasilis Dionysos (Ikaria) for helping us to wrap it all up; Lesvos Shipping Company (NEL) and Strintzis Lines for their excellent service and transport assistance; and especially Geoff Harvey of Driveaway in Sydney for enabling the best fly-drive program ever thought up. Byron and Marcus – another one bites the dust for you.

Jeanne Oliver I would like to thank Toula Chryssanthopoulou of the Greek National Tourism Office (EOT) in Athens for her valuable assistance. Haris Kakoulakis of the EOT office in Iraklion provided an extraordinary amount of advice and assistance that greatly aided the research of this chapter. In Iraklion, Motor Club and Prince Travel helped with my transportation arrangements. A special thanks to Nikos Petrakis and Georgia Stavrakaki of Sitia for their warm welcome and Antonia Karandinou of Sitia for her patience and good humour. Thanks also to David Willett and everyone at LP involved with the production of this book.

This Book

This is the 1st edition of *Greek Islands*. Coordinating author David Willett wrote the introductory chapters and Athens, Mainland Ports and the Saronic Gulf Islands. Brigitte Barta was responsible for the Cyclades; Rosemary Hall for the Dodecanese; Paul Hellander for the North-Eastern Aegean Islands, Ionian Islands and Evia & the Sporades; and Jeanne Oliver for Crete.

From the Publisher

Production of this edition of *Greek Islands* was coordinated by Susannah Farfor (editorial) and Joelene Kowalski (mapping and design). Shelley Muir, Kate Kiely, Fiona Meiers, Ada Cheung, Kalya Ryan and Susie Ashworth assisted with editing and proofing; Ann Jeffree, Jacqui Saunders, Csanád Csutoros, Celia Wood, Sarah Sloane and Trudi Canavan assisted with mapping; and Kerrie Williams helped with indexing. New illustrations were provided by Martin Harris, Quentin Frayne prepared the Language section, and the cover was designed by Jamieson Gross. The Philosophy boxed text was written by Rowan McKinnon, and the art section, originally written by Ann Moffat of the Australian National University, was revised by Virginia Maxwell. All photographs were supplied by Lonely Planet Images.

Foreword

ABOUT LONELY PLANET GUIDEBOOKS

The story begins with a classic travel adventure: Tony and Maureen Wheeler's 1972 journey across Europe and Asia to Australia. Useful information about the overland trail did not exist at that time, so Tony and Maureen published the first Lonely Planet guidebook to meet a growing need.

From a kitchen table, then from a tiny office in Melbourne (Australia), Lonely Planet has become the largest independent travel publisher in the world, an international company with offices in Melbourne, Oakland (USA), London (UK) and Paris (France).

Today Lonely Planet guidebooks cover the globe. There is an ever-growing list of books and there's information in a variety of forms and media. Some things haven't changed. The main aim is still to help make it possible for adventurous travellers to get out there – to explore and better understand the world.

At Lonely Planet we believe travellers can make a positive contribution to the countries they visit – if they respect their host communities and spend their money wisely. Since 1986 a percentage of the income from each book has been donated to aid projects and human rights campaigns.

Updates Lonely Planet thoroughly updates each guidebook as often as possible. This usually means there are around two years between editions, although for more unusual or more stable destinations the gap can be longer. Check the imprint page (following the colour map at the beginning of the book) for publication dates.

Between editions up-to-date information is available in two free newsletters – the paper *Planet Talk* and email *Comet* (to subscribe, contact any Lonely Planet office) – and on our Web site at www.lonelyplanet.com. The *Upgrades* section of the Web site covers a number of important and volatile destinations and is regularly updated by Lonely Planet authors. *Scoop* covers news and current affairs relevant to travellers. And, lastly, the *Thorn Tree* bulletin board and *Postcards* section of the site carry unverified, but fascinating, reports from travellers.

Correspondence The process of creating new editions begins with the letters, postcards and emails received from travellers. This correspondence often includes suggestions, criticisms and comments about the current editions. Interesting excerpts are immediately passed on via newsletters and the Web site, and everything goes to our authors to be verified when they're researching on the road. We're keen to get more feedback from organisations or individuals who represent communities visited by travellers.

Lonely Planet gathers information for everyone who's curious about the planet – and especially for those who explore it first-hand. Through guidebooks, phrasebooks, activity guides, maps, literature, newsletters, image library, TV series and Web site we act as an information exchange for a worldwide community of travellers.

Research Authors aim to gather sufficient practical information to enable travellers to make informed choices and to make the mechanics of a journey run smoothly. They also research historical and cultural background to help enrich the travel experience and allow travellers to understand and respond appropriately to cultural and environmental issues.

Authors don't stay in every hotel because that would mean spe ng a couple of months in each medium-sized city and, no, they don't eat at every restaurant because that would mean stretching belts beyond capacity. They do visit hotels and restaurants to check standards and prices, but feedback based on readers' direct experiences can be very helpful.

Many of our authors work undercover, others aren't so secretive. None of them accept freebies in exchange for positive write-ups. And none of our guidebooks contain any advertising.

Production Authors submit their raw manuscripts and maps to offices in Australia, USA, UK or France. Editors and cartographers – all experienced travellers themselves – then begin the process of assembling the pieces. When the book finally hits the shops, some things are already out of date, we start getting feedback from readers and the process begins again ...

WARNING & REQUEST

Things change – prices go up, schedules change, good places go bad and bad places go bankrupt – nothing stays the same. So, if you find things better or worse, recently opened or long since closed, please tell us and help make the next edition even more accurate and useful. We genuinely value all the feedback we receive. Julie Young coordinates a well travelled team that reads and acknowledges every letter, postcard and email and ensures that every morsel of information finds its way to the appropriate authors, editors and cartographers for verification.

Everyone who writes to us will find their name in the next edition of the appropriate guidebook. They will also receive the latest issue of *Planet Talk*, our quarterly printed newsletter, or *Comet*, our monthly email newsletter. Subscriptions to both newsletters are free. The very best contributions will be rewarded with a free guidebook.

Excerpts from your correspondence may appear in new editions of Lonely Planet guidebooks, the Lonely Planet Web site, *Planet Talk* or *Comet*, so please let us know if you *don't* want your letter published or your name acknowledged.

Send all correspondence to the Lonely Planet office closest to you:

Australia: PO Box 617, Hawthorn, Victoria 3122
USA: 150 Linden St, Oakland, CA 94607
UK: 10A Spring Place, London NW5 3BH
France: 1 rue du Dahomey, 75011 Paris

Or email us at: talk2us@lonelyplanet.com.au

For news, views and updates see our Web site: www.lonelyplanet.com

HOW TO USE A LONELY PLANET GUIDEBOOK

The best way to use a Lonely Planet guidebook is any way you choose. At Lonely Planet we believe the most memorable travel experiences are often those that are unexpected, and the finest discoveries are those you make yourself. Guidebooks are not intended to be used as if they provide a detailed set of infallible instructions!

Contents All Lonely Planet guidebooks follow roughly the same format. The Facts about the Destination chapters or sections give background information ranging from history to weather. Facts for the Visitor gives practical information on issues like visas and health. Getting There & Away gives a brief starting point for researching travel to and from the destination. Getting Around gives an overview of the transport options when you arrive.

The peculiar demands of each destination determine how subsequent chapters are broken up, but some things remain constant. We always start with background, then proceed to sights, places to stay, places to eat, entertainment, getting there and away, and getting around information – in that order.

Heading Hierarchy Lonely Planet headings are used in a strict hierarchical structure that can be visualised as a set of Russian dolls. Each heading (and its following text) is encompassed by any preceding heading that is higher on the hierarchical ladder.

Entry Points We do not assume guidebooks will be read from beginning to end, but that people will dip into them. The traditional entry points are the list of contents and the index. In addition, however, some books have a complete list of maps and an index map illustrating map coverage.

There may also be a colour map that shows highlights. These highlights are dealt with in greater detail in the Facts for the Visitor chapter, along with planning questions and suggested itineraries. Each chapter covering a geographical region usually begins with a locator map and another list of highlights. Once you find something of interest in a list of highlights, turn to the index.

Maps Maps play a crucial role in Lonely Planet guidebooks and include a huge amount of information. A legend is printed on the back page. We seek to have complete consistency between maps and text, and to have every important place in the text captured on a map. Map key numbers usually start in the top left corner.

Although inclusion in a guidebook usually implies a recommendation we cannot list every good place. Exclusion does not necessarily imply criticism. In fact there are a number of reasons why we might exclude a place – sometimes it is simply inappropriate to encourage an influx of travellers.

Introduction

The Greek Islands have long been one of Europe's favourite holiday destinations. It's hardly surprising: with more than 1400 islands scattered around the blue waters of the Aegean and Ionion seas, there's something for everyone. For some it's the opportunity to escape to the far-flung island paradise of their dreams, for others it's the opportunity to explore the remains of some of Europe's oldest civilisations. For most people though, the greatest attraction is the lure of sand, sea – and more than 300 days of guaranteed sunshine a year.

Until recent times, the islands were little more than remote outposts of Greece, left behind by the 20th century. Populations and economies were in serious decline as people headed to the mainland – and overseas – in search of work and opportunity.

Tourism was all but unheard of. Only the idle rich had the time or money for such exploits. All that has changed with the advent of modern transport and communications. Cheap airfares have put the islands within everyone's reach.

Tourism has boomed, breathing new life into island economies. Today the beaches of islands such as Kos, Paros and Rhodes are the prime target for millions of package holiday-makers who come to Greece every year in search of two weeks of sunshine by the sea.

Every island is different. There are party islands, quiet romantic islands, islands for

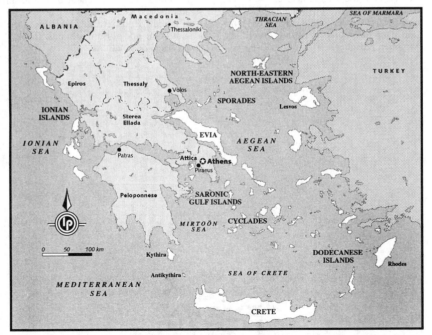

walkers, islands for windsurfers, islands for history buffs, islands for gays and islands for lesbians. There's even an island for the chronically sick (who come seeking a cure).

There's an island for everyone – the challenge is to find it. That means island-hopping, using Europe's largest ferry network. Every inhabited island has a ferry service of some sort, even if it is only a weekly supply boat.

Island-hopping is part of the fun. Like the islands themselves, the boats come in all shapes and sizes. The giant modern superferries that work the major routes have all the facilities of a luxury hotel, while the small open ferries that chug around the back blocks are more reminiscent of WWII landing craft.

Facilities these days are decidedly modern but reminders of the past are everywhere: the Minoan palaces of Crete were built by one of Europe's oldest civilisations. Mycenaean and classical Greek sites are overlooked by towering Venetian, Frankish and Turkish castles, while elaborate Byzantine churches stand alongside crumbling, forgotten mosques.

Despite tourism, islanders have retained a strong sense of tradition. Tradition and religion were the factors that kept the notion of Greek nationhood alive during hundreds of years of foreign occupation, and Greeks have clung to their traditions more tenaciously than in most European countries; even hip young people participate with enthusiasm.

The traditions manifest themselves in a variety of ways, including regional costumes – such as the embroidered dresses and floral headscarves worn by the women of Olymbos, on Karpathos, and the baggy pantaloons and high boots worn by elderly Cretan men. Young Cretans have adopted the traditional black, fringed kerchief as a fashion accessory.

Other traditions take the form of festivals, where people express their *joie de vivre* through dancing, singing and feasting.

Festival time or not, the Greek capacity for enjoyment of life is immediately evident. Food and wine are cheap by European standards, and Greeks love to eat out with family and friends. All this adds up to the islands being one of Europe's most friendly and relaxed destinations.

Facts about the Greek Islands

HISTORY

The Greek Islands were the birthplace of two of Europe's earliest civilisations, the Cycladic and the Minoan.

Both can be traced to the introduction of Bronze Age smelting techniques in about 3000 BC by settlers from Phoenicia (on the coast of modern Lebanon). The Cyclades were the first to blossom. The most impressive legacy of this civilisation is the statuettes carved from Parian marble – the famous Cycladic figurines, which depicted images of the Great Mother (the earth goddess). The finest examples were produced during the Early Cycladic period, which lasted from 3000 to 2100 BC.

The people of the Cycladic civilisation were also accomplished sailors who developed prosperous maritime trade links. They exported their wares to Asia Minor (the west of present-day Turkey), Europe and north Africa, as well as to Crete and continental Greece. The Cycladic civilisation lasted until about 1100 BC, but its later stages were increasingly dominated by the Minoan civilisation that evolved on nearby Crete.

The Minoans, named after the mythical King Minos, drew their inspiration from two great Middle Eastern civilisations: the Mesopotamian and the Egyptian. The civilisation reached its peak in the period between 2100 BC and 1500 BC, producing pottery and metalwork of remarkable beauty and a high degree of imagination and skill.

The famous palaces at Knossos, Phaestos, Malia and Zakros were built at this time. They were destroyed by a violent earthquake in about 1700 BC, but were rebuilt to a more complex, almost labyrinthine design with multiple storeys, sumptuous royal apartments, reception halls, storerooms, workshops, living quarters for staff and an advanced drainage system. The interiors were decorated with the celebrated Minoan frescoes, now on display in the archaeological museum at Iraklio.

After 1500 BC, the civilisation began to slip into decline, both commercially and militarily, against Mycenaean competition from the mainland – then reached an abrupt end around 1100 BC, when Dorian invaders and natural disasters ravaged Crete.

Some historians have suggested that the Minoan civilisation's demise was accelerated by the effects of the massive volcanic explosion on the Cycladic island of Santorini (Thira) in 1450 BC, an eruption vulcanologists believe was more cataclysmic than any on record. They theorise that the fallout of volcanic ash from the blast caused a succession of crop failures – with resulting social upheaval.

The Dorian period from 1200 to 800 BC is generally referred to as Greece's 'age of darkness', which sounds a bit unfair for a period that saw the arrival of the Iron Age and emergence of geometric pottery. The Dorians were responsible for founding the city of Lindos, on Rhodes, in around 1000 BC.

By 800 BC, when Homer's *Odyssey* and *Iliad* were first written down, Greece was undergoing a cultural and military revival with the evolution of the city-states, the most powerful of which were Athens and Sparta. Greater Greece – Magna Graecia – was created, with south Italy as an important component. The unified Greeks repelled the Persians twice, at Marathon (490 BC) and Salamis (480 BC). The period which followed was an unparalleled time of growth and prosperity, resulting in what is called the classical (or golden) age.

The Golden Age

In this period, the Parthenon was commissioned by Pericles, Sophocles wrote *Oedipus the King*, and Socrates taught young Athenians to think. At the same time, the Spartans were creating a military state. The golden age ended with the Peloponnesian War (431-404 BC) in which the militaristic Spartans defeated the Athenians. So embroiled were

Major Historical Events

3000 BC	Phoenician settlers introduce bronze smelting to the Cyclades
3000-2100 BC	Early Cycladic period, noted for its exquisite marble statuettes
2100-1500 BC	Minoan palaces built on Crete
1450 BC	Eruption of Thira; destruction of the Minoan palaces
1000 BC	Dorians found city of Lindos on Rhodes
7th Century BC	Poetess Sapho expresses her passionate love for her fellow women on Lesvos; silver turtle coins minted on Aegina
6th Century BC	Pythagoras, philosopher and sometime mathematician, born on Samos
460 BC	Hippocrates, known as the father of medicine, born on Kos
323 BC	Ptolemy I of Egypt becomes ruler of the Dodecanese following the death of Alexander the Great
305 BC	Colossus of Rhodes erected
190 BC	Romans conquer the Cyclades
88 BC	Pontian King Mithridates sacks Delos, slaughtering 10,000 inhabitants
67 BC	Gortyn, on Crete, becomes capital of the Roman province of Cyrenaica, which includes a large chunk of North Africa
70 AD	Romans capture Rhodes

they in this war that they failed to notice the expansion of Macedonia to the north under King Philip II, who easily conquered the war-weary city-states.

Philip's ambitions were surpassed by those of his son Alexander the Great, who marched triumphantly into Asia Minor, Egypt, Persia and what are now parts of Afghanistan and India. After Alexander's untimely death in 323 BC at the age of 33, his generals divided his empire between themselves. The Dodecanese became part of the kingdom of Ptolemy I of Egypt.

Roman Rule & the Byzantine Empire

Roman incursions into Greece began in 205 BC. By 146 BC the mainland had become the Roman provinces of Greece and Macedonia. Crete fell in 67 BC, and the southern city of Gortyn became capital of the Roman province of Cyrenaica, which included a large chunk of North Africa. Rhodes held out until 70 AD.

In 330 AD Emperor Constantine chose Byzantium as the new capital of the Roman Empire and renamed the city Constantinople. After the subdivision of the Roman Empire into Eastern and Western empires in 395 AD, Greece became part of the Eastern Roman Empire, leading to the illustrious Byzantine age.

In the centuries that followed Venetians, Franks, Normans, Slavs, Persians, Arabs and, finally, Turks all took their turns to chip away at the Byzantine Empire. The Persians captured Rhodes in 620, but were replaced by the Saracens (Arabs) in 653. The Arabs also captured Crete in 824.

Other islands in the Aegean remained under Byzantine control until the sack of Constantinople in 1204 by renegade Frankish crusaders in cahoots with Venice. The Venetians were rewarded with the Cyclades, and they added Crete to their possessions in 1210.

The Ottoman Empire & Independence

The Byzantine empire finally came to an end in 1453 when Constantinople fell to the

Turks. Once more Greece became a battleground, this time fought over by the Turks and Venetians. Eventually, with the exception of Corfu, Greece became part of the Ottoman Empire.

Much has been made of the horrors of the Turkish occupation in Greece. However, in the early years at any rate, people probably marginally preferred Ottoman to Venetian or Frankish rule. The Venetians in particular treated their subjects little better than slaves. But life was not easy under the Turks, not least because of the high taxation they imposed. One of their most hated practices was the taking of one out of every five male children to become janissaries, personal bodyguards of the sultan. Many janissaries became infantrymen in the Ottoman army, but the cleverest could rise to high office – including grand vizier (chief minister).

Ottoman power reached its zenith under Sultan Süleyman the Magnificent (ruled 1520-66), who expanded the empire to the gates of Vienna. His successor added Cyprus to their dominions in 1570, but his death in 1574 marked the end of serious territorial expansion.

Although they captured Crete in 1669 after a 25-year campaign and briefly threatened Vienna once more in 1683, the ineffectual sultans of the late 16th and 17th centuries saw the empire go into steady decline. They suffered a series of reversals on the battlefield, and Venice succeeded in holding on to the Peloponnese after a campaign in 1687 that saw them advancing as far as Athens. The Parthenon was destroyed in the fighting by a shell that struck a store of Turkish gunpowder.

Chaos and rebellion spread across Greece. Pirates terrorised coastal dwellers and islanders, while gangs of *klephts* (anti-Ottoman fugitives and brigands) roamed the mountains. There was an upsurge of opposition to Turkish rule by freedom fighters – who fought each other when they weren't fighting the Turks.

The long-heralded War of Independence finally began on 25 March 1821, when Bishop Germanos of Patras hoisted the Greek

Major Historical Events	
95	St John writes Book of Revelations while living in a cave on Patmos
620	Persians capture Rhodes
824	Arabs capture Crete
1204	Franks give Cyclades to the Venetians
1210	Venetians take over Crete
1309	Knights of St John arrive on Rhodes
1453	Fall of Constantinople to the Turks
1522	Turks take over the Dodecanese
1669	Turks complete conquest of Crete
1815	Corfu becomes British Protectorate
1822	25,000 people massacred on Chios following a failed uprising against Turkish rule
1827	Aegina becomes temporary capital of independent Greek state
1863	Corfu returned to Greece
1898	Great Powers make Crete a British Protectorate
1913	Crete and North-East Aegean Islands become part of Greece
1941	German forces invade Greece
1943	Italian troops occupy Corfu and Kefallonia
1947	Dodecanese returned to Greece
1953	Earthquake devastates islands of Kefallonia and Zakynthos
1976	Earthquake damages towns of Fira and Oia on Santorini

flag at the monastery of Agias Lavras in the Peloponnese. Fighting broke out almost simultaneously across most of Greece and the occupied islands, with the Greeks making big early gains. The fighting was savage, with atrocities committed on both sides. The islands weren't spared the horrors of war. In 1822, Turkish forces massacred 25,000 people on the island of Chios, while another 7000 died on Kassos in 1824.

Eventually, the Great Powers – Britain, France and Russia – intervened on the side of the Greeks, defeating the Turkish-Egyptian fleet at the Battle of Navarino in 1827. The island of Aegina was proclaimed the temporary capital of an independent Greek state, and Ioannis Kapodistrias was elected the first president. The capital was soon moved to Nafplio in the Peloponnese, where Kapodistrias was assassinated in 1831.

Amid anarchy, the European powers stepped in again and declared that Greece should become a monarchy. In January 1833, 17-year-old Prince Otto of Bavaria was installed as king of a nation (established by the London Convention of 1832) that consisted of the Peloponnese, Sterea Ellada (Central Greece), the Cyclades and the Sporades.

King Otho (as his name became) displeased the Greek people from the start, arriving with a bunch of upper class Bavarian cronies to whom he gave the most prestigious official posts. He moved the capital to Athens in 1834.

Patience with his rule ran out in 1843 when demonstrations in the capital, led by the War of Independence leaders, called for a constitution. Otho mustered a National Assembly which drafted a constitution calling for parliamentary government consisting of a lower house and a senate. Otho's cronies were whisked out of power and replaced by War of Independence freedom fighters, who bullied and bribed the populace into voting for them.

By the end of the 1850s, most of the stalwarts from the War of Independence had been replaced by a new breed of university graduates (Athens University had been founded in 1837). In 1862 they staged a bloodless revolution and deposed the king. But they weren't quite able to set their own agenda, because in 1863 Britain returned the Ionian Islands (a British protectorate since 1815) to Greece. Amid the general euphoria that followed, the British were able to push forward young Prince William of Denmark, who became King George I.

His 50-year reign brought stability to the troubled country, beginning with a new constitution in 1864, which established the power of democratically elected representatives and pushed the king further towards a ceremonial role. An uprising in Crete against Turkish rule was suppressed by the sultan in 1866-68, but in 1881 Greece acquired Thessaly and part of Epiros as the result of another Russo-Turkish war.

In 1897 there was another uprising in Crete, and the hot-headed prime minister Theodoros Deligiannis responded by declaring war on Turkey and sending help to Crete. A Greek attempt to invade Turkey in the north proved disastrous – it was only through the intervention of the Great Powers that the Turkish army was prevented from taking Athens.

Crete was made a British protectorate in 1898, and the day-to-day government of the island was gradually handed over to the Greeks. In 1905 the president of the Cretan assembly, Eleftherios Venizelos, announced Crete's union *(enosis)* with Greece, although this was not recognised by international law until 1913. Venizelos went on to become prime minister of Greece in 1910 and was the country's leading politician until his republican sympathies brought about his downfall in 1935.

Although the Ottoman Empire was in its death throes at the beginning of the 20th century, it was still clinging onto Macedonia. It was a prize sought by the newly formed Balkan countries of Serbia and Bulgaria, as well as by Greece, leading to the Balkan wars. The first, in 1912, pitted all three against the Turks; the second, in 1913, pitted Serbia and Greece against Bulgaria. The outcome was the Treaty of Bucharest (August 1913), which greatly expanded

Greek territory by adding the southern part of Macedonia, part of Thrace, another chunk of Epiros, and the North-Eastern Aegean Islands, as well as recognising the union with Crete.

In March 1913, King George was assassinated by a lunatic and his son Constantine became king.

WWI & Smyrna

King Constantine, who was married to the sister of the German emperor, insisted that Greece remain neutral when WWI broke out in August 1914. As the war dragged on, the Allies (Britain, France and Russia) put increasing pressure on Greece to join forces with them against Germany and Turkey. They made promises which they couldn't hope to fulfil, including land in Asia Minor. Venizelos, the prime minister of Greece, favoured the Allied cause, placing him at loggerheads with the king. Tensions between the two came to a head in 1916, and Venizelos set up a rebel government, first in Crete and then in Thessaloniki, while the pressure from the Allies eventually persuaded Constantine to leave Greece in June 1917. He was replaced by his more amenable second son, Alexander.

Greek troops served with distinction on the Allied side, but when the war ended in 1918 the promised land in Asia Minor was not forthcoming. Venizelos took matters into his own hands and, with Allied acquiescence, landed troops in Smyrna (present-day Izmir) in May 1919 under the guise of protecting the half a million Greeks living in that city (just under half its population). With a firm foothold in Asia Minor, Venizelos now planned to push home his advantage against a war-depleted Ottoman Empire. He ordered his troops to attack in October 1920 (just weeks before he was voted out of office). By September 1921, the Greeks had advanced as far as Ankara.

The Turkish forces were commanded by Mustafa Kemal (later to become Atatürk), a young general who also belonged to the Young Turks, a group of army officers pressing for western-style political reforms.

Kemal first halted the Greek advance outside Ankara in September 1921 and then routed them with a massive offensive the following spring. The Greeks were driven out of Smyrna and many of the Greek inhabitants were massacred. Mustafa Kemal was now a national hero, the sultanate was abolished and Turkey became a republic.

The outcome of the failed Greek invasion and the revolution in Turkey was the Treaty of Lausanne of July 1923. This gave eastern Thrace and the islands of Imvros and Tenedos to Turkey, while the Italians kept the Dodecanese (which they had temporarily acquired in 1912 and would hold until 1947).

The treaty also called for a population exchange between Greece and Turkey to prevent any future disputes. Almost 1.5 million Greeks left Turkey and almost 400,000 Turks left Greece. The exchange put a tremendous strain on the Greek economy and caused great hardship for the individuals concerned. Many Greeks abandoned a privileged life in Asia Minor for one of extreme poverty in shantytowns in Greece.

King Constantine, restored to the throne in 1920, identified himself too closely with the war against Turkey, and abdicated after the fall of Smyrna.

WWII & the Civil War

In 1930 George II, Constantine's son, became king and appointed the dictator General Metaxas as prime minister. Metaxas' grandiose ambition was to take the best from Greece's ancient and Byzantine past to create a Third Greek Civilisation, though what he actually created was more a Greek version of the Third Reich. His chief claim to fame was his celebrated *okhi* (no) to Mussolini's request to allow Italian troops to traverse Greece in 1940. Despite Allied help, Greece fell to Germany in 1941, after which followed carnage and mass starvation. Resistance movements sprang up, eventually polarising into royalist and communist factions.

A bloody civil war resulted, lasting until 1949 and leaving the country in chaos. More people were killed in the civil war than in WWII and 250,000 people were left homeless. The sense of despair that followed became the trigger for a mass exodus. Almost a million Greeks headed off in search of a better life elsewhere, primarily to Australia, Canada and the USA. Villages – whole islands even – were abandoned as people gambled on a new start in cities like Melbourne, Chicago and New York. While some have drifted back, the majority have stayed away.

The Colonels
Continuing political instability led to the colonels' coup d'etat in 1967, led by Georgos Papadopolous and Stylianos Patakos. King Constantine (son of King Paul, who succeeded George II) staged an unsuccessful counter coup, then fled the country. The colonels' junta distinguished itself by inflicting appalling brutality, repression and political incompetence upon the people.

In 1974 they attempted to assassinate Cyprus' leader, Archbishop Makarios. When Makarios escaped, the junta replaced him with the extremist Nikos Samson, a convicted murderer. The Turks, who comprised 20% of the population, were alarmed at having Samson as leader. Consequently, mainland Turkey sent in troops and occupied North Cyprus, the continued occupation of which is one of the most contentious issues in Greek politics today. The junta, by now in a shambles, had little choice but to hand power back to the civilians.

In November 1974 a plebiscite voted 69% against restoration of the monarchy, and Greece became a republic. An election brought the right-wing New Democracy (ND) party into power.

The Socialist 1980s
In 1981 Greece entered the EC (European Community, now the EU). Andreas Papandreou's Panhellenic Socialist Movement (PASOK) won the next election, giving Greece its first socialist government. PASOK promised removal of US air bases and withdrawal from NATO, which Greece had joined in 1951.

Six years into government these promises remained unfulfilled, unemployment was high and reforms in education and welfare had been limited. Women's issues had fared better however – the dowry system was abolished, abortion legalised, and civil marriage and divorce were implemented. The crunch for the government came in 1988 when Papandreou's affair with air stewardess Dimitra Liana (whom he subsequently married) was widely publicised and PASOK became embroiled in a financial scandal involving the Bank of Crete.

In July 1989 an unprecedented conservative and communist coalition took over to implement a *katharsis* (campaign of purification) to investigate the scandals. It ruled that Papandreou and four ministers should stand trial for embezzlement, telephone tapping and illegal grain sales. It then stepped down in October 1990, stating that the catharsis was complete.

The 1990s
An election in 1990 brought the ND back to power with a majority of only two seats. The tough economic reforms that Prime Minister Konstantinos Mitsotakis was forced to introduce to counter a spiralling foreign debt soon made his government deeply unpopular. By late 1992, allegations began to emerge about the same sort of government corruption and dirty tricks that had brought Papandreou unstuck. Mitsotakis himself was accused of having a secret hoard of Minoan art. He was forced to call an election in October 1993.

Greeks again turned to PASOK and the ageing, ailing Papandreou, who had been cleared of all the charges levelled in 1990. He marked his last brief period in power with a conspicuous display of the cronyism that had become his trademark. He appointed his wife as chief of staff, his son Giorgos as deputy foreign minister and his personal physician as minister of health.

Papandreou had little option but to continue with the same austerity program begun by Mitsotakis, quickly making his government equally unpopular. He was finally forced to hand over the reins in January 1996 after a lengthy spell in hospital. He was replaced by Costas Simitis, an experienced economist and lawyer and outspoken critic of Papandreou, who surprised many by calling a snap poll in September 1996, and campaigned hard in support of his Mr Clean image. He was rewarded with a comfortable parliamentary majority.

Simitis belongs to much the same school of politics as Britain's Tony Blair. Since he took power, PASOK policy has shifted right to the extent that it now agrees with the opposition New Democracy on all major policy issues. His government has focused almost exclusively on further integration with Europe, which has meant more tax reform and further austerity measures. It's rare for a day to pass without a protest of some sort from the electorate. Simitis has stuck to his guns, though, and Greece appears on track to join the Euro band in early 2000 – despite the disruption to the economy resulting from the 1999 NATO conflict with Serbia.

Foreign Policy

Greece's foreign policy is dominated by its extremely sensitive relationship with Turkey, its giant Muslim neighbour to the east. These two uneasy NATO allies seem to delight in niggling each other in an ongoing war of one-upmanship. Incidents which might appear trivial to the outsider frequently bring the two to the brink of war – such as when Turkish journalists symbolically replaced the Greek flag on the tiny rocky outcrop of Imia (Kardak to the Turks) in February 1996. Both sides poured warships into the area before being persuaded to calm down.

The massive earthquake which devastated the İzmit area of western Turkey in August 1999 sparked a remarkable turnaround in relations between the warring neighbours. According to geologists, the quake moved Turkey 1.5m closer to Greece. Greek rescue teams were among the first on the scene, a favour the Turks were quick to return after the Athens quake which followed on 7 September 1999.

Turkey remains the top priority for Greece, but recently has also had to cope with events to the north precipitated by the break-up of former Yugoslavia and the collapse of the communist regimes in Albania and Romania.

GEOGRAPHY

Greece consists of the southern tip of the Balkan Peninsula and about 1400 islands, of which 169 are inhabited. The land mass is 131,900 sq km and Greek territorial waters occupy 400,000 sq km. To the north, Greece has land borders with Albania, the Former Yugoslav Republic of Macedonia, and Bulgaria; and to the east with Turkey.

The islands are divided into six groups: the Cyclades, the Dodecanese, the islands of the North-Eastern Aegean, the Sporades, the Ionian and the Saronic Gulf Islands. The two largest islands, Crete and Evia, do not belong to any group.

Roughly four-fifths of Greece is mountainous, with most of the land over 1500m above sea level. The Pindos Mountains, which are an offshoot of the Dinaric Alps, run north to south through the peninsula, and are known as the backbone of Greece. The mountains of Crete are part of the same formation. The highest mountain is Mt Olympus (2917m). The mountainous terrain, dry climate and poor soil restricts agriculture to less than a quarter of the land. Greece is, however, rich in minerals, with reserves of oil, manganese, bauxite and lignite.

CLIMATE

Greece can be divided into a number of main climatic regions. Northern Greece has a climate similar to the Balkans, with freezing winters and very hot, humid summers; while Athens, the Cyclades, the Dodecanese and Crete have a more typically Mediterranean climate with hot, dry summers and milder winters.

Snow is very rare in the Cyclades, but the mountains of Crete are covered in snow from November until April, and it does occasionally snow in Athens. In July and August, the mercury can soar to 40°C (over 100°F) in the shade just about anywhere in the country.

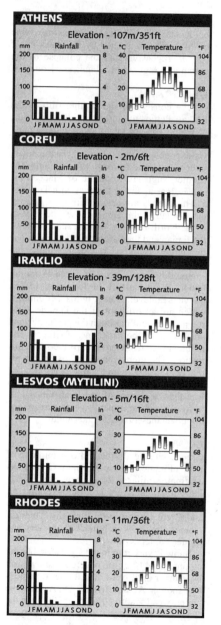

July and August are also the months of the *meltemi*, a strong northerly wind that sweeps the eastern coast of mainland Greece (including Athens) and the Aegean Islands, especially the Cyclades. The wind is caused by air pressure differences between North Africa and the Balkans. The wind is a mixed blessing: it reduces humidity, but plays havoc with ferry schedules and sends everything flying – from beach umbrellas to washing hanging out to dry.

The western part of the mainland and the Ionian Islands escape the meltemi and have less severe winters than northern Greece, but are the areas with the highest rainfall. The North-Eastern Aegean Islands fall somewhere between the Balkan-type climate of northern Greece and the Mediterranean climates. Crete stays warm the longest – you can swim off its southern coast from mid-April to November.

Mid-October is when the rains start in most areas, and the weather stays cold and wet until February – although there are also occasional winter days with clear blue skies and sunshine.

ECOLOGY & ENVIRONMENT

Greece is belatedly becoming environmentally conscious; regrettably, it is often a case of closing the gate after the horse has bolted. Deforestation and soil erosion are problems that go back thousands of years. Olive cultivation and goats have been the main culprits, but firewood gathering, shipbuilding, housing and industry have all taken their toll.

Forest fires are also a major problem, with an estimated 25,000 hectares destroyed every year. The result is that the forests of ancient Greece have all but disappeared. Epiros and Macedonia in northern Greece are now the only places where extensive forests remain. This loss of forest cover has been accompanied by serious soil erosion. The problem is finally being addressed with the start of a long overdue reafforestation program.

General environmental awareness remains at a very low level, especially where litter is concerned. The problem is particularly bad in rural areas, where roadsides are strewn with soft-drink cans and plastic packaging hurled from passing cars. Environmental education has begun in schools, but it will be some time before community attitudes change.

Water shortages are a major problem on many islands, particularly smaller islands without a permanent water supply. These islands import their water by tanker, and visitors are urged to economise on water use wherever possible: small things, like turning the tap off while you brush your teeth, can make a big difference.

FLORA & FAUNA
Flora
Greece is endowed with a variety of flora unrivalled in Europe. The wildflowers are spectacular. There are over 6000 species, some of which occur nowhere else, and more than 100 varieties of orchid. They continue to thrive because most of the land is too poor for intensive agriculture and has escaped the ravages of chemical fertilisers.

The mountains of Crete boast some of the finest displays. During spring the hillsides are carpeted with flowers, which seem to sprout even from the rocks. Spring flowers include anemones, white cyclamens, irises, lilies, poppies, gladioli, tulips, countless varieties of daisy and many more. Autumn brings flowers too, especially crocuses.

Fauna
Greece also has a large range of fauna, but you won't encounter much of interest unless you venture out into the prime habitat

Wild Flowers

The Greek countryside is the showcase for a spectacular display of wild flowers. Autumn is often described as Greece's 'second spring'.

Of Europe's 200 wild orchid species, around half grow in Greece. They flower from late February to early June. Another spring flower is the iris. The word 'iris' is Greek for rainbow – an appropriate name for these multicoloured flowers. Greece's wild irises include the white and yellow *Iris ochreoleuca* and the blue and orange *Iris cretica*. The latter is one of 120 wild flowers unique to Crete. Others include the pink Cretan ebony, the white-flowered symphyandra and the white-flowered *Cyclamen cretic*. Other unique species include the *Rhododendron luteum*, a yellow azalea which grows only on Mytilini, and a peony which is unique to Rhodes.

Spectacular plants include the coastal giant reed. You may get lost among its high, dense groves on your way to a beach. The giant fennel, which grows to 3m, and the tall yellow-horned poppy also grow by the sea. Another showy coastal plant is the magenta-flowered Hottentot fig, which was introduced from Africa. The white-flowered sea squill grows on hills above the coast.

Conspicuous thistles include the milk thistle which has green and white variegated leaves and grows in meadows and by roadsides. In rocky terrain you will see the stemless carline thistle, whose silvery-white petalled flowers are used in dried flower displays.

The beautifully perfumed sea daffodil grows along southern coasts, particularly on Crete and Corfu. The conspicuous snake's-head fritillary *(Fritillaria graeca)* has pink flowers shaped like snakes' heads, and the markings on the petals resemble a chequer board – the Latin word *fritillu* means dice box.

Interesting trees include the evergreen carob which grows to 10m. John the Baptist is said to have eaten its pods when he lived in the desert. Mineral-rich carob is sold in some countries as a healthy substitute for chocolate. The flowers of the Judas tree, unusually, appear before the leaves. According to legend they were originally white, but when Judas hanged himself from the tree they turned pink in shame.

areas of northern Greece. Bird-watchers have more chance of coming across something unusual than animal spotters. Greece has all the usual Mediterranean small birds – wagtails, tits, warblers, bee-eaters, larks, swallows, flycatchers, thrushes and chats – as well as some more distinctive species such as the hoopoe.

A large number of migratory birds, most of which are merely passing by on their way from winter feeding sites in north Africa to summer nesting grounds in Eastern Europe, can also be seen. Out of a total of 408 species of migratory birds in Europe, 240 have been sighted in Greece. One very visible visitor is the stork. Storks arrive in early spring from Africa, and return to the same nest year after year. The nests are built on electricity poles, chimney tops and church towers, and can weigh up to 50kg; look out for them in northern Greece, especially in Thrace.

MARTIN HARRIS

The hoopoe, a member of the kingfisher family, has a prominent black-tipped crest

About 350 pairs (60% of the world's population) of the rare Eleonora falcon nest on the remote island of Piperi in the Sporades.

You're unlikely to encounter much in the way of wildlife on most of the islands. The exception is on larger islands like Crete and Evia, where squirrels, rabbits, hares, foxes and weasels are all fairly common. Reptiles are well represented too. The snakes include several viper species, which are poisonous. For more information on snakes in Greece, see the Health section in the Facts for the Visitor chapter. You're more likely to see lizards, all of which are harmless.

One of the pleasures of island-hopping in Greece is watching the dolphins as they follow the boats. Although there are many dolphins in the Aegean, the striped dolphin has recently been the victim of murbilivirus – a sickness that affects the immune system. Research into the virus is being carried out in the Netherlands. You can get more information about dolphins from the Greek Society for the Protection & Study of Dolphins & Cetaceans (☎ 01-572 6612, fax 265 9917, email delphis@hol.gr), Imitou 50, Peristeri 121 32, Athens.

Endangered Species

Europe's rarest mammal, the monk seal, was once very common in the Mediterranean, but is now on the brink of extinction in Europe – it survives in slightly larger numbers in the Hawaiian islands.

There are only about 400 left in Europe, half of which live in Greece. There are about 40 in the Ionian Sea and the rest are found in the Aegean. These sensitive creatures are particularly susceptible to human disturbance, and now live only in isolated coastal caves. The majority of reported seal deaths are the result of accidental trapping, but the main threat to their survival is the continuing destruction of habitat. Tourist boats are major culprits. The Hellenic Society for the Study & Protection of the Monk Seal (☎ 01-522 2888, fax 522 2450), Solomou 53, Athens 104 32, has a seal rescue centre on Alonnisos, and the WWF funds a seal-watch project on Zakynthos.

MARTIN HARRIS

The Mediterranean monk seal, once threatened by hunters, is now threatened by tourism.

The waters around Zakynthos are also home to the last large sea turtle colony in Europe, that of the loggerhead turtle *(Careta careta)*. The loggerhead also nests in smaller numbers on the Peloponnese and on Crete. The Sea Turtle Protection Society of Greece (☎/fax 01-523 1342, email stps@compulink.gr), Solomou 57, Athens 104 32, runs monitoring programs and is always looking for volunteers.

National Parks
Visitors who expect Greek national parks to provide facilities on a par with those in countries like Australia and the US will be very disappointed. Although all have refuges and some have marked hiking trails, Greek national parks provide little else in the way of facilities.

The majority of Greece's national parks are on the mainland with the exception of Samaria Gorge National Park on Crete, a National Marine Park off the coast of Alonnisos in the Sporades, and another due to be declared for Zakynthos in the Ionians. See the respective chapters for information about these parks.

GOVERNMENT & POLITICS
Since 1975, democratic Greece has been a parliamentary republic with a president as head of state. The president and parliament, which has 300 deputies, have joint legislative power.

The PASOK party of Prime Minister Simitis holds 163 seats in the current parliament.

Greece is divided into regions and island groups. The regions of the mainland are Attica (which includes Athens), the Peloponnese, Central Greece (officially called Sterea Ellada), Epiros, Thessaly, Macedonia and Thrace. The island groups are the Cyclades, Dodecanese, North-Eastern Aegean, Sporades and Saronic Gulf, all in the Aegean Sea, and the Ionian, which is in the Ionian Sea. The large islands of Evia and Crete do not belong to any group. For administrative purposes these regions and groups are divided into prefectures (*nomoi* in Greek).

ECONOMY
Although Greece has the second-lowest income per capita of all the EU countries (after Portugal), its long-term economic future looks brighter now than for some time. Tough austerity measures imposed by successive governments have cut inflation to less than 3%, the Greek stock market has been booming since 1997 and investor confidence appears high.

Despite problems arising from the NATO war against Serbia – the fighting, combined with reports of anti-NATO sentiments in Greece have hit tourism particularly hard – the country appears on track for the second phase of European monetary union in 2000.

Tourism is Greece's biggest earner, contributing an estimated $US9 billion a year in foreign exchange. It accounts for a large part of the 50% of the workforce employed in service industries (contributing 59% of GDP). The importance of agriculture has declined rapidly since WWII, with 22% of the workforce now engaged in the agricultural sector (contributing 15%).

Three Pillars of Western Philosophy

Socrates – 'Know thyself'

Little is certain about Socrates because he committed nothing to paper. Historians and philosophers have constructed a picture of Socrates through the writings of Plato, a one-time pupil.

Socrates was born around 470 BC in Athens and fought in the First Peloponnesian War. Thereafter he gave his life over to teaching in the streets and, particularly, the gymnasia – a mission bestowed on him by his god, the *daimon*.

He was deeply religious but regarded mythology with disdain. The *daimon's* existence was demonstrated by the perfect order of nature, the universality of people's belief in the divine and the revelations that come in dreams.

Socrates' method was dialectic: he sought to illuminate truth by question and answer, responding to a pupil's question with another question, and then another, until the pupil came to answer their own inquiry.

He believed that bodily desires corrupt people's souls, and a person's soul is directly responsible for their happiness. The soul is neither good nor bad, but well or poorly realised. Accordingly, unethical actions are in some sense involuntary – people commit bad actions because they have poor conceptions of themselves. However, those who know the true good will always act in accordance with it.

Believing that a profound understanding of goodness is a prerequisite for those who govern society, Socrates held that democracy was flawed because it left the state in the hands of the unenlightened. He valued all opinion as equal.

In 399 BC, at the age of 70, Socrates was indicted for 'impiety'. He was convicted with 'corruption of the young' and 'the practice of religious novelties', and sentenced to death by the drinking of hemlock. The story of Socrates' day of execution is told in Plato's *Phaedo*.

Plato – 'Until philosophers are kings ... cities will never cease from ill, nor the human race'

Plato was born around 428 BC in Athens, or perhaps Aegina, in the early years of the First Peloponnesian War into an aristocratic family. He was a student of Socrates, who had a great influence upon him.

Around 387 BC, Plato founded the Academy in Athens as an institute of philosophical and scientific studies.

Plato's prolific writings take the form of dialogues and read like scripts. He never introduced himself as a character in his dialogues, but he did use real people as speakers, including Socrates.

Politically, Plato was an authoritarian. The *Republic* is, in part, given over to his view of the ideal state. He divided people into commoners, soldiers and rulers. Plato declared that all people should live simply and modestly; that women and men should be equal and receive the same education and prospects; that marriages should be arranged by the state and children should be removed from their parents at birth. This would minimise personal, possessive emotions, so that public spirit would be the overwhelming emotion that individuals felt.

Three Pillars of Western Philosophy

The notion of divine perfection was a central tenet in his thinking. The problem of class-ideas or 'universals' had long been a conundrum – to define the meaning of nouns like 'woman' or 'house' that can be applied to whole classes of individual instances. 'Woman' in its broadest sense is not this woman or that woman, but is greater, more real and more enduring than any individual woman.

Plato's answer was that objects in the world are merely appearances of perfect 'ideas' or 'forms'. Trees of the material world are merely copies of God's perfect tree, which bears no relation to time or space and which determines the properties of 'treeness'.

Plato held that knowledge cannot be derived from the senses. He argued that we perceive *through* our senses, not *with* them. We have knowledge of concepts that are not derived from experience: perfect symmetry has no manifestation in the material world. Plato believed that knowledge was inside everybody, and claimed that all knowledge is recollection – that it comes as revelation to the intellect.

Aristotle – 'He who exercises his reason and culti-vates it seems to be both in the best state of mind and most dear to the gods'

Aristotle was born in 384 BC in Stagira, Macedonia. In 367 BC, Aristotle went to Athens to become a pupil of Plato at the Academy. He remained there for nearly 20 years, until Plato's death.

After Plato's death a rift appeared between Aristotle and the Academy. Aristotle left and travelled widely, immersing himself in biological studies. At nearly 50, he returned to Athens and founded a rival institution, the Lyceum, working there for another 12 years and writing prolifically.

After the death of Alexander the Great in 323 BC, the strong anti-Macedonian sentiment that ensued led to Aristotle being indicted for 'impiety', ostensibly over his writings, but the real motives were political. He fled Athens and died a year later of a stomach condition.

He attacked Plato's Theory of Ideas. He regarded class-names as descriptive words, more like adjectives. For Aristotle, a universal derives its meaning from the fact that there are many individual instances of it. If there were no red things in the world, then the notion of 'redness' would be nonsensical.

Central to Aristotle's metaphysic is his distinction between 'form' and 'matter'. The sculptor of a statue confers shape (the form) onto marble (the matter). A thing's form is that which is unified about it – its *essence*. Matter without form is just potentiality, but by acquiring form its actuality increases. God has no matter, but is pure form and absolute actuality. Thus, by building houses and bridges, humans increase form in the world, making it more divine.

For Aristotle, the soul is inseparable from the body, but the mind (the rational soul) is divine and impersonal – all people should agree on issues of pure reason, like mathematics. Thus, the immortality of the mind is not a personal immortality. Rather, when exercising pure reason, people partake in the divine – in God's immortality.

Aristotle was the first thinker to look at structures of deductive arguments, or syllogisms, and for 2000 years was unsurpassed in the study of logic, until Gottlob Frege and Bertrand Russell, the 20th century's great symbolic logicians, picked up his thread.

POPULATION

A census is taken every 10 years in Greece. The 1991 census recorded a population of 10,264,156 – an increase of 5.4% on the 1981 figure. Women outnumber men by more than 200,000. Greece is now a largely urban society, with 68% of the population living in cities. By far the largest is Athens, with more than 3.1 million people living in the greater Athens area. Less than 15% of people live on the islands, the most populous of which are Crete (537,000), Evia (209,100) and Corfu (105,000).

PEOPLE

Contemporary Greeks are a mixture of all of the invaders who have occupied the country since ancient times. Additionally, there are a number of distinct ethnic minorities living in the country.

The country's small Roman Catholic population is of Genoese or Frankish origin. They live mostly in the Cyclades, especially on the island of Syros, where they make up 40% of the population. The Franks dominated the island from 1207 AD to Ottoman times.

About 300,000 ethnic Turks who were exempt from the population exchange of 1923 live in Thrace. There are also small numbers of Turks on Kos and Rhodes which, along with the rest of the Dodecanese, did not become part of Greece until 1947.

The small Jewish communities on the islands of Evia (at Halkida) and Rhodes date back to the Roman era. There are also Jewish communities in several mainland cities, including Athens, Kavala and Thessaloniki. Thessaloniki had a large Jewish community before WWII, mostly descendants of 15th century exiles from Spain and Portugal. In 1941, the Germans entered Thessaloniki and herded 46,000 Jews off to Auschwitz; most never returned. They comprised 90% of Thessaloniki's Jews and more than half the total number in Greece. Today there are only about 5000 Jews living in Greece.

You will come across Roma (Gypsies) everywhere in Greece, but especially in Macedonia, Thrace and Thessaly. There are large communities of Roma in the Thracian towns of Alexandroupolis and Didymotiho.

The collapse of the communist regimes in Albania and Romania produced a wave of economic refugees across Greece's poorly guarded northern borders, with an estimated 300,000 arriving from Albania alone. These refugees have been a vital source of cheap labour for the agricultural sector; fruit and vegetable prices have actually gone down as a result of their contribution. Albanians also have a reputation as fine stone masons, and their influence can be seen everywhere.

EDUCATION

Education in Greece is free at all levels of the state system, from kindergarten to tertiary. Primary schooling begins at the age of six, but most children attend a state-run kindergarten from the age of five. Private kindergartens are popular with those who can afford them. Primary school classes tend to be larger than those in most European countries – usually 30 to 35 children. Primary school hours are short (8 am to 1 pm), but children get a lot of homework.

At 12, children enter the *gymnasio*, and at 15 they may leave school, or enter the *lykeio*, from where they take university-entrance examinations. Although there is a high percentage of literacy, many parents and pupils are dissatisfied with the education system, especially beyond primary level. The private sector therefore flourishes, and even relatively poor parents struggle to send their children to one of the country's 5000 *frontistiria* (intensive coaching colleges) to prepare them for the very competitive university-entrance exams.

ARTS

Walk around any capital city in Europe, America or Australasia and the influence of ancient Greek art and architecture is plain to see. It's there in the civic buildings, in the monumental public sculptures, in the plan of the city streets themselves. The product of a truly extraordinary civilisation, the humanism and purity of form of Greek art has inspired artists and architects throughout history.

Ironically, the influence of Greek art has spread throughout the world due to a reality that many travellers (and indeed the Greeks themselves) find unpalatable. This is the fact that many of the greatest works of ancient Greek art haven't had a home in Greece itself for hundreds, sometimes thousands, of years. From the Parthenon frieze taken by Lord Elgin and now displayed in the British Museum to the famous *Nike (Winged Victory of Samothrace)* in Paris' Louvre museum, the work of the Greek masters is held in the collections of the great museums of the world. Many of the great ancient Greek buildings, too, are found in countries other than Greece as they date from the time of the expansive ancient Greek world, which encompassed parts or all of countries such as Italy, Iran, Turkey, Syria and Libya.

Travellers to Greece itself shouldn't despair, however. There's plenty left to see! The buildings, paintings, pots, sculptures and decorative arts of ancient Greece can be found in the country's streets, cities and islands, as well as in its wonderful museums. They may not be in their original form – it takes a stretch of the imagination to envisage the *Hermes of Praxiteles* with arms, and the magnificent and austere form of buildings such as the Parthenon overlaid with gaudily coloured paintings and sculptures – but they manage to evoke the early history of the Greek nation more powerfully than a library of history books ever could.

Architecture

Of all the ancient Greek arts, architecture has perhaps had the greatest influence. Greek temples, seen throughout history as symbols of democracy, have been the inspiration for architectural movements such as the Italian Renaissance and the British Greek Revival.

One of the earliest known architectural sites of ancient Greece is the huge palace and residential complex at Knossos on Crete, built in the Minoan period. Its excavation and reconstruction was begun by Sir Arthur Evans in 1900. Visitors today can see the ruins of the second residential palace built on this site (the first was destroyed by an earthquake in 1700 BC), with its spacious courtyards and grandiose stairways. They can also marvel at the many living rooms, storerooms and bathrooms that give us an idea of day-to-day Minoan life. Similar palaces on Crete, usually of two storeys and built around a large courtyard, have since been excavated at Phaestos, Agia Triada, Malia, Gournia and Zakros.

The Minoan period was followed by the Mycenaean. Instead of the open, labyrinthine palaces of the Minoans, the Mycenaeans used their advanced skills in engineering to build citadels on a compact, orderly plan, fortified by strong walls.

The next great advance in ancient Greek architecture came with the building of the first monumental stone temples in the Archaic and classical periods. From this time, temples were characterised by the famous orders of columns, particularly the Doric, Ionic and Corinthian. These orders were

The graceful Caryatids look out over Athens from the Erechtheion's southern portico.

applied to the exteriors of temples, which retained their traditional simple plan of porch and hall but were now regularly surrounded by a colonnade or at least a columnar facade.

Theatre design was also a hallmark of the classical period. The tragedies of Aeschylus, Sophocles and Euripides and the comedies of Aristophanes were written and first performed in the Theatre of Dionysos, built into the slope of Athens' Acropolis in the 5th century BC. Other theatres dating from this period can be found throughout Greece.

During the Hellenistic period, private houses and palaces, rather than temples and public buildings, were the main focus of building. The houses at Delos, built around peristyled (surrounded by columns) courtyards and featuring striking mosaics, are perhaps the best examples in existence.

Sculpture
Taking pride of place in the collections of the great museums of the world, the sculptures of ancient Greece have extraordinary visual power and beauty.

The prehistoric art of Greece has been discovered only recently, notably in the Cyclades and on Crete. The pared-down sculptures of this period, with their smooth and flattish appearance, were carved from the high-quality marble of Paros and Naxos in the middle of the 3rd millennium BC. Their primitive and powerful forms have inspired many artists since, particularly those of the 20th century.

In the Mycenaean period, small terracottas of women with a circular body or with arms upraised were widely produced. These are known to modern scholars as phi (φ) and psi (ψ) figurines from their resemblance to these letters of the Greek alphabet.

Displaying an obvious debt to Egyptian sculpture, the marble sculptures of the Archaic period are the true precursors of the famed Greek sculpture of the classical period. The artists of this period moved away from the examples of their Oriental predecessors and began to represent figures that were true to nature, rather than flat and stylised. Seeking to master the depiction of both the naked body and of drapery, sculptors of the period focused on figures of naked youths *(kouroi)*, with their set symmetrical stance and enigmatic smiles. At first the classical style was rather severe; later, as sculptors sought ideal proportions for the human figure, it became more animated.

Unfortunately, little original work of the classical period survives. Most freestanding classical sculpture described by ancient writers was made of bronze and survives only as marble copies made by the Romans. Looking at these copies is a bittersweet experience. On the one hand, they are marvellous works of art in their own right. On the other, they make us aware of what an extraordinary body of work has been lost. Fortunately, a few classical bronzes, lost when they were being shipped abroad in antiquity, were recovered from the sea in the 20th century and are now in the collection of the National Archaeological Museum, Athens.

The sculpture of the Hellenistic period continued the Greeks' quest to attain total naturalism in their work. Works of this period were animated, almost theatrical, in contrast to their serene Archaic and classical predecessors. The focus was on realism. Just how successful the artists of this period were is shown in the way later artists, such as Michelangelo, revered them. Michelangelo, in fact, was at the forefront of the rediscovery and appreciation of Greek works in the Renaissance. He is said to have been at the site in Rome in 1506 when the famous Roman copy of the *Laocoön* group, one of the iconic sculptural works of the Hellenistic period, was unearthed.

Pottery
Say the words 'Greek art' and many people immediately visualise a painted terracotta pot. Represented in museums and art galleries throughout the world, the pots of ancient Greece have such a high profile for a number of reasons, chief among these being that there are lots of them around!

continued on page 41

SUGGESTED ITINERARIES

One of the most difficult aspects of travel is organising an itinerary. The following list provides a choice of one-week and two-week suggested itineraries for each of the major island groups. The one-week itineraries are for people who want no more than a quick tour of the highlights of each region, while the two-week itineraries are for people with a bit more time to spend exploring the various island groups.

The list can be used to create the individual itinerary of your choice. A month in the Greek Islands, for example, could be divided up into a week on Crete, followed by a couple of weeks in the Cyclades and a week in the Dodecanese.

The list also includes shorter itineraries for Athens and the Saronic Gulf Islands.

ATHENS

If you're in Greece to visit the islands, you probably won't want to spend too much time hanging around in Athens – particularly in the middle of summer.

Athens has a lot to offer though, and it's worth making the most of your time there. However you opt to spend your time, do your walking early – or late – to avoid the heat of the day.

One Day

If one day is all you can spare, concentrate on taking in the two major sites - the Acropolis and the National Archaeological Museum.

Start off with the Acropolis – you'll appreciate it all the more if you get there before the crowds (it opens at 8 am). Allow yourself at least a couple of hours to explore the site and museum. After lunch, head over to the National Archaeological Museum. People have been known to spend all day here, but a couple of hours is enough to take in the highlights. By now, you'll be ready for a good rest in preparation for the evening.

Start the evening with dinner at a taverna with a view of the Acropolis, then take in a performance of ancient Greek drama at the Theatre of Herodes Atticus, or check out the Dora Stratou folk dancers on Filopappos Hill.

Two Days

A second day in Athens gives you time to take in some of the lesser lights. Follow the one-day tour, then start your second day with the Walking Tour of Plaka described in the Athens chapter (you can extend it by taking in the Ancient Agora if you've got the energy). After lunch, check out the excellent Goulandris Museum of Cycladic & Ancient Greek Art. For dinner, try one of the many *ouzeris* (places which serve *ouzo* and light snacks) and restaurants in the Psiri district.

Title page: Sunset Dining in Fira, Santorini, Cyclades (photograph by Diana Mayfield)

Above Left: Mesahti Beach, Ikaria, Ionian Islands (photograph by Paul Hellander)

SARONIC GULF ISLANDS

The Saronic Gulf Islands are the closest islands to Athens, and are thus a popular weekend escape for Athenians. Few travellers treat them seriously as a destination, but they are worth considering as a side trip from Athens. Five days is enough time to take in all the major attractions.

Five Days

Aegina is so close to Athens that many people pop over just for a lunch of barbecued octopus – the island specialty. It's well worth an overnight stay, though, for the chance to check out the views from the Temple of Aphaia, the group's only major archaeological site.

Poros warrants no more than a brief stopover on the way to tranquil Hydra, the Saronic Gulf Island with the most style. It's easy to spend a couple of days exploring graceful Hydra Town and walking the coastal paths. Spetses, too, has enough to offer for a couple of days – including some good beaches on the west coast.

Right: The lively waterfront of Hydra Town, Saronic Gulf Islands

ROD HYETT

CYCLADES

These are the archetypal Greek Islands as seen in the travel brochures: white-washed villages clinging to rugged hillsides, flowering geraniums in brightly-painted pots, golden beaches and blue seas.

One Week

Spend two days on Naxos, lushest of the islands. Wander around the hilltop kastro and explore the backcountry by car or moped, visiting old churches, archaeological sites, beaches, the lush Tragaea region, and the villages of Halki, Filoti and Apiranthos. Try to fit a few walks in. Catch a ferry to Santorini and oggle at the scenery as you pull in to the caldera. Spend three to four days here, staying on the cliffs in Fira or Oia to admire the spectacular sunsets. Visit Akrotiri and the museums and exhibits in Fira. Take a boat trip to Thirasia and the volcanic islets. Spend at least one day lazing by the sea, and eating at a beachside taverna. If you feel like moving on, catch a ferry or catamaran to Syros, where you can explore the graceful neoclassical city of Ermoupolis and the hilltop village of Ano Syros, or to Ios, where you can dance the night away and then recover on the beach.

Two Weeks

Spend a day and night on Syros and explore the graceful neoclassical city of Ermoupolis and the hilltop village of Ano Syros. On Mykonos, sample the nightlife and take an excursion to ancient Delos. Then follow the one-week itinerary for Naxos and Santorini. Head to Folegandros, and while away a day or two. Soak up the atmosphere of the lovely Hora, and visit one of the beaches. On the way back to Athens, stop off at Sikinos if you like quiet, or at Ios, if you want to party. Amorgos would make a good alternative to Folegandros, especially if you like walking. Make sure you visit Hora and the Moni Hozoviotissis, if you choose this route. From Amorgos you can make a side trip to the cute little island of Koufonisia before heading back to Athens.

Left: Naxos Town from the temple of Apollo, Cyclades

D I HALL

CRETE

The largest and most southerly of the islands, Crete is at its best in springtime.

One Week

Spend two days in Iraklio visiting the archaeological museum, historical museum of Crete and the Minoan site of Knossos. Allow two days in Rethymno to visit the fortress and museums and explore the old quarter. If you have time, take a day trip to the mountain town of Spili, or the resort of Plakias, if you prefer a beach. Spend three days in Hania to visit the museums, explore the old quarter and hike the Samaria Gorge. Recuperate the following day on the beach at Falassarna. Round off your trip with an evening of music and drinking at Cafe Crete.

Two Weeks

Spend two days in Iraklio visiting the archaeological museum, Historical Museum of Crete and the Minoan site of Knossos. Overnight at one of the Lassithi Plateau villages and explore the Dikteon Cave and a walk on the plateau. Spend two nights in Sitia, and use it as a base for a trip to Zakros and a walk through the Valley of the Dead to ancient Zakros. If you have time, visit Ancient Lato, otherwise travel west and stay two days in Rethymno to visit the fortress and museums and explore the old quarter. Overnight in Agia Galini to visit Phaestos and Agia Triada. Spend two nights in the mountain town of Spili, or the beach resort of Plakias and visit Moni Preveli. Spend two nights in Hania to explore the old town and visit the museums. Head down to Paleohora for two nights and spend a day hiking the Samaria Gorge. If you have time, unwind on Elafonisi beach the following day.

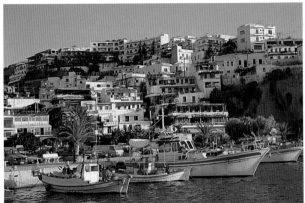

Right: The pretty port of Agia Gallini, situated in the south of Crete, is one of the island's most popular resorts.

CHRIS CHRISTO

DODECANESE

Variety is the name of the game in the Dodecanese – from the resorts of Kos and Rhodes to the uncrowded beaches of Agathonisi, Lipsi and Tilos.

One Week

Spend two days on Rhodes. Even a strong aversion to mass tourism shouldn't deter you from exploring the capital's medieval old city. Begin your exploration early in the morning. At any time of the day, away from the main thoroughfares and squares, you will find many deserted labyrinthine alleyways.

Visit either Lindos or the ancient city of Kamiros, or both if you hire a car and drive through Rhodes' unspoilt mountainous interior.

Spend two days chilling out on the beaches of tranquil Tilos – the island also offers some good opportunities for walking. You may also be able to fit in a couple of days on Nisyros, which has an extraordinary volcanic landscape, the picturesque villages of Emboreios and Nikea and an impressive ruined kastro on its ancient acropolis. Otherwise, make for Kos, birthplace of Hippocrates, to see its extensive ruins and enjoy its wild nightlife. Schedule in a day trip from Kos to Nisyros.

Two Weeks

Follow the one-week itinerary, but spend three days on Rhodes to see more of the interior. Also spend the night on Nisyros and enjoy a drink and dinner on Mandraki's delightful central square – the town undergoes a metamorphosis when the day-trippers leave.

To recuperate from the liveliness of Kos, spend three days on Lipsi to relax on its uncrowded beaches, do more walking and take a day trip to remote and traditional Arki. Or, if even Lipsi sounds too touristy for you, go to quieter Agathonisi. Finally, en route to Piraeus, spend a day on Patmos to explore its monasteries.

STELLA HELLANDER

Left: Whitewashed houses huddle around the Monastery of St John the Theologian on Patmos, Dodecanese.

NORTH-EASTERN AEGEAN ISLANDS

These islands are the perfect choice for people who want to get off the beaten track.

One Week

With only seven days, you will be a bit pushed so plan your ferry trips carefully. Fly out to Lesvos (Mytilini) or take the overnight boat. Make sure you visit Mythimna (Molyvos) and maybe Skala Eresou for some beach life. Take a boat to Chios and visit the Mastihohoria (Mastic villages) and maybe sit on Homer's stone (Daskalopetra) for some poetic inspiration. Head for Samos if you want a sub-tropical island, or Ikaria if you want a very laid-back and idiosyncratic visit and a couple of the best beaches in the Aegean. Fly or sail back to the mainland.

Two Weeks

Start your itinerary on the underrated but worthwhile island of Limnos, reached by ferry from either Kavala, Thessaloniki or Rafina. From here, try to make a two-day visit to the remote community on Agios Efstratios, one of Greece's most remote islands. Fly to Lesvos (Mytilini) and follow the one-week itinerary to Samos. Definitely include Ikaria for three to four days with perhaps a side trip to the Fourni Islands while en route from Samos. Take the overnight boat to Piraeus to finish your trip.

EVIA & THE SPORADES

The Sporades are at their best in September and early October, after the summer crowds have left – or in spring.

One Week

Starting in Athens, take the bus to Kymi in Evia and then the ferry to Linaria in Skyros. Give delectable Skyros at least two days of your time. Take a hydrofoil to Alonnisos and work your way towards Volos on the mainland, visiting the islands of Skopelos and Skiathos en route.

Two Weeks

Try this adventurous route if you have time at your disposal. From Athens head to Rafina in Attica and take the ferry to Karystos in Evia. Work your way up to Kymi in Evia, perhaps taking in Eretria on Evia's west side and walking up Mt Dirfys from the inland village of Steni. From Kymi in Evia follow the one-week itinerary, allowing two to three days on each island of the Sporades. Finally exit from Skiathos to Thessaloniki (ferry or hydrofoil) and return to Athens by train.

IONIAN ISLANDS

As the only island's off Greece's west coast, the Ionians are the odd group out. Because of ferry connections, they are best considered as two groups, north and south.

One Week - Northern Ionian Islands

Spend two days in Corfu Town; explore the narrow streets of the old town and visit the museums. Spend one night in Paleokastritsa or Lakones; walk the path between the two, visit Moni Theotokou and Angelokastro, and have a meal at one of the restaurants on the Lakones-Makrades road. If you have your own transport visit old Perithia. Spend two days at a west-coast resort and catch a sunset at Pelekas. If you have your own transport visit Lake Korission and surrounds. Spend one or two nights on Paxi.

One Week - Southern Ionian Islands

Spend one day and night on Lefkada, explore the capital and relax on one of the west coast beaches. Stay overnight on Meganisi. Spend two days on Ithaki, visiting Vathy's museums and the villages of Anogi, Frikes and Kioni. Have two days in Fiskardo on Kefallonia (in the high season stay elsewhere and visit on a day trip), to see the village of Assos and Myrtos beach. Spend one day in Sami to visit the nearby caves.

Two Weeks

Combine the above itineraries, but allow an extra day for Corfu Town, visiting Ahillion palace and the villages of Kastellani, Kamara and Agios Prokopias, and perhaps staying an extra night on Lefkada to see Lefkada Town and relax on one of the west-coast beaches. Spending only one day in Fiskardo may enable you to include Kythira – you may find it the greatest surprise in the Ionians.

STELLA HELLANDER

Left: Brightly painted fishing boats in delightful Fiskardo harbour, Kefallonia, Ionian Islands.

continued from page 32

Practised from the Stone Age, pottery is one of the most ancient arts. At first, vases were built with coils and wads of clay but the art of throwing on the wheel was introduced in about 2000 BC and was then practised with great skill by Minoan and Mycenaean artists.

Minoan pottery is often characterised by a high centre of gravity and beak-like spouts. Painted decoration was applied as a white clay slip (a thin paste of clay and water) or one which fired to a greyish black or dull red. Flowing designs with spiral or marine and plant motifs were used. The Archaeological Museum in Iraklio, on Crete, has a wealth of Minoan pots.

Mycenaean pottery shapes include a long-stemmed goblet and a globular vase with handles resembling a pair of stirrups. Decorative motifs are similar to those on Minoan pottery but are less fluid.

The 10th century BC saw the introduction of the Protogeometric style, with its substantial pots decorated with blackish-brown horizontal lines around the circumference, hatched triangles, and compass-drawn concentric circles. This was followed by the new vase shape and more crowded decoration of the pots of the Geometric period. By the early 8th century, figures were introduced, marking the introduction of the most fundamental element in the later tradition of classical art – the representation of gods, men and animals.

Painting

The lack of any comprehensive archaeological record of ancient Greek painting has forced art historians to largely rely on the painted decoration of terracotta pots as evidence of the development of this Greek art form. There are a few exceptions, such as the Cycladic frescoes in houses on Santorini, excavated in the mid-to-late 20th century. Some of these frescoes are now in the collection of the National Archaeological Museum in Athens.

These works were painted in fresco technique using yellow, blue, red and black pig-

LOUISE KLEP

Geometric detail from an urn, 750 BC

ments, with some details added after the plaster had dried. Plants and animals are depicted, as well as men and women. Figures are usually shown in profile or in a combination of profile and frontal views. Stylistically, the frescoes are similar to the paintings of Minoan Crete, which are less well preserved. Reconstructed examples of frescoes from the Minoan period can be seen at the Palace of Knossos, on Crete.

Music & Dance

The folk dances of today derive from the ritual dances performed in ancient Greek temples. One of these dances, the *syrtos*, is depicted on ancient Greek vases, and there are references to dances in Homer's works. Many Greek folk dances, including the syrtos, are performed in a circular formation; in ancient times, dancers formed a circle in order to seal themselves off from evil influences.

Each region of Greece has its own dances, but one dance you'll see performed everywhere is the *kalamatianos*, originally from Kalamata in the Peloponnese. It's the dance in which dancers stand in a row with their hands on one another's shoulders.

Singing and the playing of musical instruments have also been an integral part of life in Greece since ancient times. Cycladic figurines holding instruments resembling harps and flutes date back to 2000 BC. Musical instruments of ancient Greece included the lyre, lute, *piktis* (pipes), *kroupeza* (a percussion instrument), *kithara* (a stringed instrument), *aulos* (a wind instrument), *barbitos* (similar to a violin cello) and the *magadio* (similar to a harp).

If ancient Greeks did not have a musical instrument to accompany their songs, they imitated the sound of one. It is believed that unaccompanied Byzantine choral singing derived from this custom.

Traditional Greek Music & Dancing

Music and dancing have played an important role in Greek social life since the dawn of Hellenism. You may even think at times that Greeks live solely for the chance to sing and to participate in dancing. You wouldn't be that wrong. Whether it be at a traditional wedding, a night club, an Athenian *boîte* or a simple village *kafeneio*, a song and a dance are not far from people's minds.

The style of dancing often reflects the climate or disposition of the participants. In Epiros, the stately *tsamiko* is slow and highly emotive, reflecting the often cold and insular nature of mountain life. The Pontian Greeks, on the contrary, have a highly visual, vigorous and warlike form of dancing reflecting years of altercations with their Turkish neighbours. The *kotsari* is one of the best examples of this unique dance form. The islands with their bright and cheery atmosphere give rise to lilting music and matching dances such as the *ballos* or the *syrtos*, while the graceful *kalamatianos* circle dance, most commonly seen at Greek festive occasions, reflects years of proud Peloponnese tradition. The so-called 'Zorba's dance' or *syrtaki* is a stylised dance for two or three men or women with linked arms on shoulders, while the often spectacular solo male *zeïmbekikos* with its whirling improvisations has its roots in the Greek blues of the hashish dens and prisons of pre-war times. The women counterpoint this self-indulgent and showy male display with their own sensuous *tsifteteli*, a svelte, sinewy show of femininity evolved from the Middle Eastern belly dance.

Music is as widely divergent as dancing. The ubiquitous stringed *bouzouki* closely associated with contemporary music is a relative newcomer to the game, while the plucked strings of the bulbous *outi* (oud), the strident sound of the Cretan *lyra* (lyre) and the staccato rap of the *toumberleki* (lap drum) bear witness to a rich range of musical instruments that share many common characteristics with instruments all over the Middle East. Musical forms range from the *rembetika* – the Greek blues, to *dimotika* – humble folk poetry sung and more often than not accompanied by the *klarino* (clarinet) and *defi* (tambourine) and to the widely popular middle-of-the-road *elafrolaïka*, best exemplified by the songs of Giannis Parios. The unaccompanied, polyphonic *pogonisia* songs of northern Epiros and southern Albania are spine-chilling examples of a musical genre that owes its origins to Byzantium. At the lesser end of the scale, the curiously popular *skyladika* or 'dog songs' – presumably because they resemble a whining dog – are hugely popular in night clubs known as *bouzouxidika* where the bouzouki reigns supreme, but where musical taste sometimes takes a back seat.

MARGARET JUNG

The distinctly Greek bouzouki

The *bouzouki*, which you will hear everywhere in Greece, is a mandolin-like instrument similar to the Turkish *saz* and *baglama*. It is one of the main instruments of *rembetika* music – the Greek equivalent of the American Blues. The name rembetika may come from the Turkish word *rembet* which means outlaw. Opinions differ as to the origins of rembetika, but it is probably a hybrid of several different types of music. One source was the music that emerged in the 1870s in the 'low life' cafes, called *tekedes* (hashish dens), in urban areas and especially around ports. Another source was the Arabo-Persian music played in sophisticated Middle Eastern music cafes *(amanedes)* in the 19th century. Rembetika was popularised in Greece by the refugees from Asia Minor.

The songs which emerged from the tekedes had themes concerning hashish, prison life, gambling, knife fights etc, whereas cafe aman music had themes which centred around erotic love. These all came together in the music of the refugees, from which a subculture of rebels, called *manges*, emerged. The manges wore showy clothes even though they lived in extreme poverty. They worked long hours in menial jobs, and spent their evenings in the tekedes, smoking hashish and singing and dancing. Although hashish was illegal, the law was rarely enforced until Metaxas did his clean-up job in 1936. It was in a tekes in Piraeus that Markos Vamvakaris, now acknowledged as the greatest *rembetis*, was discovered by a recording company in the 1930s.

Metaxas' censorship meant that themes of hashish, prison, gambling and the like disappeared from recordings of rembetika in the late 1930s, but continued clandestinely in some tekedes. This polarised the music, and the recordings, stripped of their 'meaty' themes and language, became insipid and bourgeois. Recorded rembetika even adopted another name – *Laïko tragoudi* – to disassociate it from its illegal roots. Although WWII brought a halt to recording, a number of composers emerged at this time. They included Apostolos Kaldaras, Yiannis Papaïoanou, Georgos Mitsakis and Manolis

Hiotis. One of the greatest female rembe singers, Sotiria Bellou, also appeared at t time.

During the 1950s and 1960s rembetika became increasingly popular, but less and less authentic. Much of the music was glitzy and commercialised, although the period also produced two outstanding composers of popular music (including rembetika) in Mikis Theodorakis and Manos Hatzidakis. The best of Theodorakis' work is the music which he set to the poetry of Seferis, Elytis and Ritsos.

During the junta years, many rembetika clubs were closed down, but interest in genuine rembetika revived in the 1980s – particularly among students and intellectuals. There are now a number of rembetika clubs in Athens.

Since independence, Greece has followed mainstream developments in classical music. The Athens Concert Hall has performances by both national and international musicians.

Literature

The first, and greatest, ancient Greek writer was Homer, author of the *Iliad* and *Odyssey*. Nothing is known of Homer's life; where or when he lived, or whether, as it is alleged, he was blind. The historian Herodotus thought Homer lived in the 9th century BC, and no scholar since has proved nor disproved this.

Herodotus (5th century BC) was the author of the first historical work about western civilisation. His highly subjective account of the Persian Wars has, however, led him to be regarded as the 'father of lies' as well as the 'father of history'. The historian Thucydides (5th century BC) was more objective in his approach, but took a high moral stance. He wrote an account of the Peloponnesian Wars, and also the famous *Melian Dialogue*, which chronicles the talks between the Athenians and Melians prior to the Athenian siege of Melos.

Pindar (c.518-438 BC) is regarded as the pre-eminent lyric poet of ancient Greece. He was commissioned to recite his odes at the Olympic Games. The greatest writers of

appho (6th century BC)
century BC), both of
_esvos. Sappho's poetic de-
_ of her affections for other women
_e rise to the term 'lesbian'.

In Byzantine times, poetry, like all of the arts, was of a religious nature. During Ottoman rule, poetry was inextricably linked with folk songs, which were not written down but passed on by word of mouth. Many of these songs were composed by the klephts, and told of the harshness of life in the mountains and of their uprisings against the Turks.

Dionysios Solomos (1798-1857) and Andreas Kalvos (1796-1869), who were both born on Zakynthos, are regarded as the first modern Greek poets. Solomos' work was heavily nationalistic and his *Hymn to Freedom* became the Greek national anthem. At this time there were heated debates among writers, politicians and educators about whether the official language should be Demotiki or Katharevousa. Demotic was the spoken language of the people and Katharevousa was an artificial language loosely based on Ancient Greek. Almost all writers favoured demotic, and from the time of Solomos, most wrote only in that language. The highly acclaimed poet Constantine Cavafy (1863-1933) was less concerned with nationalism, being a resident of Alexandria in Egypt; his themes ranged from the erotic to the philosophical.

The best known 20th century Greek poets are George Seferis (1900-71), who won the Nobel Prize for literature in 1963, and Odysseus Elytis (1911-96), who won the same prize in 1979. Seferis drew his inspiration from the Greek myths, whereas Elytis' work is surreal. Angelos Sikelianos (1884-1951) was another poet who drew inspiration from ancient Greece, particularly Delphi. His poetry is highly evocative, and includes incantatory verses emulating the Delphic oracle. Yiannis Ritsos is another highly acclaimed Greek poet; his work draws on many aspects of Greece – its landscape, mythology and social issues. The most celebrated 20th century Greek novelist is Nikos Kazantzakis.

See the Books section in the Facts for the Visitor chapter for more information.

Drama

Drama in Greece can be dated back to the contests staged at the Ancient Theatre of Dionysos in Athens during the 6th century BC for the annual Dionysia festival. During one of these competitions, Thespis left the ensemble and took centre stage for a solo performance regarded as the first true dramatic performance. The term 'Thespian' for actor derives from this event.

Aeschylus (c.525-456 BC) is the so-called 'father of tragedy'; his best-known work is the *Oresteia* trilogy. Sophocles (c.496-406 BC) is regarded as the greatest tragedian. He is thought to have written over 100 plays, of which only seven major works survive. These include *Ajax*, *Antigone*, *Electra*, *Trachiniae* and his most famous play, *Oedipus Rex*. His plays dealt mainly with tales from mythology and had complex plots. Sophocles won first prize 18 times at the Dionysia festival, beating Aeschylus in 468 BC, whereupon Aeschylus went off to Sicily in a huff.

Euripides (c.485-406 BC), another famous tragedian, was more popular than either Aeschylus or Sophocles because his plots were considered more exciting. He wrote 80 plays of which 19 are extant (although one, *Rhesus*, is disputed). His most famous works are *Medea*, *Andromache*, *Orestias* and *Bacchae*. Aristophanes (c.427-387 BC) wrote comedies – often ribald – which dealt with topical issues. His play *The Wasp* ridicules Athenians who resorted to litigation over trivialities; *The Birds* pokes fun at Athenian gullibility; and *Plutus* deals with the unfair distribution of wealth.

You can see plays by the ancient Greek playwrights at the Athens and Epidaurus festivals (see the Athens and Peloponnese chapters), and at various other festivals around the country.

Film

Greeks are avid cinema goers, although most of the films they watch are North American or British.

The Greek film industry has long been in the doldrums, largely due to inadequate funding. The problem is compounded by the type of films the Greeks produce, which are famously slow moving, loaded with symbolism and generally too avant-garde to have mass appeal.

The leader of this school is Theodoros Angelopoulos, winner of the Golden Palm award at the 1998 Cannes Film Festival for *An Eternity and One Day*. It tells the story of a terminally ill writer who spends his last day revisiting his youth in the company of a 10-year-old boy. His other films include *The Beekeeper*, *Alexander the Great* and *The Hesitant Step of the Stork*.

Although Greece produces no action films, there is a lighter side to the Greek cinema. *Orgasmos tis Ageladas* (The Cow's Orgasm) is a comedy by Olga Malea that relates the adventures of two girls from Larissa who are frustrated by the restrictions of small-town society.

SOCIETY & CONDUCT
Traditional Culture
Greece is steeped in traditional customs. Name days, weddings and funerals all have great significance. Name days are celebrated instead of birthdays. A person's name day is the feast day of the saint after whom the person is named; on someone's name day an open-house policy is adopted and refreshments are served to well-wishers who stop by to give gifts. Birthdays hardly warrant a mention. Weddings are highly festive occasions, with dancing, feasting and drinking sometimes continuing for days.

Greeks tend to be more superstitious than other Europeans. Tuesday is considered unlucky because it's the day on which Constantinople fell to the Ottoman Turks. Many Greeks will not sign an important transaction, get married or begin a trip on a Tuesday. Greeks also believe in the 'evil eye', a superstition prevalent in many Middle Eastern countries. If someone is the victim of the evil eye, then bad luck will befall them. The bad luck is the result of someone's envy, so one should avoid being too complimentary

about things of beauty, especially newborn babies. To ward off the evil eye, Greeks often wear a piece of blue glass, resembling an eye, on a chain around their necks.

Dos & Don'ts
The Greeks' reputation for hospitality is not a myth, although it's a bit harder to find these days. In rural areas, Greece is probably the only country in Europe where you may be invited into a stranger's home for coffee, or even a meal. This can often lead to a feeling of uneasiness in the recipient if the host is poor, but to offer money is considered offensive. The most acceptable way of saying thank you is through a gift, perhaps to a child in the family. A similar situation arises if you go out for a meal with Greeks; the bill is not shared as in northern European countries, but paid by the host.

When drinking wine, it is the custom to half fill the glass. It is also bad manners to empty the glass, so it must be constantly replenished.

Personal questions are not considered rude in Greece, and if you react as if they are you will be the one causing offence. You will be inundated with queries about your age, salary, marital status etc.

If you go into a *kafeneio*, taverna, or shop, it is the custom to greet the waiters and assistants with *'kalimera'* (good day) or *'kalispera'* (good evening) – likewise if you meet someone in the street.

You may have come to Greece for sun, sand and sea, but if you want to bare all, other than on a designated nude beach, remember that Greece is a traditional country, so take care not to offend the locals.

Treatment of Animals
The Greek attitude to animals depends on whether the animal is a cat or not. It's definitely cool to be a cat. Even the mangiest-looking stray can be assured of a warm welcome and a choice titbit on approaching the restaurant table of a Greek. Most other domestic animals are greeted with a certain indifference. You don't see many pet dogs, or pets of any sort for that matter.

The main threat to animal welfare is hunting. Greek hunters are notorious for blasting anything that moves, and millions of animals are killed during the long 'open' season, from 20 August to 10 March, which encompasses the bird migratory period. The Hellenic Centre for the Rehabilitation of Wild Animals and Birds (☎ 0297-28 367), on the island of Aegina, reports that 80% of the animals it treats have been shot.

RELIGION

About 98% of Greeks belong to the Greek Orthodox Church. Most of the remainder are either Roman Catholic, Jewish or Muslim.

The Greek Orthodox Church is closely related to the Russian Orthodox Church and together with it forms the third-largest branch of Christianity. Orthodox, meaning 'right belief', was founded in the 4th century by Constantine the Great, who was converted to Christianity by a vision of the Cross.

During Ottoman times membership of the Orthodox Church was one of the most important criteria in defining a Greek, regardless of where he or she lived. The church was the principal upholder of Greek culture and traditions.

Religion is still integral to life in Greece, and the Greek year is centred on the festivals of the church calendar. Most Greeks, when they have a problem, will go into a church and light a candle to the saint they feel is most likely to help them.

Throughout the islands you will see hundreds of tiny churches dotted around the countryside. Most have been built by individual families in the name of their selected patron saint as thanksgiving for God's protection.

If you wish to look around a church, you should dress appropriately. Women should wear skirts that reach below the knees, and men should wear long trousers and have their arms covered. Regrettably, many churches are kept locked nowadays, but it's usually easy enough to locate caretakers, who will be happy to open them up for you.

Facts for the Visitor

The Best & the Worst

The Best

It's tough trying to pick just 10 of the best things about Greece. These are our personal favourites, the places, things and activities the authors of this book would most like to dedicate a lot more of their time to:

1 Swimming at uncrowded island beaches
2 Traditional Cycladic villages
3 Late night dinners at village tavernas
4 Eating fresh seafood by the sea
5 Greek music
6 Exploring the islands on foot
7 Easter festivities
8 Greek hospitality
9 Siesta time
10 Wedding feasts that include an entire village

The Worst

We'd be very happy not to experience the following again:

1 Concrete-box *domatia* spoiling island landscapes
2 The attitude to rubbish
3 Hot, mosquito-ridden hotel rooms
4 The disappearance of traditional lifestyles as every man, woman, child and dog tries to make a fast buck out of tourism
5 Aggressive restaurant touts accosting passers-by
6 Smoking
7 Demon drivers
8 Ouzo-induced hangovers
9 Athens airport
10 Poorly marked and potholed roads

PLANNING

When to Go

The best times to visit the Greek Islands are in late spring/early summer and in autumn. Winter is pretty much a dead loss. Most of the tourist infrastructure goes into hibernation from November until the beginning of April – hotels and restaurants are closed and bus and ferry services are either drastically reduced or plain cancelled.

The cobwebs are dusted off in time for Easter, when the first tourists start to arrive. Conditions are perfect between Easter and mid-June, when the weather is pleasantly warm in most places, but not too hot; beaches and ancient sites are relatively uncrowded; public transport operates on close to full schedules; and accommodation is cheaper and easy to find.

Mid-June until the end of August is the high season. It's party time on the islands and everything is in full swing. It's also very hot – in July and August the mercury can soar to 40°C (100°F) in the shade, the beaches are crowded, the ancient sites are swarming with tour groups, and in many places accommodation is booked solid.

The season starts to wind down in September, and conditions are ideal once more until the end of October.

Maps

Mapping is an important feature of this guide. Unless you are going to trek or drive, you probably won't need to buy additional maps.

Most tourist offices hand out free maps, but they are often out of date and not particularly accurate. The same applies to the cheap (400 to 500 dr) 'tourist maps' sold on every island.

The best maps are published by the Greek company Road Editions. There is a wide range of maps to suit various needs, starting with a 1:500,000 map of Greece.

Crete is covered by the company's 1:250,000 maroon-cover mainland series.

Other islands are covered by its blue-cover island series. At the time of writing, the series featured Corfu, Kea (Tzia), Kefallonia and Ithaki, Kos, Lefkada, Milos, Paxi & Antipaxi, Rhodes, Santorini, Syros and Zakynthos. Maps of Andros, Kythira, Mykonos, Naxos, Paros and Samos should be available by the time you read this. The scale of these maps ranges from 1:100,000 for larger islands like Corfu and Rhodes to 1:30,000 for Syros.

Even the smallest roads and villages are clearly marked, and the distance indicators are spot-on – important when negotiating your way around the backblocks. Useful features include symbols to indicate the location of petrol stations and tyre shops.

Freytag & Berndt's 15-map Greece series has good coverage of the islands.

What to Bring

Sturdy shoes are essential for clambering around ancient sites and wandering around historic towns and villages, which tend to have lots of steps and cobbled streets. Footwear with ankle support is preferable for trekking, although many visitors get by with trainers.

A day-pack is useful for the beach, and for sightseeing or trekking. A compass is essential if you are going to trek in remote areas, as is a whistle, which you can use should you become lost or disorientated. A torch (flashlight) is not only needed if you intend to explore caves, but comes in handy during occasional power cuts. If you like to fill a washbasin or bathtub (a rarity in Greece), bring a universal plug as Greek bathrooms rarely have plugs.

Many island camping grounds have covered areas where tourists without tents can sleep in summer, so you can get by with a lightweight sleeping bag and foam bedroll.

You will need only light clothing – preferably cotton – during the summer months. During spring and autumn you'll need a light sweater or jacket in the evening.

In summer, a broad-rimmed sun hat and sunglasses are essential (see the Health section later in this chapter). Sunscreen creams are expensive, as are moisturising and cleansing creams.

If you read a lot, it's a good idea to bring along a few disposable paperbacks to read and swap.

TOURIST OFFICES

Tourist information is handled by the Greek National Tourist Organisation, known by the initials GNTO abroad and EOT (Ellinikos Organismos Tourismou) in Greece.

Local Tourist Offices

The address of the EOT's head office is Amerikis 2, Athens 105 64 (☎ 01-322 3111). There are about 25 EOT offices throughout Greece. Most EOT staff speak English, but they vary in their enthusiasm and helpfulness. Some offices, like that in Athens, have loads of useful local information, but most have nothing more than glossy brochures, usually about other parts of the country. Some have absolutely nothing to offer.

In addition to EOT offices, there are also municipal tourist offices. They are often more helpful.

Tourist Offices Abroad

GNTO offices abroad include:

Australia
  (☎ 02-9241 1663/1664/1665) 51 Pitt St, Sydney NSW 2000
Austria
  (☎ 1-512 5317/5318) Opernring 8, Vienna A-10105
Belgium
  (☎ 2-647 5770) 172 Ave Louise Louizalaan, B-1050 Brussels
Canada
  (☎ 416-968 2220) 1300 Bay St, Toronto, Ontario M5R 3K8
Denmark
  (☎ 3-325 332) Vester Farimagsgade 1, 1606 Copenhagen
France
  (☎ 01-42 60 65 75) 3 Ave de l'Opéra, Paris 75001
Germany
  (☎ 69-237 735) Neue Mainzerstrasse 22, 60311 Frankfurt

(☎ 89-222 035/036) Pacellistrasse 5, W 80333 Munich 2
(☎ 40-454 498) Abteistrasse 33, 20149 Hamburg 13
(☎ 30-217 6262) Wittenbergplatz 3A, 10789 Berlin 30

Israel
(☎ 23-517 0501) 5 Shalom Aleichem St, Tel Aviv 61262

Italy
(☎ 06-474 4249) Via L Bissolati 78-80, Rome 00187
(☎ 02-860 470) Piazza Diaz 1, 20123 Milan

Japan
(☎ 03-350 55 911) Fukuda Building West, 5F 2-11-3 Akasaka, Minato-Ku, Tokyo 107

Netherlands
(☎ 020-625 4212/4213/4214) Leidsestraat 13, Amsterdam NS 1017

Norway
(☎ 2-426 501) Ovre Slottsgate 15B, 0157 Oslo 1

Sweden
(☎ 8-679 6480) Birger Jarlsgatan 30, Box 5298 S, 10246 Stockholm

Switzerland
(☎ 01-221 0105) Loewenstrasse 25, CH 8001 Zürich

UK
(☎ 020-7499 4976) 4 Conduit St, London W1R ODJ

USA
(☎ 212-421 5777) Olympic Tower, 645 5th Ave, New York, NY 10022
(☎ 312-782 1084) Suite 600, 168 North Michigan Ave, Chicago, Illinois 60601
(☎ 213-626 6696) Suite 2198, 611 West 6th St, Los Angeles, California 92668

Tourist Police

The tourist police work in cooperation with the regular Greek police and EOT. Each tourist police office has at least one member of staff who speaks English. Hotels, restaurants, travel agencies, tourist shops, tourist guides, waiters, taxi drivers and bus drivers all come under the jurisdiction of the tourist police. If you think that you have been ripped off by any of these, report it to the tourist police and they will investigate.

If you need to report a theft or loss of passport, the tourist police will act as interpreters between you and the regular police. The tourist police also fulfil the same functions as the EOT and municipal tourist offices, dispensing maps and brochures, and giving information on transport.

VISAS & DOCUMENTS
Passport

To enter Greece you need a valid passport or, for EU nationals, travel documents (ID cards). You must produce your passport or EU travel documents when you register in a hotel or pension in Greece. You will find that many accommodation proprietors will want to keep your passport during your stay. This is not a compulsory requirement: they need it only long enough to take down the details.

Visas

The list of countries whose nationals can stay in Greece for up to three months without a visa include Australia, Canada, all EU countries, Iceland, Israel, Japan, New Zealand, Norway, Switzerland and the USA. Other countries included are Cyprus, Malta, the European principalities of Monaco and San Marino, and most South American countries. The list changes, so contact Greek embassies for the full list. Those not on the list can expect to pay about US$20 for a three month visa.

North Cyprus Greece will refuse entry to people whose passport indicates that they have visited Turkish-occupied North Cyprus since November 1983. This can be overcome if, upon entering North Cyprus, you ask the immigration officials to stamp a piece of paper (loose-leaf visa) rather than your passport. If you enter North Cyprus from the Greek Republic of Cyprus (only possible for a day visit), an exit stamp is not put into your passport.

Visa Extensions If you want to stay in Greece for longer than three months, apply at a consulate abroad or at least 20 days in advance to the Aliens Bureau (☎ 01-770 5711), Leoforos Alexandras 173, Athens. Take your passport and four passport photographs along. You may be asked for proof that you can support yourself financially, so keep all your bank exchange slips (or the equivalent from a post office). These slips are not always automatically given – you may have to ask for them. The Aliens Bureau is open 8 am to 1 pm on weekdays. Elsewhere in Greece apply to the local police authority. You will be given a permit which will authorise you to stay in the country for a period of up to six months.

Most travellers get around this by visiting Bulgaria or Turkey briefly and then re-entering Greece.

Travel Insurance

A travel insurance policy to cover theft, loss and medical problems is a good idea. The policies handled by STA Travel and other student travel organisations are usually good value.

There is a wide variety of policies available; check the small print. Some policies specifically exclude 'dangerous activities' which can include scuba diving, motorcycling, even trekking. A locally acquired motorcycle licence is not valid under some policies.

You may prefer a policy that pays doctors or hospitals direct rather than you having to pay on the spot and claim later. If you have to claim later make sure you keep all documentation. Some policies ask you to call back (reverse charges) to a centre in your home country where an immediate assessment of your problem is made.

Check that the policy covers ambulances or an emergency flight home.

Driving Licence & Permits

Greece recognises all national driving licences, provided the licence has been held for at least one year. It also recognises an International Driving Permit, which should be obtained before you leave home.

Hostel Cards

A Hostelling International (HI) card is of limited use in Greece. The only place you will be able to use it is at the Athens International Youth Hostel.

Student & Youth Cards

The most widely recognised (and thus the most useful) form of student ID is the International Student Identity Card (ISIC). Holders qualify for half-price admission to museums and ancient sites and for discounts at some budget hotels and hostels. Several travel agencies in Athens are licensed to issue cards. They are listed in the Information section of the Athens chapter.

Student Cards

An ISIC (International Student Identity Card) is a plastic ID-style card displaying your photograph. These cards are widely available from budget travel agencies (take along proof that you are a student). In Athens you can get one from the International Student & Youth Travel Service (ISYTS; ☎ 01-323 3767), 2nd floor, Nikis 11.

Some travel agencies in Greece offer discounts on organised tours to students. However, there are no student discounts for travel within Greece (although Olympic Airways gives a 25% discount on domestic flights which are part of an international flight). Turkish Airlines (THY) gives 55% student discounts on its international flights. THY has flights from Athens to İstanbul and İzmir. Most ferries to Cyprus, Israel and Egypt from Piraeus give a 20% student discount and a few of the services between Greek and Italian ports do so also. If you are under 26 years but not a student, the Federation of International Youth Travel Organisation (FIYTO) card gives similar discounts. Many budget travel agencies issue FIYTO cards including London Explorers Club, 33 Princes Square, Bayswater, London W2 (☎ 020-7792 3770); and SRS Studenten Reise Service, Marienstrasse 23, Berlin (☎ 030-2 83 30 93).

You will need to show documents proving you are a student, provide a passport photo and cough up 2500 dr.

Air Greece and Cronus Airlines both offer student discounts on domestic flights, but there are no discounts on buses, ferries or trains.

Seniors' Cards
See the Senior Travellers section later in this chapter.

Photocopies
All important documents (passport data page and visa page, credit cards, travel insurance policy, air/bus/train tickets, driving licence etc) should be photocopied before you leave home. Leave one copy with someone at home and keep another with you, separate from the originals.

It's also a good idea to store details of your vital travel documents in Lonely Planet's free online Travel Vault in case you lose the photocopies or can't be bothered with them. Your password-protected Travel Vault is accessible online anywhere in the world – create it at www.ekno.lonelyplanet.com.

EMBASSIES & CONSULATES
Greek Embassies & Consulates
The following is a selection of Greek diplomatic missions abroad:

Australia
(☎ 02-6273 3011) 9 Turrana St, Yarralumla, Canberra ACT 2600
Bulgaria
(☎ 92-946 1027) San Stefano 33, Sofia 1504
Canada
(☎ 613-238 6271) 76-80 Maclaren St, Ottawa, Ontario K2P OK6
Cyprus
(☎ 02-441 880/8801) Byron Boulevard 8-10, Nicosia
Denmark
(☎ 33-11 4533) Borgergade 16, 1300 Copenhagen K
Egypt
(☎ 02-355 1074) 18 Aisha el Taymouria, Garden City, Cairo
France
(☎ 01-47 23 72 28) 17 Rue Auguste Vacquerie, 75116 Paris

Germany
(☎ 228-83010) An Der Marienkapelleb 10, 53 179 Bonn
Ireland
(☎ 01-676 7254) 1 Upper Pembroke St, Dublin 2
Israel
(☎ 03-605 5461) 47 Bodenheimer St, Tel Aviv 62008
Italy
(☎ 06-854 9630) Via S Mercadante 36, Rome 00198
Japan
(☎ 03-340 0871/0872) 3-16-30 Nishi Azabu, Minato-ku, Tokyo 106
Netherlands
(☎ 070-363 87 00) Koninginnegracht 37, 2514 AD, Den Hague
New Zealand
(☎ 04-473 7775) 5-7 Willeston St, Wellington
Norway
(☎ 22-44 2728) Nobels Gate 45, 0244 Oslo 2
South Africa
(☎ 12-437 351/352) 995 Pretorius Street, Arcadia, Pretoria 0083
Spain
(☎ 01-564 4653) Avenida Doctor Arce 24, Madrid 28002
Sweden
(☎ 08-663 7577) Riddargatan 60, 11457 Stockholm
Switzerland
(☎ 31-951 0814) Postfach, 3000 Berne 6, Kirchenfeld
Turkey
(☎ 312-436 8860) Ziya-ul-Rahman Caddesi 9-11, Gaziosmanpasa 06700, Ankara
UK
(☎ 020-7229 3850) 1A Holland Park, London W11 3TP
USA
(☎ 202-939 5818) 2221 Massachusetts Ave NW, Washington DC 20008

Embassies & Consulates in Greece
All foreign embassies in Greece are in Athens and its suburbs (telephone code 01). They include:

Australia
(☎ 645 0404) Dimitrou Soutsou 37, Athens 115 21
Bulgaria
(☎ 647 8105) Stratigou Kalari 33A, Psyhiko, Athens 154 52

Canada
   (☎ 727 3400) Genadiou 4, Athens 115 21
Cyprus
   (☎ 723 7883) Irodotou 16, Athens 106 75
Egypt
   (☎ 361 8613) Leoforos Vasilissis Sofias 3,
   Athens 106 71
France
   (☎ 339 1000) Leoforos Vasilissis Sofias 7,
   Athens 106 71
Germany
   (☎ 728 5111) Dimitriou 3 & Karaoli, Kolonaki,
   Athens 106 75
Ireland
   (☎ 723 2771) Leoforos Vasileos Konstantinou
   7, Athens 106 74
Israel
   (☎ 671 9530) Marathonodromou 1, Psyhiko,
   Athens 154 52
Italy
   (☎ 361 7260) Sekeri 2, Athens 106 74
Japan
   (☎ 775 8101) Athens Tower, Leoforos
   Messogion 2-4, Athens 115 27
Netherlands
   (☎ 723 9701) Vasileos Konstantinou 5-7,
   Athens 106 74
New Zealand (Consulate)
   (☎ 771 0112) Xenias 24, Athens 115 28
South Africa
   (☎ 680 6645) Kifissias 60, Maroussi, Athens
   151 25
Turkey
   (☎ 724 5915) Vasilissis Georgiou 8, Athens
   106 74
UK
   (☎ 723 6211) Ploutarhou 1, Athens 106 75
USA
   (☎ 721 2951) Leoforos Vasilissis Sofias 91,
   Athens 115 21
Yugoslavia
   (☎ 031-244 266, fax 240 412) Komninon 4,
   Thessaloniki

Generally speaking, your own country's embassy won't be much help in emergencies if the trouble you're in is remotely your own fault. Remember that you are bound by Greek laws. Your embassy will not be sympathetic if you end up in jail after committing a crime locally, even if such actions are legal in your own country.

In genuine emergencies you might get some assistance, but only if other channels have been exhausted. For example, if you need to get home urgently, a free ticket home is exceedingly unlikely - the embassy would expect you to have insurance. If you have all your money and documents stolen, it might assist with getting a new passport, but a loan for onward travel is out of the question.

CUSTOMS

There are no longer duty-free restrictions within the EU. This does not mean, however, that customs checks have been dispensed with – random searches are still made for drugs.

Upon entering the country from outside the EU, customs inspection is usually cursory for foreign tourists. There may be spot checks, but you probably won't have to open your bags. A verbal declaration is usually all that is required.

You may bring the following into Greece duty-free: 200 cigarettes or 50 cigars; 1L of spirits or 2L of wine; 50g of perfume; 250ml of eau de Cologne; one camera (still or video) and film; a pair of binoculars; a portable musical instrument; a portable radio or tape recorder; a typewriter; sports equipment; and dogs and cats (with a veterinary certificate).

Importation of works of art and antiquities is free, but they must be declared on entry, so that they can be re-exported. Import regulations for medicines are strict; if you are taking medication, make sure you get a statement from your doctor before you leave home. It is illegal, for instance, to take codeine into Greece without an accompanying doctor's certificate.

An unlimited amount of foreign currency and travellers cheques may be brought into Greece. If, however, you intend to leave the country with foreign banknotes in excess of US$1000, you must declare the sum upon entry.

Restrictions apply to the importation of sailboards into Greece. See the Activities section later in this chapter for more details.

It is strictly forbidden to export antiquities (anything over 100 years old) without an export permit. This crime is second only to drug smuggling in the penalties imposed.

It is an offence to remove even the smallest article from an archaeological site.

The place to apply for an export permit is the Antique Dealers & Private Collections Section, Archaeological Service, Polygnotou 13, Athens.

Vehicles
Cars can be brought into Greece for four months without a carnet; only a green card (international third party insurance) is required. Your vehicle will be registered in your passport when you enter Greece to prevent you from leaving the country without it.

MONEY
Currency
The unit of currency in Greece is the drachma (dr). Coins come in denominations of five, 10, 20, 50 and 100 dr. Banknotes come in 100, 200, 500, 1000, 5000 and 10,000 dr.

Exchange Rates

country	unit		drachma
Albania	100 lekë	=	231.20
Australia	A$1	=	195.35
Bulgaria	1000 leva	=	159.30
Canada	C$1	=	203.06
euro	€1	=	329.32
France	1FF	=	50.20
Germany	DM1	=	168.38
Italy	L1000	=	170.10
Japan	¥100	=	288.41
New Zealand	NZ$1	=	154.21
United Kingdom	UK£1	=	506.17
United States	US$1	=	303.15

Warning It's all but impossible to exchange Turkish lira in Greece. The only place you can change them is at the head office of the National Bank of Greece, Panepistimiou 36, Athens – and it'll give only about 75% of the going international rate.

Exchanging Money
Banks will exchange all major currencies in either cash, travellers cheques or Eurocheques. The best-known travellers cheques in Greece are Thomas Cook and American Express. A passport is required to change travellers cheques, but not cash.

Commission charged on the exchange of banknotes and travellers cheques varies not only from bank to bank but from branch to branch. It's less for cash than for travellers cheques. For travellers cheques the commission is 350 dr for up to 20,000 dr; 450 dr for amounts between 20,000 and 30,000 dr; and a flat rate of 1.5% on amounts over 30,000 dr.

Post offices can exchange banknotes – but not travellers cheques – and charge less commission than banks. Many travel agencies and hotels will also change money and travellers cheques at bank rates, but their commission charges are higher.

If there is a chance that you may apply for a visa extension, make sure you receive, and keep hold of, a bank exchange slip after each transaction.

Cash
Nothing beats cash for convenience – or for risk. If you lose it, it's gone for good and very few travel insurers will come to your rescue. Those that will, normally limit the amount to about US$300. It's best to carry no more cash than you need for the next few days, which means working out your likely needs when you change travellers cheques or withdraw cash from an ATM.

It's also a good idea to set aside a small amount of cash, say US$50, as an emergency stash.

Travellers Cheques
The main reason to carry travellers cheques rather than cash is the protection they offer against theft. They are, however, losing popularity as more and more travellers opt to put their money in a bank at home and withdraw it at ATMs as they go along.

American Express, Visa and Thomas Cook cheques are all widely accepted and have efficient replacement policies. Maintaining a record of the cheque numbers and recording when you use them is vital when it comes to replacing lost cheques. Keep this record separate from the cheques themselves. US dollars are a good currency to use.

ATMs

ATMs (automatic teller machines) are to be found in almost every town large enough to support a bank – and certainly in all the tourist areas. If you've got MasterCard or Visa/Access, there are plenty of places to withdraw money.

Cirrus and Maestro users can make withdrawals in all major towns and tourist areas.

AFEMs (Automatic Foreign Exchange Machines) are common in major tourist areas. They take all the major European currencies, Australian and US dollars and Japanese yen, and are useful in an emergency.

Credit Cards

The great advantage of credit cards is that they allow you to pay for major items without carrying around great wads of cash. Credit cards are now an accepted part of the commercial scene just about everywhere in Greece. They can be used to pay for a wide range of goods and services such as upmarket meals and accommodation, car hire and souvenir shopping.

If you are not familiar with the card options, ask your bank to explain the workings and relative merits of the various schemes: cash cards, charge cards and credit cards. Ask whether the card can be replaced in Greece if it is lost or stolen.

The main credit cards are MasterCard, Visa (Access in the UK) and Eurocard, all of which are widely accepted in Greece. They can also be used as cash cards to draw drachma from the ATMs of affiliated Greek banks in the same way as at home. Daily withdrawal limits are set by the issuing bank. Cash advances are given in local currency only. Credit cards can be used to pay for accommodation in all the smarter hotels. Some C class hotels will accept credit cards, but D and E class hotels rarely do. Most upmarket shops and restaurants accept credit cards.

The main charge cards are American Express and Diner's Club Card, which are widely accepted in tourist areas but unheard of elsewhere.

International Transfers

If you run out of money or need more for whatever reason, you can instruct your bank back home to send you a draft. Specify the city and the bank as well as the branch that you want the money sent to. If you have the choice, select a large bank and ask for the international division. Money sent by electronic transfer should reach you within 24 hours.

Security

The safest way of carrying cash and valuables (passport, travellers cheques, credit cards etc) is a favourite topic of travel conversation. The simple answer is that there is no foolproof method. The general principle is to keep things out of sight. The front pouch belt, for example, presents an obvious target for a would-be thief – only marginally less inviting than a fat wallet bulging from your back pocket.

The best place is under your clothes in contact with your skin where, hopefully, you will be aware of an alien hand before it's too late. Most people opt for a money belt, while others prefer a leather pouch hung around the neck. Whichever method you choose, put your valuables in a plastic bag first – otherwise they will get soaked in sweat as you wander around in the heat.

Costs

Greece is still a cheap country by northern European standards, but it is no longer dirt-cheap. A rock-bottom daily budget would be 6000 dr. This would mean hitching, staying in youth hostels or camping, staying away from bars, and only occasionally eating in restaurants or taking ferries. Allow at least 12,000 dr per day if you want your own room and plan to eat out regularly as well as travelling about and seeing the sights. You will still need to do a fair bit of self-catering. If you really want a holiday – comfortable rooms and restaurants all the way – you will need closer to 20,000 dr per day. These budgets are for individuals; sharing a double room will cost less.

Prices vary quite a lot between islands, particularly for accommodation. Hydra and Mykonos are the most expensive; the cheapest tend to be the most remote islands.

Tipping & Bargaining

In restaurants the service charge is included in the bill but it is the custom to leave a small tip. The practice is often just to round off the bill. Likewise for taxis – a small amount is appreciated.

Bargaining is not as widespread in Greece as it is further east. Prices in most shops are clearly marked and non-negotiable. The same applies to restaurants and public transport. It is always worth bargaining over the price of hotel rooms or *domatia* (the Greek equivalent of the British bed and breakfast, minus the breakfast), especially if you are intending to stay a few days. You may get short shrift in peak season, but prices can drop dramatically in the off season. Souvenir shops and market stalls are other places where your negotiating skills will come in handy. If you feel uncomfortable about haggling, walking away can be just as effective – you can always go back.

POST & COMMUNICATIONS
Post

Post offices *(tahydromio)* are easily identifiable by means of the yellow signs outside. Regular post boxes are also yellow. The red boxes are for express mail only.

Postal Rates The postal rate for postcards and airmail letters to destinations within the EU is 170 dr for up to 20g and 270 dr for up to 50g. To other destinations the rate is 200 dr for up to 20g and 300 dr for up to 150g. Post within Europe takes five to eight days and to the USA, Australia and New Zealand, nine to 11 days. Some tourist shops also sell stamps, but with a 10% surcharge.

Express mail costs an extra 400 dr and should ensure delivery in three days within the EU – use the special red post boxes. Valuables should be sent registered post, which costs an extra 350 dr.

Sending Mail Do not wrap a parcel until it has been inspected at a post office. In Athens, take your parcel to the Parcel Post Office (☎ 01-322 8940) in the arcade at Stadiou 4, and elsewhere to the parcel counter of a regular post office.

Receiving Mail You can receive mail at poste restante (general delivery) at any main post office. The service is free of charge, but you are required to show your passport. Ask senders to write your family name in capital letters on the envelope and underline it, and to mark the envelope 'poste restante'. It is a good idea to ask the post office clerk to check under your first name as well if letters you are expecting cannot be located. After one month, uncollected mail is returned to the sender. If you are about to leave a town and expected mail hasn't arrived, ask at the post office to have it forwarded to your next destination, c/o poste restante.

See the Post section in the Athens chapter for addresses of post offices that hold poste restante mail.

Parcels are not delivered in Greece, they must be collected from the parcel counter of a post office – or, in Athens, from the Parcel Post Office.

Telephone

The Greek telephone service is maintained by the public corporation known as Organismos Tilepikoinonion Ellados, which is always referred to by the acronym OTE (pronounced O-tay). The system is modern and efficient. Public telephones all use phonecards, which cost 1000 dr for 100 units, 1800 dr for 200 units, 4200 dr for 500 units, and 8200 dr for 1000 units. The 100-unit cards are widely available at *periptera* (street kiosks), corner shops and tourist shops; the others can be bought at OTE offices.

The phones are easy to operate and can be used for local, long distance and international calls. The 'i' at the top left of the push-button dialling panel brings up the operating instructions in English. Don't remove your card before you are told to do so or you will wipe out the remaining credit. Local calls cost one unit per minute.

It is possible to use various national card schemes, such as Telstra Australia's Telecard, to make international calls. You will still need a phonecard to dial the scheme's access number, which will cost you one unit, and the time you spend on the phone is charged at local call rates.

International calls can also be made from OTE offices. A counter clerk directs you to a cubicle equipped with a metered phone, and payment is made afterwards. Villages and remote islands without OTE offices almost always have at least one metered phone for international and long distance calls – usually in a shop, *kafeneio* (cafe) or taverna.

Reverse charge (collect) calls can be made from an OTE office. If you are using a private phone to make a reverse charge call, dial the operator (domestic ☎ 151, international ☎ 161).

To call overseas direct from Greece, dial the Greek overseas access code (☎ 00), followed by the country code for the country you are calling, then the local area code (dropping the leading zero if there is one) and then the number. The table below lists some country codes and per-minute charges:

Country	Code	Cost per minute
Australia	61	236 dr
France	33	183 dr
Germany	49	183 dr
Ireland	353	183 dr
Italy	39	183 dr
Japan	81	319 dr
Netherlands	31	183 dr
New Zealand	64	319 dr
Turkey	90	183 dr
UK	44	183 dr
USA & Canada	1	236 dr

Off-peak rates are 25% cheaper. They are available to Africa, Europe, the Middle East and India between 10 pm and 6 am; to the

Useful Phone Numbers	
Directory inquiries	☎ 131
International dialling instructions in English, French and German	☎ 169
International access code to call Greece	☎ 30
International access code from within Greece	☎ 00

Toll-free 24 hour emergency numbers:

Police	☎ 100
Tourist Police	☎ 171
Ambulance (Athens)	☎ 166
Fire Brigade	☎ 199
Roadside Assistance (ELPA)	☎ 104

Americas between 11 pm and 8 am; and to Asia and Oceania between 8 pm and 5 am.

To call Greece the international access code is ☎ 30.

Fax & Telegraph
Most post offices have fax machines; telegrams can be sent from any OTE office.

Email & Internet Access
Greece was slow to embrace the wonders of the Internet, but is now striving to make up for lost time. Internet cafes are springing up everywhere, and are listed under the Information section for cities and islands where available.

There has also been a huge increase in the number of hotels and businesses using email, and these addresses have been listed where available. Some hotels catering for travellers offer Internet access.

INTERNET RESOURCES
Predictably enough, there has also been a huge increase in the number of Web sites providing information about Greece.

A good place to start is the *500 Links to Greece* site at www.viking1.com/corfu/link.htm. It has links to a huge range of sites covering everything from accommodation to Zeus. The address takes you to www .greektravel.com, an assortment of interesting and informative sites by Matt Barrett.

The Greek Ministry of Culture has put together an excellent site, www.culture.gr, with loads of information about museums and ancient sites.

You'll find addresses of more specialist Web sites listed throughout the book.

BOOKS

Most books are published in different editions by different publishers in different countries. As a result, a book might be a hardcover rarity in one country while it's readily available in paperback in another. Fortunately, bookshops and libraries search by title or author, so your local bookshop or library is best placed to advise you on the availability of the following recommendations.

Lonely Planet

The 4th edition of Lonely Planet's guide to *Greece* has comprehensive coverage of mainland Greece as well as the islands, while the Lonely Planet guides to *Mediterranean Europe* and *Western Europe* also include coverage of Greece as does *Europe on a shoestring*. The regional titles *Corfu & the Ionian Islands*, *Crete* and *Crete Condensed* will be published in 2000. The handy *Greek phrasebook* will enrich your visit.

Katherine Kizilos vividly evokes Greece's landscapes, people and politics in her book *The Olive Grove: Travels in Greece*. She explores the islands and borderlands of her father's homeland, and life in her family's village in the Peloponnese mountains. The book is part of the Journeys travel literature series.

These titles are available at major English-language bookshops in Athens, Thessaloniki, Rhodes and Iraklio. See the Bookshop entries in these sections for more details.

Guidebooks

For archaeology buffs, the *Blue Guides* are hard to beat. They go into tremendous detail about all the major sites, and many of the lesser known ones. They have a separate guide for Crete.

Travel

English writer Lawrence Durrell, who spent an idyllic childhood on Corfu, is the best known of the 20th Century philhellenes who helped in Greece's struggle for self-determination. His evocative books *Prospero's Cell* and *Reflections on a Marine Venus* are about Corfu and Rhodes respectively. His coffee-table book *The Greek Islands* is one of the most popular books of its kind. Even if you disagree with Durrell's opinions, you will probably concede that the photographs are superb. *My Family and Other Animals* by his brother Gerald Durrell is a hilarious account of the Durrell family's chaotic and wonderful life on Corfu.

Under Mount Ida: A Journey into Crete by Oliver Burch is a compelling portrayal of this diverse and beautiful island – full of insights into its landscape, history and people.

The Colossus of Maroussi by Henry Miller is now regarded as a classic. Miller relates his travels in Greece at the outbreak of WWII with feverish enthusiasm.

People & Society

Of the numerous festivals held in Greece, one of the most bizarre and overtly pagan is the carnival held on the island of Skyros, described in *The Goat Dancers of Skyros* by Joy Coulentianou.

The Cyclades, or Life Amongst the Insular Greeks by James Theodore Bent (first published 1885) is still the greatest English-language book about the Greek Islands. It relates the experiences of the author and his wife while travelling around the Cyclades in the late 19th century. The book is now out of print but the Hellenic Book Service may have a second-hand copy; see the Bookshops section later in this chapter.

Time, Religion & Social Experience in Rural Greece by Laurie Kain Hart is a fascinating account of village traditions – many of which are alive and well beneath the tourist veneer.

History & Mythology

A Traveller's History of Greece by Timothy Boatswain & Colin Nicholson gives the layperson a good general reference on the historical background of Greece, from Neolithic times to the present day.

Modern Greece: A Short History by CM Woodhouse is in a similar vein, although it has a right-wing bent. It covers the period from Constantine the Great to 1990.

Mythology was an intrinsic part of life in ancient Greece, and some knowledge of it will enhance your visit. *The Greek Myths* by Robert Graves is regarded as the definitive book on the subject. Maureen O'Sullivan's *An Iconoclast's Guide to the Greek Gods* presents entertaining and accessible versions of the myths.

There are many translations of Homer's *Iliad* and *Odyssey*, which tell the story of the Trojan War and the subsequent adventures of Odysseus. The translations by EV Rien are among the best.

The Argonautica Expedition by Theodor Troev encompasses Greek mythology, archaeology, travel and adventure. It relates the voyage undertaken by the author and his crew in the 1980s following in the footsteps of Jason and the Argonauts.

Mary Renault's novels provide an excellent feel for ancient Greece. *The King Must Die* and *The Bull from the Sea* are vivid tales of Minoan times.

Poetry

Sappho: A New Translation by Mary Bernard is the best translation of this great ancient poet's works.

Collected Poems by George Seferis, *Selected Poems* by Odysseus Elytis and *Collected Poems* by Constantine Cavafy are all excellent translations of Greece's greatest modern poets.

Novels

The most well known and widely read Greek author is the Cretan writer Nikos Kazantzakis, whose novels are full of drama and larger-than-life characters. His most famous works are *The Last Tempta-*
tion, *Zorba the Greek*, *Christ Recrucified* and *Freedom or Death*. The first two have been made into films.

English writer Louis de Bernières has become almost a cult figure following the success of *Captain Corelli's Mandolin*, which tells the emotional story of a young Italian army officer sent to the island of Kefallonia during WWII.

Australian journalists George Johnston and Charmian Clift wrote several books with Greek themes during their 19 years as expatriates, including Johnston's novel *The Sponge Divers*, set on Kalymnos, and Clift's autobiographical *A Mermaid Singing*, which is about their experiences on Hydra.

The Mermaid Madonna and *The Schoolmistress with the Golden Eyes* are two passionate novels by Stratis Myrivilis, set in two villages on the island of Lesvos.

Botanical Field Guides

The Flowers of Greece & the Aegean by William Taylor & Anthony Huxley is the most comprehensive field guide to Greece. The Greek writer, naturalist and mountaineer George Sfikas has written many books on wildlife in Greece. Among them are *Wildflowers of Greece*, *Trees & Shrubs of Greece* and *Medicinal Plants of Greece*.

Children's Books

The Greek publisher Malliaris-Paedia puts out a good series of books on the myths, retold in English for young readers by Aristides Kesopoulos. The titles are *The Gods of Olympus and the Lesser Gods*, *The Labours of Hercules*, *Theseus and the Voyage of the Argonauts*, *The Trojan War and the Wanderings of Odysseus* and *Heroes and Mythical Creatures*.

Robin Lister's retelling of *The Odyssey* is aimed at slightly older readers (ages 10 to 12), but makes compelling listening for younger children.

Bookshops

There are several specialist English-language bookshops in Athens, and shops selling books in French, German and Italian.

There are also good foreign-language book-shops in Iraklio, Rhodes, Patras and Thessaloniki (see those sections for details).

All other major towns and tourist resorts have bookshops that sell some foreign-language books. Imported books are expensive – normally two to three times the recommended retail price in the UK and the USA. Many hotels have second-hand books to read or swap.

Abroad, the best bookshop for new and second-hand books about Greece, written in both English and Greek, is the Hellenic Book Service (☎ 020-7267 9499; fax 020-7267 9498), 91 Fortress Rd, Kentish Town, London NW5 1AG. It stocks almost all of the books recommended here.

FILMS

Greece is nothing if not photogenic, and countless films have made the most of the country's range of superb locations. The islands do, of course, figure prominently. Mykonos was the setting for the smash hit *Shirley Valentine*, featuring Pauline Collins in the title role and Tom Conti as her Greek toy boy. *Mediterraneo* (1991) is an Italian movie that achieved cult status worldwide. It was set on Kastellorizo.

Those with longer memories may recall Gregory Peck and David Niven leading the assault on the *Guns of Navarone* back in 1961. It was filmed on the island of Rhodes.

NEWSPAPERS & MAGAZINES

Greeks are great newspaper readers. There are 15 daily newspapers, of which the most widely read are *Ta Nea*, *Kathimerini* and *Eleftheros Typos*.

The main English-language newspapers are the daily (except Monday) *Athens News* (250 dr) which carries Greek and international news, and the weekly *Hellenic Times* (300 dr), with predominantly Greek news. In addition to these, the Athens edition of the *International Herald Tribune* (350 dr) includes an English-language edition of the Greek daily *Kathimerini*. All are widely available in Athens and at major resorts. You'll find the *Athens News* electronic edition on the Internet at athensnews.dolnet .gr. The site's archives date back to 1995.

Foreign newspapers are also widely available, although only between April and October on smaller islands. You'll find all the British and other major European dailies, as well as international magazines such as *Time*, *Newsweek* and the *Economist*. The papers reach Athens (Syntagma) at 3 pm on the day of publication on weekdays, and at 7 pm on weekends. They are not available until the following day in other areas.

RADIO & TV

Greece has two state-owned radio channels, ET 1 and ET 2. ET 1 runs three programs; two are devoted to popular music and news, while the third plays mostly classical music. It has a news update in English at 7.30 am Monday to Saturday, and at 9 pm Monday to Friday. It can be heard on 91.6 MHz and 105.8 MHz on the FM band, and 729 KHz on the AM band. ET 2 broadcasts mainly popular music.

Commercial radio stations tend to confine their broadcasts to major urban areas. The hills around Athens are bristling with radio transmitters, but the choice is very limited on the islands.

The best short-wave frequencies for picking up the BBC World Service are:

GMT	Frequency
3 to 7.30 am	9.41 MHz (31m band)
	6.18 MHz (49m band)
	15.07 MHz (19m band)
7.30 am to 6 pm	12.09 MHz (25m band)
	15.07 MHz (19m band)
6.30 to 11.15 pm	12.09 MHz (25m band)
	9.41 MHz (31m band)
	6.18 MHz (49m band)

As far as Greek TV is concerned, it's a case of quantity rather than quality. There are nine TV channels and various pay-TV channels. All the channels show English and US films and soapies with Greek subtitles. A bit of channel-swapping will normally turn up something in English.

VIDEO SYSTEMS

If you want to record or buy video tapes to play back home, you won't get a picture unless the image registration systems are the same. Greece uses PAL, which is incompatible with the North American and Japanese NTSC system. Australia and most of Europe use PAL.

PHOTOGRAPHY & VIDEO
Film & Equipment

Major brands of film are widely available. In Athens, expect to pay about 1500 dr for a 36 exposure roll of Kodak Gold ASA 100; less for other brands. You'll pay more on the islands, particularly in remoter areas, when old stock can also be a problem. You'll find all the gear you need in the photography shops of Athens and other major towns and tourist areas.

Because of the brilliant sunlight in summer, you'll get better results using a polarising lens filter.

As elsewhere in the world, developing film is a competitive business. Most places charge around 80 dr per print, plus a 400 dr service charge.

Restrictions

Never photograph a military installation or anything else that has a sign forbidding photography. Flash photography is not allowed inside churches, and it's considered taboo to photograph the main altar.

Greeks usually love having their photos taken, but always ask permission first. The same goes for video cameras.

TIME

Greece is two hours ahead of GMT/UTC and three hours ahead on daylight-saving time, which begins on the last Sunday in March, when clocks are put forward one hour. Daylight saving ends on the last Sunday in September.

So, when it is noon in Greece it is also noon in Istanbul, 10 am in London, 11 am in Rome, 2 am in San Francisco, 5 am in New York and Toronto, 8 pm in Sydney and 10 pm in Auckland.

ELECTRICITY

Electricity is 220V, 50 cycles. Plugs are the standard continental type with two round pins. All hotel rooms have power points and most camping grounds have supply points.

WEIGHTS & MEASURES

Greece uses the metric system. Liquids – especially barrel wine – are sold by weight rather than volume: 959g of wine, for example, is equivalent to 1000mL.

Remember that, like other continental Europeans, Greeks indicate decimals with commas and thousands with points.

LAUNDRY

Large towns and some islands have laundrettes. They charge from 2000 dr to 2500 dr to wash and dry a load whether you do it yourself or have it service-washed. Hotel and room owners will usually provide you with a washtub.

TOILETS

Most places in Greece have western-style toilets, especially hotels and restaurants which cater for tourists. You'll occasionally come across Asian-style squat toilets in older houses, *kafeneia* and public toilets.

Public toilets are rare, except at airports and bus and train stations. Cafes are the best option if you get caught short, but you'll be expected to buy something for the privilege.

One peculiarity of the Greek plumbing system is that it can't handle toilet paper, apparently the pipes are too narrow. Whatever the reason, anything larger than a postage stamp seems to cause a problem – flushing away tampons and sanitary napkins is guaranteed to block the system. Toilet paper etc should be placed in the small bin provided in every toilet.

HEALTH

Travel health depends on your predeparture preparations, your day-to-day health care while travelling and how you handle any medical problem or emergency that does develop. While the list of potential dangers can seem quite frightening, few travellers experience more than upset stomachs.

Predeparture Planning

Health Insurance Refer to Travel Insurance under Visas & Documents earlier in this chapter for information.

Warning Codeine, which is commonly found in headache preparations, is banned in Greece; check labels carefully, or risk prosecution. There are strict regulations applying to the importation of medicines into Greece, so obtain a certificate from your doctor which outlines any medication you may have to carry into the country with you.

Health Preparations Make sure you're healthy before you start travelling. If you are embarking on a long trip make sure your teeth are OK.

If you wear glasses take a spare pair and your prescription.

If you require a particular medication take an adequate supply, as it may not be available locally. Take the prescription or, better still, part of the packaging showing the generic rather than the brand name (which may not be locally available), as it will make getting replacements easier.

Immunisations No jabs are required for travel to Greece but a yellow fever vaccination certificate is required if you are coming from an infected area. There are, however, a few routine vaccinations that are recommended. These should be recorded on an international health certificate, available from your doctor or government health department. Don't leave your vaccinations until the last minute as some require more than one injection. Recommended vaccinations include:

Tetanus & Diphtheria Boosters are necessary every 10 years and protection is highly recommended.

Polio A booster of either the oral or injected vaccine is required every 10 years to maintain immunity after childhood vaccination. Polio is still prevalent in many developing countries.

Hepatitis A The most common travel-acquired illness that can be prevented by vaccination. Protection can be provided in two ways – either with the antibody gamma globulin or with

Medical Kit Check List

Following is a list of items you should consider including in your medical kit – consult your pharmacist for brands available in your country.

☐ **Aspirin** or **paracetamol** (acetaminophen in the USA) – for pain or fever

☐ **Antihistamine** – for allergies, eg hay fever; to ease the itch from insect bites or stings; and to prevent motion sickness

☐ **Antibiotics** – consider including these if you're travelling well off the beaten track; see your doctor, as they must be prescribed, and carry the prescription with you

☐ **Loperamide** or **diphenoxylate** – 'blockers' for diarrhoea; **prochlorperazine** or **metaclopramide** for nausea and vomiting

☐ **Rehydration mixture** – to prevent dehydration, eg due to severe diarrhoea; particularly important when travelling with children

☐ **Insect repellent, sunscreen, lip balm** and **eye drops**

☐ **Calamine lotion, sting relief spray** or **aloe vera** – to ease irritation from sunburn and insect bites or stings

☐ **Antifungal cream** or **powder** – for fungal skin infections and thrush

☐ **Antiseptic** (such as povidone-iodine) – for cuts and grazes

☐ **Bandages, Band-Aids (plasters)** and other wound dressings

☐ **Water purification tablets** or **iodine**

☐ **Scissors, tweezers** and a **thermometer** (note that mercury thermometers are prohibited by airlines)

☐ **Cold** and **flu tablets, throat lozenges** and **nasal decongestant**

☐ **Multivitamins** – consider for long trips, when dietary vitamin intake may be inadequate

the vaccine Havrix 1440. Havrix 1440 provides long-term immunity (possibly more than 10 years) after an initial injection and a booster at six to 12 months. Gamma globulin, a ready-made antibody, should be given as close as possible to departure because it is at its most effective in the first few weeks after administration and the effectiveness tapers off gradually between three and six months.

Rabies Pre travel rabies vaccination involves having three injections over 21 to 28 days and should be considered by those who will spend a month or longer in a country where rabies is common, especially if they are cycling, handling animals, caving, travelling to remote areas, or taking children (who may not report a bite). If someone who has been vaccinated is bitten or scratched by an animal they will require two booster injections of vaccine; those not vaccinated will require more.

Basic Rules

Care in what you eat and drink is the most important health rule. Stomach upsets are the most likely travel health problem (between 30 and 50% of travellers in a two week stay experience this) but the majority of these upsets will be relatively minor. Don't become paranoid; trying the local food is part of the experience of travel, after all.

Food & Water Tap water is safe to drink in Greece, but mineral water is widely available if you prefer it. You might experience mild intestinal problems if you're not used to copious amounts of olive oil; however, you'll get used to it and current research says it's good for you.

If you don't vary your diet, are travelling hard and fast and missing meals, or simply lose your appetite, you can soon start to lose weight and place your health at risk. Fruit and vegetables are good sources of vitamins and Greece produces a greater variety of these than almost any other European country. Eat plenty of grains (including rice) and bread. If your diet isn't well balanced or if your food intake is insufficient, it's a good idea to take vitamin and iron pills.

In hot weather make sure you drink enough – don't rely on feeling thirsty to indicate when you should drink. Not needing to urinate or very dark yellow urine is a danger sign. Always carry a water bottle with you on long trips. Excessive sweating can lead to loss of salt and therefore muscle cramping. Salt tablets are not a good idea as a preventative, but in places where salt is not used much, adding salt to food can help.

Environmental Hazards

Sunburn By far the biggest health risk in Greece comes from the intensity of the sun. You can get sunburnt surprisingly quickly, even through cloud. Using a sunscreen and taking extra care to cover the areas which don't normally see sun helps, as does zinc cream or some other barrier cream for your nose and lips. Calamine lotion is good for mild sunburn. Greeks claim that yogurt applied to sunburn is soothing. Protect your eyes with good-quality sunglasses.

Prickly Heat Prickly heat is an itchy rash caused by excessive perspiration trapped under the skin. Keeping cool but bathing often, using a mild talcum powder or even resorting to air-conditioning may help until you acclimatise.

Everyday Health

Normal body temperature is up to 37°C (98.6°F); more than 2°C (4°F) higher indicates a high fever. The normal adult pulse rate is 60 to 100 per minute (children 80 to 100, babies 100 to 140). As a general rule the pulse increases about 20 beats per minute for each 1°C (2°F) rise in fever.

Respiration (breathing) rate is also an indicator of illness. Count the number of breaths per minute: between 12 and 20 is normal for adults and older children (up to 30 for younger children, 40 for babies). People with a high fever or serious respiratory illness breathe more quickly than normal. More than 40 shallow breaths a minute may indicate pneumonia.

Heat Exhaustion Dehydration or salt deficiency can cause heat exhaustion. Take time to acclimatise to high temperatures, and drink sufficient liquids. Wear loose clothing and a broad-brimmed hat. Do not do anything too physically demanding.

Salt deficiency is characterised by fatigue, lethargy, headaches, giddiness and muscle cramps and in this case salt tablets may help. Vomiting or diarrhoea can deplete your liquid and salt levels.

Heat Stroke This serious, sometimes fatal, condition can occur if the body's heat-regulating mechanism breaks down and the body temperature rises to dangerous levels. Long, continuous periods of exposure to high temperatures can leave you vulnerable to heat stroke. You should avoid excessive alcohol consumption or strenuous activity when you first arrive in a hot climate.

The symptoms are feeling unwell, not sweating very much or at all and a high body temperature (39 to 41°C or 102 to 106°F). Where sweating has ceased, the skin becomes flushed and red. Severe, throbbing headaches and lack of coordination will also occur, and the sufferer may be confused or aggressive. Eventually the victim will become delirious or convulsive. Hospitalisation is essential, but in the interim get victims out of the sun, remove their clothing, cover them with a wet sheet or towel and then fan continually. Give fluids if they are conscious.

Fungal Infections Fungal infections, which occur with greater frequency in hot weather, are most likely to occur on the scalp, between the toes or fingers, in the groin and on the body. You get ringworm (which is a fungal infection, not a worm) from infected animals or by walking on damp areas like shower floors.

To prevent fungal infections wear loose, comfortable clothes, avoid artificial fibres, wash frequently and dry carefully. If you do get an infection, wash the infected area daily with a disinfectant or medicated soap and water, and rinse and dry well. Apply an antifungal cream or powder like the widely available Tinaderm. Try to expose the infected area to air or sunlight as much as possible and wash all towels and underwear in hot water as well as changing them often.

Motion Sickness Sea sickness can be a problem. The Aegean is very unpredictable and gets very rough when the *meltemi* wind blows. If you are prone to motion sickness, eat lightly before and during a trip and try to find a place that minimises disturbance – near the wings on aircraft, close to midships on boats, near the centre on buses. Fresh air usually helps; reading and cigarette smoke don't. Commercial motion-sickness preparations, which can cause drowsiness, have to be taken before the trip commences; when you're feeling sick it's too late. Ginger (available in capsule form) and peppermint (including mint-flavoured sweets) are natural preventatives.

Infectious Diseases
Diarrhoea Simple things like a change of water, food or climate can all cause a mild bout of diarrhoea, but a few rushed toilet trips with no other symptoms is not indicative of a major problem.

Dehydration is the main danger with any diarrhoea, particularly in children or the elderly as dehydration can occur quite quickly. Under all circumstances *fluid replacement* (at least equal to the volume being lost) is the most important thing to remember. Weak black tea with a little sugar, soda water, or soft drinks allowed to go flat and diluted 50% with clean water are all good.

Hepatitis Hepatitis is a general term for inflammation of the liver. It is a common disease worldwide. The symptoms are fever, chills, headache, fatigue, feelings of weakness and aches and pains, followed by loss of appetite, nausea, vomiting, abdominal pain, dark urine, light-coloured faeces, jaundiced (yellow) skin and the whites of the eyes may turn yellow. **Hepatitis A** is transmitted by contaminated food and drinking water. The disease poses a real threat to the western traveller. You should seek medical advice, but there is not much you can do apart from resting, drinking lots of fluids, eating lightly and avoiding fatty foods. People who have had hepatitis should avoid alcohol for some time after the illness, as the liver needs time to recover.

Hepatitis E is transmitted in the same way, and can be very serious in pregnant women.

There are almost 300 million chronic carriers of **Hepatitis B** in the world. It is spread through contact with infected blood, blood products or body fluids; for example, through sexual contact, unsterilised needles and blood transfusions, or contact with blood via small breaks in the skin. Other risky situations include having a shave, tattoo, or having your body pierced with contaminated equipment. The symptoms of type B may be more severe and may lead to long-term problems. **Hepatitis D** is spread in the same way, but the risk is mainly in shared needles.

Hepatitis C can lead to chronic liver disease. The virus is spread by contact with blood and blood products – usually via contaminated transfusions or shared needles – or bodily fluids.

Tetanus This potentially fatal disease is found worldwide. It is difficult to treat but is preventable with immunisation.

Rabies Rabies is a fatal viral infection caused by a bite or scratch by an infected animal. It's rare, but it's found in Greece. Dogs are noted carriers as are cats. Any bite, scratch or even lick from a warm-blooded, furry animal should be cleaned immediately and thoroughly. Scrub with soap and running water, and then clean with an alcohol or iodine solution. If there is any possibility that the animal is infected medical help should be sought immediately to prevent the onset of symptoms and death. Even if the animal is not rabid, all bites should be treated seriously as they can become infected or can result in tetanus. A rabies vaccination is now available and should be considered if you are in a high risk category – eg if you intend to explore caves (bat bites can be dangerous), work with animals, or travel so far off the beaten track that medical help is more than two days away.

Sexually Transmitted Diseases Sexual contact with an infected sexual partner spreads these diseases. While abstinence is the only 100% preventative, using condoms is also effective. Gonorrhoea, herpes and syphilis are among these diseases; sores, blisters or rashes around the genitals, discharges or pain when urinating are common symptoms. In some STDs, such as wart virus or chlamydia, symptoms may be less marked or not observed at all in women. Syphilis symptoms eventually disappear completely but the disease continues and can cause severe problems in later years. The treatment of gonorrhoea and syphilis is with antibiotics.

There are numerous other sexually transmitted diseases, for most of which effective treatment is available. But there is no cure for herpes and currently no cure for AIDS.

HIV/AIDS Infection with the human immunodeficiency virus (HIV) may lead to acquired immune deficiency syndrome (AIDS), which is a fatal disease. Any exposure to blood, blood products or body fluids may put the individual at risk. The disease is often transmitted through sexual contact or dirty needles - vaccinations, acupuncture, tattooing and body piercing can be potentially as dangerous as intravenous drug use.

If you do need an injection, ask to see the syringe unwrapped in front of you, or take a needle and syringe pack with you.

Fear of HIV infection should never preclude treatment for serious medical conditions.

Insect-Borne Diseases

Typhus Tick typhus is a problem from April to September in rural areas, particularly areas where animals congregate. Typhus begins with a fever, chills, headache and muscle pain, followed a few days later by a body rash. There is often a large painful sore at the site of the bite and nearby lymph nodes are swollen and painful. There is no vaccine available. The best protection is to check your skin carefully after walking in danger areas such as long grass and scrub. A strong insect repellent can help, and serious walkers in tick areas should consider having their boots and trousers impregnated with benzyl benzoate and dibutylphthalate. (See the Cuts, Bites & Stings section following for information about ticks.)

Lyme Disease Lyme disease is a tick-transmitted infection which may be acquired throughout Europe. The illness usually begins with a spreading rash at the site of the bite and is accompanied by fever, headache, extreme fatigue, aching joints and muscles and mild neck stiffness. If untreated, these symptoms usually resolve over several weeks but over subsequent weeks or months disorders of the nervous system, heart and joints may develop. The response to treatment is best early in the illness. The longer the delay, the longer the recovery period.

Cuts, Bites & Stings

Skin punctures can easily become infected in hot climates and may be difficult to heal. Treat any cut with an antiseptic such as povidone-iodine. Where possible avoid bandages and Band-Aids, which can keep wounds wet.

Although there are a lot of bees and wasps in Greece, their stings are usually painful rather than dangerous. Calamine lotion or sting relief spray will give relief and ice packs will reduce the pain and swelling.

Snakes Always wear boots, socks and long trousers when walking through undergrowth where snakes may be present. Don't put your hands into holes and crevices, and be careful when collecting firewood.

Snake bites do not cause instantaneous death and antivenenes are usually available. Keep the victim calm and still, wrap the bitten limb tightly, as you would for a sprained ankle, and attach a splint to immobilise it. Then seek medical help, if possible with the dead snake for identification. Don't attempt to catch the snake if there is even a remote possibility of being bitten again. Tourniquets and sucking out the poison are now comprehensively discredited.

Jelly Fish, Sea Urchins & Weever Fish Watch out for sea urchins around rocky beaches; if you get some of their needles embedded in your skin, olive oil will help to loosen them. If they are not removed they will become infected. Be wary also of jelly fish, particularly during the months of September and October. Although they are not lethal in Greece, their stings can be painful. Dousing in vinegar will deactivate any stingers which have not 'fired'. Calamine lotion, antihistamines and analgesics may reduce the reaction and relieve the pain.

Much more painful than either of these, but thankfully much rarer, is an encounter with the weever fish. It buries itself in the sand of the tidal zone with only its spines protruding, and injects a painful and powerful toxin if trodden on. Soaking your foot in very hot water (which breaks down the poison) should solve the problem. It can cause permanent local paralysis in the worst instance.

Bedbugs & Lice Bedbugs live in various places, but particularly in dirty mattresses and bedding. Spots of blood on bedclothes or on the wall around the bed can be read as a suggestion to find another hotel. Bedbugs leave itchy bites in neat rows. Calamine lotion or sting relief spray may help.

All lice cause itching and discomfort. They make themselves at home in your hair, your clothing or in your pubic hair. You catch lice through direct contact with infected people or by sharing combs, clothing and the like. Powder or shampoo treatment will kill the lice and infected clothing should then be washed in very hot water.

Leeches & Ticks Leeches may be present in damp areas; they attach themselves to your skin to suck your blood. Trekkers often get them on their legs or in their boots. Salt or a lighted cigarette end will make them fall off. Do not pull them off, as the bite is then more likely to become infected. An insect repellent may keep them away. You should always check your body if you have been walking through a potentially tick-infested area as ticks can cause skin infections and other more serious diseases.

Sheepdogs These dogs are trained to guard sheep, and are often underfed and sometimes ill-treated by their owners. They are almost always 'all bark and no bite', but if you are going to trek into remote areas, you should consider having rabies injections (see Rabies). You are most likely to encounter these dogs in the mountainous regions of Crete. Wandering through a flock of sheep over which one of these dogs is watching is asking for trouble.

Women's Health
Antibiotic use, synthetic underwear, sweating and contraceptive pills can lead to fungal vaginal infections, especially when travelling in hot climates. Fungal infections are characterised by a rash, itch and discharge and can be treated with a vinegar or lemon-juice douche, or with yogurt. Nystatin, miconazole or clotrimazole pessaries or vaginal cream are the usual treatment. Maintaining good personal hygiene and wearing loose-fitting clothes and cotton underwear may help prevent these infections.

Sexually transmitted diseases are a major cause of vaginal problems. Symptoms include a smelly discharge, painful intercourse and sometimes a burning sensation when urinating. Medical attention should be sought and male sexual partners must also be treated. For more details see the section on Sexually Transmitted Diseases earlier. Besides abstinence, the best thing is to practise safer sex using condoms.

Hospital Treatment
Citizens of EU countries are covered for free treatment in public hospitals within Greece on presentation of an E111 form.

Inquire at your national health service or travel agent in advance. Emergency treatment is free to all nationalities in public hospitals. In an emergency, dial ☎ 166. There is at least one doctor on every island in Greece and larger islands have hospitals. Pharmacies can dispense medicines which are available only on prescription in most European countries, so you can consult a pharmacist for minor ailments.

All this sounds fine, but although medical training is of a high standard in Greece, the health service is badly underfunded and one of the worst in Europe. Hospitals are overcrowded, hygiene is not always what it should be and relatives are expected to bring in food for the patient – which could be a problem for a tourist. Conditions and treatment are better in private hospitals, which are expensive. All this means that a good health-insurance policy is essential.

WOMEN TRAVELLERS
Many women travel alone in Greece. The crime rate remains relatively low, and solo travel is probably safer than in most European countries. This does not mean that you should be lulled into complacency; bag snatching and rapes do occur, although violent offences are rare.

The biggest nuisance to foreign women travelling alone are the guys the Greeks have nicknamed *kamaki*. The word means 'fishing trident' and refers to the kamaki's favourite pastime, 'fishing' for foreign women. You'll find them everywhere there are lots of tourists; young (for the most part), smooth-talking guys who aren't in the least bashful about sidling up to foreign women in the street. They can be very persistent, but they are a hassle rather than a threat.

The majority of Greek men treat foreign women with respect, and are genuinely helpful.

GAY & LESBIAN TRAVELLERS
In a country where the church still plays a prominent role in shaping society's views on issues such as sexuality, it should come as no surprise that homosexuality is generally

frowned upon. While there is no legislation against homosexual activity, it pays to be discreet and to avoid public displays of togetherness.

This has not prevented the Greek Islands from becoming an extremely popular destination for gay travellers. Mykonos has long been famous for its bars, beaches and general hedonism, while Paros (and Antiparos), Rhodes, Santorini and Skiathos all have their share of gay hang-outs.

The town of Eressos on the island of Lesvos (Mytilini), birthplace of the lesbian poet Sappho, has become something of a place of pilgrimage for lesbians.

Athens also has a busy gay scene, as does Thessaloniki.

Information The *Spartacus International Gay Guide*, published by Bruno Gmünder (Berlin), is widely regarded as the leading authority on the gay travel scene. The 1998/99 edition has a wealth of information on gay venues around the islands.

There's also stacks of information on the Internet. *Roz Mov* at www.geocities.com/WestHollywood/2225/index.html, is a good place to start. It has pages on travel info, gay health, the gay press, organisations, events and legal issues – and links to lots more sites.

Gayscape has a useful site at www.jwpublishing.com/gayscape.gre.html, with lots of links.

Organisations The main gay rights organisation in Greece is the Elladas Omofilofilon Kommunitas (☎ 01-341 0755, fax 883 6942, email eok@nyx.gr), upstairs at Apostolou Pavlou 31 in the Athens suburb of Thisio.

DISABLED TRAVELLERS

If mobility is a problem, visiting the Greek Islands presents some serious challenges – particularly the smaller islands without airports. The hard fact is that most hotels, ferries, museums and ancient sites are not wheelchair accessible.

If you are determined, then take heart in the knowledge that disabled people do come to the islands for holidays. But the trip needs careful planning, so get as much information as you can before you go. The British-based Royal Association for Disability and Rehabilitation (RADAR) publishes a useful guide called *Holidays & Travel Abroad: A Guide for Disabled People*, which gives a good overview of facilities available to disabled travellers in Europe. Contact RADAR (☎ 020-7250 3222, fax 020-7250 0212, email radar@radar.org.uk) at 12 City Forum, 250 City Road, London EC1V 8AF).

SENIOR TRAVELLERS

Card-carrying EU pensioners can claim a range of benefits such as reduced admission charges at museums and ancient sites and discounts on trains.

TRAVEL WITH CHILDREN

Greece is a safe and relatively easy place to travel with children. It's especially easy if you're staying by the beach or at a resort hotel. If you're travelling around, the main problem is a shortage of decent playgrounds and recreational facilities.

Don't be afraid to take children to ancient sites. Many parents are surprised by how much their children enjoy them. Young imaginations go into overdrive when let loose somewhere like the 'labyrinth' at Knossos.

Hotels and restaurants are usually very accommodating when it comes to meeting the needs of children, although highchairs are a rarity outside resorts. The service in restaurants is normally very quick, which is great when you've got hungry children on your hands.

Fresh milk is readily available in large towns and tourist areas, but hard to find on the smaller islands. Supermarkets are the best place to look. Formula is available everywhere, as is condensed and heat-treated milk.

Mobility is an issue for parents with very small children. Strollers (pushchairs) aren't much use in Greece unless you're going to spend all your time in one of the few flat spots. They are hopeless on rough stone paths and up steps, and a curse when getting on/off buses and ferries. Backpacks or front pouches are best.

Children under four travel for free on ferries and buses. They pay half fare up to the age of 10 (ferries) and 12 (buses). Full fare applies otherwise. On domestic flights, you'll pay 10% of the fare to have a child under two sitting on your knee. Kids aged two to 12 pay half fare.

USEFUL ORGANISATIONS
Automobile Associations
ELPA (☎ 01-779 1615), the Greek automobile club, has its headquarters on the ground floor of Athens Tower, Messogion 2-4, Athens 115 27. ELPA offers reciprocal services to members of national automobile associations on production of a valid membership card. If your vehicle breaks down, dial ☎ 104.

DANGERS & ANNOYANCES
Theft
Crime, especially theft, is low in Greece, but unfortunately it is on the increase. The worst area is around Omonia in central Athens – keep track of your valuables here, on the metro and at the Sunday flea market. The vast majority of thefts from tourists are still committed by other tourists; the biggest danger of theft is probably in dormitory rooms in hostels and at camp sites. So make sure you do not leave valuables unattended in such places. If you are staying in a hotel room, and the windows and door do not lock securely, ask for your valuables to be locked in the hotel safe – hotel proprietors are happy to do this.

Bar Scams
Bar scams continue to be an unfortunate fact of life in Athens, particularly in the Syntagma area. The basic scam is always some variation on the following theme: solo male traveller is lured into bar on some pretext (not always sex); strikes up conversation with friendly locals; charming girls appear and ask for what turn out to be ludicrously overpriced drinks; traveller is eventually handed an enormous bill.

Fortunately, this practice appears confined to Athens. See under Information in the Athens chapter for the full run-down on this scam and other problems.

LEGAL MATTERS
Consumer Advice
The Tourist Assistance Programme exists to help people who are having trouble with any tourism-related service. Free legal advice is available in English, French and German from July 1 to September 30. The main office (☎ 01-330 0673, fax 330 0591) is at Valtetsiou 43-45 in Athens. It's open 10 am to 2 pm Monday to Friday. Free advice is also available from the following regional offices:

Iraklio
    Consumers' Association of Crete (☎ 081-240 666), Milatou 1 and Agiou Titou
Patras
    Consumers' Association of Patras (☎ 061-272 481), Korinthou 213B
Volos
    Consumers' Association of Volos (☎ 0421-39 266), Haziagari 51

Drugs
Greek drug laws are the strictest in Europe. Greek courts make no distinction between possession and pushing. Possession of even a small amount of marijuana is likely to land you in jail.

BUSINESS HOURS
Banks are open 8 am to 2 pm Monday to Thursday, and 8 am to 1.30 pm Friday. Some banks in large towns and cities open between 3.30 and 6.30 pm in the afternoon and on Saturday morning.

Post offices are open 7.30 am to 2 pm Monday to Friday. In the major cities they stay open until 8 pm, and open from 7.30 am to 2 pm on Saturday.

The opening hours of OTE offices (for long distance and overseas telephone calls) vary according to the size of the town. In smaller towns they are usually open 7.30 am to 3 pm daily; from 6 am until 11 pm in larger towns; and 24 hours in major cities like Athens and Thessaloniki.

In summer, shops are open 8 am to 1.30 pm and 5.30 to 8.30 pm Tuesday, Thursday and Friday, and 8 am to 2.30 pm Monday, Wednesday and Saturday. They open 30 minutes later in winter. These times are not always strictly adhered to. Many shops in tourist resorts are open seven days a week. Periptera are open from early morning until late at night. They sell everything from bus tickets and cigarettes to hard-cord pornography.

Opening times of museums and archaeological sites vary, but most are closed on Monday.

PUBLIC HOLIDAYS

All banks and shops and most museums and ancient sites close public holidays. National public holidays in Greece are:

New Year's Day	1 January
Epiphany	6 January
First Sunday in Lent	February
Greek Independence Day	25 March
Good Friday	March/April
(Orthodox) Easter Sunday	March/April
Spring Festival/Labour Day	1 May
Feast of the Assumption	15 August
Ohi Day	28 October
Christmas Day	25 December
St Stephen's Day	26 December

SPECIAL EVENTS

The Greek year is a succession of festivals and events, some of which are religious, some cultural, others an excuse for a good knees-up, and some a combination of all three. The following is by no means an exhaustive list, but it covers the most important events, both national and regional. If you're in the right place at the right time, you'll certainly be invited to join the revelry.

January
Feast of Agios Vasilios (St Basil)
The year kicks off with this festival on 1 January. A church ceremony is followed by the exchanging of gifts, singing, dancing and feasting; the New Year pie *(vasilopitta)* is sliced and the person who gets the slice containing a coin will supposedly have a lucky year.

Epiphany (the Blessing of the Waters)
On 6 January, Christ's baptism by St John is celebrated throughout Greece. Seas, lakes and rivers are blessed and crosses immersed in them. The largest ceremony takes place at Piraeus.

February-March
Carnival
The Greek carnival season is the three weeks before the beginning of Lent (the 40 day period before Easter, which is traditionally a period of fasting). The carnivals are ostensibly Christian pre-Lenten celebrations, but many derive from pagan festivals. There are many regional variations, but fancy dress, feasting, traditional dancing and general merrymaking prevail. The Patras carnival is the largest and most exuberant, with elaborately decorated chariots parading through the streets. The most bizarre carnival takes place on the island of Skyros where the men transform themselves into grotesque 'half man, half beast' creatures by donning goat-skin masks and hairy jackets. Other carnivals worth catching are those on Zakynthos and Kefallonia.

Shrove Monday (Clean Monday)
On the Monday before Ash Wednesday (the first day of Lent), people take to the hills throughout Greece to have picnics and fly kites.

March
Independence Day
The anniversary of the hoisting of the Greek flag by Bishop Germanos at Moni Agias Lavras is celebrated on 25 March with parades and dancing. Germanos' act of revolt marked the start of the War of Independence. Independence Day coincides with the **Feast of the Annunciation**, so it is also a religious festival.

March-April
Easter
Easter is the most important festival in the Greek Orthodox religion. Emphasis is placed on the Resurrection rather than on the Crucifixion, so it is a joyous occasion. The festival commences on the evening of Good Friday with the *perifora epitavios*, when a shrouded bier (representing Christ's funeral bier) is carried through the streets to the local church. This moving candle lit procession can be seen in towns and villages throughout the country.

From a spectator's viewpoint, the most impressive of these processions climbs Lykavittos Hill in Athens to the Chapel of Agios Georgos. The Resurrection Mass starts at 11 pm on Saturday night. At midnight, packed churches are plunged into darkness to symbolise Christ's passing through the underworld. The ceremony of the lighting of candles which follows is the most significant moment in the Orthodox year, for it symbolises the Resurrection. Its poignancy and beauty are spellbinding. If you are in Greece at Easter you should endeavour to attend this ceremony, which ends with fireworks and a candle lit processions through the streets. The Lenten fast ends on Easter Sunday with the cracking of red-dyed Easter eggs and an outdoor feast of roast lamb followed by Greek dancing. The day's greeting is *Hristos anesti* ('Christ is risen'), to which the reply is *Alithos anesti* ('Truly He is risen'). On both Palm Sunday (the Sunday before Easter) and Easter Sunday, St Spyridon (the mummified patron saint of Corfu) is taken out for an airing and joyously paraded through the town. He is paraded again in Corfu town on 11 August.

Feast of Agios Georgos (St George)
The feast day of St George, Greece's patron saint and patron saint of shepherds, takes place on 23 April or the Tuesday following Easter (whichever comes first).

May
May Day
On the first day of May there is a mass exodus from towns to the country. During picnics, wildflowers are gathered and made into wreaths to decorate houses.

June
Navy Week
This festival celebrates the long relationship between the Greek and the sea with events in fishing villages and ports throughout the country. Volos and Hydra have unique versions of these celebrations. Volos re-enacts the departure of the *Argo*, legend has it that Iolkos (from where Jason and the Argonauts set off in search of the Golden Fleece) was near the city. Hydra commemorates Admiral Andreas Miaoulis, who was born on the island and was a hero of the War of Independence, with a re-enactment of one of his naval victories, accompanied by feasting and fireworks.

Feast of St John the Baptist
This feast day on 24 June is widely celebrated. Wreaths made on May Day are kept until this day, when they are burned on bonfires.

July
Feast of Agia Marina (St Marina)
This feast day is celebrated on 17 July in many parts of Greece, and is a particularly important event on the Dodecanese island of Kassos.

Feast of Profitis Ilias
This feast day is celebrated on 20 July at hilltop churches and monasteries dedicated to the prophet, especially in the Cyclades.

August
Assumption
Greeks celebrate Assumption Day (15 August) with family reunions. The whole population seems to be on the move either side of the big day, so it's a good time to avoid public transport. The island of Tinos gets particularly busy because of its miracle-working icon of Panagia Evangelistria. It becomes a place of pilgrimage for thousands, who come to be blessed, healed or baptised, or just for the excitement of being there. Many are unable to find hotels and sleep out on the streets.

September
Genesis tis Panagias (the Virgin's Birthday)
This day is celebrated on 8 September throughout Greece with religious services and feasting.

Exaltation of the Cross
This is celebrated on 14 September throughout Greece with processions and hymns.

October
Feast of Agios Dimitrios (St Dimitri)
This feast day is celebrated in Thessaloniki on 26 October with wine drinking and revelry.

Ohi (No) Day
Metaxas' refusal to allow Mussolini's troops free passage through Greece in WWII is commemorated on 28 October with remembrance services, military parades, folk dancing and feasting.

December
Christmas Day
Although not as important as Easter, Christmas is still celebrated with religious services and feasting. Nowadays much 'western' influence is apparent, including Christmas trees, decorations and presents.

Summer Festivals & Performances
There are cultural festivals throughout Greece in summer. The most important is the Athens Festival (June-August), with

drama and music performances in the Theatre of Herodes Atticus. Others include the Thasos Festival (July and August); the Renaissance Festival in Rethymno (July and August); the Hippocratia Festival on Kos (August); and the Patras Arts Festival (August and September).

Thessaloniki hosts a string of festivals and events during September and October, including the International Trade Fair and the Feast of Agios Dimitrios (details on the latter in the preceding list).

The nightly *son et lumière* (sound and light show) in Athens and Rhodes runs from April to October.

Greek folk dances are performed in Athens from mid-May to September and in Rhodes from May to October.

ACTIVITIES
Windsurfing
Windsurfing is the most popular water sport in Greece. Hsrysi Akti on Paros, and Vasiliki on Lefkada vie for the position of the best windsurfing beach. According to some, Vasiliki is one of the best places in the world to learn the sport.

You'll find sailboards for hire almost everywhere. Hire charges range from 2000 dr to 3000 dr an hour, depending on the gear. If you are a novice, most places that rent equipment also give lessons.

Sailboards may only be brought into Greece if a Greek national residing in Greece guarantees that it will be taken out again. To find out the procedure for arranging this, contact the Hellenic Windsurfing Association (☎ 01-323 0330), Filellinon 7, Athens.

Water-Skiing
Islands with water-ski centres are Chios, Corfu, Crete, Kythira, Lesvos, Paros, Skiathos and Rhodes.

Snorkelling & Diving
Snorkelling is enjoyable just about anywhere along the coast off Greece. Especially good places are Monastiri on Paros, Velanio on Skopelos, Paleokastritsa on Corfu, Telendos Islet (near Kalymnos) and anywhere off the coast of Kastellorizo.

Diving is another matter. Any kind of underwater activity using breathing apparatus is strictly forbidden other than under the supervision of a diving school. This is to protect the many antiquities in the depths of the Aegean. There are diving schools on the islands of Corfu, Crete (at Rethymno), Evia, Mykonos and Rhodes.

Trekking
The islands are a veritable paradise for trekkers – at the right time of the year. Trekking is no fun at all in July and August, when the temperatures are constantly up around 40°C. Spring (April-May) is the perfect time.

Some of the most popular treks, such as the Samaria Gorge on Crete, are detailed in this book. You'll find information on maps in the Planning section at the beginning of this chapter.

On small islands it's fun to discover pathways for yourself. You are unlikely to get into danger as settlements or roads are never far away. You will encounter a variety of paths: *kalderimi* are cobbled or flagstone paths which link settlements and date back to Byzantine times. Sadly, many have been bulldozed to make way for roads.

There are a number of companies running organised treks. One of the biggest is Trekking Hellas (☎ 01-323 4548, fax 325 1474, email trekking@compulink.gr), Filellinon 7, Athens 105 57. You'll find more information at its Web site, www.trekking.gr.

COURSES
Language
If you are serious about learning the language, an intensive course at the start of your stay is a good way to go about it. Most of the courses are in Athens, but there are also special courses on the islands in summer.

The Hellenic Culture Centre (☎/fax 01-360 3379 or 0275-61 482, email hccmike@netor) runs courses on the island of Ikaria from June to October. Two-week intensive courses for beginners with 40 classroom hours cost 130,000 dr. The centre also arranges accommodation. You'll find details at www.hcc.gr on the Internet.

The Athens Centre (☎ 01-701 2268, fax 701 8603, email athenscr@compulink.gr), Arhimidous 48, Mets, Athens, runs courses on the island of Spetses in June and July. It also has a Web site, www.athenscentre.gr.

Corfu's Ionian University Courses runs courses in Modern Greek and Greek Civilisation in July and August. Details are available at Deligiorgi 55-59 (☎ 01-522 9770) in Athens, or from the Secretariat of the Ionian University (☎ 0661-22 993/994) at Megaron Kapodistria 49, Corfu Town.

Dance
The Dora Stratou Dance Company (☎ 01-324 4395), in Athens, holds folk dancing workshops for amateurs during July and August. The *Hellenic Times* carries information about this and other workshops.

The Skyros Centre, on Skyros, runs courses on subjects ranging from yoga and dancing to massage and windsurfing. The emphasis is on learning to develop a holistic approach to life. For details of its fortnightly programs, contact the Skyros Centre (☎ 020-7267 4424, fax 020-7284 3063, email skyros@easynet.co.uk), 92 Prince of Wales Rd, London NW5 3NE.

WORK
Permits
EU nationals don't need a work permit, but they need a residency permit if they intend to stay longer than three months. Nationals of other countries are supposed to have a work permit.

Bar & Hostel Work
The bars of the Greek Islands could not survive without foreign workers and there are thousands of summer jobs up for grabs every year. The pay is not fantastic, but you get to spend a summer in the islands. April/May is the time to go looking. Hostels and travellers' hotels are other places that regularly employ foreign workers.

Summer Harvest
Seasonal harvest work seems to be monopolised by migrant workers from Albania, and is no longer a viable option for travellers.

Volunteer Work
The Hellenic Society for the Study & Protection of the Monk Seal (☎ 01-522 2888, fax 522 2450), Solomou 53, Athens 104 32, and the Sea Turtle Protection Society of Greece (☎/fax 01-523 1342, email stps@compulink.gr), Solomou 57, Athens 104 32, both use volunteers for their monitoring programs on the Ionian Islands and the Peloponnese.

Street Performers
The richest pickings are to be found on the islands, particularly Mykonos, Paros and Santorini. Plaka is the place to go in Athens.

Other Work
There are often jobs advertised in the classifieds of the English-language newspapers, or you can place an advertisement yourself. EU nationals can also make use of the OAED (Organismos Apasholiseos Ergatikou Dynamikou), the Greek National Employment Service, in their search for a job.

ACCOMMODATION
There is a range of accommodation available in Greece to suit every taste and pocket. All places to stay are subject to strict price controls set by the tourist police. By law, a notice must be displayed in every room, which states the category of the room and the price charged in each season.

Accommodation owners may add a 10% surcharge for a stay of less than three nights, but this is not mandatory. A mandatory charge of 20% is levied if an extra bed is put into a room. During July and August, accommodation owners will charge the maximum price, but in spring and autumn, prices will drop by up to 20%, and perhaps by even more in winter. These are the times to bring your bargaining skills into action.

Rip-offs rarely occur, but if you suspect you have been exploited by an accommodation owner, report it to either the tourist police or regular police and they will act swiftly.

Mountain Refuges

You're unlikely to have much need of Greece's network of mountain refuges – unless you're going trekking in the mountains of Crete. See the Crete chapter for details of the refuges at Mt Ida and in the Lefka Ori.

Camping

There are almost 200 camping grounds dotted around the islands. A few are operated by the EOT, but most are privately run. Very few are open outside the high season (April-October). The Panhellenic Camping Association (☎/fax 01-362 1560), Solonos 102, Athens 106 80, publishes an annual booklet listing all the camp sites and their facilities.

Camping fees are highest from 15 June to the end of August. Most camping grounds charge from 1200 dr to 1500 dr per adult and 600 dr to 800 dr for children aged four to 12. There's no charge for children aged under four. Tent sites cost from 900 dr per night for small tents, and from 1200 dr per night for large tents. Caravan sites start at around 2500 dr.

Between May and mid-September it is warm enough to sleep out under the stars, although you will still need a lightweight sleeping bag to counter the pre-dawn chill. It's a good idea to have a foam pad to lie on and a waterproof cover for your sleeping bag.

Freelance (wild) camping is illegal, but the law is not always strictly enforced. It's more likely to be tolerated on islands that don't have camp sites, but it's wise to ask around before freelance camping anywhere in Greece.

Apartments

Self-contained family apartments are available in some hotels and domatia. There are also a number of purpose-built apartments, particularly on the islands, available for either long or short-term rental. Prices vary considerably according to the amenities offered.

Domatia

Domatia are the Greek equivalent of the British bed and breakfast, minus the breakfast. Once upon a time domatia comprised little more than spare rooms in the family home which could be rented out to travellers in summer; nowadays, many are purpose-built appendages to the family house. Some come complete with fully equipped kitchens. Standards of cleanliness are generally high. The decor runs the gamut from cool grey marble floors, coordinated pine furniture, pretty lace curtains and tasteful pictures on the walls, to so much kitsch, you are almost afraid to move in case you break an ornament.

Domatia remain a popular option for budget travellers. They are classified A, B or C. Expect to pay from 4000 dr to 9000 dr for a single, and 6000 dr to 15,000 dr for a double, depending on the class, whether bathrooms are shared or private, the season and how long you plan to stay. Domatia are found on almost every island which has a permanent population. Many domatia are open only between April and October.

From June to September domatia owners are out in force, touting for customers. They meet buses and boats, shouting 'Room, room!' and often carrying photographs of their rooms. In peak season, it can prove a mistake not to take up an offer – but be wary of owners who are vague about the location of their accommodation. 'Close to town' can turn out to be way out in the sticks. If you are at all dubious, insist they show you the location on a map.

Hostels

There is only one youth hostel in Greece affiliated to Hostelling International (HI), the excellent Athens International Youth Hostel (☎ 01-523 4170). You don't need a membership card to stay there; temporary membership costs 600 dr per day.

Most other youth hostels are run by the Greek Youth Hostel Organisation (☎ 01-751 9530, fax 751 0616, email y-hostels@ otenet.gr), Damareos 75, 116 33 Athens. There are affiliated hostels in Athens, Patras and Thessaloniki on the mainland, and on the islands of Crete and Santorini.

Hostel rates vary from 1600 dr to 2000 dr and you don't have to be a member to stay in any of them. Few have curfews.

There is a XEN (YWCA) hostel for women in Athens.

Traditional Settlements

Traditional settlements are old buildings of architectural merit that have been renovated and converted into tourist accommodation. You'll find them on many of the islands; Hania (Crete) and Rhodes Town are two places with a good range of possibilities. Most are equivalent in price to an A or B class hotel.

Pensions

Pensions in Greece are virtually indistinguishable from hotels. They are classed A, B or C. An A class pension is equivalent in amenities and price to a B class hotel, a B class pension is equivalent to a C class hotel, and a C class pension is equivalent to a D or E class hotel.

Hotels

Hotels in Greece are divided into six categories: deluxe, A, B, C, D and E. Hotels are categorised according to the size of the room, whether or not they have a bar, and the ratio of bathrooms to beds, rather than standards of cleanliness, comfort of the beds and friendliness of staff – all elements which may be of greater relevance to guests.

As one would expect, deluxe, A and B class hotels have many amenities, private bathrooms and constant hot water. C class hotels have a snack bar, rooms have private bathrooms, but hot water may only be available at certain times of the day. D class hotels may or may not have snack bars, most rooms will share bathrooms, but there may be some with private bathrooms, and they may have solar heated water, which means hot water is not guaranteed. E classes do not have a snack bar, bathrooms are shared and you may have to pay extra for hot water – if it exists at all.

Prices are controlled by the tourist police and the maximum rate that can be charged for a room must be displayed on a board behind the door of each room. The classification is not often much of a guide to price. Rates in D and E class hotels are generally comparable with domatia. You can pay anywhere from 10,000 dr to 20,000 dr for a single in high season in C class and 15,000 dr to 25,000 dr for a double. Prices in B class range from 15,000 dr to 25,000 dr for singles, and from 25,000 to 35,000 dr for doubles. A class prices are not much higher.

FOOD

Greek food does not enjoy a reputation as one of the world's great cuisines. Maybe that's because many travellers have experienced Greek cooking only in tourist resorts. The old joke about the Greek woman who, on summer days, shouted to her husband 'Come and eat your lunch before it gets hot' is based on truth.

Until recently, food was invariably served lukewarm – which is how Greeks prefer it. Most restaurants that cater to tourists have now cottoned on to the fact that foreigners expect cooked dishes to be served hot, and improved methods of warming meals (including the dreaded microwave) have made this easier. If your meal is not hot, ask that it be served *zesto*, or order grills, which have to be cooked to order. Greeks are fussy about fresh ingredients, and frozen food is rare.

Greeks eat out regularly, regardless of socioeconomic status. Enjoying life is paramount to Greeks and a large part of this enjoyment comes from eating and drinking with friends.

By law, every eating establishment must display a written menu including prices. Bread will automatically be put on your table and usually costs between 100 dr and 200 dr, depending on the restaurant's category.

Where to Eat

Tavernas Traditionally, the taverna is a basic eating place with a rough-and-ready ambience, although some are more upmarket, particularly in Athens, and resorts and big towns. All tavernas have a menu, often displayed in the window or on the door, but it's usually not a good guide as to what's actually available on the day. You'll be told about the daily specials – or ushered into the kitchen to peer into the pots and point to what you want. This is not merely a privilege for tourists; Greeks also do it because they want to see the taverna's version of the dishes on offer. Some tavernas don't open until 8 pm, and then stay open until the early hours. Some are closed on Sunday.

Greek men are football (soccer) and basketball mad, both as spectators and participants. If you happen to be eating in a taverna on a night when a big match is being televised, expect indifferent service.

Psistaria These places specialise in spit roasts and charcoal-grilled food – usually lamb, pork or chicken.

Restaurants A restaurant *(estiatorio)* is normally more sophisticated than a taverna or psistaria – damask tablecloths, smartly attired waiters and printed menus at each table with an English translation. Ready-made food is usually displayed in a *bain-marie* and there may also be a charcoal grill.

Ouzeria An *ouzeri* serves ouzo. Greeks believe it is essential to eat when drinking alcohol so, in traditional establishments, your drink will come with a small plate of titbits or *mezedes* (appetisers) – perhaps olives, a slice of feta and some pickled octopus. Ouzeria are becoming trendy and many now offer menus with both appetisers and main courses.

Galaktopoleia A *galaktopoleio* (literally 'milk shop') sells dairy produce including milk, butter, yogurt, rice pudding, cornflour pudding, custard, eggs, honey and bread. It may also sell home-made ice cream. Look for the sign *'pagoto politiko'* displayed outside. Most have seating and serve coffee and tea. They are inexpensive for breakfast

and usually open from very early in the morning until evening.

Zaharoplasteia A *zaharoplasteio* (patisserie) sells cakes (both traditional and western), chocolates, biscuits, sweets, coffee, soft drinks and, possibly, bottled alcoholic drinks. They usually have some seating.

Kafeneia Kafeneia are often regarded by foreigners as the last bastion of male chauvinism in Europe. With bare light bulbs, nicotine-stained walls, smoke-laden air, rickety wooden tables and raffia chairs, they are frequented by middle-aged and elderly Greek men in cloth caps who while away their time fiddling with worry beads, playing cards or backgammon, or engaged in heated political discussion.

It was once unheard of for women to enter a kafeneia but in large cities this situation is changing.

In rural areas, Greek women are rarely seen inside kafeneia. When a female traveller enters one, she is inevitably treated courteously and with friendship if she manages a few Greek words of greeting. If you feel inhibited about going into a kafeneio, opt for outside seating. You'll feel less intrusive.

Kafeneia originally only served Greek coffee but now, most also serve soft drinks, Nescafé and beer. They are generally fairly cheap, with Greek coffee costing about 150 dr and Nescafé with milk 250 dr or less. Most kafeneia are open all day every day, but some close during siesta time (roughly from 3 to 5 pm).

Meals
Breakfast Most Greeks have Greek coffee and perhaps a cake or pastry for breakfast. Budget hotels and pensions offering breakfast generally provide it continental-style (rolls or bread with jam, and tea or coffee), while more upmarket hotels serve breakfast buffets (western and continental-style). Otherwise, restaurants and galaktopoleia serve bread with butter, jam or honey; eggs; and the budget travellers' favourite, yogurt *(yiaourti)* with honey. In tourist areas, many

menus offer an 'English' breakfast – which means bacon and eggs.

Lunch This is eaten late – between 1 and 3 pm – and may be either a snack or a complete meal. The main meal can be lunch or dinner – or both. Greeks enjoy eating and often have two large meals a day.

Dinner Greeks also eat dinner late. Many people don't start to think about food until about 9 pm, which is why some restaurants don't bother to open their doors until after 8 pm. In tourist areas dinner is often served earlier.

A full dinner in Greece begins with appetisers and/or soup, followed by a main

---

A Greek Feast

Greek dishes are easy to prepare at home. Here's a simple lunch or dinner to share with friends. Recipes serve four people.

Tzatziki (Cucumber and Yoghurt Dip) Peel and grate a medium cucumber. Add a cup of yoghurt, a tablespoon of olive oil, a pinch of salt, a teaspoon of vinegar, a teaspoon of freshly chopped dill and a minced garlic clove and refrigerate for two hours. Garnish with an olive and serve with fresh crusty bread or as an accompaniment to vegetables or fried fish.

Soupa Avgolemono (Egg and Lemon Soup) Add six tablespoons of uncooked rice to six cups of boiling chicken, fish or beef stock, then cover and simmer until the rice is tender. Beat two eggs, adding a pinch of salt and the juice of a large lemon. Add the stock to this mixture slowly, so that it doesn't curdle, then pour the mixture into a pot for reheating. Stir and ensure it does not boil.

Soutzoukakia (Sausages from Smyrna) This hearty dish originated in Smyrna (İzmir) in the days of Greek occupation and has subsequently been adopted by the cooks of Thessaloniki. Soak two slices of white bread in half a cup of water, mash and add three finely chopped garlic cloves, half a teaspoon of pepper and a dessertspoon of cumin.

Add 500g (1lb) of minced lamb or beef and a beaten egg, mix well and form into small sausages. Place in an oiled roasting pan and bake in a medium to hot oven until the sausages brown on the base side. Turn the sausages and add 500g (1lb) of tomatoes, a dollop of butter and teaspoon of sugar and return to the oven for about 15 minutes – or until the tomatoes are soft and the *soutzoukakia* are brown on the other side. Serve with fried potatoes or rice, and salad.

Halvas tou Fournou (Baked Halva) Here's a delightful dessert that is simple to make. Sift half a cup of flour with two teaspoons of baking powder and a pinch of salt. Add two cups of semolina and a cup of finely chopped nuts. Cream ¾ of a cup of butter or margarine with a cup of sugar and add three beaten eggs and grated lemon peel. Combine the mixtures well, then pour into a greased 25cm (10 inch) square pan. Bake in a medium oven until golden.

Boil three cups of water with three cups of sugar, add four cloves and a half stick of cinnamon, then pour over the rest of the dessert. Leave it to stand until the cinnamon and clove mixture has been absorbed, then serve with or without cream, warm or cold. It's filling and keeps for days.

course of either ready-made food, grilled meat, or fish. Only very posh restaurants or those pandering to tourists include western-style desserts on the menu. Greeks usually eat cakes separately in a galaktopoleio or zaharoplasteio.

Greek Specialities

Snacks Favourite Greek snacks include pretzel rings sold by street vendors, *tyro-pitta* (cheese pie), *bougatsa* (custard-filled pastry), *spanakopitta* (spinach pie) and *san-douits* (sandwiches). Street vendors sell various nuts and dried seeds such as pumpkin for 200 dr to 400 dr a bag.

Mezedes In a simple taverna, possibly only three or four mezedes (appetisers) will be offered – perhaps taramasalata (fish-roe dip), tzatziki (yogurt, cucumber and garlic dip), olives and feta (sheep or goat cheese). Ouzeria and restaurants usually offer wider selections.

Mezedes include *ohtapodi* (octopus), *garides* (shrimps), *kalamaria* (squid), dolmades (stuffed vine leaves), *melitzanos-alata* (aubergine or eggplant dip) and *mavromatika* (black-eyed beans). Hot mezedes include *keftedes* (meatballs), *faso-lia* (white haricot beans), *gigantes* (lima beans), *loukanika* (little sausages), tyro-pitta, spanakopitta, *bourekaki* (tiny meat pie), *kolokythakia* (deep-fried zucchini), *melitzana* (deep-fried aubergine) and *saganaki* (fried cheese).

It is quite acceptable to make a full meal of these instead of a main course. Three plates of mezedes are about equivalent in price and quantity to one main course. You can also order a *pikilia* (mixed plate).

Soups Soup is normally eaten as a starter, but can be an economical meal in itself with bread and a salad. *Psarosoupa* is a filling fish soup with vegetables, while *kakavia* (Greek bouillabaisse) is laden with seafood and more expensive. *Fasolada* (bean soup) is also a meal in itself. *Avgolemano soupa* (egg and lemon soup) is usually prepared from a chicken stock. If you're into offal,

don't miss the traditional Easter soup *mayiritsa* at this festive time.

Salads The ubiquitous (and no longer inexpensive) Greek or village salad, *horiatiki salata*, is a side dish for Greeks, but many drachma-conscious tourists make it a main dish. It consists of peppers, onions, olives, tomatoes and feta cheese, sprinkled with oregano and dressed with olive oil and lemon juice. A tomato salad often comes with onions, cucumber and olives, and, with bread, makes a satisfying lunch. In spring, try *radikia salata* (dandelion salad).

Main Dishes The most common main courses are *moussaka* (layers of eggplant or zucchini, minced meat and potatoes topped with cheese sauce and baked), *pastitsio* (baked cheese-topped macaroni and bechamel, with or without minced meat), dolmades and *yemista* (stuffed tomatoes or green peppers). Other main courses include *giouvetsi* (casserole of lamb or veal and pasta), *stifado* (meat stewed with onions), *soutzoukakia* (spicy meatballs in tomato sauce) and *salingaria* (snails in oil with herbs). *Melizanes papoutsakia* is baked eggplant stuffed with meat and tomatoes and topped with cheese, which looks, as its Greek name suggests, like a little shoe. Spicy *loukanika* (sausage) is a good budget choice and comes with potatoes or rice. Lamb fricassee, cooked with lettuce, *arni fricassée me maroulia*, is usually filling enough for two to share.

Fish is usually sold by weight in restaurants, but is not as cheap nor as widely available as it used to be. Calamari (squid), deep-fried in batter, remains a tasty option for the budget traveller at 1000 dr to 1400 dr for a generous serve. Other reasonably priced fish (about 1000 dr a portion) are *marides* (whitebait), sometimes cloaked in onion, pepper and tomato sauce, and *gopes*, which are similar to sardines. More expensive are *ohtapodi* (octopus), *bakaliaros* (cod), *xifias* (swordfish) and *glossa* (sole). Ascending the price scale further are *syna-grida* (snapper) and *barbounia* (red mullet).

Astakos (lobster) and *karabida* (crayfish) are top of the range at about 10,000 dr per kg.

Fish is mostly grilled or fried. More imaginative fish dishes include shrimp casserole and mussel or octopus saganaki (fried with tomato and cheese).

Desserts Greek cakes and puddings include baklava, *loukoumades* (puffs or fritters with honey or syrup), *kataïfi* (chopped nuts inside shredded wheat pastry or filo soaked in honey), *rizogalo* (rice pudding), *loukoumi* (Turkish delight), *halva* (made from semolina or sesame seeds) and *pagoto* (ice cream). Tavernas and restaurants usually only have a few of these on the menu. The best places to go for these delights are galaktopoleia or zaharoplasteia.

Island Specialities

Greek food is not all moussaka and souvlaki. Every region has its own specialities and it need not be an expensive culinary adventure to discover some of these. Corfu, for example, which was never occupied by the Turks, retains traditional recipes of Italian, Spanish and ancient Greek derivations. Corfiot food is served in several restaurants and includes *sofrito* (lamb or veal with garlic, vinegar and parsley), *pastitsada*, (beef with macaroni, cloves, garlic, tomatoes and cheese) and *burdeto* (fish with paprika and cayenne).

Santorini's baby tomatoes flavour distinctive dishes, not least a rich soup as thick and dark as blood. The *myzithra* (soft ewe's-milk cheese) of Ios is unique, and the lamb pies of Kefallonia and Crete are worth searching for. Andros' speciality is *froutalia*, a spearmint-flavoured potato and sausage omelette, while a Rhodes omelette is loaded with meat and zucchini.

Vegetarian Food

Greece has few vegetarian restaurants. Unfortunately, many vegetable soups and stews are based on meat stocks. Fried vegetables are safe bets as olive oil is always used – never lard. The Greeks do wonderful things with artichokes *(aginares)*. They can be served stuffed, as a salad, as a meze (particularly with *raki* in Crete) or used as the basis of a vegetarian stew.

Vegetarians who eat eggs can rest assured that an economical omelette can be whipped up anywhere. Salads are cheap, fresh, substantial and nourishing. Other options are yogurt, rice pudding, cheese and spinach pies, and nuts.

Lent, incidentally, is a good time for vegetarians because the meat is missing from many dishes.

Fast Food

Western-style fast food has arrived in Greece in a big way – creperies, hamburger joints and pizza places are to be found in all the major towns and resort areas.

It's hard, though, to beat eat-on-the-street Greek offerings. Foremost among them are the *gyros* and the souvlaki. The gyros is a giant skewer laden with slabs of seasoned meat which grills slowly as it rotates and the meat is trimmed steadily from the outside; souvlaki are small individual kebab sticks. Both are served wrapped in pitta bread, with salad and lashings of tzatziki.

Another favourite is *tost*, which is a bread roll cut in half, stuffed with the filling(s) of your choice, buttered on the outside and then flattened in a heavy griddle iron. It's the speciality of the Everest fast-food chain, which has outlets nationwide.

Fruit

Greece grows many varieties of fruit. Most visitors will be familiar with *syka* (figs), *rodakina* (peaches), *stafylia* (grapes), *karpouzi* (watermelon), *milo* (apples), *portokalia* (oranges) and *kerasia* (cherries).

Many will not, however, have encountered the *frangosyko* (prickly pear). Also known as the Barbary fig, it is the fruit of the opuntia cactus, recognisable by the thick green spiny pads that form its trunk. The fruit are borne around the edge of the pads in late summer and autumn and vary in colour from pale orange to deep red. They are delicious but need to be approached with extreme caution because of the thousands of tiny prickles (invisible to the naked eye) that cover their skin. Never pick one up with your bare hands. They must be peeled before you can eat them. The simplest way to do this is to trim the ends off with a knife and then slit the skin from end to end.

Another fruit that will be new to many people is the *mousmoula* (loquat). These small orange fruit are among the first of summer, reaching the market in mid-May. The flesh is juicy and pleasantly acidic.

Self-Catering

Eating out in Greece is as much an entertainment as a gastronomic experience, so to self-cater is to sacrifice a lot. But if you are on a low budget you will need to make the sacrifice – for breakfast and lunch at any rate. All towns and villages of any size have supermarkets, fruit and vegetable stalls and bakeries.

Only in isolated villages and on remote islands is food choice limited. There may only be one all-purpose shop – a *pantopoleio* which will stock meat, vegetables, fruit, bread and tinned foods.

Markets Most larger towns have huge indoor *agora* (food markets) which feature fruit and vegetable stalls, butchers, dairies and delicatessens, all under one roof. They are lively places that are worth visiting for the atmosphere as much as for the shopping. The markets at Hania (Crete) are a good example.

Smaller towns have a weekly *laïki agora* (street market) with stalls selling local produce.

DRINKS
Nonalcoholic Drinks

Coffee & Tea Greek coffee is the national drink. It is a legacy of Ottoman rule and, until the Turkish invasion of Cyprus in 1974, the Greeks called it Turkish coffee. It is served with the grounds, without milk, in a small cup. Connoisseurs claim there are at least 30 variations of Greek coffee, but most people know only three – *glyko* (sweet), *metrio* (medium) and *sketo* (without sugar).

After Greek coffee, the next most popular coffee is instant, called Nescafé (which it usually is). Ask for Nescafé *me ghala* (me-**ga**-la) if you want it with milk. In summer, Greeks drink Nescafé chilled, with or without milk and sugar – this version is called *frappé*.

Espresso and filtered coffee, once sold only in trendy cafes, are now also widely available.

Tea is inevitably made with a tea bag.

Fruit Juice & Soft Drinks Packaged fruit juices are available everywhere. Fresh orange juice is also widely available, but doesn't come cheap.

The products of all the major soft-drink multinationals are available everywhere in cans and bottles, along with local brands.

Milk Fresh milk can be hard to find on the islands and in remote areas. Elsewhere, you'll have no problem. A litre costs about 350 dr. UHT milk is available almost everywhere, as is condensed milk.

Water Tap water is safe to drink in Greece, although sometimes it doesn't taste too good – particularly on some of the islands. Many tourists prefer to drink bottled spring water, sold widely in 500mL and 1.5L plastic bottles. If you're happy with tap water, fill a container with it before embarking on ferries or you'll wind up paying through the nose for bottled water. Sparkling mineral water is rare.

Alcoholic Drinks

Beer Beer lovers will find the market dominated by the major northern European breweries. The most popular beers are Amstel and Heineken, both brewed locally under licence. Other beers brewed locally are Henniger, Kaiser, Kronenbourg and Tuborg.

The only local beer is *Mythos*, launched in 1997 and widely available. It has proved popular with drinkers who find the northern European beers a bit sweet.

Imported lagers, stouts and beers are found in tourist spots such as music bars and discos. You might even spot Newcastle Brown, Carlsberg, Castlemaine XXXX and Guinness.

Supermarkets are the cheapest place to buy beer, and bottles are cheaper than cans. A 500mL bottle of Amstel or Mythos costs about 200 dr (including 25 dr deposit on the bottle), while a 500mL can costs about 260 dr. Amstel also produces a low-alcohol beer and a bock, which is dark, sweet and strong.

Wine According to mythology, the Greeks invented or discovered wine and have produced it in Greece on a large scale for more than 3000 years.

The modern wine industry, though, is still very much in its infancy. Until the 1950s, most Greek wines were sold in bulk and were seldom distributed any farther afield than the nearest town. It wasn't until industrialisation (and the resulting rapid urban

Retsina

A holiday in Greece would not be the same without a jar or three of retsina, the famous – some might say notorious – resinated wine that is the speciality of Attica and neighbouring areas of central Greece.

Your first taste of retsina may well leave you wondering whether the waiter has mixed up the wine and the paint stripper, but stick with it – it's a taste that's worth acquiring. Soon you will be savouring the delicate pine aroma, and the initial astringency mellows to become very moreish. Retsina is very refreshing consumed chilled at the end of a hot day, when it goes particularly well with tzatziki.

Greeks have been resinating wine, both white and rosé, for millennia. The ancient Greeks dedicated the pine tree to Dionysos, also the god of wine, and held that land that grew good pine would also grow good wine.

No-one seems quite sure how wine and pine first got together. The consensus is that it was an inevitable accident in a country with so much wine and so much pine. The theory that resin entered the wine-making process because the wine was stored in pine barrels does not hold water, since the ancients used clay amphora rather than barrels. It's more likely that it was through pine implements and vessels used elsewhere in the process. Producers discovered that wine treated with resin kept for longer, and consumers discovered that they liked it.

Resination was once a fairly haphazard process, achieved by various methods such as adding crushed pine cones to the brew and coating the insides of storage vessels. The amount of resin also varied enormously. One 19th century traveller wrote that he had tasted a wine 'so impregnated with resin that it almost took the skin from my lips'. His reaction was hardly surprising; he was probably drinking a wine with a resin content as high as 7.5%, common at the time. A more sophisticated product awaits the modern traveller, with a resin content no higher than 1% – as specified by good old EU regulations. That's still enough to give the wine its trademark astringency and pine aroma.

The bulk of retsina is made from two grape varieties, the white *savatiano* and the red *roditis*. These two constitute the vast majority of vine plantings in Attica, central Greece and Evia. Not just any old resin will do; the main source is the Aleppo pine *(Pinus halepensis)*, which produces a resin known for its delicate fragrance.

Retsina is generally cheap and it's available everywhere. Supermarkets stock retsina in a variety of containers ranging from 500mL bottles to 5L casks and flagons. Kourtaki and Cambas are both very good, but the best (and worst) still flows from the barrel in traditional tavernas. Ask for *heema*, which means 'loose'.

growth) that there was much call for bottled wine. Quality control was unheard of until 1969, when appellation laws were introduced as a precursor to applying for membership of the European Community. Wines have improved significantly since then.

Don't expect Greek wines to taste like French wines. The grape varieties grown in Greece are quite different. Some of the most popular and reasonably priced labels include Rotonda, Kambas, Boutari, Calliga and Lac des Roches.

The most expensive wines are the Kefallonian Robola de Cephalonie, a superb dry white, and those produced by the Porto Carras estate in Halkidiki. Good wines are produced on Rhodes (famous in Greece for its champagne) and Crete. Other island wines worth sampling are those from Samos (immortalised by Lord Byron), Santorini, Kefallonia and Paros. *Aspro* is white, *mavro* is red and *kokkinelli* is rosé.

Spirits Ouzo is the most popular aperitif in Greece. Distilled from grape stems and flavoured with anise, it is similar to the Middle Eastern *arak*, Turkish *raki* and French Pernod. Clear and colourless, it turns white when water is added. A 700mL bottle of a popular brand like Ouzo 12, Olympic or Sans Rival costs about 1200 dr in supermarkets. In an ouzeri, a glass costs from 250 to 500 dr. It will be served neat, with a separate glass of water to be used for dilution.

The second-most popular spirit is Greek brandy, which is dominated by the Metaxa label. Metaxa comes in a wide choice of grades, starting with three star – a high-octane product without much finesse. You can pick up a bottle in a supermarket for about 1500 dr. The quality improves as you go through the grades: five star, seven star, VSOP, Golden Age and finally the top-shelf Grand Olympian Reserve (5600 dr). Other reputable brands include Cambas and Votrys. The Cretan speciality is raki, a fiery clear spirit that is served as a greeting (regardless of the time of day).

If you're travelling off the beaten track, you may come across *chipura*. Like ouzo,

it's made from grape stems but without the anise. It's an acquired taste, much like Irish poteen – and packing a similar punch. You'll most likely encounter chipura in village kafeneia or private homes.

ENTERTAINMENT
Cinemas
Greeks are keen movie-goers and almost every town of consequence has a cinema. English-language films are shown in English with Greek subtitles. Admission ranges from 1000 dr in small-town movie houses to 1800 dr at plush big-city cinemas.

Discos & Music Bars
Discos can be found in big cities and resort areas, though not in the numbers of a decade ago.

Most young Greeks prefer to head for the music bars that have proliferated to fill the void. These bars normally specialise in a particular style of music – Greek, modern rock, 60s rock, techno and, very occasionally, jazz.

Ballet, Classical Music & Opera
Unless you're going to be spending a bit of time in Athens or Thessaloniki, you're best off forgetting about ballet, classical music and opera while in Greece. See the Entertainment section of the Athens chapter for information on venues.

Theatre
The highlight of the Greek dramatic year is the staging of ancient Greek dramas at the Theatre of Herodes Atticus in Athens during the Athens Festival from late June to early September. See the Special Events section of the Athens chapter for more information.

Rock
Western rock music continues to grow in popularity, but live music remains a rarity outside Athens and Thessaloniki.

Traditional Music
Most of the live music you hear around the resorts is tame stuff laid on for the tourists.

If you want to hear music played with a bit of passion, the *rembetika* clubs in Athens are strongly recommended.

Folk Dancing

The pre-eminent folk dancers in Greece are the ones who perform at the Dora Stratou Theatre on Filopappos Hill in Athens, where performances take place nightly in summer. Another highly commendable place is the Old City Theatre, Rhodes City, where the Nelly Dimoglou Dance Company performs during the summer months. Folk dancing is an integral part of all festival celebrations and there is often impromptu folk dancing in tavernas.

SPECTATOR SPORTS

Soccer (football) remains the most popular spectator sport, although basketball is catching up fast following the successes of Greek sides in European club competition in recent years. Greek soccer teams, in contrast, have seldom had much impact on European club competition, and the national team is the source of constant hair-wrenching. The side's only appearance in the World Cup finals, in the USA in 1994, brought a string of heavy defeats.

The two glamour clubs of Greek soccer are Olympiakos of Piraeus and Panathinaikos of Athens (see Spectator Sports in the Athens chapter for more information). The only island team in the first division is OFI, from the Cretan capital of Iraklio. The season lasts from September to mid-May; cup matches are played on Wednesday night and first division games on Sunday afternoon. Games are often televised. Entry to a match costs around 1500 dr for the cheapest terrace tickets, or 3000 dr for a decent seat. Fixtures and results are given in the *Athens News*.

Olympiakos and Panathinaikos are also the glamour clubs of Greek basketball. Panathinaikos was European champion in 1996, and Olympiakos followed suit in 1997.

SHOPPING

Greece produces a vast array of handicrafts.

Antiques

It is illegal to buy, sell, possess or export any antiquity in Greece (see Customs earlier in this chapter). However, there are antiques and 'antiques'; a lot of items only a century or two old are regarded as junk, rather than part of the national heritage. These items include handmade furniture and odds and ends from rural areas in Greece, ecclesiastical ornaments from churches and items brought back from far-flung lands. Good hunting grounds for this 'junk' are Monastiraki and the flea market in Athens, and the Piraeus market held on Sunday morning.

Ceramics

You will see ceramic objects of every shape and size – functional and ornamental – for sale throughout Greece. The best places for high-quality handmade ceramics are Athens, Rhodes and the islands of Sifnos and Skyros.

There are a lot of places selling plaster copies of statues, busts, grave stelae and so on.

Leather Work

There are leather goods for sale throughout Greece; most are made from leather imported from Spain. The best place for buying leather goods is Hania on Crete. Bear in mind that the goods are not as high quality nor as good value as those available in Turkey.

Jewellery

You could join the wealthy North Americans who spill off the cruise ships onto Mykonos to indulge themselves in the high-class gold jewellery shops there. But although gold is good value in Greece, and designs are of a high quality, it is priced beyond the capacity of most tourists' pockets. If you prefer something more reasonably priced, go for filigree silver jewellery – a speciality of the town of Ioannina in Epiros.

Bags

Tagari bags are woven wool bags – often brightly coloured – which hang from the shoulder by a rope. Minus the rope, they make attractive cushion covers.

Getting There & Away

AIR

Most travellers arrive in Greece by air, the cheapest and quickest way to get there.

Airports & Airlines

Greece has 16 international airports, but only those in Athens, Thessaloniki and Iraklio (Crete) take scheduled flights.

Athens handles the vast majority of flights, including all intercontinental traffic. Thessaloniki has direct flights to Berlin, Brussels, Copenhagen, Dusseldorf, Frankfurt, İstanbul, Cyprus, London, Milan, Moscow, Munich, Paris, Stuttgart, Tirana, Vienna and Zürich. Most of these flights are with Greece's national airline, Olympic Airways, or the flag carrier of the country concerned. Iraklio's sole scheduled connection is to Amsterdam with Transavia.

Greece's other international airports are at Mykonos, Santorini (Thira), Hania (Crete), Kos, Karpathos, Samos, Skiathos, Hrysoupolis (for Kavala), Preveza (for Lefkada), Kefallonia and Zakynthos. These airports are used exclusively for charter flights, mostly from the UK, Germany and Scandinavia. Charter flights also fly to all of Greece's other international airports.

Olympic Airways is no longer Greece's only international airline. Cronus Airlines flies direct from Athens to London and Paris, and via Thessaloniki to Cologne, Dusseldorf, Frankfurt and Stuttgart. Air Manos operates cheap charter flights to London and Manchester, and Air Greece flies to the Italian port of Bari.

Buying Tickets

If you are flying to Greece from outside Europe, the plane ticket will probably be the most expensive item in your travel budget, and buying it can be an intimidating business. There will be a multitude of airlines and travel agents hoping to separate you from your money, so take time to research the options. Start early – some of the cheapest tickets must be bought months in advance, and popular flights tend to sell out early.

Discounted tickets fall into two categories – official and unofficial. Official discount schemes include advance-purchase tickets, budget fares, Apex, Super-Apex and a few other variations on the theme. These tickets can be bought from travel agents or direct from the airline. They often have restrictions – advance purchase being the usual one. There might also be restrictions on the period you must be away, such as a minimum of 14 days and a maximum of one year.

Unofficial tickets are simply discounted tickets the airlines release through selected travel agents.

Return tickets can often be cheaper than a one-way ticket. Generally, you can find discounted tickets at prices as low as, or even lower than, Apex or budget tickets. Phone around travel agents for bargains.

If you are buying a ticket to fly out of Greece, Athens is one of the major centres in Europe for budget airfares.

In Greece, as everywhere else, always remember to reconfirm your onward or return bookings by the specified time – usually 72 hours before departure on international flights. If you don't, there's a risk you'll turn up at the airport only to find you've missed your flight because it was rescheduled, or that the airline has given the seat to someone else.

Charter Flights

Charter flight tickets are for seats left vacant on flights which have been block-booked by package companies. Tickets are cheap but conditions apply on charter flights to Greece. A ticket must be accompanied by an accommodation booking. This is normally circumvented by travel agents issuing accommodation vouchers which are not meant to be used – even if the hotel named on the voucher actually exists. The

Air Travel Glossary

Baggage Allowance This will be written on your ticket and usually includes one 20kg item to go in the hold, plus one item of hand luggage.

Bucket Shops These are unbonded travel agencies specialising in discounted airline tickets.

Bumped Just because you have a confirmed seat doesn't mean you're going to get on the plane (see Overbooking).

Cancellation Penalties If you have to cancel or change a discounted ticket, there are often heavy penalties involved; insurance can sometimes be taken out against these penalties. Some airlines impose penalties on regular tickets as well, particularly against 'no-show' passengers.

Check-In Airlines ask you to check in a certain time ahead of the flight departure (usually one to two hours on international flights). If you fail to check in on time and the flight is over-booked, the airline can cancel your booking and give your seat to somebody else.

Confirmation Having a ticket written out with the flight and date you want doesn't mean you have a seat until the agent has checked with the airline that your status is 'OK' or confirmed. Meanwhile you could just be 'on request'.

Courier Fares Businesses often need to send urgent documents or freight securely and quickly. Courier companies hire people to accompany the package through customs and, in return, offer a discount ticket which is sometimes a phenomenal bargain. In effect, what the companies do is ship their freight as your luggage on regular commercial flights. This is a legitimate operation, but there are two shortcomings – the short turnaround time of the ticket (usually not longer than a month) and the limitation on your luggage allowance. You may have to surrender all your allowance and take only carry-on luggage.

Full Fares Airlines traditionally offer 1st class (coded F), business class (coded J) and economy class (coded Y) tickets. These days there are so many promotional and discounted fares available that few passengers pay full economy fare.

ITX An ITX, or 'independent inclusive tour excursion', is often available on tickets to popular holiday destinations. Officially it's a package deal combined with hotel accommodation, but many agents will sell you one of these for the flight only and give you phoney hotel vouchers in the unlikely event that you're challenged at the airport.

Lost Tickets If you lose your airline ticket an airline will usually treat it like a travellers cheque and, after inquiries, issue you with another one. Legally, however, an airline is entitled to treat it like cash and if you lose it then it's gone forever. Take good care of your tickets.

MCO An MCO, or 'miscellaneous charge order', is a voucher that looks like an airline ticket but carries no destination or date. It can be exchanged through any International Association of Travel Agents (IATA) airline for a ticket on a specific flight. It's a useful alternative to an onward ticket in those countries that demand one, and is more flexible than an ordinary ticket if you're unsure of your route.

No-Shows No-shows are passengers who fail to show up for their flight. Full-fare passengers who fail to turn up are sometimes entitled to travel on a later flight. The rest are penalised (see Cancellation Penalties).

Air Travel Glossary

On Request This is an unconfirmed booking for a flight.

Onward Tickets An entry requirement for many countries is that you have a ticket out of the country. If you're unsure of your next move, the easiest solution is to buy the cheapest onward ticket to a neighbouring country or a ticket from a reliable airline which can later be refunded if you do not use it.

Open Jaw Tickets These are return tickets where you fly out to one place but return from another. If available, this can save you backtracking to your arrival point.

Overbooking Airlines hate to fly empty seats and since every flight has some passengers who fail to show up, airlines often book more passengers than they have seats. Usually excess passengers make up for the no-shows, but occasionally somebody gets 'bumped' onto the next available flight. Guess who it is most likely to be? The passengers who check in late.

Point-to-Point Tickets These are discount tickets that can be bought on some routes in return for passengers waiving their rights to a stopover.

Promotional Fares These are officially discounted fares, available from travel agencies or direct from the airline.

Reconfirmation If you don't reconfirm your flight at least 72 hours prior to departure, the airline may delete your name from the passenger list. Ring to find out if your airline requires reconfirmation.

Restrictions Discounted tickets often have various restrictions on them – such as needing to be paid for in advance and incurring a penalty to be altered. Others are restrictions on the minimum and maximum period you must be away, such as a minimum of 14 days or a maximum of one year.

Round-the-World Tickets RTW tickets give you a limited period (usually a year) in which to circumnavigate the globe. You can go anywhere the carrying airlines go, as long as you don't backtrack. The number of stopovers or total number of separate flights is decided before you set off and they usually cost a bit more than a basic return flight.

Stand-by This is a discounted ticket where you only fly if there is a seat free at the last moment. Stand-by fares are usually available only on domestic routes.

Transferred Tickets Airline tickets cannot be transferred from one person to another. Travellers sometimes try to sell the return half of their ticket, but officials can ask you to prove that you are the person named on the ticket. This is less likely to happen on domestic flights, but on an international flight tickets are compared with passports.

Travel Agencies Travel agencies vary widely and you should choose one that suits your needs. Some simply handle tours, while full-service agencies handle everything from tours and tickets to car rental and hotel bookings. If all you want is a ticket at the lowest possible price, then go to an agency specialising in discounted fares.

Travel Periods Ticket prices vary with the time of year. There is a low (off-peak) season and a high (peak) season, and often a low-shoulder season and a high-shoulder season as well. Usually the fare depends on your outward flight – if you depart in the high season and return in the low season, you pay the high-season fare.

law requiring accommodation bookings was introduced in the 1980s to prevent budget travellers flying to Greece on cheap charter flights and sleeping rough on beaches or in parks. It hasn't worked.

The main catch for travellers taking charter flights involves visits to Turkey. If you fly to Greece with a return ticket on a charter flight, you will forfeit the return portion if you visit Turkey. Greece is one of several popular charter destination countries which have banded together to discourage tourists from leaving the destination country during the duration of the ticket. The countries involved want to ensure people don't flit off somewhere else to spend their tourist cash. The result is that if you front up at the airport for your return charter flight with a Turkish stamp in your passport, you will be forced to buy another ticket.

This does not apply if you take a day excursion into Turkey, because the Turkish immigration officials will not stamp your passport. Neither does it apply to regular or excursion-fare flights.

Charter flight tickets are valid for up to four weeks, and usually have a minimum-stay requirement of at least three days. Sometimes it's worth buying a charter return even if you think you want to stay for longer than four weeks. The tickets can be so cheap that you can afford to throw away the return portion.

The travel section of major newspapers is the place to look for cheap charter deals. More information on charter flights is given later in this chapter under specific point-of-origin headings.

Courier Flights

Another budget option (sometimes even cheaper than a charter flight) is a courier flight. This deal entails accompanying freight or a parcel that will be collected at the destination. The drawbacks are that your time away may be limited to one or two weeks, your luggage is usually restricted to hand luggage (the parcel or freight you carry comes out of your luggage allowance), and you may have to be a resident of the country

that operates the courier service and apply for an interview before they'll take you on.

Travel Agents

Many of the larger travel agents use the travel pages of national newspapers and magazines to promote their special deals. Before you make a decision, there are a number of questions you need to ask about the ticket. Find out the airline, the route, the duration of the journey, the stopovers allowed, any restrictions on the ticket and – above all – the price. Ask whether the fare quoted includes all taxes and other possible inclusions.

You may discover when you start ringing around that those impossibly cheap flights, charter or otherwise, are not available, but the agency just happens to know of another one that 'costs a bit more'. Or the agent may claim to have the last two seats available for Greece for the whole of July, which will hold for a maximum of two hours only. Don't panic – keep ringing around.

If you are flying to Greece from the USA, South-East Asia or the UK, you will probably find the cheapest flights are being advertised by obscure agencies whose names haven't yet reached the telephone directory – the proverbial bucket shops. Many such firms are honest and solvent, but there are a few rogues who will take your money and disappear, only to reopen elsewhere a month or two later under a new name. If you feel suspicious about a firm, don't give them all the money at once – leave a small deposit and pay the balance when you get the ticket. If they insist on cash in advance, go somewhere else or be prepared to take a big risk. Once you have booked the flight with the agency, ring the airline to check you have a confirmed booking.

It can be easier on the nerves to pay a bit more for the security of a better-known travel agent. Firms such as STA Travel, with offices worldwide, Council Travel in the USA or Travel CUTS in Canada offer good prices to Europe (including Greece), and are unlikely to disappear overnight.

The fares quoted in this book are intended as a guide only. They are approximate and are based on the rates advertised by travel agents at the time of writing.

Travel Insurance

The kind of cover you get depends on your insurance and type of ticket, so ask both your insurer and your ticket-issuing agency to explain where you stand. Ticket loss is usually covered.

Buy travel insurance as early as possible. If you buy it just before you fly, you may find you're not covered for such problems as delays caused by industrial action. Make sure you have a separate record of all your ticket details – preferably a photocopy.

Paying for your ticket with a credit card sometimes provides limited travel insurance, and you may be able to reclaim the payment if the operator doesn't deliver. In the UK, for instance, credit card providers are required by law to reimburse consumers if a company goes into liquidation and the amount in contention is more than UK£100.

Travellers with Special Needs

If you've broken a leg, require a special diet, are travelling in a wheelchair, are taking a baby, or have some other special need, let the airline staff know as soon as possible – preferably when booking your ticket. Check that your request has been registered when you reconfirm your booking (at least 72 hours before departure) and again when you check in at the airport.

Children under two years of age travel for 10% of the standard fare (or free on some airlines) as long as they don't occupy a seat. But they do not get a baggage allowance. 'Skycots' should be provided by the airline if requested in advance. These will take a child weighing up to about 10kg. Olympic Airways charges half-fare for accompanied children aged between two and 12 years, while most other airlines charge two-thirds.

Departure Tax

There is an airport tax of 6800 dr on all international departures from Greece. This is paid when you buy your ticket, not at the airport.

The USA

The North Atlantic is the world's busiest long-haul air corridor, and the flight options to Europe – including Greece – are bewildering.

Microsoft's popular Expedia.com Web site at www.expedia.msn.com gives a good overview of the possibilities. Other sites worth checking out are the ITN (www.itn.net) and Travelocity (www.travelocity.com) sites.

The *New York Times*, *LA Times*, *Chicago Tribune* and *San Francisco Chronicle Examiner* all publish weekly travel sections in which you'll find any number of advertisements for travel agents'. Council Travel (www.counciltravel.com) and STA Travel (www.sta-travel.com) have offices in major cities nationwide.

New York has the most number of direct flights to Athens. Olympic Airways has at least one flight a day, and Delta Airlines has three a week. Apex fares range from US$960 to US$1600, depending on the season and how long you want to stay away.

Boston is the only other east coast city with direct flights to Athens – on Saturday with Olympic Airways. Fares are the same as for flights from New York.

There are no direct flights to Athens from the west coast. There are, however, connecting flights to Athens from many US cities, either linking with Olympic Airways in New York or flying with one of the European national airlines to their home country, and then on to Athens. These connections usually involve a stopover of three or four hours.

One-way fares can work out very cheap on a stand-by basis. Airhitch (☎ 212-864 2000) specialises in this. It can get you to Europe one way for US$159 from the east coast and US$239 from the west coast, plus tax. Its Web site is www.airhitch.org.

Courier flights are another possibility. The International Association of Air Travel Couriers (☎ 561-582 8320, fax 582 1581) has flights from six US cities to a range of European capitals – but not Athens. Check out its Web site at www.courier.org.

If you're travelling from Athens to the USA, the travel agents around Syntagma offer the following one-way fares (prices do not include airport tax): Atlanta 110,000 dr, Chicago 110,000 dr, Los Angeles 125,000 dr and New York 85,000 dr.

Canada

Olympic Airways has two flights weekly from Toronto to Athens via Montreal. There are no direct flights from Vancouver, but there are connecting flights via Toronto, Amsterdam, Frankfurt and London on Canadian Airlines, KLM, Lufthansa and British Airways.

Travel CUTS (☎ 1-888-838 CUTS) has offices in all major cities and is a good place to ask about cheap deals. You should be able to get to Athens from Toronto and Montreal for about C$1150 or from Vancouver for C$1500. The *Toronto Globe & Mail*, the *Toronto Star*, the *Montreal Gazette* and the *Vancouver Sun* all carry advertisements for cheap tickets.

For courier flights originating in Canada, contact FB On Board Courier Services in Montreal (☎ 514-631 2677). They can get you to London for C$575 return.

At the time of writing, budget travel agencies in Athens were advertising flights to Toronto for 105,000 dr and to Montreal for 100,000 dr, plus airport tax.

Australia

Olympic Airways has two flights weekly from Sydney and Melbourne to Athens. Return fares are normally priced from about A$1799 in low season to A$2199 in high season.

Thai International and Singapore Airlines also have convenient connections to Athens, as well as a reputation for good service. If you're planning on doing a bit of flying around Europe, it's worth checking around for special deals from the major European airlines. Alitalia, KLM and Lufthansa are three likely candidates with good European networks.

STA Travel and Flight Centres International are two of Australia's major dealers in cheap fares. The Sunday tabloid newspapers and the travel sections of the *Sydney Morning Herald* and Melbourne's *Age* are a good place to look for cheap flights.

If you're travelling from Athens to Australia, a one-way ticket to Sydney or Melbourne costs about 180,000 dr, plus airport tax.

New Zealand

There are no direct flights from New Zealand to Athens. There are connecting flights via Sydney, Melbourne, Bangkok and Singapore on Olympic Airways, United Airlines, Qantas Airways, Thai Airways and Singapore Airlines.

The UK

British Airways, Olympic Airways and Virgin Atlantic operate daily flights between London and Athens. Pricing is very competitive, with all three offering return tickets for around UK£200 in high season, plus tax. These prices are for midweek departures; you will pay about UK£40 more for weekend departures.

There are connecting flights to Athens from Edinburgh, Glasgow and Manchester. Greek newcomer Cronus Airlines (☎ 020-7580 3500) flies the London-Athens route five times a week for £210, and offers connections to Thessaloniki on the same fare. Olympic Airways has four direct London-Thessaloniki flights weekly. Most scheduled flights from London leave from Heathrow.

The cheapest scheduled flights are with no-frills specialist EasyJet (☎ 0870 6 000 000), which has two Luton-Athens flights daily. One-way fares range from UK£89 to UK£139 in high season, and from a bargain UK£39 to UK£69 at other times. Its Web site is www.easyjet.com.

There are numerous charter flights between the UK and Greece. Typical London-Athens charter fares are UK£79/129 one way/return in the low season and UK£99/189 in the high season. These prices are for advance bookings, but even in high season it's possible to pick up last-minute deals for

to Athens. Most island destinations cost about UK£109/209 in high season. Charter flights to Greece also fly from Birmingham, Cardiff, Glasgow, Luton, Manchester and Newcastle. Contact the Air Travel Advisory Bureau (☎ 020-7636 5000) for information about current charter flight bargains; try its Web site www.atab.co.uk.

London is Europe's major centre for discounted fares. Some of the most reputable agencies selling discount tickets are:

Usit Campus
   (☎ 020-7730 3402)
   52 Grosvenor Gardens, London SW1
   www.usitcampus.co.uk
Council Travel
   (☎ 020-7287 3337)
   28A Poland St, London W1V 3DB
   www.counciltravel.com
STA Travel
   (☎ 020-7361 6161)
   86 Old Brompton Rd, London SW7
   www.statravel.co.uk
Trailfinders
   (☎ 020-7937 5400)
   215 Kensington High St, London W8

Listings publications such as *Time Out*, the Sunday papers, the *Evening Standard* and *Exchange & Mart* carry advertisements for cheap fares. The *Yellow Pages* is worth scanning for travel agents' ads, and look out for the free magazines and newspapers widely available in London, especially *TNT*, *Footloose*, *Southern Cross* and *LAM* – you can pick them up outside the main train and tube stations.

Some travel agents specialise in flights for students aged under 30 and travellers aged under 26 (you need an ISIC card or an official youth card). Whatever your age, you should be able to find something to suit your budget.

Most British travel agents are registered with ABTA (Association of British Travel Agents). If you have paid for your flight through an ABTA-registered agent who then goes out of business, ABTA will guarantee a refund or an alternative. If an agency is registered with ABTA, its advertisements will usually say so.

If you're flying from Athens to the UK, budget fares start at 25,000 dr to London or 30,000 dr to Manchester, plus airport tax.

Continental Europe

Athens is linked to every major city in Europe by either Olympic Airways or the flag carrier of each country.

London is the discount capital of Europe, but Amsterdam, Frankfurt, Berlin and Paris are also major centres for cheap airfares.

France Air France (☎ 0802 802 802) and Olympic Airways (☎ 01 42 65 92 42) have at least four Paris-Athens flights daily between them. Expect to pay from 2950FF to 3300FF in high season, dropping to about 2100FF at other times. Cronus Airlines (☎ 01 47 42 56 77) flies the same route four times weekly. Olympic Airways also has three flights weekly to Athens from Marseille.

Charter flights are much cheaper. You'll pay around 2000FF in high season for a return flight from Paris to Athens, and 2050FF to Rhodes or Santorini. The fare to Athens drops to 1500FF in low season. Reliable travel agents include:

Air Sud
   (☎ 01 40 41 66 66) 18 Rue du Pont-Neuf, 75001 Paris
Atsaro
   (☎ 01 42 60 98 98) 9 Rue de l'Echelle, 75001 Paris
Bleu Blanc
   (☎ 01 40 21 31 31) 53 Avenue de la République, 75011 Paris
Héliades
   (☎ 01 53 27 28 21) 24-27 Rue Basfroi, 75011 Paris
La Grèce Autrement
   (☎ 01 44 41 69 95) 72 Boulevard Saint Michel, 75006 Paris
Nouvelles Frontières
   (☎ 08 03 33 33) 87 Boulevard de Grenelle, 75015 Paris
Planète Havas
   (☎ 01 53 29 40 00) 26 Avenue 75001 Paris

Germany Atlas Rei＿ throughout Germany an＿ start checking prices.

In Berlin, Alternativ Tours (☎ 030-8 81 20 89), Wilmersdorfer Strasse 94, has discounted fares to just about anywhere in the world. SRS Studenten Reise Service (☎ 030-28 59 82 64), at Marienstrasse 23 near Friedrichstrasse station, offers special student (under 35) and youth (under 26) fares. Travel agents offering unpublished cheap flights advertise in *Zitty*, Berlin's fortnightly entertainment magazine.

In Frankfurt, try SRID Reisen (☎ 069-43 01 91), Berger Strasse 118.

The Netherlands Reliable travel agents in Amsterdam include:

Budget Air
   (☎ 020-627 12 51) Rokin 34
Malibu Travel
   (☎ 020-626 32 20) Prinsengracht 230
NBBS Reizen
   (☎ 020-624 09 89) Rokin 66

If you're travelling from Athens to Europe, budget fares to a host of European cities are widely advertised by the travel agents around Syntagma. Following are some typical one-way fares (not including airport tax):

Destination	One Way Fare
Amsterdam	57,500 dr
Copenhagen	59,500 dr
Frankfurt	55,000 dr
Geneva	54,000 dr
Hamburg	52,000 dr
Madrid	73,000 dr
Milan	48,000 dr
Munich	55,000 dr
Paris	55,500 dr
Rome	42,000 dr
Zürich	53,500 dr

Turkey

lympic Airways and Turkish Airlines
  ʳe the İstanbul-Athens route, with at
   one flight a day each. The full fare is
     ʲ0 one way. Olympic Airways also
     ˙ice weekly between İstanbul and

Thessaloniki (US$190). Students qualify for a 50% discount on both routes.

There are no direct flights from Ankara to Athens; all flights go via İstanbul.

Cyprus

Olympic Airways and Cyprus Airways share the Cyprus-Greece routes. Both airlines have three flights daily from Larnaca to Athens, and there are five flights weekly to Thessaloniki. Cyprus Airways also flies from Paphos to Athens once a week in winter, and twice a week in summer.

Travel agents in Athens charge 50,000 dr one way to Larnaca and Paphos, or 83,000 dr return.

LAND
Turkey

Bus The Hellenic Railways Organisation (OSE) operates Athens-İstanbul buses (22 hours) daily except Wednesday, leaving the Peloponnese train station in Athens at 7 pm and travelling via Thessaloniki and Alexandroupolis. One-way fares are 21,800 dr from Athens, 14,300 dr from Thessaloniki and 5600 dr from Alexandroupolis. Students qualify for a 15% discount and children under 12 travel for half-fare. See the Getting There & Away sections for each city for information on where to buy tickets.

Buses from İstanbul to Athens leave the Anadolu Terminal (Anatolia Terminal) at the Topkapı *otogar* (bus station) at 10 am daily except Sunday.

Train There are daily trains between Athens and İstanbul (19,000 dr) via Thessaloniki (13,000 dr) and Alexandroupolis (6350 dr). The service is incredibly slow and the train gets uncomfortably crowded. There are often delays at the border and the journey can take much longer than the supposed 22 hours.

Car & Motorcycle If you're travelling between Greece and Turkey by private vehicle, the crossing points are at Kipi, 43km north-east of Alexandroupolis, and at Kastanies, 139km north-east of Alexandroupolis. Kipi is more convenient if you're heading for İstanbul, but the route through Kastanies goes via the fascinating towns of Soufli and Didymotiho, in Greece, and Edirne (ancient Adrianople) in Turkey.

Bulgaria

Bus The OSE operates two Athens-Sofia buses (15 hours, 13,400 dr) daily except Monday, leaving at 7 am and 5 pm. It also operates Thessaloniki-Sofia buses (7½ hours, 5600 dr, three daily).

Train There is an Athens-Sofia train daily (18 hours, 10,330 dr) via Thessaloniki (nine hours, 6700 dr).

Car & Motorcycle The Bulgarian border crossing is at Promahonas, 145km northeast of Thessaloniki and 50km from Serres.

Albania

Bus There is a daily OSE bus between Athens and Tirana (12,600 dr) via Ioannina and Gjirokastër. The bus departs Athens (Larisis train station) at 7 pm arriving in Tirana the following day at 5 pm. It leaves Ioannina at 7.30 am and passes through Gjirokastër at 10.30 am. On the return trip, the bus departs Tirana at 7 am. There are buses from Thessaloniki to Korça (Korytsa in Greek) daily at 8 am. The fare is 6600 dr.

Car & Motorcycle There are two crossing points between Greece and Albania. The main one is at Kakavia, 60km north-west of Ioannina; the other is at Krystallopigi, north-west of Kastoria. Kapshtica is the closest town on the Albanian side.

Former Yugoslav Republic of Macedonia

Train There are Thessaloniki-Skopje trains (three hours, 4200 dr, two daily), which cross the border between Idomeni and Gevgelija. They leave Thessaloniki at 6 am and 5.30 pm. Both trains continue to the Serbian capital of Belgrade (12 hours, 11,500 dr). The 5.30 pm service goes all the way to Budapest (21 hours, 20,000 dr).

Car & Motorcycle There are two border crossings between Greece and FYROM. One is at Evzoni, 68km north of Thessaloniki. This is the main highway to Skopje which continues to Belgrade. The other border crossing is at Niki, 16km north of Florina.

Western Europe

Overland travel between western Europe and Greece is almost a thing of the past. Airfares are so cheap that land transport cannot compete. Travelling from the UK to Greece through Europe means crossing various borders, so check whether any visas are required before setting out.

Bus There are no bus services to Greece from the UK, nor from anywhere else in northern Europe. Bus companies can no longer compete with cheap airfares.

Train Unless you have a Eurail pass or are aged under 26 and eligible for a discounted fare, travelling to Greece by train is prohibitively expensive. For example, the full one-way/return fare from London to Athens is UK£265/521, including the Eurostar service from London to Paris.

Greece is part of the Eurail network. Eurail passes can only be bought by residents of non-European countries and are supposed to be purchased before arriving in Europe. They can, however, be bought in Europe as long as your passport proves that you've been there for less than six months. In London, head for the Rail Europe Travel Centre (☎ 08705 848 848), 179 Piccadilly, W1. Sample fares include UK£461 for an adult Eurail Flexipass, which permits 10 days 1st class travel in two months, and UK£323 for the equivalent youth pass.

If you are starting your European travels in Greece, you can buy your Eurail pass from the Hellenic Railways Organisation offices at Karolou 1 and Filellinon 17 in Athens, and at the train station in Patras and Thessaloniki.

Greece is also part of the Inter-Rail Pass system, but the pass for those aged over 26 is not valid in France, Italy and Switzerland

– rendering it useless if you want to get to Greece. Inter-Rail Youth Passes for those under 26 are divided into zones. A Global Pass (all zones) costs UK£259 and is valid for a month. You need to be under 26 on the first day of travel and to have lived in Europe for at least six months.

Car & Motorcycle Before the troubles in the former Yugoslavia began, most motorists driving from the UK to Greece opted for the direct route: Ostend, Brussels, Salzburg and then down the Yugoslav highway through Zagreb, Belgrade and Skopje and crossing the border to Evzoni.

These days most people drive to an Italian port and get a ferry to Greece. Coming from the UK, this means driving through France, where petrol costs and road tolls are exorbitant.

SEA
Turkey
There are five regular ferry services between Turkey's Aegean coast and the Greek Islands. Tickets for all ferries to Turkey must be bought a day in advance. You will almost certainly be asked to turn in your passport the night before the trip but don't worry, you'll get it back the next day before you board the boat. Port tax for departures to Turkey is 3000 dr.

See the relevant sections under individual island entries for more information about the following services.

Rhodes to Marmaris There are three ferries daily from Rhodes to Marmaris between April and October and less frequent services in winter. Prices vary, so shop around. There are also daily hydrofoils to Marmaris (weather permitting) from April to October for 10,000/14,000 dr one way/return plus Turkish port tax.

Chios to Çeşme There are daily Chios-Çeşme boats from July to September, dropping steadily back to one boat a week in winter. Tickets cost 15,000/20,000 dr one way/return, including port taxes.

Kos to Bodrum There are daily ferries in summer from Kos to Bodrum (ancient Halicarnassus) in Turkey. Boats leave at 8.30 am and return at 4 pm. The one hour journey costs 13,000 dr return, including port taxes.

Lesvos to Ayvalık There are up to five boats weekly on this route in high season. Tickets cost 16,000/21,000 dr one way/return.

Samos to Kuşadası There are two boats daily to Kuşadası (for Ephesus) from Samos in summer, dropping to one or two boats weekly in winter. Tickets cost 5000/9000 dr one way/return plus 5000 dr Greek port tax and US$10 Turkish port tax.

Italy
There are ferries to Greece from the Italian ports of Ancona, Bari, Brindisi, Trieste and Venice.

The ferries can get very crowded in summer. If you want to take a vehicle across it's a good idea to make a reservation. In the UK, reservations can be made on almost all of these ferries at Viamare Travel Ltd (☎ 020-7431 4560, fax 7431 5456, email ferries@viamare.com), 2 Sumatra Rd, London NW6 IPU.

You'll find all the latest information about ferry routes, schedules and services on the Internet. For a good overview try www.ferries.gr. Most of the ferry companies have their own Web sites, including:

Adriatica: www.adriatica.it
ANEK Lines: www.anek.gr
Hellenic Mediterranean Lines: www.hml.it
Minoan Lines: www.minoan.gr
Strintzis: www.strintzis.gr
Superfast: www.superfast.com
Ventouris: www.ventouris.gr

The following ferry services are for high season (July and August), and prices are for one way deck class. Deck class on these services means exactly that. If you want a reclining, aircraft-type seat, you'll be up for another 10 to 15% on top of the listed fares. Most companies offer discounts for return travel. Prices are about 30% less in the low season.

Ancona to Patras This route has become increasingly popular in recent years. There can be up to three boats daily in summer, and at least one a day year-round.

Superfast Ferries (☎ 071-20 28 05) provides the fastest and most convenient service, but it's also the most expensive. It has boats daily (20 hours, L148,000). Minoan Lines (☎ 071-20 17 08) has ferries to Patras (20 hours, L124,000) via Igoumenitsa (15 hours) daily except Tuesday. ANEK Lines (☎ 071-20 59 99) runs two direct boats weekly (24 hours, L115,000) and three via Igoumenitsa (34 hours). Strintzis (☎ 071-20 10 68) sails direct to Patras (23 hours, L96,000) three times weekly, twice via Igoumenitsa and Corfu.

All ferry operators in Ancona have booths at the *stazione marittima* (ferry terminal) off Piazza Candy, where you can pick up timetables and price lists and make bookings.

Bari to Corfu, Igoumenitsa & Patras Superfast Ferries (☎ 080-52 11 416) operates daily to Patras (15 hours, L88,000) via Igoumenitsa (9½ hours). Marlines (☎ 080-52 31 824) has daily boats to Igoumenitsa (12 hours, L70,000), while Ventouris (☎ 080-521 7118) goes to Igoumenitsa (13½ hours, L65,000) via Corfu.

Brindisi to Corfu, Igoumenitsa & Patras The route from Brindisi to Patras (18 hours) via Corfu (nine hours) and Igoumenitsa (10 hours) is the cheapest and most popular of the various Adriatic crossings. There can be up to five boats daily in high season.

Companies operating ferries from Brindisi are: Adriatica di Navigazione (☎ 0831-52 38 25), Corso Garibaldi 85-87, and on the 1st floor of the stazione marittima, where you must go to check in; Five Star Lines (☎ 0831-52 48 69), represented by Angela Gioia Agenzia Marittima, Via F Consiglio 55; Fragline (☎ 0831-59 01 96), Corso Garibaldi

88; Hellenic Mediterranean Lines (☎ 0831-52 85 31), Corso Garibaldi 8; and Med Link Lines (☎ 0831-52 76 67), represented by Discovery Shipping, Corso Garibaldi 49.

Adriatica and Hellenic Mediterranean are the most expensive at around L100,000 for deck class passage to Corfu (7½ hours), Igoumenitsa (nine hours) or Patras (15½ hours), but they are the best. They are also the only lines which accept Eurail passes. You will still have to pay port tax and a high-season loading in summer – usually about L15,000. If you want to use your Eurail pass, it is important to reserve some weeks in advance, particularly in summer. Even with a booking, you must still go to the Adriatica or Hellenic Mediterranean embarkation office in the stazione marittima to have your ticket checked.

The cheapest crossing is with Five Star Lines, which charges L46,000 to either Igoumenitsa (7½ hours) or Patras (15½ hours). Med Link charges L62,000 to Igoumenitsa and L65,000 to Patras, while Fragline charges L68,000 to Corfu and Igoumenitsa. Fares for cars range from L65,500 to L120,000 in the high season, depending on the line.

From 1 July to 19 September, Italian Ferries (☎ 0831-59 03 05), Corso Garibaldi 96, operates a daily high-speed catamaran to Corfu (3¼ hours, L154,000) leaving Brindisi at 2 pm. The service continues to Paxi (4¾ hours, L190,000 dr).

Brindisi to Kefallonia & Zakynthos Hellenic Mediterranean Lines has daily services to the port of Sami on Kefallonia from late June to early September. The trip takes 15 hours and costs L110,000 for deck class. Med Link also stops occasionally at Sami on its Brindisi-Patras run during July and August.

Hellenic Mediterranean Lines stops at Zakynthos (17 hours, L110,000) two or three times weekly in July and August.

Trieste to Patras ANEK Lines (☎ 40-30 28 88), Stazione Marittima di Trieste, has three boats weekly to Patras travelling via

Igoumenitsa. The trip takes 37 hours and costs L106,000 for deck class.

Venice to Patras Minoan Lines (☎ 41-27 12 345), Magazzino 17, Santa Marta, has boats from Venice to Patras (40 hours, L132,000). All services go via Corfu and Igoumenitsa, and from mid-May until late September two boats weekly call at Kefallonia.

Cyprus & Israel

Two companies ply the route between Piraeus and the Israeli port of Haifa, via Lemesos on Cyprus. These boats also stop at Rhodes and various other Greek islands.

During July and August, Salamis Lines leaves Haifa at 8 pm on Sunday and Lemesos at 4 pm on Monday, reaching Rhodes at noon on Tuesday, Tinos at 6 am on Wednesday, and Piraeus at 3 pm. The return service departs Piraeus at 7 pm on Thursday, and stops at Patmos on the way to Rhodes, Lemesos and Haifa. For the rest of the year, the boat leaves Haifa at 8 pm on Monday and skips Tinos. Bookings in Haifa are handled by Rosenfeld Shipping (☎ 04-861 3670), 104 Ha'Atzmaut St, and in Lemesos by Salamis Tours (☎ 05-355 555), Salamis House, 28 October Ave.

Poseidon Lines operates a similar service. In July and August, it sails from Haifa at 8 pm on Thursday and Lemesos at 1 pm on Friday, and then calls at Rhodes, Santorini and Tinos on the way to Piraeus. It leaves Piraeus at 7 pm on Monday, stopping at Santorini and Patmos on the way to Rhodes, Lemesos and Cyprus. It operates virtually the same timetable for the rest of the year, but stops only at Rhodes and Lemesos. Bookings in Haifa are handled by Caspi Travel (☎ 04-867 4444), 76 Ha'Atzmaut St, and in Lemesos by Poseidon Lines Cyprus (☎ 05-745 666), 124 Franklin Roosevelt St.

Both lines charge the same. Deck-class fares from Haifa are US$101 to Rhodes and US$106 to Piraeus. Fares from Lemesos are US$68 to Rhodes and US$72 to Piraeus. If you want a seat you'll be up for an extra US$10 more, while the cheapest shared cabins cost an extra US$30.

You'll find the latest information on these services on the Internet: www.ferries.gr for Poseidon Lines, and www.viamare.com/ Salamis for Salamis Lines.

ORGANISED TOURS

A lot of UK companies specialise in package holidays to unspoilt areas of Greece. They include: Laskarina (☎ 01629-824 881, www.laskarina.co.uk), Greek Islands Club (☎ 020-8232 9780), Greek Options (☎ 020-7233 5233), and Simply Ionian (☎ 020-8995 9323). Island Holidays (0176-477 0107) specialises in cultural holidays on Crete.

Warning

The information in this chapter is particularly vulnerable to change: prices for international travel are volatile, routes are introduced and cancelled, schedules change, special deals come and go, and rules and visa requirements are amended. Airlines and governments seem to take a perverse pleasure in making price structures and regulations as complicated as possible. You should check directly with the airline or a travel agent to make sure you understand how a fare (and ticket you may buy) works. In addition, the travel industry is highly competitive and there are many lurks and perks.

The upshot of this is that you should get opinions, quotes and advice from as many airlines and travel agents as possible before you part with your hard-earned cash. The details given in this chapter should be regarded as pointers and are not a substitute for your own careful, up-to-date research.

Getting Around

Greece is an easy place to travel around thanks to a comprehensive public transport system.

Buses are the mainstay of land transport, with a network that reaches out to the smallest villages. Trains are a good alternative on the mainland – where available. To most visitors, though, travelling in Greece means island-hopping on the multitude of ferries that criss-cross the Adriatic and the Aegean. If you're in a hurry, Greece also has an extensive domestic air network.

The information in this chapter was for the 1999 high season. You'll also find lots of travel information on the Internet. A useful general site is ellada.com, which has lots of links and includes airline timetables.

AIR
Domestic Air Services
Olympic Airways The vast majority of domestic flights are handled by the country's much-maligned national carrier, Olympic Airways, together with its offshoot, Olympic Aviation.

Olympic Airways has offices wherever there are flights, as well as in other major towns. The head office in Athens (☎ 01-966 6666) is at Leoforos Syngrou 96, and its Web site is at www.olympic-airways.gr.

The free-baggage allowance on domestic flights is 15kg. However, this does not apply when the domestic flight is part of an international journey. The international free-baggage allowance of 20kg is then extended to the domestic sector. This allowance applies to all tickets for domestic travel sold and issued outside Greece. Olympic offers a 25% student discount on domestic flights, but only if the flight is part of an international journey.

Olympic lost its monopoly on domestic routes in 1993. It took a while for any serious opposition to emerge, but there are now three established competitors on the scene and newcomers appearing all the time.

Air Greece This Crete-based airline was the first newcomer to show any sign of permanence. It has been around since 1995, offering a cheaper alternative to Olympic on some of the major routes. It flies the Athens-Iraklio route four times daily; Athens-Thessaloniki, Athens-Rhodes and Iraklio-Thessaloniki twice daily; Athens-Hania once a day; Rhodes-Thessaloniki four times weekly; and Iraklio-Rhodes three times weekly. It also offers youth discounts (under 26).

Air Manos Discount and package specialist Air Manos flies from Athens to Chios, Hania, Mykonos, Samos, Santorini, Syros and Thessaloniki. It also flies from Thessaloniki to Mykonos, Samos and Santorini. It offers some very cheap flight and accommodation packages, and has a reputation for good service.

Cronus Airlines Cronus is another popular company new to the local scene. It flies Athens-Thessaloniki return four times a day; Athens-Iraklio twice a day; and Athens-Rhodes, Iraklio-Thessaloniki and Rhodes-Thessaloniki once a day. The Saturday flight from Rhodes to Thessaloniki goes via Kavala.

Cronus offers discounts for students and for travellers aged over 60, and special rates for advance purchase. Its Web site, www.cronus.gr, has for more information on routes and fares.

Aegean Air Aegean is the latest addition to the line-up. It flies from Athens to Hania, Iraklio and Rhodes.

Mainland Flights
There's hot competition among all the airlines on the Athens-Thessaloniki route. Olympic Airways leads the way with seven flights daily (55 mins, 22,000 dr). Cronus Airlines (19,400 dr) has four flights daily and Air Greece (20,400 dr) has two.

Air Services Within Greece

Summer Flights from Athens to the Greek Islands

Destination	Flights/Week	Duration	Price (dr)	Destination	Flights/Week	Duration	Price (dr)
Astypalea	4	65 mins	20,100	Lesvos	35	50 mins	17,100
Chios	34	50 mins	15,800	Limnos	16	60 mins	15,000
Corfu	26	50 mins	20,700	Milos	7	45 mins	14,900
Crete (Hania)	25	50 mins	19,900	Mykonos	37	45 mins	19,100
Crete (Iraklio)	42	60 mins	21,900	Naxos	10	45 mins	20,100
Crete (Sitia)	3	85 mins	23,100	Paros	41	45 mins	18,900
Ikaria	4	50 mins	17,100	Rhodes	43	60 mins	24,900
Karpathos	3	120 mins	26,000	Samos	31	60 mins	17,000
Kassos	1	130 mins	24,700	Santorini	44	50 mins	22,200
Kefallonia	10	60 mins	17,900	Skiathos	8	40 mins	16,700
Kos	21	55 mins	21,400	Skyros	2	50 mins	14,200
Kythira	6	45 mins	14,400	Syros	9	35 mins	15,200
Leros	7	65 mins	21,200	Zakynthos	7	35 mins	17,400

This information is for flights between 14 June and 26 September. Outside these months, the number of flights to the islands drops dramatically – especially to Mykonos, Paros, Skiathos and Santorini.

Summer Flights from Thessaloniki to the Greek Islands

Destination	Flights/Week	Duration	Price (dr)	Destination	Flights/Week	Duration	Price (dr)
Chios	2	50 mins	22,400	Limnos	4	50 mins	15,200
Corfu	3	50 mins	20,900	Mykonos	3	75 mins	27,900
Crete (Hania)	2	75 mins	29,900	Rhodes	2	115 mins	31,900
Crete (Iraklio)	3	110 mins	29,900	Samos	2	80 mins	25,400
Lesvos	6	60 mins	20,900	Santorini	3	90 mins	30,400

Inter-Island Flights

Route	Flights/Week	Duration	Price (dr)	Route	Flights/Week	Duration	Price (dr)
Chios – Lesvos	2	30 mins	10,900	Kastellorizo – Rhodes	7	45 mins	10,900
Iraklio – Rhodes	4	45 mins	21,900	Lesvos – Limnos	1	35 mins	13,400
Iraklio – Santorini	2	40 mins	15,400	Mykonos – Rhodes	2	60 mins	22,900
Karpathos – Rhodes	14	40 mins	12,800	Mykonos – Santorini	5	30 mins	15,400
Kassos – Rhodes	3	40 mins	13,400	Rhodes – Santorini	5	60 mins	22,900

Olympic Airways and Air Greece both fly the Iraklio-Rhodes route; all other scheduled flights are operated by Olympic. See the table above for details.

Other routes are operated solely by Olympic. They include two flights a day to Alexandroupolis (65 mins, 18,600 dr) and Kavala (one hour, 18,300 dr) and five flights a week to Preveza (one hour, 13,900 dr). Preveza serves the island of Lefkada.

Mainland to Island Flights

Olympic Airways operates a busy schedule to the islands, particularly in summer. Athens has flights to a total of 22 islands, with services to all the island groups as well as to three destinations on Crete – Hania, Iraklio and Sitia. Thessaloniki also has flights to all the island groups except the Sporades. See the tables of summer flights from Athens and Thessaloniki to the Greek Islands below for details (fares given are one-way). Olympic's competitors offer cheaper fares on some of the more popular routes, so check around.

In spite of the number of flights, it can be hard to find a seat during July and August. Early bookings are recommended. Flight schedules are greatly reduced in winter.

Inter-Island Flights

Olympic Airways and Air Greece both fly the Iraklio-Rhodes route; all other scheduled flights are operated by Olympic. See the accompanying table for details.

Domestic Departure Tax

The airport tax for domestic flights is 3400 dr, paid as part of the ticket. All prices quoted in this book include this tax.

BUS

Buses are the mainstay of the country's public transport system. Fares are fixed by the government, and are very reasonable by European standards.

Mainland Services

Buses are operated by regional collectives known as KTEL (Koino Tamio Eispraxeon Leoforion). Every prefecture has its own KTEL, which operates local services within the prefecture and services to the main towns of other prefectures.

The network is comprehensive. With the exception of towns in Thrace, which are serviced by Thessaloniki, all the major towns have frequent connections to Athens. The islands of Corfu, Kefallonia and Zakynthos can also be reached directly from Athens by bus – the fares include the price of the ferry ticket.

Larger towns usually have a central, covered bus station with seating, waiting rooms, toilets, and a snack bar selling pies, cakes and coffee. Big cities like Athens, Patras and Thessaloniki have several bus stations, each serving different regions.

Most booking offices have timetables in both Greek and Roman script. They show both the departure and return times – useful if you are making a day trip. Times are listed using the 24-hour-clock system.

When you buy a ticket you will be allotted a seat number, noted on the ticket. The seat number is indicated on the back of each seat of the bus, not on the back of the seat in front; this causes confusion among Greeks and tourists alike. You can board a bus without a ticket and pay on board, but on a popular route, or during the high season, this may mean having to stand. Keep your ticket for the duration of the journey; it will be checked several times en route.

Buses do not have toilets on board and they don't have refreshments available, so make sure you are prepared on both counts. Buses stop about every three hours on long journeys. Smoking is prohibited on all buses in Greece; only the chain-smoking drivers dare to ignore the no-smoking signs.

Sample fares and journey times include: Athens-Thessaloniki, 7½ hours, 8200 dr; Athens-Patras, three hours, 3650 dr; Athens-Volos, five hours, 5250 dr; and Athens-Corfu, 11 hours, 8150 dr (including ferry).

Island Buses

Island bus services are less simple to summarise! There's an enormous difference in the level of services. Crete (which is split into three prefectures) is organised in the same way as the mainland – each prefecture has its own KTEL providing local services and services to the main towns of other prefectures. Most islands have just one bus company, operating out of the main town; some have just one bus.

As on the mainland, larger towns usually have a central, covered bus station with seating, waiting rooms, toilets, and a snack bar selling pies, cakes and coffee. In small towns and villages the 'bus station' may be no more than a bus stop outside a *kafeneio* or taverna which doubles as a booking office.

On islands where the capital is inland rather than a port, buses normally meet the boats. Some of the more remote islands have not yet acquired a bus, but most have some sort of motorised transport – even if it is only a bone-shaking, three-wheeled truck.

TRAIN

Most Greeks regard train travel as a poor alternative to road travel.

For starters, the rail network is limited. There are two main services: a standard-gauge line north from Athens to Thessaloniki and Alexandroupolis, and a narrow-gauge line from Athens to the Peloponnese.

There are also two very distinct levels of service: slow, stopping-all-stations services that crawl around the countryside, and express intercity trains that link the major cities.

The slow trains represent the country's cheapest form of public transport. The fares haven't changed for years; 2nd class fares are absurdly cheap, and even 1st class is much cheaper than bus travel. The downside is that the trains are painfully slow, uncomfortable and unreliable. There seems to be no effort to upgrade the dilapidated rolling stock. Unless you are travelling on a very tight budget, they are best left alone. Sample journey times and fares include Athens-Thessaloniki, 7½ hours, 5580/3720 dr (1st/2nd class); Athens-Patras, five hours, 2370/1580 dr; and Thessaloniki-Alexandroupolis, seven hours, 4490/2990 dr.

The Intercity trains are a much better way to travel. The services are not really express – the Greek terrain is too mountainous for that – but the trains are modern and comfortable. There are 1st and 2nd-class smoking/non-smoking seats and there is a cafe-bar on board. On some services, meals can be ordered and delivered to your seat.

Ticket prices for intercity services are subject to a distance loading on top of the normal fares. Seat reservations should be made as far in advance as possible, especially in summer. Sample journey times and fares include Athens-Thessaloniki, six hours, 10,480/8250 dr (1st/2nd class); Thessaloniki-Alexandroupolis, 5½ hours, 6770/4970 dr; and Athens-Patras, 3½ hours, 3970/2980 dr.

A comfortable night service runs between Athens and Thessaloniki with a choice of couchettes (from 1750 dr) and sleeping cars (from 3000 dr).

Eurail and Inter-Rail cards are valid in Greece, but it's not worth buying one if Greece is the only place you plan to use it. The passes can be used on intercity services without paying the loading, although you still need to make a seat reservation.

Tickets can be bought from OSE booking offices in a few major towns, otherwise from train stations. There is a 20% discount on return tickets, and a 30% discount for groups of 10 or more.

You'll find information on fares and schedules on the Hellenic Railways Organisation Web site (www.ose.gr).

CAR & MOTORCYCLE

Many of the islands are plenty big enough to warrant having your own vehicle. Roads have improved enormously in recent years, particularly on the larger, more visited islands like Crete. Few people bother to bring their own vehicle from Europe; there are plenty of places to hire both cars and motorcycles.

Almost all islands are served by car ferries, but they are expensive. Sample prices for small vehicles include Piraeus-Mykonos, 18,570 dr; Piraeus-Crete (Hania and Iraklio), 19,610 dr; Piraeus-Rhodes, 23,960 dr; and Piraeus-Lesvos, 22,230 dr. The charge for a large motorbike is about the same as the price of a 3rd class passenger ticket.

Petrol in Greece is also expensive, and the farther you get from a major city the more it costs. Prices vary from petrol station to petrol station. Super can be found as cheaply as 199 dr per litre at big city discount places, but 225 dr to 235 dr is the normal range. You may pay closer to 245 dr per litre on the islands. The price range for unleaded – available everywhere – is from 200 dr to 225 dr per litre. Diesel costs about 170 dr per litre.

See the Documents section in the Facts for the Visitor chapter for information on licence requirements.

See the Useful Organisations section in the Facts for the Visitor chapter for information about the Greek automobile club (ELPA).

Road Rules

In Greece, as throughout Continental Europe, you drive on the right and overtake on the left. Outside built-up areas, traffic on a main road has right of way at intersections. In towns, vehicles coming from the right have right of way. Seat belts must be worn in front seats, and in back seats if the car is fitted with them. Children under 12 years of age are not allowed in the front seat. It is compulsory to carry a first-aid kit, fire extinguisher and warning triangle, and it is forbidden to carry cans of petrol. Helmets are compulsory for motorcyclists if the motorbike is 50cc or more.

Outside residential areas the speed limit is 120km/h on highways, 90km/h on other roads and 50km/h in built-up areas. The speed limit for motorbikes up to 100cc is 70km/h and for larger motorbikes, 90km/h.

Drivers exceeding the speed limit by 20% are liable for a fine of 20,000 dr; and by 40%, 50,000 dr. Other offences and fines include:

illegal overtaking – 100,000 dr
going through a red light – 100,000 dr
driving without a seat belt – 50,000 dr
motorcyclist not wearing a helmet – 50,000 dr
wrong way down one-way street – 50,000 dr
illegal parking – 10,000 dr

The police have also cracked down on drink-driving laws – at last. A blood-alcohol content of 0.05% is liable to incur a fine of 50,000 dr, and over 0.08% is a criminal offence.

The police can issue traffic fines, but payment cannot be made on the spot – you will be told where to pay.

If you are involved in an accident and no-one is hurt, the police will not be required to write a report, but it is advisable to go to a nearby police station and explain what happened. A police report may be required for insurance purposes. If an accident involves injury, a driver who does not stop and does not inform the police may face a prison sentence.

Warning If you are planning to use a motorcycle or moped, check that your travel insurance covers you for injury resulting from a motorbike accident. Many insurance companies don't offer this cover; so check the fine print!

Rental

Car Most of the big multinational car hire companies have branches in Athens and on the major tourist islands. High-season weekly rates with unlimited mileage start at about 110,000 dr for the smallest models, such as a 900cc Fiat Panda. The rate drops to about 90,000 dr per week in winter. To these prices must be added VAT of 18%, or 13% on the islands of the Dodecanese, the North-Eastern Aegean and the Sporades. Then there are the optional extras, such as a collision damage waiver of 3300 dr per day (more for larger models), without which you will be liable for the first 1,500,000 dr of the repair bill (much more for larger models). Other costs include a theft waiver of at least 1000 dr per day and personal accident insurance. It all adds up to an expensive exercise. Some companies offer much cheaper prebooked and prepaid rates.

The many local companies are normally more open to negotiation, especially if business is slow. Their advertised rates are about 25% cheaper than those offered by the multinationals. Smaller islands may have only one car hire outlet.

If you want to take a hire car onto a ferry, you will need advance written authorisation from the hire company. Unless you pay with a credit card, most hire companies will require a minimum deposit of 20,000 dr per day.

The minimum driving age in Greece is 18 years, but most car hire firms require you to be at least 23, although some will rent to 21-year-olds.

See the Getting Around sections of cities and islands for details of places to rent cars.

Motorcycle Mopeds and motorcycles are available for hire wherever there are tourists to rent them. In many cases their maintenance has been minimal, so check the machine thoroughly before you hire it – especially the brakes: you'll need them!

Motorbikes are a cheap way to travel around. Rates range from 2500 dr to 4000 dr per day for a moped or 50cc motorbike to 6000 dr per day for a 250cc motorbike. Out of season these prices drop considerably, so use your bargaining skills. By October it is sometimes possible to hire a moped for as little as 1500 dr per day.

The islands can be a dangerous place for novices. Dozens of tourists have accidents every year on the many steep, poorly maintained roads. Most motorcycle hirers include third party insurance in the price, but it is wise to check this. This insurance will not include medical expenses.

BICYCLE
Cycling has not caught on in Greece, which isn't surprising considering the hilly terrain. Tourists are beginning to cycle in Greece, but you'll need strong leg muscles. You can hire bicycles in most tourist places, but they are not as widely available as cars and motorbikes. Prices range from 1000 dr to 3000 dr per day, depending on the type and age of the bike. Bicycles are carried free on ferries.

HITCHING
Hitching is never entirely safe in any country in the world, and we don't recommend it. Travellers who decide to hitch should understand that they are taking a small but potentially serious risk. People who do choose to hitch will be safer if they travel in pairs and should let someone know where they are planning to go. Greece has a reputation for being a relatively safe place for women to hitch, but it is still unwise to do it alone. It's better for women to hitch with a companion, preferably a male one.

Some parts of Greece are much better for hitching than others. Getting out of major cities tends to be hard work, and Athens is notoriously difficult. Hitching is much easier in remote areas and on islands with poor public transport. On country roads, it is not unknown for someone to stop and ask if you want a lift even if you haven't stuck a thumb out. You can't afford to be fussy about the mode of transport – it may be a tractor or a spluttering old truck.

WALKING
Unless you have come to Greece just to lie on a beach, the chances are you will do quite a bit of walking. You don't have to be a trekker to start clocking up the kilometres. The narrow, stepped streets of many towns and villages can only be explored on foot, and visiting the archaeological sites involves a fair amount of legwork. See the What to Bring, Health and Trekking sections in the Facts for the Visitor chapter for more information about walking.

BOAT
Ferry
For most people, travel in Greece means island-hopping. Every island has a ferry service of some sort, although in winter services to some of the smaller islands are fairly skeletal. Services start to pick up again from April onwards, and by July and August there are countless services criss-crossing the Aegean. Ferries come in all shapes and sizes, from the giant 'superferries' that work the major routes to the small, ageing open ferries that chug around the backwaters.

Routes The hub of Greece's ferry network is Piraeus, the port of Athens. Ferries leave here for the Cyclades, Dodecanese, the North-Eastern Aegean Islands, Saronic Gulf Islands and Crete. Athens' second port is Rafina, 70km east of the city and connected by an hourly bus service. It has ferries to the northern Cyclades, Evia, Lesvos and Limnos. The port of Lavrio, in southern Attica, is the main port for ferries to the Cycladic island of Kea. There are regular buses from Athens to Lavrio.

Ferries for the Ionian Islands leave from the Peloponnese ports of Patras (for Kefal-

lonia, Ithaki, Paxi and Corfu) and Kyllini (for Kefallonia and Zakynthos); from Astakos (for Ithaki) in Sterea Ellada; and from Igoumenitsa in Epiros (for Corfu).

Ferries for the Sporades leave from Volos, Thessaloniki, Agios Konstantinos, and Kymi on Evia. The latter two ports are easily reached by bus from Athens.

Some of the North-Eastern Aegean Islands have connections with Thessaloniki as well as Piraeus. The odd ones out are Thasos, which is reached from Kavala, and

GREECE - HYDROFOIL & CATAMARAN ROUTES

ROUTES
· · · · · · · · Catamaran
– – – – – Hydrofoil

Samothraki, which can be reached from Alexandroupolis year-round and also from Kavala in summer.

Schedules Ferry timetables change from year to year and season to season, and ferries are subject to delays and cancellations at short notice due to bad weather, strikes or boats simply conking out. No timetable is infallible, but the comprehensive weekly list of departures from Piraeus put out by the EOT in Athens is as accurate as humanly possible. The people to go to for the most up-to-date ferry information are the local port police (limenarheio), whose offices are usually on or near the quay side.

There's lots of information about ferry services on the Internet. Try www.ferries.gr, which has a useful search program and links. Many of the larger ferry companies now have their own sites, including:

Agapitos Lines: www.agapitos-ferries.gr
ANEK: www.anek.gr
Minoan Lines: www.minoan.gr
Strintzis: www.strintzis.gr
Superfast: www.superfast.com
Ventouris: www.ventouris.gr

Throughout the year there is at least one ferry a day from a mainland port to the major island in each group, and during the high season (from June to mid-September) there are considerably more. Ferries sailing from one island group to another are not so frequent, and if you're going to travel in this way you'll need to plan carefully, otherwise you may end up having to backtrack to Piraeus.

Travelling time can vary considerably from one ferry to another, depending on the ship and the route it takes. For example, the Piraeus-Rhodes trip can take between 14 and 18 hours. Before buying your ticket, check how many stops the boat is going to make, and its estimated arrival time.

Costs Prices are fixed by the government, and are determined by the distance travelled rather than by the facilities of a particular boat. There can be big differences in the size, comfort and facilities of boats offering rival services on a given route, but the fares will be the same. The small differences in price you may find at ticket agencies are the result of some agents sacrificing part of their designated commission to qualify as a 'discount service'. The discount is seldom more than 50 dr.

Classes The large ferries usually have four classes: 1st class has air-con cabins and a posh lounge and restaurant; 2nd class has smaller cabins and sometimes a separate lounge; tourist class gives you a berth in a shared four-berth cabin; and 3rd (deck) class gives you access to a room with 'airline' seats, a restaurant, a lounge/bar and, of course, the deck.

Deck class remains an economical way to travel, while a 1st class ticket can cost almost as much as flying on some routes. Children under four travel for free, while children between four and 10 pay half fare. Full fares apply for children over 10. Unless you state otherwise when purchasing a ticket, you will automatically be given deck class. Prices quoted in this book are for deck class as this is what most tourists opt for.

Ticket Purchase Ferries are prone to delays and cancellations in bad weather, so it's best not to buy a ticket until it has been confirmed that the ferry is operating. If you need to reserve a car space, you may need to pay in advance. If the service is cancelled, you can transfer your ticket to the next available service with that company.

Agencies selling tickets line the waterfront of most ports, but rarely is there one that sells tickets for every boat, and often an agency is reluctant to give you information about a boat they do not sell tickets for. This means you have to check the timetables displayed outside each agency to find out which ferry is next to depart – or ask the port police. In high season, a number of boats may be due at a port at around the same time, so it is not beyond the realms of possibility that you might get on the wrong boat. The crucial thing to look out for is the name of the boat; this will be printed on your ticket, and in large English letters on the side of the vessel.

If for some reason you haven't purchased a ticket from an agency, makeshift ticket tables are put up beside a ferry about an hour before departure. Tickets can also be purchased on board the ship after it has sailed. If you are waiting at the quay side for a delayed ferry, don't lose patience and wander off. Ferry boats, once they turn up, can demonstrate amazing alacrity – blink and you may miss the boat.

Ferry Travel Once on board, the fun really begins. It can be absolute chaos in high season. No matter how many passengers are already on the ferry, more will be crammed on. Bewildered, black-shrouded grannies are steered through the crowd by teenage grandchildren, children get separated from parents, people stumble over backpacks, dogs get excited and bark – and everyone rushes to grab a seat. As well as birds in cages and cats in baskets there is almost always at least one truck of livestock on board – usually sheep, goats or cattle, vociferously making their presence known.

Greeks travelling deck class usually make a beeline for the indoor lounge/snack bar, while tourists make for the deck where they can sunbathe. Some ferry companies have allegedly attempted to capitalise on this natural division by telling backpackers and non-Greeks that they are barred from the deck-class saloon and indoor-seating area, directing them instead to the sun deck. There is no such thing as 'deck only' class on domestic ferries, although there is on international ferries.

You'll need strong nerves and lungs to withstand the lounge/snack bar, though. You can reckon on at least two TVs turned up full blast, tuned to different channels and crackling furiously from interference. A couple of other people will have ghetto blasters pumping out heavy metal, and everyone will be engaged in loud conversation. Smoke-laden air adds the final touch to this delightful ambience. Unlike other

Meeting the Ferry

At a few remote islands, the arrival of a ferry boat is a once or twice-weekly occurrence which provides a lifeline for the inhabitants. Witnessing the arrival of a ferry at such an island is an interesting spectacle, as it is one of the most exciting events of the week. It seems as if the whole population – including at least one tail-wagging dog – turns out to meet the ferry. Arriving and departing relations are warmly embraced, sacks of vegetables and crates of drinks are unloaded quickly and haphazardly, and high-tech and industrial appliances are carried off with the utmost care. All this takes place amid frantic arm waving, shouting and general pandemonium in the rush to ensure that the ferry arrives on time at the next island – which invariably it does not. It serves to remember on such occasions that chaos is a Greek word and that the Greeks invented drama. Eventually, the task completed, the ferry departs and the island slips back into its customary tranquillity.

public transport in Greece, smoking is not prohibited on ferries.

On overnight trips, backpackers usually sleep on deck in their sleeping bags – you can also roll out your bag between the 'airline' seats. If you don't have a sleeping bag, claim an 'airline' seat as soon as you board. Leave your luggage on it – as long as you don't leave any valuables in it. The noise on board usually dies down around midnight so you should be able to snatch a few hours of sleep.

The food sold at ferry snack bars ranges from mediocre to inedible, and the choice is limited to packets of biscuits, sandwiches, very greasy pizzas and cheese pies. Most large ferries also have a self-service restaurant where the food is OK and reasonably priced, with main courses starting at around 1500 dr. If you are budgeting, have special dietary requirements, or are at all fussy about what you eat, take food with you.

Inter-Island Boat

In addition to the large ferries which ply between the large mainland ports and island groups, there are smaller boats which link islands within a group, and occasionally, an island in one group with an island in another. In the past these boats were always caïques – sturdy old fishing boats – but gradually these are being replaced by new purpose-built boats, which are usually called express or excursion boats. Tickets tend to cost more than those for the large ferries, but the boats are very useful if you're island-hopping.

Hydrofoil

Hydrofoils offer a faster alternative to ferries on some routes, particularly to islands close to the mainland. They take half the time, but cost twice as much. They do not take cars or motorbikes. Most routes operate only during high season, and according to demand, and all are prone to cancellations if the sea is rough. The ride can be bumpy at the best of times.

The biggest operator is Minoan Flying Dolphin, which runs the busy Argosaronic network linking Piraeus with the Saronic Gulf Islands and the ports of the eastern Peloponnese (plus occasional services south to the Ionian island of Kythira). Minoan also operates services from Piraeus to the western and central Cyclades, and from Agios Konstantinos, Thessaloniki and Volos to Evia and the Sporades.

Hydrofoil services in the eastern and southern Cyclades are operated by Speed Lines out of Santorini. These Santorini Dolphins operate daily between Santorini, Ios, Naxos, Paros, Tinos and Syros, with services to Folegandros, Sikinos and Milos once or twice a week – and occasional services to Iraklio on Crete.

The Dodecanese has its own network, centred on Rhodes, with connections to the North-East Aegean islands of Ikaria and Samos. Other routes are between Kavala

and Thasos, and from Alexandroupolis to Samothraki and Limnos.

Tickets cannot be bought on board hydrofoils – you must buy them in advance from an agent. You will be allocated a seat number.

Catamaran

High-speed catamarans have rapidly become an important part of the island travel scene. They are just as fast as the hydrofoils – if not faster – and much more comfortable. They are also much less prone to cancellation in rough weather.

Minoan Flying Dolphin again is the major player. Its giant *Highspeed 1* runs daily between Piraeus, Syros, Mykonos, Paros and Naxos, and it uses smaller cats on many of the routes around the Saronic Gulf.

Catamarans have now taken over from hydrofoils on the routes from Rafina to the central and northern Cyclades. Strintzis Lines uses the *Seajet 1* for the daily run to Syros, Paros, Naxos, Ios and Santorini, and the *Seajet 2* to Tinos and Mykonos, stopping once a week at Andros, Syros, Paros, Naxos and Amorgos. Goutos Lines operates its *Athina 2004* on a similar schedule.

These services are very popular; book as far in advance as possible, especially if you want to travel on weekends.

Taxi Boat

Most islands have taxi boats – small speedboats which operate like taxis, transporting people to places that are difficult to get to by land. Some owners charge a set price for each person, others charge a flat rate for the boat, and this cost is divided by the number of passengers. Either way, prices are usually quite reasonable.

Yacht

Despite the disparaging remarks among backpackers, yachting is *the* way to see the Greek Islands. Nothing beats the peace and serenity of sailing the open sea, and the freedom of being able to visit remote and uninhabited islands.

The free EOT booklet *Sailing the Greek Seas*, although long overdue for an update, contains lots of information about weather conditions, weather bulletins, entry and exit regulations, entry and exit ports and guidebooks for yachties. You can pick up the booklet at any GNTO/EOT office either abroad or in Greece. The Internet is the place to look for the latest information. The Hellenic Yachting Server site, www.na.biznet.com.gr/sail, has general information on sailing around the islands and lots of links.

The sailing season lasts from April until October. The best time to go depends on where you are going. The most popular time is between July and September, which ties in with the high season for tourism in general. Unfortunately, it also happens to be the time of year when the *meltemi* is at its strongest. The meltemi is a northerly wind that affects the Aegean throughout the summer. It starts off as a mild wind in May and June, and strengthens as the weather hots up – often blowing from a clear blue sky. In August and September, it can blow at gale force for days on end.

The meltemi is not an issue in the Ionian Sea, where the main summer wind is the *maistros*, a light to moderate north-westerly that rises in the afternoon. It usually dies away at sunset.

If your budget won't cover buying a yacht there are several other options open to you. You can hire a bare boat (a yacht without a crew) if two crew members have a sailing certificate. Prices start at US$1300 per week for a 28-footer that will sleep six. It's an option only if two crew members have a sailing certificate; otherwise you can hire a skipper for an extra US$100 per day.

Most of the hire companies are based in and around Athens. They include:

Aegean Tourism
 (☎ 01-346 6229, fax 342 2121)
 Kadmias 8, Athens
Alpha Yachting
 (☎ 01-968 0486, fax 968 0488,
 email mano@ otenet.gr)
 Poseidonos 67, Glyfada

Ghiolman Yachts & Travel
 (☎ 01-323 3696, fax 322 3251,
 email ghiol man@travelling.gr)
 Filellinon 7, Athens
Hellenic Charters
 (☎/fax 01-988 5592,
 email hctsa@ath.forth net.gr)
 Poseidonos 66, Alimos
Kostis Yachting
 (☎ 01-895 0657, fax 895 0995)
 Epaminonda 61, Glyfada
 www.kostis-yachting.com
Vernicos Yachts
 (☎ 01-985 0122, fax 985 0120)
 Poseidonos 11, Alimos
 www.vernicos.gr

There are many more yacht charter companies in Greece; the EOT can provide addresses.

LOCAL TRANSPORT
To/From the Airports
Olympic Airways operates buses to a few domestic airports (see individual entries in the appropriate chapters). Where the service exists, buses leave the airline office about 1½ hours before departure. In many places, the only way to get to the airport is by taxi.

Check-in is an hour before departure for domestic flights. Transport to and from international airports in Greece is covered in the Getting Around section of the relevant city.

Bus
Most Greek towns are small enough to get around on foot. The only places where you may need to use local buses are Athens, Piraeus and Thessaloniki. The procedure for buying tickets for local buses is covered in the Getting Around section for each city.

Metro
Athens is the only city in Greece large enough to warrant an underground system. See the Athens chapter for news on the metro extension program: at the time of writing two new lines were due to start operations in late 1999.

Taxi

Taxis are widely available in Greece except on very small or remote islands. They are reasonably priced by European standards, especially if three or four people share costs.

Yellow city cabs are metered. Flagfall is 200 dr, followed by 62 dr per kilometre (120 dr per kilometre outside town). These rates double between midnight and 5 am. Additional costs (on top of the per-kilometre rate) are 300 dr from an airport, 150 dr from a bus, port or train station and 55 dr for each piece of luggage. Grey rural taxis do not have meters, so you should always settle on a price before you get in.

The taxi drivers of Athens are legendary for their ability to part locals and tourists alike from their drachma – see the 'Dangers & Annoyances' section in the Athens chapter. If you have a complaint about a taxi driver, take the cab number and report your complaint to the tourist police. Taxi drivers in other towns in Greece are, on the whole, friendly, helpful and honest.

ORGANISED TOURS

Tours are worth considering only if your time is very limited, in which case you'll find countless companies vying for your money. See the respective island chapters for more information.

Organised Treks

Trekking Hellas (☎ 01-325 0853, fax 323 4548, email trekking@compulink.gr), at Filellinon 7, Athens 105 57, specialises in treks and other adventure activities for small groups throughout Greece. Its program includes walks on the Ionian island of Ithaki and on the Cycladic islands of Andros and Tinos.

See the Hania and Rethymno sections of the Crete chapter for information about organised treks on Crete.

MYTHOLOGY

Mythology was an integral part of life in ancient times. The myths are accounts of the lives of the deities whom the Greeks worshipped and of the heroes they idolised.

The myths are all things to all people – a ripping good yarn, expressions of deep psychological insights, words of spine-tingling poetic beauty and food for the imagination. They have inspired great literature, art and music – as well as the odd TV show.

The myths we know are thought to be a blend of Dorian and Mycenaean mythology. Most accounts derive from the works of the poets Hesiod and Homer, produced in about 900 BC. The original myths have been chopped and changed countless times – dramatised, moralised and even adapted for ancient political propaganda – so numerous versions exist.

The Greek Myths by Robert Graves is regarded as being the ultimate book on the subject. It can be heavy going, though. *An Iconoclast's Guide to the Greek Gods* by Maureen O'Sullivan makes more entertaining reading.

The Twelve Deities

The main characters of the myths are the 12 deities who lived on Mt Olympus – which the Greeks thought to be at the exact centre of the world.

The supreme deity was **Zeus**, who was also god of the heavens. His job was to make laws and keep his unruly family in order by brandishing his thunderbolt. He was also the possessor of an astonishing libido and vented his lust on just about everyone he came across, including his own mother. Mythology is littered with his offspring.

Zeus was married to his sister, **Hera**, the protector of women and the family. Hera was able to renew her virginity each year by bathing in a spring. She was the mother of Ares, Hephaestus and Hebe.

Ares, god of war, was the embodiment of everything warlike. Strong and brave, he was definitely someone to have on your side in a fight – but he was also hot-tempered and violent, liking nothing better than a good massacre. Athenians, who fought only for such noble ideals as liberty, thought that Ares must be a Thracian – whom they regarded as bloodthirsty barbarians.

Hephaestus was worshipped for his matchless skills as a craftsman. When

Zeus decided to punish man, he asked Hephaestus to make a woman. So Hephaestus created Pandora from clay and water, and, as everyone knows, she had a box, from which sprang all the evils afflicting humankind.

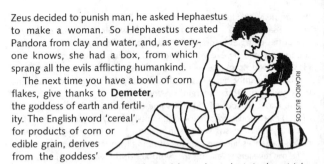

RICARDO BUSTOS

The next time you have a bowl of corn flakes, give thanks to **Demeter**, the goddess of earth and fertility. The English word 'cereal', for products of corn or edible grain, derives from the goddess' Roman name, Ceres. The Greek word for such products is *demetriaka*.

The goddess of love (and lust) was the beautiful **Aphrodite**. Her *tour de force* was her magic girdle which made everyone fall in love with its wearer. The girdle meant she was constantly pursued by both gods and goddesses – the gods because they wanted to make love to her, the goddesses because they wanted to borrow the girdle. Zeus became so fed up with her promiscuity that he married her off to Hephaestus, the ugliest of the gods.

Athena, the powerful goddess of wisdom and guardian of Athens, is said to have been born (complete with helmet, armour and spear) from Zeus' head, with Hephaestus acting as midwife. Unlike Ares, she derived no pleasure from fighting, preferring to use her wisdom to settle disputes peacefully. If need be, however, she went valiantly into battle.

Poseidon, the brother of Zeus, was god of the sea and preferred his sumptuous palace in the depths of the Aegean to Mt Olympus. When he was angry (which was often) he would use his trident to create massive waves and floods. His moods could also trigger earthquakes and volcanic eruptions. He was always on the lookout for some real estate on dry land and challenged Dionysos for Naxos, Hera for Argos and Athena for Athens.

Apollo, god of light, was the son of Zeus by the nymph Leto. He was the sort of person everybody wanted to have around. The ancient Greeks associated sunshine with spiritual and intellectual illumination. Apollo was also worshipped as the god of music and song, which the ancients believed were heard only where there was light and security. His twin sister, **Artemis**, seems to have been a bit confused by her portfolio. She was worshipped as the goddess of childbirth, yet she asked Zeus to grant her eternal virginity; she was also the protector of suckling animals, but loved hunting!

Hermes, messenger of the gods, was another son of Zeus – this time by Maia, daughter of Atlas. He was a colourful character who smooth-talked his way into the top ranks of the Greek pantheon. Convicted of rustling Apollo's cattle while still in his cradle, he emerged from the case as the guardian of all divine property. Zeus then made Hermes his messenger, and fitted him out with a pair of winged golden sandals to speed

MYTHOLOGY

him on his way. His job included responsibility for commerce, treaties and the safety of travellers. He remained, however, the patron of thieves.

Hermes completes the first XI – the gods whose position in the pantheon is agreed by everyone. The final berth is normally reserved for **Hestia**, goddess of the hearth. She was as pure as driven snow, a symbol of security, happiness and hospitality. She spurned disputes and wars and swore to be a virgin forever.

She was a bit too virtuous for some, who relegated her to the ranks of the Lesser Gods and promoted the fun-loving **Dionysos**, god of wine, in her place. Dionysos was a son of Zeus by another of the supreme deity's dalliances. He had the job of touring the world with an entourage of fellow revellers spreading the word about the vine and wine.

Lesser Gods

After his brothers Zeus and Poseidon had taken the heavens and seas, **Hades** was left with the underworld (the earth was common ground). This vast and mysterious region was thought by the Greeks to be as far beneath the earth as the sky was above it. The underworld was divided into three regions: the Elysian Fields for the virtuous, Tartarus for sinners and the Asphodel Meadows for those who fitted neither category. Hades was also the god of wealth, in the form of the precious stones and metals found deep in the earth.

Pan, the son of Hermes, was the god of the shepherds. Born with horns, beard, tail and goat legs, his ugliness so amused the other gods that eventually he fled to Arcadia where he danced, played his famous pipes and watched over the pastures, shepherds and herds.

Other gods included: **Asclepius**, god of healing; **Eros**, god of love; **Hypnos**, god of sleep; **Helios**, god of the sun; and **Selene**, goddess of the moon.

Mythology & the Islands

The Gods may have lived on Mt Olympus, but their influence extended to the farthest reaches of Greek territory and the islands feature prominently in mythology.

The sacred island of **Delos** was the birthplace of the twins Apollo and Artemis, while Zeus himself was raised in a cave on the island **Crete**.

The island of **Ikaria** is named after Icarus, who plunged into the sea after he flew too close to the sun. **Aegina** is named after a daughter of the river god, Asopus. She was taken to the island by Zeus on another of his lecherous sorties.

RICARDO BUSTOS

Olympian Creation Myth

According to mythology, the world was formed from a great shapeless mass called Chaos. From Chaos came forth Gaea, the earth goddess. She bore a son, Uranus, the Firmament, and their subsequent union produced three 100-handed giants and three one-eyed Cyclopes. Gaea dearly loved her hideous offspring, but not so Uranus, who hurled them into Tartarus (the underworld).

The couple then produced the seven Titans, but Gaea still grieved for her other children. She asked the Titans to take vengeance upon their father, and free the 100-handed giants and the Cyclopes. The Titans did as they were requested, castrating the hapless Uranus, but Cronos (the head Titan), after setting eyes on Gaea's hideous offspring, hurled them back into Tartarus, whereupon Gaea foretold that Cronos would be usurped by one of his own offspring.

Cronos married his sister Rhea, but wary of his mother's warning, he swallowed every child Rhea bore him. When Rhea bore her sixth child, Zeus, she smuggled him to Crete, and gave Cronos a stone in place of the child, which he duly swallowed. Rhea hid the baby Zeus in the Dikteon cave in the care of three nymphs.

On reaching manhood, Zeus, determined to avenge his swallowed siblings, became Cronos' cupbearer and filled his cup with poison. Cronos drank from the cup, then disgorged first the stone and then his children Hestia, Demeter, Hera, Poseidon and Hades, all of whom were none the worse for their ordeal. Zeus, aided by his regurgitated brothers and sisters, deposed Cronos, and went to war against the Titans who wouldn't acknowledge him as chief god. Gaea, who still hadn't forgotten her imprisoned, beloved offspring, told Zeus he would only be victorious with the help of the Cyclopes and the 100-handed giants, so he released them from Tartarus.

The Cyclopes gave Zeus a thunderbolt, and the three 100-handed giants threw rocks at the Titans, who eventually retreated. Zeus banished Cronos, as well as all of the Titans except Atlas (Cronos' deputy), to a far-off land. Atlas was ordered to hold up the sky.

Mt Olympus became home-sweet-home for Zeus and his family. Zeus soon took a fancy to his sister Hera. He tricked the unsuspecting Hera into holding him to her bosom by turning himself into a dishevelled cuckoo, then violated her. Hera reluctantly agreed to marry him and they had three children: Ares, Hephaestus and Hebe.

RICARDO BUSTOS

Athens Αθήνα

☎ 01 • postcode 102 00 (Omonia),
103 00 (Syntagma) • pop 3.7 million

Ancient Athens ranks alongside Rome and
Jerusalem for its glorious past and its influence on western civilisation, but the modern
city is a place few people fall in love with.

However inspiring the Acropolis might
be, most visitors have trouble coming to
terms with the surrounding urban sprawl,
the traffic congestion and the pollution.

The city is not, however, without its re-
deeming features. The Acropolis is but one of
many important ancient sites, and the National Archaeological Museum has the
world's finest collection of Greek antiquities.

Culturally, Athens is a fascinating blend
of east and west. King Otho and the middle
class that emerged after Independence may
have been intent on making Athens a European city, but the influence of Asia Minor is
everywhere – the coffee, the kebabs, the
raucous street vendors and the colourful
markets.

HISTORY

The early history of Athens is so interwoven
with mythology that it's hard to disentangle
fact from fiction.

According to mythology, the city was
founded by a Phoenician called Cecrops,
who came to Attica and decided that the
Acropolis was the perfect spot for a city.
The gods of Olympus then proclaimed that
the city should be named after the deity who
could produce the most valuable gift to
mortals. Athena and Poseidon contended.
Poseidon struck the ground with his trident
and a magnificent horse sprang forth, sym-
bolising the warlike qualities for which he
was renowned. Athena produced an olive
tree, the symbol of peace and prosperity,
and won hands down.

According to archaeologists, the Acropolis has been occupied since Neolithic
times. It was an excellent vantage point, and
the steep slopes formed natural defences on

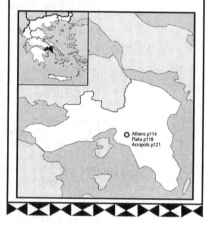

HIGHLIGHTS

- The inspirational Acropolis (and
  outdoor dining below it)
- The treasures of the National
  Archaeological Museum
- The panoramic view from Lykavittos Hill
- The lively *rembetika* clubs

⊙ Athens p114
✕ Plaka p118
Acropolis p121

three sides. By 1400 BC the Acropolis was
a powerful Mycenaean city.

Its power peaked during the so-called
golden age of Athens in the 5th century BC,
following the defeat of the Persians at the
Battle of Salamis. It fell into decline after its
defeat by Sparta in the long-running Peloponnesian War, but rallied again in Roman
times when it became a seat of learning.
The Roman emperors, particularly Hadrian,
graced Athens with many grand buildings.

After the Roman Empire split into east
and west, power shifted to Byzantium and
the city fell into obscurity. By the end of Ottoman rule, Athens was little more than a dilapidated village (the area now known as
Plaka).

Then, in 1834, Athens became the capital of independent Greece. The newly crowned King Otho, freshly arrived from Bavaria, began rebuilding the city along neoclassical lines, featuring large squares and tree-lined boulevards with imposing public buildings. The city grew steadily and enjoyed a brief heyday as the 'Paris of the Mediterranean' in the late 19th and early 20th centuries.

The hisorical event which, more than any other, shaped the Athens of today was the compulsory population exchange between Greece and Turkey that followed the Treaty of Lausanne in 1923. The huge influx of refugees from Asia Minor virtually doubled the population overnight, forcing the hasty erection of the first of the concrete apartment blocks that dominate the city today.

The belated advent of Greece's industrial age in the 1950s brought another wave of migration, this time of rural folk looking for jobs. The city's infrastructure, particularly road and transport, could not keep pace with such rapid and unplanned growth, and by the end of the 80s the city had developed a sorry reputation as one of the most traffic-clogged and polluted in Europe.

The 1990s appear to have been a turning point in the city's development with politicians finally accepting the need for radical solutions. Jolted into action by the failed bid to stage the 1996 Olympics, authorities embarked on an ambitious program to prepare the city for the 21st century. Two key elements in this program have been a major expansion of the Metro network, and the construction of a new international airport at Spata, east of Athens (see the Getting Around section later in this chapter).

These projects played an important role in the city's successful bid to stage the 2004 Olympics. The Olympics have now created a momentum of their own; confidence is riding high and billions are being poured into city centre redevelopment.

You can check out the latest Olympic news on the official Web site www.athens 2004.gr.

ORIENTATION

Although Athens is a huge, sprawling city, nearly everything of interest to travellers is located within a small area bounded by Omonia Square (Plateia Omonias) to the north, Monastiraki Square (Plateia Monastirakiou) to the west, Syntagma Square (Plateia Syntagmatos) to the east and the Plaka district to the south. The city's two major landmarks, the Acropolis and Lykavittos Hill, can be seen from just about everywhere in this area.

Syntagma is the heart of modern Athens; it's flanked by luxury hotels, banks and fast-food outlets and dominated by the old royal palace – home of the Greek parliament since 1935.

The Olympics Come Home

While much of central Athens has disappeared behind construction hoardings amid a frenzy of renovation and reconstruction in the lead-up to the 2004 Olympics, most of the facilities for the games themselves are already completed and operational.

The centrepiece is the 80,000-seat Olympic Stadium, in the northern suburb of Maroussi, which will stage the athletic events as well as the opening and closing ceremonies. The stadium has doubled as the city's No 1 soccer venue since it was completed in 1996.

The stadium is part of the Athens Olympic Sports Complex, next to Irini metro station, which also includes an indoor sports hall for gymnastics and basketball, a swimming complex and diving pool, a velodrome and a tennis centre.

The other major area of Olympic activity is in the coastal suburb of Faliro. Karaïskaki Stadium, home ground of the Olympiakos soccer club, will host the hockey competition, while the nearby Peace and Friendship Stadium will be used for volleyball and handball as well as wrestling and judo. The yachting will be held in Faliro Bay.

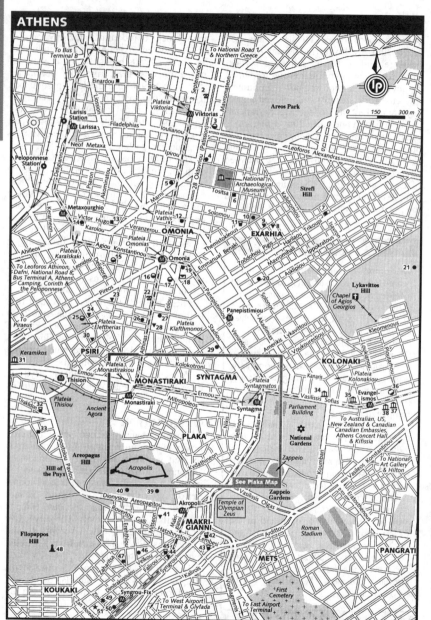

ATHENS

To Bus
Terminal B
To National Road 1
& Northern Greece

Einardou
Areos Park

Larisis
Station
Plateia
Viktorias
Viktorias

Larissa
Filadelphias

Neof Metaxa
Leoforos Alexandras

Peloponnese
Station
Ipirou
Strefi
Hill

National
Archaeological
Museum
Tositsa

Metaxourghio
Victor Hugo
Plateia
Vathis
OMONIA
EXARHIA

Ahilleos
Plateia
Omonias
Plateia
Karaiskaki
Agiou Konstantinou
Omonia
Panepistimiou
Lykavittos
Hill

To Leoforos Athinon,
Dafni, National Road 8,
Bus Terminal A, Athens
Camping, Corinth &
the Peloponnese
Pireos
Panepistimiou
Chapel
of Agios
Georgios

To
Piraeus
Plateia
Eleftherias
Plateia
Klafthmonos
KOLONAKI

Plateia
Kolonakiou

Keramikos
Plateia
Monastirakiou
Kolokotroni
SYNTAGMA
Plateia
Syntagmatos
Evangel-
ismos

Thision
Ermou
MONASTIRAKI
Ermou

Plateia
Thisiou
Monastiraki
Mitropoleos
Syntagma
Parliament
Building
To Australian, US,
New Zealand & Canadian
Canadian Embassies,
Athens Concert Hall
& Kifissia

Ancient
Agora
PLAKA
National
Gardens
To National
Art Gallery
& Hilton

Areopagus
Hill
Zappeio

Hill of
the Pnyx
Acropolis
See Plaka Map

Zappeio
Gardens

Dionysiou Areopagitou
Akropoli
Temple of
Olympian
Zeus

Fllopappos
Hill
MAKRI-
GIANNI
Roman
Stadium
PANGRATI

METS

KOUKAKI
Syngrou-Fix
To West Airport
Terminal & Glyfada
To East Airport
Terminal
First
Cemetery

PLACES TO STAY		
1	Hostel Aphrodite	
6	Museum Hotel	
13	Athens International Youth Hostel	
33	Hotel Erechthion	
47	Art Gallery Pension	
49	Marble House Pension	

PLACES TO EAT		
8	Taverna Barbargiannis	
9	Ouzeri I Gonia	
23	Restaurant Nargis	
24	Bengal Garden	
28	Meat Market Tavernas	
30	Embros	
41	Socrates Prison Taverna	
44	To 24 Hours	

OTHER		
2	OTE	

3	Mavromateon Bus Terminal
4	Museum Internet Cafe
5	Rodon Club
7	Supermarket
10	Plateia Exarchion
11	AN Club & Rembetika Boemissa
12	Astor Internet Cafe
14	Laundrette
15	Bus 051 to Bus Terminal A
16	Bus 049 to Piraeus
17	Bus 091 to Airport
18	Main Post Office
19	Bazaar Discount Supermarket
20	Info Cafe
21	Lykavittos Theatre
22	OTE
25	Bus A16 to Dafni

26	Fruit & Vegetable Market
27	Rembetika Stoa Athanaton
29	Basilopoulou Delicatessen
31	Keramaikos Museum
32	Stavlos Bar
34	Benaki Museum
35	Goulandris Museum of Cycladic & Ancient Greek Art
36	UK Embassy
37	War Museum
38	Byzantine Museum
39	Ancient Theatre of Dionysos
40	Theatre of Herodes Atticus
42	Lamda Club
43	Granazi Bar
45	Porta Bar
46	Hellaspar Supermarket
48	Monument of Filopappos
50	Olympic Airways
51	Tourist Police

Omonia has developed a sorry reputation for sleaze in recent years, and is now better known for its prostitutes and pickpockets than its neoclassical architecture. Since the Metro construction hoardings went up in 1994, it's been more of a transport hub than a square. The major streets of central Athens all meet here. Panepistimiou (El Venizelou) and Stadiou run parallel south-east to Syntagma, while Athinas leads south to the market district of Monastiraki. Monastiraki is in turn linked to Syntagma by Ermou – home to some of the city's smartest shops – and Mitropoleos.

Mitropoleos skirts the northern edge of Plaka, the delightful old Turkish quarter which was virtually all that existed when Athens was declared the capital of independent Greece. Its labyrinthine streets are nestled on the north-eastern slope of the Acropolis, and most of the city's ancient sites are close by. It may be touristy, but it's the most attractive and interesting part of Athens and the majority of visitors make it their base.

Just south of Plaka is the trendy residential suburb of Makrigianni, which occupies the southern slope of the Acropolis between Filopappos Hill and Syngrou. It has a smattering of upmarket hotels and restaurants, and is also home to the city's main gay area – occupying the belt between Makrigianni (the street) and Syngrou. Further south is the less risqué residential district of Koukaki.

Streets are clearly signposted in Greek and English. If you do get lost, it's very easy to find help. A glance at a map is often enough to draw an offer of assistance. Anyone you ask will be able to direct you to Syntagma (**sin**-tag-mah).

INFORMATION
Tourist Offices

The main EOT tourist office (☎ 331 0561/0562, fax 325 2895, email gnto@eexi.gr) is close to Syntagma at Amerikis 2. It has a useful free map of Athens, which has most of the places of interest clearly marked and also shows the trolleybus routes. It also has information about public transport prices and schedules from Athens, including ferry departures from Piraeus. The office is open 9 am to 7 pm Monday to Friday and 9.30 am to 2 pm Saturday.

The EOT office (☎ 969 4500) at the East airport terminal is open 9 am to 7 pm Monday to Friday and 11 am to 5 pm Saturday.

Earthquake!

On 7 September 1999, the Greek capital was struck by the most powerful earthquake to hit the region for almost 200 years. It killed 120 people and left 70,000 homeless.

The quake, measuring 5.9 on the Richter scale, was centred some 40km north of the city centre at Menidi, near Mt Parnitha. The jolt flattened many buildings in Menidi and the surrounding areas of Aharnes, Ano Liosia and Metamorphosi, where dozens died in a factory collapse. Buildings throughout the capital and Piraeus were damaged, including the National Archaeological Museum. The tremor left minor cracks in the building, and large cracks in the 2nd floor pottery collection, which is expected to remain closed for some time. The Parthenon, which has survived many quakes in its 2500 year history, suffered minor damage to one of its columns.

The tourist police (☎ 924 2700) at Dimitrakopoulou 77, Koukaki, are open 24 hours a day. Take trolleybus No 1, 5 or 9 from Syntagma. They also have a 24-hour information service (☎ 171).

Money

Most of the major banks have branches around Syntagma, open 8 am to 2 pm Monday to Thursday and 8 am to 1.30 pm Friday. The National Bank of Greece on Stadiou has an automatic exchange machine.

American Express (☎ 324 4975), Ermou 2, Syntagma, is open 8.30 am to 4 pm Monday to Friday, and 8.30 am to 1.30 pm Saturday.

Eurochange (☎ 322 0155) has an office at Karageorgi Servias 4, Syntagma, open 8.30 am to 8 pm Monday to Friday, 9.30 am to 4 pm Saturday and 10 am to 4 pm Sunday. Eurochange changes Thomas Cook travellers' cheques without commission.

In Plaka, Acropole Foreign Exchange, Kydathineon 23, is open 9 am to midnight every day.

The banks at the East and West airport terminals are open from 7 am to 9 pm.

Post

The main post office is at Eolou 100, Omonia (postcode 102 00). Unless specified otherwise mail addressed to poste restante will be sent here. If you're staying in Plaka, it's best to get mail sent to the post office on Plateia Syntagmatos (postcode 103 00). Both are open 7.30 am to 8 pm Monday to Friday, 7.30 am to 2 pm Saturday, and 9 am to 1.30 pm Sunday.

Parcels for abroad that weigh over 2kg must be posted from the parcels office at Stadiou 4 (in the arcade), in Syntagma. They should not be wrapped until they've been inspected.

Telephone

The OTE telephone office at 28 Oktovriou-Patission 85 is open 24 hours a day. There are also offices at Stadiou 15, Syntagma, and at Athinas 50, south of Omonia. They are open 7 am to 11.30 pm every day.

Email & Internet Access

Internet cafes are popping up like mushrooms all over Athens. Most charge from 1000 dr to 1500 dr per hour of computer time, whether you log on or not. They include:

Skynet Internet Centre
  At the corner of Voulis and Apollonos, Plaka, open 9.30 am to 8.30 pm Monday to Friday and 10 am to 8.30 pm Saturday.
Sofokleus.com Internet Cafe
  Stadiou 5, Syntagma, behind the Flocafé, open 10 am to 10 pm Monday to Saturday and 1pm to 9 pm Sunday.
Astor Internet Cafe
  Oktovriou-Patission 27, Omonia, open from 10 am to 10 pm every day.
Info Cafe
  Ippocratous 31, Exarhia, open 8 am to 12.30 am Monday to Saturday.
Museum Internet Cafe
  Oktovriou-Patission 46, next to the National Archaeological Museum, open 9 am to 2.30 am every day.

Travel Agencies

The bulk of the city's travel agencies are around Plateia Syntagmatos, particularly in the area just south of the square on Filellinon, Nikis and Voulis.

Reputable agencies include STA Travel (☎ 321 1188, 321 1194, email robissa@spark.net.gr), Voulis 43, and Etos Travel (☎ 324 1884, fax 322 8447, email usit@usitetos.gr), Filellinon 1, which is the Athens representative of the international group USIT. Both places also issue International Student Identity Cards (ISIC), as does the International Student & Youth Travel Service (ISYTS) (☎ 323 3767), Nikis 11 (1st floor).

Bookshops

Athens has three good English-language bookshops. The biggest is Eleftheroudakis, which has branches at Panepistimiou 17 and at Nikis 4 in Syntagma. The others are Pantelides Books, Amerikis 11, Syntagma, and Compendium Books, Nikis 28, Plaka. Compendium also has a second-hand books section.

Cultural Centres

The British Council (☎ 363 3215), Plateia Kolonaki 17, Kolonaki, and the Hellenic American Union (☎ 362 9886), Massalias 22, Pefkakia, hold frequent concerts, film shows, exhibitions etc. Both also have libraries.

Laundry

Plaka has a convenient laundry at Angelou Geronta 10, just off Kydathineon near the outdoor restaurants.

Emergency

For emergency medical treatment ring the tourist police (☎ 171) and they will tell you where the nearest hospital is. Don't wait for an ambulance – get a taxi. Hospitals give free emergency treatment to tourists. For hospitals with outpatient departments on duty, ring ☎ 106; for first-aid advice, call ☎ 166. US citizens can ring ☎ 721 2951 for emergency medical aid.

Some travellers have recommended SOS Doctors (☎ 322 0046/0015), a 24-hour callout service employing doctors who speak English and a range of other languages. They charge about 20,000 dr for a call.

Dangers & Annoyances

Athens is a big city, and it has its fair share of the problems found in all major cities. Fortunately, violent street crime remains very rare, but travellers should be alert to the following traps:

Pickpockets Pickpockets have become a major problem in Athens. Their favourite hunting grounds are the metro system and the crowded streets around Omonia, particularly Athinas. The Sunday Flea Market on Ermou is another place where it pays to take extra care of your valuables.

Taxi Drivers Many Athens residents will tell you that their taxi drivers are the biggest bunch of bastards in the world. It seems that they have as much trouble getting a fair deal as tourists do.

Most (but not all) rip-off stories involve cabs picked up late at night from the taxi ranks at the city's main arrival and departure points: the airport, the train stations, the two bus terminals – particularly Terminal A at Kifissou, and the port of Piraeus. Paying by the meter, the fare from any of the above places to the city centre shouldn't be more than 2500 dr at any time of day.

The trouble is that the cabbies who work these ranks don't like to bother with the meter, especially after midnight when most public transport stops. They prefer to demand whatever they think they can get away with. If you insist on using the meter, many will simply refuse to take you. You can either negotiate a set fare, or attempt to find a taxi elsewhere.

Every now and again, the police conduct well-publicised clamp-downs. One such purge turned up an airport cabby who was well prepared for tourists who want to see the meter working – he was equipped with a handy remote-controlled device that could make the meter spin round at 2000 dr per minute!

A more common trick is to set the meter on night rate (tariff 2) during the day. Between 6 am and midnight the day rate (tariff 1) should be charged.

If there is a dispute over the fare, take the driver's number and report it to the tourist police.

Taxi Touts Taxi drivers working in league with some of the overpriced C class hotels around Omonia are another problem. The scam involves taxi drivers picking up late night arrivals, particularly at the airport and Bus Terminal A, and persuading them that the hotel they want to go to is full – even if they have a booking. The taxi driver will pretend to phone the hotel of choice, announce that it's full and suggest an alternative. You can ask to speak to your chosen hotel yourself, or simply insist on going where you want.

Bar Scams Lonely Planet continues to receive a steady flow of letters from readers who have been taken in by one of the various bar scams that operate around central Athens, particularly around Syntagma.

The basic scam runs something like this: friendly Greek approaches solo male traveller and discovers that the traveller knows little about Athens; friendly Greek then reveals that he, too, is from out of town. Why don't they go to this great little bar that he's just discovered and have a beer? They order a drink, and the equally friendly owner then offers another drink. Women appear, more drinks are provided and the visitor relaxes as he realises that the women are not prostitutes, just friendly Greeks. The crunch comes at the end of the evening when the traveller is presented with an exorbitant bill and the smiles disappear. The con men who cruise the streets playing the role of the friendly

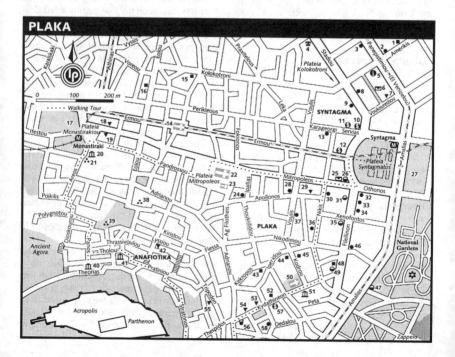

Greek can be very convincing: some people have been taken in more than once.

Other bars don't bother with the acting. They target intoxicated males with talk of sex and present them with outrageous bills.

Travel Agents Several travel agents in the Plaka/Syntagma area employ touts to patrol the streets promoting 'cheap' packages to the islands. These touts like to hang out at the bus stops on Amalias, hoping to find naive new arrivals who have no idea of prices in Greece.

Potential customers are then taken back to the agency, where slick salespeople then pressure them into buying outrageously overpriced packages. Lonely Planet regularly receives complaints from victims of this scam.

There is no need to buy a package; you will always be able to negotiate a better deal yourself when you get to the island of your choice. If you are worried that everywhere will be full, select a place from the pages of this guide and make a booking.

THINGS TO SEE
Walking Tour

This walk takes in most of Plaka's main sites. Without detours, it will take about 45 minutes. The route is marked with a dotted line on the Plaka map.

From **Plateia Syntagmatos**, walk along Mitropoleos and take the first turning left onto Nikis. Continue along here to the junction with Kydathineon, Plaka's main thoroughfare, and turn right. Opposite the **Church of Metamorphosis** is the **Museum of Greek Folk Art**, which houses an excellent collection of embroidery, weaving and jewellery. It is open 10 am to 2 pm Tuesday to Sunday; admission is 500 dr. After passing the square with the outdoor tavernas, take the second turning left onto Adrianou. A right turn at end of Adrianou leads to the small square with the **Choregic Monument of Lysicrates**, erected in 334 BC to commemorate victory in a choral festival.

Turn left and then right onto Epimenidou; at the top, turn right onto Thrasilou, which

PLAKA

PLACES TO STAY			
1	XEN (YWCA) Hostel	4	OTE
15	Hotel Carolina	5	Tourist Office (EOT)
16	Hotel Tempi	6	Parcel Post Office
43	Hotel Nefeli	8	Athens Festival
44	Acropolis House Pension		Box Office
45	Hotel Adonis	9	Sofokleos.com
48	Festos Youth & Student		Internet Cafe
	Guest House	10	National Bank of Greece
52	Student & Travellers' Inn	11	Eurochange
		12	American Express
PLACES TO EAT		13	Eleftheroudakis Books
7	Brazil Coffee Shop	14	Church of Kapnikarea
18	Savas	17	Flea Market
19	Thanasis	20	Museum of Traditional
29	Furin Kazan Japanese		Greek Ceramics
	Fast-Food Restaurant	21	Library of Hadrian
42	Eden Vegetarian	22	Athens Cathedral
	Restaurant	23	Church of Agios Eleftherios
53	Byzantino	24	National Welfare
54	Plaka Psistaria		Organisation
55	Ouzeri Kouklis	25	Syntagma Post Office
		26	Buses to Airport
OTHER		27	Parliament
2	Pantelides Books	28	Skynet Internet Cafe
3	Eleftheroudakis Books	30	International Student &
			Youth Travel Service

31	Bus 040 to Piraeus
32	Etos Travel
33	Flying Dolphin Office
34	Olympic Airways
35	Buses to Cape Sounion
36	Compendium Books
37	STA Travel
38	Tower of the Winds
39	Roman Agora
40	Paul & Alexandra
	Kanellopoulos Museum
41	Museum of the
	University
46	OSE Office
	(Train Tickets)
47	Bus 024 to Bus
	Terminal B
49	Trolley Stop for Plaka
50	Church of
	Metamorphosis
51	Museum of Greek
	Folk Art
56	Brettos
57	Acropole Foreign
	Exchange
58	Laundrette

skirts the Acropolis. Where the road forks, veer left into the district of **Anafiotika**. Here the little white cubic houses resemble those of the Cyclades, and olive-oil cans brimming with flowers bedeck the walls of their tiny gardens. The houses were built by the people of Anafi, who were used as cheap labour in the rebuilding of Athens after independence.

The path winds between the houses and comes to some steps on the right. At the bottom is a curving pathway leading downhill to Pratiniou. Turn left onto Pratiniou and veer right after 50m onto Tholou. The yellow-ochre Venetian building with brown shutters at No 5 is the old university, now the **Museum of the University**. It is open 2.30 to 7 pm Monday and Wednesday, and 9.30 am to 2.30 pm Tuesday, Thursday and Friday. Admission is free.

At the end of Tholou, turn left onto Panos. At the top of the steps on the left is a restored 19th century mansion which is now the **Paul & Alexandra Kanellopoulos Museum**, open 8 am to 2.30 pm Tuesday to Sunday; admission 500 dr. Retracing your steps, go down Panos to the ruins of the **Roman Agora**, then turn left onto Polygnotou and walk to the crossroads. Opposite, Polygnotou continues to the **Ancient Agora**. At the crossroads, turn right and then left onto Poikilis, then immediately right onto Areos. On the right are the remains of the **Library of Hadrian** and next to it is the **Museum of Traditional Greek Ceramics**, open 10 am to 2 pm every day, except Tuesday. Admission is 500 dr. The museum is housed in the **Mosque of Tzistarakis**, built in 1759. After Independence it lost its minaret and was used as a prison.

Ahead is **Plateai Monastirakiou**, named after the small church. To the left is the metro station and the **flea market**. Monastiraki is Athens at its noisiest, most colourful and chaotic; it's teeming with street vendors.

Turn right just beyond the mosque onto Pandrossou, a relic of the old Turkish bazaar. At No 89 is Stavros Melissinos, the 'poet sandalmaker' of Athens who names the Beatles, Rudolph Nureyev and Jackie

Onassis among his customers. Fame and fortune have not gone to his head – he still makes the best sandals in Athens, costing from 3800 dr per pair.

Pandrossou leads to Plateia Mitropoleos and the **Athens Cathedral**. The cathedral was constructed from the masonry of over 50 razed churches and from the designs of several architects. Next to it stands the much smaller, and far more appealing, **Church of Agios Eleftherios**. Turn left after the cathedral, and then right onto Mitropoleos and back to Syntagma.

Acropolis

Most of the buildings now gracing the Acropolis were commissioned by Pericles during the golden age of Athens in the 5th century BC. The site had been cleared for him by the Persians, who destroyed an earlier temple complex on the eve of the Battle of Salamis.

The entrance to the Acropolis is through the **Beule Gate**, a Roman arch added in the 3rd century AD. Beyond this is the **Propylaia**, the monumental gate that was the entrance in ancient times. It was damaged by Venetian bombing in the 17th century, but has since been restored. To the south of the Propylaia is the small, graceful **Temple of Athena Nike**, which is not accessible to visitors.

Standing supreme over the Acropolis is the monument which more than any other epitomises the glory of ancient Greece: the **Parthenon**. Completed in 438 BC, this building is unsurpassed in grace and harmony. To achieve perfect form, its lines were ingeniously curved to counteract unharmonious optical illusions. The base curves upwards slightly towards the ends, and the columns become slightly narrower towards the top, with the overall effect of making them both look straight.

Above the columns are the remains of a Doric frieze, which was partly destroyed by Venetian shelling in 1687. The best surviving pieces are the famous Elgin Marbles, carted off by Lord Elgin in 1801 and now in the British Museum.

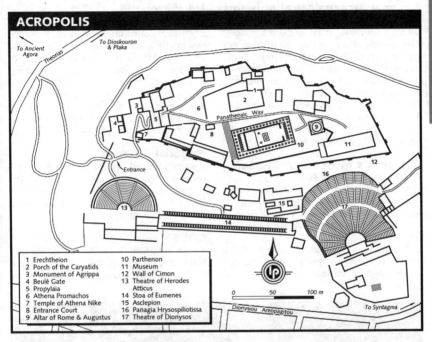

ACROPOLIS

To Ancient Agora

To Dioskouron & Plaka

Theorias

Panathenaic Way

Entrance

To Syntagma

Dionysiou Areopagitou

0   50   100 m

1	Erechtheion	10	Parthenon
2	Porch of the Caryatids	11	Museum
3	Monument of Agrippa	12	Wall of Cimon
4	Beulé Gate	13	Theatre of Herodes
5	Propylaia		Atticus
6	Athena Promachos	14	Stoa of Eumenes
7	Temple of Athena Nike	15	Asclepion
8	Entrance Court	16	Panagia Hrysospiliotissa
9	Altar of Rome & Augustus	17	Theatre of Dionysos

The Parthenon, dedicated to Athena, contained an 11m-tall gold and ivory statue of the goddess completed in 438 BC by Phidias of Athens; only the statue's foundations remain today.

To the north is the **Erechtheion** with its much-photographed Caryatids, the six maidens who support its southern portico. These are copies – the originals (except for one taken by Lord Elgin) are in the site's museum. The Erechtheion was dedicated to Athena and Poseidon and supposedly built on the spot where they competed for possession of ancient Athens. The **Acropolis Museum** has sculptures from the temples.

The site and museum are open 8 am to 8 pm every day. The combined admission fee is 2000 dr.

Ancient Agora

The Agora was the marketplace of ancient Athens and the focal point of civic and social life. Socrates spent much time here expounding his philosophy.

The main monuments are the well-preserved **Temple of Hephaestus**, the 11th century **Church of the Holy Apostles** and the reconstructed **Stoa of Attalos**, which houses the site's museum.

The site is open 8 am to 8 pm (to 5 pm in winter) Tuesday to Sunday; admission is 1200 dr.

Changing of the Guard

At 11 am every Sunday a platoon of traditionally costumed *evzones* (guards) marches down Vasilissis Sofias, accompanied by a band, to the Tomb of the Unknown Soldier in front of the parliament building on Syntagma. Some find the costumes (skirts and pom-pom shoes) and marching style comic, but the ceremony is colourful and entertaining.

National Archaeological Museum

This is the most important museum in the country, with finds from all the major sites. The crowd-pullers are the magnificent, exquisitely detailed gold artefacts from Mycenae and the spectacular **Minoan frescoes** from Santorini (Thira), which are here until a suitable museum is built on the island. The museum is at 28 Oktovriou-Patission 44, open 8 am to 7 pm Tuesday to Friday; 8.30 am to 3 pm Saturday, Sunday and holidays; and 12.30 to 7 pm Monday.

Goulandris Museum of Cycladic & Ancient Greek Art

This private museum was custom-built to display a fabulous collection of Cycladic art, with an emphasis on the Early Bronze Age. Particularly impressive are the beautiful marble figurines.

The museum is at Neofytou Douka 4, 10 am to 4 pm open every day except Tuesday and Sunday; admission is 1000 dr.

Lykavittos Hill

Pine-covered Lykavittos is the highest of eight hills dotted around Athens. From the summit there are all-embracing views of the city, the Attic basin and the islands of Salamis and Aegina – pollution permitting.

The southern side of the hill is occupied by the posh residential suburb of Kolonaki. The main path to the summit starts at the top of Loukianou, or you can take the funicular railway from the top of Ploutarhou (500 dr).

National Gardens

Formerly named the Royal Gardens, these offer a welcome shady retreat from the summer sun, with subtropical trees, peacocks, water fowl, ornamental ponds and a botanical museum.

COURSES

The Athens Centre (☎ 701 2268, fax 701 8603, email athenscr@compulink.gr), Archimidous 48, Mets, has a very good reputation.

CHRISTINE COSTA

View across Athens from Plaka towards Lykavittos Hill, the highest point in Athens

Its courses cover five levels of proficiency from beginners to advanced. There are five immersion courses a year for beginners.

The Hellenic American Union (☎ 362 9886, email dtolias@hau.gr), Massalias 22, Pefkakia, has courses lasting from one to three months for 90,000 dr.

ORGANISED TOURS

Key Tours (☎ 923 3166), Kallirois 4; CHAT Tours (☎ 322 3137), Stadiou 4; and GO Tours (☎ 322 5951), Athanassiou 20, are the main operators. You'll see their brochures everywhere, offering identical tours and prices. They include a half-day bus tour (10,000 dr), which does no more than point out the major sights.

SPECIAL EVENTS

The Athens Festival is the city's most important cultural event, running from mid-June to the end of August. The main attraction is the performance of ancient Greek drama at the Theatre of Herodes Atticus. The setting is superb, backed by the floodlit Acropolis. There are also performances at the nearby Stoa of Eumenes, the Hill of the Pnyx, the Lykavittos Theatre and at a new theatre in Piraeus near the junction of Pireos and Kifissou streets.

Tickets can be bought at the festival box office (☎ 322 1459), in the arcade at Stadiou 4, Syntagma. They sell out quickly so try to buy them early.

PLACES TO STAY
Camping

The closest camp site is *Athens Camping* (☎ 581 4114), 7km west of the city centre at Athinon 198 – on the road to Corinth.

Hostels

There are several places around town making a pitch for the hostelling market by tagging 'youth hostel' onto their name. There are some real dumps among them.

There are only a couple of youth hostels worth knowing about. They include the excellent HI-affiliated *Athens International Youth Hostel* (☎ 523 4170, fax 523 4015,

Victor Hugo 16,) in Omonia. Location is the only drawback, otherwise the place is almost too good to be true. The spotless rooms, with bathroom, sleep two to four people. Rates are 1620 dr per person for HI members. If you're not a member, you can either pay 4200 dr to join or 700 dr for a daily stamp.

XEN (YWCA) (☎ 362 4291, fax 362 2400, Amerikis 11, Syntagma) is an option for women only. It has singles/doubles with shared bathroom for 6000/9000 dr, or 7000/9500 dr with private bathroom. There are laundry facilities and a snack bar. Annual membership is 600 dr.

Hotels

Athens is a noisy city and Athenians keep late hours, so an effort has been made to select hotels in quiet areas. Plaka is the most popular place to stay, and it has a good choice of accommodation right across the price spectrum. Rooms fill up quickly in July and August, so it's wise to make a reservation.

Plaka *Student & Travellers' Inn* (☎ 324 4808, fax 321 0065, email students-inn@ath.forthnet.gr, Kydathineon 16) is hard to look past. It's a well run place with spotless rooms. The dormitories are particularly good value with beds in triple/quad rooms for 4000/3500 dr. Rooms with bunk beds are 3000 dr and singles/doubles are 7000/9000 dr. All rooms share communal bathrooms. The place stays open all year, and rooms are heated in winter.

Festos Youth & Student Guest House (☎ 323 2455, consolas@hol.gr, Filellinon 18), is a popular place with travellers despite being on one of the noisiest streets in Athens. It has dorm beds priced from 3000 dr to 3500 dr, but tends to cram beds into the rooms in summer. There are a couple of doubles for 7500 dr. A popular feature is the bar on the 1st floor, which also serves meals, including several vegetarian options.

Plaka also has some good mid-range accommodation. *Acropolis House Pension* (☎ 322 2344, fax 322 6241, Kodrou 6-8) is a beautifully preserved 19th century house. Singles/doubles with shared bathroom are

12,800/15,300 dr, or 15,000/18,000 dr with private bathroom. There's a 20% discount for stays of more than two days. All rooms have central heating.

Hotel Adonis (☎ *324 9737, fax 323 1602, Kodrou 3)*, opposite, is a comfortable modern hotel with air-con rooms from 12,000/17,000 dr. It has good views of the Acropolis from the 4th floor rooms, and from the rooftop bar.

Just around the corner from Acropolis House Pension is *Hotel Nefeli* (☎ *322 8044, fax 322 5800, Iperidou 16)* which has air-con rooms for 16,000/20,500 dr, including breakfast. To get there from Syntagma, head south down Voulis and turn right into Iperidou.

Monastiraki There are a couple of good budget options around Plateia Monastirakiou.

The friendly, family-run *Hotel Tempi* (☎ *321 3175, fax 321 4179, Eolou 29)* is the best of them. The rooms at the front have balconies overlooking a little square with a church and a flower market on the pedestrian precinct part of Eolou. Rates are 5500/8000/9500 dr for singles/doubles/triples with shared bathroom, or 10,000/11,500 dr for doubles/triples with private bathroom. Credit cards are accepted – unusual for a budget hotel.

The nearby *Hotel Carolina* (☎ *324 3551/3552, fax 324 3550, Kolokotroni 55)* has singles/doubles with outside bathroom for 6000/9000 dr, or 9000/11,000 dr with inside bathroom. All the rooms have air-con.

Thisio *Hotel Erechthion* (☎ *345 9606, fax 346 2756, Flammarion 8)* has spotless singles/doubles with TV and private bathroom for 8000/13,000 dr. The rooms at the front have superb views of the Acropolis.

Koukaki There are a couple of good options in the residential suburb of Koukaki, south of the Acropolis.

Marble House Pension (☎ *923 4058, fax 922 6461, Zini 35A)* is a quiet place tucked away on a small cul-de-sac. Rates are 5500/9500 dr for singles/doubles with shared bathroom, or 6500/10,800 dr with

private bathroom. All rooms come equipped with bar fridge, ceiling fans and safety boxes for valuables.

Art Gallery Pension (☎ *923 8376, fax 923 3025, email ecotec@otenet.gr, Erehthiou 5)* is a small, friendly place that's always brimming with fresh flowers. It has comfortable singles/doubles/triples for 12,000/15,200/18,000 dr with balcony and private bathroom.

To get to both of these places from Syntagma catch trolleybus Nos 1, 5, 9 or 18. Coming from Syntagma, they travel along Veïkou. Get off at the Drakou stop for Art Gallery Pension, and at Zini for Marble House.

Omonia & Surrounds Most of the hotels around Omonia are either bordellos masquerading as cheap hotels or uninspiring, overpriced C class hotels. Only a couple of places are worth a mention – and both are a fair way north of Omonia.

The excellent *Hostel Aphrodite* (☎ *881 0589, fax 881 6574, email hostel-aphrodite@ath.forthnet.gr, Einardou 12)*, is 10 minutes from the train stations. It has dorm beds for 2500 dr, singles/doubles/triples for 5000/7000/9000 dr and with private bathroom 6000/8000/10,000 dr. The hostel also offers Internet access.

Museum Hotel (☎ *380 5611, fax 380 0507, Bouboulinas 16)*, behind the National Archaeological Museum, has singles/doubles with private bathroom for 7000/10,500 dr.

PLACES TO EAT
Plaka

For most people, Plaka is the place to be. It's hard to beat the atmosphere of dining out beneath the floodlit Acropolis. You do, however, pay for the privilege – particularly at the outdoor restaurants around the square on Kydathineon.

The best of this bunch is *Byzantino*, which has reasonable prices and is popular with Greek family groups. One of the best deals in the Plaka is the nearby *Plaka Psistaria (Kydathineon 28)*, with a range of gyros and souvlakia to eat in or take away.

Ouzeri Kouklis (Tripodon 14), is an old-style ouzeri with an oak-beamed ceiling, marble tables and wicker chairs. It serves only mezedes, which are brought round on a large tray for you to take your pick. They include flaming sausages – ignited at your table – and cuttlefish for 1200 dr, as well as the usual dips for 600 dr. The whole selection, enough for four hungry people, costs 9800 dr.

Vegetarian restaurants are thin on the ground in Athens. *Eden Vegetarian Restaurant (Lyssiou 12)*, has been around for years, substituting soya products for meat in tasty vegetarian versions of moussaka (1600 dr) and other Greek favourites.

Syntagma

Fast food is the order of the day around busy Syntagma with an assortment of Greek and international offerings.

Anyone suffering from a surfeit of Greek salad and souvlakis should head for the *Furin Kazan Japanese Fast-Food Restaurant (Apollonos 2, Syntagma)*. It offers yakisoba noodle dishes from 1400 dr and rice dishes from 1250 dr. It's open 11.30 am to 5.30 pm Monday to Friday.

Follow your nose to the *Brazil Coffee Shop* on Voukourestiou for the best coffee in town.

Makrigianni

To 24 Hours (Syngrou 44) is a great favourite with Athenian night owls. As the name suggests, it's open 24 hours. It calls itself a *patsadakia*, which means that it specialises in *patsas* (tripe soup), but a wide selection of taverna dishes are always available.

Socrates Prison (Mitseon 20), is not named after the philosopher, but after the owner (also called Socrates) who reckons the restaurant is his prison. It's a stylish place with an imaginative range of mezedes from 850 dr and main dishes from 1500 dr.

Monastiraki

There are some excellent cheap eats around Monastiraki, particularly for gyros and souvlaki fans. *Thanasis* and *Savas*, opposite each other at the bottom end of Mitropoleos, are the places to go.

The best taverna food in this part of town is at the *meat market*, 400m along Athinas from Monastiraki Square on the right. The place must resemble a vegetarian's vision of hell, but the food is great and the tavernas are open 24 hours, except Sunday. Soups start at 800 dr and main dishes at 1350 dr.

Opposite the meat market is the main *fruit & vegetable market*.

Psiri

There are loads of possibilities in Psiri, just north-west of Monastiraki. Once rated as 'Athens at its most clapped out', the district has undergone an amazing transformation in the past two years. The narrow streets are now dotted with numerous trendy ouzeris, tavernas and music bars, particularly the central area between Plateia Agion Anargyron and Plateia Iroön.

If none of these places grab your attention as you wander around, try *Embros (Plateia Agion Anargyron 4)*. It's a popular spot with seating in the square, and a choice of about 20 mezedes, they include delicious cheese croquettes (1150 dr) and chicken livers wrapped in bacon (1600 dr).

The renovators have yet to reach the streets just north of Psiri, around Plateia Eletherias, but the area has recently been adopted by the city's Bangladeshi community and it's the place to head for a good cheap curry and a cold beer. The *Bengal Garden (Korinis 12)* turns out a spicy chicken curry and rice for 800 dr, as well as side dishes like chick peas (400 dr) and spicy samozas (100 dr). The tiny *Restaurant Nargis (Sofokleous 60)*, tucked away down a very dodgy-looking alleyway, specialises in Indian food. There are more than 100 items on the menu – like a plate of tandoori chicken wings (1000 dr).

Exarhia

There are lots of ouzeria and tavernas to choose from in the lively suburb of Exarhia, just east of Omonia. Prices here are tailored to suit the pockets of the district's student clientele. It's quite a hike to the area from

Syntagma. An alternative is to catch bus No 230 from Amalias to Harilau Trikoupi and walk across.

The *Ouzeri I Gonia*, at the corner of Emmanual Benaki and Arahovis, has a good range of tasty mezedes priced between 600 dr and 1800 dr. *Taverna Barbargiannis*, farther up the hill on the corner of Emmanual Benaki and Dervenion, is also good. Most meat dishes are priced around 1500 dr, and draught retsina is 700 dr for a litre.

Self-catering

Supermarkets are few and far between in central Athens. Those that do exist are marked on the main Athens map. *Basilopoulou (Stadiou 19, Syntagma)* is an excellent delicatessen with a good selection of cold meats and cheeses. The *fruit and vegetable markets* on Athinas have the best range of fresh produce.

ENTERTAINMENT

The best source of entertainment information is the weekly listings magazine *Athenorama*, but you'll need to be able to read some Greek to make much sense of it. It's available from kiosks all over the city.

English-language listings appear daily in the *Kathimerini* supplement that accompanies the *International Herald Tribune*, while Friday's edition of the *Athens News*, carries a 16-page weekly entertainment guide.

Discos & Bars

Discos operate in central Athens only between October and April. In summer, the action moves to the coastal suburbs of Glyfada and Ellinikon.

Most bars around Plaka and Syntagma are places to avoid, especially if there are guys outside touting for customers.

Brettos (Kydathineon 41), is a delightful old family-run place right in the heart of Plaka. Huge old barrels line one wall, and the shelves are stocked with an eye-catching collection of coloured bottles. It's open 10 am to 1 am daily.

Most bars in Athens have music as a main feature. Thisio is a good place to look,

particularly on Iraklidon. *Stavlos (Iraklidon 10)* occupies an amazing old rabbit warren of a building.

Gay Bars

The greatest concentration of gay bars is to be found on the streets off Syngrouin Makrigianni, south of the Temple of Olympian Zeus. Popular spots include the long-running *Granazi Bar (Lembesi 20)*, and the more risqué *Lamda Club (Lembesi 15)*. Lesbians should check out the lively *Porta Bar*, nearby at Falirou 10.

Live Music

Rodon Club (☎ 524 7427) at Marni 24, north of Omonia, is the main rock venue and hosts touring international rock bands, while local bands play at the *AN Club (Solomou 20, Exarhia)*.

Rembetika Clubs

Rembetika is the music of the working classes and has its roots in the sufferings of the refugees from Asia Minor in the 1920s. Songs are accompanied by bouzouki, guitar, violin and accordion. It was banned during the junta years, but has since experienced a resurgence, especially in Athens.

Rembetika Stoa Athanaton (☎ 321 4362), Sofokleous 19 (above the meat market), is a good place to check out; it's open 3 to 7.30 pm and from midnight to 6 am every day except Sunday. It closes from mid-May until the end of September. *Boemissa (☎ 384 3836, Solomou 19)*, in Exarhia, operates all year. It's open 11 pm to 4 am every day except Monday. Neither place charges for admission, but drinks are expensive.

Greek Folk Dances

The *Dora Stratou Dance Company* performs at its theatre on Filopappos Hill at 10.15 pm daily from mid-May to October, with additional performances at 8.15 pm on Wednesday. Tickets are 1500 dr. Filopappos Hill is west of the Acropolis, off Dionysiou Areopagitou. Bus No 230 from Syntagma will get you there.

Nes Frappé

You can hardly miss the forest of straws sprouting from glasses of frothy-topped black liquid at countless street cafes throughout Greece. Nes(café) frappé has almost universally overtaken the traditional Greek (or Turkish) coffee as the nation's favourite beverage. But what could possibly be the attraction of a glass of cold water, flavoured with a spoonful of instant coffee and sugar, processed to resemble a glass of Guinness stout and then chilled with ice cubes?

Nes frappé is not a beverage to be taken in a hurry; it is certainly not a beverage to be drunk for the caffeine hit that you might expect from traditional coffee. Its primary role is that of a 'ticket' to sit at a street cafe in order to idly chat and smoke. Its arrival at the table, however, is treated with almost reverential ceremony. Firstly the imbiber will dutifully stir the ice cubes to ensure that every molecule of Nes frappé is equally chilled, and then the first minuscule sip is taken. It is considered extremely bad form to drink the mixture quickly, so never order one if you intend to quench your thirst in Greek company. The next sip may follow between five and 10 minutes later; in fact, the whole drinking procedure may take up to an hour.

The drink's universal popularity throughout the country and at all times of the year may be a puzzle to observers, for its appeal as a beverage is surely limited. The cafe owners, however, are not complaining: at 500 dr a shot, it is a sure-fire money spinner.

Cinema

Athenians are avid cinema-goers and there are cinemas everywhere. The *Athens News* has listings. Admission is about 1600 dr.

Sound-and-Light Show

Athens' endeavour at this spectacle is not one of the world's best. There are shows in English at 9 pm daily from the beginning of April until the end of October at the theatre on the *Hill of the Pnyx (☎ 322 1459)*. Tickets are 1500 dr. The Hill of the Pnyx is opposite Filopappos Hill, and the show is timed so that you can cross straight to the folk dancing.

SPECTATOR SPORTS

Soccer is the most popular sport in Greece. Almost half of the 18 teams in the Greek first division are based in Athens or Piraeus. Olympiakos (Piraeus) is the most popular team. Its success in the 1998/99 Greek championship was its 28th in 74 years. Its main rival is Athens club Panathinaikos. Both teams play at the Olympic Stadium in Maroussi – a short walk from Irini station on metro Line 1. Schedules (and results) are listed in the *Athens News*.

SHOPPING

The National Welfare Organisation shop, on the corner of Apollonos and Ipatias, Plaka, is a good place to go shopping for handicrafts. It has a wide range of knotted carpets, kilims, flokatis, needle-point rugs and embroidered cushion covers as well as a small selection of pottery, copper and woodwork.

GETTING THERE & AWAY

Air

Athens' dilapidated airport, Ellinikon, is 9km south of the city. There are two main terminals: West for all Olympic Airways flights, and East for all other flights. The airport's old military terminal is dusted off for charter flights in peak season.

Facilities are equally dreadful at all the terminals, but nothing is likely to change until the new international airport at Spata (21km east of Athens) opens for business in 2002. Ellinikon will then handle only domestic flights.

The Olympic Airways head office (☎ 926 7251/7254) is at Syngrou 96. The office at Filellinon 13, near Syntagma, is more convenient.

Flokati

There are few better souvenirs of a visit to Greece than the luxuriant woollen flokati rugs produced in the mountain areas of central and northern Greece. They make beautiful, cosy floor coverings.

The process by which these rugs are produced has changed little over the centuries. The first step is to weave a loose woollen base. Short lengths of twisted wool are then looped through it, leaving the two ends on top to form the pile – the more loops, the denser the pile.

At this point, the rug looks like a scalp after stage one of a hair transplant – a series of unconvincing little tufts. The twisted threads can easily be pulled through.

A transformation takes place during the next stage, the 'waterfall treatment'. The rugs are immersed in fast-running water for between 24 and 36 hours, unravelling the twisted wool and shrinking the base so that the pile is held fast. They can then be dyed.

The main production areas are the villages of Epiros, around the town of Tripolis in the Peloponnese and around the towns of Trikala and Karditsa in Thessaly. All these villages have plenty of the running water required for the waterfall treatment.

The rugs are sold by weight. A rug measuring 150 x 60cm will cost from 12,000 dr to 45,000 dr, depending on the length and density of the pile.

Bus

Athens has two main intercity bus stations. The EOT gives out comprehensive schedules for both with departure times, journey duration and fares.

Terminal A is north-west of Omonia at Kifissou 100 and has departures to the Peloponnese, the Ionian Islands and western Greece. To get there, take bus No 051 from the junction of Zinonos and Menandrou, near Omonia. This service runs every 15 minutes from 5 am to midnight.

Terminal B is north of Omonia off Liossion and has departures to central and northern Greece as well as to Evia. To get there, take bus No 024 from outside the main gate of the National Gardens on Amalias. The EOT misleadingly gives the terminal's address as Liossion 260, which turns out to be a small workshop. Liossion 260 is where you should get off the bus. Turn right onto Gousiou and you'll see the terminal at the end of the road.

Buses to Rafina and Lavrio leave from the Mavromateon terminal at the junction of Leoforos Alexandras and 28 Oktovriou-Patission.

Train

Athens has two train stations, located about 200m apart on Deligianni, which is about 1km north-west of Omonia. Trains to the Peloponnese leave from the Peloponnese station, while trains to the north leave from Larisis station – as do all international trains.

Services to the Peloponnese include eight trains to Patras, four of which are intercity express (3½ hours, 2980 dr), while services north include 10 trains a day to Thessaloniki, five of which are intercity express (six hours, 8250 dr). The 7 am service from Athens is express right through to Alexandroupolis, arriving at 7 pm. There are also trains to Volos and Halkida, Evia.

The easiest way to get to the stations is on metro Line 2 to Larissa, outside Larisis station. The Peloponnese station is across the footbridge at the southern end of Larisis Station. Tickets can be bought at the stations or at the OSE offices at Filellinon 17, Sina 6 and Karolou 1.

Car & Motorcycle

National Rd 1 is the main route north from Athens. It starts at Nea Kifissia. To get there

RICK GERHARTER

The Parthenon, Athens, epitomises the glory of ancient Greece.

DIANA MAYFIELD

DIANA MAYFIELD

Evzones outside Parliament House, Athens

Athens' quaint Panagia Hrysospiliotissa chapel

MARK DAFFEY

Aaagh!

CHRIS MELLOR

Street vendor, Athens

DIANA MAYFIELD

Atmospheric outdoor dining beneath the Acropolis, Plaka, Athens

JON DAVISON

Pick up some colourful homewares in the Plaka, Athens

MARK HONAN

Lottery ticket seller, Athens

from central Athens, take Vasilissis Sofias from Syntagma and follow the signs. National Rd 8, which begins beyond Dafni, is the road to the Peloponnese. Take Agiou Konstantinou from Omonia.

The northern reaches of Syngrou, just south of the Temple of Olympian Zeus, are packed solid with car-rental firms. Local companies offer much better deals than their international rivals.

Ferry

See the Piraeus section of the Mainland Ports chapter for information on ferries to/from the islands.

GETTING AROUND
To/From the Airport

There is a 24-hour express bus service between central Athens and both the East and West terminals, also calling at the special charter terminal when in use.

Service No 091 leaves Stadiou, near Omonia, every 20 minutes from 6 am to 9 pm, every 40 minutes from 9 pm until 12.20 am, and then hourly through the night. Buses stop at Syntagma (outside the post office) five minutes later; allow between 30 minutes and an hour for the journey, depending on traffic. The reverse run to the city is service No 092. The fare is 250 dr (500 dr from midnight to 6 am), and you pay the driver. There are also express buses between the airport and Plateia Karaïskaki in Piraeus.

A taxi from the airport to Syntagma should cost from 1500 dr to 2500 dr – depending on the time of day – no more.

Bus & Trolleybus

You probably won't need to use the normal blue-and-white suburban buses. They run every 15 minutes from 5 am to midnight. Important routes are listed on the free EOT map. The map also marks the routes of the yellow trolleybuses, which also run from 5 am to midnight.

There are special buses that operate 24 hours a day to Piraeus. Bus No 040 leaves from the corner of Syntagma and Filellinon,

and No 049 leaves from the Omonia end of Athinas. They run every 20 minutes from 6 am to midnight, and then hourly.

All these services cost a flat rate of 120 dr. Tickets can be bought from ticket kiosks and periptera. They must be validated when you board a bus; the penalty for failing to do so is 4800 dr.

Metro

At the time of writing, the first phase of the metro extension program was on track to begin passenger services in November 1999. This will add two new lines and 21 new stations to the old Kifissia-Piraeus line – now known as Line 1.

Line I remains unchanged. Useful stops include Piraeus (Great Harbour), Monastiraki and Omonia (city centre) and Plateia Viktorias (National Archaeological Museum).

Line 2 runs from Agios Antonios in the north-west to Dafni in the south-east. Useful stops include Larissa (for the train stations), Omonia, Panepistimiou and Syntagma (city centre) and Akropoli (Makrigianni).

Line 3 runs north-east from Monastiraki to Ethniki Amyna via Syntagma. Other useful stops into Evangelismos (for the museums on Vasilissis Sofias) and Megaro Musikis (Athens Concert Hall).

Ticket prices can be expected to remain at 120 dr for most journeys, including Monastiraki-Piraeus. There are ticket machines and ticket booths at all stations, and validating machines at platform entrances. The penalty for travelling without a validated ticket is 4800 dr.

Trains operate between 5 am and midnight. They run every three minutes during peak periods, dropping to every 10 minutes at other times.

Taxi

Athenian taxis are yellow. The flag fall is 200 dr, with a 160 dr surcharge from ports and railway and bus stations, and a 300 dr surcharge from the airport. After that, the day rate (tariff 1 on the meter) is 66 dr per km. The rate doubles between midnight and 5 am (tariff 2 on the meter).

Baggage is charged at the rate of 55 dr per item over 10kg. The minimum fare is 500 dr, which covers most journeys in central Athens.

To hail a taxi, stand on a pavement and shout your destination as they pass. If a taxi is going your way the driver may stop even if there are already passengers inside. This does not mean the fare will be shared: each person will be charged the fare shown on the meter.

If it is absolutely imperative that you get somewhere on time, it's advisable to spend an extra 600 dr to book a taxi. Radio taxis operating out of central Athens include Athina 1 (☎ 921 7942), Kosmos (☎ 1300) and Parthenon (☎ 532 330).

Mainland Ports

Piraeus Πειραιάς

☎ 01   • postcode 185 01   • pop 171,000
Piraeus (pir-ay-**ahs**) is the port of Athens,
the main port of Greece and one of the
major ports of the Mediterranean.

Piraeus has been the port of Athens since
classical times, when the two were linked
by defensive walls. Nowadays, Athens has

expanded sufficiently to meld imperceptibly into Piraeus. The road linking the two
passes through a grey, urban sprawl of factories, warehouses and concrete apartment
blocks. The streets are every bit as traffic-
clogged as Athens, and behind the veneer of
banks and shipping offices most of Piraeus
is pretty seedy. The only reason to come
here is to catch a ferry or hydrofoil.

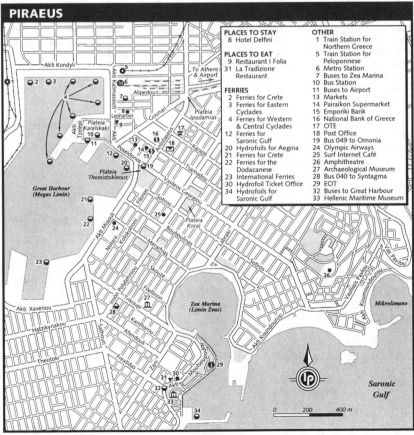

PIRAEUS

PLACES TO STAY	OTHER
8 Hotel Delfini	1 Train Station for Northern Greece
PLACES TO EAT	5 Train Station for Peloponnese
9 Restaurant I Folia	6 Metro Station
31 La Tradizione Restaurant	7 Buses to Zea Marina
	10 Bus Station
FERRIES	11 Buses to Airport
2 Ferries for Crete	13 Markets
3 Ferries for Eastern Cyclades	14 Pairaikon Supermarket
4 Ferries for Western & Central Cyclades	15 Emporiki Bank
	16 National Bank of Greece
12 Ferries for Saronic Gulf	17 OTE
20 Hydrofoils for Aegina	18 Post Office
21 Ferries for Crete	19 Bus 049 to Omonia
22 Ferries for the Dodacanese	24 Olympic Airways
23 International Ferries	25 Surf Internet Café
30 Hydrofoil Ticket Office	26 Amphitheatre
34 Hydrofoils for Saronic Gulf	27 Archaeological Museum
	28 Bus 040 to Syntagma
	29 EOT
	32 Buses to Great Harbour
	33 Hellenic Maritime Museum

Orientation

Piraeus is 10km south-west of central Athens. The largest of its three harbours is the Great Harbour (Megas Limin) on the western side of the Piraeus Peninsula. All ferries leave from here, as well as hydrofoil and catamaran services to Aegina and the Cyclades. There are dozens of shipping agents around the harbour, as well as banks and a post office. Zea Marina (Limin Zeas), on the other side of the peninsula, is the main port for hydrofoils to the Saronic Gulf Islands (except Aegina). East of here is the picturesque, small harbour Mikrolimano.

The metro line from Athens terminates at the north-eastern corner of the Great Harbour on Akti Kalimassioti. Most ferry departure points are a short walk from here. A left turn out of the metro station leads after 250m to Plateia Karaïskaki, which is the terminus for buses to the airport.

South-east of Plateia Karaïskaki, the waterfront becomes Akti Poseidonos, which leads into Vasileos Georgiou beyond Plateia Themistokleous. Vasileos Georgiou is one of the two main streets of Piraeus, running south-east across the peninsula; the other main street is Iroön Polytehniou, which runs south-west along the ridge of the peninsula, meeting Vasileos Georgiou by the main square, Plateia Korai.

Information

EOT has a fairly useless office (☎ 452 2586/2591) overlooking the harbour at Zea Marina. For the record, it's open 8 am to 3 pm Monday to Friday. The telephone number of Piraeus' port police is ☎ 412 2501.

Money There are lots of places to change money at the Great Harbour, including virtually all the ticket and travel agencies. The Emporiki Bank, just north of Plateia Themistokleous on the corner of Antistaseos and Makras Stoas, has a 24-hour automatic exchange machine. The National Bank of Greece has a Great Harbour branch at the corner of Antistaseos and Tsamadou, and another branch above the maritime museum at Zea Marina.

Post & Communications The main post office is on the corner of Tsamadou and Filonos, just north of Plateia Themistokleous. It's open 7.30 am to 8 pm Monday to Friday and 7.30 am to 2 pm Saturday. The OTE is just north of here at Karaoli 19 and is open 24 hours.

You can check your email at the Surf Internet Café at Platanos 3, just off Iroön Polytehniou. It's open 8 am to 9 pm Monday to Friday and 8 am to 3 pm Saturday.

Archaeological Museum

If you have time to spare in Piraeus, the archaeological museum is a good place to spend it. It's well laid out and contains some important finds from classical and Roman times. The star attraction is a magnificent statue of Apollo, the Piraeus Kouros – the oldest larger-than-life, hollow bronze statue yet found. The museum is at Trikoupi 31 and is open 8.30 am to 3 pm Tuesday to Sunday. Admission is 500 dr.

Hellenic Maritime Museum

The museum's collection spans the history of the Greek navy from ancient times to the present day, with drawings and plans of battles, models of ships, battle scenes, uniforms and war memorabilia. The museum (☎ 451 6822) is on Akti Themistokleous at Zea Marina, very close to the hydrofoil quay. It's open 9 am to 2 pm Tuesday to Saturday. Admission is 400 dr.

Places to Stay

There's no reason to stay at any of the shabby, cheap hotels around Great Harbour when Athens is so close.

If you're desperate, the C class *Hotel Delfini* (☎ 412 9779, Leoharous 7) has singles/doubles for 7000/10,000 dr with private bathroom. Make sure you don't get taken there by one of the touts who hang around the port or you will wind up paying the official prices of 14,000/16,000 dr.

Places to Eat

Great Harbour There are dozens of cafes, restaurants and fast-food places along the waterfront. The tiny *Restaurant I Folia*, opposite Plateia Karaïskaki on Akti Poseidonos, is a rough and ready place that does a bowl of gigantes beans for 600 dr, calamari for 750 dr and moussaka for 850 dr.

If you want to stock up on supplies before a ferry trip, head for the area just inland from Poseidonos. You'll find fresh fruit and vegetables at the *markets* on Demosthenous. Opposite the markets is the *Pairaikon Supermarket*, open 8am to 8 pm Monday to Friday, and 8am to 4 pm Saturday.

Zea Marina The choice is more limited over at Zea Marina. You'll find pasta dishes priced from 900 dr and pizzas at *La Tradizione*, next to the Flying Dolphin office on Akti Moutsoupoulou.

Getting There & Away

Bus There are two 24-hour bus services between central Athens and Piraeus. Bus No 049 runs from Omonia to the Great Harbour, and bus No 040 runs from Syntagma to the tip of the Piraeus peninsula. This is the service to catch for Zea Marina – get off at the Hotel Savoy on Iroön Polytehniou – and leave plenty of time as the trip can take over an hour in bad traffic. The fare is 120 dr on each service.

Buses to the airport leave from the southwestern corner of Plateia Karaïskaki. The fare is 250 dr, or 500 dr from 11.30 pm to 6 am. There are no intercity buses to or from Piraeus.

Metro The metro is the fastest and easiest way of getting from the Great Harbour to central Athens (see the Getting Around section of the Athens chapter). The station is at the northern end of Akti Kalimassioti.

Train Railway services to the Peloponnese actually start and terminate at Piraeus, although most schedules don't mention it. There are about 15 trains a day to Athens – enough to make them a reasonable option if you want to stay close to the stations.

Getting Around

Local bus Nos 904 and 905 run between the Great Harbour and Zea Marina. They leave from the bus stop beside the metro at Great Harbour, and drop you by the maritime museum at Zea Marina.

Getting to the Islands

Ferry Piraeus is the busiest port in Greece with a bewildering array of departures and destinations, including daily services to all the island groups except the Ionians and the Sporades. See the Ferries from Piraeus table in this section for a complete list of destinations.

For the latest departure information, pick up a weekly ferry schedule from the tourist office in Athens.

The departure points for the various ferry destinations are shown on the map of Piraeus. Note that there are two departure points for Crete. Ferries for Iraklio leave from the western end of Akti Kondyli, but ferries for other Cretan ports occasionally dock there as well. It's a long way to the other departure point for Crete on Akti Miaouli, so check where to find your boat when you buy your ticket.

Hydrofoil & Catamaran Minoan Lines operates Flying Dolphins (hydrofoils) and high-speed catamarans to the Cyclades and the Saronic Gulf from early April to the end of October. It also has occasional services to the Ionian island of Kythira.

All services to the Cyclades and Aegina leave from Great Harbour, near Plateia Themistokleous. Some services to Poros, Hydra and Spetses also leave from here, but most leave from Zea Marina.

See the Hydrofoils from Piraeus table in this section for a complete list of destinations. For the latest departure information, pick up a timetable from the Flying Dolphin office at Filellinon 3 (Syntagma) in Athens. There are also offices quayside at Great Harbour and overlooking the maritime museum at Zea Marina.

Tickets to Aegina can be bought quayside; tickets to other destinations should be bought in advance from Flying Dolphin offices. Phone (☎ 428 0001) for reservations; you can make credit card payments by phone.

MAINLAND PORTS

Ferries from Piraeus

Destination	Duration	Price (dr)	Frequency	Destination	Duration	Price (dr)	Frequency
Cyclades							
Amorgos	10 hours	4500	daily	Naxos	6 hours	4320	8 daily
Anafi	11 hours	6700	4 weekly	Paros	5 hours	4950	6 daily
Folegandros	9 hours	5150	daily	Santorini	9 hours	6000	5 daily
Ios	7½ hours	5300	4 daily	Serifos	4½ hours	4000	daily
Kimolos	6 hours	4800	daily	Sifnos	5½ hours	4400	daily
Kythnos	2½ hours	2300	daily	Sikinos	8-10 hours	6000	daily
Milos	7 hours	5050	daily	Syros	4 hours	4400	3 daily
Mykonos	5½ hours	5100	daily	Tinos	4½ hours	4700	2 daily
Crete							
Agios Nikolaos	12 hours	7200	3 weekly	Iraklio	10 hours	7000	2 daily
				Rethymno	10-12 hours	7000	daily
Hania	10 hours	5900	daily	Sitia	14 hours	7600	3 weekly
Dodecanese							
Astypalea	12 hours	7000	2 weekly	Lipsi	16 hours	7800	weekly
Halki	22 hours	9700	weekly	Nissiros	20 hours	7600	weekly
Kalymnos	16½ hours	7200	2 daily	Patmos	10 hours	7200	daily
Karpathos	19 hours	8000	3 weekly	Rhodes	14-18 hours	9000	daily
Kassos	17½ hours	7800	3 weekly	Symi	22½ hours	8800	weekly
Kos	11-18 hours	7700	2 daily	Tilos	20½ hours	8800	weekly
Leros	11 hours	6500	daily				
North-Eastern Aegean Islands							
Chios	8 hours	5800	daily	Limnos	13 hours	7000	2 weekly
Fournoi	10 hours	5300	weekly	Samos	13 hours	6700	daily
Ikaria	9 hours	5300	daily				
Lesvos (Mytilini)	12 hours	6700	daily				
Saronic Gulf Islands							
Aegina	1½ hours	1400	hourly	Poros	3 hours	2100	3 daily
Hydra	3½ hours	2300	2 daily	Spetses	4½ hours	3200	daily

Rafina Ραφήνα

☎ 0294 • postcode 190 09 • pop 10,000
Rafina, on Attica's east coast, is Athens'
main fishing port and second port for passenger ferries. The port is much smaller
than Piraeus and less confusing – and fares

are about 20% cheaper, but you have to
spend at least an hour on the bus and 460 dr
to get there.

The port police (☎ 22 888) occupy a
kiosk near the quay, which is lined with fish
restaurants and ticket agents. The main
square, Plateia Plastira, is at the top of the
ramp leading to the port.

Hydrofoils from Piraeus

Destination	Duration	Price (dr)	Frequency	Destination	Duration	Price (dr)	Frequency
Cyclades (*from Zea Marina)				Naxos	3½ hours	9300	daily
Kea*	1½ hours	4600	5 weekly	Paros	3 hours	9300	daily
Kimolos	3½ hours	8400	1 weekly	Serifos	2½ hours	7400	daily
Kythnos	1½ hours	6000	daily	Sifnos	3 hours	8500	daily
Milos	4¼ hours	9800	daily	Syros	2¼ hours	8200	daily
Mykonos	3 hours	9500	daily				
Saronic Gulf Islands (*most from Zea Marina)							
Aegina	35 mins	2700	hourly	Poros*	1 hour	4000	9 daily
Hydra*	1¼ hours	4600	9 daily	Spetses*	2 hours	6400	9 daily
Ionian Islands (from Zea Marina)				Kythira	4 hours	10,000	4 weekly

Places to Stay

There's no reason to hang about in Rafina, but there are a couple of hotels if you want to stay the night and catch an early ferry or hydrofoil. The D class *Hotel Koralli* (☎ 22 477), on Plateia Plastira, has basic singles/doubles for 5500/8000 dr. The C class *Hotel Avra* (☎ 22 781, fax 23 320) overlooks the port just south of the square. It has large singles/doubles with sea views for 13,500/21,000 dr, including breakfast.

Getting There & Away

Bus There are frequent buses from the Mavromateon terminal in Athens to Rafina (one hour, 460 dr) between 5.40 am and 10.30 pm. The first bus leaves Rafina at 5.45 am and the last at 10.15 pm.

Ferry Goutos Lines and Strintzis Lines both operate ferries to the Cycladic islands of Andros (two hours, 2400 dr), Tinos (3½ hours, 3600 dr) and Mykonos (4½ hours, 4100 dr). Strintzis has departures to all three every morning at 8.05 am, and a 7 pm service to Andros only. Goutos has departures to Andros, Tinos and Mykonos at 7.15 am every day except Wednesday. The Tuesday service continues from Mykonos to Syros (5¾ hours, 3400 dr), Paros (7¼ hours, 4100 dr), Naxos (8½ hours, 4200 dr) and Amorgos (11¾ hours, 4700 dr), returning the next day.

The Maritime Company of Lesvos has four boats a week to Limnos (10 to 13 hours, 5500 dr), two of them stopping at Lesvos (8½ hours, 4450 dr).

There are also ferries to the ports of Karystos and Marmari on the island of Evia. There are three services a day to Marmari (1¼ hours, 1230 dr) and two to Karystos (1¾ hours, 1710 dr).

Catamaran High-speed catamarans have now completely taken over from hydrofoils on the routes from Rafina to the Cyclades.

Strintzis Lines' *Seajet I* leaves daily at 8.15 am for Syros (1¾ hours, 6900 dr), Paros (2½ hours, 8200 dr), Naxos 3¼ hours, 8500 dr), Ios (four hours, 8200 dr) and Santorini (4¾ hours, 9600 dr). Strintzis also operates the *Seajet II* to Tinos (1½ hours, 7200 dr) and Mykonos (two hours, 8200 dr) every day at 7.40 am, and at 4 pm every day except Tuesday. The Tuesday morning service also calls at Andros (one hour, 4700 dr), and continues from Mykonos to Syros (three hours, 6900 dr), Paros (3¾ hours, 8200 dr), Naxos (4¼ hours, 8500 dr) and finally Amorgos (5½ hours, 9500 dr).

Goutos has departures to Tinos and Mykonos every day at 8 am and 4.15 pm.

The Thursday morning service calls at Andros, and continues from Mykonos to Paros, Naxos and Amorgos.

Thessaloniki
Θεσσαλονίκη

☎ 031 • postcode 541 00 • pop 750,000

Thessaloniki, also known as Salonica, is Greece's second-largest city. It's a bustling, sophisticated place with good restaurants and a busy nightlife. It was once the second city of Byzantium, and there are some magnificent Byzantine churches, as well as a scattering of Roman ruins.

Orientation

Thessaloniki is laid out on a grid system. The main thoroughfares – Tsimiski, Egnatia and Agiou Dimitriou – run parallel to Nikis, on the waterfront. Plateias Eleftherias and Aristotelous, both on Nikis, are the main squares. The city's most famous landmark is the White Tower (no longer white) at the eastern end of Nikis. The train station is on Monastiriou, the westerly continuation of Egnatia beyond Plateia Dimokratias, and the airport is 16km to the south-east. The old Turkish quarter is north of Athinas.

Information

Tourist Office The EOT (☎ 271 888, 263 112), Plateia Aristotelous 8, is open 8.30 am to 8 pm Monday to Friday and 8.30 am to 2 pm Saturday.

Money Most banks around town are equipped with ATMs. There is an automatic exchange machine and an ATM at the train station. American Express (☎ 269 521) is at Tsimiski 19.

Midas Exchange, at the western end of Tsimiski close to the Ladadika district, is handy for people using the ferry terminal. It's open from 8.30 am to 8.30 pm Monday to Friday, 8.30 am to 2 pm Saturday and 9 am to 1.30 pm Sunday.

Post & Communications The main post office is at Aristotelous 26. It's open 7.30 am to 8 pm Monday to Friday, 7.30 am to 2.15 pm Saturday and 9 am to 1.30 pm Sunday. The OTE is at Karolou Dil 27 and is open 24 hours a day.

The most convenient Internet cafe is Globus Internet Cafe (☎ 232 901), near the Roman Agora at Amynta 12. However, it is closed for one month during summer.

Laundry Bianca Laundrette, on Antoniadou (just east of the Arch of Galerius, off Gournari), charges 1500 dr to wash and dry a load. The laundrette is open 8 am to 8.30 pm Monday to Friday.

Emergency There is a first aid centre (☎ 530 530) at Navarhou Koundourioti 6. The tourist police (☎ 554 871) are on the 5th floor at Dodekanisiou 4. The office is open every day from 7.30 am to 11 pm all year round.

Things to See

The **archaeological museum**, at the eastern end of Tsimiski, houses a superb collection of treasures from the royal tombs of Philip II of Macedon. It is open 12.30 to 7 pm Monday and 8 am to 7 pm Tuesday to Sunday; admission is 1500 dr.

The imposing **Arch of Galerius** at the eastern end of Egnatia is the finest of the city's remaining Roman monuments. It was erected in 303 AD to celebrate Emperor Galerius' victories over the Persians in 297 AD.

Just north of here is the **Rotonda**, the oldest of Thessaloniki's churches. It was built in the 3rd century as a mausoleum for Galerius, but never fulfilled this function. Constantine the Great transformed it into a church. The minaret was erected during its days as a mosque.

Places to Stay

The *youth hostel (☎ 225 946, fax 262 208, Alex Svolou 44)* has dorm beds for 2000 dr. The dorms are open all day.

The best budget hotel in town is the friendly, family-run *Hotel Acropol (☎ 536 170, Tantalidou 4)*, close to the central police

THESSALONIKI

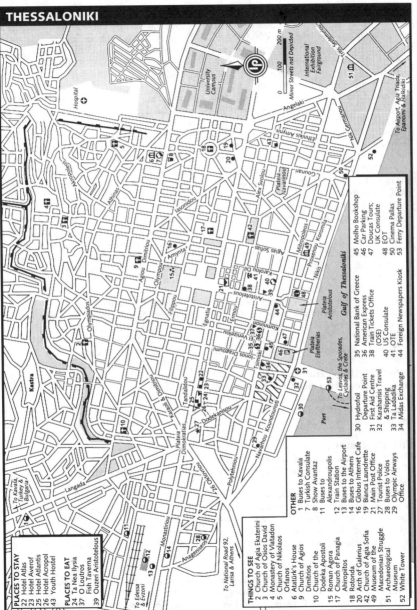

0   100   200 m

Minor Streets not Depicted

PLACES TO STAY
22   Hotel Atlas
23   Hotel Averof
25   Hotel Atlantis
26   Hotel Acropol
43   Youth Hostel

PLACES TO EAT
24   Ta Nea Ilysia
37   O Loutros
   Fish Taverna
39   Ouzeri Aristotelous

THINGS TO SEE
2   Church of Agia Ekaterini
3   Church of Osios David
4   Monastery of Vlatadon
5   Church of Nikolaos
   Orfanos
6   Atatürk's House
9   Church of Agios
   Dimitrios
10   Church of the
   Dodeka Apostoli
15   Roman Agora
17   Church of Panagia
   Ahiropitos
18   Rotonda
20   Arch of Galerius
42   Church of Agia Sofia
49   Museum of the
   Macedonian Struggle
51   Archaeological
   Museum
52   White Tower

OTHER
1   Buses to Kavala
7   Turkish Consulate
8   Show Avantaz
11   Buses to
   Alexandroupolis
12   Train Station
13   Buses to the Airport
14   Buses to Athens
16   Globus Internet Cafe
19   Bianca Laundrette
21   Main Post Office
27   Tourist Police
28   Buses to Volos
29   Olympic Airways
   Office
30   Hydrofoil
   Departure Point
31   First Aid Centre
32   Karahanis Travel
   & Shipping
33   Ta Ladadika
34   Midas Exchange
35   National Bank of Greece
36   American Express
38   Train Tickets Office
   (OSE)
40   US Consulate
41   OTE
44   Foreign Newspapers Kiosk
45   Molho Bookshop
46   Car Parking
47   Doucas Tours;
   UK Consulate
48   EOT
50   Cinema Pallas
53   Ferry Departure Point

station. The clean singles/doubles with shared bathroom are listed at 6000/9000 dr, but most of the time it charges a bargain 5000 dr per room. *Hotel Atlantis* (☎ *540 131, Egnatia 14*), has tiny but clean rooms with shared bathroom for 5500/8600 dr.

Hotel Atlas (☎ *537 046, Egnatia 40*), has singles/doubles with shared bathroom for 8000/11,000 dr and good doubles with bathrooms for 14,000 dr. The rooms at the front get a lot of traffic noise. Just around the corner from the Atlas is the quiet *Hotel Averof* (☎ *538 498, Leontos Sofou 24*). Pleasant rooms with shared bathroom are 6000/9000 dr.

Rooms can be hard to find during the international trade fair in September.

Places to Eat

Ta Nea Ilysia, opposite the Hotel Averof on Leontos Sofou, is a popular place with main dishes priced from 1050 dr.

A place full of local colour is the lively *O Loutros Fish Taverna*, which occupies an old Turkish hammam near the flower market on Komninon. Most dishes cost from 2000 dr to 3000 dr.

Ouzeri Aristotelous (*Aristotelous 8*) has first-rate mezedes, which include cuttlefish stuffed with cheese, grilled eggplant with garlic, and prawns in red sauce. The restaurant is in the Vosporion Megaron arcade off Aristotelous. It's open Monday to Saturday all day until late, but closes on Sunday at 6 pm.

Entertainment

Music bars abound in *Ta Ladadika*, an area of renovated warehouses and shops behind the port.

Live bouzouki and Greek folk are played at *Show Avantaz*, Agiou Dimitriou 156. There is no cover charge but spirits cost 1800 dr. The club is open 11 pm to 4 am nightly, but closes from June to September.

Getting There & Away

Air There are at least 13 flights a day to Athens – seven with Olympic Airways (22,000 dr), four with Cronus (19,400 dr) and two with Air Greece (20,400 dr).

See the Getting There & Away chapter at the start of this book for information on international flights, and the following Getting to the Islands section for flights to the islands.

Bus There are numerous bus terminals, most of them near the train station. Frequent buses for Athens leave from Monastiriou 65 and 67, opposite the train station; buses for Alexandroupolis leave from Koloniari 17 behind the train station; buses for Volos leave from Anageniseos 22. Kavala buses leave from Langada 59, on the main road north out of Thessaloniki.

Train There are eight trains a day to Athens and five to Alexandroupolis. All international trains from Athens stop at Thessaloniki. You can get more information from the OSE office at Aristotelous 18 or from the train station.

Getting Around

To/From the Airport Thessaloniki's airport is 16km south-east of town. You can get there on public bus No 78, which leaves from in front of the train station and stops in front of the ferry terminal. It costs 140 dr. A taxi to or from the airport costs around 2000 dr.

Bus There is a flat fare of 100 dr on city buses, paid either to a conductor at the rear door or to coin-operated machines on driver-only buses.

Getting to the Islands

Air Olympic Airways has daily flights to Limnos (15,200 dr), six flights a week to Mytilini (20,900 dr), three a week to Corfu (20,900 dr), Iraklio (29,900 dr) and Mykonos (27,900 dr), and two a week to Hania (29,900 dr), Chios (22,400 dr) and Samos (25,400 dr).

Cronus Airlines has daily flights to Iraklio and Rhodes; Air Greece flies to Iraklio twice a day, and to Rhodes four times a week; Air Manos flies to Mykonos, Samos and Santorini.

Ferry There's a Sunday ferry to Chios (18 hours, 8300 dr) via Limnos (eight hours, 5300 dr) and Lesvos (13 hours, 8300 dr) throughout the year. In summer there are three to six boats a week to Iraklio, on Crete (12,000 dr). All ferries go via Paros and Santorini; some also stop at Tinos and Mykonos.

There are ferries to the Sporades islands of Skiathos, Skopelos and Alonnisos three times a week (5½-seven hours, 3800 dr) in July and August. One ferry a week goes to Rhodes (21 hours, 14,800 dr), via Samos and Kos, throughout the year.

Karaharisis Travel & Shipping Agency (☎ 524 544, fax 532 289), on Navarhou Koundourioti 8, handles tickets. The telephone number of Thessaloniki's port police is ☎ 531 504.

Hydrofoil In summer there are daily hydrofoils to the Sporades islands of Skiathos (3¼ hours, 8500 dr), Skopelos (four hours, 9300 dr) and Alonnisos (4½ hours, 11,700 dr). Karaharisis Travel & Shipping Agency also sells hydrofoil tickets.

Gythio Γύθειο

☎ 0733   • postcode 232 00   • pop 4900
Gythio (**yee**-thih-o), once the port of ancient Sparta, is an attractive fishing town at the head of the Lakonian Gulf. It is the most convenient port of departure for the Ionian island of Kythira, and also has services to Kastelli-Kissamos on Crete.

Orientation
Most things of importance to travellers are along the seafront on Akti Vasileos Pavlou. The bus station is at the northern end, next to the small triangular park known as the Perivolaki. Vasileos Georgiou runs inland from here past the main square Plateia Panagiotou Venetzanaki, and becomes the road to Sparta.

The square at the southern end of Akti Vasileos Pavlou is Plateia Mavromihali, hub of the old quarter of Marathonisi. The

ferry quay is opposite this square. Beyond it, the waterfront road becomes Kranais, which leads south to Areopoli. A causeway leads out to Marathonisi Islet at the southern edge of town.

Information
The EOT (☎/fax 24 484) is about 500m north of the waterfront at Vasileos Georgiou 20, open 11 am to 3 pm Monday to Friday.

The post office is on Ermou, in the newer part of the town two blocks north of the bus station, and the OTE office is between the two at the corner of Herakles and Kapsali.

The tourist police (☎ 22 271) share lodgings with the regular police (☎ 22 100) on the waterfront between the bus station and Plateia Mavromihali.

Things to Do
According to mythology, the island of **Marathonisi** is ancient Cranae, where Paris (a prince of Troy) and Helen (the wife of Menelaus of Sparta) consummated the love affair that sparked the Trojan War. An 18th century **tower** at the centre of the island has been restored and converted into a **museum**.

Gythio's small but well-preserved **ancient theatre** is next to an army camp on the northern edge of town. Most of ancient Gythio lies beneath the nearby Lakonian gulf.

Places to Stay & Eat
You'll find plenty of domatia signs around town. ***Kontogiannis Rooms to Rent*** (☎ 22 518), up the steps next to the police station on Akti Vasileos Pavlou, has spotless singles/doubles with bathroom for 7000/ 10,000 dr. ***Saga Pension*** (☎ 23 220, fax 24 370), on the seafront south of Plateia Mavromihali, charges the same rates.

The waterfront is lined with countless fish tavernas with very similar menus. For something completely different, head inland to the tiny ***General Store & Wine Bar*** (☎ 24 113, Vasileos Georgiou 67). You'll find an unusually varied and imaginative menu featuring dishes like orange and pumpkin soup (600 dr) and fillet of pork with black pepper and ouzo (2800 dr).

Self-caterers can stock up at *Kourtakis supermarket*, around the corner from the bus station on Heracles.

Getting There & Away
There are five buses a day to Athens (4¼ hours, 4500 dr) via Sparta (one hour, 750 dr).

Getting to the Islands
There are daily ferries to Kythira (two hours, 1600 dr) in summer, continuing twice a week to Antikythira and Kastelli-Kissamos on Crete (seven hours, 5100 dr). Tickets are sold at Golden Ferries (☎ 22 996, fax 22 410) opposite the tourist office on Vasileos Pavlou.

There are also ferries to Kythira from Neapoli. For more information, see the Other Ports to the Ionians section later in this chapter.

Other Ports to the Saronic Gulf Islands

There are hydrofoil connections to the Saronic Gulf Islands from a host of minor ports dotted around the eastern coast of the Peloponnese. Many of these ports are hard to get to by land, and cannot be considered as options for getting to the islands. Others represent a viable alternative, but only for travellers who want to travel via **Nafplio** – main town and transport hub of the Argolis Peninsula. There are hourly buses to Nafplio (2½ hours, 2550 dr) from Terminal A in Athens.

Porto Heli, at the south-western tip of the Argolis, has at least six hydrofoils a day to Spetses (10 minutes, 1400 dr) and Hydra (one hour, 2500 dr). There are three buses a day to Porto Heli (two hours, 1400 dr) from Nafplio. These buses also stop at the tiny village of **Costa**, right opposite Spetses. There are caïques and water taxis across the intervening straits.

Galatas, on the eastern side of the Argolis, is just across the water from the island of Poros. There are three buses a day from Nafplio (two hours, 1450 dr), travelling via the site of ancient Epidaurus.

Ports like **Gerakas**, **Kyparissi**, **Leonidio** and **Monemvasia** are best considered as day trips from the islands.

Other Ports to the Cyclades

LAVRIO Λαύριο
☎ 0292   • postcode 195 00   • pop 2500
Lavrio is an unattractive industrial town on the east coast of Attica, 10km north of Sounion. It is worth a mention only because it is the departure point for ferries to the islands of Kea and Kythnos.

Getting There & Away
Bus There are buses every 30 minutes to Lavrio from the Mavromateon terminal in Athens (1½ hours, 950 dr).

Ferry Goutos Lines runs the F/B *Myrina Express* from Lavrio to Kea (1600 dr) and Kythnos (2300 dr). From mid-June, there are ferries to Kea every morning and evening from Monday to Friday, and up to six a day at weekends. Three ferries a week continue to Kythnos. In winter there are ferries to Kea every day except Monday, returning every day except Wednesday. One service a week continues to Kythnos. The EOT in Athens stocks a timetable for this route.

The ticket office at Lavrio is opposite the quay.

Other Ports to the Ionians

PATRAS Πάτρα
☎ 061   • postcode 260 01   • pop 153,300
Patras is Greece's third-largest city and the principal port for ferries to the Ionian Islands, as well as for international services to Italy. It's not particularly exciting and most travellers hang around only long enough for transport connections.

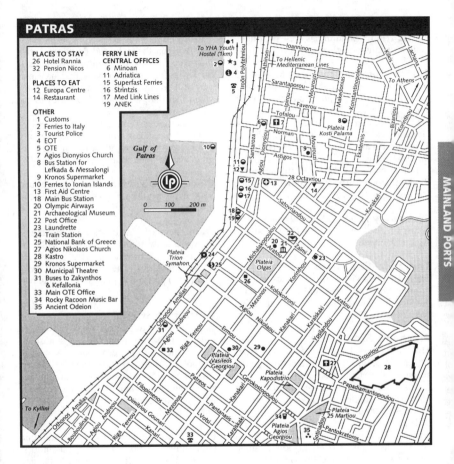

PATRAS

PLACES TO STAY
26 Hotel Rannia
32 Pension Nicos

PLACES TO EAT
12 Europa Centre
14 Restaurant

OTHER
1 Customs
2 Ferries to Italy
3 Tourist Police
4 EOT
5 OTE
7 Agios Dionysios Church
8 Bus Station for
   Lefkada & Messalongi
9 Kronos Supermarket
10 Ferries to Ionian Islands
13 First Aid Centre
18 Main Bus Station
20 Olympic Airways
21 Archaeological Museum
22 Post Office
23 Laundrette
24 Train Station
25 National Bank of Greece
27 Agios Nikolaos Church
28 Kastro
29 Kronos Supermarket
30 Municipal Theatre
31 Buses to Zakynthos
   & Kefallonia
33 Main OTE Office
34 Rocky Racoon Music Bar
35 Ancient Odeion

**FERRY LINE
CENTRAL OFFICES**
6 Minoan
11 Adriatica
15 Superfast Ferries
16 Strintzis
17 Med Link Lines
19 ANEK

*Gulf of
Patras*

0   100   200 m

Plateia
Trion
Symahon

Plateia
Olgas

Plateia
Vasileos
Georgiou

Plateia
Kapodistriou

Plateia
25 Martiou

Plateia
Agios
Georgiou

To Kyllini

To YHA Youth
Hostel (1km)

To Hellenic
Mediterranean Lines

To Athens

MAINLAND PORTS

Orientation

The city is easy to negotiate and is laid out on a grid stretching uphill from the port to the old *kastro* (castle). Most services of importance to travellers are along the waterfront, known as Othonos Amalias, in the middle of town and Iroön Politehniou to the north. The various shipping offices are to be found along here. The main thoroughfares of Agiou Dionysiou, Riga Fereou, Mezones, Korinthou and Kanakari run parallel to the waterfront. The train station is in the middle of

town on Othonos Amalias, and the main bus station is close by.

Information

Tourist Offices The EOT (☎ 620 353) is outside the international arrivals terminal at the port. In theory, it's open 8 am to 10 pm Monday to Friday; in practice, it's often closed. The most useful piece of information is an arrow pointing to the helpful tourist police (☎ 451 833), upstairs in the embarkation hall, who are open 7.30 am to 11 pm daily.

Money The National Bank of Greece on Plateia Trion Symahon has a 24-hour automatic exchange machine.

Post & Communications The post office, on the corner of Zaïmi and Mezonos, is open 7.30 am to 8 pm Monday to Friday and 7.30 am to 2 pm Saturday. The main OTE office, on the corner of Dimitriou Gounari and Kanakari, is open 24 hours. There is also an OTE office at the port, near the EOT office.

For Internet access, head inland to the Rocky Racoon Music Bar, Gerokostopoulou 56. It's open 9 am to 3 am daily.

Emergency There is a first-aid centre (☎ 27 7386) on the corner of 28 Octavriou and Agiou Dionysiou.

Things to See & Do

There are great views of Zakynthos and Kefallonia from the Venetian **kastro**, which is reached by the steps at the top of Agiou Nikolaou.

Places to Stay & Eat

Most travellers head for *Pension Nicos* *(☎ 623 757)*, up from the waterfront on the corner of Patreos and Agiou Andreou 121. It has doubles with shared facilities for 6500 dr, and singles/doubles with bathroom for 4000/7000 dr.

The C class *Hotel Rannia (☎ 220 114, fax 220 537, Riga Fereou 53)*, facing Plateia Olgas, has comfortable air-con singles/doubles with TV for 10,000/15,000 dr.

Europa Centre, Othonos Amalias 10, is a convenient cafeteria-style place close to the international ferry dock. It has a range of taverna dishes as well as spaghetti (from 900 dr) and a choice of vegetarian meals (900 dr).

Locals prefer the nameless *restaurant* at Michalakopoulou 3, which specialises in traditional dishes like *entosthia arnisia* – translated as lamb bowels on the menu! Travellers will probably be happier with a large bowl of fish soup (1100 dr) or roast chicken with potatoes (700 dr).

Getting There & Away

The bus from Patras is faster, but is more expensive than the train and drops you off a long way from the city centre at Terminal A on Kifissou. This can be a real hassle if you're arriving in Athens after midnight – when there are no connecting buses to the city centre, leaving newcomers at the mercy of the notorious Terminal A taxi drivers.

The train takes you close to the city centre, within easy walking distance of good accommodation.

Bus There are buses to Athens (three hours, 3500 dr) every 30 minutes, with the last at 9.45 pm.

Train There are nine trains a day to Athens. Four are slow trains (4½ hours, 1580 dr) and five are express intercity trains (3½ hours, 2980 dr). The last intercity train leaves at 6 pm, and the last slow train leaves at 8 pm.

Getting to the Islands

Bus There are two buses a day to Lefkada (3450 dr), leaving from the bus station on the corner of Faverou and Konstantinopoleos. Buses to Zakynthos (3½ hours, 2900 dr) and Kefallonia leave from the bus station at the corner of Othonos Amalias and Gerokostopoulou. They travel via the port of Kyllini.

Ferry There are daily ferries to Kefallonia (four hours, 3200 dr), Ithaki (six hours, 3500 dr) and Corfu (10 hours, 5800 dr). Services to Italy are covered in the Getting There & Away chapter at the start of this book. Ticket agents line the waterfront.

KYLLINI Κυλλήνη

The tiny port of Kyllini (kih-**lee**-nih), 78km south-west of Patras, warrants a mention only as the jumping-off point for ferries to Kefallonia and Zakynthos. Most people pass through Kyllini on buses from Patras that board the ferries. If you get stuck, the port police (☎ 0623-92 211) at the quay can suggest accommodation.

Getting There & Away

There are regular buses to Kyllini (1¼ hours, 1500 dr) from the Zakynthos bus station in Patras.

Getting to the Islands

There are up to five boats a day to Zakynthos (1½ hours, 1160 dr), as well as four boats a day to Poros (1¼ hours, 1620 dr) and two to Argostoli (2¼ hours, 2310 dr) on Kefallonia.

NEAPOLI Νεάπολη

☎ 0734 • postcode 230 70 • pop 2500

Neapoli (nih-**ah**-po-lih), close to the southern tip of the eastern prong of the Peloponnese, is the 'other' port serving Kythira – which is clearly visible to the south.

Few travellers come this way; the ferries from Gythio are much more convenient – see the Gythio section earlier in this chapter. Neapoli is popular enough with local holiday-makers to have three seafront *hotels* and several *domatia*.

Getting There & Away

There are 11 buses a day from Athens to Sparta (3¼ hours, 3700 dr), and four buses a day from Sparta to Neapoli (three hours, 2550 dr).

Getting to the Islands

There are three ferries a week from Neapoli to Agia Pelagia on Kythira (one hour, 1500 dr). Tickets are sold at Vatika Bay Travel (☎/fax 22 660), Agios Traidos 3, opposite the ferry quay. In July and August, there is a Sunday afternoon hydrofoil service to Kythira (20 minutes, 3000 dr) and four hydrofoils a week to Piraeus (five hours, 9400 dr).

IGOUMENITSA Ηγουμενίτσα

☎ 0665 • postcode 461 00 • pop 6800

Igoumenitsa, opposite the island of Corfu, is the main port of north-western Greece. Few people stay any longer than it takes to buy a ticket out. The bus station is on Kyprou. To get there from the ferries, follow the waterfront (Ethnikis Antistasis) north for 500m and turn right up 23 Fevrouariou. After two blocks turn left onto Kyprou and the bus station is on the left.

Places to Stay & Eat

If you get stuck for the night, you'll find signs for *domatia* around the port. The D class *Egnatia* (☎ 23 648, fax 23 63, Eleftherias 2) has comfortable rooms for 8500/11,500 dr with private bathroom. Turn right from the bus station and walk 100 metres. You will see it across the square on your left.

Bilis (☎ 26 214, Agion Apostolon 15) is right opposite the Corfu ferry quay and is handy for a quick meal.

Getting There & Away

Bus Services include three buses a day to Athens (eight hours, 8300 dr).

Getting to the Islands

Ferry There are ferries to Corfu Town every hour between 5 am and 10 pm (1½ hours, 1300 dr), and six a day to Lefkimmi (one hour, 750 dr) in southern Corfu. They are also three boats a week to Paxi (1½ hours, 1600 dr). Tickets are sold at booths opposite the quay. See the introductory Getting There & Away chapter for information on ferries to Italy.

ASTAKOS Αστακός

The small resort of Astakos (as-tah-**kos**), in Sterea Ellada (Central Greece), makes a handy stepping stone to the island of Ithaki. From June to September, there's a boat every day at 1 pm to Piso Aetos on Ithaki (three hours, 1300 dr). There are two buses a day to Astakos from Terminal A in Athens (five hours, 5200 dr). If you need to stay overnight, there's one hotel – the C class *Hotel Stratos* (☎ 0646-41 096) – and domatia.

Other Ports to the Sporades

VOLOS Βόλος

☎ 0421 • postcode 380 01 • pop 110,000

Volos is a bustling city attractively positioned on the northern shores of the Pagasitic

Gulf, and the principal port for ferry and hydrofoil services to the Sporades.

According to mythology, Volos was the ancient Iolkos from where Jason and the Argonauts set sail on their quest for the Golden Fleece.

Orientation & Information

Volos is laid out on an easy grid system stretching inland parallel to the waterfront (called Argonafton), which is where most things of importance to travellers are to be found. The main square, Plateia Riga Fereou, is at the north-western end of Argonafton.

The EOT (☎ 23 500, fax 24 750) is on the northern side of the square. It has maps and hotel information as well as bus, ferry and hydrofoil schedules. In summer, the office is open 7.30 am to 2.30 pm and 6 to 8.30 pm Monday to Friday, and 9.30 am to 1.30 pm weekends and holidays. The tourist police (☎ 72 421) are in the same building as the regular police at 28 Oktovriou 179.

The National Bank of Greece on Argonafton has an ATM.

Places to Stay

The D class **Hotel Avra** (☎ 25 370, Solonos 5), on the corner of Iasonos, is the best of the cheap hotels. It charges 5000/7000 dr for singles/doubles with shared bathroom, and 6500/9000 dr bathroom. Nearby is the C class **Hotel Jason** (☎ 26 075, fax 26 975, Pavlou Mela 1), which charges 6500/10,000 dr with bathroom.

The B class **Aigli** (☎ 24 471, fax 33 006, Argonafton 24), with its impressive neoclassical facade and warm interior, is a good option if you want more style. Rooms cost 15,000/23,000 dr, including breakfast.

Places to Eat

Volos is famous for its food, particularly for the range and quality of the mezedes (literally 'tastes') found at its many ouzeria. There are places all over town, but the main concentration is on Argonafton. You'll find *ohtapodi* (octopus) prepared a dozen different ways, *htypiti* (a mixed feta cheese and hot pepper dip); *spetsofaï* (chopped sausages and peppers in a rich sauce); and many more. **Ouzeri Naftilia**, at the north-western end of

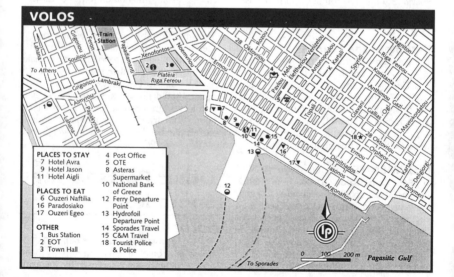

VOLOS

PLACES TO STAY	4	Post Office
7 Hotel Avra	5	OTE
9 Hotel Jason	8	Asteras
11 Hotel Aigli		Supermarket
	10	National Bank
PLACES TO EAT		of Greece
6 Ouzeri Naftilia	12	Ferry Departure
16 Paradosiako		Point
17 Ouzeri Egeo	13	Hydrofoil
		Departure Point
OTHER	14	Sporades Travel
1 Bus Station	15	C&M Travel
2 EOT	18	Tourist Police
3 Town Hall		& Police

Pagasitic Gulf

To Sporades

The Ouzeri

An *ouzeri* (strictly speaking, a *tsipouradiko*), if you have not already come across one, is a type of small restaurant where you eat from various plates of *mezedes* (tasty titbits) and drink bottles of *tsipouro*. Tsipouro is a distilled spirit similar to ouzo, but stronger. You can dilute it with water if you prefer it weaker, or want it to last a little longer. When you have finished one round of mezedes or tsipouro, you order another and so on, until you are full, or can't stand up.

The ouzeri is not purely a Volos institution, but Volos is famous throughout Greece for the quality and quantity of its ouzeria. The institution came about as a result of refugees from Asia Minor who established themselves in Volos after the exchange of populations in 1923, when Greeks and Turks were forced to swap homelands. Most of the refugees who came to Volos were seafarers who would gather on the harbour at lunchtime and drink tsipouro accompanied by various mezedes. As this eating and drinking routine flourished, demand for more exotic mezedes grew and so too did the repertoire of the establishments serving them. Seafood mezedes were the mainstay of the Volos ouzeri.

Argonafton, and *Ouzeri Egeo* towards the middle, are both very popular.

At *Paradosiako* (*Kartali 8*) you can listen to live *rembetica* music while you dine. The taverna is open all day, but the live music doesn't start till 10.30 pm. The food is traditional Greek and low-priced.

Getting There & Away
Bus There are nine buses a day to Athens (five hours, 5250 dr) and five to Thessaloniki (three hours, 3500 dr).

Train Most services to Volos involve changing trains at Larissa, on the main Athens-Thessaloniki line. However, there are two direct intercity (IC) trains a day to Athens (five hours, 5820 dr).

Getting to the Islands
Ferry There are one to two ferries daily from Volos to Skiathos (three hours, 2750 dr), Glossa (Skopelos; 3½ hours, 2750 dr), Skopelos Town (4½ hours, 3400 dr) and Alonnisos (five hours, 3750 dr). Buy tickets from Sporades Travel (☎/fax 35 846), Argonafton 33.

Hydrofoil In summer, there are five or six hydrofoils a day to Skiathos (1½ hours, 5500 dr), Glossa (1¾ hours, 6200 dr), Skopelos Town (two hours, 6800 dr) and

Alonnisos (three hours, 7500 dr). Tickets are available from C&M Travel (☎ 39 786, fax 24 388), Antonopoulou 11.

AGIOS KONSTANTINOS
Αγιος Κωνσταντίνος
☎ 0235   • postcode 350 06   • pop 2360
Agios Konstantinos, on the main Athens-Thessaloniki route, is one of the three mainland ports that serve the Sporades Islands (the other two are Thessaloniki and Volos).

With judicious use of buses from Athens to the port, you probably won't need to stay overnight before catching a Sporades-bound ferry or hydrofoil. If you get stuck, the *Hotel Poulia* (☎ 31 663) charges 6000/8000 dr for singles/doubles. A more comfortable option is the A class *Motel Levendi* (☎ 32 251, fax 32 255), where singles/doubles are 16,000/20,000 dr.

Getting There & Away
Bus There are hourly buses to Agios Konstantinos from Athens Terminal B (2½ hours, 3000 dr).

Getting to the Islands
Ferry There is at least one ferry a day to Skiathos (3½ hours, 3200 dr) and one or two to Skopelos Town (4½ hours, 4000 dr) and Alonnisos (six hours, 4300 dr).

Hydrofoil There are at least three hydrofoils a day to Skiathos (1½ hours, 6600 dr), Skopelos Town (2½ hours, 8200 dr) and Alonnisos (three hours, 8800 dr). Two services a day travel via Glossa (1¾ hours, 7600 dr) on Skopelos.

Other Ports to the North-East Aegean

KAVALA Καβάλα
☎ 051 • postcode 655 00 • pop 57,000

Modern Kavala, 163km east of Thessaloniki, is built over ancient Neopolis and serves as the main port for the island of Thasos. It's an attractive city, spilling gently down the foothills of Mt Symvolon to a large harbour. The old quarter of Panagia nestles under a massive Byzantine fortress.

Orientation & Information
Kavala's focal point is Plateia Eleftherias. The two main thoroughfares, Eleftheriou Venizelou and Erythrou Stavrou run west from here parallel with the waterfront.

The EOT (☎ 222 425), on the west side of Plateia Eleftherias, has information on hotel prices and transport. It's open 8 am to 2 pm Monday to Friday.

The National Bank of Greece, on the corner of Megalou Alexandrou and Dragoumi, has an automatic exchange machine and an ATM. Midas Exchange, next to the EOT, is open 8.30 am to 8 pm Monday to Friday and 9 am to 8 pm Saturday.

Things to See
If you've got time to spare, spend it exploring the streets of **Panagia**, the old Turkish quarter occupying the promontory south-east of Plateia Eleftherias. Its most conspicuous

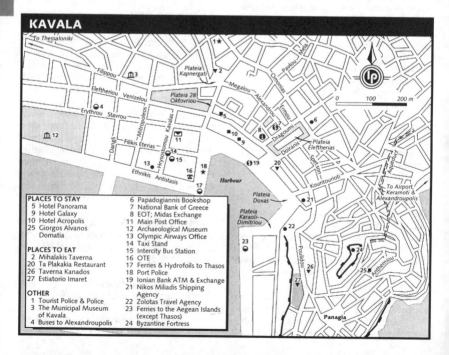

KAVALA

PLACES TO STAY
5 Hotel Panorama
9 Hotel Galaxy
10 Hotel Acropolis
25 Giorgos Alvanos Domatia

PLACES TO EAT
2 Mihalakis Taverna
20 Ta Plakakia Restaurant
26 Taverna Kanados
27 Estiatorio Imaret

OTHER
1 Tourist Police & Police
3 The Municipal Museum of Kavala
4 Buses to Alexandroupolis
6 Papadogiannis Bookshop
7 National Bank of Greece
8 EOT; Midas Exchange
11 Main Post Office
12 Archaeological Museum
13 Olympic Airways Office
14 Taxi Stand
15 Intercity Bus Station
16 OTE
17 Ferries & Hydrofoils to Thasos
18 Port Police
19 Ionian Bank ATM & Exchange
21 Nikos Miliadis Shipping Agency
22 Zolotas Travel Agency
23 Ferries to the Aegean Islands (except Thasos)
24 Byzantine Fortress

building is the **Imaret**, a huge structure with 18 domes, which overlooks the harbour from Poulidou. In Turkish times the Imaret was a hostel for theology students. It has recently been restored and is now a pleasant cafe and restaurant (see Places to Eat). Within the cafe are some cabinets displaying memorabilia from Mehmet Ali's time.

The imposing **aqueduct** which once supplied water to Panagia was built during the reign of Süleyman the Magnificent (1520-66).

Places to Stay
The best deal for budget travellers, and perhaps the cosiest environment in Kavala, is at the *domatia* run by Giorgos Alvanos (☎ 228 412, Anthemiou 35). The address is a beautiful 300-year-old house in Panagia. Singles/doubles are 5000/7000 dr with shared bathroom.

The C class *Hotel Acropolis* (☎ 223 543, fax 830 752, Eleftheriou Venizelou 29), is the closest thing to a budget hotel. It has singles with shared bathroom for 7500 dr and doubles with private bathroom for 14,000 dr.

The B class *Hotel Galaxy* (☎ 224 812, fax 226 754, email galaxy@hol.gr, Eleftheriou Venizelou 27) is Kavala's best hotel, with spacious single/double rooms for a very reasonable 13,200/19,400 dr.

Places to Eat
Ta Plakakia Restaurant (*Doïranis 4*), near Plateia Eleftherias, is a convenient place with a huge choice of low-priced dishes. *Mihalakis Taverna* (*Kassandrou 3*), on Plateia Kapnergati, is more upmarket. Don't be put off by the tacky murals – the food is good.

Taverna Kanados, opposite the Imaret on Poulidou, specialises in fish – try their mussels in tomato sauce. *Estiatorio Imaret*, inside the Imaret, is Kavala's most atmospheric location.

Getting There & Away
Air Olympic Airways has two flights a day to Athens (18,300 dr). The airport is 29km east of Kavala. The local KTEL operates buses to the airport from the intercity bus station, timed to connect with flights.

Bus There are three buses a day to Athens (9½ hours, 11,100 dr) from the intercity bus station on the corner of Hrysostomou Kavalas and Filikis Eterias, near the Thasos ferry quay, as well as hourly buses to Keramoti (one hour, 900 dr) and Thessaloniki (two hours, 2850 dr).

Buses to Alexandroupolis (2½ hours, 3100 dr) leave from outside the Dore Café (☎ 227 601), on Erythrou Stavrou 34.

Getting to the Islands
Ferry and hydrofoil schedules are posted in the window of the port police near the hydrofoil departure point.

Ferry There are ferries every hour from Kavala to Skala Prinou on Thasos (1¼ hours, 850 dr, 4400 dr for a car).

In summer there are ferries from Kavala to Samothraki (four hours, 3000 dr). Times and frequency vary month by month. Zolotas Travel (☎ 835 671), near the entrance to the Aegean Islands ferry departure point, sells tickets.

There are ferries to Limnos (4½ hours, 3100 dr), Agios Efstratios (six hours, 3700 dr) and Lesvos (11½ hours, 5200 dr). Some services also go through to Rafina (in Attica) and Piraeus via Chios and Samos. Nikos Miliadis Shipping Agency (☎ 226 147, fax 838 767), on Karaoli-Dimitriou 36, handles tickets.

Hydrofoil There are about nine hydrofoils a day to Limenas (30 minutes, 1500 dr), and a further two per day to Potos (2500 dr), via Kallirahi, Maries and Limenaria. Purchase tickets at the departure point at the port.

KERAMOTI
In summer, there are frequent ferries to Limenas on Thasos (35 minutes, 330 dr, 2700 for a car) from the small port of **Keramoti**, 46km south-east of Kavala. There are hourly buses to Keramoti (one hour, 900 dr) from Kavala.

ALEXANDROUPOLIS

Αλεξανδρούπολη

☎ 0551 • postcode 681 00 • pop 37,000

Alexandroupolis, 328km east of Thessaloniki, is the main port for the island of Samothrace. It's a lively town with a sizeable student population, but with few attractions.

Orientation & Information

The town is laid out on a grid system stretching back from the waterfront, which is Karaoli Dimitriou at the eastern end and Megalou Alexandrou at the western end. The two main squares are Plateia Eleftherias and Plateia Polytehniou. Both are just one block north of Karaoli Dimitriou. The town's most prominent landmark is the large 19th century lighthouse on the middle of the waterfront.

The main post office is on the waterfront on the corner of Nikiforou Foka and Megalou Alexandrou. The OTE is inland on the corner of Mitropolitou Kaviri and Eleftheriou Venizelou. Internet access is available at the Internet Cafe (☎ 81 811), on Koletti 4.

The National Bank of Greece at Dimokratias 246 has an ATM.

Places to Stay

Hotel Lido (☎ 28 808, Paleologou 15) is an outstanding D class hotel with comfortable single/double rooms for 4000/5000 dr with shared bathroom, and doubles/triples with private bathroom for 5500/6500 dr. The hotel is one block north of the bus station. The C class *Hotel Okeanis* (☎ 28 830, fax 34 118, Paleologou 20), almost opposite the Lido, has very comfortable single/double rooms for 12,500/15,500 dr.

Places to Eat

Neraïda Restaurant, in the Plateia Polytehniou where Kyprou widens to form a small square, is a good choice and has a

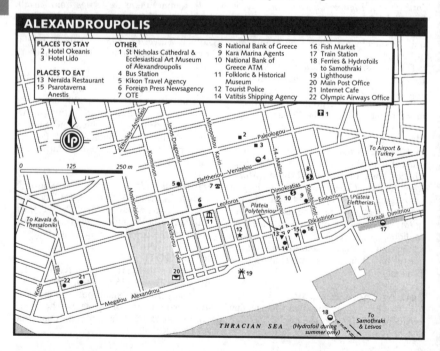

ALEXANDROUPOLIS

PLACES TO STAY	OTHER	8 National Bank of Greece	16 Fish Market
2 Hotel Okeanis	1 St Nicholas Cathedral &	9 Kara Marina Agents	17 Train Station
3 Hotel Lido	Ecclesiastical Art Museum	10 National Bank of	18 Ferries & Hydrofoils
	of Alexandroupolis	Greece ATM	to Samothraki
PLACES TO EAT	4 Bus Station	11 Folkloric & Historical	19 Lighthouse
13 Neraïda Restaurant	5 Kikon Travel Agency	Museum	20 Main Post Office
15 Psarotaverna	6 Foreign Press Newsagency	12 Tourist Police	21 Internet Cafe
Anestis	7 OTE	14 Vatitsis Shipping Agency	22 Olympic Airways Office

range of standard fare and some local specialities for 1600 dr to 2200 dr.

Psarotaverna Anestis (*Athanasiou Diakou 5*), right opposite the fish market, is an unassuming place with a fine choice of mezedes and very reasonable prices. *Mydiasaganaki* (chilli mussels) are highly recommended.

Getting There & Away

Air There are two flights a day to Athens (18,600 dr). The airport is 7km east of town – about 1200 dr by taxi. There are six buses a day to Thessaloniki (six hours, 6000 dr) and five trains – two of which are intercity (5½ hours, 4970 dr).

Getting to the Islands

Ferry There are two or three boats a day to Samothraki (two hours, 2300 dr) in summer, dropping to one a day in winter. For tickets and schedules, contact Vatitsis Shipping Agency (☎ 26 721, fax 32 007, email saos@orfeasnet.gr), opposite the port at Kyprou 5.

There is a weekly ferry to Rhodes (11,500 dr), via Limnos (3300 dr) and Lesvos (5000 dr). This currently leaves on Tuesday. On Friday there is a ferry to Limnos, Agios Efstratios and Rafina (7500 dr). Contact Kikon Travel Agency (☎ 25 455, fax 34 755), on Eleftheriou Venizelou 68, for tickets and reservations.

Hydrofoil In summer there are hydrofoil services to Samothraki (4700 dr) and Limnos (5400 dr). Kaga Marina (☎/fax 81 700), on Emboriou 70, handles tickets.

Saronic Gulf Islands
(Νησιά του Σαρωνικού)

The five Saronic Gulf Islands are the closest group to Athens. The closest, Salamis, is little more than a suburb of the sprawling capital. Aegina is also close enough to Athens for people to commute to work. Along with Poros, the next island south, it is a popular package-holiday destination. Hydra, once famous as the rendezvous of artists, writers and beautiful people, manages to retain an air of superiority and grandeur. Spetses, the most southerly island in the group, receives an inordinate number of British package tourists.

Spetses has the best beaches, but these islands are not the place to be if long stretches of golden sand are what you want. And with the exception of the Temple of Aphaia, on Aegina, the islands have no significant archaeological remains.

Nevertheless, the islands are a very popular escape for Athenians. Accommodation can be nigh on impossible to find between mid-June and mid-September, and weekends are busy all year round. If you plan to go at these times, it's a good idea to reserve a room in advance.

The islands have a reputation for high prices, which is a bit misleading. What is true is that there are very few places for budget travellers to stay – no camp sites and only a couple of cheap hotels. There is plenty of good accommodation available if you are happy to pay 10,000 dr or more for a double. Midweek visitors can get some good deals. Food is no more expensive than anywhere else.

The Saronic Gulf is named after the mythical King Saron of Argos, a keen hunter who drowned while pursuing a deer that had swum into the gulf to escape.

Getting There & Away

Ferry At least 10 ferries daily sail from Piraeus' Great Harbour to Aegina Town (1½

HIGHLIGHTS

- The rambling ruins of the old town of Paleohora on Aegina
- Views over the Saronic Gulf from the Temple of Aphaia on Aegina
- Staying in Hydra's gracious old stone mansions
- Exploring the back roads of Spetses by motorcycle

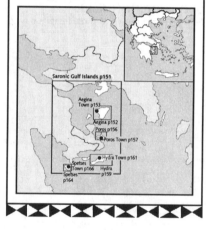

hours, 1400 dr). Three continue to Poros (three hours, 2100 dr), two keep going to Hydra (3½ hours, 2300 dr), and one goes all the way to Spetses (4½ hours, 3200 dr).

Hydrofoil & Catamaran Minoan Lines operates a busy schedule to the islands and nearby Peloponnesian ports with its Flying Dolphin hydrofoils. Services to Aegina leave from Piraeus' Great Harbour, while services to Hydra, Poros and Spetses leave from both the Great Harbour and Zea Marina – be sure to note the departure point.

SARONIC GULF ISLANDS

Minoan Lines also operates high-speed catamarans on some routes. These Flying Cats, as the company calls them, have both economy and VIP class. Economy fares are the same as for hydrofoils; VIP class costs twice as much – and gets you a plush red-leather seat, free drinks and headphone music.

Getting Around

There is a comprehensive network of ferries and hydrofoils linking the Saronic Gulf Islands. See individual island entries for details.

Organised Tours The *Aegean Glory* offers a daily cruise from Piraeus to the islands of Aegina, Poros and Hydra. Passengers get to spend about an hour on shore at each island – long enough to buy a souvenir and take the obligatory 'been there, done that photo'.

You'll see the cruise advertised all over Athens for 19,000 dr, which includes a buffet lunch. The cruises operate all year.

Aegina Αίγινα

☎ 0297 • postcode 180 10 • pop 11,000

Unassuming Aegina (**eh-yee-nah**) was once a major player in the Hellenic world, thanks largely to its strategic position at the mouth of the Saronic Gulf. It began to emerge as a commercial centre in about 1000 BC.

By the 7th century BC, it was the premier maritime power in the region and amassed great wealth through its trade with Egypt and Phoenicia. The silver 'turtle' coins minted on the island at this time are thought to be the first coins produced in Europe. The Aeginian fleet made a major contribution on the Greek side at the Battle of Salamis.

Athens, uneasy about Aegina's maritime prowess, attacked the island in 459 BC. Defeated, Aegina was forced to pull down its city walls and surrender its fleet. It did not recover.

The island's other brief moment in the spotlight came during 1827 to 1829, when it was declared the temporary capital of partly liberated Greece. The first coins of the modern Greek nation were minted here.

Aegina has since slipped into a more humble role as Greece's premier producer of pistachio nuts. The writer Nikos Kazantzakis was fond of the island and wrote *Zorba the Greek* while living in a house in Livadi, just north of Aegina Town.

Aegina was named after the daughter of the river god, Asopus. According to mythology, Aegina was abducted by Zeus and taken to the island. Her son by Zeus, Aeacus, was the grandfather of Achilles of Trojan War fame.

Getting There & Away

Ferry In summer there are at least 10 ferries daily from Aegina Town to Piraeus (1½ hours, 1400 dr) as well as services from Agia Marina (1000 dr) and Souvala (950 dr).

There are at least three boats daily to Poros (1½ hours, 1100 dr) via Methana (40 minutes, 1000 dr), two daily to Hydra (two hours, 1600 dr), and one to Spetses (three hours, 2400 dr). The ferry companies have ticket offices at the quay, where you'll find a full list of the day's sailings.

Hydrofoil Hydrofoils operate almost hourly from 7 am to 8 pm between Aegina Town and the Great Harbour at Piraeus (35 minutes, 2700 dr). Services south are restricted to two daily to Poros (40 minutes,

2400 dr) via Methana (20 minutes, 1900 dr). Tickets are sold at the quay in Aegina Town.

Services from Piraeus to Agia Marina (30 minutes) and Souvala (25 minutes) are operated by Sea Falcon Lines. Both trips cost 2200 dr one way, 3600 dr return.

Getting Around
There are frequent buses from Aegina Town to Agia Marina (30 minutes, 400 dr), via Paleohora and the Temple of Aphaia. Other buses go to Perdika (15 minutes, 230 dr) and Souvala (20 minutes, 300 dr). Departure

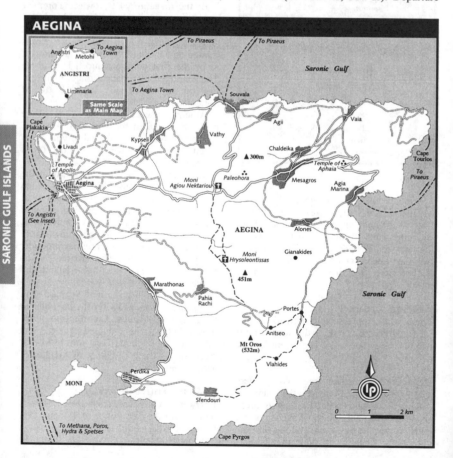

times are displayed outside the ticket office in Plateia Ethnegersias.

There are numerous places to hire motorcycles.

AEGINA TOWN

Aegina Town, on the west coast, is the island's capital and main port. The town is a charming and bustling, if slightly ramshackle, place; its harbour is lined with colourful caïques. Several of the town's crumbling neoclassical buildings survive from its days as the Greek capital.

Orientation & Information

The ferry dock and nearby small quay used by hydrofoils are on the western edge of town. A left turn at the end of the quay leads to Plateia Ethnegersias, where you'll find the bus terminal and post office. The town beach is 200m farther along. A right turn at the end of the quay leads to the main harbour.

Aegina doesn't have an official tourist office. The 'tourist offices' you'll see advertised on the waterfront are booking agencies, which will do no more than add a 25% commission to the price of whatever

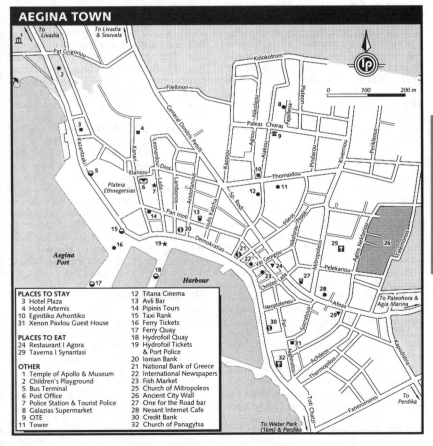

AEGINA TOWN

PLACES TO STAY
3 Hotel Plaza
4 Hotel Artemis
10 Eginitiko Arhontiko
31 Xenon Pavlou Guest House

PLACES TO EAT
24 Restaurant I Agora
29 Taverna I Synantasi

OTHER
1 Temple of Apollo & Museum
2 Children's Playground
5 Bus Terminal
6 Post Office
7 Police Station & Tourist Police
8 Galazias Supermarket
9 OTE
11 Tower

12 Titana Cinema
13 Avli Bar
14 Pipinis Tours
15 Taxi Rank
16 Ferry Tickets
17 Ferry Quay
18 Hydrofoil Quay
19 Hydrofoil Tickets & Port Police
20 Ionian Bank
21 National Bank of Greece
22 International Newspapers
23 Fish Market
25 Church of Mitropoleos
26 Ancient City Wall
27 One for the Road bar
28 Nesant Internet Cafe
30 Credit Bank
32 Church of Panagytsa

SARONIC GULF ISLANDS

service you care to nominate. The tourist police (☎ 27 777) are on Leonardou Lada, opposite the hydrofoil quay. The port police (☎ 22 328) are next to the hydrofoil ticket office at the entrance to the hydrofoil quay.

The OTE is off Aiakou, which heads inland next to the port authority building. The National Bank of Greece is on the waterfront just past Aiakou, and the Credit Bank is 150m farther around the harbour. You can check your email at the Nesant Internet Cafe, Afeas 13, which is open 10 am to 2 am daily.

Temple of Apollo

'Temple' is a bit of a misnomer for the one Doric column which stands at this site. The column is all that's left of the 5th century Temple of Apollo which once stood on the Hill of Koloni. The hill was the site of the ancient acropolis, and there are remains of a Helladic (early) settlement. The site, on the far side of the town beach, also has a **museum**. Both are open 8.30 am to 3 pm Tuesday to Sunday. Admission is 500 dr.

Places to Stay

The best place to head for is *Hotel Plaza* (*☎ 25 600, fax 28 404*), on the waterfront 100m past Plateia Ethnegersias. It has good singles/doubles overlooking the sea for 4500/7500 dr with bathroom. There are several *domatia* at the top of Leonardou Lada offering rooms with bathroom for 6000/9000 dr.

Hotel Artemis (*☎ 25 195, fax 28 466, email pipinis@otenet.gr*), north of Plateia Ethnegersias, is virtually unrecognisable following a change of management and a complete refit. It has a wide range of rooms and offers good discounts for midweek visitors. Rooms with bathroom cost 7500/8500 dr, with air-con an extra 2000 dr.

The most interesting rooms in town are at *Eginitiko Arhontiko* (*☎ 24 968, fax 24 156*), located 100m from the harbour at the junction of Aiakou and Thomaïdou. This fine 19th century sandstone *arhontiko* has beautifully furnished rooms for

10,000/15,000 dr, and a splendid, ornate two-room suite for 28,000 dr. The drawback here is the constant ringing of the church bells next door.

Xenon Pavlou Guest House (*☎ 22 795*) is popular, even if the prices are a bit steep at 9000/13,000 dr. The guesthouse is on the far side of the harbour from the ferry dock, at the back of the square next to the church.

Places to Eat

The harbourfront is lined with countless cafes and restaurants – good for relaxing and soaking up the atmosphere, but not particularly good value.

Locals prefer to head for the cluster of small *ouzeria* and restaurants around the fish markets at the southern end of the harbour. The tiny *Restaurant I Agora (Pan Irioti 47)*, behind the fish market, is a good place to start. You'll find the local speciality, barbecued octopus (1000 dr), as well as fresh calamari (1200 dr) and sardines (900 dr).

Taverna I Synantasis (Afeas 40) has live music on Friday and Saturday night.

Local pistachio nuts are on sale everywhere, priced from 1000 dr for 500g.

Entertainment

There are dozens of music bars dotted around the maze of small streets behind the waterfront. *One For The Road (Afeas 3)* plays a mixture of modern Greek and rock and is popular with young people. *Avli (Pan Irioti 17)* attracts an older audience with a mixture of 60s music and Latin.

AROUND AEGINA
Temple of Aphaia

The splendid, well preserved Doric Temple of Aphaia, a local deity of pre-Hellenic times, is the major ancient site of the Saronic Gulf Islands. It was built in 480 BC when Aegina was at its most powerful.

The temple's pediments were decorated with outstanding Trojan War sculptures, most of which were spirited away in the 19th century and eventually fell into the hands of Ludwig I (father of King Otho).

They now have pride of place in Munich's Glyptothek. The temple is impressive even without these sculptures. It stands on a pine-covered hill and commands imposing vistas of the Saronic Gulf and Cape Sounion.

The site (☎ 32 398) is open 8.30 am to 7 pm Monday to Friday and 8.30 am to 3 pm Saturday and Sunday. Admission is 800 dr. Aphaia is 10km east of Aegina Town. Buses to Agia Marina stop at the site. A taxi from Aegina Town costs about 2000 dr.

Paleohora Παλαιοχώρα

The ruins of Paleohora, on a hillside 6.5km east of Aegina Town, are fascinating to explore. The town was the island's capital from the 9th century to 1826, after pirate attacks forced the islanders to flee the coast and settle inland. It didn't do them much good when the notorious pirate Barbarossa arrived in 1537, laid waste to the town and took the inhabitants off into slavery.

The ruins are far more extensive than they first appear. The only buildings left intact are the churches. There are more than two dozen of them, in various states of disrepair, dotted around the hillside. Beautiful frescoes can be seen in some of them.

In the valley below Paleohora is **Moni Agiou Nektariou**, an important place of pilgrimage. The monastery contains the relics of a hermit monk, Anastasios Kefalas, who died in 1920. When his body was exhumed in 1940 it was found to have mummified – a sure sign of sainthood in Greek Orthodoxy, especially after a lifetime of performing miracle cures. Kefalas was canonised in 1961 – the first Orthodox saint of the 20th century. The enormous new church that has been built to honour him is a spectacular sight beside the road to Agia Marina. A track leads south from here to the 16th century **Moni Hrysoleontissas**, in a lovely mountain setting.

The bus from Aegina Town to Agia Marina stops at the turn-off to Paleohora.

Beaches

Beaches are not Aegina's strong point. The east coast town of **Agia Marina** is the island's premier tourist resort, but the beach is not great – if you can see it for package tourists. There are a couple of sandy patches that almost qualify as beaches between Aegina and Perdika, at the southern tip of the west coast.

MONI & ANGISTRI ISLETS

Νήσος Μονή & Νήσος Αγκίστρι

The Moni and Angistri islets lie off the west coast of Aegina, opposite Perdika. Moni, the smaller of the two, is a 10 minute boat ride from Perdika – frequent boats make the trip in summer.

Angistri is much bigger with around 500 inhabitants. There's a sandy beach at the port and other smaller beaches around the coast. Both package-holiday tourists and independent travellers find their way to Angistri, which has *tavernas*, *hotels* and *domatia*. There are regular boats to Angistri from Aegina Town (600 dr) and from Piraeus (1100 dr).

Poros Πόρος

☎ 0298 • postcode 180 20 • pop 4000

The island of Poros is little more than a stone's throw from the mainland. The slender passage of water that separates it from the Peloponnesian town of Galatas is only 360m wide at its narrowest point.

Poros was once two islands, Kalavria and Sferia. These days they are connected by a narrow isthmus, cut by a canal for small boats and rejoined by a road bridge. The vast majority of the population lives on the small volcanic island of Sferia, which is more than half-covered by the town of Poros. Sferia hangs like an appendix from the southern coast of Kalavria, a large, well forested island that has all the package hotels. The town of Poros is not wildly exciting, but it can be used as a base for exploring the ancient sites of the adjacent Peloponnese.

Getting There & Away

Ferry There are up to eight ferries daily to Piraeus (three hours, 2100 dr), via Methana

SARONIC GULF ISLANDS

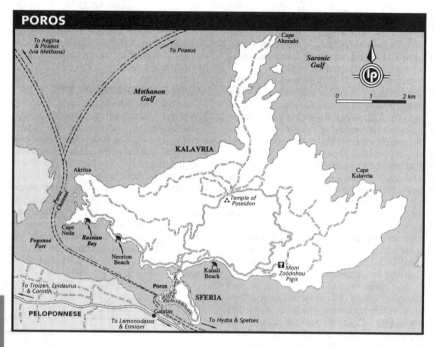

and Aegina (1½ hours, 1200 dr), two daily to Hydra (one hour, 1000 dr), and one to Spetses (two hours, 1600 dr). Ticket agencies are opposite the ferry dock.

Small boats shuttle constantly between Poros and Galatas (80 dr) on the mainland. They leave from the quay opposite Plateia Iroön in Poros Town. Car ferries to Galatas leave from the dock on the road to Kalavria.

Hydrofoil Services from Poros to Piraeus (one hour, 4000 dr) are evenly split between the Great Harbour and Zea Marina, with up to five daily to each. Two daily travel via Methana and Aegina (40 minutes, 2400 dr). There are also seven hydrofoils south to Hydra (30 minutes, 2000 dr) and five to Spetses (one hour, 3300 dr) and Porto Heli. The Flying Dolphin agency is on Plateia Iroön, and has a timetable of departures outside.

Getting Around

The Poros bus operates almost constantly along a route that starts near the hydrofoil dock on Plateia Iroön in Poros Town. It crosses to Kalavria and goes east along the south coast as far as Moni Zoödohou Pigis (150 dr), then turns around and heads west as far as Neorion Beach.

Some of the caïques operating between Poros and Galatas switch to ferrying tourists to beaches in summer. Operators stand on the waterfront and call out their destinations.

There are several places on the road to Kalavria offering bikes for hire, both motorised and pedal-powered. They include Kostas Bikes, near Cinema Diane.

POROS TOWN

Poros Town is the island's main settlement. It's a pretty place of white houses with terracotta-tiled roofs, and there are wonderful views over to the mountains of Argolis. It is a popular weekend destination for Athenians as well as for package tourists and cruise ships.

Orientation & Information

The main ferry dock is at the western tip of Poros Town, overlooked by the striking blue-domed clock tower. A left turn from the dock puts you on the waterfront road leading to Kalavria. The OTE building is on the right after 100m. A right turn at the ferry dock leads along the waterfront facing Galatas. The first square (triangle actually) is Plateia Iroön, where the hydrofoils dock. The bus leaves from next to the kiosk at the eastern end of the square.

The next square along is Plateia Karamis, where the post office is located. The National Bank of Greece is 500m farther along the waterfront. There are branches of the Credit Bank and the Bank Emporiki on Plateia Iroön.

Poros does not have a tourist office. The tourist police (☎ 22 462/256) are at Dimosthenous 10 – behind the Poros high

POROS TOWN

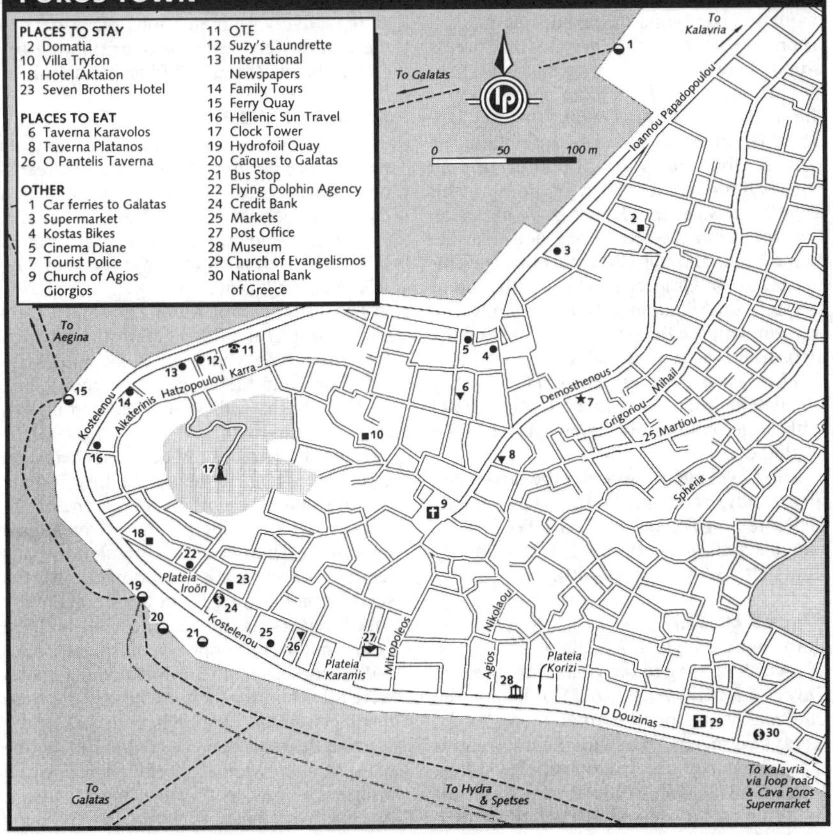
PLACES TO STAY
2 Domatia
10 Villa Tryfon
18 Hotel Aktaion
23 Seven Brothers Hotel
PLACES TO EAT
6 Taverna Karavolos
8 Taverna Platanos
26 O Pantelis Taverna
OTHER
1 Car ferries to Galatas
3 Supermarket
4 Kostas Bikes
5 Cinema Diane
7 Tourist Police
9 Church of Agios Giorgios
11 OTE
12 Suzy's Laundrette
13 International Newspapers
14 Family Tours
15 Ferry Quay
16 Hellenic Sun Travel
17 Clock Tower
19 Hydrofoil Quay
20 Caïques to Galatas
21 Bus Stop
22 Flying Dolphin Agency
24 Credit Bank
25 Markets
27 Post Office
28 Museum
29 Church of Evangelismos
30 National Bank of Greece
To Kalavria
To Galatas
0 50 100 m
Ioannou Papadopoulou
To Aegina
Hatzopoulou Karra
Aikaterinis
Kostelenou
Demosthenous
Grigoriou
Mihail
25 Martiou
Spheria
Plateia Iroön
Kostelenou
Mitropoleos
Plateia Karamis
Nikolaou
Agios
Plateia Korizi
D Douzinas
To Kalavria via loop road & Cava Poros Supermarket
To Galatas
To Hydra & Spetses

school. Dimosthenous runs inland from the road to Kalavria, starting just beyond the small supermarket.

Suzi's Laundrette Service, next to the OTE, charges 2000 dr to wash and dry a 5kg load.

Places to Stay

Poros has very little cheap accommodation. The cheapest rooms are at **Hotel Aktaion** (☎ 22 281) on Plateia Iroön, which charges 6300/7200 dr for basic singles/doubles.

If things are not too hectic, you may be offered a room by one of the domatia owners when you get off the ferry. Otherwise, head left along the waterfront and turn right after about 400m, beyond the small supermarket. There are lots of **domatia** on the streets around here.

The place to be for a room with a view is the charming **Villa Tryfon** (☎ 22 215, 25 854), on top of the hill overlooking the port. Double rooms are 11,000 dr, and all have bathroom and kitchen facilities as well as great views over to Kalavria. To get there, turn left from the ferry dock and take the first right up the steps 20m past the Agricultural Bank of Greece. Turn left at the top of the steps on Aikaterinis Hatzopoulou Karra, and you will see the place signposted up the steps to the right after 150m.

The Seven Brothers Hotel (☎ 23 412), on Plateia Iroön, is a smart C class hotel with large, comfortable rooms for 12,000/16,000 dr.

The travel agents opposite the ferry dock also handle accommodation. They include Hellenic Sun Travel (☎ 22 636, fax 25 653, email sungr1@compulink.gr) and Family Tours (☎ 23 743, fax 24 480).

Places to Eat

Poros has a couple of excellent restaurants. It's worth coming to the island just to eat at **Taverna Karavolos** (☎ 26 158), behind the Cinema Diana on the road to Kalavria. Karavolos means 'big snail' in Greek and is the nickname of cheerful owner Theodoros. Sure enough, snails (1000 dr) are a speciality of the house – served in a delicious thick

tomato sauce. You'll find a range of imaginative *mezedes* like *taramokeftedes* (fish roe balls) priced from 800 dr, and a daily selection of main courses like pork stuffed with garlic (1500 dr). The place is open from 7 pm daily. Bookings are advisable because Theodoros has only a dozen tables – and a strong local following.

Equally popular with locals is **Taverna Platanos**, on the small square at the top of Dimosthenous. Owner Tassos is a butcher by day and the restaurant specialises in spit-roast meats. You'll find specialities like *kokoretsi* (offal) and *gouronopoulo* (suckling pig), both 1400 dr.

For more basic fare, try **O Pantelis Taverna**, a lively, unpretentious place next to the markets on the backstreet running between Plateia Iroön and Plateia Karamis.

AROUND POROS

Poros has few places of interest and its beaches are no great shakes. **Kanali Beach**, on Kalavria 1km east of the bridge, is a mediocre pebble beach. **Neorion Beach**, 3km west of the bridge, is marginally better. The best beach is reputedly at **Russian Bay**, 1.5km past Neorion.

The 18th century **Moni Zoödohou Pigis** has a beautiful gilded iconostasis which came from Asia Minor and is decorated with paintings from the gospels. The monastery, on Kalavria, is well signposted and is 4km east of Poros Town.

From the road below the monastery you can strike inland to the 6th century **Temple of Poseidon**. The god of the sea and earthquakes was the principal deity worshipped on Poros. There's very little left of this temple, but the walk is worthwhile for the scenery on the way. From the site there are superb views of the Saronic Gulf and the Peloponnese. The orator Demosthenes, after failing to shake off the Macedonians who were after him for inciting the city-states to rebel, committed suicide here in 322 BC.

From the ruins you can continue along the road, which eventually winds back to the bridge. The road is drivable, but it's also a fine 6km walk that will take around 1½ hours.

PELOPONNESIAN MAINLAND

The Peloponnesian mainland opposite Poros can easily be explored from the island.

The vast citrus groves of **Lemonodasos** are 2km south-east of **Galatas**. About 9km north-west of Galatas is the ancient site of **Troizen**, legendary birthplace of Theseus. Take a bus to Dhamala, 6km from Galatas, and walk to the site from there. Alternatively, a Methana-bound bus will let you off at Agios Georgios, from where it is a 3km walk inland to the site.

Camping Kyragelo is about 1km north-west of Galatas. There are also a couple of *hotels* and *domatia* in town.

Getting There & Around

Small boats do the five minute run between Galatas and Poros (80 dr) every 10 minutes. A couple of buses daily depart for Nafplio (two hours, 1300 dr) and can drop you off at the ancient site of Epidaurus (see the Peloponnese chapter for details on this site).

The district around Galatas is ideal for exploring by bicycle. These can be hired on the seafront in Galatas.

Hydra Υδρα

☎ 0298 • postcode 180 10 • pop 3000

Hydra (**ee**-drah) is the Saronic Gulf island with the most style. The gracious stone, white and pastel mansions of Hydra Town are stacked up the rocky hillsides that surround the fine natural harbour. Film-makers were the first foreigners to be seduced by the beauty of Hydra. They began arriving in the 1950s when the island was used as a location for the film *Boy on a Dolphin*, among others. The artists and writers moved in next, followed by the celebrities, and now-adays it seems the whole world is welcomed ashore.

If you've been in Greece for some time you may fall in love with Hydra for one reason alone – the absence of kamikaze motorcyclists. Hydra has no motorised transport except for sanitation and construction vehicles. Donkeys (hundreds of them) are the only means of transport.

The name Hydra suggests that the island once had plenty of water. Legend has it that the island was once covered with forests, which were destroyed by fire. Whatever the

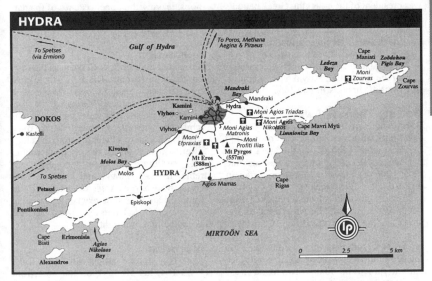

HYDRA

story, these days the island is almost totally barren and imports its water from the Peloponnese.

History

Like many of the Greek islands, Hydra was ignored by the Turks, so many Greeks from the Peloponnese settled on the island to escape Ottoman suppression and taxes. The population was further boosted by an influx of Albanians. Agriculture was impossible, so these new settlers began building boats. By the 19th century, the island had become a great maritime power. The canny Hydriots made a fortune by running the British blockade of French ports during the Napoleonic Wars. The wealthy shipping merchants built most of the town's grand old arhontika from the considerable profits. It became a fashionable resort for Greek socialites, and lavish balls were a regular feature.

Hydra made a major contribution to the War of Independence. Without the 130 ships supplied by the island, the Greeks wouldn't have had much of a fleet with which to blockade the Turks. It also supplied leadership in the form of Georgios Koundouriotis, who was president of the emerging Greek nation's national assembly from 1822 to 1827, and Admiral Andreas Miaoulis, who commanded the Greek fleet. Streets and squares all over Greece are named after these two.

A mock battle is staged in Hydra harbour during the Miaoulia Festival held in honour of Admiral Miaoulis in late June.

Getting There & Away

Ferry There are two ferries daily to Piraeus (3½ hours, 2300 dr), sailing via Poros (1000 dr), Methana (1500 dr) and Aegina (1600 dr). There's also a daily boat to Spetses (one hour, 1200 dr). Departure times are listed on a board at the ferry dock.

You can buy tickets from Idreoniki Travel (☎ 54 007), just off the waterfront on the street leading to the post office and market.

Hydrofoil Hydra is well served by the Flying Dolphin fleet with up to nine services daily to Piraeus (4600 dr) – two to the Great Harbour, the rest to Zea Marina. Direct services take 1¼ hours, but most go via Poros (30 minutes, 2000 dr) and take 1½ hours. There are also frequent services to Spetses (30 minutes, 2300 dr), some of which call at Ermioni, adding 20 minutes to the trip. Many of the services to Spetses continue to Porto Heli (50 minutes, 2500 dr). There are also occasional services to Kyparissi, Leonidio and Monemvasia.

The Flying Dolphin office (☎ 53 814) is on the waterfront opposite the ferry dock.

Getting Around

In summer, there are caïques from Hydra Town to the island's beaches. There are also water taxis (☎ 53 690) which will take you anywhere you like. A water taxi to Kamini costs 1600 dr, and 2500 dr to Mandraki and Vlyhos.

The donkey owners clustered around the port charge around 2500 dr to transport your bags to the hotel of your choice.

HYDRA TOWN

Most of the action in Hydra Town is concentrated around the waterfront cafes and shops, leaving the upper reaches of the narrow, stepped streets virtually deserted – and a joy to explore.

Orientation

Ferries and hydrofoils both dock on the eastern side of the harbour. The town's three main streets all head inland from the waterfront at the back of the harbour. Walking around from the ferry dock, the first street you come to is Tombazi, at the eastern corner. The next main street is Miaouli, on the left before the clock tower, which is the town's main thoroughfare. The third is Lignou, at the western extreme. It heads inland and links up with Kriezi, which runs west over the hills to Kamini. Lignou is best reached by heading up Votsi, on the left after the clock tower, and taking the first turn right.

Information

There is no tourist office, but Saitis Tours (☎ 52 184, fax 53 469), on the waterfront

Hydra, Saronic Gulf

A quiet word, Hydra, Saronic Gulf

MARK DAFFEY

ROD HYETT

JON DAVISON

The sheer cliffs of Santorini's caldera make a dramatic coastline, Cyclades.

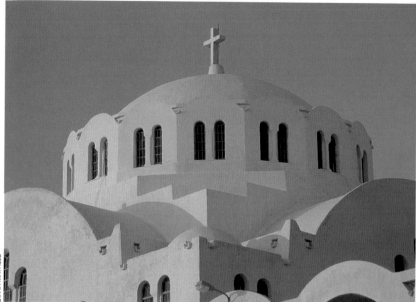

Cathedral, Fira, Cyclades

Fira town at dusk, Santorini, Cyclades

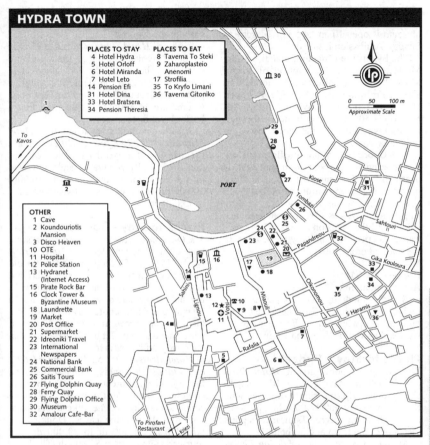

HYDRA TOWN

PLACES TO STAY
4 Hotel Hydra
5 Hotel Orloff
6 Hotel Miranda
7 Hotel Leto
14 Pension Efi
31 Hotel Dina
33 Hotel Bratsera
34 Pension Theresia

PLACES TO EAT
8 Taverna To Steki
9 Zaharoplasteio Anenomi
17 Strofilia
35 To Kryfo Limani
36 Taverna Gitoniko

OTHER
1 Cave
2 Koundouriotis Mansion
3 Disco Heaven
10 OTE
11 Hospital
12 Police Station
13 Hydranet (Internet Access)
15 Pirate Rock Bar
16 Clock Tower & Byzantine Museum
18 Laundrette
19 Market
20 Post Office
21 Supermarket
22 Idreoniki Travel
23 International Newspapers
24 National Bank
25 Commercial Bank
26 Saitis Tours
27 Flying Dolphin Quay
28 Ferry Quay
29 Flying Dolphin Office
30 Museum
32 Amalour Cafe-Bar

To Kavos

PORT

To Pirofani Restaurant

0   50   100 m
Approximate Scale

SARONIC GULF ISLANDS

near Tombazi, puts out a useful free guide called *Holidays in Hydra*. You can find information about the island on the Internet at www.compulink.gr/hydranet.

Most things of importance are close to the waterfront. The post office is on a small side street between the Commercial (Emporiki) Bank and the National Bank of Greece. The tourist police (☎ 52 205) can be found at the police station opposite the OTE on Votsi from mid-May until the end of September.

You can check your email at Hydranet, 100m from the waterfront on Lignou. It's open 10.30 to 2.30 pm daily.

There's a laundry service in the small market square just past the post office. It's open 9 am to 9 pm daily (4 to 9 pm on Sunday) and charges 2200 dr to wash and dry a load.

Things to See

The **Historical Archives Museum of Hydra** is close to the ferry dock on the eastern side of the harbour. It houses a collection of portraits and naval oddments, with an emphasis on the island's role in the War of Independence. The museum is open 10 am to 5 pm Tuesday to Sunday. Admission is 500 dr.

The **Byzantine Museum**, upstairs at the Monastery of the Assumption of Virgin Mary, houses a collection of icons and assorted religious paraphernalia. It's open 10 am to 5 pm Tuesday to Sunday. Admission is 500 dr. The entrance is through the archway beneath the clock tower on the waterfront.

The **Georgios Koundouriotis mansion**, overlooking the harbour from the west, is destined to become the town's third museum once renovation work has been completed. Koundouriotis was a wealthy shipowner as well as a War of Independence leader, and the mansion houses a large portrait collection. It's unlikely to be open to the public before 2001.

Places to Stay
Accommodation in Hydra is generally of a very high standard, and you pay accordingly for it. The prices listed here are for the high season, which in Hydra means every weekend as well as July and August.

Places to Stay – Budget
The cheapest rooms are at *Hotel Dina* (☎ 52 248) on Stavrou Tsipi. It's a small, cheery place offering singles/doubles with bathroom for 10,000/12,000 dr. The location, high up on Stavrou Tsipi, means great views over the town and harbour.

Another popular place is *Pension Theresia* (☎ 53 984, fax 53 983), about 300m from the waterfront on Tombazi. It has clean, comfortable rooms with bathroom for 10,000/15,000 dr.

You'll find similar prices at *Pension Efi* (☎ 52 371), close to the harbour at the junction of Lignou and Sahini.

Places to Stay – Mid-Range
Hotel Hydra (☎ 52 102) has a great setting overlooking the town from the west. It has large, comfortable rooms for 12,000/17,000 dr with bathroom. It's a fair haul to get there

– more than 100 steps up Sahini from Lignou – but the views over the town and harbour are worth it.

Finding *Hotel Leto* (☎ 53 385, fax 53 806) involves no more than a gentle stroll up Miaouli to the first square, and then a left turn up the steps. It's a stylish place with beautiful polished timber floors. Rooms are 16,400/22,000 dr, including a buffet breakfast.

A little bit further up Miaouli is *Hotel Miranda* (☎ 52 230, fax 53 510), originally the mansion of a wealthy Hydriot sea captain. Beautifully renovated and converted into a very smart hotel, it costs 16,000/20,000 dr with breakfast; a two-room suite is 33,000 dr.

Places to Stay – Top End
The two hotels at the top of the comfort scale both offer something special. *Hotel Orloff* (☎ 52 564, fax 53 532) is a beautiful old mansion with a cool, vine-covered courtyard at the back. The furnishings are elegant without being overstated, and each of the 10 rooms has a character of its own. Single/double rooms are priced from 28,000/32,000 dr, which includes a buffet breakfast – served in the courtyard in summer.

Hotel Bratsera (☎ 53 971, fax 53 626, email tallos@hol.gr) is a converted sponge factory. The architects have left the rich stonework and solid timbers and have added some nice touches like doors made up from old packing cases. Doubles are priced from 31,000 dr to 39,000 dr, and four-bed suites start at 50,000 dr. The Bratsera has the town's only swimming pool. It's for guests only, but you'll qualify if you eat at their restaurant.

Places to Eat – Budget
Hydra has dozens of tavernas and restaurants. Unlike the hotels, there are plenty of cheap places around – especially if you're prepared to head away from the waterfront.

Taverna Gitoniko, on Spilios Haramis, is better known by the names of its owners, Manolis and Christina. The menu is nothing special, but they have built up an enthusiastic local following through the simple formula of turning out consistently good traditional taverna food. Try their beetroot salad – a bowl of baby beets and boiled greens with a dollop of cold, very garlicky, mashed potato on top. The flavours complement each other perfectly. You can eat well for 2500 dr per person, including a jug of *retsina*, but get in early or you'll have a long wait.

Nearby, tucked away on a small alleyway, is *To Kryfo Limani* (The Secret Port). It's a charming spot with seating beneath a large lemon tree, and delicious specials like hearty fish soup (1600 dr).

Other possibilities include the popular *Taverna To Steki* on Miaouli. *Zaharoplasteio Anenomi*, opposite the hospital on Votsi, has a great selection of cakes as well as ice cream.

Places to Eat – Mid-Range

Strofilia is an excellent ouzeri just up from the waterfront on Miaouli. It specialises in mezedes, including *spetsofai* (sausages in spicy sauce) for 1450 dr, mussels saganaki for 1500 dr and vegetable croquettes for 1000 dr.

For something special, head out to the excellent *Pirofani Restaurant* (☎ 53 175) at Kamini. Owner Theo specialises in desserts – so be sure to leave room for a slice of lemon meringue pie or chocolate and pear cake. The easiest way to get there is to follow Kriezi over the hill from Hydra Town.

Entertainment

Hydra boasts a busy nightlife. The action is centred on the bars on the western side of the harbour, where the *Pirate* rock bar is a long-standing favourite. *Amalour*, 100m up Tombazi, is a more sophisticated cafe-bar that sells a wide range of fresh juices as well as alcohol.

Discos operate only during the summer months. The most popular is *Disco Heaven*, overlooking the harbour on the western side and accessed from the coastal path to Kamini. *Kavos*, with its sign made up of nautical oddments, is a popular disco just west of town on the coastal path to Kamini,

but there is no point heading out there before 11 pm.

AROUND HYDRA

It's a strenuous but worthwhile one hour walk up to **Moni Profiti Ilias**, starting from Miaouli. Monks still live in the monastery, which has fantastic views down to the town. It's a short walk from here to the convent of **Moni Efpraxias**.

The beaches on Hydra are a dead loss, but the walks to them are enjoyable. **Kamini**, about 20 minutes walk along the coastal path from town, has rocks and a very small pebble beach. **Vlyhos**, 20 minutes farther on, is an attractive village with a slightly larger pebble beach, two tavernas and a ruined 19th century stone bridge. There are *domatia* at Vlyhos as well as *Antigoni's Apartments* (☎ 53 228), which has self-catering apartments to sleep four/six for 16,000/24,000 dr.

From here, walkaholics can continue to the small bay at **Molos**, or take a left fork before the bay to the inland village of **Episkopi**. There are no facilities at Episkopi or Molos.

An even more ambitious walk is the three hour stint from Hydra Town to **Moni Zourvas**, in the north-east of the island. Along the way you will pass **Moni Agias Triadas** and **Moni Agios Nikolaos**.

A path leads east from Hydra Town to the pebble beach at **Mandraki**. The beach is the exclusive reserve of *Hotel Miramare* (☎ 52 300, fax 52 301), which has doubles with breakfast for 28,000 dr. There's a range of water sports equipment for hire, including windsurfers.

Spetses Σπέτσες

☎ 0298　•　postcode 180 50　•　pop 3700

Pine-covered Spetses, the most distant of the group from Piraeus, has long been a favourite with British holiday makers.

Spetses' history is similar to Hydra's. It became wealthy through shipbuilding, ran the British blockade during the Napoleonic

Wars and refitted its ships to join the Greek fleet during the War of Independence. Spetsiot fighters achieved a certain notoriety through their pet tactic of attaching small boats laden with explosives to the enemy's ships, setting them alight and beating a hasty retreat.

The island was known in antiquity as Pityoussa (meaning 'pine-covered'), but the original forest cover disappeared long ago. The pine-covered hills that greet the visitor today are a legacy of the far-sighted and wealthy philanthropist Sotirios Anargyrios.

Anargyrios was born on Spetses in 1848 and emigrated to the USA, returning in 1914 an exceedingly rich man. He bought two-thirds of the then largely barren island and planted the Aleppo pines that stand today. He also financed the island's road system and commissioned many of the town's grand buildings, including the Hotel Possidonion. He was a big fan of the British public (ie private) school system, and established Anargyrios & Korgialenios College, a boarding school for boys from all over Greece. British author John Fowles taught English at the college in 1950-51, and used the island as a setting for his novel *The Magus*.

Getting There & Away

Ferry There is one ferry daily to Piraeus (4½ hours, 3200 dr), via Hydra (1200 dr), Poros (1600 dr) and Aegina (2400 dr). Two companies operate the service on alternate days. You'll find departure times on the waterfront outside Alasia Travel (☎ 74 098), which sells tickets. The port police (☎ 72 245) are opposite the quay.

Between July and September, there are also caïques to Kosta, 25 minutes away on the Peloponnese. The ferries depart at 7.15

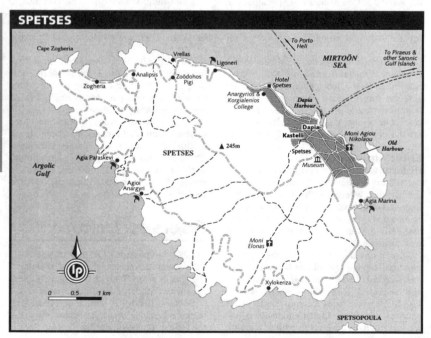

and 10 am, and at 1 and 4.30 pm; they return half an hour later. Get your ticket (130 dr) on the boat. Water taxis do the trip in 10 minutes for 3000 dr. There are three buses daily from Kosta to Nafplio (2¼ hours, 1500 dr).

Hydrofoil There are up to nine Flying Dolphins daily to Piraeus (6400 dr). Most services travel via Hydra (30 minutes, 2300 dr) and Poros (70 minutes, 3300 dr) and take about 2½ hours. In high season, there are also daily connections to Leonidio (one hour, 2400 dr) and Monemvasia (1½ hours, 4200 dr).

Getting Around
Spetses has two bus routes. There are three or four buses daily from Plateia Agias Mamas in Spetses Town to Agioi Anargyri (800 dr return), via Agia Marina and Xylokeriza. Departure times are displayed on a board by the bus stop. There are hourly buses to Ligoneri (160 dr) departing from in front of Hotel Possidonion.

No cars are permitted on the island. Unfortunately this ban has not been extended to motorbikes, resulting in there being more of the critters here than just about anywhere else.

The colourful horse-drawn carriages are a pleasant but expensive way of getting around. Prices are displayed on a board where the carriages gather by the port.

Boat Water taxis (☎ 72 072) go anywhere you care to nominate from opposite the Flying Dolphin office at Dapia Harbour. Fares are displayed on a board. Samples include 5000 dr to Agia Marina and 9000 dr to Agioi Anargyri. In summer, there are caïques from the harbour to Agioi Anargyri (1500 dr return) and Zogheria (1000 dr return).

SPETSES TOWN
Spetses Town sprawls along almost half the north-east coast of the island, reflecting the way in which the focal point of settlement has changed over the years.

There's evidence of an early Helladic settlement near the old harbour, about 1.5km

Lascarina Bouboulina

Spetses contributed one of the most colourful figures of the War of Independence, the dashing heroine Lascarina Bouboulina. Her exploits on and off the battlefield were the stuff of legend. She was widowed twice by the time the war began – both her ship-owning husbands had been killed by pirates, leaving her a very wealthy woman – and she used her money to commission her own fighting ship, the *Agamemnon*, which she led into battle during the blockade of Nafplio.

Bouboulina was known for her fiery temperament and her countless love affairs, and her death was in keeping with her flamboyant lifestyle – she was shot during a family dispute in her Spetses home. Bouboulina was featured on the old 50 drachma note in a dramatic portrayal of her directing cannon fire.

The Bouboulina mansion is on the western side of the square behind the OTE building. It houses a small museum, which is open 9 am to 5 pm Tuesday to Sunday. Admission is 700 dr.

east of the modern commercial centre and port of Dapia. Roman and Byzantine remains have been unearthed in the area behind Moni Agios Nikolaos, halfway between the two.

The island is thought to have been uninhabited for almost 600 years before the arrival of Albanian refugees fleeing fighting between the Turks and the Venetians in the 16th century. They settled on the hillside just inland from Dapia, the area now known as Kastelli.

The Dapia district has a few impressive arhontika, but the prettiest part of town is around the old harbour.

Orientation & Information
The quay at Dapia Harbour serves both ferries and hydrofoils. A left turn at the end of the quay leads east along the waterfront on

Sotirios Anargyris, skirting a small square where the horse-drawn carriages wait. The road is flanked by a string of uninspiring, concrete C class hotels, and emerges after 200m on Plateia Agias Mamas, next to the town beach. The bus stop for Agioi Anargyri is next to the beach. The post office is on the street running behind the hotels; coming from the quay, turn right at Hotel Soleil and then left.

The waterfront to the right of the quay is also called Sotirios Anargyris. It skirts Dapia Harbour, passes the decaying shell of the once-grand Hotel Possidonion and continues west around the bay to Hotel Spetses.

The main road inland from Dapia is N Spetson, which runs off the small square where the horse-drawn carriages wait. It soon becomes Botassi, which continues inland to Kastelli. These two streets are among the very few on Spetses with street signs.

There is no tourist office on Spetses. The tourist police (☎ 73 100) are based in the police station – on the well signposted road to the museum – from mid-May to September.

The OTE is behind Dapia Harbour, opposite the National Bank of Greece. Internet access is available at Cafe Delfinia on Plateia Agias Mamas.

Things to See

The **old harbour** is a delightful place to explore. It is ringed by old Venetian buildings, and filled with boats of every shape and size – from colourful little fishing boats to sleek luxury cruising yachts. The shipbuilders of Spetses still do things the traditional way and the shore is dotted with the hulls of emerging caïques. The walk from Dapia Harbour takes about 20 minutes. **Moni Agios Nikolaos** straddles a headland at the halfway mark.

The **museum** is housed in the arhontiko of Hadzigiannis Mexis, a shipowner who became the island's first governor. While most of the collection is devoted to folklore items and portraits of the island's founding fathers, there is also a fine collection of ships' figureheads. It's open 8.30 am to 3 pm

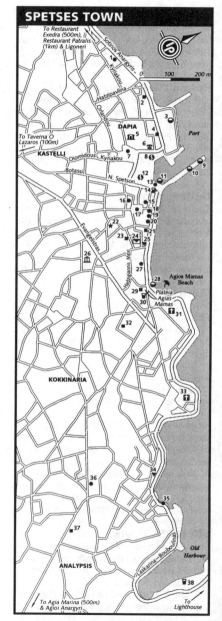

SPETSES TOWN

PLACES TO STAY	6	OTE	19	Fish Market
2	Nissia	7	Children's	20	Kritikos
4	Hotel Possidonion		Playground		Supermarket
21	Hotel Soleil	8	National Bank	22	Police Station
23	Zoe's Club		of Greece	24	Post Office
29	Villa Marina	9	Ferry Dock	26	Museum
32	Hotel Kamelia	10	Hydrofoil Dock	27	Cafe Delfinia
37	Orloff Apartments	11	Taxis Boals & Caïques	28	Buses to Agioi
		12	Ionian Bank		Anargyri
PLACES TO EAT	13	Hydrofoil Ticket Office	30	Bar Spetsa
25	Restaurant Stelios	14	Petrol Station	31	Moni Agios Mamas
34	Byzantino	15	International	33	Moni Agios
			Newspapers		Nikolaos
OTHER	16	Laundry	35	Caique Building
1	Town Hall	17	Plateia Orologiou	36	Children's
3	Buses to Ligoneri	18	Alasia Travel &		Playground
5	Bouboulinas Mansion		Meledon Travel	38	Le Figaro Night Club

Tuesday to Sunday. Admission is 500 dr. The museum is clearly signposted from Plateia Orologiou.

Places to Stay – Budget
The best budget option is *Orloff Apartments* (☎ 72 246, fax 74 470), above the old harbour on the road leading out to Agioi Anargyri – about 1.5km from the port. Manager Christos has a dozen or so well equipped studio rooms set in the gardens of the family home. Rates for singles/doubles are 8000/12,000 dr, dropping to 6000/8000 dr outside July and August.

The friendly *Villa Marina* (☎ 72 646), just off Plateia Agias Mamas beyond the row of restaurants, is another popular place. It has good rooms with bathroom for 10,000/16,000 dr – available most of the year for 7000/10,000 dr. All rooms have refrigerators and there is a well equipped communal kitchen downstairs.

If these two are full try *Hotel Kamelia* (☎ 72 415), signposted to the right at the supermarket, 100m past Plateia Agias Mamas on the road that leads inland to Agioi Anargyri. The place is almost hidden beneath a sprawling burgundy bougainvillea. Spotless rooms with bathroom are 10,000/12,000 dr.

Otherwise, you might be forced to fall back on one of the uninspiring C and D

class places that line the waterfront between the ferry dock and Plateia Agias Mamas, or seek help from one of the travel agents.

Places to Stay – Top End
If money is no object, there are some good places at the luxury end of the market. *Zoe's Club* (☎ 74 447, fax 72 841) and *Nissia* (☎ 75 000, fax 75 012, email nissia@ otenet.gr) are a couple of stylish resorts with accommodation spread around large swimming pools. Both charge close to 45,000 dr for doubles with buffet breakfast.

Zoe's is up the steps next to the post office, while Nissia is on the waterfront west of Hotel Possidonion (closed).

Places to Eat
Restaurant Stelios, between Plateia Agias Mamas and the post office, is a popular taverna that pitches for the tourist trade with a series of set menus. Prices start at 2600 dr for three courses.

Getting away from the tourist hype involves a bit of walking. The place to head for is the excellent *Taverna O Lazaros* (☎ 72 600) in the district of Kastelli, about 600m inland at the top end of Spetson. Treat yourself to a plate of *taramasalata* (800 dr); their home-made version of this popular fish roe dip is unrecognisable from the pink, food colouring-filled muck served at most Greek restaurants. The speciality of the house is baby goat in lemon sauce (1600 dr).

Restaurant Exedra, halfway around the bay on the road to Hotel Spetses, has seating on a small platform built out over the beach. Surprisingly, given its location, fish hardly features on the menu.

Fish fans should keep walking around the bay to *Restaurant Patralis*. It has a great setting, a good menu and fish supplied by the restaurant's own boat. The fish à la Spetses (2000 dr), a large tuna or swordfish steak baked with vegetables and lots of garlic, goes down perfectly with a cold beer.

If character is what you want, you won't find a better place than *Byzantino*, halfway to the old harbour on the other side of town. The early 19th century port-authority building has been converted into a stylish restaur-ant specialising in mezedes. Reckon on about 9000 dr for two, with drinks.

Self-caterers can head to *Kritikos Supermarket*, next to Hotel Soleil on the waterfront near Plateia Agias Mamas. There is a very well stocked bottle shop across the alleyway behind it.

Entertainment

For a quiet beer and a great selection of music from the 60s and 70s, try *Bar Spetsa*, 50m beyond Plateia Agias Mamas on the road to Agioi Anargyri. Look out for the sign that announces 'No disco, house, acid, rap or crap in here'. If that's what you're after, though, try one of the discos at the old harbour.

AROUND SPETSES

Spetses' coastline is speckled with numerous coves with small, pine-shaded beaches. A 24km road (part sealed, part dirt) skirts the entire coastline, so a motorcycle is the ideal way to explore the island.

The beach at **Ligoneri**, west of town, has the attraction of being easily accessible by bus. **Agia Marina**, to the south of the old harbour, is a small resort with a crowded beach. **Agia Paraskevi** and **Agioi Anargyri**, on the south-west coast, have good, albeit crowded, beaches; both have water sports of every description. A large mansion between the two beaches was the inspiration for the Villa Bourani in John Fowles' *The Magus*.

The small island of **Spetsopoula** to the south of Spetses is owned by the family of the late shipping magnate Stavros Niarchos.

Cyclades Κυκλάδες

The Cyclades (kih-**klah**-dez) are the quint-essential Greek islands – rugged outcrops of rock dotted with brilliant white buildings offset by vividly painted balconies and bright blue church domes, all bathed in daz-zling light and fringed with golden beaches lapped by aquamarine seas.

Goats and sheep are raised on the moun-tainous, barren islands, as well as some pigs and cattle. Naxos is the most fertile island, producing potatoes and other crops for export to Athens and neighbouring islands. Many islanders still fish, but tourism is becoming the dominant source of income.

Some islands, especially Mykonos, Santorini (Thira) and Ios, have eagerly em-braced tourism – their shores are spread with sun lounges, umbrellas and water sports equipment. Other islands, such as Andros, Syros, Kea, Serifos and Sifnos, are less vis-ited by foreigners but, thanks to their prox-imity to the mainland, are popular weekend and summer retreats for Athenians.

Tinos is not a holiday island but the coun-try's premier place of pilgrimage – a Greek Lourdes. Other islands, such as Anafi and the Little Cyclades east of Naxos, are little more than clumps of rock with tiny depopu-lated villages.

The Cyclades are so named because they form a circle *(kyklos)* around the island of Delos, one of the country's most significant ancient sites.

The islands are small and closely grouped, making them ideal for island-hopping. It's best to avoid them in high season (July and August), when accommo-dation can be scarce. Most places are open only from April to October. Accommoda-tion prices quoted throughout this chapter are for high season; expect to pay a lot less at other times.

The Cyclades are more exposed to the north-westerly *meltemi* wind than other island groups, but this usually provides a welcome respite from the heat.

HIGHLIGHTS

- Spectacular sunsets over Santorini's submerged volcano
- Walks though the verdant country-side of Naxos and Andros
- Unspoilt whitewashed villages on Amorgos and Folegandros
- Ouzo and freshly grilled fish at beachside tavernas
- Uncrowded island beaches with crystal-clear water
- The island-size archaeological site of ancient Delos
- Nightlife on Mykonos, Santorini and Ios
- Island-hopping by ferry

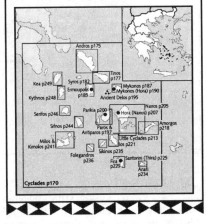

History

The Cyclades have been inhabited since at least 7000 BC, and there is evidence that the obsidian on Milos was exploited as early as 7500 BC. Around 3000 BC, the Cycladic civilisation, a culture famous for its seafar-ers, appeared. During the Early Cycladic

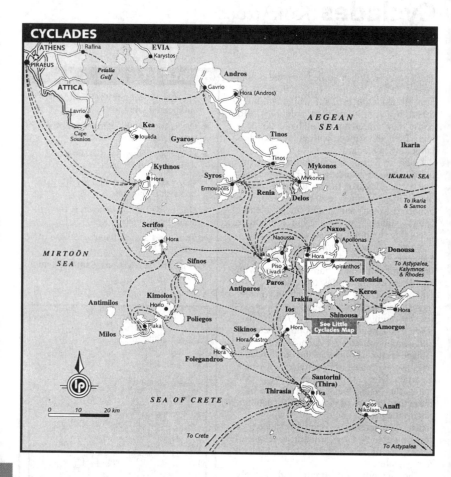

CYCLADES

period (3000-2000 BC) there were settlements on Keros, Syros, Milos, Naxos, Milos, Sifnos and Amorgos. It was during this time that the famous Cycladic marble figurines were sculpted.

In the Middle Cycladic period (2000-1500 BC), many of the islands were occupied by the Minoans – at Akrotiri on Santorini, a Minoan town has been excavated. At the beginning of the Late Cycladic period (1500-1100 BC), the Cyclades passed to the Mycenaeans. The Dorians

followed in the 8th century BC, bringing their Archaic culture with them.

Most of the Cyclades joined the Delian League in 478 BC, and by the middle of the 5th century the islands were members of a fully fledged Athenian empire. In the Hellenistic era (323-146 BC) the islands fell under the control of Egypt's Ptolemies, and, later, the Macedonians. In 146 BC, the islands became a Roman province and trade links were established with many parts of the Mediterranean, bringing prosperity.

After the division of the Roman Empire into western and eastern entities in 395 AD, the Cyclades were ruled from Byzantium (Constantinople). Following the fall of Byzantium in 1204, the Franks gave the Cyclades to Venice, which parcelled the islands out to opportunistic aristocrats. The most powerful was Marco Sanudo (self-styled Duke of Naxos), who acquired Naxos, Paros, Ios, Santorini, Anafi, Sifnos, Milos, Amorgos and Folegandros.

The islands came under Turkish rule in 1537. Neglected by the Ottomans, they became backwaters prone to pirate raids, hence the labyrinthine, hilltop character of their towns – the mazes of narrow lanes were designed to disorientate invaders. On many islands, people moved inland to escape pirates. Nevertheless, the impact of piracy led to massive depopulation; in 1563 only five out of 16 islands were still inhabited.

In 1771 the Cyclades were annexed by the Russians during the Russian-Turkish War, but were reclaimed by the Ottomans a few years later.

The Cyclades' participation in the Greek War of Independence was minimal but they became havens for people fleeing islands where insurrections against the Turks had led to massacres. During WWII the islands were occupied by the Italians.

The fortunes of the Cycladic islands have been revived by the tourism boom that began in the 1970s. Until then, many islanders lived in abject poverty and many more gave up the battle and headed for the mainland in search of work.

Getting There & Away

For information on travel within the Cyclades, see this chapter's Getting Around section and individual island entries.

Air Olympic Airways links Athens with Naxos, Syros, Santorini, Mykonos, Paros and Milos. Santorini has direct flights to/from Mykonos, Thessaloniki, Iraklio (Crete) and Rhodes, and Mykonos has flights to/from Thessaloniki and Rhodes.

At the time of writing, a few new airlines were also offering flights to the islands; see individual island entries for details.

Ferry – Domestic Ferry routes tend to separate the Cyclades into western, northern, central and eastern subgroups. Most ferries serving the Cyclades connect one of these subgroups with Piraeus, Lavrio or Rafina on the mainland.

The central Cyclades (Paros, Naxos, Ios and Santorini) are the most visited and have the best links with the mainland, usually Piraeus.

The northern Cyclades (Andros, Tinos, Syros and Mykonos) also have very good connections with the mainland. The jumping-off point for Andros is Rafina, but it's possible to access it from Piraeus by catching a ferry to Syros, Tinos or Mykonos and connecting from there.

The western Cyclades (Kea, Kythnos, Milos, Serifos, Sifnos, Folegandros and Sikinos) have less frequent connections with the mainland. Lavrio is the mainland port for ferries serving Kea.

The eastern Cyclades (Anafi, Amorgos, Iraklia, Shinousa, Koufonisia and Donousa) are the least visited and have the fewest links with the mainland. They are best visited from Naxos and Santorini.

Ferries from Paros and Naxos connect the Cyclades with Ikaria and Samos in the North-Eastern Aegean and with Rhodes in the Dodecanese. There are also a couple of boats a week from Santorini to Rhodes and one a week to Astypalea, also in the Dodecanese.

The central and northern Cyclades are linked a few times a week with Thessaloniki and once a week with Volos.

Boats from the Cretan ports of Agios Nikolaos and Sitia depart for Milos three times weekly, while ferries from Rethymno head for Sifnos twice weekly. Iraklio has frequent connections with Santorini and other islands in the central Cyclades.

The following table gives an overview of high-season ferry services to the Cyclades from the mainland and Crete.

Ferry Connections to the Cyclades

Origin	Destination	Duration	Price	Frequency
Agios Nikolaos (Crete)	Milos	7 hours	4850 dr	3 weekly
Iraklio (Crete)	Mykonos	10 hours	7100 dr	2 weekly
Iraklio	Ios	6 hours	4180 dr	1 weekly
Iraklio	Naxos	4¼-7½ hours	5000 dr	4 weekly
Iraklio	Paros	7-8 hours	4950 dr	6 weekly
Iraklio	Santorini	4 hours	3700 dr	7 weekly
Iraklio	Syros	8½ hours	5400 dr	3 weekly
Iraklio	Tinos	9 hours	6100 dr	3 weekly
Lavrio	Kea	1¼ hours	1600 dr	2 daily
Lavrio	Kythnos	3½ hours	2300 dr	2 weekly
Piraeus	Amorgos	10 hours	4500 dr	6 weekly
Piraeus	Anafi	11 hours	6700 dr	4 weekly
Piraeus	Folegandros	6-9 hours	5150 dr	8 weekly
Piraeus	Ios	7 hours	5300 dr	4 daily
Piraeus	Kythnos	2½ hours	2300 dr	1 daily
Piraeus	Milos	5-7 hours	5050 dr	10 weekly
Piraeus	Mykonos	6 hours	5100 dr	1 daily
Piraeus	Naxos	6 hours	5000 dr	8 daily
Piraeus	Paros	5 hours	4950 dr	6 daily
Piraeus	Santorini	9 hours	6100 dr	5 daily
Piraeus	Serifos	4½ hours	4000 dr	1 daily
Piraeus	Sifnos	5 hours	4400 dr	1 daily
Piraeus	Sikinos	10 hours	6000 dr	7 weekly
Piraeus	Syros	4 hours	4400 dr	3 daily
Piraeus	Tinos	5 hours	4700 dr	1 daily
Rafina	Amorgos	10¾ hours	4700 dr	1 weekly
Rafina	Andros	2 hours	2400 dr	4 daily
Rafina	Kea	1¼ hours	1900 dr	1 weekly
Rafina	Mykonos	5 hours	4100 dr	1 daily
Rafina	Paros	7 hours	4150 dr	5 weekly
Rafina	Syros	5¾ hours	3400 dr	3 weekly
Rafina	Tinos	3¾ hours	3600 dr	2 daily
Rethymno (Crete)	Sifnos	5½ hours	5100 dr	2 weekly
Sitia (Crete)	Milos	9 hours	5100 dr	3 weekly
Thessaloniki	Mykonos	18 hours	9100 dr	2 weekly
Thessaloniki	Naxos	14¾ hours	7100 dr	4 weekly
Thessaloniki	Paros	12-15 hours	9350 dr	4 weekly
Thessaloniki	Santorini	17¾ hours	10,100 dr	5 weekly
Thessaloniki	Syros	13 hours	8400 dr	2 weekly
Thessaloniki	Tinos	13 hours	9100 dr	4 weekly
Volos	Paros	8 hours	6950 dr	1 weekly
Volos	Santorini	14 hours	8100 dr	1 weekly
Volos	Tinos	9 hours	6000 dr	1 weekly

CYCLADES

From early June to mid-October you can buy a 20-day island pass that offers round-trip travel from Piraeus to Paros, Naxos, Ios and Santorini for 16,500 dr. The passes are issued by Agapitos Express Ferries for use on their ships only, and are available from most Athens travel agents.

Ferry – International Ferries from Piraeus to Cyprus and Israel stop at Santorini and Tinos.

Hydrofoil Although hydrofoils can travel faster than ferries, they often take longer to get to their destination because of their sensitivity to bad weather and the many stops made.

Minoan is the major operator in the Cyclades. In summer, there are daily hydrofoils from the main harbour at Piraeus to Kythnos, Serifos, Sifnos and Milos, and five weekly to Kea from Zea Marina at Piraeus. There are daily hydrofoils from Iraklio (Crete) to Santorini.

Catamaran Large high-speed cats are now major players on Cyclades routes. The travel time is usually half that of regular ferries. Tickets cost about twice as much as deck-class ferry fares. Catamarans are very popular and seats fill fast – it's worth booking your ticket a day or so in advance.

Minoan operates *Highspeed 1*, which travels daily between Piraeus, Syros, Mykonos, Paros and Naxos. Strintzis Lines runs *Seajet 1* daily from Rafina to Syros, Paros, Naxos, Ios and Santorini, and *Seajet 2* daily from Rafina to Tinos and Mykonos. Once a week, *Seajet 2* continues to Syros, Paros, Naxos and Amorgos. Goutos Lines' *Athina 2004* also makes daily runs between Rafina, Tinos and Mykonos, continuing to Andros twice weekly and to Paros, Naxos and Amorgos once a week.

Getting Around
Air Olympic Airways flights between Mykonos and Santorini (15,400 dr) provide the only inter-island link within the Cyclades.

Ferry There are usually relatively good connections within each of the western, northern, central and eastern subgroups, but infrequent connections between the different subgroups. When you plan your island-hopping, it pays to bear this pattern of ferry routes in mind. However, Paros is the ferry hub of the Cyclades, and connections between different groups are usually possible via Paros if not direct.

The central Cyclades (Paros, Naxos, Ios and Santorini) have the best links with the other subgroups and each other. The northern Cyclades (Andros, Tinos, Syros and Mykonos) have very good connections with each other and with the central Cyclades.

The western Cyclades (Kea, Kythnos, Milos, Serifos, Sifnos, Folegandros and Sikinos) have less frequent connections with other Cyclades subgroups. Kea is only liked a few times a week (in high season) to Kythnos and the other islands in the western Cyclades.

The eastern Cyclades (Anafi, Amorgos, Iraklia, Shinous, Koufonisia and Donousa) are the least visited and have the fewest links with other islands. Naxos is the best jumping-off point for the Little Cyclades (Iraklia, Shinousa, Koufonisia and Donousa) and Amorgos, while Santorini has the most ferries to Anafi.

Hydrofoil Minoan is the major operator in the Cyclades. In summer, there are daily hydrofoils between Kythnos, Serifos, Sifnos and Milos, as well as frequent connections between Mykonos, Naxos, Paros and Syros.

Santorini Dolphins runs daily hydrofoils from Santorini to Ios, Naxos, Paros, Tinos and Syros, with services to Folegandros, Sikinos, Amorgos and the Little Cyclades once or twice weekly.

Catamaran There are daily cats between Syros, Mykonos, Tinos, Paros, Naxos, Ios and Santorini. Cats link Andros and Amorgos to other islands in the group twice weekly.

Andros Ανδρος

☎ 0282 • postcode 845 00 • pop 8781

Andros is the northernmost island of the
Cyclades and the second largest after
Naxos. It is also one of the most fertile, producing citrus fruit and olives, and is unusual in that it has retained its pine forests
and mulberry woods. There is plentiful
water – indeed, Andros is famous for its
water, which is bottled at Sariza.

More distinctive features are its dovecotes (although Tinos has more of them)
and elaborate stone walls. Many of the old
water mills are now being restored. If you
have a sweet tooth, seek out the island's
walnut and almond sweets: *kalsounia* and
amygdolota.

Getting There & Away

Ferry At least four ferries daily leave
Andros' main port of Gavrio for Rafina
(two hours, 2400 dr), Tinos (1½ hours, 1700
dr) and Mykonos (2½ hours, 2600 dr).
There are ferries to Paros (four hours, 2700
dr, three weekly) and Syros (four hours,
1800 dr, weekly).

Catamaran Four catamarans weekly go
to Rafina (one hour, 4700 dr), Tinos (30
minutes, 3500 dr), Mykonos (1¼ hours,
5200 dr), Paros (three hours, 5500 dr) and
Naxos (3½ hours, 6000 dr), and three go to
Amorgos (4¼ hours, 8100 dr). A catamaran also runs once a week to Syros (two
hours, 3700 dr).

Getting Around

Around nine buses daily (fewer on weekends) link Gavrio and Hora (750 dr) via
Batsi (250 dr); if there's no schedule posted,
call ☎ 22 316 for information. A taxi
(☎ 22 171) from Batsi to Hora costs 4000
dr. Caïques from Batsi go to some of the
island's nicest beaches.

GAVRIO Γαύριο

Gavrio, on the west coast, is the main port
of Andros. Nothing much happens in
Gavrio, but there are lovely beaches nearby.

Orientation & Information

The ferry quay is in the middle of the waterfront and the bus stop is next to it. Turn left
from the quay and walk along the waterfront
for the post office. The tourist office opposite
the quay is rarely open. The telephone number of the port police is ☎ 71 213.

Places to Stay & Eat

If you decide to stay in town, look for
domatia signs along the waterfront or try
Hotel Galaxy (☎ 71 005) to the left of the
quay. It has reasonable singles/doubles for
6000/7000 dr with bathroom. The B class
Andros Holiday Hotel (☎ 71 384), overlooking the beach, has a restaurant, bar,
tennis court, sauna, jacuzzi and gym. Air-
con singles/doubles/triples cost 22,000/
25,000/33,500 dr with breakfast.

Veggera and *Neraida* are both nice eateries with tables on a large plateia one block
back from the waterfront. Turn left from the
quay and take the first right after the Batsi
road.

BATSI Μπατσί

Batsi, 8km south of Gavrio, is Andros'
major resort. The attractive town encircles a
bay with a fishing harbour at one end and a
nice sandy beach at the other. There is no
EOT, but Greek Sun Holidays (☎ 41 198,
fax 41 239) and Andros Travel (☎ 41 252,
fax 41 608), near the car park, are very helpful and can handle everything from accommodation to sightseeing and ferry tickets.

The post office is near the large car park.
The taxi rank, bus stop and Ionian Bank
(with ATM) are all on the main square near
the fishing boats. A stepped path leads up
from behind the square through lush vegetation sprouting along a watercourse. Car
hire is available at Auto Europe (☎ 41 995,
fax 41 239).

Organised Tours

Andros Travel (see preceding section) offers an interesting range of walks and an
island tour (6000 dr) that takes in Menites,
Apikia, Moni Agiou Nikolaou, Korthi and
Paleopolis. Guided half and full-day walks

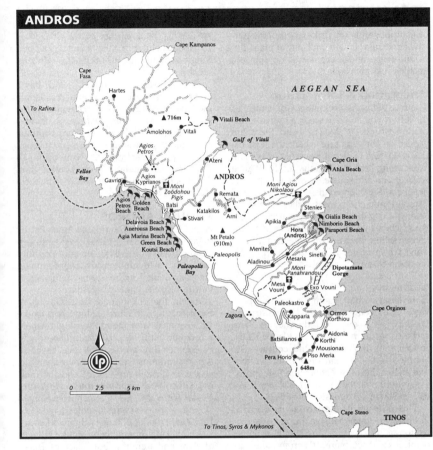

ANDROS

Cape Kampanos

Cape Fasa

Hartes

AEGEAN SEA

To Rafina

▲ 716m

Vitali Beach

Amolohos   Vitali

Agios Petros

Gulf of Vitali

Ateni

Fellos Bay   Agios Kyprianos   **ANDROS**   Cape Gria

Gavrio   *Moni Zoödohou Pigis*   Ahla Beach

Remata

Moni Agiou Nikolaou

Agios Petros Beach   Golden Beach   Batsi

Delavoia Beach   Katakilos   Arni   Stenies

Anerousa Beach   Stivari   Apikia   Gialia Beach

Agia Marina Beach   Nimborio Beach

Green Beach   **Hora (Andros)**   Paraporti Beach

Koutsi Beach   ▲   *Paleopolis*   Menites   Sineti

Mt Petalo (910m)   Aladinou   Mesaria

Paleopolis Bay   *Moni Panahrandou*   **Dipotamata Gorge**

Mesa Vouni   Exo Vouni

Paleokastro   Cape Orginos

Zagora ∴   Kapparia   Ormos Korthiou

Aidonia

Batsilianos   Korthi

Mousionas

Pera Horio   Piso Meria

▲ 648m

0   2.5   5 km

Cape Steno   **TINOS**

To Tinos, Syros & Mykonos

following old paths through beautiful countryside range from 4100 dr to 5200 dr.

Places to Stay & Eat

Scan the waterfront and side streets for domatia signs. *Cavo d'Oro* (☎ 41 776) at the beach end of the waterfront, above the pizzeria of the same name, has doubles for 10,000 dr with telephone and bathroom. *Scouna Hotel* (☎ 41 165), overlooking the beach, has singles/doubles for 7500/10,000 dr with bathroom. *Karanassos Hotel*

(☎ 41 480), 50m from the beach, has pleasant rooms for 12,000/14,000 dr with bathroom. *Hotel Chryssi Akti* (☎ 41 237), right on the beach, has a pool and charges 13,000/15,000 dr for rooms with TV, fridge, phone and balcony. *Likio Studios* (☎ 41 050) is set back from the beach amid masses of geraniums. Spotless double studios with kitchen, TV, phone and balcony cost 16,500 dr.

There are a few decent tavernas along the waterfront, including *Oti Kalo*, *Stamatis* and *Esthesis*.

CYCLADES

HORA (ANDROS)
Hora (Χώρα) is on the east coast, 35km east of Gavrio, and is set strikingly along a narrow peninsula. It's an enchanting place full of surprises, and there are some fine old neoclassical mansions.

Orientation & Information
The bus station is on Plateia Goulandri. To the left as you face the sea is a tourist information office (☎ 25 162) and the main pedestrian thoroughfare where the post office, OTE and National Bank of Greece are. Walk along here towards the sea for Plateia Kaïri, the central square, beyond which is the headland. Steps descend from the square to Paraporti and Nimborio beaches. The street leading along the promontory ends at Plateia Riva, where there is a bronze statue of an unknown sailor. The ruins of a Venetian fortress stand on an island joined to the tip of the headland by an old, steeply arched bridge.

Museums
Hora has two outstanding museums; both were endowed by Vasili Goulandris, a wealthy ship owner and Andriot. The **archaeological museum** is on Plateia Kaïri. Its contents include the 2nd century BC Hermes of Andros and finds from Andros' two ancient cities of Zagora and Paleopolis. The museum is open 8 am to 2.30 pm Tuesday to Sunday. Admission is 500 dr.

The **museum of modern art** is a small, intimate museum with an impressive collection of 20th century Greek and European paintings and sculpture. It's around the corner immediately left of the archaeological museum and is open 10 am to 2 pm and 6 to 8 pm Saturday to Monday (closed Sunday afternoon). Admission is 200 dr.

There is also a **nautical museum** near the end of the promontory, open 10 am till 1 pm and 6 to 8 pm Saturday to Monday (closed Sunday afternoon).

Places to Stay & Eat
Hotel Egli (☎ 22 303), between the two squares, off the right side of the main road as you head towards the sea, has doubles for 14,000/18,000 dr with shared/private bathroom, including breakfast. *Paradise Hotel* (☎ 22 187) is a partner of the St George Lycabettus Hotel in Athens and has a pool. Singles/doubles are 17,000/28,000 dr with breakfast.

Parea Taverna, on Plateia Kaïri, has a commanding beach view and reasonable food. *Nonnas* is a lovely *mezedes* place in the old port area known as Plakoura, on the way to Nimborio Beach; to get there continue down the steps past the modern art museum.

On the waterfront at Nimborio, *Ta Delfinia* has excellent home-cooked fare. *Cabo del Mar*, at the far end of Nimborio Beach, has a lovely setting.

AROUND ANDROS
About 2.5km from Gavrio, the **Agios Petros** tower is an imposing circular watchtower, dating from Hellenistic times – possibly earlier. It's a 30 minute walk from Camping Andros. Look for the signpost for Agios Petros, also the name of a village.

Along the coast road from Gavrio to Batsi is a turn-off left leading 5km to the 12th century **Moni Zoödohou Pigis**, where a few nuns still live. Between Gavrio and Paleopolis Bay are several nice beaches: **Agios Kyprianos** (where a former church is now a beachfront *taverna*), **Delavoia** (nudist), **Green Beach** and **Anerousa**. *Anerousa Beach Hotel* (☎ 41 044), open from May to October, offers singles/doubles/triples for 15,500/18,500/22,000 dr with breakfast.

An old path running between the villages of **Arni** and **Remata**, both east of Batsi, passes water mills. **Paleopolis**, 9km south of Batsi on the coast road, is the site of Ancient Andros, where the Hermes of Andros was found. There is little to see, but the mountain setting is lovely. **Menites**, southwest of Hora, has springs and a row of drinking fountains with spouts shaped like lions' heads.

From the pretty village of **Mesaria**, it's a strenuous two hour walk to the 12th century **Moni Panahrandou**, the island's largest and most important monastery. **Apikia**, northwest of Hora, is famous for its mineral springs. Near **Sineti**, the wild **Dipotamata Gorge** and its water mills are now EU-protected. An old cobbled path, once the main route from Korthi to Hora, leads along the gorge.

The pretty blue-green bay and holiday hamlet at **Ormos Korthiou**, in the southeast, has a lot of faded charm. *Hotel Korthion (☎ 61 218)*, on the shore, has singles/doubles for 8000/9000 dr with bath.

Tinos Τήνος

☎ 0283 • postcode 842 00 • pop 7747

Tinos is green and mountainous, like nearby Andros. The island is a Greek Orthodox place of pilgrimage, so it's hardly surprising that churches feature prominently among the attractions. The celebrated Church of Panagia Evangelistria dominates the un-interesting capital, while unspoilt hill villages and ornate whitewashed dovecotes are rural attractions.

Tinos also has a large Roman Catholic population – the result of its long Venetian occupation. The Turks didn't succeed in wresting the island from the Venetians until 1715, long after the rest of the country had surrendered to Ottoman rule.

Getting There & Away

Ferry At least six ferries daily go to Mykonos (30 minutes, 1100 dr), and around two daily go to Rafina (3¾ hours, 3600 dr) and Andros (1½ hours, 1700 dr). There is at least one daily to Syros (45 minutes, 1100 dr) and Piraeus (five hours, 4700 dr).

Four ferries weekly go to Thessaloniki (13 hours, 9100 dr), three weekly go to Paros (1½ to three hours, 1700 dr), Santorini (4¾ hours, 4000 dr), Crete (nine

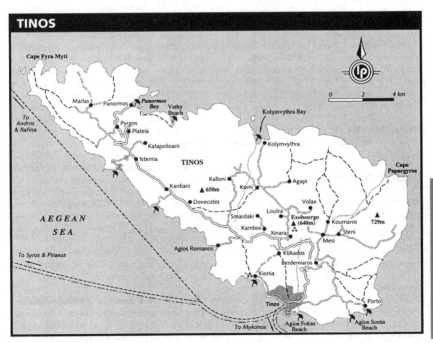

TINOS

hours, 6100 dr) and Skiathos (7¼ hours, 5300 dr). There are also weekly services to Naxos (4¼ hours, 1900 dr), Iraklia (8¾ hours, 2600 dr), Shinousa (8¼ hours, 2600 dr), Koufonisia (7¾ hours, 2800 dr) and Donousa (2½ hours, 3200 dr), Amorgos (3½ hours, 2600 dr), Ios (6¼ hours, 2900 dr) and Volos (nine hours, 6000 dr).

Twice weekly there are ferries to Lemesos (Limassol) in Cyprus (38 hours) and the port of Haifa in Israel (58 hours).

Hydrofoil There are daily hydrofoils to Syros (15 minutes, 2100 dr), Mykonos (15 minutes, 2400 dr), Paros (1¼ hours, 3500 dr) and Santorini (at least 3¼ hours, 8400 dr). Five hydrofoils weekly go to Ios (3½ hours, 7100 dr) and Naxos (two hours, 3200 dr), and two go to Amorgos (5½ hours, 5100 dr), Folegandros (4½ to six hours, 5700 dr), Milos (3¼ to six hours, 6300 dr) and Sifnos (2½ hours, 6200 dr).

Catamaran There are around four catamarans daily to Mykonos (15 minutes, 2400 dr) and three to Rafina (1½ hours, 6000 dr). There are at least six weekly to Paros (1¼ hours, 3500 dr), Naxos (two hours, 3200 dr) and Andros (one hour, 3500 dr), and two weekly to Syros (two hours, 2100 dr) and Amorgos (2¾ hours, 5100 dr).

Excursion Boat Excursion boats run most days to Delos (5000 dr) from June to September.

Getting Around

There are frequent buses from Tinos (Hora) to Kionia and several daily to Panormos via Pyrgos and Kambos, and to Porto. Buses leave from the station on the waterfront, opposite the National Bank of Greece. The travel agent next to the bank has a timetable in its front window.

However, by far the best way to explore the island is by motorcycle (prices start at 3000 dr a day) or car (7000 dr a day); the roads are generally pretty good. Motorcycles and cars can be hired along the waterfront at Hora.

TINOS (HORA)

Tinos, also known as Hora, is the island's rather shabby capital and port. The waterfront is lined with cafes and hotels, while the little streets behind have shops and stalls catering to pilgrims and tourists. The Church of Panagia Evangelistria is uphill in the centre of town.

Orientation

The new ferry quay is at the north-western end of the waterfront, about 300m from the main harbour, but there are two other, more central, quays where catamarans and smaller ferries dock. When you buy your ticket, check which quay your boat departs from.

Leoforos Megaloharis, straight ahead from the main harbour, is the route pilgrims take to the church. The narrow Evangelistria, to the right facing inland, also leads to the church.

Information

Tinos has no tourist office, but there are many travel agencies supplying information as well as providing accommodation and car hire services. Windmills Travel (☎ 23 398), at Kionion 2 above the new ferry quay, and Malliaris Travel (☎ 24 241), on the waterfront near Hotel Posidonion, are both helpful. There are plans to establish an information booth on the waterfront, probably near the bus station.

The post office is at the south-eastern end of the waterfront, past the bus station and the National Bank of Greece (with ATM), next door to Hotel Tinion – turn right from the quay. The OTE is on Megaloharis, not far from the church. The town beach of Agios Fokas is a 10 minute walk south from the waterfront.

The port police (☎ 22 348) are on the waterfront, near the Hotel Oceanis, but the staff don't speak English.

Church of Panagia Evangelistria

This surprisingly small church is a neoclassical marble confection of white and cream, with a high bell tower. The ornate facade

Beware the Evil Eye

When travelling through Greece – particularly in rural areas – you may notice that some bus drivers keep a chain bearing one or two blue stones dangling over the dashboard. Or you may spot a small, plastic blue eye attached to the cross hanging around someone's neck. Or maybe you'll wonder why there is a string of blue beads hanging from the front fender of a tractor.

Puzzle no longer. The Greeks are not sporting colours in support of their favourite soccer team or to show a particular political leaning. No – they are warding off the evil eye.

The evil eye is associated with envy, and can be cast – apparently unintentionally – upon someone or something which is praised or admired (even secretly). So those most vulnerable to the evil eye include people, creatures or objects of beauty, rarity and value. Babies are particularly vulnerable, and those who admire them will often spit gently on them to repel any ill effects. Adults and older children who are worried about being afflicted by the evil eye will wear blue.

Who then is responsible for casting the evil eye? Well, most culprits are those who are already considered quarrelsome or peculiar in some way by the local community. And folk with blue eyes are regarded with extreme suspicion – no doubt more than partly because being blue-eyed is a trait Greeks associate with Turks. All these quarrelsome, peculiar or blue-eyed folk have to do is be present when someone or something enviable appears on the scene – and then the trouble starts.

If, during your travels, someone casts the evil eye on you, you'll soon know about it. Symptoms include dizziness, headaches, a feeling of 'weight' on the head or of tightening in the chest. Locals will point you in the direction of someone, usually an old woman, who can cure you.

The cure usually involves the curer making the sign of the cross over a glass of water; then praying silently, at the same time dropping oil into the glass. If the oil disappears from the surface, it proves you have the evil eye – but also cures it, for the 'blessed' water will be dabbed on your forehead, stomach and at two points on your chest (at the points of the crucifix).

Apparently, the cure works. But you know the old adage about prevention being better than cure. If you're worried about the evil eye, don't take any chances – wear blue.

has graceful white upper and lower colonnades. The final approach is up carpeted steps, doubtless a relief to pious souls choosing to crawl. Inside, the miracle-working icon is draped with gold, silver, jewels and pearls, and surrounded by gifts from the hopeful.

A lucrative trade in candles, icon copies, incense and evil-eye deterrents is carried out on Evangelistria. The largest candles, which are about 2m long, cost 1000 dr; after an ephemeral existence burning in the church, the wax remains are gathered, melted and resold.

Within the church complex, several **museums** house religious artefacts, icons and secular artworks. Below the church, a crypt marks the spot where the icon was found. Next to it is a memorial to the sailors killed on the *Elli*, a Greek ship torpedoed by an Italian submarine in Tinos' harbour on Assumption Day, 1940. The church and museums are open 8 am to 8 pm daily.

Archaeological Museum

This somewhat disappointing museum (☎ 22 670), below the church on Leoforos Megaloharis, has a small collection that includes impressive clay *pithoi* (large storage jars), a few Roman sculptures, and a 1st century sundial. It's open 8 am to 3 pm Tuesday to Sunday. Admission is 500 dr.

CYCLADES

Places to Stay

Avoid Tinos on 25 March (Annunciation), 15 August (Feast of the Assumption) and 15 November (Advent), unless you want to join the huddled masses who sleep on the streets.

Camping Tinos (☎ *22 344*) is a lovely site with good facilities south of the town, near Agios Fokas. It charges 1500 dr per adult (children 850 dr) and 900 dr to 1100 dr per tent, depending on size. Tents can be rented for 1250 dr. Cute little bungalows are 6000/4500 dr with/without bathroom. A minibus meets ferries. The camp site is signposted from the waterfront.

Look for domatia signs along Evangelistria and other streets leading inland from the waterfront. *Rooms to Rent Giannis* (☎ *22 575*), on the waterfront next to Hotel Oceanis and five minutes from the beach, is a lovely, clean, homy place run by friendly people. There's a shared kitchen (free Greek coffee) and fridge, and a laundry tub made from the local green marble. Doubles are 10,000/7000 dr with/without bathroom. There are also nice triple apartments for 15,000 dr.

Hotel Posidonion (☎ *23 123*), on the waterfront opposite the bus station, has bright doubles for 14,000 dr, with balcony and bathroom. The B class *Hotel Tinion* (☎ *22 261*), at the southern end of the waterfront near the roundabout, is a grand old place with marble staircase and balconies overlooking the harbour. Spacious doubles with bathroom are 14,500 dr.

Places to Eat

The waterfront is lined with places serving the usual fare – none of them outstanding. *P Pallada Taverna*, just off the waterfront, behind Hotel Lito, is popular with the locals. It serves hearty, if somewhat oily, traditional dishes; the wine is poured from huge barrels overhead. It's opposite the only bakery on Tinos that still uses wood ovens. *Mixhalis Taverna*, in the first lane to the right off Evangelistria, is noted for high-quality meat. *Kypos Taverna*, behind Hotel Posidonion, also has decent food.

AROUND TINOS

Unless you've come solely to visit the church, you'll need to explore the countryside and its villages to make the most of Tinos. Most of the island is still farmed in one way or another, and you should look out for livestock (including piglets, goats and donkeys) wandering onto roads.

Kionia, 3km north-west of Hora, has several small beaches, the nearest overlooked by Tinos Beach Hotel. The site of the **Sanctuary of Poseidon & Amphitrite**, before the hotel, dates from the 4th century BC. Poseidon was worshipped because he banished the snakes that once infested the island.

At **Porto**, 6km east of Hora, there's a sandy, uncrowded beach. **Kolymvythra Bay**, beyond Komi, has two beautiful sandy beaches; a lovely road leads through reed beds and vegetable gardens to the bay.

Farther along the coast there's a small beach at **Panormos** from where distinctive green marble quarried in nearby **Marlas** was once exported. **Pyrgos** is a picturesque village where marble is still carved. There's a sculpture school and several little workshops with traditional items such as lintels and plaques (which both adorn houses around the village) and figurines for sale. About three buses per day run to Pyrgos; from there it's a pleasant 2km walk to Panormos.

The ruins of the Venetian fortress of **Exobourgo**, atop a 640m-high hill, stand sentinel over a cluster of unspoilt villages. At the fortress, built on an ancient acropolis, the Venetians made their last stand against the Turks in 1715. The ascent can be made from several villages; the shortest route is from Xinara. It's a steep climb, but the views are worth it.

The famous basket weavers of Tinos are based in the tiny, traditional village of **Volax**, nestled on a spectacular rocky plain in the centre of the island. You can usually buy direct from the workshops, but if they're shut for siesta, a cafe sells baskets as well. There is a small folkloric museum (free entry) and an attractive Catholic chapel. *O Rokos* (☎ *41 989*) is one of the best tavernas on the island, serving home-produced meat and vegetables. Everything is delicious, right down to the olives and capers in the Greek salad. Make sure you try the artichokes. Buses to Volax are rare indeed, so get a taxi, or hire a car or motorcycle.

Syros Σύρος

☎ 0281 • postcode 841 00 • pop 19,870
Many tourists come to Syros merely to change ferries. This is a pity because the capital, Ermoupolis (named after Hermes, god of trade, messengers and thieves), is a beautiful city with inhabitants who have not become tourist-weary.

Syros' economy depends little on tourism, and though its ship-building industry (once the most vigorous in Greece) has declined, it has textile factories, dairy farms and a horticultural industry that supplies the rest of the Cyclades with plants and flowers.

If you have a sweet tooth, don't miss the famous *loukoumia* (Turkish delight) and *halvadopites* (nougat). It's so popular that vendors race aboard ferries in the few minutes between arrival and departure.

History

Excavations of an Early Cycladic fortified settlement and burial ground at Kastri in the island's north-east, dating from the period 2800-2300 BC, reveal that the inhabitants farmed, fished, and had close connections with other communities.

In the Middle Ages, Syros was the only Greek island with an entirely Roman Catholic population, the result of conversions by the Franks who took over the island in 1207. This gave it the support and protection of the west (particularly the French) during Turkish rule.

Syros remained neutral during the War of Independence and thousands of refugees from islands ravaged by the Turks fled here, bringing the Orthodox religion. They built a new settlement (now called Vrodado), and the port town of Ermoupolis. After inde-

pendence, Ermoupolis became the commercial, naval and cultural centre of Greece.

Today, Syros' population is 40% Catholic and 60% Orthodox. Ermoupolis' ornate churches and neoclassical mansions are testimonies to its former grandeur.

Getting There & Away

Air Olympic Airways operates at least one flight daily to/from Athens (15,200 dr). Air Manos flies between Athens and Syros (14,200 dr) at least three times weekly; TEA flies the same route (16,400 dr) at least four times weekly. Tickets for all three airlines can be bought from most travel agents in Ermoupolis.

The Olympic Airways office (☎ 88 018, 82 634) is on the waterfront, around the corner from Naxou. Air Manos is represented by Gaviotis Tours (☎ 86 606, fax 83 445), on the waterfront near Kythnou. TEA is represented by Team Work Holidays (☎ 83 400, fax 83 508), on the waterfront near Dodekanisou.

Ferry There are at least three ferries daily from Syros to Piraeus (four hours, 4400 dr), Tinos (50 minutes, 1100 dr) and Mykonos (1¼ hours, 1500 dr); and at least one daily to Paros (1½ hours, 1500 dr) and Naxos (three hours, 2100 dr).

Four ferries weekly go to Amorgos (4½ hours, 3400 dr), Ios (2¾ hours, 3700 dr) and Santorini (six hours, 4100 dr); and three weekly serve Crete (8½ hours, 5400 dr), Rafina (5¾ hours, 3400 dr) and Skiathos (seven hours, 5200 dr).

At least twice weekly there are boats to Andros (1¾ hours, 1800 dr), Donousa (3½ hours, 2700 dr), Kea (three hours, 2300 dr), Kythnos (two hours, 1950 dr), Iraklia (4¾ hours, 2400 dr), Shinousa (five hours, 2500 dr), Koufonisia (5½ hours, 2800 dr), Thessaloniki (13 hours, 8400 dr), Sifnos (5½ hours, 2000 dr) and Serifos (three to five hours, 2000 dr).

There are weekly ferries to Sikinos (six hours, 2700 dr), Folegandros (six hours, 2900 dr), Patmos (five hours), Leros (seven hours), Kalymnos (two hours, 5300 dr),

CYCLADES

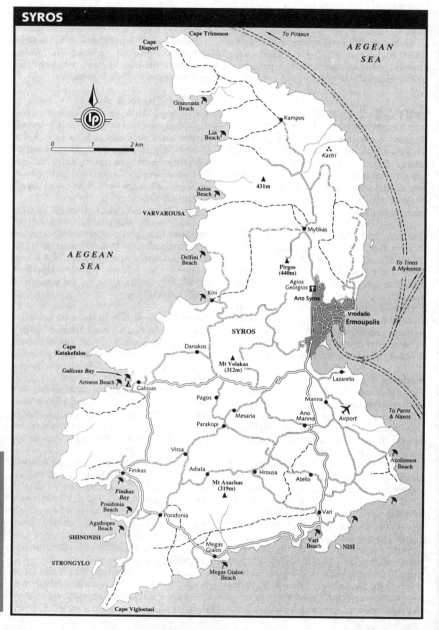

SYROS

To Piraeus

Cape Trimeson

Cape Diapori

AEGEAN SEA

Grammata Beach

Lia Beach

Kampos

Kastri

431m

Aetos Beach

VARVAROUSA

Mytikas

AEGEAN SEA

Delfini Beach

Pirgos (440m)

Kini

Agios Georgios

Ano Syros

To Tinos & Mykonos

SYROS

Vrodado

Ermoupolis

Cape Katakefalos

Danakos

Mt Volakas (312m)

Galissas Bay

Lazareto

Armeos Beach

Galissas

Pagos

Manna

To Paros & Naxos

Mesaria

Ano Manno

Parakopi

Airport

Vissa

Azolimnos Beach

Finikas

Adiata

Hrousa

Atelio

Mt Axachas (319m)

Finikas Bay

Posidonia Beach

Posidonia

Vari

Agathopes Beach

SHINONISI

Vari Beach

NISI

STRONGYLO

Megas Gialos

Megas Gialos Beach

Cape Viglostasi

0   1   2 km

CYCLADES

Kos, Nisyros (11 hours), Tilos (12 hours), Symi and Rhodes (15½ hours, 7100 dr).

Hydrofoil There are daily hydrofoils to Mykonos (35 minutes, 3000 dr), Paros (45 minutes, 3100 dr), Naxos (1½ hours, 4100 dr), Ios (2¼ hours, 7300 dr), Santorini (three hours, 8300 dr) and Crete (five hours, 12,200 dr). There are six hydrofoils weekly to Folegandros (five hours, 8300 dr), Milos (4½ hours, 5800 dr) and Sifnos (3½ hours, 4000 dr), and three weekly to Amorgos (6¼ hours, 6800 dr).

Catamaran High-speed catamarans depart daily for Piraeus (2½ hours, 8600 dr), Rafina (1½ hours, 6900 dr), Paros (45 minutes, 3100 dr), Naxos (1½ hours, 4100 dr), Ios (two hours, 7300 dr), Santorini (three hours, 8300 dr), Mykonos (30 minutes, 3000 dr) and Tinos (15 minutes, 2100 dr). There are weekly services to Amorgos (2½ hours, 6800 dr) and Andros (one hour, 5200 dr).

Getting Around
Frequent buses do a southern loop around the island from Ermoupolis, calling at all beaches mentioned in the text.

There is a bus to Ano Syros every morning. Taxis (☎ 86 222) charge about 600 dr for the ride up to Ano Syros from the port.

Cars can be hired for about 10,000 dr a day, and there are numerous moped hire outlets; try Dream Rent a Bike (☎ 84 707), on the waterfront near Sifnou, which also rents out bicycles (2500 dr per day).

ERMOUPOLIS Ερμούπολη
During the 19th century, a combination of fortuitous circumstances resulted in Ermoupolis becoming Greece's major port. It was superseded by Piraeus in the early 20th century but is still the Cyclades' capital and largest city, with a population of 13,030.

It's a very affluent, lively town; its wealth evident in the many restored neoclassical mansions, the marble-paved streets, and the chic little backstreet boutiques. Unlike most of the Cyclades, the occupants of Ermoupolis are busy with things other than

tourism, which in itself adds immeasurable real-life charm to the place.

As the boat sails into the port you will see the Catholic settlement of Ano Syros to the left, and the Orthodox settlement of Vrodado to the right, both set on hills. Spilling down from each and skirting the harbour is Ermoupolis – it's an impressive sight.

Orientation
Most boats dock at the south-western end of the bay, but ferries occasionally berth closer to the centre of town, near Hiou. The bus station is also by the quay.

To reach the central square, Plateia Miaouli, turn right from the quay, and then left into El Venizelou. There are public toilets around the bay to the east, and on the corner of Protopapadaki and Antiparou.

Information
In summer there is an information booth on the waterfront, near the corner of Nikolaou Filini, about 100m north-east of the quay. The post office is on Protopapadaki and the useless EOT is on Dodekanisou. The OTE is on the eastern edge of Plateia Miaouli.

There are ATMs at the Ionian Bank on El Venizelou, the Commercial Bank on Vokotopoulo, the Alpha Credit Bank on Protopapadaki, and the Agricultural Bank of Greece on the corner of El Venizelou at the waterfront. Kafe Net, on the waterfront below the Hotel Aktaion, provides Internet access; it's 1500 dr for the first hour (500 dr minimum) and 1000 dr for each subsequent hour.

The police station (☎ 82 610) is beside the Apollon Theatre, just north of the OTE. Syros' port police (☎ 82 690, 88 888) are on the eastern side of the waterfront.

Things to See
Plateia Miaouli is the hub of bustling Ermoupolis. It's flanked by palm trees and open-air cafes and dominated by the magnificent neoclassical **town hall**, designed by the German architect Ernst Ziller. Climb the marble steps to take a look at the airy interior. The small **archaeological museum** inside, founded in 1834 and one of the oldest

in Greece, houses a tiny collection of ceramic and marble vases, grave stelae, and Cycladic figurines. The entrance is around the corner on Benaki; opening hours are 8.30 am to 3 pm Tuesday to Sunday (free).

The **Apollon Theatre**, on Plateia Vardaki, was designed by the French architect Chabeau and is a replica of La Scala in Milan. There are terrific views from the church of **Anastasis**, on top of Vrodado Hill; head north from Plateia Miaouli to get there.

Vrodado and Ermoupolis merge fairly seamlessly, but **Ano Syros** – a medieval settlement with narrow alleyways and whitewashed houses – is quite different. It's a fascinating place to wander around and has views of neighbouring islands. On the way up check out the **cemetery**, which has ostentatious mausoleums reminiscent of Athens' First Cemetery. The finest of the Catholic churches is the 13th century **Agios Georgios** cathedral. Close by is the **Agios Ioannis** Capuchin monastery, founded in 1535 to minister to the poor.

Ano Syros was the birthplace of Markos Vamvakaris, the celebrated *rembetika* singer. A small **museum** on Piatsa, the town's main thoroughfare, houses his personal effects and records.

Places to Stay

Domatia owners are discouraged from meeting ferries, but there are plenty of rooms in the centre of town. *Rooms Central (☎ 28 509)* on Plateia Miaouli has spacious singles/doubles/triples for 8000/10,000/ 12,000 dr with a large lounge area and shared fridge. It's a colourful place that has made no attempt to upgrade its decor in the past 30 years – quite a treat. The faded but characterful *Hotel Aktaion (☎ 82 675)*, by the waterfront, has rooms for 6000/8000/ 12,000 dr; most have private bathroom.

Villa Nefeli (☎ 87 076), on Hiou, is newer and has doubles with bathroom for 10,000 dr. *Ariadne (☎ 80 245)*, behind the waterfront near the corner of Agios Proiou and Nikolaou Filini, has nice rooms for 10,000 dr. *Kastro Rooms to Let (☎ 88 064, 093-850 401, Kalomenopoulou 12)*, in an old house east of Plateia Miaouli, has rooms for 12,000 dr.

Ipatia Guesthouse (☎ 83 575), overlooking Agios Nikolaos Bay, is a beautiful, exquisitely restored neoclassical mansion. Spacious doubles/triples with original ceiling frescoes and antique furniture are a steal at 15,000/18,000 dr. At the southern end of the waterfront about 100m from the bus station and quay, the clean and tidy *Esperance Rooms & Studios (☎ 81 671)* has doubles for 16,000 dr, with TV, air-con and port view. *Villa Nostos (☎ 84 226, 2 Spartiaton)*, an old mansion west of the Agios Nikolaos church, has spacious, simple rooms for 18,700/14,700 dr with/without bathroom.

The spiffy B class *Hotel Hermes (☎ 83 011)*, on the waterfront at Plateia Kanari, has comfortable singles/doubles starting at 15,000/24,000 dr, with TV, bathroom, air-con, telephone and breakfast. A few doors away from Esperance Rooms & Studios, the over-renovated *Diogenis Hotel (☎ 86 301)* charges 17,000/22,000 dr for rooms with TV and minibar.

North-east of the port, *Sea Colours Apartments (☎ 83 400, 81 183, fax 83 508)* has two-person studios for 16,500 dr and four-person apartments for 35,000 dr. To find it, descend the steps after Agios Nikolaos church; it's on the right, perched above lovely Agios Nikolaos Bay.

Syrou Melathron (☎ 85 963, fax 87 806), on the bay just past Agios Nikolaos church, is rather ostentatious and borders on kitsch, despite its neoclassical shell. It has doubles with/without sea view for 35,000/29,000 dr.

Vourlis Luxury Hotel (☎/fax 88 440, Mavrokordatou 5) is a beautifully restored neoclassical mansion about 100m beyond Syrou Melathron. Suites with antique furniture and spectacular sea view start at 37,400 dr a double, but there are also doubles out the back for 24,000 dr. Make sure you book well in advance – it has only eight rooms.

Places to Eat

The waterfront is lined with restaurants and cafes. *Psistaria Giannena*, at the eastern end of the waterfront, specialises in *kokoretsi*

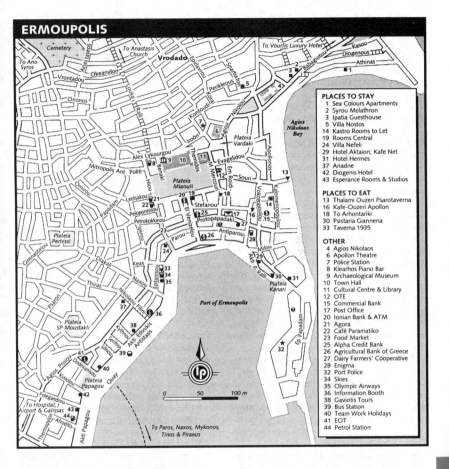

ERMOUPOLIS

PLACES TO STAY
1 Sea Colours Apartments
2 Syrou Melathron
3 Ipatia Guesthouse
5 Villa Nostos
14 Kastro Rooms to Let
19 Rooms Central
24 Villa Nefeli
29 Hotel Aktaion; Kafe Net
31 Hotel Hermes
37 Ariadne
42 Diogenis Hotel
43 Esperance Rooms & Studios

PLACES TO EAT
13 Thalami Ouzeri Psarotaverna
16 Kafe-Ouzeri Apollon
18 To Arhontariki
30 Psistaria Giannena
33 Taverna 1935

OTHER
4 Agios Nikolaos
6 Apollon Theatre
7 Police Station
8 Klearhos Piano Bar
9 Archaeological Museum
10 Town Hall
11 Cultural Centre & Library
12 OTE
15 Commercial Bank
17 Post Office
20 Ionian Bank & ATM
21 Agora
22 Café Paramatiko
23 Food Market
25 Alpha Credit Bank
26 Agricultural Bank of Greece
27 Dairy Farmers' Cooperative
28 Enigma
32 Port Police
34 Skies
35 Olympic Airways
36 Information Booth
38 Gaviotis Tours
39 Bus Station
40 Team Work Holidays
41 EOT
44 Petrol Station

(spit-roasted lamb's entrails) for 1650 dr, and spiced rolled pork for 1850 dr. *Taverna 1935*, near Olympic Airways, is one of the better waterfront places, with moderately priced traditional fare, including fresh fish. *Kafe-Ouzeri Apollon*, a couple of blocks in from the port on Stefanou, is a great place to sample octopus and fish grilled over hot coals.

To Arhontariki, on Vikela, one block south-east of Plateia Miaouli, is deservedly popular. Its extensive menu features all the regular fare plus unusual and delicious dishes such as parsley salad for 700 dr, oriental pie with *bastourma* (spiced, cured meat) for 1000 dr, mushrooms baked with cheese for 1700 dr and veal with plums for 1800 dr. Meals come with warm, freshly baked bread, and the wine list includes regional favourites from all over Greece.

Thalami Ouzeri Psarotaverna (☎ 85 331) looks out over the crystalline waters of Agios Nikolaos Bay. Fresh fish is sold by the kilo, and *kakavia*, a local fish soup, is available. The setting is spectacular and the

CYCLADES

food pretty good, but the service is a little indifferent. To get there, follow Souri (which runs along the southern side of Plateia Miaouli) east to its end.

Frankosyriani, up in Ano Syros near the Vamvakaris museum, is a great place to stop for a drink and mezedes. The view from the terrace is superb and you can sing along with Vamvakaris as you sup.

The best place for fresh produce is the *food market* on Hiou. The tiny Dairy Farmers' Cooperative on Protopapadaki, near Androu, sells local cheese and yogurt.

Entertainment

There are plenty of bars around Plateia Miaouli and along the waterfront. *Cafe Piramatiko*, on the western edge of the plateia, is definitely a hot spot, with crowds spilling outside. Next door, *Agora* is a bit more subdued but also fairly classy.

A few door up, *Klearhos Piano Bar* (☎ 81 441) is a groovy but well established place with Gustav Klimt cushions and good music, catering to an eclectic crowd. Klearhos, the owner, is partial to getting up and cranking out a tune or two most nights. There's no sign, so follow your ears.

Enigma, a metal hang-out with an interesting edgy atmosphere, is on Androu, a few doors back from the waterfront. If bouzouki is your cup of tea, there are quite a few places. Try *Skies*, on the waterfront near Taverna 1935.

GALISSAS Γαλησσάς

The west coast resort of Galissas has one of the island's best beaches: a 900m crescent of sand, shaded by tamarisk trees. **Armeos**, a walk round the rocks to the left of the bay, is an official nudist beach.

Places to Stay

Syros' two camping grounds are both here. The bizarrely named *Two Hearts Camping* (☎ 42 052, 42 321), set in a pistachio orchard, has most facilities and charges 1500 dr per person, and 900 dr per tent; a minibus meets ferries in high season. The other site is *Yianna Camping* (☎ 42 418), but it has minimal facilities and is a barren, dusty place despite a forest of tamarisk trees.

There are plenty of domatia available, mostly much of a muchness in standard concrete box style. *Rooms P Sicala* (☎ 42 643), on the way to Two Hearts Camping, is a cute little traditional place shaded by jasmine, grapevines and bougainvillea. Doubles are 8700 dr. On the right of the main road, not far from the branch road to the beach, *Karmelina Rooms* (☎ 42 320) has clean rooms for 7000 dr with communal kitchen. Close by, *Pension Blue Sky* (☎ 43 410, fax 43 411) has double/quad studios and apartments for 16,000/19,000 dr.

Hotel Benois (☎ 42 833), close to the beach, has singles/doubles/triples with fridge, TV, air-con and bathroom for 15,000/19,000/24,000 dr, including breakfast.

The A class *Dolphin Bay Resort* (☎ 42 924, fax 42 843) is a large white cluster of buildings left of the beach as you face the sea. Doubles with satellite TV, private safe and other amenities are 32,000 dr, including breakfast.

Places to Eat

Markos O Psilos, next to the minimarket, serves good, cheap meals, as do most of the other *tavernas*. *Argo Café*, next to Hotel Benois, is a bar-cafe serving breakfast, juices, shakes and snacks. It's a nice relaxing place to hang out, with comfy cushions and deck chairs on the patio.

AROUND SYROS

The beaches south of Galissas all have domatia and some have hotels. The first is **Finikas**, with a nice, tree-lined beach and a shop selling interesting old things as well as local crafts. The next, **Posidonia**, has a sand and pebble beach shaded by tamarisk trees.

Farther south, **Agathopes** has a nice, tree-bordered sandy beach. On the south coast, tranquil **Megas Gialos** has two sand beaches.

Vari, the next bay, has a sandy beach, but is more developed. *Hotel Domenica* (☎ 61 216) has air-con doubles for 13,500 dr and *Hotel Kamelo* (☎ 61 217) has singles/doubles for 10,000/16,000 dr.

Azolimnos, the next beach along, has a few *fish tavernas*.

Mykonos Μύκονος

☎ 0289 • postcode 846 00 • pop 6170

Mykonos is perhaps the most visited and expensive of all Greek islands (although these days Santorini runs a pretty close second) and it has the most sophisticated nightlife. Despite its reputation as the gay capital of Greece, this shouldn't – and doesn't – deter others. The days when Mykonos was the favourite rendezvous for the world's rich and famous may be over, but the island probably still has more poseurs per square metre than any other Mediterranean resort.

Depending on your temperament, you'll either be captivated or take one look and stay on the ferry. Barren, low-lying Mykonos would never win a beauty contest, but it has some decent beaches and is the jumping-off point for the sacred island of Delos.

Getting There & Away

Air There are at least five flights daily to and from Athens (19,100 dr), as well as flights to Santorini (15,400 dr, five weekly), Thessaloniki (27,900 dr, three weekly) and Rhodes (22,900 dr, two weekly).

Ferry Mykonos has daily services to Rafina (five hours, 4100 dr) via Tinos (30 minutes, 1100 dr) and Andros (2½ hours, 2600 dr); to Piraeus (six hours, 5100 dr) via Tinos and Syros (1½ hours, 1500 dr); and to Naxos (three hours, 1900 dr), Paros (two hours, 1800 dr), Ios (five hours, 3100 dr) and Santorini (six hours, 3600 dr).

There are six ferries weekly to Amorgos (six hours, 3100 dr), five to Iraklia (five to

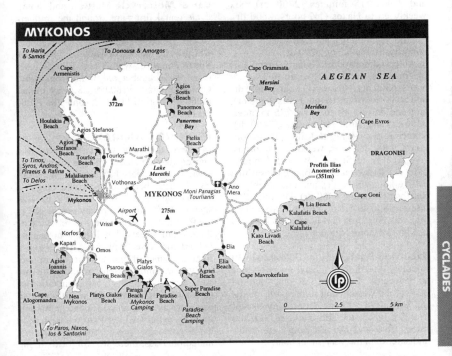

MYKONOS

eight hours, 2100 dr), Shinousa (4½ to 7½ hours, 2500 dr) and Koufonisia (5½ to seven hours, 2500 dr), and two to Samos (3½ to 5¾ hours, 5300 dr), Patmos (four to 10 hours, 5000 dr), Lipsi (five to 11 hours, 4900 dr) and Crete (10 hours, 7100 dr). There are two weekly to Skiathos (8½ hours, 5100 dr), Thessaloniki (18 hours, 9100 dr) and Ikaria (2¾ hours, 3100 dr), and one weekly to Fourni (four hours), Leros (6¼ hours, 4300 dr), Kalymnos (seven hours, 5000 dr), Kos (eight hours, 5000 dr), Nisyros (10 hours, 4800 dr), Tilos (11 hours, 5000 dr), Symi (13 hours, 5600 dr), Rhodes (14½ hours, 6700 dr), Megisti (19 hours, 7900 dr) and Donousa (two hours, 2400 dr).

Hydrofoil & Catamaran There are daily catamarans connecting Mykonos with Andros (1¼ hours, 5300 dr), Paros (45 minutes, 3400 dr), Syros (35 minutes, 3100 dr) and Tinos (15 minutes, 2400 dr). Six weekly go to Naxos (1½ hours, 3600 dr), Piraeus (three hours, 10,000 dr) and Rafina (2½ hours, 8300 dr), and two weekly go to Amorgos (three hours, 6200 dr).

At least three hydrofoils daily go to Paros (45 minutes, 3400 dr), two go to Ios (2¾ hours, 6300 dr), Naxos (1½ hours, 3600 dr) and Santorini (three to four hours, 6800 dr), and one daily goes to Syros (35 minutes, 3100 dr) and Tinos (15 minutes, 2400 dr). There are six weekly to Milos (2¾ to four hours, 9900 dr), three weekly to Amorgos, five weekly to Sifnos (2½ to 3½ hours, 6100 dr), four weekly to Folegandros (three to five hours, 5700 dr), and one weekly to Serifos (2½ hours, 6300 dr), Donousa (2½ hours, 5800 dr), Koufonisia (two hours, 5000 dr), Shinousa (1¾ hours, 5000 dr) and Iraklia (1½ hours, 5000 dr).

Excursion Boat Boats for Delos (20 to 30 minutes, 1900 dr return) leave every hour or so between 8.30 am and 1.20 pm, from the quay at the western end of the port, returning between 12.20 and 3 pm daily except Monday (when the site is closed). Of the three, *Hera* and *Delos Express* are faster and safer than the very small boat.

Between May and September, guided tours (8000 dr, including boat fare and site entrance) are conducted in English, French and German. Tickets are available from several travel agencies.

A boat also departs for Delos from Platys Gialos at 10.15 am daily.

Getting Around
To/From the Airport Buses no longer serve Mykonos' airport, 3km south-east of the town centre. A taxi is around 1300 dr.

Bus Mykonos (Hora) has two bus stations. The northern station has frequent departures to Ornos, Agios Stefanos (via Tourlos), Ano Mera, Elia, Kato Livadi and Kalafatis. The southern station serves Agios Ioannis Beach, Paraga, Psarou, Platys Gialos, Paradise Beach, and, sometimes, Ornos.

Car & Motorcycle Most car and motorcycle rental firms are around the southern bus station.

Caïque Caïques leave Mykonos (Hora) for Super Paradise, Agrari and Elia beaches (June to September only) and from Platys Gialos to Paradise (800 dr), Super Paradise (1000 dr), Agrari (1200 dr) and Elia (1200 dr) beaches.

MYKONOS (HORA)
Mykonos, the island's port and capital, is a warren-like Cycladic village turned toy town. It can be very hard to find your bearings – just when you think you've got it worked out, you'll find yourself back at square one. Throngs of pushy people add to the frustration. Familiarise yourself with the three main streets that form a horseshoe behind the waterfront and you'll have a fighting chance of finding your way around.

Even the most disenchanted could not deny that Mykonos – a conglomeration of chic boutiques, houses with brightly painted balconies and bougainvillea and geraniums growing against whiter than white walls – has a certain charm. And, somehow, against incredible odds, there are still locals living here; chances are you'll glimpse an old Greek granny watering the plants on her balcony while the club next door pumps out throbbing disco.

Orientation
The waterfront is to the right of the ferry quay (facing inland), beyond the tiny town beach. The central square is Plateia Manto Mavrogenous (usually called Taxi Square), south along the waterfront.

The northern bus station is near the OTE, while the southern bus station is on the road to Ornos. The quay for boats to Delos is at the western end of the waterfront. South of here is Mykonos' famous row of windmills and the Little Venice quarter, where balconies overhang the sea.

Information
Mykonos has no tourist office. When you get off the ferry, you will see a low building with four numbered offices. No 1 is the Hotel Reservation Department (☎ 24 540), open 8 am to midnight daily; No 2 is the Association of Rooms & Apartments (☎ 26 860), open 10 am to 6 pm daily; No 3 has camping information (☎ 22 852); and No 4 houses the tourist police (☎ 22 482), with variable opening times.

The National Bank of Greece is on the waterfront and has an ATM. Two doors away, Delia Travel (☎ 22 322) represents American Express.

The post office is in the southern part of town, with the police (☎ 22 235) next door. The OTE is beside the northern bus station. The Mykonos Cyber Cafe, on the road between the southern bus station and the windmills, provides email access and connections for laptops; it also rents mobile phones. The Public Medical Center of Mykonos (☎ 23 994, 23 996) is on the road to Ano Mera. The port police (☎ 22 218) are on the waterfront, above the National Bank.

Museums
There are five museums. The **archaeological museum**, near the quay, houses pottery from Delos and some grave stelae and jewellery from the island of Renia (Delos' necropolis). Chief exhibits are a pithos featuring a Trojan War scene in relief, and a statue of Heracles. It's open 8 am to 2.30 pm Tuesday to Sunday. Admission is 500 dr.

The **Aegean Maritime Museum** has a fantastic collection of nautical paraphernalia from all over the Aegean, including fascinating models of ancient vessels. It's open 10.30 am to 1 pm and 6.30 to 9 pm daily. Admission is 500 dr.

Next door, **Lena's House** is a 19th century, middle class Mykonian house with furnishings intact. It's open 6 to 9 pm daily (from 7 pm Sunday). Entrance is free.

The **folklore museum**, housed in an 18th century sea captain's house, features a large collection of memorabilia, a reconstructed 19th century kitchen and a bedroom with a four-poster bed. The museum, near the Delos quay, is open 5.30 to 8.30 pm daily. Entrance is free.

The **windmill museum** is on Agiou Ioannou, near the road to Ano Mera. Entrance is free but opening times are very erratic.

Church of Panagia Paraportiani
The Panagia Paraportiani is the most famous of Mykonos' many churches. It is actually four little churches amalgamated into one beautiful, white, lumpy, asymmetrical building. It could do with some paint, but even so, the interplay of light and shade on the multifaceted structure make it a photographer's delight.

Activities
Dive Adventures (☎ 26 539), on Paradise Beach, offers the full range of scuba diving courses right up to instructor level. The Aphrodite Diving School is owned by Aphrodite Beach Hotel (☎ 71 367) on Kalafatis Beach. Other activities include tennis and horse riding, and there's a gym and aerobics.

Organised Tours
Excursion boats run day trips to Delos. See the Mykonos Getting There & Away section for details.

CYCLADES

MYKONOS (HORA)

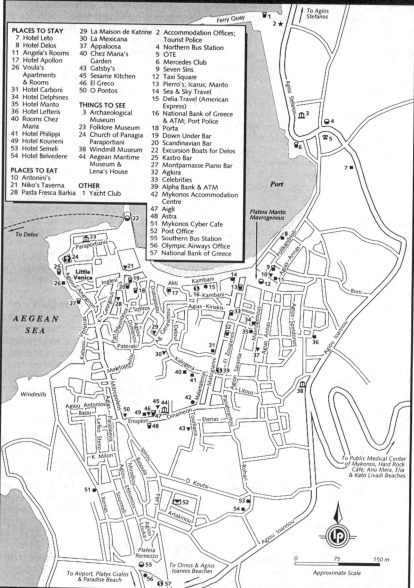

PLACES TO STAY
7 Hotel Leto
8 Hotel Delos
11 Angela's Rooms
17 Hotel Apollon
26 Voula's
   Apartments
   & Rooms
31 Hotel Carboni
34 Hotel Delphines
35 Hotel Manto
36 Hotel Lefteris
40 Rooms Chez
   Maria
41 Hotel Philippi
49 Hotel Kouneni
53 Hotel Semeli
54 Hotel Belvedere

PLACES TO EAT
10 Antonini's
21 Niko's Taverna
28 Pasta Fresca Barkia

29 La Maison de Katrine
30 La Mexicana
37 Appaloosa
40 Chez Maria's
   Garden
43 Gatsby's
45 Sesame Kitchen
46 El Greco
50 O Pontos

THINGS TO SEE
3 Archaeological
   Museum
23 Folklore Museum
24 Church of Panagia
   Paraportiani
38 Windmill Museum
44 Aegean Maritime
   Museum &
   Lena's House

OTHER
1 Yacht Club

2 Accommodation Offices;
   Tourist Police
4 Northern Bus Station
5 OTE
6 Mercedes Club
9 Seven Sins
12 Taxi Square
13 Pierro's; Icarus; Manto
14 Sea & Sky Travel
15 Delia Travel (American
   Express)
16 National Bank of Greece
   & ATM; Port Police
18 Porta
19 Down Under Bar
20 Scandinavian Bar
22 Excursion Boats for Delos
25 Kastro Bar
27 Montparnasse Piano Bar
32 Agkira
33 Celebrities
39 Alpha Bank & ATM
42 Mykonos Accommodation
   Centre
47 Aigli
48 Astra
51 Mykonos Cyber Cafe
52 Post Office
55 Southern Bus Station
56 Olympic Airways Office
57 National Bank of Greece

Places to Stay – Budget

If you arrive without a reservation between June and September and manage to find suitably priced accommodation, take it. Otherwise seek the assistance of the accommodation organisations mentioned in the Information section, or ask John at the Mykonos Accommodation Centre (☎ 23 408), on the corner of Enoplon Dinameon and Malamatenias. If you choose domatia from owners meeting ferries, ask if they charge for transport – some do.

Angela's Rooms (☎ 22 967), on Taxi Square, has doubles with bathroom for 15,000 dr. For a place with a bit of character, try the old-world D class *Hotel Apollon* (☎ 22 223, fax 24 237), on the waterfront. It's been around since 1930 and most of the furniture looks older, but it is very well kept and the owner is sweet. Clean and tidy singles/doubles go for 12,000/15,000 dr. *Hotel Delphines* (☎ 24 505, fax 27 307), on Mavrogenous, is also run by friendly people and charges 13,000/16,500 dr for rooms with TV, fridge and bathroom.

Hotel Philippi (☎ 22 294, 24 680), on Kalogera, has an agrarian feel; the garden out the back has fruit trees and a motley assortment of flowers planted in rows as if they were vegetables. Doubles (one of which seems to occupy an old stable) with bathroom go for 16,000 dr. Next door, *Rooms Chez Maria* (☎ 22 480) is a pretty place with potted geraniums out the front and lovely doubles/triples for 15,000/20,000 dr with bathroom.

Hotel Lefteris (☎ 27 117, Apollonos 9), in the residential backstreets away from the hubbub, also has geraniums on its steps. Singles/doubles, some with balcony, go for 16,000/21,000 dr. Signs point the way from Taxi Square. The D class *Hotel Carboni* (☎ 22 217, fax 23 264), on Andronikou Matogianni, has plain but clean doubles/triples for 17,000/21,000 dr with TV and bathroom.

Places to Stay – Mid-Range

The C class *Hotel Delos* (☎ 22 517, fax 22 312), on the town beach, charges 18,000/23,000 dr for doubles/triples, including bathroom. *Hotel Manto* (☎ 22 330, fax 26 664), just off Mavrogenous, has singles/doubles for 18,000/27,000 dr with bathroom.

Little Venice's only seafront accommodation is *Voula's Apartments & Rooms* (☎ 22 951, 0945-223 026). Its balconied rooms are above a club and taverna, so bring earplugs if you're not prepared to party. Doubles/triples are 15,000/20,000 dr with bathroom, more with balcony. Voula meets boats and does not charge for transport.

Hotel Kouneni (☎ 22 301), on Enoplon Dinameon, has a charming garden; doubles with bathroom cost 28,000 dr.

Places to Stay – Top End

The time-worn *Hotel Leto* (☎ 22 207, fax 23 985), facing the town beach, has singles/doubles/triples for a whopping 59,000/70,000/93,000 dr, with breakfast.

Much better value can be found at *Hotel Belvedere* (☎ 25 122, fax 25 126) and *Hotel Semeli* (☎ 27 466, fax 27 467), next to each other on Rohari, away from the centre of town. The hotels, run by the same family (the Belvedere by a brother, the Semeli by a sister), are built around the old family house that has been converted into a very good traditional restaurant.

Both places are stylish and have made an effort to combine old-world charm with modern comforts. The Belvedere has jacuzzis, steam room, fitness studio, DVD, Internet corner (no access charge) and a large and lovely conference room. Both hotels have a pool, bar and lounge areas and all rooms in both have balconies with a view over town. Semeli charges 55,000 dr a double, including breakfast. Belvedere charges 59,000 dr for a double; suites are also available.

For more top-end listings, see the Beaches and Ano Mera sections.

Places to Eat

The high prices charged in many eating establishments are not always indicative of quality. The fish served in most of the tavernas is cheap frozen stuff imported from Asia which often tastes like warmed up old boots. If you want good fish, try another island.

Antonini's, on Taxi Square, is where the locals go. It serves reliably good Greek food and is reasonably priced – try the moussaka. At *Niko's Taverna*, up from the Delos quay, waiters take your order on a palmtop, which seems to make service pretty efficient. The food is nothing great, but it's better than what's on offer in a lot of the other 'traditional' places. Avoid *Restaurant Klimataria*: its food is dreadful.

Pasta Fresca Barkia, on Georgouli, serves pizza and fresh pasta made on the premises; *tagliatelle siciliana* is 2100 dr. *Gatsby's* has a slightly refined atmosphere and serves some interesting food, including shrimp with spinach and green apple in a hot black sauce (3300 dr) and *spaghetti alla fornala* (with garlic, walnuts and parmesan; 2500 dr). *Appaloosa* is a cute little Mexican-inspired place that has guacamole (1500 dr) and nachos (2000 dr), as well as more substantial burgers (2800 dr) and pasta dishes (from 2700 dr).

El Greco, next to Hotel Kouneni, offers dishes such as stuffed fresh anchovies with white *tarama* and fresh herbs (1650 dr), zucchini stuffed with Mykonos cheese and fennel (1850 dr), *sofrito* (Corfu-style veal with parsley, garlic and vinegar; 2450 dr) and mountain goat (2300 dr). Some of their fish is local. *Sesame Kitchen*, a few doors up, serves innovative fare, much of it vegetarian, including Delos salad with arugula, fresh asparagus, Mykonos goat's cheese and sesame seeds (3000 dr), and veal fillet with radicchio and balsamic vinegar (6200 dr).

Chez Maria's Garden has a lovely outdoor candlelit setting. It's a bit pricey (set menus are 6000 dr per person – and that's considerably less than a la carte) and a tad pretentious, but the food isn't at all bad. *La Maison de Katrine* (☎ 22 169), probably the classiest restaurant, serves Greek food with a French twist. It's been open since 1971 and has diligent service and a relaxed, unfussy atmosphere. The white taramasalata is superb, as is the *coq au vin*, but make sure you leave room for the *tarte tatin* with caramelised calvados cream. Expect to pay at least 15,000 dr per person for a full meal including wine. It's on Gerasimou at Nikou.

There's a cluster of cheap fast-food outlets and creperies in the centre of town; *O Pontos* serves gyros for 400 dr. There are several supermarkets and fruit stalls, particularly around the southern bus station.

Entertainment

Seven Sins, the oldest bar in Mykonos (established 1965), is a cosy little place with background music by, appropriately enough, the Stones and other 60s outfits. For classy ambience and a mature but not necessarily sedate crowd, try *Montparnasse Piano Bar* in Little Venice.

On Enaplon Dinameon is a cluster of large bars playing dance music, including *Astra* and *Aigli*. *Agkira* ('anchor') and *Celebrities* (pity about the name) on Matogianni are in a similar vein, but rather more chic.

Gay venues include *Porta*, which has a reputation for being the best pick-up bar in town; *Kastro Bar* in Little Venice; and *Pierro's*, which is the place for late-night dancing. Adjoining it, *Icarus* and *Manto* are popular haunts.

Mercedes Club, near the archaeological museum, attracts an older clientele. *Cavo Paradiso* (☎ 26 124), 300m above Paradise Beach, has all-night raves with international DJs; doors open at 3 am.

The cheap alcohol at *Down Under Bar* and *Scandinavian Bar* attracts hordes of backpackers and kids on Kontiki Tours; go for it if that's your thing. *Hard Rock Cafe*, about 4km along the Ano Mera road, has a restaurant, nightclub and pool. If you're roomless or an insomniac, head for the *Yacht Club*, by the quay, which is open 24 hours. A pink shuttle bus runs from the Yacht Club to the Hard Rock every half-hour between noon and 4 am.

AROUND MYKONOS
Beaches

The nearest beaches to Hora are **Malaliamos** and the tiny, crowded **Tourlos**, 2km to the north. **Agios Stefanos**, 2km beyond, is larger but just as crowded. To the south, beyond

Old tunnel in Antoniou winery, Santorini, Cyclades

DIANA MAYFIELD

Windmills, Mykonos, Cyclades

JOHN ELK III

Catching the sun's last rays, Amorgos, Cyclades

JON DAVISON

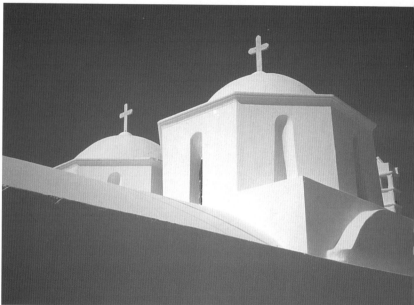

Hora, Amorgos, Cyclades

Black sand beach at Kamari, Santorini, Cyclades

Moni Hozoviotissas, Amorgos, Cyclades

It's a Cat's Life

Cats are everywhere in Greece: stalking plump pigeons around Athens' parliament house; congregating under restaurant tables in the hope of scavenging scraps; and looking cute on tourist-geared calendars and postcards. Most of the cats are strays, but sometimes you'll see a domestic cat – sporting a collar and bell – out hunting with them.

Greece is swarming with cats because the expense of having them spayed is prohibitive. Owners allow their female cats to produce litter after litter.

Although Greeks recognise that the mighty cat population keeps the rodent numbers down, the cats are still regarded as a major problem. To keep them at bay, some restaurateurs display signs requesting that patrons do not feed the cats. Other restaurant owners will discourage cats from bothering diners by feeding the cats leftovers themselves.

Travellers should take care when feeding the cats – although many of them are friendly, hunger can make them snatch at food with their paws, sometimes scratching or puncturing the skin. And people with a phobia about cats may feel very uneasy in a country which has so many!

Whatever Greeks and tourists feel about the cats, the population is likely to increase until the cost of desexing them comes down.

Ornos, is **Agios Ioannis**, where *Shirley Valentine* was filmed. **Psarou**, east of Ornos, is a pretty little cove. **Platys Gialos**, on the south-west coast, is bumper to bumper sun lounges backed by very ordinary package tour hotels – really not nice at all.

From here, caïques call at the island's best beaches farther around the south coast: **Paradise**, **Super Paradise**, **Agrari** and **Elia**. Nudism is accepted on all these beaches. Elia is the last caïque stop, so is the least crowded. The next beach along, **Kato Livadi**, is also relatively quiet. North-coast beaches are exposed to the meltemi, but **Panormos** and **Agios Sostis** are sheltered and uncrowded.

Places to Stay Mykonos has two camping grounds: *Paradise Beach Camping* (☎ 22 852) on Paradise Beach and *Mykonos Camping* (☎ 24 578) on Paraga Beach (10 minutes walk from Platys Gialos). Both have good facilities and charge 1800 dr per person per day, plus 1000 dr per tent per day. Paradise Beach Camping also has two-person bungalows for 10,000 dr. Minibuses from the camping grounds meet ferries.

There are many top end places around the coast. *Ornos Beach Hotel* (☎ 23 216) has great sea views and a swimming pool; doubles are 36,000 dr. *Villa Katerina* (☎ 23 414), a quiet, romantic place, 300m up the hill above Agios Ioannis, has a garden and pool. Double studios cost 24,500 dr. Close by, the A class *Apollonia Bay* (☎ 27 890) charges 52,000 dr for doubles, including breakfast. At Agios Stefanos, the A class *Princess of Mykonos* (☎ 23 806) was once a Jane Fonda hang-out. Singles/doubles are 40,000/46,000 dr with breakfast.

On Kalafatis Beach, the A class *Aphrodite Beach Hotel* (☎ 71 367) has masses of facilities including water sports and scuba diving. Doubles/triples cost 58,000/71,000 dr with breakfast. The deluxe *Tharroe of Mykonos* (☎ 27 370) in Vrissi has singles/doubles for 60,000/88,000 dr, including breakfast. The A class *Kivotos* (☎ 24 094) in Ornos has its own private beach, as well as fitness centre, restaurants, bars etc. Rooms are 72,000/79,000 dr; superior rooms go for 86,000/98,000 dr.

Ano Mera Ανω Μέρα

The village of Ano Mera, 7km east of Hora, is the island's only inland settlement. On its central square is the sumptuous 6th century

CYCLADES

Moni Panagias Tourlianis, which has a fine carved marble bell tower, an ornate wooden iconostasis carved in Florence in the late 1700s, and 16th century icons painted by members of the Cretan School. Speakers turned up to 11 crank out beautiful Orthodox hymns, which makes for a powerful experience. It's open 9 am to 1 pm and 2 to 7.30 pm daily.

The A class *Ano Mera Hotel (☎ 71 215, fax 71 276)* has a pool, restaurant and disco. Singles/doubles/triples are 24,300/30,400/40,700 dr with breakfast, but there's no real reason why you should stay up here. The central square is edged with tavernas. *O Apostolis*, near the bus stop, has decent traditional food.

Delos Δήλος

Despite its diminutive size, Delos is one of the most important archaeological sites in Greece, and certainly the most important in the Cyclades. Lying a few kilometres off the west coast of Mykonos, this sacred island is the mythical birthplace of the twins Apollo and Artemis. The site is World Heritage-listed, and, like most archaeological sites, it is closed on Mondays.

History
Delos was first inhabited in the 3rd millennium BC. In the 8th century BC, a festival in honour of Apollo was established; the oldest temples and shrines on the island (many donated by Naxians) date from this era. For a long time, the Athenians coveted Delos, seeing its strategic position as one from where they could control the Aegean. By the 5th century BC, it had come under their jurisdiction.

Athens' power grew during the Persian Wars, and in 478 BC it established an alliance known as the Delian League that kept its treasury on Delos. Athens carried out a number of 'purifications', decreeing that no-one could be born or could die on Delos, thus strengthening its control over the island by removing the native population.

Delos reached the height of its power in Hellenistic times, becoming one of the three most important religious centres in Greece and a flourishing centre of commerce. It traded throughout the Mediterranean and was populated with wealthy merchants, mariners and bankers from as far away as Egypt and Syria. These inhabitants built temples to the various gods worshipped in their homelands, although Apollo remained the principal deity.

The Romans made Delos a free port in 167 BC, which brought even greater prosperity – due largely to a lucrative slave market that sold up to 10,000 people a day. Later, Delos was prey to pirates and to looters of antiquities.

Getting There & Away
See Excursion Boats in the Mykonos section for schedules and prices of services from Mykonos. Boats also operate to Delos from Tinos and Paros.

ANCIENT DELOS
Orientation & Information
The quay where excursion boats dock is south of the tranquil Sacred Harbour. Many of the most significant finds from Delos are in the National Archaeological Museum in Athens. The site museum has a modest collection.

Overnight stays on Delos are forbidden, and boat schedules allow a maximum of six or seven hours there (depending on which boat you're with). Bring water and food, as the cafeteria is poor value. Wear a hat and sensible shoes. Entrance to the site costs 1200 dr (museum included). If you hire a guide once you get to Delos, you'll need to fork out more cash.

Exploring the Site
Following is an outline of some significant archaeological remains on the site. For further details, buy a guidebook at the ticket office, or – even better – take a guided tour.

If you have the energy, climb Mt Kythnos (113m), which is south-east of the harbour, to see the layout of Delos. There are terrific

ANCIENT DELOS

1 Stadium	16 Stoa of Antigonas	31 Wall of the Triarus
2 Gymnasium	17 Sanctuary of Dionysos	32 House of Cleopatra
3 House of Comedians	18 Museum	33 House of Dionysos
4 Sanctuary of Archegetes	19 Temple of Artemis	34 House of Hermes
5 House of Diadumenos	20 Poros Temple	35 Sanctuary of the Syrian Gods
6 Lake House	21 Temple of the Athenians	36 House of the Trident
7 Hill House	22 Keraton	37 Shrine to the Samothracian
8 Institution of the Poseidoniasts	23 Temple of Apollo	Great Gods
9 Palaestra	24 Stoa of the Naxiots	38 Shrine to the Egyptian Gods
10 Terrace of the Lions	25 House of the Naxiots	39 Cistern
11 Roman Wall	26 Monument of the Bulls	40 Theatre
12 Agora of the Italians	27 Agora of the Competialists	41 House of the Dolphins
13 Stoa of Poseidon	28 Stoa of Philip V	42 House of the Masks
14 Dodecatheon	29 South Stoa	43 Sacred Cave
15 Tourist Pavillion	30 Agora of the Delians	44 Warehouses

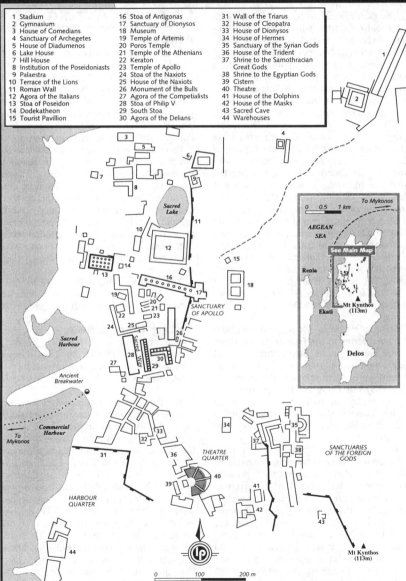

CYCLADES

views of the surrounding islands on clear days.

The path is reached by walking through the **Theatre Quarter**, where Delos' wealthiest inhabitants built their houses. These houses surrounded peristyle courtyards, with mosaics (a status symbol) the most striking feature of each house. These colourful mosaics were exquisite art works, mostly representational and offset by intricate geometric borders. The most lavish dwellings were the **House of Dionysos**, named after the mosaic depicting the wine god riding a panther; and the **House of Cleopatra**, where headless statues of the owners were found. The **House of the Trident** was one of the grandest. The **House of the Masks**, probably an actors' hostelry, has another mosaic of Dionysos resplendently astride a panther, and the **House of the Dolphins** has another exceptional mosaic.

The **theatre** dates from 300 BC and had a large cistern, the remains of which can be seen. It supplied much of the town with water. The houses of the wealthy had their own cisterns – essential as Delos was almost as parched and barren then as it is today.

Descending from Mt Kythnos, explore the **Sanctuaries of the Foreign Gods**. Here, at the **Shrine to the Samothracian Great Gods**, the Kabeiroi (the twins Dardanos and Aeton) were worshipped. At the **Sanctuary of the Syrian Gods** are the remains of a theatre where an audience watched ritual orgies. There is also an area where Egyptian deities, including Serapis and Isis, were worshipped.

The **Sanctuary of Apollo**, to the north of the harbour, contains temples dedicated to him. It is also the site of the much-photographed **Terrace of the Lions**. These proud beasts, carved from marble, were offerings from the people of Naxos, presented to Delos in the 7th century BC to guard the sacred area. To the north-east is the **Sacred Lake** (dry since it was drained in 1925 to prevent malarial mosquitoes breeding) where, according to legend, Leto gave birth to Apollo and Artemis.

Paros & Antiparos
Πάρος & Αντίπαρος

PAROS
☎ 0284 • postcode 844 00 • pop 9591

Paros is an attractive island with softly contoured, terraced hills culminating in Mt Profitis Ilias (770m). The island is famous for the pure white marble from which it prospered from the Early Cycladic period onwards – the *Venus de Milo* was carved from Parian marble, as was Napoleon's tomb.

Paros is now the main ferry hub for the Greek islands. The port town of Parikia is the busiest on the island, largely because of the volume of people waiting for ferry connections. The hubbub surrounding the ferry quay is countered by the remarkably charming and peaceful old hora that lies one block back from the waterfront. The other major settlement, Naoussa, on the north coast, is a pretty resort with a colourful fishing village at its core.

The relatively unspoilt island of Antiparos, 1km south-west of Paros, is easily accessible by car ferry and excursion boat.

Getting There & Away
Air Olympic has at least five flights daily to/from Athens (18,900 dr). The Olympic Airways office (☎ 21 900) is on Plateia Mavrogenous in Parikia.

Ferry Paros offers a comprehensive array of ferry connections. It has frequent links to all of the Cyclades, and is also a regular stop for boats en route from the mainland to the Dodecanese, the North-Eastern Aegean islands of Ikaria and Samos, and Crete.

There are around six boats daily to Piraeus (five hours, 4950 dr), Naxos (one hour, 1350 dr), Ios (2½ hours, 2450 dr) and Santorini (three to four hours, 3050 dr), and two daily to Mykonos (1¾ hours, 1750 dr). There are daily services to Syros (1½ hours, 1550 dr), Tinos (2½ hours, 1750 dr), Amorgos (three to 4½ hours, 2750 dr), Ikaria (four hours, 3350 dr) and Samos (7½ hours, 4250 dr), and six weekly to Sikinos (three to four hours, 1750 dr) and Crete (seven to eight hours, 4950 dr).

There are five ferries weekly to Folegandros (3½ hours, 1950 dr) and Rhodes (12 to 15 hours, 6950 dr), and four to Thessaloniki (12 to 15 hours, 9350 dr), Rafina (seven hours, 4150 dr), Andros (4½ hours, 2750 dr) and Anafi (six hours, 3550 dr). Three weekly go to Astypalea (six hours, 4850 dr) and Koufonisia (4½ hours, 2750 dr).

Two boats weekly serve Skiathos (six hours, 6450 dr), Fourni (five hours, 4050 dr), Kalymnos (6½ hours, 3750 dr), Kos (six to eight hours, 4350 dr), Serifos (three hours, 1000 dr), Sifnos (two hours, 1000 dr), Milos (4½ hours, 2900 dr), Kimolos (four hours, 2250 dr) and Donousa (two to four hours, 2350 dr). Only one weekly connection goes to poor old Patmos (four hours, 3950 dr), Leros (4450 dr), Shinousa (four hours, 2150 dr) and Volos (eight hours, 6950 dr).

There is also a half-hourly car ferry from Pounta on the west coast of Paros to Antiparos (10 minutes, 170 dr – car extra); the first ferry runs to Antiparos at around 7 am, and the last boat back leaves Antiparos at 12.30 am.

Hydrofoil There are at least four hydrofoils daily to Naxos (30 minutes, 2700 dr) and Mykonos (one hour, 3300 dr), and three to Ios (1¼ hours, 4950 dr), Santorini (two hours, 6100 dr), Tinos (1¼ hours, 3500 dr) and Syros (45 minutes, 3100 dr). They run almost daily to Amorgos (1½ hours, 5500 dr), Crete (four hours, 10,000 dr), Folegandros (1½ hours, 3800 dr), Milos (two hours, 5700 dr) and Sifnos (one hour, 1900 dr).

Hydrofoils also serve Andros (three hours, 5500 dr, two weekly), Sikinos (two hours, 3500 dr, two weekly) and Serifos (one hour, 3800 dr, one weekly).

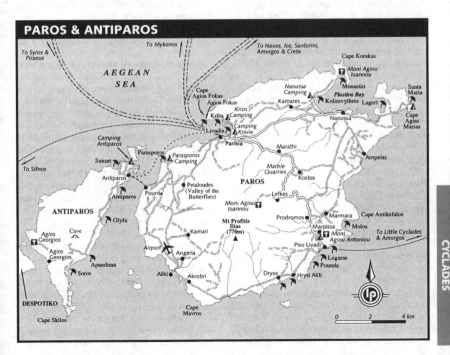

PAROS & ANTIPAROS

Catamaran There are at least two catamarans daily to Naxos (30 minutes, 2700 dr), one or two daily to Rafina (2½ hours, 8200 dr), and one to Syros (45 minutes, 3100 dr), Ios (1¼ hours, 4950 dr) and Santorini (two hours, 6100 dr). There are six services weekly to Piraeus (three hours, 9700 dr), and two weekly to Mykonos (one hour, 3300 dr), Tinos (1¼ hours, 3500 dr), Andros (three hours, 5500 dr) and Amorgos (1¾ hours, 5500 dr).

Excursion Boat In summer, frequent excursion boats depart for Antiparos from Parikia on Paros (45 minutes, 460 dr one way).

Getting Around

Bus There are around seven buses daily from Parikia to Naoussa via Dryos, Hrysi Akti, Marpissa, Marmara, Prodromo, Kosto, Marathi and Lefkes, and frequent buses to Pounta (for Antiparos), Aliki (for Petaloudes) and the airport. Around 12 buses daily link Parikia and Naoussa directly.

Car, Motorcycle & Bicycle There are numerous rental outlets all around the island. Parai Rent-a-Car-Motorcycle (☎ 21 1771), south along the waterfront in Parikia, rents cars, motorcycles and bicycles as well as tandem bikes. Paros Rent-a-Car (☎ 24 408) is north of the quay.

Taxi Boat Taxi boats leave from the quay for beaches around Parikia. Tickets are available on board.

Parikia Παροικία

The island's capital and port is Parikia. The waterfront conceals an attractive and typically Cycladic old quarter with a 13th century Venetian kastro.

Orientation & Information The main square, Plateia Mavrogenous, is straight ahead from the quay. The road on the left leads around the northern waterfront to the beach at Livadia and is lined with modern hotels. On the left, heading inland from the quay, Prombona leads to the famous Church of Ekatontapyliani, which lies within a walled courtyard. The road to the right follows the cafe-lined south-western waterfront, a pedestrian precinct in high season.

Market St (Agora in Greek, but also known by other names) is the main commercial thoroughfare running south-west from Plateia Mavrogenous through the old town, which is all narrow pedestrian streets.

Kiosks on the quay give out information on domatia and hotels (see Places to Stay). Praxis Tours (☎ 24 415), opposite the quay, can help with accommodation and sells ferry tickets.

The National Bank of Greece, the Commercial Bank of Greece and the police (☎ 23 333) are all on Plateia Mavrogenous. The bus station is 50m left of the quay (looking inland), and the post office is 300m farther along. The OTE is on the waterfront, to the right of the ferry quay (facing inland). The Wired Cafe, on Market St, and Memphis.net, near the bus station, both provide Internet access.

The port police (☎ 21 240) are back from the northern waterfront, near the post office.

Things to See & Do The **Panagia Ekatontapyliani** church, which dates from 326 AD, is one of the most splendid in the Cyclades. The building is actually three distinct churches: Agios Nikolaos, the largest, with lovely columns of Parian marble and carved iconostasis, is in the east of the compound; the others are the Church of Our Lady and the Baptistery. The name translates as Our Lady of the Hundred Gates, although only 99 doors have been counted. It is said that when the 100th is found, İstanbul will return to Greek jurisdiction. It's open 8 am to 1 pm and 4 to 9 pm daily.

Next to a school behind the Panagia Ekatontapyliani, the **Archaeological Museum** has some interesting reliefs and statues, but the most important exhibit is a fragment of the 4th century Parian Chronicle, which lists the most outstanding artistic achievements of ancient Greece. It was discovered in the 17th century by the Duke of Arundel's cleric, and most of it ended up in the Ashmolean Museum, Oxford. The museum is open 9 am to 2.30 pm daily except Monday and public holidays. Admission is 500 dr.

North along the waterfront there is a fenced **ancient cemetery** dating from the 7th century BC; it was excavated in 1983. Roman graves, burial pots and sarcophagi are floodlit at night. Photographs and other finds are exhibited in an attached building, but it's rarely open.

The **Frankish kastro** was built on the remains of a temple to Athena by Marco Sanudo, Venetian Duke of Naxos, in 1260 AD. Not much remains, save an impressively large wall with cross-sectional chunks of columns from the temple embedded in it. To find it, head west along Market St and take the first right.

Eurodivers Club (☎ 92 071), down the coast at Pounta, offers **scuba diving** courses.

Places to Stay All camping grounds have minibuses that meet the ferries. *Camping Koula* (☎ 22 081), 1km along the northern waterfront at Livadia, is the most central. It charges 1000 dr per person and 500 dr for tent hire. *Parasporos Camping* (☎ 22 268), 2km south of Parikia, charges 1400 dr per person. *Krios Camping* (☎ 21 705) is on Krios Beach, beyond Livadia Beach. It charges 1200/700 dr per person/tent, and runs a taxi boat across the bay to Parikia every 10 minutes for 400 dr per person (return). It also has a restaurant and minimarket.

The Rooms Association (☎/fax 24 528) on the quay has information on domatia; if it's closed, call Giorgos Epitropakis, the president, on ☎ 22 220. He will collect you from the port at all hours and deliver you safely to a suitable domatio. Alternatively, you can haggle with some of the owners right outside the port. For hotel details, call ☎ 24 555 (Parikia) or ☎ 41 333 (around the island).

Right in the midst of the atmospheric old Kastro, *Jane's Rooms* (☎ 21 338) have sea views and balconies; doubles cost 13,000 dr. She also has an apartment nearby, as well as some farther out of town. There's no sign identifying the rooms, but Jane will meet you at the port if you book ahead.

Rooms Rena (☎ 22 220, ☎/fax 21 427) has spotless singles/doubles/triples for 10,000/13,000/15,000 dr with bath, balcony and fridge. To find it, turn left at the quay and walk 300m along the waterfront, then turn right at the ancient cemetery. Around the corner, *Mariza Rooms* (☎ 22 629) has similar doubles/triples for 15,000/18,000 dr.

Rooms Mike (☎ 22 856) is popular with backpackers; rooms cost 15,000/18,000 dr, with TV, shared kitchen and a roof terrace. To get there, walk 50m left from the quay – it's next to Memphis.net, not far from the bus station. Mike also has self-contained studios for 19,000/21,000 dr around the corner near Ephesus restaurant.

Angie's Studios (☎ 23 909), out in the back blocks but a nice walk from the centre of town, are dripping with bougainvillea and have a pleasant patio and lawn. Rooms cost 21,000/24,000 dr. Close by, *Asteriou Rooms* (☎ 23 584) has well kept, spacious rooms for 15,000/18,000 dr.

Hotel Dina (☎ 21 325), in the old town on Market St, charges 15,000 dr for doubles with bathroom; some have a balcony. The lovely, central C class *Hotel Argonauta* (☎ 21 440), on the main square, has sparkling singles/doubles for 14,000/17,000 dr with bathroom, air-con and balcony.

For something a bit more rural and quiet, *Denis Apartments* (☎ 22 466), near Livadia, has spacious doubles/triples for 13,000/15,000 dr with bathroom. Take the first major road on the right after Camping Koula to get there, or telephone in advance to be picked up from the boat. Not far away, *Maggie's Studios* (☎ 24 370) are nicely designed and have a great view; there's also a pool. Double studios cost 22,000 dr. There are also plenty of run-of-the-mill hotels to choose from along the waterfront at Livadia, near Camping Koula.

The fine A class *Yria Hotel Bungalows* (☎ 24 154), 2.5km south of Parikia, open April to October, overlooks pretty Parasporos Beach. It has a restaurant, bar, pool and water sports. Singles/doubles/triples cost 33,000/39,000/50,000 dr. There are also four-person maisonettes for 69,000 dr.

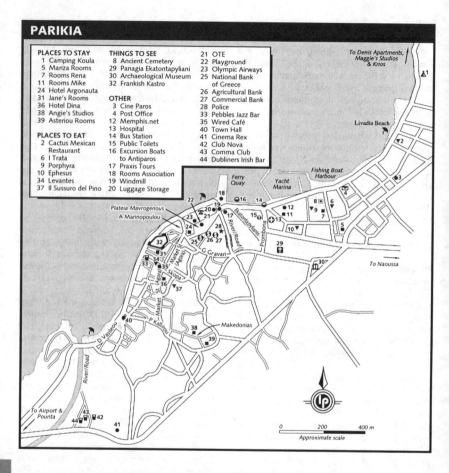

PARIKIA

PLACES TO STAY
1 Camping Koula
5 Mariza Rooms
7 Rooms Rena
11 Rooms Mike
24 Hotel Argonauta
31 Jane's Rooms
36 Hotel Dina
38 Angie's Studios
39 Asteriou Rooms

PLACES TO EAT
2 Cactus Mexican Restaurant
6 I Trata
9 Porphyra
10 Ephesus
34 Levantes
37 Il Sussuro del Pino

THINGS TO SEE
8 Ancient Cemetery
29 Panagia Ekatontapyliani
30 Archaeological Museum
32 Frankish Kastro

OTHER
3 Cine Paros
4 Post Office
12 Memphis.net
13 Hospital
14 Bus Station
15 Public Toilets
16 Excursion Boats to Antiparos
17 Praxis Tours
18 Rooms Association
19 Windmill
20 Luggage Storage
21 OTE
22 Playground
23 Olympic Airways
25 National Bank of Greece
26 Agricultural Bank
27 Commercial Bank
28 Police
33 Pebbles Jazz Bar
35 Wired Café
40 Town Hall
41 Cinema Rex
42 Club Nova
43 Comma Club
44 Dubliners Irish Bar

Places to Eat *I Trata*, next to the ancient cemetery, has very good seafood, not least shrimp saganaki, and a stimulating array of mezedes, fresh fish and salads. On the opposite side of the cemetery, *Porphyra* (named after a shellfish famed for its purple dye and ability to drill a hole into its prey) specialises in unusual seafood delicacies, including raw shellfish. Tamer offerings include fresh fish, calamari and prawns cooked to perfection, and various mixed platters (2300 dr). The service is a little

chilly but the good food makes up for this. *Ephesus*, an Anatolian place behind the hospital, has delicious, herb-laden home-made dips and appetisers (500 dr to 700 dr), a large selection of kebabs (around 2000 dr), and bread and stuffed pizzas (around 1700 dr) cooked in a wood-fired oven. Halfway down Market St, *Levantes* is an interesting place with creative international cuisine. *Il Sussuro del Pino*, in a shady garden, has fresh fish and unusual dishes such as artichokes with calamari, and octopus with macaroni (both 1400 dr). Follow the signs from Skopa, which runs off Market St.

Cactus Mexican Restaurant, by the beach at Livadia, has fajitas, tacos and enchiladas for around 2500 dr. It also has a wide variety of Greek and international fare.

Entertainment Most bars are along the south-west waterfront. *Pebbles Jazz Bar* is a good place to watch the sunset and sometimes has live music. Farther south, before the bend, is a cluster of rowdy discos – *Nova, Comma Club* and *Dubliners Irish Bar*. Avoid bars offering very cheap cocktails (invariably made from the local hooch).

Parikia's popular open-air cinemas are *Cine Paros*, in Livadia's backstreets, and *Cinema Rex*, not far from the discos at the southern end of the waterfront.

Naoussa Νάουσσα

Naoussa, on the north coast, has metamorphosed from pristine fishing village into popular tourist resort. For many visitors, Naoussa *is* Paros; its popularity is due in part to its proximity to nice beaches and to its slightly upmarket, French Riviera feel. It's certainly a lot less hectic than Parikia. Despite an incursion by package tourists, Naoussa remains relaxed.

Naoussa is still a working harbour with piles of yellow fishing nets, bright caïques, and little ouzeria with rickety tables and raffia chairs. Behind the central square (where the bus terminates) is a picturesque village, with narrow alleyways whitewashed with fish and flower motifs.

There is an information booth near the bus station. The post office is a tedious uphill walk from the central square. Nissiotissa Tours has a book exchange.

Naoussa's **Byzantine museum**, open 10 am to noon and 7 to 9 pm Tuesday, Thursday and weekends, and the **folklore museum**, open 7 to 9 pm daily, are both near the post office. Admission to each is 400 dr.

The best beaches are **Kolimvythres**, which has interesting rock formations, and **Monastiri**. **Santa Maria**, on the other side of the eastern headland, is good for windsurfing.

Activities & Organised Tours The Santa Maria Diving Club (☎ 094 385 307) offers scuba diving courses. Kokou Riding Centre offers morning, afternoon and evening horse rides, starting from the central square, for 7000/9000/10,000 dr for one/two/three hours; the one hour ride is recommended for children. Book with Cathy at Nissiotissa Tours (☎ 51 480), left off the main square.

Nissiotissa Tours can also organise caïque fishing trips (2500 dr), boats to nearby beaches, windsurfing and scuba outings, and excursions to Naxos, Delos, Mykonos, Santorini and Amorgos.

Places to Stay There are two camping grounds: *Naoussa Camping* (☎ 51 595), at Kolimvythres, charges 1300/500 dr per person/tent, and *Surfing Beach* (☎ 51 013), at Santa Maria, has a surfing and water-ski school. Minibuses from both meet ferries.

Anna's Rooms (☎ 51 538) has simple, clean doubles with bathroom and patio for 12,000 dr. To get there, turn right off the main road into town at Hotel Atlantis (just before the main square). The E class *Hotel Madaky* (☎ 51 475), off the central square, has doubles/triples for 8000/9000 dr with fridge, and singles/doubles for 13,000/ 15,000 dr with bathroom.

In the heart of town, *Pension Stella* (☎ 51 317) has a shady garden and doubles with bathroom for 15,000 dr. To reach it, turn left from the central square at Café Naoussa, then take the first right; continue past a small church on the left.

There is no shortage of good self-contained accommodation. *Sunset Apartments* (☎ 51 733), has nice double apartments for 18,500 dr and two-bedroom apartments for four costing 24,000 dr. Face inland from the main square, follow the one way street uphill, and turn right at the T-junction – it's on the left. *Katerina's* (☎ 51 642) is a stunning place with red shutters and a beautiful patio with views over town and beach; two-person apartments are 14,000 dr. *Isabella Apartments* (☎ 51 090) next door and *Senia Apartments* (☎ 51 971) charge similar prices. As you come into town, these are all off the main road to the right, behind the OTE. The attractive *Spiros Apartments* (☎ 51 210), right on the beach at Kolimvythres, has doubles/triples for 15,000/16,000 dr.

The elegant B class *Hotel Fotilia* (☎ 52 581, fax 52 583), near the big church 200m uphill from the town centre, has spacious, traditional doubles for 21,000 dr, including breakfast. There is an old windmill in its courtyard, as well as a jacuzzi and pool. *Hotel Papadakis* (☎ 51 643, fax 51 269), also with a pool, has stylish double suites and apartments for 25,000 dr. To get there, turn right off the main road (coming into town) at Hotel Atlantis and continue for about 200m. The B class *Kondiratos Hotel* (☎ 51 693) at Agia Anagyri Beach is also nice and has doubles for 29,600 dr, with breakfast.

Head for Nissiotissa Tours (☎ 51 480) if you need help with accommodation.

Places to Eat *Moshonas Ouzeri* (pronounced 'moskonas'), at the harbour, serves great fish; most dishes cost between 1500 dr and 2000 dr. Don't miss Argyro Barbarigou's *Papadakis*, on the waterfront near the caïques. The food is traditional but inventive, and prices are very reasonable. The octopus and onion stew is luscious, and there are refreshing salads with fennel, soft local cheese and an assortment of olives and greens. Even the bread, which is rolled in fennel and sesame seeds, is very good. Home-made syrupy fruits are served for dessert.

Barbarossa Ouzeri, also by the port, has great char-grilled octopus and fish. *Perivolaria* garden restaurant, on the left, along from the bus stop, and *Christos Taverna*, on the way to the post office, are both fine, upmarket places.

Around Paros

Marathi (Μαράθι) In antiquity Parian marble was considered the world's finest. The **marble quarries** have been abandoned, but it's exciting to explore the three shafts by torchlight. Take the Lefkes bus and get off at Marathi village, where you'll find a signpost to the quarries.

Lefkes to Moni Agiou Antoniou Lefkes (Λεύκες), 12km south-east of Parikia, is the island's highest and loveliest village, and was its capital during the Middle Ages. It boasts the magnificent **Agias Trias** cathedral, as well as the **Museum of Popular Aegean Civilisation** (open in summer), an amphitheatre and an interesting library.

The only accommodation is *Hotel Pantheon* (☎ 41 646), with doubles for 13,500 dr, but there are some *domatia* on the road into town.

From the central square, a signpost points to a well preserved Byzantine paved path which leads to the village of **Prodromos**. Just below the village the path takes a sharp left which is easy to miss because there isn't a sign – don't take the wider route straight ahead. The walk through beautiful countryside takes about an hour.

From Prodromos, it's a short walk to either **Marmara** or **Marpissa**. From Marmara, it's a stroll to the sandy beach at **Molos**; from Marpissa you can puff your way up a steep paved path to the 16th century **Moni Agiou Antoniou** atop a 200m-high hill. On this fortified summit, the Turks defeated Paros' Venetian rulers in 1537. Although the monastery and its grounds are generally locked, there are breathtaking views to neighbouring Naxos.

After this exertion, you'll probably feel like having a swim at the nice little beach at **Piso Livadi**. This pretty fishing village is well on the way to becoming a resort and there are plenty of places to stay and eat overlooking the harbour. There's a *camping ground* on the outskirts of town.

Petaloudes (Πεταλούδες) In July and August, butterflies almost enshroud the copious foliage at Petaloudes (Valley of the Butterflies), 8km south of Parikia. They're actually tiger moths, but spectacular all the same. Travel agents organise tours from both Parikia and Naoussa; or take the Aliki bus and ask to be let off at the Petaloudes turn-off. Petaloudes is open only in July and August, 9 am to 8 pm Monday to Saturday and 9 am to 1 pm and 4 to 8 pm Sunday.

Beaches Apart from the beaches already mentioned, there is a good beach at **Krios**, accessible by taxi boat (400 dr return) from Parikia. Paros' most talked about beach, **Hrysi Akti** (Golden Beach), on the south-east coast, is nothing spectacular, but it's popular with windsurfers. Equipment for various water sports, including sailing, water-skiing and windsurfing, is available here.

The coast between Piso Livadi and Hrysi Akti has some decent, empty beaches. Some of the attempts to concoct beach resorts along here are heartbreaking – at **New Golden Beach** you can watch the bulldozers create a beach from scratch while builders work overtime to erect the usual box-style accommodation compounds.

ANTIPAROS
☎ 0284   • postcode 840 07   • pop 819

Antiparos was once regarded as the quiet alternative to Paros, but development is increasing. The permanent inhabitants live in an attractive village (also called Antiparos) that is rapidly becoming obscured by tourist accommodation. It's still a very pleasant place and is a popular holiday spot for families with young kids. No cars are allowed in the village, which makes it even nicer.

Getting There & Around
For details on boats from Paros, see Getting There & Away under Paros.

The only bus service on Antiparos runs to the cave in the centre of the island. In summer, this bus continues to Agios Georgios.

Captain Yannis runs caïque day trips (20,000 dr for up to six people) to secluded beaches. Ask for the friendly old captain at Smiles Cafe on the main square in Antiparos village or at the port.

Orientation & Information
To reach the village centre if you've come from Pounta, turn right from the quay, walk along the waterfront and turn left into the main street at Anarghyros restaurant. If you've come by excursion boat, walk straight ahead from the quay.

The post office is a fair way down on the left. The OTE, with currency exchange and ferry information, is just beyond. The central square is left at the top of the main street and then right, behind Smiles Cafe.

To reach the kastro, another Marco Sanudo creation, go under the stone arch that leads north off the central square.

Beach bums will direct you to the decent beaches. Nudism is only permitted on the camp-site beach.

Cave of Antiparos
Despite previous looting of stalactites and stalagmites, this cave is still awe-inspiring. In 1673, the French ambassador, Marquis de Nointel, organised a Christmas Mass (enhanced by a large orchestra) inside the cave for 500 Parians. In summer, the cave is open 10 am to 4 pm daily; admission is 600 dr.

There are buses every half-hour from the village of Antiparos (220 dr one way) or you can take an excursion boat (high season only) from Antiparos village (1200 dr) or Parikia (2500 dr); the price includes the 1.5km bus ride from the landing stage to the cave.

Places to Stay & Eat
The well equipped camp site, *Camping Antiparos* (☎ 61 221), is on a beach 1km north of the quay; signs point the way. It charges 1000/300 dr per person/tent.

Domatia are prevalent and there are several hotels. On the waterfront, *Anarghyros* (☎ 61 204) has doubles with bathroom for 10,000 dr. The newish *Hotel Mantalena* (☎ 61 206), farther along to the left, has doubles/triples for 17,000/20,000 dr with bathroom. All rooms have a balcony overlooking the port and there's a nice terrace. Nearby, *Margarita Studios* (same telephone) has good doubles for 17,000 dr.

The main street has many cafes. The popular *Taverna Yorgis*, on the right, serves Greek family staples and specialises in fish. *O Damis*, about 100m west of the main square (go under the stone archway that leads to the beach – not the one that goes into the kastro), is the oldest taverna on the island. It has a large menu of home-cooked traditional food and the service is friendly. Prices are very reasonable. Ask about *tsikoudia*, the local firewater.

Agios Georgios, in the south, has several *tavernas*.

Naxos Νάξος

☎ 0285 • postcode 843 00 • pop 16,703

According to legend, it was on Naxos that Theseus abandoned Ariadne after she helped him find his way out of the Cretan labyrinth. She didn't pine long – she was soon ensconced in the arms of Dionysos, the god of wine and ecstasy and the island's favourite deity. Ever since, Naxian wine has been considered a fine remedy for a broken heart.

The island is the Cyclades' largest and most fertile, producing olives, grapes, figs, citrus, corn and potatoes. Rugged mountains and lush green valleys also make it one of the most beautiful. Mt Zeus (1004m; also known as Mt Zas or Zefs) is the archipelago's highest peak.

Naxos was an important Byzantine centre and boasts about 500 churches and monasteries, many containing interesting frescoes. Some of the early Christian basilicas were originally ancient temples.

The island is a wonderful place to explore on foot and walking is now a major draw for many visitors, especially Germans. Many old paths linking villages, churches and other sights still survive. For detailed route information, consult Christian Ucke's excellent *Walking Tours on Naxos*, available from local bookshops.

Getting There & Away

Air There is at least one flight daily to Athens (20,100 dr). Olympic Airways is represented by Naxos Tours (☎ 22 095, 23 043).

Ferry Naxos has around eight ferry connections daily with Piraeus (six hours, 5000 dr); seven with Paros (one hour, 1350 dr); six with Ios (1¼ hours, 2100 dr) and Santorini (three hours, 3100 dr); and two with Mykonos (three hours, 1900 dr).

There are daily boats to Iraklia (1¼ to 5¼ hours, 1300 dr), Shinousa (1¾ to five hours, 1400 dr), Koufonisia (2½ to 4¼ hours, 1500 dr) and Amorgos (two to 5½ hours, 2300 dr), and a few every week to Donousa (one to four hours, 1500 dr). Six boats weekly go to Sikinos (three hours, 1600 dr), five go to Folegandros (three hours, 2300 dr), Anafi (four hours, 2800 dr) and Samos (4¾ to 7½ hours, 4000 dr), four go to Syros (three hours, 3000 dr), Thessaloniki (14¾ hours, 7100 dr) and Iraklio on Crete (4¼ to 7½ hours, 5000 dr), and three go to Astypalea (5½ hours, 4000 dr), Rhodes (10 hours, 5000 dr) and Skiathos (8½ hours, 5300 dr).

There are two ferries weekly to Ikaria (2½ hours, 2500 dr) and Tinos (4¼ hours, 1900 dr), and one to Fourni (four hours, 3000 dr) and Kos (15 hours, 4000 dr).

Zas Travel (☎ 23 330) sells tickets for all ferries.

Hydrofoil There are around two hydrofoils daily to Paros (30 minutes, 2700 dr), Santorini (1¾ hours, 6100 dr) and Mykonos (1¼ hours, 3600 dr), one daily to Ios (50 minutes, 4200 dr), six weekly to Sifnos (1½ hours, 5800 dr), five weekly to Milos (three hours, 8200 dr) and Syros (1½ hours, 4100 dr), four weekly to Tinos (two hours, 3200 dr), three weekly to Amorgos (2¼ to 3¼ hours, 4000 dr), two weekly to Folegandros (1½ hours, 4600 dr) and Sikinos (one hour, 3000 dr), and one a week to Serifos (1½ hours, 5700 dr), Iraklia (30 minutes, 2200 dr), Shinousa (50 minutes, 2300 dr), Koufonisia (one hour, 2600 dr) and Donousa (1½ hours, 2500 dr).

The hydrofoil representative is Passenger Tours (☎ 25 329).

Catamaran There are at least two catamarans daily to Paros (30 minutes, 2700 dr) and Rafina (3¼ hours, 7000 dr), one daily to Syros (1½ hours, 4100 dr), Ios (50 minutes, 4200 dr) and Santorini (1½ hours, 6100 dr), six weekly to Piraeus (3¾ hours, 8000 dr), Mykonos (1½ hours, 3600 dr) and Tinos (two hours, 3200 dr), three weekly to Andros (3½ hours, 6000 dr), and two weekly to Amorgos (one to two hours, 3800 dr).

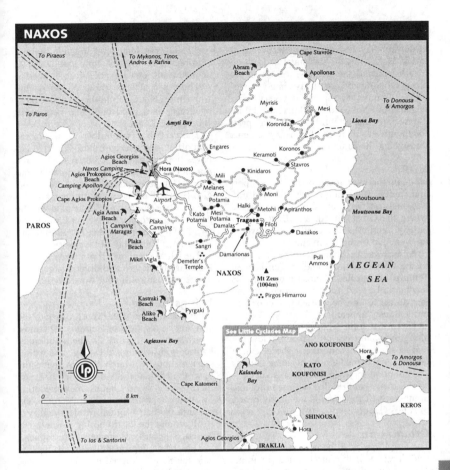

NAXOS

Naxos Tours sells Goutos and Minoan tickets and Kykladikon Travel (☎ 23 830) is the official agent for Strintzis Lines.

Excursion Boat There are daily excursions to Mykonos (9000 dr) and frequent excursions to Delos.

Getting Around
To/From the Airport There is no shuttle bus, but buses to Agios Prokopios and Agia Anna pass close by. A taxi costs 1500 dr.

Bus Frequent buses run to Agia Anna (300 dr) from Hora. Five buses daily serve Filoti (400 dr) via Halki (340 dr), four serve Apiranthos (600 dr) via Filoti and Halki, three serve Apollonas (1100 dr), and two serve Pyrgaki (400 dr) and Melanes (300 dr). There are less frequent departures to other villages.

Buses leave from the end of the wharf; timetables are posted outside the bus station and the Naxos Tourist Information Centre in Hora.

CYCLADES

Car, Motorcycle & Bicycle You can hire cars and motorcycles as well as 21-speed all-terrain bicycles from the waterfront outlets in Hora. Bicycle hire starts at 1500 dr. You'll need all the gears – the roads are steep, winding and not always in good condition. Remember that it is a very large island: from Naxos to Apollonas it's 35km.

Pay particular attention to the small print for liability as there are frequent accidents throughout the summer.

HORA

Hora, on the west coast, is the island's port and capital. It's a large town, divided into two historic neighbourhoods – Bourgos, where the Greeks lived, and Kastro (now largely derelict), on the hill above, where the Venetian Catholics lived.

A causeway to the north of the port leads to the islet of Palatia and the unfinished **Temple of Apollo**, Naxos' most famous landmark. Legend has it that when İstanbul is returned to Greece, the temple door will miraculously appear.

There are some good swimming areas along the waterfront promenade below the temple. The town's northern shore, called Grotta – nicknamed Grotty by some tourists – is not good for swimming as it's very exposed, rocky, and riddled with sea urchins. South-west of the town is the sandy beach of Agios Georgios.

Orientation

The ferry quay is at the northern end of the waterfront, with the bus terminal in front. The busy waterfront is lined with cafes and restaurants and is the focus of most of the action. Behind the waterfront, a warren of little laneways and steps leads up to the Kastro.

Information

There is no EOT, but the privately owned Naxos Tourist Information Centre (NTIC; ☎ 25 301, emergency 24 525, fax 25 200), opposite the quay, provides advice on accommodation, excursions and rental cars. Despina Kitini and her staff have an amazing knowledge of the island and are more

than willing to share it. Other services include reverse-charge phone calls, laundry for 2500 dr a load, and luggage storage starting at 500 dr a day. Note that the NTIC does not sell ferry tickets.

There are at least three ATMs on the waterfront. Not far from the National Bank of Greece is a good book and newspaper shop called Zoom.

The OTE is 150m farther south. For the post office, continue past the OTE, cross Papavasiliou and take the left branch where the road forks. Internet access is available from Naxos Computers, inland from Agios Georgios Beach; there are plans to open an additional office closer to the centre of town. The police are south-east of Plateia Protodikiou (☎ 22 100). The port police (☎ 23 300) are in the town hall, south of the quay.

The island is endowed with many springs; look for public taps and drinking fountains where you can refill your water bottle.

Things to See

After leaving the waterfront, turn into the winding backstreets of Bourgos. The most alluring part of Hora is the residential **Kastro**, with winding alleyways and white-washed houses. Marco Sanudo made the town the capital of his duchy in 1207, and there are some handsome Venetian dwellings, many with well kept gardens and insignia of their original residents. Take a stroll around the kastro during siesta to experience its hushed, medieval atmosphere.

The **archaeological museum** (☎ 22 725) is in the Kastro, housed in a former school where author Nikos Kazantzakis was briefly a pupil. The contents include the usual collection of vases, torsos and funerary stelae, as well as Hellenistic and Roman terracotta figurines. There are, more interestingly, also some Early Cycladic figurines. The museum is open 8 am to 2.30 pm Tuesday to Sunday; admission is 1000 dr.

Close by, **Sanudo's Palace**, near the kastro ramparts, and the Roman Catholic **cathedral** (open daily at 6.30 pm) are worth seeing. The nearby **Naxos Cultural Centre** has art exhibits in summer.

HORA (NAXOS)

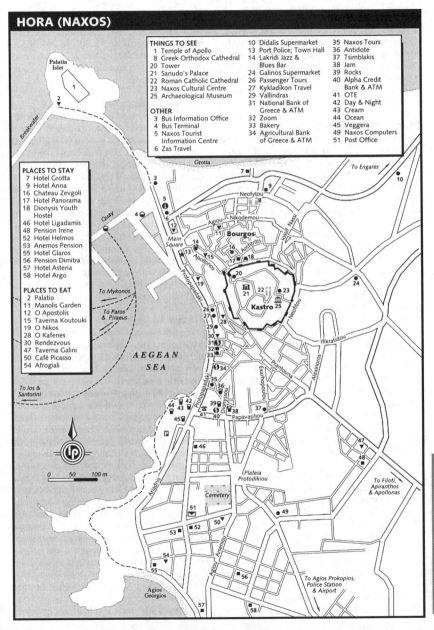

THINGS TO SEE
1 Temple of Apollo
8 Greek Orthodox Cathedral
20 Tower
21 Sanudo's Palace
22 Roman Catholic Cathedral
23 Naxos Cultural Centre
25 Archaeological Museum

OTHER
3 Bus Information Office
4 Bus Terminal
5 Naxos Tourist
  Information Centre
6 Zas Travel

10 Didalis Supermarket
13 Port Police; Town Hall
14 Lakridi Jazz &
   Blues Bar
24 Galinos Supermarket
26 Passenger Tours
27 Kykladikon Travel
29 Vallindras
31 National Bank of
   Greece & ATM
32 Zoom
33 Bakery
34 Agricultural Bank
   of Greece & ATM

35 Naxos Tours
36 Antidote
37 Tsimblakis
38 Jam
39 Rocks
40 Alpha Credit
   Bank & ATM
41 OTE
42 Day & Night
43 Cream
44 Ocean
45 Veggera
49 Naxos Computers
51 Post Office

PLACES TO STAY
7 Hotel Grotta
9 Hotel Anna
16 Chateau Zevgoli
17 Hotel Panorama
18 Dionysis Youth
   Hostel
46 Hotel Ligadamis
48 Pension Irene
52 Hotel Helmos
53 Anemos Pension
55 Hotel Glaros
56 Pension Dimitra
57 Hotel Asteria
58 Hotel Argo

PLACES TO EAT
2 Palatio
11 Manolis Garden
12 O Apostolis
15 Taverna Koutouki
19 O Nikos
28 O Kafenes
30 Rendezvous
47 Taverna Galini
50 Café Picasso
54 Afrogiali

Palatia Islet

Breakwater

To Engares

Grotta

Neofytou

Quay

Agiou Nikodemou

Main Square

Bourgos

Iosif Nassi

To Mykonos

To Paros & Piraeus

Apollonos

Amfitritis

Protopapadaki

Kastro

Neofitou

Ifikratidou

AEGEAN SEA

To Ios & Santorini

Pantouni

Exarhopoulou

Alexinoros

nostou

Protopapadaki

Papavasiliou

Ariadnis

0   50   100 m

Plateia Protodikiou

Cemetery

To Filoti, Apiranthos & Apollonas

Agiou Arseniou

Agios Georgios

To Agios Prokopios, Police Station & Airport

Organised Tours
The Naxos Tourist Information Centre offers day tours of the island by bus (5000 dr) or caïque (13,000 dr, including barbecue). There is also a daily excursion to Apollonas (2000 dr). One-day walking tours (15,000 dr for two people) of the back country are offered three times weekly.

Places to Stay – Budget
There are four camp sites near Hora: *Naxos Camping* (☎ 23 500), 1km south of Agios Georgios Beach; *Camping Maragas* (☎ 24 552), at Agia Anna Beach; *Camping Apollon* (☎ 24 417), 700m from Agios Prokopios Beach; and *Plaka Camping* (☎ 42 700), 6km from town at Plaka Beach. All sites have good facilities and some offer walking tours of the back country. Officially they all charge the same rates, but there is fierce competition in high season. Minibuses meet ferries.

Dionysos Youth Hostel (☎ 22 331) is only open in July and August. It's a good place to meet other travellers, and has dorm beds for 2000 dr; simply furnished singles/doubles are 3000/4000 dr with bathroom. The hostel is signposted from Agiou Nikodemou, Bourgos' main street.

Many domatia owners meet ferries, but don't feel pressured to go with them as there are plenty of better options. The NTIC is the best place for information about rooms.

Pension Dimitra (☎ 24 922), right on Agios Georgios Beach, has doubles/triples for 12,000/15,000 dr with fridge and balcony. Both *Pension Irene* (☎ 23 169), south-east of the town centre, and *Anemos Pension* (☎ 25 098), near the post office, have doubles for around 14,000 dr. Anemos also has two-person apartments starting from 12,000 dr.

Near the Kastro, *Hotel Panorama* (☎ 24 404) has a roof garden with superb views; lovely quiet doubles are 14,000 dr. *Hotel Anna* (☎ 25 213), near the Orthodox cathedral, is also a nice place with singles/doubles for 10,000/12,000 dr, and triples for 15,000 dr with kitchenette.

Hotel Helmos (☎ 22 455), next to the post office, has characterful and cosy singles/ doubles/triples for 8000/10,000/ 13,000 dr with balcony and bathroom; two/four-person apartments are 12,000/18,000 dr. Opposite the waterfront park, *Hotel Ligdamis* (☎ 23 745) has double rooms/studios for 10,000/15,000 dr.

Places to Stay – Mid-Range
The well furnished and quiet *Hotel Grotta* (☎ 22 215) has splendid sea views; singles/ doubles/triples are 12,000/16,000/ 20,000 dr with bathroom. If you telephone, the owner will pick you up at the quay. In Bourgos, *Chateau Zevgoli* (☎ 24 525, fax 25 200) has traditionally furnished doubles for 22,000 dr. The owner is Despina from the NTIC, who also has large, restored homes for two/four people at 16,000/18,000 dr.

On Agios Georgios Beach, *Hotel Argo* (☎ 25 330) has air-con singles/doubles for 10,000/12,000 dr, *Hotel Glaros* (☎ 23 101) has rooms with sea view for 13,000/17,500 dr including breakfast, and *Hotel Asteria* (☎ 23 002) has rooms for 14,000/18,000 dr.

Places to Eat
Lively *O Apostolis* on the waterfront is a great place for mezedes, fresh fish and grilled octopus (a local speciality); prices are very reasonable. Just behind Apollonos, *Taverna Koutouki* is also very popular. Nearby, *Manolis Garden* specialises in chicken in yogurt and wine and has a nice outdoor setting. It's next to a traditional wood-fired bakery. *Taverna Galini*, south-east of the town centre, is the locals' favourite. *Palatio*, a bar-cafe at the end of the promenade below the temple, serves light meals and fresh seafood, including grilled octopus. But the best fish restaurant in town has to be *O Nikos* on the waterfront. It's not cheap, but it's well worth a splurge.

If you're desperate for a change, *O Kafenes*, on the way to the Kastro, has real Indian food. *Café Picasso*, just off Arseniou, has burritos, tacos and quesadillas from 1200 dr to 2300 dr.

For breakfast, cakes and coffee, head to *Rendezvous* patisserie on the waterfront, next to the National Bank. *Afrogiali*, near

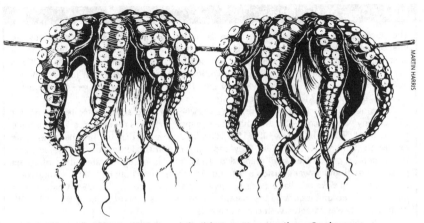

MARTIN HARRIS

Octopus *(ohtapodi)* drying; seafood features prominently on Greek menus

Agios Georgios Beach, is the best place for gyros (350 dr).

Immediately adjacent to Zoom bookshop is the town's best **bakery**. The cheapest **supermarkets** are Galinos and Didalis, both a little way out of town.

Naxian specialities include *kefalotyri* (hard cheese), honey, *citron* (a liqueur made from the leaves of the citron tree), *raki*, ouzo, and fine white wine. *Tsimblakis* olive and cheese shop, on Papavasilou, is a fascinating, cavernous old place selling local produce. You'll see rabbit and partridge on restaurant menus in spring.

Entertainment
One block back from the waterfront, *Rocks* and *Jam* are popular late-night bars. *Day & Night*, *Cream*, *Ocean* and *Veggera*, all at the end of the waterfront near the OTE, are the places to go disco dancing. On the Grotta road, not far from the waterfront, is a collection of *clubs* that change name each year.

Antidote bar has at least 55 different types of beer from around the world, ranging from 400 dr to 4500 dr for Belgian Trappist. *Lakridi Jazz & Blues Bar*, behind the waterfront, on the way to the Kastro, is a nice, laid-back little place.

Shopping
You can find citron liqueur in beautiful French and Italian bottles at the Vallindras shop on the waterfront. The green citron is the sweetest; the yellow is a bit stronger and has more citron aroma, and the clear stuff is reminiscent of Cointreau and quite potent indeed. Vallindras also makes very good ouzo untainted by additives. Samples are available at the shop. The citron fruit itself is bottled in a sugary syrup for 'spoon sweets'; the preserved fruit is a little bit lemony but quite subtle and almost quince-like. Take-home jars are available at Vallindras.

In the streets heading up to the Kastro you can find beautiful embroidery and hand-made silver jewellery. Most of the gold and silver baubles here are the same as those available on Mykonos, but 30% cheaper.

AROUND NAXOS
Beaches
Agios Georgios is just a typical town beach, but you can windsurf here on water so shallow that it seems you could wade to Paros, visible in the distance; the beach becomes so crowded that you may develop an uncontrollable desire to do so. The next beach south is **Agios Prokopios**, a sheltered bay,

CYCLADES

Glory Days of the Citron

The citron (Citrus medica) looks like a very large, lumpy lemon. It has a thick rind and an interior yielding little juice. This seemingly useless fruit was introduced to the Mediterranean area in about 300 BC, probably by Alexander the Great, and up until the Christian era it was the only citrus fruit cultivated in Europe. In antiquity the citron was known for its medicinal qualities and was also a symbol of fertility and affluence. The ancient Greeks called it the 'median' apple (from Media, the ancient Greek name for Persia).

Citron trees are fussy about where they'll grow – they need abundant water and do not tolerate any wind or cold – but they have been happy on Naxos for centuries. Although the fruit is barely edible in its raw state, the Naxians discovered that the rind becomes quite exquisite when preserved in syrup. They also put the aromatic leaves to good use by creating kitroraki, a raki distilled from grape skins and citron leaves. By the late 19th century the preserved fruits and a sweet version of kitroraki known as citron both had cult followings outside Greece and were popular exports to Russia, Austria, France and the USA. Citron was so much in demand that it became the mainstay of the island's economy and by the early 20th century Naxos was carpeted with citron orchards.

Alas, citron went out of vogue after WWII; even the islanders abandoned it, seduced by the invasion of exotic alcohols from the outside world. In the 1960s most citron trees were uprooted to make way for more useful, more profitable crops.

This might seem like a sad story, but fear not: the citron is on the rise. On Naxos there are currently two distilleries producing citron liqueur. At Vallindras distillery in Halki they still distil citron the old-fashioned way, using leaves collected from the orchards in the autumn and winter. The harvesting of leaves is an arduous, time-consuming task, due to the trees' thorns, and if too many leaves are taken this can destroy the tree. The leaves are laid out in a dry room, dampened with water, and then placed with alcohol and water in a boiler fuelled by olive wood. The distillate is added to water and sugar, and citron is born.

These days approximately 13,000 to 15,000L of citron are produced each year at Vallindras. Still, this is nowhere near enough to meet current demand, and nothing can be done about this until more citron trees are planted. As the 20th century draws to a close it is nearly impossible to get hold of citron outside Greece, so make sure you track some down while visiting its island home. It comes in three strengths and sweetnesses: the green is the traditional Naxian liqueur and has the most sugar and least alcohol; the yellow has little sugar, more aroma and more alcohol; the white falls somewhere in between and resembles Cointreau. Citron is very good after dinner, especially after fish.

If you want to see citron trees in action, look for orchards around Hora and in Engares, Melanes, Halki and Apollonas.

followed by **Agia Anna** – a lovely long arc of sand. Sandy beaches continue down as far as **Pyrgaki**. There are **domatia** and **tavernas** aplenty along this stretch, and any of these beaches would make a good spot to stop for a few days. Other worthy beaches are **Plaka**, **Aliko**, **Mikri Vigla** and **Kastraki**. **Abram**, north of Hora, is also a nice spot.

Tragaea Τραγαία

The lovely Tragaea region is a vast plain of olive groves and unspoilt villages harbouring numerous little Byzantine churches. **Filoti**, on the slopes of Mt Zeus, is the region's largest village; the Maharis butcher shop sells all you'll need for a perfect picnic, including fresh cheese and bread, wine and fruit. On the outskirts of the village (coming from Hora), an asphalt road leads off right into the heart of the Tragaea. This road brings you to the isolated hamlets of **Damarionas** and **Damalas**.

The picturesque village of **Halki** has several tower houses built by aristocratic families as refuges and lookouts in the days of pirate raids and feuds between the islanders and the Venetians and Turks. The best preserved is the **Gratsia Pyrgos**; to reach it turn right at **Panagia Protothronis** church, which is itself worth checking out for its fine frescoes. It is on the main road near the bus stop. The **Vallindras distillery**, housed in a lovely old building in the centre of town, offers citron tastings and impromptu tours.

Agii Apostoli (Holy Apostles) church in Metohi is famous for its odd triple storey architecture, while **Agios Mamas**, near Potamia, is known for its early 'cross in a square' layout. The **Panagia Drosiani** at **Moni**, north of Halki, is one of the oldest and most important churches in the Balkans. Successive layers of frescoes have been uncovered, some dating back to the 7th century. If it's locked, seek out the priest's wife and ask for the key.

South-west of the Tragaea, near **Sangri**, an impressive **Temple to Demeter** (also known as Dimitra's Temple) is being restored. The small church next to the temple was originally built from remnants of the temple and was recently demolished and rebuilt so that the temple material could be salvaged. Signs point the way from Sangri.

Melanes Μέλανες

Near the hillside villages of Melanes and Mili, there is a large unfinished 6th century BC **kouros** (male statue), abandoned in a quarry that is now encircled by orchards. The Kondylis family, who own the land, are the official guardians. Near the site, next to a large goldfish pond, they have a little *cafe* of sorts where the old lady serves Greek coffee, wine, omelettes and salads. Another, less famous, kouros was found nearby a few years ago; ask at the cafe for directions.

Taverna Xenaki (☎ 62 374) in Melanes has rabbit and free-range chicken; if you order an hour in advance, it will prepare a feast. From Melanes you can walk down to **Kato Potamia**, **Mesi Potamia** and **Ano Potamia**, where there are more orchards and lovely tavernas. From there, it's not far to Halki, where you can catch the bus back to town.

Pirgos Himarrou Πύργος Χειμάρρου

South of Filoti, in the island's remote southeast, the Pirgos Himarrou is a well preserved cylindrical marble tower dating from Hellenistic times. It is three storeys high with an internal spiral staircase. One theory holds that it was a lookout post used to warn of approaching pirates, but the position of the tower in a place with limited views discounts this. It was more likely a fortified house on a prosperous farmstead – the marble base of a large olive or wine press lies nearby.

After checking out the tower, continue south for a swim at **Kalandos Bay**. Take food and water as there are no shops or tavernas.

Apiranthos Απείρανθος

Apiranthos is a handsome village of stone houses and marble-paved streets. Its inhabitants are descendants of refugees who fled Crete to escape Turkish repression. The village is known for its communist tendencies – its most famous son is Manolis Glezos, the resistance fighter who during WWII replaced the Nazi flag atop the Acropolis with the Greek one. He later became the parliamentary representative for the Cyclades.

On the right of the village's main thoroughfare (coming from the Hora-Apollonas road) is a **museum of natural history**. Just before the museum a path on your left leads to the centre of town, past the **women's handcrafts co-op**, which has looms and textiles, the **geology museum** and the **archaeology museum**. The museums are open 9 am to 2 pm (sometimes later in summer) Tuesday to Sunday. Admission to the archaeology museum is 1000 dr.

Just before the beautiful main square dominated by a huge plane tree is the famous

Taverna Lefteris, where you can eat in the garden overlooking the valley. Apiranthos has no accommodation.

Moutsouna Μουτσούνα

The road from Apiranthos to Moutsouna winds through spectacular mountain scenery. Formerly a busy port shipping the emery mined in the region, Moutsouna is now something of a ghost town. It feels peaceful rather than spooky and there are some nice beaches with superbly clear water. *Pension Ostria (☎ 094-148 904)* is a lovely place and has singles/doubles for 12,000/15,000 dr, and there's also a couple of *tavernas*.

Apollonas Απόλλωνας

Apollonas, on the north coast, was once a tranquil fishing village but is now a popular resort. It has a small sandy beach and a larger pebble one.

Hordes of day-trippers come to see the gargantuan 7th century BC **kouros** which lies in an ancient quarry a short walk from the village. The largest of three on the island (the other two are in the Melanes region), it is signposted to the left as you approach Apollonas on the main inland road from Hora. This 10.5m statue was apparently abandoned unfinished because it cracked. Apollonas has several *domatia* and *tavernas*.

The inland route from Hora to Apollonas winds through spectacular mountains – a worthwhile trip. With your own transport you can return to Hora via the west-coast road, passing through wild and sparsely populated country with awe-inspiring sea views. Several tracks branch down to secluded beaches.

Little Cyclades
Μικρές Κυκλάδες

The chain of small islands between Naxos and Amorgos is variously called the Little Cyclades, Minor Islands, Back Islands and Lesser Islands. Only four – Donousa, Koufonisia, Iraklia and Shinousa – have permanent populations.

All were densely populated in antiquity, as evident from the large number of graves found. In the Middle Ages, the islands were uninhabited except by pirates and goats. After independence, intrepid souls from Naxos and Amorgos re-inhabited them, and now each island has a small population. Until recently, their only visitors were Greeks returning to their roots. These days they receive a few tourists, mostly backpackers looking for splendid beaches and a laid-back lifestyle.

Donousa is the northernmost of the group and farthest from Naxos. The others are clustered near the south-east coast of Naxos. Each has a public telephone and post agency. Money can usually be changed at the general store or post agency, but rates are lousy – bring drachmas with you.

Getting There & Away

Links with the Little Cyclades are regular but tenuous, so make sure you have plenty of time before embarking on a visit – these islands do not make a convenient last stop a few days before you're due to fly home!

At least a few times a week the F/B *Express Skopelitis* provides a lifeline service between Naxos and Amorgos via the Little Cyclades (see the Naxos and Amorgos sections for details of prices and times), but it's small, extremely slow, and susceptible to bad weather. In high season it does a daily run from Amorgos to Koufonisia, Shinousa, Iraklia, Naxos, Paros and Mykonos, returning by the same route.

Twice a week the F/B *Express Hermes* sails from Piraeus to each of the Little Cyclades via Paros and Naxos, continuing to Amorgos and Astypalea. A few other large ferries call at the islands in high season, often at ungodly hours.

Once a week there is a hydrofoil from Naxos to Iraklia (30 minutes, 2200 dr), Shinousa (50 minutes, 2300 dr), Koufonisia (one hour, 2600 dr) and Donousa (1½ hours, 2500 dr).

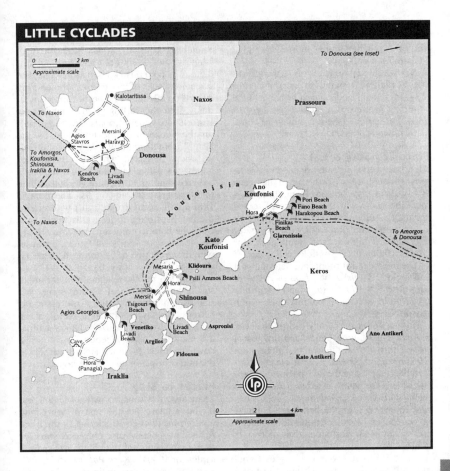

LITTLE CYCLADES

Because of its northerly position, it is sometimes easier to get to Donousa from Mykonos than from Naxos.

IRAKLIA Ηράκλεια
☎ 0285   • postcode 843 00   • pop 110
This rather barren island has a couple of tiny villages, a nice beach and not much else, save a small clique of Germans who return each year. The island's only sight as such is a **cave** with fine stalactites. Tourism is increasing, but amenities (including

rooms) are few. The port and main village is **Agios Georgios**. It's very quiet and not particularly scenic, although the deep cove-like harbour is rather pretty. The way into town is to the right, around the port beach, and then left up the hill. From here the town's two main roads fork around a cactus-filled ravine.

The right fork leads to Melissa, the general store that sells ferry tickets. Melissa also has a cardphone, serves as the island's post office and has domatia. The left fork leads past the second minimarket (which is also Perigiali restaurant) and more domatia. You can exchange money at Melissa and at Maistrali bar-cafe.

A new sealed road leads off to the left (as you face inland from the harbour). This runs to **Livadi** – the island's nicest beach, and the stomping ground of a picturesque herd of goats. Farther on is the tiny village of **Hora**, also known as Panagia.

Places to Stay & Eat

All domatia and tavernas are in Agios Georgios, although a few spring up on the beach at Livadi in high season. Domatia owners meet the boats, but the shortage of rooms makes it a sellers' market – take whatever you can get and don't bother looking for bargains. In high season doubles go for around 10,000 dr. If possible, call ahead.

The most central rooms are near the port and include *Melissa* (☎ 71 539), *Anthi & Angelo's* (☎ 71 486), and *Manolis* (☎ 71 569), which is open only during high season.

Rooms up on the windy hill on the way to Livadi have nice patios and are just a stone's throw from the beach. The best are *Alexandra* (☎ 71 482), with clean, comfortable rooms, and the swish *Anna's Place* (☎/fax 71 145), which also has deluxe apartments with a view. *Marietta* (☎ 71 252) has nice rooms right on the beach at Livadi. A large sign at Livadi declares that nudism and camping are forbidden, but neither is unheard of.

There are three tavernas in Agios Georgios, all serving fresh fish and the usual fare. *Perigiali* is a popular place with a large marble table encircling an old pine tree. *O Pevkos*, also known as Dimitri's, is more traditional and shaded by an even larger pine. You'll be led into the kitchen to choose your meal; for breakfast try the yogurt served with the local thyme honey. *Maistrali*, opposite Pevkos, is the local bar; it also sells tickets for Ventouris Sea Lines' *Georgios Express* and Agapitos Lines' *Naias Express*, both of which call about once a week.

SHINOUSA Σχοινούσα
☎ 0285 • postcode 843 00 • pop 120

Shinousa (skih-**noo**-sah) is a little gem of an island with a lively **hora** and smiling residents. The hora (also known as Panagia) has sweeping views of the sea and neighbouring islands on all sides, and nestles inconspicuously into the rolling golden landscape. Unfortunately, new 'rooms' are being built on the outskirts of the hora and by the beaches, but there's still a very pastoral feeling about the island, which has its share of happy cows, chickens, donkeys and goats.

Ferries pull in at **Mersini** Harbour, home to the island's fishing boats. The hora is 1km uphill, so try to get a lift with one of the locals offering rooms. Dirt tracks lead from the hora to numerous beaches around the coast; take food and water, because, with the exception of **Tsigouri**, there are no shops or tavernas at the beaches.

There's a public telephone in the main square and a couple of general stores sell stamps. Unfortunately, ferry information is hard to come by; your best bet is to ask the people you're staying with. Or try calling the Central Travel Agency (☎ 71 950), down the hill at Tsigouri. Tickets are sold at the port a few minutes before boats arrive.

Places to Stay

There are a few rooms down at Mersini, but if you want to see the rest of the island you're much better off staying in the hora. At the budget end, *Kafe-Ouzeri Rooms for Rent* in the centre of the village has spartan triples for 5000 dr. *Kyra Pothiti* (☎ 71 184), a bit farther along the main street, has nice, cosy doubles for 7000 dr with balcony and bathroom. On the road to Mesaria, *Anna Domatia* (☎ 71 161) has good, clean singles/doubles for 7000/8000 dr. *Hotel Sunset* (☎ 71 948) is a brand new, comfortable but impersonal complex with rooms for 8000/12,000 dr; it's run by the folk at Anna Domatia.

Ghrispos Tsigouri Beach Villas (☎ 71 930, fax 71 176) is a crazy family affair about 500m away from the hora, down by the beach at Tsigouri. Doubles go for

16,500 dr, including breakfast. It's close to the beach (though the path to the beach is unfinished and access is difficult), but if you want to pop into the hora occasionally, you're faced with a long, dusty walk uphill. Similarly isolated is *Panorama (☎ 71 160)*, by the beach at Livadi, where doubles with bathroom are 9000 dr, or 13,000 dr with kitchen.

Places to Eat
You're unlikely to have any very uplifting culinary adventures on Shinousa, an island where you might want to do a bit of self-catering. Outside high season the only establishment open for lunch is *Kyra Pothiti*. All drinks and meals come with obligatory serves of her home-made *myzithra*, which isn't bad the first time. Steer clear of the greasy-spoon *giouvetsi* (meat with macaroni) and stick to fish and baked vegetables. *Panorama* has good salads and charcoal grilled fish, and *tavernas* at the port serve freshly caught fish and lobster. The *bakery* just past Anna Domatia on the road to Mesaria is a good place to have breakfast.

To Kentro kafeneio is the most popular and nicest looking bar, but is pretty much a male-only domain; brave women may wish to transgress its boundaries. The only other bar is the *Cafe-Pub Margarita* down the steps just around the corner.

KOUFONISIA (Κουφονήσια)
☎ 0285 • postcode 843 00 • pop 284
Koufonisia is the only one of the Little Cyclades that's anywhere near the tourist trail, and it has a lot to offer. It's really two islands, Ano Koufonisi and Kato Koufonisi, but only the latter is permanently inhabited.

Despite being the smallest of the Little Cyclades, Koufonisia is the most densely populated, which adds quite a bit of life to its hora. Every family is involved with fishing – the island boasts the largest fishing fleet in Greece in proportion to its population. And because it's so attractive, it hasn't suffered from an exodus of young people to the mainland and the consequent ghost-town effect seen on many of the Cyclades;

in fact, it's brimming with happy children and teenagers.

The beaches are picture-perfect swathes of golden sand lapped by crystal-clear turquoise waters; the locals are hospitable and friendly; and food and accommodation options are far more plentiful and refined than on neighbouring islands.

A caïque ride away, **Kato Koufonisi** has beautiful beaches and a lovely church. Archaeological digs on **Keros**, the large lump of rock that looms over Koufonisia to the south, have uncovered over 100 Early Cycladic figurines, including the famous harpist and flautist now on display in Athens' archaeological museum. There are no guides at the site.

Orientation & Information
Koufonisia's only settlement extends behind the ferry quay and around the pretty harbour filled with the island's fishing flotilla. The older part of town, the hora, is on the low hill behind the quay.

From the quay head right towards the town beach, and take the first road to the left. Continue to the crossroads, then turn left onto the village's main pedestrian thoroughfare, decorated with flower motifs.

Along here you'll find a small minimarket and an inconspicuous ticket agency (look for the dolphins painted above the door). Also here is the tiny, one-phone OTE, complete with straw ceiling; the old guy standing by obviously doesn't see much action now that the island has cardphones. The post office is on the first road to the left as you come from the ferry quay.

The town beach sees a few swimmers but mostly serves as a football field (fishing nets are strung up on the goal posts) for the local kids. Cars and pedestrians heading to the south coast road also traverse it.

Beaches
Koufonisia is blessed with some outstanding beaches and a wild coastal landscape of low sand dunes punctuated by rocky coves and caves. The dunes are covered in wild flowers and hardy shrubs.

CYCLADES

A walk along the south coast road is the nicest way to access the island's beaches. The road extends a couple of kilometres from the eastern end of the town beach to **Finikas**, **Harakopou** and **Fano** beaches.

However, the best beaches and swimming places are farther along the path that follows the coast from Fano to the superb stretch of sand at **Pori**. There are no facilities at Pori, so take food and water. Pori can also be reached by an inland road that heads east from the crossroads in the hora.

Organised Tours

Koufonisia Tours (☎ 71 671, fax 74 091) at Villa Ostria can organise caïque trips to Keros (6000 dr for two people) and Kato Koufonisi (7000 dr for two).

Places to Stay

The *camping ground (☎ 71 683)* is by the beach at Harakopou; it's a bit shadeless but otherwise adequate.

At the western end of the village, *Rooms Maria (☎ 71 778)* has cute two-person apartments overlooking the small fishing harbour for 10,000 dr. To get there, walk along the main pedestrian street and take the first left after Scholeio bar. *Rooms to Let Akrogiali (☎ 71 685)* has nice rooms with sea views at the eastern end of the town beach; doubles with fridge are 10,300 dr. *Lefteris Rooms (☎ 71 458)*, on the town beach, has doubles/triples/quads for 10,000/12,000/14,000 dr. *Katerina's (☎ 71 670)*, on the road leading from the port to the hora, has nice clean doubles with balcony and shared kitchen for 12,000 dr.

Villa Ostria (☎/fax 71 671) is a cosy little hotel with very comfortable rooms with telephone, fridge and veranda for 18,000/16,000 dr with/without breakfast. To get there, walk along the town beach and take the first left. *Keros Studios (☎ 71 600)*, near the post office, also has nice rooms for 16,000 dr.

On the beach at Finikas, *Hotel Finikas (☎ 71 368)* has simple rooms for around 8000 dr and fancier new ones for 13,000 dr. All have a balcony and bathroom.

Places to Eat

Giorgos, at the eastern end of the waterfront on the road to the beaches, has excellent fish and good wines from all over Greece. Everything at *Capitan Nikolas* is delicious and beautifully presented, but the grilled fresh fish, which comes hidden under a veil of finely chopped parsley, is hard to beat. The restaurant looks out over the small harbour at the western end of the village; to get there, follow the main pedestrian street to the end and turn left.

Nikitouri, past Keros Studios, also has good fish. *Lefteris*, below the rooms of the same name, has fine, reasonably priced Greek standards and is one of the few places open for lunch. *Fanari*, next to the windmills above the quay, has good wood-fired pizzas, *pastitsio* and gyros.

Scholeio is a cosy little bar occupying an old schoolhouse at the far end of the main pedestrian street.

Out of town, there's a *taverna* by the beach at Finikas and a good fish *restaurant* on Kato Koufonisi.

DONOUSA (Δονούσα)

☎ 0285 • postcode 843 00 • pop 110

Donousa is the least accessible of the Little Cyclades because it's too far north to be a convenient stop for ferries en route to more popular islands. The main attraction here, as on Iraklia, is that there is nothing much to do except lie on the beach.

Agios Stavros is the main settlement and the island's port. It has a reasonably nice beach, which also serves as a thoroughfare for vehicles and foot traffic. Behind the beach there are lush vegetable gardens and vineyards.

Kendros, over the hill to the west, is a sandy and secluded beach. **Livadi**, the next beach along, sees even fewer visitors. As on many of the other small islands, a frenzy of road construction is currently under way on Donousa, making many of the walks, which used to be so pleasurable, a lot less attractive.

There is one public telephone, up the hill two streets back from the waterfront; look for the large satellite dish above the OTE shack. Stamps are sold at the minimarket on the street running behind the beach.

There is a ticket agency on the waterfront, but it is rarely open and the posted schedule is years out of date; buy your ticket on board from the purser if the agency is closed. Be aware that no-one on the island has much of an idea when the next boat is due or where it's going; unless you are happy to be marooned here for weeks on end, it's worth establishing – before you set out for Donousa – how you're going to leave. Some of the boats to Naxos go via Astypalea, a 12 hour detour you may wish to avoid.

Places to Stay & Eat
Camping is tolerated at Kendros, but you'll need to hike into town for food and water.

The following domatia all charge around 9000 dr for a double. *Spiros Skopelitis Rooms* (☎ 51 586), halfway along the town beach, are neat bungalows, decorated with oriental rugs, set in a shady garden. *Nikitas Markoulis Rooms*, near the kafeneio, and *To Ilio Vasilema* (☎ 51 570), the taverna at the far end of the town beach, also have reasonable rooms.

Aposperitis taverna is next to Spiros Skopelitis and, along with To Ilio Vasilema, serves the usual fare. The hub of village life is the little *Kafeneio To Kyma* by the quay. Everyone seems to pass through here at least once a day and in the evenings it gets rather lively.

Amorgos Αμοργός

☎ 0285 • postcode 840 08 • pop 1630
Elongated Amorgos (ah-mor-**goss**) is the most easterly Cycladic island. With rugged mountains and an extraordinary monastery clinging to a cliff, Amorgos is an enticing island for those wishing to venture off the well worn Mykonos-Paros-Santorini route. It also offers excellent walking.

Amorgos has two ports, Katapola and Aegiali; boats from Naxos usually stop at Katapola first. The beautiful, unspoilt capital, Hora (also known as Amorgos), is up high, north-east of Katapola.

Getting There & Away
Ferry Most ferries stop at both Katapola and Aegiali, but check if this is the case with your ferry. There are daily boats to Naxos (two to 5¾ hours, 2300 dr), Koufonisia (one hour, 1500 dr), Shinousa (1½ hours, 2000 dr), Iraklia (two hours, 2100 dr) and Paros (three hours, 2750 dr), but some of these go to the resort of Piso Livadi (three to 4½ hours, 2750 dr) rather than Parikia. There are at least six ferries weekly to Piraeus (10 hours, 4500 dr).

Ferries also serve Mykonos (six hours, 3100 dr, five weekly), Donousa (30 minutes, 1400 dr, four weekly), Astypalea (2½ hours, 2700 dr, three weekly) and Syros (4½ to 9½ hours, 3400 dr, two weekly). There is a weekly boat to Rafina (10¾ hours, 4700 dr) via Tinos and Andros, and to Kalymnos (three hours, 3400 dr), Kos (4¼ hours, 4100 dr) and Rhodes (eight hours, 4600 dr).

Hydrofoil Four hydrofoils weekly go to Naxos (2¼ to 3¼ hours, 4000 dr) and Mykonos (three to five hours, 6200 dr), and three to Syros (6¼ hours, 6800 dr), Santorini (1½ hours, 4620 dr) and Ios (two hours, 4200 dr). Two weekly serve Paros (1½ hours, 5500 dr), Tinos (six hours, 5100 dr), Syros (2¾ to 4¾ hours, 6800 dr), Koufonisia (one hour, 2600 dr), Iraklia (two hours, 3500 dr) and Shinousa (1½ hours, 3300 dr). A weekly service goes to Donousa (one hour, 2400 dr).

Catamaran Goutos Lines and Strintzis both have weekly fast cats from Katapola to Rafina (five to seven hours, 9500 dr), via Naxos (one to two hours, 3800 dr), Paros (1½ to 2½ hours, 5500 dr), Mykonos (2¼ to four hours, 6200 dr), Tinos (2¾ hours, 5100 dr) and Andros (3½ to 6¼ hours, 8100 dr). Strintzis also stops at Aegiali.

Getting Around
Regular buses go from Katapola to Hora (15 minutes, 220 dr), Moni Hozoviotissis

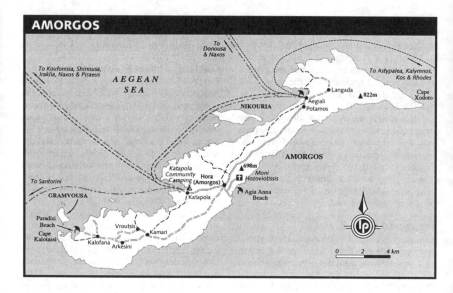

(15 minutes, 220 dr), Agia Anna Beach (20 minutes, 220 dr) and Aegiali (30 minutes, 450 dr), but services are few on weekends. There are also buses from Aegiali to the picturesque village of Langada. Schedules are posted on bus windscreens.

Motorcycles are available for rent in both Katapola and Aegiali. Aegialis Tours (☎ 73 107, fax 73 394), in Aegiali, is the only car hire agency.

KATAPOLA Κατάπολα

Katapola, the principal port, is a pretty town occupying a large, dramatic bay in the most verdant part of the island. A smattering of remains from the ancient Cretan city of Minoa, as well as a Mycenaean cemetery, lie above the port. Amorgos has also yielded many Cycladic finds; the largest figurine in the National Archaeological Museum in Athens was found in the vicinity of Katapola. Boats dock either in front of the central square or to the right (facing inland). The bus station is on the waterfront, near the square.

There is no tourist office or tourist police. Contact Aegialis Tours (see Getting Around) for information. The regular police (☎ 71 210) are on the central square. There is a post office on the square and an ATM on the waterfront nearby.

It can be difficult to extract information about ferries despite the existence of a number of ticket agencies; the old guy at the ouzeri ticket agency (see Places to Stay & Eat) is the most helpful.

Places to Stay & Eat

Katapola Community Camping (☎ 71 257) is back from the northern end of the waterfront. Turn left from the quay (as you face inland).

Domatia owners usually meet the ferries. *Pension Maroussa* (☎ 71 038), just past Katapola Camping, has a beautiful garden; doubles with fridge and bathroom start from 10,000 dr. The C class *Hotel St George* (☎ 71 228) is tucked away up the steps behind the northern end of the harbour and charges 14,900 dr. Spotless studios at *Pension Amorgos* (☎ 71 814), on the waterfront near the square, cost 15,000 dr. The C class *Hotel Minoa* (☎ 71 480), on the square, has comfortable doubles for 17,500 dr. *Vitsentzos*, at the northern end of the waterfront beyond Pension Maroussa, has good, reasonably priced daily specials and serves delicious, freshly squeezed lemon juice. *Psaropoula*, nearby, is the best for fish. *Mouragio*, on the waterfront near the square, is a good traditional place. *Idiston*, around the corner from Hotel Minoa, has local sweets and liqueurs.

The nicest place to have a drink is the laid-back *Moon Bar*, with tables under a large tree on the waterfront; it's just beyond Pension Maroussa. On the waterfront near the square, *Naftilia E Preka*, doubling as a ferry ticket agency, is a beautiful old ouzeri with an ornately tiled floor, green ceiling and impressive collection of defunct TVs.

HORA (AMORGOS)

This amazingly well preserved Cycladic village is 400m above sea level, so high that it's often shrouded in clouds when the rest of the island is sunny. It's an impressive sight, all white and capped with a 13th century kastro atop a large lump of rock.

The bus stop is on a square at the edge of town. The post office is on the main square, reached by a pedestrian laneway from the bus stop. The OTE is in a new building on the main road near the high school. There are no hotels, but domatia are available. *Pension Ilias* (☎ 71 277) and *Pension Panorama* are both close to the bus stop.

MONI HOZOVIOTISSIS

A visit to the 11th century Moni Hozoviotissis is unreservedly worthwhile, as much for the spectacular scenery as for the monastery itself. The dazzling white building clings precariously to a cliff face above the east coast. A few monks still live there and, if you're lucky, one will show you around.

The monastery contains a miracle-working icon found in the sea below the monastery, having allegedly arrived unaided from Asia Minor, Cyprus or Jerusalem, depending on which legend you're told. Modest dress is required – long trousers for men, and a long skirt or dress and covered shoulders for women. The monastery is open 8 am to 1 pm and 5 to 7 pm daily.

The walk to the monastery down the steep hillside from Hora is breathtaking; an old stepped path winds down from near the radio tower. There's also a bus; the monastery bus stop is at the Agia Anna road junction, about 500m uphill from the monastery itself.

AEGIALI Αιγιάλη

Aegiali is Amorgos' other port. The atmosphere is much more laid-back than Katapola and there is a good beach stretching left of the quay.

Organised Tours Aegialis Tours organises some interesting outings, including boat trips around the island with stops at remote beaches (8000 dr, including picnic), and bus tours of the island (7000 dr). Afternoon donkey-riding expeditions cost 5000 dr, and guided explorations of the island's wild herbs cost 3500 dr for a relaxed half-day outing or 5000 dr for a more strenuous full day of clambering about.

Places to Stay & Eat As in Katapola, domatia owners meet ferries. Right on the beach, *Lakki Pension* (☎ 73 253) has immaculate singles/doubles/triples for 12,000/14,000/17,500 dr with bathroom and breakfast; and two/four-person apartments for 17,000/22,000 dr. Luxury two-person apartments with air-con, view and traditional furniture are 20,000 dr, including breakfast. The pension has a delightful garden, a taverna and a bar.

Rooms Irini (☎ 73 237), at the top of the steps after the terrace restaurants, is a pretty place with doubles for 12,500 dr. *Grispos Hotel* (☎ 73 502), up the hill behind the waterfront, has spacious studios for two/four people for 15,000/21,000 dr. *Pension Nostos* (☎ 73 528), across the road, has triple studios with kitchen for 15,000 dr. *Aegialis Hotel* (☎ 73 393, fax 73 395) sits above two sandy beaches and is the

CYCLADES

classiest place around. It has a seawater pool, two bars and a restaurant known for excellent seafood. Singles/doubles cost 23,500/26,500 dr with phone and balcony.

Liminaki, on the waterfront, and *To Steki*, behind Aegialis Tours, both serve good Greek food, but the best place is *Restaurant Lakki*, on the beach at the pension of the same name. Home-grown ingredients make all the difference – the food is simple yet fragrant and delicious. The moussaka is surprisingly delicate, and the stuffed vine leaves and zucchini flowers are plump and aromatic. Interesting wines are also available.

AROUND AMORGOS

Pebbled **Agia Anna Beach**, on the east coast south of Moni Hozoviotissis, is the nearest decent beach to both Katapola and Hora. It has no facilities, so take water and food.

Langada is the most picturesque of the villages inland from Aegiali.

Ios Ιος

☎ 0286   • postcode 840 01   • pop 2000

Ios – the apogee of sun, sea and sex – is the *enfant terrible* of the Greek islands. There's no denying that most visitors come to party hard, but for those who are looking for a more relaxing stay, the island also offers plenty to explore: beautiful beaches, a pretty capital and an interesting rocky, Mars-like landscape. Ios also has a tenuous claim to being Homer's burial place; his tomb is supposedly in the island's north, although no-one seems to know exactly where.

Getting There & Away

Ferry There are at least four daily connections with Piraeus (seven hours, 5300 dr), Paros (2½ hours, 2450 dr) and Naxos (1¼ hours, 2100 dr). There are daily boats to Mykonos (four hours, 3100 dr) and Santorini (one hour, 1500 dr), five weekly to Sikinos (20 minutes, 1100 dr) and Folegandros (1½ hours, 1500 dr), four weekly to Anafi (two hours, 1900 dr) and two weekly

to Syros (2¾ hours, 3700 dr). There are weekly boats to Crete (six hours, 4180 dr), Amorgos (2½ hours, 2115 dr), Kimolos (2½ hours, 1900 dr), Milos (3½ hours, 2800 dr), Sifnos (five hours, 2600 dr) and Serifos (six hours, 2900 dr).

Hydrofoil There are at least three hydrofoils daily to Santorini (30 minutes, 3100 dr) and Naxos (50 minutes, 4200 dr); two to three daily to Paros (1½ hours, 4900 dr), Mykonos (2¾ hours, 6300 dr) and Tinos (3½ hours, 7100 dr); and one or two to Syros (2¼ hours, 7300 dr).

There are six services weekly to Sikinos (10 minutes, 2200 dr) and Folegandros (45 minutes, 3000 dr), four weekly to Amorgos (two hours, 4200 dr), three to Anafi (one hour, 3900 dr), two to Koufonisia (3½ hours, 3300 dr), Shinousa (three hours, 3300 dr), Iraklia (3½ hours, 4400 dr) and Crete (2¼ hours, 8400 dr), and one weekly to Donousa (2½ hours, 4100 dr). Hydrofoil and catamaran tickets are available from Acteon Travel.

Catamaran There are daily cats to Santorini (30 minutes, 3100 dr), Naxos (50 minutes, 4200 dr), Paros (1½ hours, 4900 dr), Syros (2¼ hours, 7300 dr) and Rafina (four hours, 8200 dr).

Getting Around

In summer, crowded buses run between Ormos, Hora (230 dr) and Milopotas (230 dr) about every 15 minutes. Private excursion buses go to Manganari Beach (2000 dr); inquire at Acteon Travel.

Caïques from Ormos to Manganari cost around 2500 dr per person. Ormos and Hora both have car and motorcycle rental firms.

WARNING

Ios' roads are rough and steep. Don't hire an underpowered motorcycle or attempt to ride on unsealed roads unless you are an experienced rider.

HORA, ORMOS & MILOPOTAS

Ios has three population centres, all very close together on the west coast: the port (Ormos); the capital, Hora (also known as the 'village'), 2km inland from the port; and Milopotas, the beach 1km downhill from Hora. Gialos Beach stretches west of the port.

Orientation

The bus terminal in Ormos is straight ahead from the ferry quay on Plateia Emirou. If you want to walk from the port to Hora, turn left from Plateia Emirou, then immediately right and you'll see the stepped path leading up to the right after about 100m. The walk takes about 30 minutes.

In Hora, the church is the main landmark. It's opposite the bus stop, across the car park. To reach the central square of Plateia Valeta from the church, head in to the vil-

lage and turn left at the junction. There are public toilets up the hill behind the main square. The road straight ahead from the bus stop leads to Milopotas Beach.

Information

There is no EOT but Acteon Travel (☎ 91 343), on the square near the quay, is very helpful and is also the American Express representative. At the port, travel agents offer free luggage storage, including free safes. There is a hospital (☎ 91 227) 250m north-west of the quay, on the way to Gialos. The port police (☎ 91 264) are at the southern end of the waterfront, just before Ios Camping.

In Hora, the National Bank of Greece, behind the church, and the Commercial Bank nearby both have ATMs. To get to the post office from the church, continue uphill along the edge of the village, past the bakery, and take the second left.

The OTE is in Hora, along the street that leads right (east) from the top of the port steps; a signpost points the way. It's a difficult uphill walk. The office is open 7.30 am to 3.10 pm daily, closed weekends and public holidays. Internet access is available at Plakiotis Travel and Acteon Travel.

Things to See

Hora itself is a very lovely Cycladic village with myriad laneways and cute houses and shops. Its charm is most evident during daylight hours when the bars are shut and the locals come out of the woodwork.

The only real 'cultural' attraction is the new **archaeological museum** in Hora. The building is immaculately decked out, but the exhibits are a tad disappointing. It's in the yellow building by the bus stop and is open 8 am to 2 pm Tuesday to Sunday (free).

The views from the top of the hill in Hora are worth the climb, especially at sunset. On the way, pause at **Panagia Gremiotissa**, the large church next to the palm tree.

Activities

Ios Diving Centre (☎ 0932-638 646) and Meltemi Watersports (☎/fax 91 680) have outlets at both Milopotas and Manganari. A range of diving courses is offered and wind-surfing and water-skiing equipment is available for hire. There are also some very strange innovations, including the 'banana' – an inflatable yellow object which thrill-seekers cling to as they are pulled along behind a speedboat.

Places to Stay – Budget

Far Out Camping (☎ 91 468) at Milopotas is a slick, somewhat overhyped operation. It has a 24 hour bar, restaurant and two swimming pools, as well as volleyball and basketball courts, and, of course, water sports facilities. All facilities but the accommodation are open to everyone. Charges are 1200/1000 dr per person, with/without tent hire. Basic 'bungalows' that look like dog kennels cost 1500 dr per person; larger ones with double and single beds cost 1800 dr per person. There's little tree cover and roofed areas provide most of the shade. A minibus makes frequent runs to Hora and Ormos.

Purple Pig Camping Stars (☎ 91 302), also at Milopotas, is a smaller, friendlier place shaded by tall trees. It has a swimming pool, disco and restaurant, as well as refreshingly low-key activities such as darts and pool. Internet access is also available. Camping/bungalows cost 1000/2500 dr per person. *Ios Camping* (☎ 91 329) in Ormos has a pool, restaurant, house doctor, travel agency and minimarket, and it also hosts film nights. It charges 1500 dr per person. Turn right at Plateia Emirou and walk along the waterfront to find it.

Backpackers who aren't camping tend to stay at the friendly *Francesco's* (☎/fax 91 223) in the village. Dorm beds cost 3000 dr; doubles/triples are 12,000/15,000 dr with bathroom and 6000/9000 dr without. It's a lively meeting place with a bar and terrace and a wonderful view of the bay. Internet access, free safety deposit boxes, and laundry facilities are also offered. Port transfers are free – call from the port if the van is not there. To get there from the church, head for the central square and turn left at the Second Skin boutique;

Francesco's is about 50m farther along. *Pension Panorama* (☎ 91 592), nearby, offers great views and has doubles/triples for 12,000/15,000 dr with bathroom.

There are lots of domatia signs on the route towards Milopotas Beach from the Hora bus stop. *Rooms Helena* (☎ 91 595) is an old-style place with a bit of character; it's on the left, halfway between Hora and the beach. Basic rooms are 5000/6000 dr. Over the road, *Hermes Rooms* (☎ 91 471), has rooms for 14,000/20,000 dr with bathroom.

Farther along is *Katerina Rooms to Let* (☎ 91 614), with a lovely garden full of flowers. Rooms are 15,000/18,000 dr with bathroom. Home-made breakfast is served on its terrace. *Petradi Rooms* (☎ 91 510), opposite, offers rooms for 18,000/21,000 dr with balcony and bathroom. There is a bar-restaurant and a nice terrace.

Straight ahead from the quay in Ormos is *Zorba's Rooms* (☎ 91 871). Neat singles/doubles/triples are 4000/8000/12,000 dr, or 5000/10,000/15,000 dr with bathroom. *Irene Rooms* (☎ 91 023), signposted nearby, has doubles/triples for 14,000/16,000 dr with balcony and bathroom.

There are also some nice options at Gialos Beach, a short walk from the port. Set back a bit from the beach, *Pension O Kampos* (☎ 91 424) is a great, old-fashioned place with red shutters and green doors. Simple doubles go for 8000/12,000 dr without/with bath. Next door, *Galini Pension* (☎ 91 115) has a lovely shady garden; rooms cost 12,000 dr with bathroom, some with fridge.

Hotel Glaros (☎/fax 91 876) is a relaxed, family-run place on the beach with rooms for 15,000 dr. *Galaxy Hotel* (☎ 91 922), near Purple Pig Camping Stars at Milopotas, has rooms with bath and fridge for 15,000 dr.

Places to Stay – Mid-Range & Top End

Hotel Yialos Beach (☎ 91 421), in Gialos, is a friendly new place with nicely designed Cycladic-style units around a pool. Doubles with air-con, phone, bathroom and balcony go for 18,000 dr.

In Ormos, *Hotel Poseidon (☎ 91 091)* is a nice quiet place with a view over the port and a pool; singles/doubles/triples are 15,000/18,000/22,000 dr with phone. From the waterfront, turn left at Enigma Bar and climb the steps on the left.

Hotel Ios Plage (☎/fax 91 301) is a beautiful, French-run place at the far end of Milopotas Beach, with quite a different feel from the other hotels. Rooms are simply decorated, with large mosquito nets over the beds; doubles cost 18,000 dr. There is a lively bar and a French restaurant.

Sun Club (☎ 92 140), on the road to Hora, has immaculate rooms for 24,000 dr, with bath, TV, phone and view. There's also a pool and bar.

The plush B class *Ios Palace (☎ 91 269)* is a cluster of traditional Cycladic cubes rising up the hill at the Hora end of Milopotas Beach. Singles/doubles/triples are 22,000/27,000/31,000 dr, including breakfast. Four-person suites with private pool go for 70,000 dr. The classy *Far Out Village Hotel (☎ 92 305)*, right on the beach at Milopotas, is the newest addition to the Far Out empire. Traditional rooms go for 18,100/24,800/35,500 dr, with breakfast.

Places to Eat
Fishermen's Restaurant, in Ormos on the way to Ios Camping, is known for its excellent fish. *Corner Cafe*, also at the port, serves good breakfasts and coffee.

In Hora, *Zorba's* and *Nest* are both good value. *Pithari Taverna*, behind the large church, serves cheap, traditional Greek dishes. Close by, *Lord Byron* is a *meze-dopolion* with a very cosy atmosphere augmented by rembetika music; different mezedes are served every day.

Pinocchio Pizzeria has good pizza and pasta, and *panna cotta* for dessert. Look for the signs and Pinocchio standing outside. *La Buca*, next to the bus stop, also has reasonably authentic Italian food, including wood-fired pizza and nice salads. There are also numerous gyros stands where you can get a cheap bite. *Fiesta*, on the Ormos-Hora road, serves good Greek food.

Restaurant Polydoros on Koumbara Beach is popular, and *Filippos*, a huge place on the left-hand side of the road as you head to Koumbara, has spectacular seafood. The legendary *Drakos Taverna* at Milopotas is not be missed. *Harmony*, at the village end of Milopotas beyond Ios Palace, has a lovely terrace dotted with deckchairs and hammocks. Aside from the laid-back atmosphere, the Mexican food is the main attraction, although the pizza, pasta, grills and breakfasts are also pretty good.

Entertainment
At night Hora's tiny central square is transformed into a noisy crowded open-air party so packed it can take half an hour to get from one side to the other. The crowd is mostly made up of alcohol-swilling backpackers in their teens and early twenties – if you're older, the fun wears thin quite quickly.

Popular bars and clubs on the square include *Disco 69*, *Slammer Bar* and *Red Bull*. There is also a gauntlet of Scandinavian bars scattered around town, including *Blue Note*, *Scandinavians* and *Scandinavian Bar*.

Other famous drinking cultures are also well represented, especially the Irish, who claim *Dubliner's*, opposite the bus stop, and *Sweet Irish Dream* across the road. *Upside Down* and *Scorpion's*, both on the Milopotas road, are also popular.

Ios Club provides sweeping views and is a relaxed, quiet place for a drink. It's signposted from the top of the steps down to the port. *Orange Bar*, 150m beyond the central square, is a good, laid-back escape hatch.

The nightlife down at Ormos is pretty lame in comparison to Hora's. *Frog's Club*, on the waterfront, caters mainly to a yachtie

> ### WARNING
> There's no such thing as a free cocktail. The cheap local moonshine used in mixed drinks and cocktails is bad news, particularly for the unwary.

CYCLADES

clientele and sometimes has a live guitarist. Nearby, *Enigma* is also worth a look. *Marina Bar*, overlooking Gialos Beach, has good Greek music.

AROUND IOS

Apart from the nightlife, the beaches are what lure travellers to Ios. From Ormos, it's a 10 minute walk past the little church of Agia Irini for **Valmas Beach**. **Kolitzani Beach**, south of Hora, down the steps by Scorpion's, is also nice. **Koubara**, a 30 minute walk north-west of Ormos, is the official nudist beach. **Tsamaria**, nearby, is nice and sheltered when it's windy elsewhere.

Vying with Milopotas for best beach is **Manganari**, a long swathe of fine white sand on the south coast, reached by bus or by excursion boat in summer. There are several domatia, including *Dimitri's* (☎ 91 483), which has lovely doubles for 10,000 dr. *Cristos Taverna* (☎ 0932-411 547), 200m away, has a very good restaurant – they catch their own fish – and doubles for 10,000 dr. *Hotel Manganari* (☎ 91 200) is accessible only by boat and has villas for two at 32,000 dr, including breakfast and dinner. *Antonio's Restaurant* has incredibly fresh fish and calamari, and good grills; make sure you sample the different home-made cheeses made with milk from their goats.

Agia Theodoti, **Psathi** and **Kalamos** beaches, all on the north-east coast, are more remote. **Moni Kalamou**, on the way to Manganari and Kalamos, stages a huge religious festival in late August and a festival of music and dance on 7 September.

Santorini (Thira)
Σαντορίνη (Θήρα)

☎ 0286 • postcode 847 00 • pop 9360

Santorini, officially known as Thira, is regarded by many as the most spectacular of all the Greek islands. Thousands visit annually to gaze in wonder at the submerged caldera (crater), a vestige of what was probably the biggest volcanic eruption in recorded history. Although it gets crowded and is overly commercial, Santorini is unique and should not be missed. The caldera is a real spectacle – it's worth arriving by ferry rather than catamaran or hydrofoil if you want to experience the full dramatic impact. The main port is Athinios. Buses meet all ferries and cart passengers to Fira, the capital, which teeters on the lip of the caldera, high above the sea.

History

Greece is susceptible to eruptions and earthquakes – mostly minor – but on Santorini these have been so violent as to change the shape of the island several times.

Dorians, Venetians and Turks occupied Santorini, as they did all other Cycladic islands, but its most influential early inhabitants were the Minoans. They came from Crete some time between 2000 and 1600 BC, and the settlement at Akrotiri dates from the height of their great civilisation.

The island then was circular and called Strongili (the Round One). Around 1650 BC, a colossal volcanic eruption caused the centre of Strongili to sink, leaving a caldera with high cliffs – one of the world's most dramatic geological sights. Some archaeologists have speculated that this catastrophe destroyed not only Akrotiri but the whole Minoan civilisation as well. Another theory that has fired the imaginations of writers, artists and mystics since ancient times postulates that the island was part of the mythical lost continent of Atlantis. See the following boxed text for more details on the volcano.

Getting There & Away

Air Olympic Airway operates at least six flights daily to Athens (22,200 dr), five weekly to Rhodes (22,900 dr) and Mykonos (15,400 dr), three weekly to Thessaloniki (30,400 dr) and two weekly to Iraklio (15,400 dr). The Olympic Airways office (☎ 22 493) is in Fira, on the road to Kamari, one block east of 25 Martiou. Air Manos flies to Athens (21,200 dr) six days a week, and also to Mykonos (14,400 dr), Samos (16,400 dr) and

Mending nets, Kamari beach, Santorini, Cyclades

What's for lunch? Cafe menu, Loutro, Crete

Neoclassical mansions, Ermoupolis, Syros, Cyclades

Scorching black-sand beaches become so hot that using a mat is essential, Perissa Beach, Santorini, Cyclades

TREVOR CREIGHTON

Coffee house remains, Crete

JEANNE OLIVER

Glistening 'Cretan Blue' ceramics

DIANA MAYFIELD

Retail therapy to cure those 'Cretan Blues', Hania, Crete

KIMBERLY GRANT

The beautiful Venetian quarter, Hania, Crete

KIMBERLY GRANT

Santorini, Cyclades

Thessaloniki (18,400 dr) twice weekly. TransEuropean flies to Athens (23,400 dr) at least twice weekly. Various travel agencies in Fira sell tickets for these airlines.

Ferry Santorini is the southernmost island of the Cyclades, and as a major tourist destination it has good connections with Piraeus and Thessaloniki on the mainland, as well as with Crete. Santorini also has useful services to Anafi, Folegandros and Sikinos. No travel agent sells tickets for all the ferries, so make sure you check schedules with at least three before you hand over your cash.

There are at least seven boats daily to Naxos (three hours, 3100 dr) and Paros (three to four hours, 3050 dr), six daily to Ios (1¼ hours, 1700 dr), five to Piraeus (nine hours, 6100 dr), two to Mykonos (six hours, 3600 dr), and one to Crete (four hours, 3700 dr), Tinos (five hours, 4200 dr) and Syros (5¼ hours, 4300 dr).

Five boats weekly go to Anafi (one hour, 1900 dr), Thessaloniki (17¾ hours, 10,100 dr) and Folegandros (1½ to 2½ hours, 1900 dr), and four weekly depart for Amorgos (2½ hours, 2350 dr).

There are three ferries weekly to Sikinos (2½ hours, 1700 dr), and two weekly to Milos (four hours, 3650 dr), Kimolos (3½ hours, 3000 dr), Sifnos (six hours, 3060 dr), Serifos (seven hours, 3600 dr), Rhodes (seven to eight hours, 6400 dr) and Skiathos (11¾ hours, 8200 dr).

There are weekly ferries to Volos (14 hours, 8100 dr) and Astypalea (four hours, 3350 dr), and, outside high season, usually two weekly to Karpathos (4900 dr) and Kassos (4100 dr). Once a week there is a ferry to Lemesos (Limassol) in Cyprus (38 hours) and Haifa in Israel (58 hours).

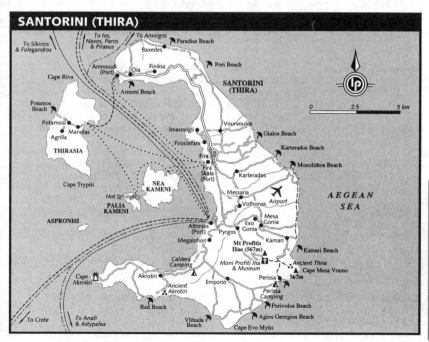

SANTORINI (THIRA)

Santorini's Unsettling Past

Santorini's violent upheaved volcanic history is visible everywhere you look – in black sand beaches, in raw lava-layered cliffs that plunge into the sea, in earthquake-damaged dwellings, and in fertile soil that supports coiled-up grape vines. The volcano may be dormant but it's not dead. Santorini's caldera ('cauldron'), which often has a surface as calm and glassy as a backyard fish pond, could start to boil at any moment...

Santorini first appeared when the landmass known as Aegis, which joined the European and Asian continents, was gradually flooded around one million years ago, leaving only the highest peaks above water. Profitis Ilias and Monolithos are both ancient rocks dating back to this time. At some point a complex of submarine, overlapping shield volcanoes began to toil and trouble, eventually erupting and filling in the area between Santorini's mountains with lava. This process continued for thousands of years and over time the island took on a conical shape.

Eventually the volcanoes quieted, and vegetation established itself in the fertile ash. Around 3000 BC the first human settlers arrived and, from evidence found at Akrotiri, it appears that they led very idyllic lives and fashioned a highly evolved culture.

But peace and harmony never last long enough, and around 1650 BC a chain of earthquakes and eruptions culminated in one of the largest explosions in the history of the planet. Thirty cubic kilometres of magma spewed forth and a column of ash 36km high jetted into the atmosphere. So much magma was ejected that the magma chambers of the volcano gave way and the centre of the island collapsed, producing a caldera that the sea quickly filled. It's hard to imagine the magnitude of the explosion, but it is often compared to thousands of

Hydrofoil There are at least three hydrofoils daily to Ios (30 minutes, 3100 dr) and Mykonos (three hours, 6800 dr), and at least two daily to Naxos (1¾ hours, 6100 dr), Paros (two hours, 6100 dr), Tinos (3¼ hours, 8400 dr) and Syros (3½ hours, 9000 dr).

There are also services to Iraklio on Crete (2¾ hours, 7200 dr, daily), Folegandros (one hour, 3350 dr, six weekly), Sikinos (30 minutes, 3400 dr, five weekly) and Amorgos (1½ hours, 4650 dr, four weekly). A couple a week serve Donousa (two hours, 3650 dr), Koufonisia (2½ hours, 3650 dr), Shinousa (2¾ hours, 3650 dr), Iraklia (three hours, 3650 dr), Sifnos (three hours, 6200 dr) and Milos (3½ hours, 7450 dr). There are occasional services to Anafi (30 minutes, 3500 dr) and Karystos (3½ hours) on Evia.

Catamaran Daily cats go to Ios (30 minutes, 3100 dr), Naxos (1½ hours, 6100 dr), Paros (2¼ hours, 6100 dr), Syros (three hours, 9000 dr) and Rafina (4¾ hours, 9600 dr).

Getting Around

To/From the Airport There are frequent bus connections in summer between Fira's bus station and the airport. Enthusiastic hotel and domatia staff meet flights and some also return guests to the airport.

Bus In summer, buses leave Fira's bus station hourly for Akrotiri (370 dr) and every half-hour for Oia (270 dr), Monolithos (250 dr), Kamari (260 dr) and Perissa (390 dr). There are less frequent buses to Exogonia (250 dr), Perivolos (390 dr) and Vlihada (450 dr).

Buses leave Fira, Kamari and Perissa for the port of Athinios (370 dr) 1½ hours before most ferry departures. Buses for Fira meet all ferries, even late at night.

Car, Motorcycle & Bicycle Fira has many car, motorcycle and bicycle rental firms. Hired wheels are the best way to explore the island as the buses are intolerably

Santorini's Unsettling Past

atomic bombs all having their pins pulled simultaneously. The event sent ash all over the Mediterranean, and it also generated huge tsunamis (tidal waves) that travelled with dangerous force all the way to Crete and Israel. Anafi was hit by a wave 250m high. The fall-out from the explosion was more than just dust and pumice – it's widely believed that the catastrophe was responsible for the demise of Crete's Minoan culture, one of the most powerful civilisations in the Aegean at that time. After the Big One, Santorini once again settled down for a time and allowed plants, animals and humans to recolonise it. In 286 BC the rumbles from the deep resumed and volcanic activity separated Thirasia from the main island. Further changes to the landscape continued intermittently. In 197 BC the islet now known as Palia Kameni appeared in the caldera, and in 726 AD there was a major eruption that catapulted pumice all the way to Asia Minor. The south coast of Santorini collapsed in 1570, taking the ancient port of Eleusis with it. In 1650 earthquakes and explosions caused tsunamis and killed and blinded many people on the island. An eruption of lava in 1707 created Nea Kameni islet next to Palia Kameni, and further eruptions in 1866-70, 1925-26, 1928, 1939-41 and 1950 augmented it. A major earthquake measuring 7.8 on the Richter scale savaged the island in 1956, killing scores of people and destroying most of the houses in Fira and Oia.

Volcanic activity has been pretty low-key since 1956, but minor tremors are quite common and the ground shakes, usually imperceptibly, almost every day. A major earthquake is due at any moment, but the locals don't seem worried – they seem to like living on the edge. For lovers of impermanence, precariousness and drama, no other place even comes close.

overcrowded in summer and you'll be lucky to get on one at all.

Taxi Call ☎ 23 951 or 22 555 for a taxi.

Cable Car & Donkey Cable cars shunt passengers from cruise ships and excursion boats up to Fira from the small port below known as Fira Skala. Tickets cost 800 dr one way. Or you can go by donkey, for the same price.

FIRA Φήρα

The commercialism of Fira has not diminished its all-pervasive, dramatic aura. Walk to the edge of the caldera for spectacular views of the cliffs and their multicoloured strata of lava and pumice.

Orientation

The central square is Plateia Theotokopoulou. The main road, 25 Martiou, runs north-south, intersecting the square and is lined with travel agencies. The bus station is on 25 Martiou, 50m south of Plateia Theotokopoulou. West of 25 Martiou the streets are old pedestrian laneways; Erythrou Stavrou, one block west of 25 Martiou, is the main commercial thoroughfare.

Another block west, Ypapantis runs along the crest of the caldera and provides staggering panoramic views. Head north on Nomikou for the cable car station. If you keep walking along the caldera – and it's well worth it – you'll come to the Nomikos Convention Centre and, eventually, the cliff-top villages of Firostefani and Imerovigli.

Information

Fira doesn't have an EOT or tourist police. Dozens of travel agencies offer tourist information. The staff at Dakoutros Travel (☎ 22 958, fax 22 686) are particularly helpful and can organise accommodation, ferry tickets and excursions. The National Bank of Greece is between the bus station and Plateia Theotokopoulou, on the caldera side

CYCLADES

of the road. American Express is represented by Alpha Credit Bank on Plateia Theotokopoulou. Both banks have ATMs. The post office is about 150m south of the bus station. Lava Internet Cafe, just up from the main square, provides Internet access at 600/900/1800 dr for 15/30/60 minutes.

There is a laundrette and dry cleaner 200m north of Plateia Theotokopoulou, underneath Pension Villa Maria, and another laundrette next to Pelican Hotel.

The hospital (☎ 222 37) is on the road to Karterados, near the Olympic Airways office. The police station (☎ 22 649) is south of Plateia Theotokopoulou; the port police (☎ 22 239) are north of the square.

Museums

Megaron Gyzi museum, behind the Catholic cathedral, has local memorabilia, including fascinating photographs of Fira before and immediately after the major 1956 earthquake. Theoretically, it's open 10.30 am to 1.30 pm and 5 until 8 pm Monday to Saturday, 10.30 am to 4.30 pm Sunday (closed holidays). In practice, opening times are erratic. Entrance is 400 dr.

The **archaeological museum**, opposite the cable car station, houses finds from Akrotiri and Ancient Thira, some Cycladic figurines, and Hellenistic and Roman sculpture. It's open 8 am to 2.30 pm Tuesday to Sunday. Admission is 400 dr. At the time of writing, a new archaeological museum (opposite the bus station) was nearing completion.

For the past few years the **Nomikos Convention Centre** (☎ 23 016), also known as the Thera Foundation, has displayed fascinating three-dimensional photographic reproductions of the Akrotiri frescoes, which offer a glimpse of what life was like on the island in the 16th century BC. Saffron had an important religious and symbolic role and many of the paintings show young women collecting it. The exhibit is open 10 am to 9 pm Tuesday to Sunday; admission is 1000 dr, but before you go, call to see if it is still running. To get there, follow the old Byzantine path along the caldera, past the cable car station.

The **Bellonio Cultural Centre & Library**, next to the post office, has a large collection of books about Santorini. It's open 9 am to 2 pm and 6 to 9 pm daily.

Organised Tours

Tour agencies operate trips to Thirasia, the volcanic island of Nea Kameni, Palia Kameni's hot springs and Oia. See the Thirasia & Volcanic Islets section for details.

Places to Stay – Budget

Camping Santorini (☎ 22 944) is a nice site with many facilities, including a restaurant and pool. The cost is 1500/800 dr per person/tent. It's 400m east of Plateia Theotokopoulou – look for the sign.

Accommodation owners meeting boats and buses are fairly aggressive but are now confined to 'official' information booths; this doesn't mean that you'll get impartial information or the best accommodation available, so don't jump at the first offer. Some owners of rooms in Karterados (3km south-east of Fira) claim that their rooms are in town; ask to see a map showing the location.

The massive *Thira Hostel* (☎ 23 864), 300m north of Plateia Theotokopoulou, is a beautiful old place that was formerly part of the Catholic monastery. Some of the rooms have remnants of antique furniture and there's a lovely secret garden. The hostel has a variety of small dorms with up to 10 beds for 2500 dr per person, plus doubles/triples for 9000/10,000 dr with bath. Beds on the roof cost 2000 dr.

Hotel Keti (☎ 22 324) is a real gem with lovely traditional rooms dug into the cliffs; doubles with terrace overlooking the caldera go for 14,000 dr. *Argonaftis Villas* (☎ 22 055), near the school , is run by a talented painter who is also a port policeman. His folksy paintings, most with nautical themes, decorate many of the rooms. Doubles with bath are 16,000 dr, and apartments for two/four are 17,000/25,000 dr – one of these is a traditional cave house.

A short walk north-east of the town centre takes you to Kontohori, a peaceful, vaguely rural area with plenty of domatia.

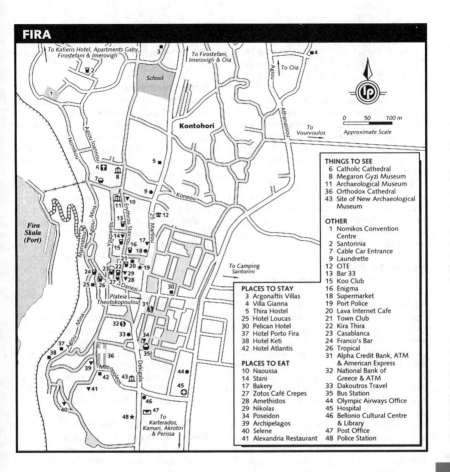

FIRA

*To Kafieris Hotel, Apartments Gaby,
Firostefani & Imerovigli*

*To Firostefani,
Imerovigli & Oia*

To Oia

School

Kontohori

*To
Vourvoulos* *Approximate Scale*

0   50   100 m

To Oia

Nomikou

Agiou Ioannou

**Fira
Skala
(Port)**

Marinatou

Agiou Mina

Agiou Mina

Ypapatis

Erythrou Stavrou

25 Martiou

Koneou

Danezi

Plateia
Theotokopoulou

Mitropoleos

Dekigala

*To Camping
Santorini*

*To
Karterados,
Kamari, Akrotiri
& Perissa*

THINGS TO SEE
6 Catholic Cathedral
8 Megaron Gyzi Museum
11 Archaeological Museum
36 Orthodox Cathedral
43 Site of New Archaeological
     Museum

OTHER
1 Nomikos Convention
    Centre
2 Santorinia
7 Cable Car Entrance
9 Laundrette
12 OTE
13 Bar 33
15 Koo Club
16 Enigma
18 Supermarket
19 Port Police
20 Lava Internet Cafe
21 Town Club
22 Kira Thira
23 Casablanca
24 Franco's Bar
26 Tropical
31 Alpha Credit Bank, ATM
     & American Express
32 National Bank of
     Greece & ATM
33 Dakoutros Travel
35 Bus Station
44 Olympic Airways Office
45 Hospital
46 Bellonio Cultural Centre
     & Library
47 Post Office
48 Police Station

PLACES TO STAY
3 Argonaftis Villas
4 Villa Gianna
5 Thira Hostel
25 Hotel Loucas
30 Pelican Hotel
37 Hotel Porto Fira
38 Hotel Keti
42 Hotel Atlantis

PLACES TO EAT
10 Naoussa
14 Stani
17 Bakery
27 Zotos Café Crepes
28 Amethistos
29 Nikolas
34 Poseidon
39 Archipelagos
40 Selene
41 Alexandria Restaurant

Among these is **Villa Gianna** (☎ 23 367), which has a pool and air-con; doubles/triples are 21,000/28,000 dr.

On the path up to Firostefani, not far from the convention centre, **Kafieris Hotel** (☎ 22 189) has lovely doubles on the caldera for 10,000 dr. Nearby, **Apartments Gaby** (☎ 22 057) is a great place with doubles for 18,000 dr and four-person apartments for 32,000 dr. Gaby also has some rooms closer to the main road with a view of the eastern side of the island, for 12,000 dr.

Farther up the hill, near Firostefani's main square, **Hotel Sofia Sigala** (☎ 22 802) has nice doubles for 16,000 dr with bathroom and fridge. **Hotel Mylos** (☎ 23 884), opposite, has similar rooms for 15,000 dr. Nearby, **Ioaniss Roussos Rooms** (☎ 22 611) has doubles for 14,000 dr.

Places to Stay – Mid-Range &
Top End
Pelican Hotel (☎ 23 113), right in the centre of town, has comfortable singles/doubles/

CYCLADES

triples for 23,000/29,000/36,000 dr, including breakfast.

Hotels perched on the caldera's edge in Fira are naturally a bit more expensive. Among them, *Hotel Loucas* (☎ 22 480), with a pool, has rooms for 25,000/32,500/41,000 dr, with breakfast. Also on the caldera, *Hotel Porto Fira* (☎ 22 849) charges 27,500/35,000/40,000 dr. The spacious, airy A class *Hotel Atlantis* (☎ 22 232) has singles/doubles for 40,000/60,000 dr with all comforts, a view over the caldera, and breakfast.

Up in Firostefani, *Eterpi Villas* (☎ 22 541) has traditional abodes dug into the caldera; two-person studios/apartments go for 35,000/48,000 dr. *Dana Villas* (☎ 22 566), also in Firostefani, is similar and charges 48,600/51,600 dr.

Places to Eat
Fira has many terrible tourist-trap eateries, so it's worth being picky. *Nikolas*, opposite Kira Thira, has tasty traditional food and friendly service. *Naoussa*, upstairs (and not to be confused with the very average establishment at ground level), beyond Bar 33, serves excellent, reasonably priced Greek classics. *Stani*, upstairs next to Koo Club, has good home-cooked food. *Poseidon*, below the bus station, has reasonable, inexpensive food and is open 24 hours.

Archipelagos is a classy place with nice simple dishes like spaghetti with sage and walnuts (2200 dr). *Selene* is one of the best restaurants and has a lovely romantic atmosphere; creative main courses start at 3700 dr. *Kukumavlos* has an innovative menu featuring local and imported exotica, including ostrich fillet with caramelised onions in merlot sauce (5200 dr).

The best places for juices, coffee, cake and crepes are *Zotos Cafe Crepe* and *Amesthistos*, opposite each other on Erythrou Stavrou. The *bakery* up from the main square sells pies as well as bread and is open 24 hours.

On the main square in Firostefani, *To Aktaion* is a nice little taverna serving traditional food. Farther up the caldera in Imerovigli, *Skaros Fish Tavern* has excellent mezedes and fish as well as a spectacular view.

Entertainment
Kira Thira, the oldest bar in Fira and a favourite haunt of both locals and travellers, is a funky little candlelit dive with an eclectic selection of sounds and occasional live music. *Tropical* is another long-established bar with a loyal clientele. *Franco's Bar* is a good place to watch the sun set.

After midnight, *Koo Club*, the superkitsch *Town Club*, *Casablanca* and *Enigma* are the best places to go disco dancing.

Santorinia, not far from the cable car station and the convention centre, has traditional live music, including *rembetika* and *laïko*; outside high season it opens only on weekends. *Bar 33*, past Koo Club, is a lively bouzouki place.

Shopping
Grapes thrive in Santorini's volcanic soil, and the island's wines are famous all over Greece and beyond. Local wines are widely available in Fira and elsewhere. Try 50-50 from Canava Nomikos, and the wines from Oia. Cava Sigalas in Firostefani sells local fava beans, capers, caper leaves (a delicacy), wines and thyme honey.

AROUND SANTORINI
Ancient Akrotiri Παλαιό Ακρωτήρι
Ancient Akrotiri was a Minoan outpost; excavations begun in 1967 have uncovered an ancient city beneath the volcanic ash. Buildings, some three storeys high, date to the late 16th century BC. The absence of skeletons and treasures indicates that inhabitants were forewarned of the eruption and escaped.

The most outstanding finds are the stunning frescoes, many of which are now on display at the National Archaeological Museum in Athens. (Very accurate replicas are on display at the Nomikos Convention Centre; see Fira.) The site is open 8 am to 8 pm Tuesday to Sunday. Admission is 1200 dr.

Caldera View Camping (☎ 82 010) near Akrotiri doesn't really have a view over the caldera and it's a long way from any nightlife, but it's a nice enough spot. It charges 1500 dr per person and 600 dr per tent. There are also two-person bungalows from 15,000 dr, including breakfast.

There are some nice little fish *tavernas* on the beach below the archaeological site. On the way to Akrotiri, pause at the enchanting traditional settlement of **Megalohori**.

Ancient Thira Αρχαία Θήρα

Ancient Thira, first settled by the Dorians in the 9th century BC, has Hellenistic, Roman and Byzantine ruins. These include temples, houses with mosaics, an agora, a theatre and a gymnasium. The site has splendid views. It's open 9 am to 2.30 pm Tuesday to Sunday (free).

It takes about 30 minutes to walk to the site along the path from Perissa. If you're driving, take the road from Kamari.

Moni Profiti Ilia
Μονή Προφήτη Ηλία

This monastery crowns Santorini's highest peak, Mt Profitis Ilias (567m). Although it now shares the peak with radio and TV pylons and a radar station, it's worth the trek for the stupendous views. The monastery has an interesting **folk museum**. You can walk there from Pyrgos (1½ hours) or from Ancient Thira (one hour).

Oia Οία

The village of Oia (**ee**-ah) was devastated by the 1956 earthquake and has never fully recovered, but it's dramatic, striking and quieter than Fira. Built on a steep slope of the caldera, many of its dwellings nestle in niches hewn into the volcanic rock. Oia is famous for its sunsets and its narrow passageways get crowded in the evenings.

From the bus turnaround, go left (following signs for the youth hostel), turn immediately right, take the first left, ascend the steps and walk across the central square to the main street, Nikolaou Nomikou,

which skirts the caldera. You can get information and book hotels through Ecorama (☎ 71 507, fax 71 509), by the bus turnaround, and Kargounas Tours (☎ 71 290) on Nikolaou Nomikou.

The last bus for Fira leaves Oia at 10.20 pm in summer. After that, three to four people can bargain for a shared taxi for about 3000 dr. Six buses daily connect Oia with Baxedes Beach.

The **maritime museum** is open 12.30 to 4 pm and 5 to 8.30 pm daily except Tuesday; admission is 800 dr.

You can swim at **Ammoudi**, the tiny port with tavernas that lies 300 steps below. In summer at least two boats daily go from Ammoudi to Thirasia (1000 dr per person); check the times at Kargounas Tours.

The traditional settlement of **Finikia**, just east of Oia, is a beautiful, quiet place to wander around.

Places to Stay Oia's exceptional *youth hostel (☎ 71 465)* has dorm beds for 3500 dr, including breakfast. The hostel has a bar, laundry facilities and a nice terrace, but is open in summer only.

A little farther on there are several domatia with reasonable prices. *Irini Halari (☎ 71 226)*, on the main road near the pink church, has singles/doubles/triples for 5000/10,000/12,000 dr with bathroom. Next door, *Antonis* has similar rooms and prices.

Lauda Traditional Pension (☎ 71 157), on the main pedestrian thoroughfare overlooking the caldera, has singles/doubles for 12,000/15,000 dr and double/triple studios for 18,000/24,000 dr.

If you can afford to splurge, Oia is the place to do it. For lovingly restored traditional cave dwellings, contact *Chelidonia (☎ 71 287, fax 71 649)*. The office is in the centre of town (the Web address is www.chelidonia.com); apartments for two/four cost 28,000/42,000 dr. *Restaurant Lotza (☎ 71 357)*, on the same street, has traditional houses at similar prices. *Zoe-Aegeas (☎ 71 466)* has lovely two-person studios in traditional houses with shared/private courtyard for 25,000/30,000 dr.

CYCLADES

Katikies (☎ 71 401) is one of the most beautiful hotels on the island and has a spectacular pool filled to the brim and balanced on the lip of the caldera. Doubles rooms cost 43,000 dr and apartments for four cost 100,000 dr. Double studios (51,000 dr), two-person apartments (58,000 dr) and a honeymoon suite (79,000 dr) are also available.

Places to Eat *Anemomylos*, at the eastern edge of the town, serves traditional food at reasonable prices. For fish, locals eat at *Thalami* in the centre of town, and at *Dimitri's* and *Sunset*, gorgeous little tavernas at the port of Ammoudi. There is no shortage of restaurants with a view; *Skala*, on the caldera, has excellent lamb, salads and hors d'oeuvres. *1800*, in a restored sea captain's house complete with original furniture, is an upmarket place serving contemporary Greek cuisine. Expect to pay at least 10,000 dr a head, including wine.

Karterados Καρτεράδος
There's not a lot to see here, and the old village with houses dug into a ravine is very neglected now that new apartments have been built on its periphery. However, accommodation is cheaper than in Fira and it makes a good base, providing you don't mind the 20 minute walk to town.

Agapi & Stavros Filitsis (☎ 22 694, 23 720), at Taverna Neraïda, have 65 rooms to choose from. Singles/doubles are 8000/15,000 dr with bathroom; two-person apartments at a nearby beach are 24,000 dr. Turn left off the main approach road from Fira, and it's the last in a row of tavernas on the left.

The comfortable *Pension George (☎ 22 351)* has singles/doubles for 12,000/14,000 dr with bathroom. George will collect guests from Fira, the ferry port or the airport if phoned. Otherwise, walk or take a bus to the village turn-off. Follow the road and turn right after a church on your left. The pension is on the left, cloaked in bougainvillea.

Messaria Μεσσαριά
Situated at a shady junction between Karterados and Kamari, Messaria has a few tavernas and domatia. The main attraction is the **Arhontiko Argirou** (☎ 31 669), a sumptuously restored neoclassical mansion that dates from 1888. It's open 10 am to 1 pm and 5 to 7 pm daily. You can also stay here: doubles with bathroom are 14,000 dr, while apartments with kitchen are 24,000 dr.

Wineries
There are five commercial wineries that hold tastings in summer: **Canava Roussos** and **Lava**, both on the way to Kamari; **Santo Wines**, near Pyrgos; and **Antoniou** and **Boutari**, both in Megalohori.

Antoniou winery is an old place with dungeons that descend down the cliffs; wine is no longer made at this site, but it's a fascinating place to visit. Santo Wines is the local vine growers' cooperative and worth supporting.

Beaches
Santorini's black sand beaches become so hot that a mat is essential. The nicest beaches are on the east coast. **Perissa** gets quite busy, but **Perivolos** and **Agios Georgios**, farther south, are more relaxed. The Mediterranean Dive Club (☎ 83 080), based at Perissa, offers diving certification, wreck dives and volcano dives.

Perissa Camping (☎ 81 343) charges 1500 dr per person and 800 dr per tent. *Hostel Anna (☎ 82 182)*, also in Perissa, has a free bus from the port. Dorm beds cost 1800 dr, and nearby double/quad rooms with pool are 10,000/20,000 dr. Plenty of *domatia* are available in Perissa and at Perivolos.

Leonidas taverna at Agios Georgios is a nice place to kick back and have a relaxing ouzo or raki and a bite to eat. *The Nets*, closer to Perissa, serves exquisite, delicate mezedes and seafood and is open year-round. Nearby, *Perivolos* also serves superb seafood. *Taverna Lava*, on the beachfront at Perissa, is a well established, low-key place with deliciously simple mezedes and excellent, unfussy traditional food.

Kamari is a long strand now covered by beach umbrellas and backed by package tour hotels. There are a few *domatia* in the backstreets. If you're tired of the bland eateries along the beach, *Ouzeria Pontios*, which is festooned with Chinese lanterns and other paraphernalia, can provide a bit of local colour. Try the mezedes or the grilled fish. It's up in Kamari village, near the football ground. To get there, turn off the main road at the large church and take the first street on the right.

Kamari Cinema, on the main road coming into Kamari, is a great open-air theatre set in a thicket of trees and showing recent releases; entry is 1800 dr. In July it hosts the Santorini Jazz Festival.

Monolithos Beach, farther along the coast near an abandoned tomato cannery, is less crowded and there are sometimes sizable waves to splash about in. *Galini Fish Taverna (☎ 32 924)* has good fresh seafood and is set right on the beach. *Mythos Mezedopoleio* is another nice place to stop for ouzo and a nibble. North of Monolithos, the beaches are almost deserted.

Red Beach, near Ancient Akrotiri, has some novelty value but is overrated. **Vlihada**, also on the south coast, is much nicer. On the north coast near Oia, **Paradise** and **Pori** are both worth a stop. *Captain John*, at Pori, is a good spot for lunch. At **Armeni** and **Ammoudi**, down the cliffs below Oia, you can plunge right into the caldera. Contact Atlantis Diving (☎ 0932-778 411) at Ammoudi if you're interested in exploring the depths.

THIRASIA & VOLCANIC ISLETS

Unspoilt Thirasia (Θηρασιά) was separated from Santorini by an eruption in 236 BC. The cliff-top hora, **Manolas**, has *tavernas* and *domatia*. It's a pretty place that gives some idea of what Santorini was like before tourism took over.

The *Nisos Thirasia* leaves Athinios port for Thirasia on Monday and Friday at the inconveniently early hour of 7 am, returning at 2 pm. On Wednesday it leaves Athinios at 1.30 pm but does not return to Santorini. Tickets are available only at the port. There are also morning and afternoon boats to Thirasia from Oia's port of Ammoudi; see the Oia section for details.

The islets of **Palia Kameni** and **Nea Kameni** are still volcanically active and can be visited on half-day excursions from Fira Skala and Athinios for around 3500 dr. A two hour trip to Nea Kameni costs around 2000 dr. A day's excursion taking in Nea Kameni, the hot springs at Palia Kameni, Thirasia and Oia is about 5000 dr. A tour around the caldera by glass-bottomed boat costs 5000 dr. Tours that include Akrotiri as well are 7000 dr. Shop around Fira's travel agencies for the best deals and the nicest boats.

The very bella *Bella Aurora*, an exact copy of an 18th century schooner, scoots around the caldera every afternoon on a sunset tour (8000 dr), stopping for sight-seeing at Nea Kameni and for ouzo at Thirasia.

Anafi Ανάφη

☎ 0286   • postcode 840 09   • pop 250

Unpretentious Anafi is a one hour ferry ride east of Santorini. The main attractions are the beaches, the slow-paced, traditional lifestyle and the lack of commercialism – it's an ideal place to unwind. In mythology, Anafi emerged at Apollo's command when Jason and the Argonauts were in dire need of refuge during a storm. The island's name means 'no snakes'.

Its little port is **Agios Nikolaos**. The main town, the **hora**, is a 10 minute bus ride or steep 30 minute walk from the port. To get to the hora's main pedestrian thoroughfare, head up the hill behind the ouzeri at the first bus stop. This street has most of the domatia, restaurants and minimarkets, and there is also a post office that opens occasionally.

There are several lovely beaches near Agios Nikolaos; palm-lined **Klissidi**, a 10 minute walk east of the port, is the closest and most popular.

Anafi's main sight, **Moni Kalamiotissas**, is a three hour walk from the hora in the extreme east of the island, near the meagre remains of a sanctuary to Apollo. **Monastery Rock** (584m) is the highest rock formation in the Mediterranean Sea. There is also a ruined Venetian kastro at **Kastelli**, east of Klissidi.

Jeyzed Travel (☎ 61 253), down at the port, sells tickets, exchanges money, can help with accommodation and organises Monastery Rock climbs.

Getting There & Away

There are five ferries weekly to Ios (two to 3½ hours, 1900 dr), Naxos (four hours, 2800 dr) and Paros (6½ hours, 3500 dr). Four ferries weekly go to Santorini (one hour, 1700 dr) and Piraeus (11 hours, 6700 dr), and one goes to Syros (eight hours, 4100 dr), Folegandros (five hours, 2450 dr), Sikinos (four hours, 1850 dr) and Astypalea (1½ hours, 2500 dr). Twice weekly there's a post boat to Santorini (3½ hours, 2000 dr). Two hydrofoils weekly serve Ios (1½ hours, 4000 dr) and Santorini (30 minutes, 3500 dr).

Getting Around

An undersized bus carts passengers from the port up to the hora (200 dr). Caïques serve various beaches and nearby islands.

Places to Stay & Eat

Camping is tolerated at Klissidi Beach, but the only facilities are at nearby tavernas.

Rooms in the hora are overpriced and pretty much of a muchness. Shop around if you can, but be careful not to miss out altogether. Domatia owners are looking for long stays – if you're only staying one night you should take whatever you can get. Contact Jeyzed Travel (☎ 61 253) in advance to be sure of a room. *Rooms Rent Paradise*

(☎ 61 243), on the main street, has clean doubles with a nice view for 8000 dr. *Panorama* (☎ 61 292), next door, has similar rooms for the same price. *Anafi Rooms* (☎ 61 271), nearby, charges 9000 dr. *Villa Apollon* at Klissidi Beach is the nicest and priciest place, charging around 12,000 dr for traditional rooms with a few extra modern comforts such as telephones. *Rooms to Let Artemis* (☎ 61 235), also at Klissidi, has rooms for around 10,000 dr. Places at Klissidi fill fast, so book well in advance.

Tavernas in the hora are all reasonably priced and have nice views. These include *Alexandra's*, *Astrakan* and *To Steki*. *Taverna Armenaki*, below the main street, past To Steki, has a nice atmosphere and a menu that includes Cretan tacos, local greens and cheeses, and lamb. It also has raki with honey.

Klissidi has a few *tavernas* as well.

Sikinos Σίκινος

☎ 0286 • postcode 840 10 • pop 287

If a quiet, unspoilt island is what you're looking for, Sikinos fits the bill. It has some nice beaches and a beautiful terraced landscape that drops dramatically down to the sea. The port of Alopronia, and the contiguous villages of Hora and Kastro that together comprise the hilltop capital, are the only settlements. Hora/Kastro has a combined post office and OTE, but no banks. Ferry tickets are sold at Koundouris Travel (☎ 51 168) in Hora/Kastro and at a booth at the port before departures. If you're bringing a car or motorcycle, bring petrol too – there's no petrol station on the island.

Getting There & Around

Ferry Seven ferries weekly go to Piraeus (10 hours, 6000 dr) and Ios (30 minutes, 1100 dr), six to Naxos (three hours, 1600 dr) and Paros (four hours, 1700 dr), five to Folegandros (45 minutes, 1200 dr), four to Santorini (2½ hours, 1700 dr), two to Kimolos (2½ hours, 1700 dr), Milos (three hours, 2800 dr), Sifnos (four hours, 1800 dr), Serifos (five hours, 2700 dr), Kythnos (seven hours,

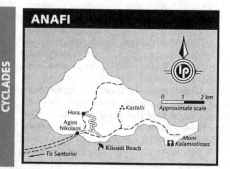

ANAFI

Hora
Agios
Nikolaos
Kastelli
Klissidi Beach
Moni
Kalamiotissas
To Santorini

0   1   2 km
Approximate scale

CYCLADES

SIKINOS

AEGEAN SEA

Moni Zoödohou Pigis
Malta Beach
Kastro
Agios Georgios
Agios Beach
Hora
Nikolaos Beach
To Naxos, Paros, Tinos & Syros
▲552m
Alopronia
SIKINOS
Katergo
Episkopi
To Ios, Paros, Naxos & Piraeus
Kalogeri
▲432m
Kardiotissa
Karra Beach
0   2   4 km
To Folegandros, Milos & Piraeus
To Santorini

3100 dr) and Thirasia (2½ hours, 1700 dr), and one weekly to Syros (six hours, 2700 dr).

Hydrofoil Santorini Dolphins go twice weekly to Ios (10 minutes, 2200 dr), Naxos (one hour, 3000 dr), Paros (1¼ hours, 3500 dr), Tinos (three hours, 5500 dr) and Syros (six hours, 5500 dr), and weekly to Folegandros (30 minutes, 2500 dr) and Santorini (30 minutes, 3400 dr).

The local bus meets all ferries and runs between Alopronia and Hora/Kastro every half-hour in August. A timetable is sometimes posted near the minimarket.

Things to See & Do
The **Kastro** is a cute and compact place with some lovely old houses and friendly locals. In the centre there's a pretty square that was created in the 40s by the occupying Italians, who apparently planned to stay. The fortified **Moni Zoödohou Pigis** stands on a hill above the town.

Sikinos' main excursion is a one hour scenic trek (or five minute drive along a rather silly new road) south-west to **Episkopi**. When ruins there were investigated by 19th century archaeologists, the Doric columns and inscriptions led them to believe it had originally been a shrine to Apollo, but the remains are now believed to be those of a 3rd century AD Roman mausoleum. In the 7th century the ruins were transformed into a church, which was extended in the 17th century to become **Moni**

Episkopis. The church and monastery are open 6.30 to 8.30 pm daily. From here it's possible to climb up to a little church and ancient ruins perched on a precipice to the south, from where the views are spectacular.

Caïques run to nice beaches at **Agios Georgios, Malta** – with ancient ruins on the hill above – and **Karra**. **Katergo**, a swimming place with interesting rocks, and **Agios Nikolaos Beach** are both within easy walking distance of Alopronia.

Places to Stay & Eat
Alopronia has the bulk of accommodation. *Lucas Rooms to Let* (☎ 51 075), near the restaurant of the same name, has doubles for 9000 dr with fridge and bathroom, and three to four-person apartments for 13,000 dr. Bougainvillea-covered *Tasos Rooms* (☎ 51 005), past the Rock Café, has doubles with bathroom, fridge and balcony for 10,000 dr. The stylish B class *Porto Sikinos* (☎/fax 51 220), on the port beach, has doubles with bathroom for 15,000 dr, including breakfast. This traditional Cycladic-style establishment has a bar and restaurant.

In Hora/Kastro, *To Steki tou Garbi* is a good grill house. There is also a good *taverna* at Agio Georgios. Down at the port, *Lucas* serves the best food. In high season a lovely *bar* opens over the water at the northern end of Alopronia's bay; at other times the *Rock Café*, above the quay, suffices.

Folegandros
Φολέγανδρος

The happiest man on earth is the man with fewest needs. And I also believe that if you have light, such as you have here, all ugliness is obliterated.
Henry Miller

☎ 0286 • postcode 840 11 • pop 650
Folegandros (fo-**leh**-gan-dross) is one of Greece's most enticing islands, bridging the gap between tourist traps and small, under-populated islands on the brink of total abandonment. The number of visitors is

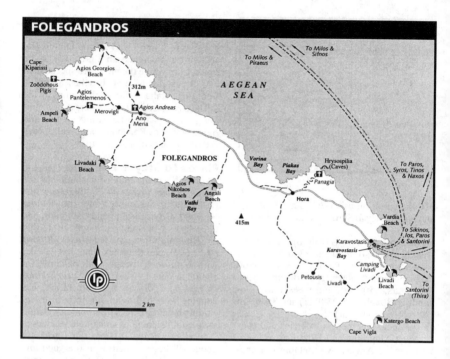

FOLEGANDROS

increasing, but most locals still make a living from fishing and farming.

Tourists tend to come in search of unspoilt island life and, except for July and August, the island is uncrowded and blissful. The island has several good beaches – be prepared for strenuous walking to reach some of them – and a striking landscape of cultivated terraces that give way to precipitous cliffs.

The capital is the concealed cliff-top Hora, one of the prettiest capitals in the Cyclades. All boats dock at the small harbour of Karavostasis, on the east coast. The only other settlement is Ano Meria, 4km northwest of Hora.

Getting There & Away

Ferry There are eight services weekly to Piraeus (six to nine hours, 5150 dr), seven to Santorini (1½ to 2½ hours, 1700 dr), and six to Ios (1½ hours, 1500 dr), Paros (four hours, 1900 dr) and Naxos (three hours, 2300 dr). There are also five boats weekly to Sikinos (40 minutes, 1200 dr), three weekly to Milos (2½ hours, 1700 dr), Sifnos (four hours, 1600 dr) and Kythnos (six hours, 2900 dr), and two weekly to Kimolos (1½ hours, 1200 dr) and Serifos (five hours, 1600 dr). Once weekly there are ferries to Thirasia (1½ hours, 1700 dr), Syros (six hours, 2900 dr) and Anafi (five hours, 2450 dr).

Hydrofoil There are four hydrofoils weekly to Paros (one to four hours, 3800 dr), Syros (seven hours, 5700 dr), Mykonos (five hours, 5700 dr) and Tinos (six hours, 5700 dr). There are three services weekly to Santorini (one hour, 3315 dr), two weekly to Naxos (two hours, 4600 dr), Milos (one hour, 3400 dr) and Sifnos (two hours, 3200 dr), and one weekly to Ios (one to two hours, 3000 dr), Sikinos (20 minutes, 2400 dr) and Thirasia (one hour, 3400 dr).

Getting Around

The local bus meets all boats and takes passengers to Hora (240 dr). From Hora there are buses to the port one hour before all ferry departures, even late at night. Buses from Hora run hourly to Ano Meria (300 dr), stopping at the road leading to Angali Beach. The bus stop for Ano Meria is on the western edge of town, next to the Sottovento Tourist Office. There is one overworked taxi (☎ 41 048, 0944-693 957) on the island.

In July and August, excursion boats make separate trips from Karavostasis to Angali and Agios Nikolaos (both 2500 dr return) and from Angali to Livadaki Beach (1000 dr return).

KARAVOSTASIS Καραβοστάσις

This port town lacks charm but makes a convenient base from which to explore the island's beaches.

Places to Stay & Eat

Camping Livadi (☎ *41 204*) is at Livadi Beach, 1km from Karavostasis. Turn left onto the cement road skirting Karavostasis Beach. It charges 1200 dr per person and 600 dr for tent hire.

Karavostasis has several domatia and hotels – look for the signs when you get off the ferry. The C class *Aeolos Beach Hotel* (☎ *41 205*), on the beach, has clean singles/doubles/suites for 8000/14,000/20,000 dr with bathroom.

Restaurant Kati Allo, by Poseidon Hotel, has one of the best reputations for top quality traditional food and fresh fish. There are two bars, *Evangelos* and *Sirma*, on the beach, which are good for snacks and mezedes.

HORA Χώρα

The captivating Hora, complete with a medieval kastro filled with little houses draped in bougainvillea, is perhaps the most beautiful capital in the Cyclades.

Orientation & Information

From the bus turnaround, facing away from the port, turn left and follow the curving road. An archway on the right leads into the kastro, the walls of which have been incorporated into dwellings. A left turn leads to a row of three shady squares. The third is the central plateia.

There is no EOT or tourist police. The post office is 200m downhill from the bus turnaround, on the port road. There are cardphones, but no OTE.

There is no bank, but Maraki Travel (☎ 41 273), by the first square, exchanges currency, as does the Sottovento Tourism Office (☎/fax 41 430), by the bus stop for Ano Meria and Angali. Note that, except for a couple of boutiques, credit cards are not usually accepted on Folegandros.

Ferry tickets can be purchased from Maraki Travel; there is no ticket booth at the port.

The police (☎ 41 249) are beyond the third plateia, past Nikos' Restaurant.

Things to See

The Hora is a well preserved Cycladic village with aspirin-white churches, sugar cube houses and shady squares. The medieval **kastro**, a tangle of narrow streets spanned by low archways, dates from when Marco Sanudo ruled the island in the 13th century. The houses' wooden balconies blaze with bougainvillea and hibiscus.

The newer village, outside the kastro, is just as pretty. From the first bus stop, a steep path leads up to the large church of the **Panagia**, which is perched on a cliff top above the town. It's open between 6 and 8 pm daily.

Courses

The Cycladic School (founded on Folegandros in 1984) offers one and two-week courses in drawing, painting, Greek cookery, folk dancing and hatha yoga. Accommodation is included. For details, contact Anne and Fotis Papadopoulos (☎ 41 137).

Organised Tours

Three times weekly in summer, Sottovento Tourism Office (see the Hora Orientation &

CYCLADES

Information section) operates day trips by caïque to hidden bays and the little-known **Hrysospilia Caves** on the east coast for 6000 dr, including lunch.

A tour of the island by jeep, departing at 10 am and returning at 3 pm, costs 13,000 dr for up to four people.

Places to Stay

In July and August most domatia and hotels are booked solid; unless you're happy to join the homeless overspill down at Camping Livadi, make sure you book well in advance.

Pavlos' Rooms (☎ *41 232*) are comfortable, converted stables on the main road, five minutes walk uphill from the village. Doubles are 11,000 dr, or 15,000 dr with bathroom. Rooftop sleeping is available in summer if there are no rooms. A bus meets the boats.

There are reasonably priced domatia near the police station, including *Spyridoula Rooms* (☎ *41 078*), where doubles with bathroom and fridge are 13,000 dr. *Nikos Rooms* (☎ *41 055*) has clean rooms with kitchen and bathroom for 16,000 dr. Turn right at Piatsa Restaurant on the central square – the rooms are on the right. The atmospheric *Hotel Castro* (☎ *41 414*) has

cosy doubles/triples for 17,000/25,000 dr with en suite. Some rooms have incredible views straight down the cliffs to the sea. Walk straight ahead from the entrance to the kastro and you'll find the hotel on the left. Opposite, *Rooms Margarita* (☎ *41 321*) has doubles for 12,000 dr.

The C class *Folegandros* (☎ *41 276*), where the port bus terminates, has large, well equipped apartments priced from 24,000 dr for two people. Views don't come any better than from the top-of-the-range *Anemomilos Apartments* (☎ *41 309*), by the bus station. Traditional Cycladic-style apartments are furnished with pottery and antiques and there is one unit for the disabled. Rates for doubles/triples overlooking the sea are 31,000/37,000 dr.

Places to Eat

Pounta, at the port-Hora bus turnaround, has tables in a lovely little garden out the back. Excellent breakfast, *spanakopita*, rabbit *stifado*, lamb and vegetarian dishes are served at very reasonable prices. *Apanemos*, next to the Sottovento Tourism Office, is run by the same crew and is also worth a visit. *Melissa*, on the main square, has very good home-cooked food.

The Caper Caper

Capers are the unopened buds of the caper bush *Capparis spinosa*, which grows wild throughout the Mediterranean region. They have a radishy, pungent taste and are usually pickled in vinegar. Capers were known to the ancient Greeks, and carbon dating of fossilised seeds and buds has shown that they were eaten as far back as 6000 BC in Iraq and Turkey.

Folegandros, Santorini and Anafi are all very proud of their capers, and Andros even has a town named after them – Kapparia. The bushes, which are small, fleshy and sprawling, often inhabit the stone walls that line old paths and divide fields. The harvesting of the buds and the leaves (a delicacy) from the low-lying plants is a laborious process that must be done by hand. Spring is caper-collecting season, although you can still find buds in abundance in early summer. Any buds not collected blossom into surprisingly showy pink and white flowers, which are, of course, also edible. The torpedo-shaped fruit is packed in salt or pickled in vinegar and eaten as well.

Capers are experiencing a comeback in Greek cuisine, especially on the islands. Many tavernas, notably those that take pride in serving traditional local food, are spiking salads and mezedes with liberal sprinklings of these tasty buds.

Piatsa Restaurant is one of the best on the island and has interesting daily specials including rabbit with onions (1900 dr) and beef in lemon sauce with green peas (2000 dr), as well as vegetarian dishes. It's on the second square past the kastro. On the third square, *O Kritikos*, with the rotisserie in front, has succulent grilled meat.

Entertainment

Astarti, on the main square, is a good place to go after dinner for Greek music. In the kastro, *Kellari* is a moody little wine bar. *Anihto* is the place to go for a late-night drink; it's on the road that leads west off the third square towards the Ano Meria bus stop and the Sottovento office. *Rakendia Sunset Bar*, signposted from the road to Ano Meria, has a fabulous view over the cliffs and is also open late.

AROUND FOLEGANDROS
Ano Meria Άνω Μεριά
The settlement of Ano Meria stretches for several kilometres because small farms surround most of the dwellings. Agriculture is still very much alive at this end of the island and you'll see haystacks, market gardens, goats and donkeys.

The folklore museum, near the eastern end of the village, is open 10 am to noon and 6 to 8 pm daily; admission is 400 dr. Ask the bus driver to drop you off nearby.

There are several excellent tavernas, including *I Synantisi*, which specialises in fresh swordfish and *matsada* – a type of handmade pasta served with rabbit or rooster; and *Mimi's*, which has good grilled meat as well as matsada. *Barbakosta*, a very old and authentic kafeneio frequented by locals, is well worth a stop.

Beaches
Karavostasis has a pebbled beach. For **Livadi Beach**, follow the signs for Camping Livadi. The sandy and pebbled **Angali Beach** has a lovely aspect but gets a bit dirty before its annual clean-up in mid-May. There are a few domatia; try *Panagiotis Rooms* (☎ 41 116).

There are other good beaches at **Agios Nikolaos** and **Livadaki**, both west of Angali. The steep path to the beach at Agios Nikolaos is only for those with strong boots and a head for heights, but it's worth it if you plan to stop for lunch – don't miss the octopus in wine sauce at *Taverna Papalagi*. **Agios Georgios** is north of Ano Meria. A path from Agios Andreas church in Ano Meria leads to Agios Georgios Beach. The walk takes about an hour.

Most of the beaches have no shops or tavernas, so make sure you take food and water.

Milos & Kimolos
Μήλος & Κίμωλος

MILOS
☎ 0287 • postcode 848 00 • pop 4390

Volcanic Milos (**mee**-loss), the most westerly island of the Cyclades, is overlooked by most foreign tourists. While not as visually dramatic as the volcanic islands of Santorini and Nisyros, it does have some weird rock formations, hot springs and pleasant beaches. A boat trip around the island allows you to visit most of Milos' stunning beaches (many inaccessible by road), coves and geologically interesting places.

Filakopi, the ancient Minoan city in the north-east of the island, was one of the earliest settlements in the Cyclades. During the Peloponnesian Wars, Milos remained neutral and was the only Cycladic island not to join the Athenian alliance. It paid dearly in 416 BC when avenging Athenians massacred the adult males and enslaved the women and children.

The island's most celebrated asset, the beautiful *Venus de Milo* (a 4th century BC statue of Aphrodite) is far away in the Louvre (apparently having lost its arms on the way to Paris in the 19th century).

Since ancient times, the island has been quarried for minerals, resulting in huge gaps and fissures in the landscape. Obsidian (hard, black volcanic glass used for manufacturing sharp blades) was mined on the island and exported throughout the Mediterranean. These days, about a third of the working population is employed in the mining industry.

Getting There & Away

Air There is a daily flight to Athens (14,900 dr). The Olympic Airways office (☎ 22 380) is in Adamas, just past the main square, on the road to Plaka.

Ferry There are at least 10 ferries weekly to Piraeus (five to seven hours, 5050 dr), six weekly to Sifnos (1¼ hours, 1550 dr), five weekly to Serifos (two hours, 1650 dr) and Kythnos (3½ hours, 2550 dr), four weekly to Kimolos (one hour, 1220 dr), three weekly to Folegandros (two hours, 1750 dr) and Santorini (four hours, 3650 dr), two weekly to Sikinos (three hours, 2850 dr), and one weekly to Ios (three hours, 2850 dr). Three times weekly the *Vitsentsos Kornaros* sails to the Cretan ports of Agios Nikolaos (seven hours, 4850 dr) and Sitia (nine hours, 5100 dr), sometimes continuing on to Kassos (11 hours, 5850 dr), Karpathos (12 hours, 7150 dr) and Rhodes (13 hours, 8450 dr).

Hydrofoil Minoan Flying Dolphins and Santorini Dolphins run daily to Piraeus (four hours, 9800 dr), daily except Friday to Sifnos (45 minutes, 3000 dr) and Serifos (one hour, 3300 dr), five times weekly to Paros (two hours, 5200 dr), Mykonos (3½ hours, 9100 dr), Naxos (2½ hours, 8200 dr) and Syros (four hours, 5800 dr), four times weekly to Kythnos (two hours, 5100 dr), twice weekly to Folegandros (one hour, 3400 dr), Santorini (3½ hours, 7900 dr) and Tinos (six hours, 6300 dr), and once weekly to Kimolos (30 minutes, 2400 dr).

A boat that transports mine workers between Pollonia and Kimolos (20 minutes, 600 dr) has a tourist-unfriendly schedule linked to shift times, usually running at 6 or 7 am and returning at 9 pm, after the last bus back to Adamas has departed. If you're staying in Pollonia it might suit.

Getting Around

There are no buses to the airport, so you'll need to take a taxi (1500 dr from Adamas).

Buses leave Adamas for Plaka and Trypiti (both 350 dr) every hour or so. Four buses daily go to Pollonia (250 dr) and Paleohori (350 dr), and three go to Provatas (350 dr). Taxis can be ordered on ☎ 22 219. Cars, motorcycles and mopeds can be hired along the waterfront.

Adamas Αδάμας

Although Plaka is the capital, the rather plain port of Adamas has most of the accommodation.

To get to the town centre from the quay, turn right at the waterfront. The central square, with the bus stop, taxi rank and outdoor cafes, is at the end of this stretch of waterfront. Just past the square is a road to the right that skirts the town beach. Straight ahead is the town's main thoroughfare and the road to Plaka.

There is no EOT; Milos' municipal tourist office (☎ 22 445) is opposite the quay and open only in summer. For the post office, turn right just after the square and take the third street on the left. Note that Adamas has its own postcode: 848 01. There are ATMs on the main square. The police (☎ 21 378) are on the main square, next to the bus stop; the port police (☎ 22 100) are on the waterfront.

Mining Museum This new museum has some interesting geological exhibits and traces the island's long history of mining, which dates back to Neolithic times. It's open 9.30 am to 1 pm and 5 to 8 pm daily and is free. To get there, take the first right after the central square and continue along the waterfront for about 500m.

Organised Tours The *Delphina* tour boat chugs around the island, stopping at beaches and Kleftiko, and pausing at Kimolos for lunch. It leaves Adamas at 9 am, and returns at 6.30 pm; the tour costs 4000 dr and tickets are available from most travel agents.

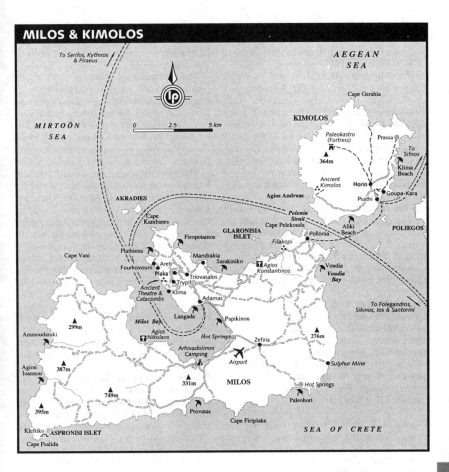

MILOS & KIMOLOS

Terry's Travel (☎ 22 640), up the steps from the quay, has a range of tours, including a sailing trip to the island's nicest beaches and coves. It costs 13,000 dr per person and features a seafood lunch caught by the captain.

Places to Stay Adamas' *camping ground* (☎ 31 410) is 6.5km east of town at Arhivadolimni; to get there, follow the signs along the waterfront from the central square.

In summer, lists of domatia are given out at the tourist office on the quay, but decent accommodation is quite thin on the ground – make sure you call ahead. Options include the excellent *Ethelvina's Rooms* (☎ 22 169), uphill from the bakery on the main square, where singles/doubles/triples are 7000/15,000/18,000 dr; most have refrigerator and bathroom. *Langada Beach Hotel* (☎ 23 411), left of the ferry quay, behind Langada Beach, is a huge complex with a pool; rooms with fridge cost 12,000/15,000/

18,000 dr. *Hotel Delfini (☎ 22 001)*, behind Langada Beach Hotel, has friendly owners and nice simple doubles for 10,000/15,000 dr with shared/private bathroom.

Hotel Dionysis (☎ 23 118), just up from the square, opposite Olympic Airways, has comfortable double/triple studios for 20,000/24,000 dr with TV, phone and air-con. *Portiani Hotel (☎ 22 940)*, on the waterfront at the square, is by far the best value. Singles/doubles/triples with TV, air-con, phone, balcony and terrace cost 20,000/24,000/34,500 dr, including an exceptional buffet breakfast featuring fresh figs, comb honey, cheeses and home-made jams.

Villa Ilios (☎ 22 258), on the hill behind the quay, has beautifully furnished, spacious two-person apartments with phone, TV and air-con for 20,000 dr. If you're after something different, ask Terry's Travel about accommodation in a *windmill*. It sleeps up to six people and costs 35,000 dr per night.

Places to Eat *Vedema*, on the first staircase up from the port as you head into town, has local delicacies such as *peltes* (sun-dried tomato paste) and *pittarakia* (small cheese pies). On the waterfront, *O Kinigos* has superb Greek staples. *Trapetselis Restaurant* and *Navagio*, overlooking the water beyond Portiani Hotel, are both excellent fish places.

Plaka & Trypiti Πλάκα & Τρυπητή
Plaka, 5km uphill from Adamas, is a typical Cycladic town with white houses and labyrinthine laneways. It merges with the settlement of Trypiti to the south.

The **Milos Folk & Arts Museum** is located in a 19th century house in Plaka and contains household items, furniture, tools, embroidery and weavings. It's open 10 am to 2 pm and 6 to 8 pm (closing 2 pm Sunday) daily except Monday; admission is 500 dr. It's signposted at the bus turnaround in Plaka.

At the bus turnaround, turn right for the path to the Frankish **kastro** built on the ancient acropolis. The 13th century church, **Thalassitras**, is inside the walls. The final battle between the ancient Melians and Athenians was fought on this hill. The kastro offers panoramic views of most of the island.

The **archaeology museum** is in Plaka, near the junction with the road leading to the much signposted catacombs. Don't miss the perfectly preserved terracotta figurine of Athena (unlabelled) in the middle room. The room on the left has charming figurines from Filakopi. The museum opens 8 am to 2.30 pm, Tuesday to Sunday. Entry is 500 dr.

Plaka is built on the site of Ancient Milos, which was destroyed by the Athenians and rebuilt by the Romans. There are some Roman ruins near Trypiti, including Greece's only Christian **catacombs**, open 8 am to 1 pm daily except Monday. On the road to the catacombs, a sign points right to the well preserved **ancient theatre**, which hosts the Milos Festival every July. On the track to the theatre, a sign points to where a farmer found the *Venus de Milo* in 1820. Opposite are remains of massive Doric walls. Fifty metres farther along on the cement road is a sign to the 1st century catacombs. A passage leads to a large chamber flanked by tunnels that contained the tombs.

Places to Stay & Eat Both Plaka and Trypiti have *domatia*; your best bet is to ask at tavernas. *Arhontoula*, left from the bus turnaround in Plaka, is a friendly family-run place, with a large selection of appetisers, including cod with *skordalia* (garlic sauce) and interesting salads. *Alisahni*, just around the corner, is also very good.

Around Milos

Klima, once the port of ancient Milos, is now a charming, unspoilt fishing village skirting a narrow beach below Trypiti and the catacombs. Whitewashed buildings, with bright blue, green and red doors and balconies, have boat houses on the ground floor and living quarters on the 1st floor. Klima's one hotel, 2km from the village, is *Hotel Panorama (☎ 21 623)*, where double rooms are 18,000 dr, with breakfast; there's also a restaurant.

Plathiena is a lovely sandy beach below Plaka. On the way to Plathiena you can detour to the tiny fishing villages of **Areti** and **Fourkovouni**. The beaches of **Provatas** and **Paleohori**, on the south coast, are long and sandy, and there are hot springs at Paleohori.

Pollonia, on the north coast, is a fishing village-cum-resort with a small beach and domatia. It serves as the jumping-off point for the boat to Kimolos. **Mandrakia** is a lovely fishing hamlet north-east of Plaka.

The Minoan settlement of **Filakopi** is 2km inland from Pollonia. Three levels of cities have been uncovered here – Early, Middle and Late Cycladic.

The islet of **Glaronisia**, off the north coast, is a rare geological phenomenon composed entirely of hexagonal volcanic stone bars.

KIMOLOS

This small island lies just north-east of Milos. It receives few visitors, although there are *domatia*, *tavernas*, and decent beaches.

Those who do make the effort tend to be day-trippers arriving on the boat from Pollonia, on the north-eastern tip of Milos. The boat docks at the port of **Psathi**, from where it's 3km to the pretty capital of **Horio**. There's no petrol station on Kimolos – if you're bringing a car or moped from Milos, make sure you've got enough fuel.

Donkeys are still the principal mode of transport, and there are tracks all around the island. There are thermal springs at the settlement of **Prassa** on the north-east coast. **Beaches** can be reached by caïque from Psathi. At the centre of the island is the 364m-high cliff on which sits the fortress of **Paleokastro**.

Day-trippers should try the local speciality, *ladenia*, a pizza-like pie with tomato, onion and olives.

Getting There & Away

Ferry There are seven ferries weekly to Adamas (one hour, 1220 dr). Twice weekly ferries go to Folegandros (1½ hours, 1200 dr), Sikinos (2½ hours, 1700 dr), Santorini (four hours, 2987 dr), Sifnos (1½ hours, 1460 dr), Serifos (two hours, 1750 dr) and Kythnos (three hours, 2000 dr) and Piraeus (six hours, 4800 dr). One ferry weekly goes to Ios (2½ hours, 1900 dr). Boats go daily to/from Pollonia on Milos (see the Milos Getting There & Away section for details).

Hydrofoil Once a week Minoan Flying Dolphins go to Milos (30 minutes, 2400 dr), Sifnos (25 minutes, 2800 dr), Serifos (one hour, 3500 dr), Kythnos (two hours, 4800 dr) and Piraeus (3½ hours, 8800 dr).

Sifnos Σίφνος

☎ 0284   • postcode 840 03   • pop 2900

Sifnos coyly hides its assets from passing ferry passengers. At first glance it looks barren, but the port is in the island's most arid area. Explore and you'll find an abundantly attractive landscape of terraced olive groves and almond trees, with oleanders in the valleys and hillsides covered in wild juniper, which used to fuel potters' kilns. There are numerous dovecotes, whitewashed houses and chapels. Plenty of old paths link the villages, which makes it an ideal island for walking.

During the Archaic period the island was very wealthy due to its gold and silver resources. To protect their loot the islanders constructed an elaborate communications network of watchtowers that used fire and smoke signals to warn of attack. The ruins of 55 towers have been located to date. By the 5th century BC the mines were exhausted and Sifnos' fortunes were reversed – the island became so poor that it was the butt of endless jokes in Athens and elsewhere.

The island has a long history of producing superior pottery because of the quality of its clay, and many shops sell local ceramics. Some potters' workshops are open to the public – it's quite mesmerising to watch their work.

Sifniot olive oil is highly prized throughout Greece, which might have something to

CYCLADES

do with the island's reputation for producing some of the country's best chefs. Local specialities include *revithia* (baked chickpeas), *revithokeftedes* (falafel-like vegetable balls), *xynomyzithra* (a sharpish fresh cheese) and almond sweets flavoured with orange flowers.

Getting There & Away
No travel agency sells all ferry and hydrofoil tickets, so you'll probably be shunted from one office to another.

Ferry There are daily ferries to Milos (two hours, 1560 dr), Piraeus (five hours, 4400 dr) via Serifos (one hour, 1460 dr), and Kythnos (2½ hours, 1960 dr). There are three ferries weekly to Kimolos (1½ hours, 1460 dr), Folegandros (four hours, 1660 dr), Sikinos (five hours, 1860 dr) and Santorini (six hours, 3060 dr), two weekly to Paros (three hours, 1000 dr), Syros (5½ hours, 2000 dr) and Rethymno on Crete (5½ hours, 5100 dr), and one weekly to Mykonos (4½ hours, 3100 dr).

Hydrofoil At least one hydrofoil daily serves Piraeus (three hours, 8500 dr), Serifos (25 minutes, 2800 dr), Kythnos (1¼ hours, 3800 dr), Paros (one hour, 1900 dr) and Mykonos (2½ to 3½ hours, 6100 dr), and two daily go to Milos (one hour, 3000 dr). There are five weekly to Naxos (1½ hours, 5800 dr), and two weekly to Santorini (three hours, 6000 dr), Folegandros (1½ hours, 3100 dr), Syros (3½ hours, 4000 dr) and Tinos (2½ hours, 6200 dr).

Getting Around
Frequent buses link Apollonia (stopping at Artemonas) with Kamares (240 dr), Kastro (240 dr), Vathi (290 dr), Faros (240 dr) and Platys Gialos (290 dr); inquire at the municipal tourist office at the port for timetables.

Taxis (☎ 094-761 210) hover around the port and Apollonia's main square. Cars can be hired from Hotel Kamari (☎ 33 383) in Kamares, and from Apollo Rent a Car (☎ 32 237) in Apollonia.

KAMARES Καμάρες
Unlike most villages on the island, the port of Kamares is a newish resort-style town. It has a nice enough 'holiday' feel about it, with lots of waterfront cafes and tavernas, and a reasonable sandy beach. The bus stop is the stand of tamarisk trees outside the municipal tourist office.

Opposite the quay there is a very helpful municipal tourist office (☎ 31 977) with staff who can find you accommodation anywhere on the island. It also offers free luggage storage and has copies of the bus schedule.

Places to Stay & Eat
Camping Makis (☎ 32 366) just behind the beach north of the port charges 1600 dr per person, including tent. Domatia owners rarely meet the boats and in high season it's best to book ahead. The C class *Stavros*

Hotel (☎ *31 641)*, in the middle of the waterfront, has basic, clean doubles with bathroom for 10,000 dr. *Hotel Kamari* (☎ *33 383)*, 400m up the road to Apollonia, has attractive doubles with bathroom and telephone for 15,000 dr.

Restaurant Simos and *I Meropi*, next to each other on the waterfront, serve well prepared traditional Greek fare. *Ouzeri Kamares*, also on the waterfront, has good mezedes. Nearby, *Captain Andreas* is the best place for fish.

APOLLONIA Απολλώνια

The capital, situated on a plateau 5km uphill from the port, is a conglomeration of six pretty whitewashed villages: Artemonas, Apollonia, Ano Petali, Kato Petali, Katavati and Exambelas.

The bus stop for Kamares is on the lively central square where the post office and OTE are located; all other buses stop outside Hotel Anthousa. The main pedestrian thoroughfare – with jewellery and clothes shops, restaurants and bars – is to the right behind the museum. The National Bank of Greece, which has an ATM, is a bit farther out on the road to Artemonas, and the police are about 50m beyond.

The interesting little **Museum of Popular Art**, on the central square, contains old costumes, pots and textiles, and is open 9 am to 1.30 pm and 6 to 11 pm daily; admission is 300 dr.

Courses

Greek-language courses take place in Apollonia during the summer. Two weeks' tuition costs around US$700/400 with/ without accommodation. For details contact Dr Anna Kyritsi on ☎/fax 01-775 5021.

Places to Stay & Eat

The C class *Hotel Sofia* (☎ *31 238)*, north of the central square, has basic singles/ doubles for 8000/11,000 dr with bathroom.

Hotel Anthousa (☎ *31 431)*, around the corner, has nice rooms for 12,000/15,000 dr with bathroom, TV and telephone. It also has laundry facilities. Downstairs there's a lovely patisserie that sells local produce as well as sweets, coffee and snacks. There are a few bars nearby and it can get a bit noisy at night, especially on weekends.

A better option is the C class *Hotel Sifnos* (☎ *31 629, 33 067)* on the main pedestrian street that leads off to the right behind the museum; it has immaculate singles/doubles/triples for 13,000/16,000/ 19,000 dr with bathroom. *Peristeronas Apartments* (☎ *71 288)*, downhill from Hotel Anthousa, is a new Sifnos-style house overlooking terraced fields with doubles/ triples/quads for 23,000/25,000/27,000 dr. *Hotel Petali* (☎ *33 024)*, about 100m along the footpath to Artemonas, is a newer, more upmarket place with spacious doubles/ triples for 30,000/33,000 dr with air-con, TV and telephone.

Apostoli tou Koutouki on the main pedestrian street serves very good meat, while *Restaurant Sifnos*, a bit farther along, below the hotel of the same name, has excellent vegetable balls and other local fare. In Artemonas, try *Manganas* and *Margarita*.

Shopping

As well as fine ceramics and jewellery, you can also find beautiful hand-woven textiles. On the main pedestrian thoroughfare, Margarita Baki has a tiny workshop where she weaves on a loom and sells tablecloths, cushion covers, curtains, shawls and kilims, all at reasonable prices.

AROUND SIFNOS

The pretty village of **Artemonas** is a short walk or bus ride north of Apollonia. Not to be missed is the walled cliff-top village of **Kastro**, 3km from Apollonia. The former capital, it is a magical place of buttressed alleys and whitewashed houses. Its small archaeological museum is open 8 am to 2.30 pm Tuesday to Sunday (free).

The pretty downhill walk along old paths from Apollonia to Kastro takes under an hour and you can return by bus. The serene village of **Exambelas**, south of Apollonia, is said to be the birthplace of most of Sifnos' accomplished chefs.

The resort of **Platys Gialos**, 10km south of Apollonia, has a long sandy beach. The spectacularly situated **Moni Hrysopigis**, near Platys Gialos, was built to house a miraculous icon of the Virgin found in the sea by two fishermen. A path leads from the monastery to a beach with a *taverna*. **Vathi**, on the west coast, is a gorgeous sandy bay. **Faros** is a cosy little fishing hamlet with a couple of nice beaches.

Places to Stay & Eat

Platys Gialos has quite a few accommodation options. *Camping Platys Gialos* (☎ 31 786) is in an olive grove behind the beach. *Angeliki Rooms* (☎ 71 288), right on the beach, has doubles/triples for 14,000/16,500 dr with fridge and bathroom. The lodge-like *Platys Gialos Beach Hotel* (☎ 71 324) has doubles with air-con, TV, minibar and sea view for 40,000 dr. In Faros, *Fabrika* (☎ 71 427) has rooms in an old flour mill for 13,500 dr.

Dimitri's, at the sweet little beach of Fasolou, up the stairs and over the headland from the bus stop in Faros, has very good home-cooked food. *Faros*, in Faros, is the place to go for fish.

Serifos Σέριφος

☎ 0281 • postcode 840 05 • pop 1020

Serifos is a barren, rocky island with a few pockets of greenery that are the result of tomato and vine cultivation. Livadi, the port, is on the south-east coast; the whitewashed capital, Hora, clings onto a hillside 2km inland.

Getting There & Away

Ferry There are daily ferries from Serifos to Piraeus (4½ hours, 4000 dr), Sifnos (one hour, 1460 dr), Milos (two hours, 1650 dr) and Kimolos (2½ hours, 1750 dr). Four times weekly the Piraeus ferry stops at Kythnos (1½ hours, 1750 dr), and twice weekly boats go to Paros (two hours, 2000 dr), Mykonos (three hours, 3000 dr), Syros (three to five hours, 2000 dr) and Folegandros (five hours, 1600 dr).

There are weekly boats to Santorini (seven hours, 3587 dr), Ios (six hours, 2900 dr) and Sikinos (five hours, 2700 dr).

Hydrofoil Flying Dolphin hydrofoils travel daily to Piraeus (2½ hours, 7400 dr), Kythnos (45 minutes, 3500 dr), Sifnos (25 minutes, 2800 dr) and Milos (1½ hours, 3300 dr). There is a weekly service to Paros (one hour, 3800 dr), Naxos (1½ hours, 5700 dr), Mykonos (2½ hours, 6300 dr) and Kimolos (one hour, 3500 dr).

Getting Around

There are frequent buses between Livadi and Hora (240 dr); a timetable is posted at the bus stop by the yacht marina. Motorcycles and cars can be hired from Krinas Travel (☎ 51 488, fax 51 073), upstairs next to Captain Hook Bar, 50m from the quay.

LIVADI Λιβάδι

This rather scrappy port is at the top end of an elongated bay. Continue around the bay for the ordinary town beach or climb over the headland that rises from the ferry quay for the pleasant, tamarisk-fringed beach at **Livadakia**. **Karavi Beach**, a walk farther south over the next headland, is the unofficial nudist beach. There is an Ionian Bank, with ATM, on the waterfront. Krinas Travel (see Getting Around) offers a wide range of services. The port police (☎ 51 470) are up steps from the quay.

Places to Stay & Eat
The excellent, shady *Coralli Camping (☎ 51 500)* at sandy Livadakia Beach charges 1500 dr per person and 700 dr for a tent. The bungalows – probably the nicest accommodation on the island – have bathroom, phone and fridge and cost 15,000/18,000 dr for doubles/triples. There's also a restaurant, bar and minimarket, and a minibus meets all ferries.

Anna Domatia (☎ 51 263), about 500m along the waterfront next to Hotel Asteria, has airy doubles with fridge for 10,000 dr. The light and bright *Hotel Areti (☎ 51 479)*, on the hill above the ferry quay, has lovely singles/doubles for 11,000/14,000 dr. *Rooms to Let Marianna (☎ 51 338)* is a nice, secluded, shady place set back a little from the waterfront; doubles go for 15,000 dr with bathroom and fridge. *Hotel Albatros (☎ 51 148)*, on the waterfront, has singles/doubles for 12,000/14,000 dr. Next door, the C class *Maistrali Hotel (☎ 51 381, fax 51 298)* has good doubles for 16,800/18,500 dr without/with sea views.

Mokka, near the quay, is a good place specialising in seafood. *Perseus*, farther along the waterfront, serves the best Greek standards. There are also a couple of reasonable *tavernas* on the beach at Livadakia.

Those with a sweet tooth should check out the almond versions of baklava and other pastries that are an island speciality.

AROUND SERIFOS
The dazzling white **Hora**, clinging to a crag above Livadi, is one of the most striking Cycladic capitals. It can be reached either by bus or by walking up the steps from Livadi. More steps lead to a ruined 15th century Venetian fortress above the village.

The post office is by the first bus stop; the OTE is farther uphill, off the central square. There is no bank. For a journey back in time, visit ye olde medieval cobbler near the square. He makes sturdy – occasionally bizarre – leather shoes and sandals to order.

About an hour's walk north of Livadi along a track (negotiable by moped) is **Psili Ammos Beach**. A path from Hora heads north to the pretty village of **Kendarhos** (also called Kallitsos), from where you can continue to the 17th century fortified **Moni Taxiarhon**, which has impressive 18th century frescoes. The walk from the town to the monastery takes about two hours, but you will need to take food and water as there are no facilities in Kendarhos.

Kythnos Κύθνος

☎ 0281 • postcode 840 06 • pop 1632
Kythnos, the next island north of Serifos, is virtually barren. It is popular mainly with Athenian holiday-makers, and there is little to enthuse about unless you're looking for a cure for rheumatism at the thermal baths.

The main settlements are the port of Merihas and the capital, Hora, also known as Kythnos. Merihas has an OTE, and there is an agency of the National Bank of Greece at Cava Kythnos travel agency and minimarket, which also sells Flying Dolphin tickets, and ferry tickets to Kea and Lavrio. Hora has the island's post office, police station and OTE.

Getting There & Away
There are daily boats to Piraeus (2½ hours, 2300 dr). Most services coming from Piraeus continue to Serifos (1½ hours, 1750 dr), Sifnos (2½ hours, 1750 dr), Kimolos (three hours, 2000 dr) and Milos (3½ hours, 2550 dr). There are four ferries weekly to Kea (1¼ hours, 1500 dr), two weekly to Folegandros (six hours, 2900 dr), Sikinos (seven hours, 3100 dr), Santorini (eight hours, 4000 dr), Syros (two hours, 2000 dr) and Lavrio (3½ hours, 2300 dr), and one weekly to Ios (7½ hours, 3400 dr).

In summer, hydrofoils travel daily to Piraeus (1½ hours, 6000 dr), Serifos (45 minutes, 3500 dr) and Sifnos (1¼ hours, 3800 dr). They continue to Milos (two hours, 5100 dr) six days a week and to Kimolos (two hours, 4800 dr) once a week.

Getting Around

There are regular buses from Merihas to Dryopida (300 dr) and Hora (300 dr), occasionally continuing to Loutra (500 dr). The buses supposedly meet the ferries, but usually they leave from the turn-off to Hora in Merihas.

Taxis are a better bet, except at siesta time. There are two motorcycle rental outlets on the waterfront.

MERIHAS Μέριχας

Merihas does not have a lot going for it other than a small, dirty-brown beach. But it's a reasonable base and has most of the island's accommodation. There are better beaches within walking distance north of the quay (turn left facing inland).

Places to Stay & Eat

Domatia owners usually meet the boats, but if no-one is waiting, wander around the waterfront and backstreets and you'll see plenty of signs advertising rooms.

If you want to stay in the town's one hotel – *Kythnos Hotel* (**☎** 32 092) – you'd best book ahead. It's up the first set of steps on the way into town from the harbour and has decent doubles/triples overlooking the harbour for 8500/10,000 dr.

There are no especially exciting eateries. *Ostria* and *Restaurant Kissos* provide reasonable standard stuff, while *Taverna to Kantouni*, near the abandoned Hotel Posidonion, has good grilled meat.

AROUND KYTHNOS

The capital, **Hora** (also known as Kythnos), lacks the charm of other Cycladic capitals. The main reason for visiting is the walk south to **Dryopida**, a picturesque town of red-tiled roofs and winding streets that was the island's capital in the Middle Ages. It takes about 1½ hours to cover the 6km. From Dryopida, you can either walk the 6km back to Merihas or catch a bus or taxi.

Loutra offers the only accommodation outside Merihas. There are several *domatia* as well as *Hotel Porto Klaras* (**☎**/fax 31 276), reportedly the best on the island, with doubles/self-contained studios for 13,000/ 16,000 dr.

The **thermal baths** at Loutra in the north-east are reputedly the most potent in the Cyclades. The best **beaches** are on the south-east coast, near the village of Kanala.

KYTHNOS

To Syros — Cape Kefalos

AEGEAN SEA

297m

Loutra

To Kea

KYTHNOS

Fikiado Beach — Apokrousi Beach

Episkopi Beach

308m

Hora

To Piraeus

Merihas

Dryopida

Cape Tzoulis

302m

Flambouria Beach

Kanala

To Serifos

0   2   4 km

Cape Berou

Kea Κέα or Τζία

☎ 0288 • postcode 840 02 • pop 1800

Kea, to the north of Kythnos, is the closest of the Cyclades to the mainland. The island is a popular summer weekend escape for

Athenians, but remains relatively untouched by tourism. While it appears largely barren from a distance, there is ample water and the bare hills hide fertile valleys filled with orchards, olive groves, and almond and oak trees (acorns, a raw material used by the tanneries, made the inhabitants rich in the 18th century). The main settlements are the port of Korissia, and the capital, Ioulida, 5km inland.

Getting There & Away
The F/B *Myrina Express* connects Kea with Lavrio (1¼ hours, 1600 dr) on the mainland at least twice daily and also with Kythnos (1¼ hours, 1500 dr) twice weekly. In addition, the F/B *Georgios Express* goes twice weekly to Kythnos and Syros (four hours, 2250 dr).

On Sunday, the supercat *Haroula* goes to the mainland port of Rafina (1¼ hours, 1900 dr). In summer, there are at least five hydrofoils weekly to Zea Marina at Piraeus (1¼ hours, 4800 dr).

Getting Around
In July and August there are, in theory, regular buses from Korissia to Vourkari (150 dr), Otzias (300 dr), Ioulida (300 dr) and Pisses (500 dr). In practice, however, the bus driver operates at his own whim; if there isn't a bus waiting for the boat, you're better off catching one of the taxis (☎ 21 021/228) that hang about near the port. Alternatively, there are three expensive motorcycle rental outlets.

KORISSIA Κορησσία
The port of Korissia is an uninspiring place in spite of its setting on a large bay with a long, sandy beach.

The tourist police (☎ 22 100) can be found one block back from the waterfront between June and September. The fairly useless tourist information office opposite the ferry quay has lists of domatia. Stefanos Lepouras, next door at Stegali bookshop (☎ 21 435, fax 21 012) and Minoan Flying Dolphin agency, is a good source of information. He also changes money.

Places to Stay & Eat
The C class *Hotel Karthea* (☎ 21 222) is a large concrete box at the corner of the bay with ordinary singles/doubles for 12,000/16,000 dr. There are better places along the road that runs behind the beach, including a couple of *domatia*. The recently renovated *Hotel Tzia* (☎ 21 305) has lovely doubles that open right onto the beach for 13,000 dr with bathroom and telephone. *Hotel Korissia* (☎ 21 484) has large, modern singles/doubles for 11,000/14,000 dr, and double/triple studios for 18,000/21,000 dr. Turn right off the beach road at the creek and the hotel is on the right after about 150m.

Lagoudera, near the tourist office, has good home-cooked local specialities.

IOULIDA Ιουλίδα
Ioulida is a delightful higgledy-piggledy hillside town, full of alleyways and steps

CYCLADES

that beg to be explored. The architecture here is quite different from other Cycladic capitals – the houses have red-tiled roofs.

The bus turnaround is on a square at the edge of town. An archway leads to Ioulida proper, and Ilia Malavazou, the main thoroughfare, leads uphill to the right. The post office is along here on the right. The pathway continues uphill and crosses a small square, just beyond which, on the right, is an agency of the National Bank of Greece, signposted above a minimarket.

Things to See
The **archaeological museum**, on the main thoroughfare, houses local finds, mostly from Agia Irini. It's open 8.30 am to 3 pm Tuesday to Sunday (free).

The celebrated **Kea Lion**, chiselled from a huge chunk of slate in the 6th century BC, lies on the hillside an easy, pleasant 10 minute walk north-east of town. The path to the lion leads off to the left (the main path goes sharp right) about 150m past the bank agency. Keep walking past the cemetery and you'll find the gate that leads downhill to the lion, which is surrounded by white-washed rocks.

Places to Stay & Eat
Apart from a couple of *domatia*, the only option is *Hotel Filoxenia* (☎ *22 057*), a tiny old place with lots of character. Singles/doubles are 8000/10,000 dr. To get there, head up the stairs straight ahead from the square; it's on the right above the shoe shop.

There are a couple of decent tavernas. *Estiatorio I Piatsa*, just inside the archway, serves a generous plate of fresh fish for

1500 dr. Carnivores should not dilly-dally: go directly to *Kalofagadon* on the main square and order the lamb chops (2000 dr).

AROUND KEA
The beach road from Korissia leads past nice but slightly suburban **Gialiskari Beach** to the trendy resort of **Vourkari**, 2.5km away. Just north of Vourkari is the ancient site of **Agia Irini** (named after a nearby church), where a Minoan palace has been excavated.

The road continues for another 3km to a sandy beach at **Otzias**. A dirt road continues beyond here for another 5km to the 18th century **Moni Panagias Kastriani**, with a commanding position and terrific views.

The island's best beach, 8km south-west of Ioulida, has the unfortunate name of **Pisses**. It is long and sandy and backed by a verdant valley of orchards and olive groves. **Flea**, also with an interesting name, occupies a lush valley and makes a nice walking destination from either Korissia or Ioulida.

Places to Stay
The island's camping ground, *Kea Camping* (☎ *31 302*), is at Pisses Beach and has a shop, bar and restaurant. It costs 1200 dr per person and 1200 dr per tent, and there are additional charges for cars and motorcycles. There are also *domatia* and *tavernas* here.

Kea Beach Hotel (☎ *31 230, fax 31 234*) is on a headland overlooking Koundouros Beach, 2km south of Pisses. The hotel complex has a bar, restaurant, disco and swimming pool. Doubles/triples are 19,000/20,500 dr with breakfast.

CYCLADES

Crete Κρήτη

Crete is Greece's largest and most southerly island, and arguably the most beautiful. A spectacular mountain chain runs from east to west across the island, split into three ranges: the Mt Dikti Range in the east, the Mt Ida (or Mt Psiloritis) Range in the centre and the Lefka Ori (white mountains) in the west. The mountains are dotted with agricultural plains and plateaus, and sliced by numerous dramatic gorges. Long, sandy beaches speckle the coastline, and the east coast boasts Europe's only palm-tree forest.

Administratively, the island is divided into four prefectures: Lassithi, Iraklio, Rethymno and Hania. Apart from Lassithi, with its capital of Agios Nikolaos, the prefectures are named after their major cities. The island's capital is Iraklio with a population of 127,600. It's Greece's fifth-largest city. Nearly all Crete's major population centres are on the north coast. Most of the south coast is too precipitous to support large settlements.

Crete is famous for its wildflowers. You'll find *Wild Flowers of Crete* by George Sfikas a comprehensive field guide, but *Flowers of Crete* by Yanoukas Iatrides may be a better bet for the layperson.

Scenery and beaches aside, the island is also the birthplace of Europe's first advanced civilisation, the Minoan. If you intend to spend much time at the many Minoan sites, *Palaces of Minoan Crete* by Gerald Cadogan is an excellent guide.

Crete's size and its distance from the rest of Greece allowed an independent culture to evolve. Vibrant Cretan weavings are sold in many of the island's towns and villages. The traditional Cretan songs differ from those heard elsewhere in Greece. Called *mantinades*, these songs are highly emotive, expressing the age-old concerns of love, death and the yearning for freedom. You will still come across a few old men wearing the traditional dress of breeches tucked into knee-high leather boots, and black-fringed kerchiefs tied tightly around their heads.

HIGHLIGHTS

- Iraklio's archaeological museum and the historical museum of Crete
- The ancient Minoan site of Knossos
- The stunning expanse of the Lassithi Plateau
- Walking the gorge between Zakros and Kato Zakros, site of ancient Zakros
- Hania's beautiful old Venetian quarter
- Trekking the spectacular Samaria Gorge
- The lovely sand beaches and coves at Elafonisi

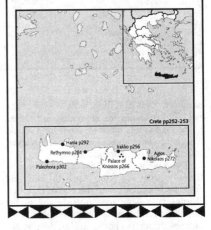

Crete pp252-253

Hania p292
Rethymno p284
Paleohora p302
Iraklio p256
Palace of Knossos p266
Agios Nikolaos p272

The attractions of Crete have not gone unnoticed by tour operators, and the island has the dubious honour of playing host to almost a quarter of Greece's tourists. The result is that much of the north coast is packed solid with hastily constructed hotels for package tourists, particularly between Iraklio and Agios Nikolaos and west of Hania. The tour operators have also taken over several of the

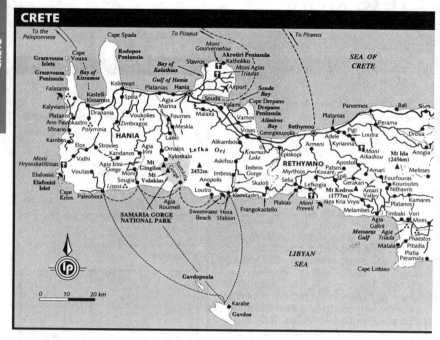

CRETE

southern coastal villages that were once backpacker favourites. If you haven't visited Crete for a while, brace yourself for a shock. The wild and rugged west coast, however, remains relatively untouched.

If you want to avoid the crowds, the best times to visit are from April to June and from mid-September to the end of October. Winter is a dead loss outside the major population centres, as most hotel owners and restaurateurs choose to shut their establishments and recharge their batteries in preparation for the next tourist onslaught.

History

Although Crete has been inhabited since Neolithic times (7000 to 3000 BC), as far as most people are concerned its history begins with the Minoan civilisation. The glories of Crete's Minoan past remained hidden until British archaeologist Sir Arthur Evans made

his dramatic discoveries at Knossos in the early 1900s. The term 'Minoan' was coined by Evans and derived from the King Minos of Greek mythology. Nobody knows what the Minoans called themselves.

Among the ruins unearthed by Evans, were the famous Knossos frescoes. Artistically, the frescoes are superlative; the figures that grace them have a naturalism lacking in contemporary Cycladic figurines, ancient Egyptian artwork (which they resemble in certain respects), and the Archaic sculpture that came later. Compared with candle-smoke-blackened Byzantine frescoes, the Minoan frescoes, with their fresh, bright colours, look as if they were painted yesterday. See the following boxed text 'The Mysterious Minoans' for more details.

But no matter how much speculation the frescoes inspire about the Minoans, all we really know is that early in the 3rd millen-

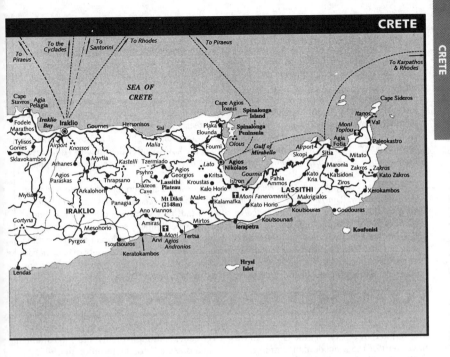

nium BC, an advanced people migrated to Crete and brought with them the art of metallurgy. Many elements of Neolithic culture lived on in the Early Minoan period (3000 to 2100 BC), but the Middle Minoan period (2100 to 1500 BC) saw the emergence of a society with unprecedented artistic, engineering and cultural achievements. It was during this time that the famous palace complexes were built at Knossos, Phaestos, Malia and Zakros.

Also during this time, the Minoans began producing their exquisite Kamares pottery (see Archaeological Museum in the Iraklio section) and silverware, and became a maritime power trading with Egypt and Asia Minor.

Around 1700 BC, all four palace complexes were destroyed by an earthquake. Undeterred, the Minoans built bigger and better palaces on the sites of the originals,

as well as new settlements in other parts of the island.

Around 1500 BC, when the Minoan civilisation was at its peak, the palaces were destroyed again, signalling the start of the Late Minoan period (1500 to 1100 BC). This destruction was probably caused by Mycenaean invasions, although the massive volcanic eruption on the island of Santorini (Thira) may also have had something to do with it. The Knossos palace was the only one to be salvaged. It was finally destroyed by fire around 1400 BC.

The Minoan civilisation was a hard act to follow. The war-orientated Dorians, who arrived in 1100 BC, were pedestrian by comparison. The 5th century BC found Crete, like the rest of Greece, divided into city-states. The glorious classical age of mainland Greece had little impact on Crete, and the Persians bypassed the island. It was

The Mysterious Minoans

Of the many finds at Knossos and other sites, it is the celebrated frescoes that have captured the imagination of experts and amateurs alike, shedding light on a civilisation hitherto a mystery. The message they communicate is of a society that was powerful, wealthy, joyful and optimistic.

Gracing the frescoes are white-skinned women with elaborately coiffured glossy black locks. Proud, graceful and uninhibited, these women had hourglass figures and were dressed in stylish gowns that revealed perfectly shaped breasts. The bronze-skinned men were tall, with tiny waists, narrow hips, broad shoulders and muscular thighs and biceps; the children were slim and lithe. The Minoans also seemed to know how to enjoy themselves. They played board games, boxed and wrestled, played leap-frog over bulls and over one another, and performed bold acrobatic feats.

As well as being literate, they were religious, as frescoes and models of people partaking in rituals testify. The Minoans' beliefs, like many other aspects of their society, remain an enigma, but there is sufficient evidence to confirm that they worshipped a nature goddess, often depicted with serpents and lions. Male deities were distinctly secondary.

From the frescoes it appears that women enjoyed a respected position in society, leading religious rituals and participating in games, sports and hunting. Minoan society may have had its dark side, however. There is evidence of human sacrifice being practised on at least one occasion, although probably in response to an extreme external threat.

also ignored by Alexander the Great, so was never part of the Macedonian Empire.

By 67 BC, Crete had fallen to the Romans. The town of Gortyna in the south became the capital of Cyrenaica, a province that included large chunks of North Africa. Crete, along with the rest of Greece, became part of the Byzantine Empire in 395 AD. In 1210 the island was occupied by the Venetians, whose legacy is one of mighty fortresses, ornate public buildings and monuments, and the handsome dwellings of nobles and merchants.

Despite the massive Venetian fortifications, which sprang up all over the island, by 1669 the whole of the Cretan mainland was under Turkish rule. The first uprising against the Turks was led by Ioannis Daskalogiannis in 1770. This set the precedent for many more insurrections, and in 1898 the Great Powers intervened and made the island a British protectorate. It was not until the signing of the Treaty of Bucharest in 1913 that Crete officially became part of

Greece, although the island's parliament had declared a de facto union in 1905.

The island saw heavy fighting during WWII. Germany wanted to use the island as an air base in the Mediterranean, and on 20 May 1941 German parachutists landed on Crete. It was the start of 10 days of fierce fighting that became known as the Battle of Crete. For two days the battle hung in the balance until Germany won a bridgehead for its air force at Maleme, near Hania. The Allied forces of Britain, Australia, New Zealand and Greece then fought a valiant rearguard action which enabled the British Navy to evacuate 18,000 of the 32,000 Allied troops trapped on the island. Most were picked up from the rugged southern coast around Hora Sfakion. The German occupation of Crete lasted until the end of WWII.

During the war a large active resistance movement drew heavy reprisals from the Germans. Many mountain villages were temporarily bombed 'off the map' and their occupants were shot. Among the bravest members of the resistance were the 'runners' who relayed messages on foot over the mountains. One of these runners, George Psychoundakis, wrote a book based on his experiences entitled *The Cretan Runner*.

Getting There & Away

The following section provides a brief overview of air and boat options to and from Crete. For more comprehensive information, see the relevant sections under specific town entries.

Air Crete has two international airports. The principal one is at Iraklio and there is a smaller one at Hania. In addition there is a domestic airport at Sitia. All three airports have flights to Athens. Iraklio and Hania have flights to Thessaloniki; Iraklio also has flights to Rhodes and Santorini.

Ferry Crete has ports at Iraklio, Hania, Agios Nikolaos, Sitia, Kastelli-Kissamos and Rethymno. The following are high season schedules; services are reduced by about half during low season.

Direct daily ferries travel to Piraeus from Iraklio, Hania and Rethymno. There are three ferries weekly from Iraklio to Santorini, and from Sitia via Agios Nikolaos to Piraeus, stopping once a week at Milos. Three ferries weekly go from Iraklio to Thessaloniki via Santorini stopping twice a week at Paros, Tinos and Skiathos and once a week at Naxos, Syros and Volos. There's also a weekly boat to Rhodes from Iraklio, and from Agios Nikolaos via Sitia stopping at Karpathos and Halki. Two ferries weekly sail from Kastelli-Kissamos to Antikythira, Kythira and Githio.

Getting Around

A four lane national highway skirts the north coast from Hania in the west to Agios Nikolaos in the east, and is being extended farther west to Kastelli-Kissamos. There are frequent buses linking all the major northern towns from Kastelli-Kissamos to Sitia.

Less frequent buses operate between the north coast towns and resorts and places of

interest on the south coast, via the mountain villages of the interior. These routes are Hania to Paleohora, Omalos (for the Samaria Gorge) and Hora Sfakion; Rethymno to Plakias, Agia Galini, Phaestos and Matala; Iraklio to Agia Galini, Phaestos, Matala and the Lassithi Plateau; Agios Nikolaos to Ierapetra; and Sitia to Ierapetra, Vaï, Paleokastro and Kato Zakros.

There is nothing comparable to the national highway on the south coast and parts of this area have no roads at all. There is no road between Paleohora and Hora Sfakion, the most precipitous part of the south coast; a boat (daily from June through August) connects the two resorts via Sougia and Agia Roumeli.

As well as the bus schedules given in each section in this chapter, clapped-out 'village buses' travel to just about every village which has a road to it. These buses usually leave in the early morning and return in the afternoon.

Central Crete

Central Crete is occupied by Iraklio prefecture, named after the island's burgeoning major city and administrative capital. The area's major attractions are the Minoan sites of Knossos, Malia and Phaestos. The north coast east of Iraklio has been heavily exploited by the package tourism industry, particularly around Hersonisos.

IRAKLIO Ηράκλειο
☎ 081 • postcode 710 01 • pop 127,600
The Cretan capital of Iraklio is a bustling modern city and the fifth largest in Greece. It has none of the charm of Hania or Rethymno, but it is a dynamic city boasting the highest average per capita income in Greece. That wealth stems largely from Iraklio's position as the island's trading capital, but also from the year-round flow of visitors who flock to nearby Knossos.

History
The Arabs who ruled Crete from 824 to 961 AD were the first people to govern from the

CRETE

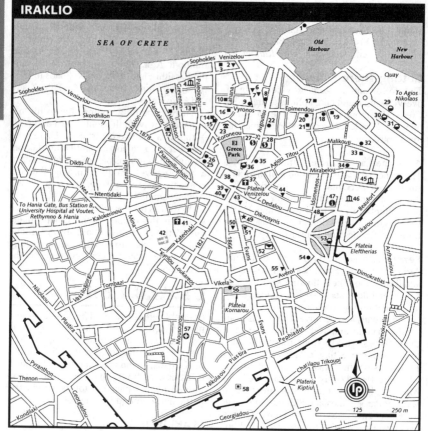

IRAKLIO

SEA OF CRETE

Old Harbour

New Harbour

Quay

To Agios Nikolaos

El Greco Park

Plateia Venizelou

Plateia Eleftherias

Plateia Kornarou

Plateia Kiptiu

To Hania Gate, Bus Station B, University Hospital at Voutes, Rethymno & Hania

0   125   250 m

site of modern Iraklio. It was known then as El Khandak, after the moat that surrounded the fortified town, and was reputedly the slave trade capital of the eastern Mediterranean.

El Khandak became Khandakos, after Byzantine troops finally dislodged the Arabs, and then Candia under the Venetians who ruled the island from here for more than 400 years. While the Turks quickly overran the Venetian defences at Hania and Rethymno, Candia's fortifications proved as effective as they looked – an unusual

combination. They withstood a siege of 21 years before the garrison finally surrendered in 1669.

Hania became the capital of independent Crete at the end of Turkish rule in 1898, and Candia was renamed Iraklio. Because of its central location, Iraklio became a commercial centre, and resumed its position as the island's administrative centre in 1971.

The city suffered badly in WWII, when most of the old Venetian and Turkish town was destroyed by bombing.

IRALKLIO

PLACES TO STAY		39	Ta Leontaria 1922	20	Summerland Travel
3	Hotel Kronos	40	Bougatsa Serraikon	22	Adamis Travel Bureau
10	Hotel Lena	43	Loukoumades Cafe	23	OTE
11	Vergina Rooms	44	Giovanni Taverna	25	Laundry Washsalon
12	Hotel Rea	50	Giakoumis Taverna	26	Planet International
14	Hotel Mirabello	51	Restaurant Ionia		Bookshop
15	Hotel Kastro	55	Bella Casa	27	Credit Bank
16	Youth Hostel			28	National Bank of Greece
17	Hotel Lato	**THINGS TO SEE**		29	Buses to Hania
19	Hotel Ilaira	1	Venetian Fortress		& Rethymno
21	Hotel Irini	4	Historical Museum of Crete	30	Buses to Knossos & Airport
24	Youth Hostel	37	Basilica of San Marco	31	Bus Station A
	(Rent Rooms Hellas)	38	Morosini Fountain	32	Istos Cyber Cafe
33	Atlantis Hotel	41	Church of Agia Ekaterini	34	Wash-O-Mate
48	Astoria Hotel	42	Agios Minos Cathedral	35	Venetian Loggia
		45	Battle of Crete Museum	36	Buses to Knossos
PLACES TO EAT		46	Archaeological Museum	47	EOT
2	Ippokampos Ouzeri	56	Bembo Fountain	49	Tourist Police
5	Garden of Deykaliola			52	Post Office
	Taverna	**OTHER**		53	Buses to Airport
6	Vareladika Ouzeri	8	Prince Travel	54	Olympic Airways
7	Katsina Ouzeri	9	Grecomar Holidays	57	Apollonia Hospital
13	Baxes	18	Crete Travel	58	Kazantzakis' Tomb

Orientation

Iraklio's two main squares are Plateia Venizelou and Plateia Eleftherias. Plateia Venizelou, instantly recognisable by its famous Morosini fountain (better known as the Lion fountain), is the heart of Iraklio and the best place from which to familiarise yourself with the layout of the city. The city's major intersection is a few steps south of the square. From here, 25 Avgoustou runs north-east to the harbour; Dikeosynis runs south-east to Plateia Eleftherias; Kalokerinou runs west to the Hania Gate; 1866 (the market street) runs south; and 1821 runs to the south-west. To reach Plateia Venizelou from the New Harbour, turn right, walk along the waterfront and turn left onto 25 Avgoustou.

Iraklio has three intercity bus stations. Station A, on the waterfront between the port and 25 Avgoustou, serves eastern Crete. A special bus station for Hania and Rethymno only is opposite Station A. Station B, just beyond the Hania Gate, serves Phaestos, Agia Galini and Matala. To reach the city centre from Station B walk through the Hania Gate and along Kalokerinou. For details on bus schedules, see the Iraklio Getting There & Away section.

Information

Tourist Offices The EOT (☎ 22 8225/6081/8203, fax 22 6020) is just north of Plateia Eleftherias at Xanthoudidou 1. The staff at the information desk are often work-experience students from a local tourism training college. They can give you photocopied lists of ferry and bus schedules, plus a map of the city. Opening times are 8 am to 2 pm Monday to Friday. In high season they also open on Saturday and Sunday.

The tourist police (☎ 28 3190), at Dikeosynis 10, are open 7 am to 11 pm.

Money Most of the city's banks are on 25 Avgoustou, including the National Bank of Greece at No 35. It has a 24 hour automatic exchange machine, as does the Credit Bank at No 94.

American Express (☎ 24 6202, 22 2303) is represented by Adamis Travel Bureau,

25 Avgoustou 23. Opening hours are 8 am to 2 pm Monday to Saturday. Thomas Cook (☎ 24 1108/1109) is represented by Summerland Travel, Epimenidou 30.

Post & Communications The central post office is on Plateia Daskalogianni. Coming from Plateia Venizelou, turn right off Dikeosynis opposite Hotel Petra, and you will see the post office across the square. Opening hours are 7.30 am to 8 pm Monday to Friday, and 7.30 am to 2 pm Saturday. From June through August there is a mobile post office at El Greco Park, just north of Plateia Venizelou, open 8 am to 6 pm Monday to Friday, and 8 am to 1.30 pm Saturday. The OTE, on Theotokopoulou just north of El Greco Park, opens 7.30 am to 11 pm daily. Istos Cyber Cafe (☎ 22 2120), Malikouti 2, charges 1300 dr an hour for computer access and can also scan, print and fax documents. It's open 9 am to 1 am daily.

Bookshops The huge Planet International Bookshop (☎ 28 1558) on the corner of Hortatson and Kidonias stocks most of the books recommended in this guide and has a large selection of Lonely Planet titles.

Laundry There are two laundrettes: Laundry Washsalon, Handakos 18, and Wash-O-Mate, Merabelou 25, near the archaeological museum. A wash and dry costs 2000 dr.

Left Luggage The left-luggage office at Bus Station A charges 300 dr per day and is open 6.30 am to 8 pm daily. Other options include Prince Travel (☎ 28 2706), 25 Avgoustou 30, which charges 500 dr, Washsalon (see Laundry) which charges 450 dr and the youth hostel at Vyronos 5 which charges 500 dr.

Emergency The new University Hospital (☎ 39 2111) at Voutes, 5km south of Iraklio, is the city's best equipped medical facility. The Apollonia Hospital (☎ 22 9713), inside the old walls on Mousourou, is more convenient.

Archaeological Museum

This outstanding museum (☎ 22 6092) is second in size and importance only to the National Archaeological Museum in Athens. If you are seriously interested in the Minoans you will want more than one visit, but even a fairly superficial perusal of the contents requires half a day.

The exhibits, arranged in chronological order, include pottery, jewellery, figurines and sarcophagi as well as some famous frescoes, mostly from Knossos and Agia Triada. All testify to the remarkable imagination and advanced skills of the Minoans. Unfortunately, the exhibits are not very well explained. If they were, there would be no need to part with 2200 dr for a copy of the glossy illustrated museum guide.

Room 1 of Iraklio's Archaeological Museum is devoted to the Neolithic and Early Minoan periods. Room 2 has a collection from the Middle Minoan period. Among the most fascinating exhibits here are the tiny glazed reliefs of Minoan houses from Knossos.

Room 3 covers the same period with finds from Phaestos, including the famous **Phaestos disc**. The symbols inscribed on the disc have not been deciphered. Here also are the famous **Kamares pottery vases**, named after the sacred cave of Kamares where the pottery was first discovered. The four large vases in case 43 were part of a royal banquet set. They are of exceptional quality and are some of the finest examples of Kamares pottery.

Exhibits in Room 4 are also from the Middle Minoan period. Most striking is the 20cm black stone **Bull's Head**, which was a libation vessel. The bull has a fine head of curls, from which sprout horns of gold. The eyes of painted crystal are extremely lifelike. Also in this room are relics from a shrine at Knossos, including two fine figurines of **snake goddesses**. Snakes symbolised immortality for the Minoans.

Pottery, bronze figurines and seals are some of the exhibits displayed in Room 5. These include vases imported from Egypt and some Linear A and B tablets. The

Mycenaean Linear B script has been deciphered, and the inscriptions on the tablets displayed here have been translated as household or business accounts from the palace at Knossos.

Room 6 is devoted to finds from Minoan cemeteries. Especially intriguing are two small clay models of grouped figures which were found in a *tholos* (Mycenaen tomb shaped like a beehive). One depicts four male dancers in a circle, their arms around each other's shoulders. The dancers may have been participating in a funeral ritual. The other model depicts two groups of three figures in a room flanked by two columns. Each group features two large seated figures being offered libations by a smaller

figure. It is not known whether the large figures represent gods or departed mortals. On a more grisly level, there is a display of the bones of a horse sacrificed as part of Minoan worship.

Finds in Room 7 include the beautiful **bee pendant** found at Malia. It's a remarkably fine piece of gold jewellery depicting two bees dropping honey into a comb. Also in this room are the three celebrated vases from Agia Triada. The **Harvester Vase**, of which only the top part remains, depicts a light-hearted scene of young farm workers returning from olive picking. The **Boxer Vase** depicts Minoans indulging in two of their favourite pastimes – wrestling and bull grappling. The **Chieftain Cup** depicts a

Linear B Script

The methodical decipherment of the Linear B script by English architect and part-time linguist Michael Ventris was the first tangible evidence that the Greek language had a recorded history longer than any scholar had previously believed. The decipherment demonstrated that the language disguised by these mysterious scribblings was an archaic form of Greek 500 years older than the Ionic Greek used by Homer.

Linear B was written on clay tablets that lay undisturbed for centuries until they were unearthed at Knossos in Crete. Further clay tablets were unearthed later on the mainland at Mycenae, Tiryns and Pylos on the Peloponnese and at Thebes in Boeotia.

The clay tablets, found to be mainly inventories and records of commercial transactions, consist of about 90 different signs and date from the 14th to the 13th century BC. Little of the social and political life of these times can be deduced from the tablets, though there is enough to give a glimpse of a fairly complex and well organised commercial structure.

For linguists, the script did not provide a detailed image of the actual language spoken, since the symbols were used primarily as syllabic clusters designed to give an approximation of the pronunciation of the underlying language. Typically, the syllabic cluster 'A-re-ka-sa-da-ra' is the woman's name Alexandra, but the exact pronunciation remains unknown.

Importantly, what is clear is that the language is undeniably Greek, thus giving the modern-day Greek language the second-longest recorded written history, after Chinese. The language of an earlier script, Linear A, remains to this day undeciphered. It is believed to be of either Anatolian or Semitic origin, though even this remains pure conjecture.

more cryptic scene: a chief holding a staff and three men carrying animal skins.

Room 8 holds finds from the palace at Zakros. Don't miss the gorgeous little crystal vase which was found in over 300 pieces and was painstakingly reconstructed by museum staff. Other exhibits include a beautiful elongated libation vessel decorated with shells and other marine life.

Room 10 covers the postpalatial period (1350 to 1100 BC) when the Minoan civilisation was in decline and being overtaken by the warrior-like Mycenaeans. Nevertheless, there are still some fine exhibits, including a child (headless) on a swing.

Room 13 is devoted to Minoan sarcophagi. However, the most famous and spectacular of these, the **sarcophagus from Agia Triada**, is upstairs in Room 14 (the Hall of Frescoes). This stone coffin, painted with floral and abstract designs and ritual scenes, is regarded as one of the supreme examples of Minoan art.

The most famous of the Minoan frescoes are also displayed in Room 14. Frescoes from Knossos include the **Procession Fresco**, the **Griffin Fresco** (from the Throne Room), the **Dolphin Fresco** (from the Queen's Room) and the amazing **Bull-Leaping Fresco**, which depicts a seemingly double-jointed acrobat somersaulting on the back of a charging bull. Other frescoes here include the two lovely **Frescoes of the Lilies** from Amisos and fragments of frescoes from Agia Triada. More frescoes can be

El Greco

One of the geniuses of the Renaissance, El Greco (meaning 'The Greek' in Spanish; his real name was Domeniko Theotokopoulos) was born and educated on Crete but had to travel to Spain to earn recognition.

El Greco was born in the Cretan capital of Candia (present-day Iraklio) in 1541 during a time of great artistic activity in the city. Many of the artists, writers and philosophers who fled Constantinople after it was conquered by the Turks in 1453 had settled on Crete, leading to the emergence of the Cretan school of icon painters. The painters had a formative influence upon the young El Greco, giving him the early grounding in the traditions of late Byzantine fresco painting that was to give such a powerful spiritual element to his later paintings.

Because Candia was a Venetian city it was a logical step for El Greco to head to Venice to further his studies, and he set off when he was in his early twenties to join the studio of Titian. It was not, however, until he moved to Spain in 1577 that he really came into his own as a painter. His highly emotional style struck a chord with the Spanish, and the city of Toledo was to become his home until his death in 1614. To view the most famous of his works like his masterpiece *The Burial of Count Orgaz* (1586), you will have to travel to Toledo. The only El Greco work on display in Crete is *View of Mt Sinai and the Monastery of St Catherine* (1570), painted during his time in Venice. It hangs in Iraklio's Historical Museum of Crete.

A white marble bust of the painter stands in Iraklio's Plateia El Greco, and streets are named after him throughout the island.

seen in Rooms 15 and 16. In Room 16 there is a large wooden model of Knossos.

The museum is on Xanthoudidou, just north of Plateia Eleftherias. Opening times are 8 am to 7 pm Tuesday to Sunday, and 12.30 to 7 pm Monday. The museum closes at 5 pm from late October to early April. Admission is 1500 dr.

Historical Museum of Crete

This museum (☎ 28 3219), just back from the waterfront, houses a fascinating range of bits and pieces from Crete's more recent past. The ground floor covers the period from Byzantine to Turkish rule, with plans, charts, photographs, ceramics and maps. On the 1st floor is the only **El Greco painting** on display in Crete. Other rooms contain fragments of 13th and 14th century frescoes, coins, jewellery, liturgical ornaments and vestments, and medieval pottery.

The 2nd floor has a reconstruction of the **library of author Nikos Kazantzakis**, with displays of his letters, manuscripts and books. Another room is devoted to Emmanual Tsouderos, who was born in Rethymno and who was prime minister in 1941. There are some dramatic photographs of a ruined Iraklio in the **Battle of Crete** section. On the 3rd floor there is an outstanding **folklore collection**.

The museum is open 9 am to 5 pm Monday to Friday, and 9 am to 2 pm Saturday, from June through August. From December through February it opens 9.30 am to 2.30 pm Monday to Saturday. Admission is 1000 dr.

Other Attractions

Iraklio burst out of its **city walls** long ago but these massive fortifications, with seven bastions and four gates, are still very conspicuous, dwarfing the concrete structures of the 20th century. Venetians built the defences between 1462 and 1562. The 16th century **Rocca al Mare**, another Venetian fortress, stands at the end of the Old Harbour's jetty. The fortress (☎ 24 6211) is open 8 am to 6 pm Monday to Saturday, and 10 am to 3 pm Sunday. Admission is 500 dr.

Several other notable vestiges from Venetian times survive in the city. Most famous is the **Morosini fountain** on Plateia Venizelou. The fountain, built in 1628, was commissioned by Francesco Morosini while he was governor of Crete. Opposite is the three-aisled 13th century **Basilica of San Marco**. It has been reconstructed many times and is now an exhibition gallery. A little north of here is the attractively reconstructed 17th century **Venetian loggia**. It was a Venetian version of a gentleman's club where the male aristocracy came to drink and gossip.

The delightful **Bembo fountain**, at the southern end of 1866, is shown on local maps as the Turkish fountain, but it was actually built by the Venetians in the 16th century. It was constructed from a hotchpotch of building materials including an ancient statue. The ornate edifice next to the fountain was added by the Turks, and now functions as a snack bar.

The former Church of Agia Ekaterini, next to Agios Minos Cathedral, is now a **museum** (☎ 28 8825) housing an impressive collection of icons. Most notable are those painted by Mihail Damaskinos, the mentor of El Greco. The museum is open 9 am to 1.30 pm Monday to Saturday. In addition it is open 5 to 8 pm on Tuesday, Thursday and Friday afternoons. Admission is 500 dr.

The **Battle of Crete Museum**, on the corner of Doukos Dofor and Hatzidaki, chronicles this historic battle through photographs, letters, uniforms and weapons. It is open 9 am to 1 pm daily. Admission is free.

You can pay homage to Crete's most acclaimed contemporary writer, Nikos Kazantzakis (1883-1957), by visiting his **tomb** at the Martinenga Bastion (the best preserved bastion) in the southern part of town. The epitaph on his grave, 'I hope for nothing, I fear nothing, I am free', is taken from one of his works.

Trekking

The Iraklio branch of the EOS (☎ 22 7609) is at Dikeosynis 53. It operates the Prinos Refuge on Mt Ida, a 1½ hour walk from the village of Melisses, 25km south-west of Iraklio.

CRETE

Organised Tours

Iraklio's travel agents run coach tours the length and breadth of Crete. Creta Travel (☎ 22 7002), Epimenidou 20-22, has a good range.

Places to Stay – Budget

The nearest *camp sites* are 26km away at Hersonisos.

Iraklio has two youth hostels. Although stripped of its official status, the *youth hostel (☎ 28 6281, Vyronos 5)* is a clean, well run place, where a bed in a single-sex dorm costs 1500 dr and basic doubles/triples cost 4000/5000 dr. Many prefer the livelier atmosphere at the hostel called *Rent Rooms Hellas (☎ 28 8851, Handakos 24)* where there's a roof garden and a bar. Rates are 1800 dr for a dorm bed and 5200/6700/8200 dr for doubles/triples/quads.

There are few *domatia* in Iraklio and not enough cheap hotels to cope with the number of budget travellers who arrive in high season. One of the nicest budget places is the spiffy *Hotel Mirabello (☎ 28 5052, Theotokopoulou 20)* which has clean singles/doubles for 6500/8500 dr, or 8000/10,000 dr with bathroom. *Hotel Lena (☎ 22 3280, fax 24 2826, Lahana 10)* has basic rooms for 6500/9000 dr, and doubles with bathroom for 11,000 dr.

The pleasant *Vergina Rooms (☎ 24 2739, Hortatson 32)* is a characterful, century-old house with a small courtyard and spacious high-ceilinged rooms. Doubles/triples/quads are 5000/6500/8500 dr. Bathrooms are on the terrace and hot water is available upon request.

Hotel Rea (☎ 22 3638), at the junction of Hortatson and Kalimeraki, is clean, quiet and friendly. Singles/doubles are 5000/6500 dr, while doubles/triples with bathroom are 7500/8000 dr.

Places to Stay – Mid-Range

One of the cheapest B class hotels is *Hotel Kastro (☎ 28 4185/5020, Theotokopoulou 22)*, where singles/doubles cost 13,000/16,000 dr. The best value C class hotel is *Hotel Kronos (☎ 28 2240, fax 28 5853,* Venizelou 2), which has large rooms in excellent condition for 9,000/12,000 dr. Try to get a room overlooking the sea. You could also try *Hotel Ilaira (☎ 22 7103/7125, Ariadnis 1)*, which has a roof garden and rooms for 10,000/14,000 dr. Nearby *Hotel Irini (☎ 22 6561, fax 22 6407, Idomeneos 4)* has large airy rooms with TV and telephone for 13,500/18,000 dr.

Places to Stay – Top End

The best place in town is the A class *Astoria Hotel (☎ 34 3080, fax 22 9078, Plateia Eleftherias 11)* which has rates of 28,500/36,000 dr. Facilities include a glorious outdoor swimming pool. The A class *Atlantis Hotel (☎ 22 9103/4023, fax 22 6265, Igias 2)* also offers comfortable rooms with air-conditioning. Rates are 24,000/34,000 dr and facilities include a health studio, sauna and indoor swimming pool. *Hotel Lato (☎ 22 8103, fax 24 0350, Epimenidou 15)* has rooms with spectacular sea views for 22,700/28,500 dr.

Places to Eat – Budget

Iraklio has some excellent restaurants, and there's something to suit all tastes and budgets.

If you're after traditional taverna food the place to look is Theodasaki, a little street between 1866 and Evans. Choices include *Giakoumis Taverna*, a popular spot turning out a big bowl of tasty bean stew for 900 dr. *Restaurant Ionia*, 20m away on the corner of Evans and Giannari, serves similar food in fancier surroundings for a few drachma more.

Ippokampos Ouzeri, on the waterfront just west of 25 Avgoustou, is as good as this style of eating gets. It has a huge range of *mezedes* on offer, priced from 400 dr. The fish dishes are especially recommended. They include grilled octopus (1100 dr), calamari (1000 dr) and sea urchin salad (1500 dr). The place is always busy, so it's a good idea to get in early. It's closed between 3.30 and 7 pm and on Sunday. The stylish *Vareladika Ouzeri* on Moni Agarathou has similar fare at about the same price.

The simple little *Katsina Ouzeri (Marineli 12)* has tasty main dishes from 700 dr to 1200 dr. The cosy *Baxes (Gianni Chroaki 14)* offers hearty Cretan meat dishes to a mostly local crowd that appreciates lamb and pork roasted in a brick oven as well as excellent stewed goat and rabbit.

In the charming *Garden of Deykaliola Taverna (Kalokerinou 8)* you'll soon forget you're in Crete's largest and least picturesque city. It offers a wide range of reasonably priced, imaginative mezedes and main dishes. It's open evenings only and really gets rolling around 11 pm when the tourists leave and the Cretans arrive.

If you haven't yet tried *loukoumades* (fritters with syrup), then *Loukoumades Cafe* on Dikeosynis is a good place to sample this gooey confection. For a meal on the move, try the tiny *Bougatsa Serraikon*, on Idis in the city centre. It makes excellent sweet (custard filled) or savoury (cheese filled) *bougatsa* for 380 dr. The more leisurely paced can while away some time people-watching at *Ta Leontaria 1922*, beside the Morosini fountain. The delicious bougatsa here costs 450 dr.

Whether you're self-catering or not, you'll enjoy a stroll up 1866 (the market street). This narrow street is always packed, and stalls spill over with produce of every description, including ornate Cretan wedding loaves. These loaves (smaller versions of the one on display at the Historical Museum of Crete) are not meant to be eaten; rather, they make an attractive kitchen decoration.

Places to Eat – Top End
Giovanni Taverna (Korai 12) is a splendid place with elegant antique furniture. In summer there is outdoor eating on a quiet pedestrian street. The food is a very Mediterranean combination of Greek and Italian specialities. A meal for two people, including a carafe of house red, costs about 12,000 dr.

Bella Casa, on the corner of Zografou and Averof, serves the same style food at more moderate prices. The restaurant is set in a stunning early 20th century villa with a verdant terrace.

Getting There & Away
Air – Domestic Olympic Airways has at least six flights daily to Athens (21,900 dr) from Iraklio's Nikos Kazantzakis airport. It also has flights to Thessaloniki (29,900 dr, three weekly), Rhodes (21,900 dr, four weekly) and Santorini (15,400 dr, two weekly). The Olympic Airways office (☎ 22 9191) is at Plateia Eleftherias 42.

Air Greece has flights to Athens (20,400 dr, four daily), Thessaloniki (28,400 dr, two daily) and, from June through August, Rhodes (21,900 dr, three weekly). The Air Greece office (☎ 33 0729/0739) is at Ethnikis Antistaseos 67.

Aegean Airlines has flights to Athens (18,500 dr, three daily) and Thessaloniki (29,700 dr, one daily). Its office is at the airport (☎ 33 0475).

Air – International The KLM associate Transavia flies direct between Amsterdam and Iraklio on Monday and Friday. Transavia is represented by Sbokos Tours (☎ 22 9712), Dimokratias 51.

Iraklio has lots of charter flights from all over Europe. Prince Travel (☎ 28 2706), 25 Avgoustou 30, advertises cheap last-minute tickets on these flights. Sample fares include London for 28,000 dr and Munich for 41,000 dr.

Bus There are buses every half-hour (hourly from December through February) to Rethymno (1½ hours, 1550 dr) and Hania (three hours, 2900 dr) from the Rethymno/ Hania bus station opposite Bus Station A. Buses from Bus Station A are:

Destination	Duration	Price	Frequency
Agia Pelagia	45 mins	650 dr	5 daily
Agios Nikolaos	1½ hours	1400 dr	half-hourly
Arhanes	30 mins	340 dr	15 daily
Hersonisos/Malia	1 hour	750 dr	half-hourly
Ierapetra	2½ hours	2100 dr	7 daily
Lassithi Plateau	2 hours	1400 dr	2 daily
Milatos	1½ hours	1000 dr	1 daily
Sitia	3½ hours	2850 dr	5 daily

Buses from Bus Station B are:

Destination	Duration	Price	Frequency
Agia Galini	2½ hours	1500 dr	7 daily
Anogia	1 hour	750 dr	6 daily
Matala	2 hours	1500 dr	9 daily
Phaestos	2 hours	1250 dr	8 daily

Taxi Long-distance taxis (☎ 21 0102) leave from Plateia Eleftherias and Bus Station B for all parts of Crete. Sample fares include Agios Nikolaos (9700 dr), Rethymno (12,000 dr) and Hania (20,000 dr).

Ferry Minoan Lines and ANEK Lines operate ferries every evening each way between Iraklio and Piraeus (10 hours). They depart from both Piraeus and Iraklio between 7.45 and 8 pm. Fares are 7000 dr deck class and 14,100 dr for cabins. Minoan Lines' boats are more modern and more comfortable than their ANEK Lines rivals. ANEK Lines, though, is a better bet for deck class travellers. It has dorm beds with plastic-covered mattresses, while Minoan Lines has only seats.

GA Ferries has three boats weekly to Santorini (four hours, 3700 dr), continuing to Paros (8½ hours, 5200 dr) and Piraeus, stopping at Naxos. GA also has three ferries weekly to Rhodes (11 hours, 6400 dr) via Karpathos (3800 dr). Minoan Lines runs three boats weekly to Thessaloniki (12,100 dr) via Santorini, Paros, Volos, Tinos and the Sporades. The travel agencies on 25 Avgoustou are the place to get information and buy tickets. Iraklio's port police can be contacted on ☎ 24 4912.

Getting Around

To/From the Airport Bus No 1 goes to and from the airport every 15 minutes between 6 am and 1 am (170 dr). It leaves the city from outside the Astoria Hotel on Plateia Eleftherias.

Bus Bus No 2 goes to Knossos every 10 minutes from Bus Station A (20 minutes, 240 dr). It also stops on 25 Avgoustou and 1821.

Car, Motorcycle & Bicycle Most of the car and motorcycle rental outlets are on 25 Avgoustou. You'll get the best deal from local companies like Sun Rise (☎ 22 1609) at 25 Avgoustou 46, Loggeta Cars & Bikes (☎ 28 9462) at Plateia Kallergon 6, next to El Greco Park, or Ritz Rent-A-Car at Hotel Rea (see Places to Stay), which offers discounts for hotel guests. There are also many car rental outlets at the airport.

Mountain bicycles can be hired from Porto Club Travel Services (☎ 28 5264), 25 Avgoustou 20.

KNOSSOS Κνωσσός

Knossos (no-**sos**), 5km from Iraklio, was the capital of Minoan Crete. Nowadays it's the island's major tourist attraction.

The ruins of Knossos were uncovered in 1900 by the British archaeologist Sir Arthur Evans. Heinrich Schliemann, who had earlier uncovered the ancient cities of Troy and Mycenae, had had his eye on the spot (a low, flat-topped mound), believing an ancient city was buried there, but was unable to strike a deal with the local landowner.

Evans was so enthralled by his discovery that he spent 35 years and £250,000 of his own money excavating and reconstructing sections of the palace. Some archaeologists have disparaged Evans' reconstruction, believing he sacrificed accuracy to his overly vivid imagination. However, most non-specialists agree that Sir Arthur did a good job and that Knossos is a knockout. Without these reconstructions it would be impossible to visualise what a Minoan palace looked like.

You will need to spend about four hours at Knossos to explore it thoroughly. The cafe at the site is expensive – you'd do better to bring a picnic along. Between April and October the site (☎ 081-23 1940) is open 8 am to 7 pm daily. In winter it closes at 5 pm. Admission is 1500 dr.

History

The first palace at Knossos was built around 1900 BC. In 1700 BC it was destroyed by an earthquake and rebuilt to a grander and more sophisticated design. It is this palace that Evans reconstructed. It was partially destroyed again sometime between 1500 and 1450 BC. It was inhabited for another 50 years before it was devastated once and for all by fire.

The city of Knossos consisted of an immense palace, residences of officials and priests, the homes of ordinary people, and burial grounds. The palace comprised royal domestic quarters, public reception rooms, shrines, workshops, treasuries and storerooms, all built around a central court. Like all Minoan palaces, it also doubled as a city hall, accommodating all the bureaucracy necessary for the smooth running of a complex society.

Until early 1997 it was possible to enter the royal apartments, but it was decided to cordon this area off before it disappeared altogether under the continual pounding of tourists' feet. Extensive repairs are under way but it is unlikely to open to the public again.

Exploring the Site

Numerous rooms, corridors, dog-leg passages, nooks and crannies, and staircases prohibit a detailed walk-through description of the palace. However, Knossos is not a site where you'll be perplexed by heaps of rubble, trying to fathom whether you're looking at the throne room or a workshop. Thanks to Evans' reconstruction, the most significant parts of the complex are instantly recognisable (if not instantly found). On your wanders you will come across many of Evans' reconstructed columns, most painted deep brown-red with gold-trimmed black capitals. Like all Minoan columns, they taper at the bottom.

It is not only the vibrant frescoes and mighty columns which impress at Knossos; keep your eyes open for the little details which are evidence of a highly sophisticated society. Things to look out for include the drainage system, the placement of light wells, and the relationship of rooms to passages, porches, light wells and verandahs, which kept rooms cool in summer and warm in winter.

The usual entrance to the palace complex is across the Western Court and along the **Corridor of the Procession Fresco**. The fresco depicted a long line of people carrying gifts to present to the king; only fragments remain. A copy of one of these fragments, called the **Priest King Fresco**, can be seen to the south of the Central Court.

If you leave the Corridor of the Procession Fresco and walk straight ahead to enter the site from the northern end, you will come to the **theatral area**, a series of steps, the function of which remains unknown. The area could have been a theatre where spectators watched acrobatic and dance performances, or the place where people gathered to welcome important visitors arriving by the Royal Road.

The **Royal Road** leads off to the west. The road, Europe's first (Knossos has lots of firsts), was flanked by workshops and the houses of ordinary people. The **lustral basin** is also in this area. Evans speculated that this was where the Minoans performed a ritual cleansing with water before religious ceremonies.

Entering the **Central Court** from the north, you pass the relief **Bull Fresco** which depicts a charging bull. Relief frescoes were made by moulding wet plaster, and then painting it while still wet.

Also worth seeking out in the northern section of the palace are the **giant pithoi**. Pithoi were ceramic jars used for storing olive oil, wine and grain. Evans found over 100 of these huge jars at Knossos, some 2m high. The ropes used to move them inspired the raised patterns decorating the jars.

Once you have reached the Central Court, which in Minoan times was surrounded by the high walls of the palace, you can begin exploring the most important rooms of the complex.

From the northern end of the west side of the Central Court, steps lead down to the **throne room**. This room is fenced off but you can still get a good view of it. The centrepiece, the simple, beautifully proportioned throne, is flanked by the **Griffin Fresco**. (Griffins were mythical beasts regarded as

CRETE

PALACE OF KNOSSOS

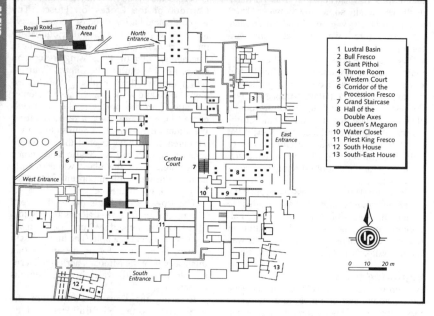

- 1 Lustral Basin
- 2 Bull Fresco
- 3 Giant Pithoi
- 4 Throne Room
- 5 Western Court
- 6 Corridor of the Procession Fresco
- 7 Grand Staircase
- 8 Hall of the Double Axes
- 9 Queen's Megaron
- 10 Water Closet
- 11 Priest King Fresco
- 12 South House
- 13 South-East House

sacred by the Minoans.) The room is thought to have been a shrine, and the throne the seat of a high priestess, rather than a king. Certainly, the room seems to have an aura of mysticism and reverence rather than pomp and ceremony. The Minoans did not worship their deities in great temples but in small shrines, and each palace had several.

On the 1st floor of the west side of the palace is the section Evans called the **Piano Nobile**, for he believed the reception and state rooms were here. A room at the northern end of this floor displays copies of some of the frescoes found at Knossos.

Returning to the Central Court, the impressive **grand staircase** leads from the middle of the eastern side of the palace to the royal apartments, which Evans called the Domestic Quarter. This section of the site is now cordoned off. Within the royal apartments is the **Hall of the Double Axes**.

This was the king's *megaron*, a spacious double room in which the ruler both slept and carried out certain court duties. The room had a light well at one end and a balcony at the other to ensure air circulation.

The room takes its name from the double axe marks on its light well. These marks appear in many places at Knossos. The double axe was a sacred symbol to the Minoans. *Labrys* was Minoan for 'double axe' and the origin of our word 'labyrinth'.

A passage leads from the Hall of the Double Axes to the **queen's megaron**. Above the door is a copy of the **Dolphin Fresco**, one of the most exquisite Minoan artworks, and a blue floral design decorates the portal. Next to this room is the queen's bathroom, complete with terracotta bathtub and **water closet**, touted as the first ever to work on the flush principle; water was poured down by hand.

Getting There & Away

Regular buses operate from Iraklio. See Iraklio's Getting Around section for details.

MYRTIA Μυρτιά

Myrtia (mir-tih-**ah**, also called Varvari), 22km south of Iraklio, makes the most of being the village that spawned Crete's favourite literary son, Nikos Kazantzakis. Kazantzakis was born in Iraklio and lived most of his life abroad, but his father was born here – and the writer himself did live here for a time. The **Nikos Kazantzakis Museum**, on the central square of the village, has a collection of the writer's personal mementoes. A video compiled from film clippings of the author's life is shown in Greek, German, French and English.

The museum is open 9 am to 1 pm and 4 to 8 pm Monday, Wednesday and weekends, and 9 am to 1 pm Tuesday and Friday. Admission is free.

The Myth of the Minotaur

King Minos of Crete invoked the wrath of Poseidon when he failed to sacrifice a magnificent white bull sent to him for that purpose. Poseidon's revenge was to cause Pasiphae, King Minos' wife, to fall in love with the animal.

In order to attract the bull, Pasiphae asked Daedalus, chief architect at Knossos and all-round handyman, to make her a hollow, wooden cow structure. When she concealed herself inside it, the bull found her irresistible. The outcome of their bizarre association was the Minotaur: a hideous monster who was half-man and half-bull.

King Minos asked Daedalus to build a labyrinth in which to confine the Minotaur and demanded that Athens pay an annual tribute of seven youths and seven maidens to satisfy the monster's huge appetite.

Minos eventually found out that Daedalus had been instrumental in bringing about the union between his wife and the bull, and threw the architect

Theseus killing the Minotaur

and his son Icarus into the labyrinth. Daedalus made wings from feathers stuck together with wax, and father and son made their getaway. As everyone knows, Icarus flew too close to the sun, the wax on his wings melted, and he plummeted into the sea off the island of Ikaria.

Athenians, meanwhile, were enraged by the tribute demanded by King Minos. The Athenian hero, Theseus, vowed to kill the Minotaur and sailed off to Crete posing as one of the sacrificial youths. On arrival, he fell in love with Ariadne, the daughter of King Minos, and she promised to help him if he would take her away with him afterwards. She provided him with the ball of twine that he unwound on his way into the labyrinth and used to retrace his steps after slaying the monster. Theseus fled Crete with Ariadne. The two married, but Theseus abandoned Ariadne on the island of Naxos on his way back to Athens.

On his return to Athens, Theseus forgot to unfurl the white sail that he had promised to display to announce that he was still alive. This prompted his distraught father, Aegeus, to hurl himself to his death from the Acropolis. This, incidentally, is how the Aegean sea got its name.

TYLISOS Τύλισος

The minor Minoan site at the village of Tylisos (**til**-is-os), 13km from Iraklio, is only for the insatiable enthusiast. Three villas dating from different periods have been excavated. The site (☎ 081-22 6092) is open 8.30 am to 3 pm daily. Admission is 400 dr. Buses from Iraklio to Anogia go through Tylisos. They also go past another Minoan site at **Sklavokambos**, 8km closer to Anogia. The ruins date from 1500 BC and were probably the villa of a district governor.

ARHANES Αρχάνες

The attractive village of Arhanes, 16km from Iraklio, lies in the heart of Crete's principal grape-producing region. Several Minoan remains have been unearthed in the vineyards surrounding the village. The most noteworthy is the elaborate **Vathypetro Villa**, the home of a prosperous Minoan noble.

The villa complex included storerooms where wine and oil presses, a weaving loom and a kiln were discovered. The villa is 5km from Arhanes, on the road south – look for a signpost to the right. Admission is free.

Getting There & Away

It's a pleasant outing from Iraklio to Arhanes if you have your own transport. Otherwise, there are 15 buses daily (fewer on weekends) from Iraklio's Bus Station A to Arhanes (30 minutes, 340 dr). There are no buses to Vathypetro, but Creta Travel in Iraklio has a tour which includes a visit to the villa.

GORTYNA Γόρτυνα

The archaeological site of Gortyna (**gor**-tih-nah, also called Gortys) lies 46km southwest of Iraklio, and 15km from Phaestos, on the plain of Mesara. It's a vast and wonderfully intriguing site with bits and pieces from various ages strewn all over the place. The site was a settlement from Minoan to Christian times. In Roman times, Gortyna was the capital of the province of Cyrenaica.

The most significant find at the site was the massive stone tablets inscribed with the **Laws of Gortyna**, dating from the 5th century BC. The laws deal with just about every imaginable offence. The tablets are on display at the site.

The 6th century **basilica** is dedicated to Agios Titos, a protege of St Paul and the first bishop of Crete.

Other ruins at Gortyna include the 2nd century AD **praetorin**, which was the residence of the governor of the province, a **nymphaeum**, and the **Temple of Pythian Apollo**. The site (☎ 0892-31 144) is open 8 am to 6 pm daily. Admission is 800 dr. The ruins are on both sides of the main Iraklio-Phaestos road.

PHAESTOS Φαιστός

The Minoan site of Phaestos (fes-**tos**), 63km from Iraklio, was the second most important palace city of Minoan Crete. Of all the Minoan sites, Phaestos has the most awe-inspiring location, with all-embracing views of the Mesara Plain and Mt Ida. The layout of the palace is identical to Knossos, with rooms arranged around a central court.

In contrast to Knossos, Phaestos has yielded very few frescoes. It seems the palace walls were mostly covered with a layer of white gypsum. Perhaps, with such inspiring views from the windows, the inhabitants didn't feel any need to decorate their walls. Evans didn't get his hands on the ruins of Phaestos, so there has been no reconstruction. Like the other palatial period complexes, there was an old palace here which was destroyed at the end of the Middle Minoan period. Unlike the other sites, parts of this old palace have been excavated and its ruins are partially superimposed upon the new palace.

The entrance to the new palace is by the 15m-wide **Grand Staircase**. The stairs lead to the west side of the **Central Court**. The best preserved parts of the palace complex are the reception rooms and private apartments to the north of the Central Court; excavations continue here. This section was entered by an imposing portal with half columns at either side, the lower parts of which are still *in situ*. Unlike the Minoan freestanding columns, these do not taper at the base. The celebrated Phaestos disc was found in a building to the north of the palace. The disc is in Iraklio's archaeologic-al museum. The site is open 8 am to 7 pm daily. Admission is 1200 dr.

Getting There & Away

There are buses to Phaestos from Iraklio's Bus Station B (1½ hours, 1250 dr, eight daily). There are also buses from Agia Galini (40 minutes, 400 dr, six daily) and Matala (30 minutes, 300 dr, five daily). Services are halved from December through February.

AGIA TRIADA Αγία Τριάδα

Agia Triada (ah-**yee**-ah trih-**ah**-dah) is a small Minoan site 3km west of Phaestos. Its principal building was smaller than the other royal palaces but built to a similar design. This, and the opulence of the objects found at the site, indicate that it was a royal residence, possibly a summer palace of Phaestos' rulers. To the north of the palace is a small town where remains of a *stoa* (long colonnaded building) have been unearthed.

Finds from the palace, now in Iraklio's archaeological museum, include a sarcophagus, two superlative frescoes and three vases: the Harvester Vase, Boxer Vase and Chieftain Cup.

The site is open 8.30 am to 3 pm daily. Admission is 500 dr. The road to Agia Triada takes off to the right about 500m from Phaestos on the road to Matala. There is no public transport to the site.

MATALA Μάταλα

☎ 0892 • postcode 702 00 • pop 300

Matala (**mah**-tah-lah), on the coast 11km south-west of Phaestos, was once one of Crete's best-known hippie hang-outs.

It was the old Roman caves at the northern end of the beach that made Matala famous in the 1960s. There are dozens of them dotted over the cliff-face. They were originally tombs, cut out of the sandstone rock in the 1st century AD. In the 1960s, they were discovered by hippies, who turned the caves into a modern troglodyte city – moving ever higher up the cliff to avoid sporadic attempts by the local police to evict them. Joni Mitchell was among the visitors, and she sang the praises of life under a Matala moon in *Carey*.

These days, Matala is a decidedly tacky tourist resort packed out in summer and bleak and deserted in winter. The sandy beach below the caves is, however, one of Crete's best, and the resort is a convenient base from which to visit Phaestos and Agia Triada.

Orientation & Information

Matala's layout is easy to fathom. The bus stop is on the central square, one block back from the waterfront. There is a mobile post office near the beach, on the right of the main road as you come into Matala. The OTE is beyond here in the beach car park.

Places to Stay

Matala Community Camping (☎ 42 340) is a reasonable site just back from the beach. There is another *camp site* near Komos Beach (☎ 42 596), about 4km before Matala on the road from Phaestos.

There are several pleasant options in Matala proper. Walk back along the main road from the bus station and turn right at Zafiria Hotel. This street is lined with budget accommodation. One of the cheapest is *Fantastic Rooms to Rent (☎ 45 362)*, on the right. The comfortable doubles/triples cost 6000/7000 dr with bathroom. *Pension Antonios (☎ 45 123/438)*, opposite, has attractively furnished rooms with bathroom for 4000/6000/7000 dr, and double/triple apartments for 8000/9000 dr.

The C class *Hotel Fragiskos (☎ 45 380/135)*, on the left as you head out of town, charges 8000/14,500 dr for singles/doubles with bathroom, including breakfast. It has a swimming pool.

If you don't like the sound of Matala, **Pitsidia Village**, 4.5km inland and 7km from Phaestos, is a quieter alternative. There are no hotels but plenty of *domatia*.

Places to Eat

Most of the restaurants in Matala are poor value. An exception is *Taverna Giannis*, where a huge plate of calamari, chips and salad costs 1200 dr, while a bowl of tasty lentil soup is 800 dr. Walk towards the southern headland and the taverna is on the right.

Restaurant Mystical View, high above Komos Beach about 3km from Matala, has views that live up to its name and serves good food to boot. The restaurant is signposted off the road to Phaestos.

Getting There & Away

There are buses between Iraklio and Matala (two hours, 1500 dr, five daily), and between Matala and Phaestos (30 minutes, 300 dr, five daily).

MALIA Μάλια

The Minoan site of Malia is the only cultural diversion on the stretch of coast east of Iraklio, which otherwise has surrendered lock, stock and barrel to the package tourist industry. Malia is smaller than Knossos and Phaestos, but like them consisted of a palace complex and a town. Unlike Knossos and Phaestos, the palace was built on a flat, fertile plain, not on a hill.

Entrance to the ruins is from the **West Court**. At the extreme southern end of this court there are eight circular pits which archaeologists think were used to store grain. To the east of the pits is the main entrance to the palace which leads to the southern end of the **Central Court**. At the south-west corner of this court you will find the **Kernos Stone**, a disc with 34 holes around its edge. Archae-ologists still don't know what it was used for.

The **central staircase** is at the north end of the west side of the palace. The **loggia**, just north of the staircase, is where religious ceremonies took place.

The site (☎ 0897-31 597), 3km east of the resort of Malia, is open 8.30 am to 3 pm Tuesday to Sunday. Admission is 800 dr.

Any bus going to or from Iraklio along the north coast can drop you at the site.

Eastern Crete

The eastern quarter of the island is occupied by the prefecture of Lassithi, named after the quaint plateau tucked high in the Mt Dikti Ranges rather than its uninspiring administrative capital of Agios Nikolaos, which is becoming something of a monument to package tourism. The main attractions, apart from the Lassithi Plateau, are the palm forest and beach at Vaï and the remote Minoan palace site of Zakros.

AGIOS NIKOLAOS Αγιος Νικόλαος

☎ 0841 • postcode 721 00 • pop 9000

The manifestations of package tourism gather momentum as they advance east from Iraklio, reaching their peak at Agios Nikolaos (ah-**yee**-os nih-**ko**-laos). In July and August the town's permanent population is increased by 11,000 tourists. The result is that there is very little to attract the independent traveller. It's pointless trying to squeeze into Agios Nikolaos in the peak season between July and mid-September, and the place just about closes down entirely from December through February.

Orientation

The town centre is Plateia Venizelou, 150m up Sofias Venizelou from the bus station. The most interesting part of town is around the picturesque Voulismeni Lake, which is ringed with tavernas and cafes. The lake is 200m from Plateia Venizelou. Walk northeast along Koundourou and turn left at the bottom and you will come to a bridge that separates the lake from the harbour. The tourist office is at the far side of the bridge.

Once over the bridge, if you turn right and follow the road as it veers left, you will come to the northern stretch of waterfront which is the road to Elounda. A number of large and expensive hotels are along here.

Alternatively, if you turn right at the bottom of Koundourou you will come to a stretch of waterfront with steps leading up to the right. These lead to the streets that have the highest concentration of small hotels and pensions.

Information

The municipal tourist office (☎ 22 357, fax 82 354), by the bridge, is open 8 am to 9.30 pm daily from the start of April to mid-November. The tourist police (☎ 26 900), Kondogianni 34, open between 7.30 am and 2.30 pm daily.

The National Bank of Greece on Nikolau Plastira has a 24 hour automatic exchange machine. The tourist office also changes money. The post office, 28 Oktovriou 9, is open 7.30 am to 2 pm Monday to Friday. The OTE is on the corner of 25 Martiou and K Sfakianaki. It is open 7 am to 11 pm daily.

Internet access is available at the pleasant Polychoros (☎ 24 876), Oktovoriou 28, open 9 am to 2 am daily. There is a well stocked English-language bookshop at Koundourou 5 next to the bank.

The general hospital (☎ 25 221) is between Lassithiou and Paleologou.

Things to See

The **folk museum**, next to the tourist office, has a well displayed collection of traditional handcrafts and costumes. It's open 10 am to 3 pm Sunday to Friday. Admission is 250 dr.

The **archaeological museum** (☎ 22 462), on Paleologou, is a modern building housing a large, well displayed collection from eastern Crete. It's open 8.30 am to 3 pm Tuesday to Sunday. Admission is 500 dr.

The **Local Aquarium of Agios Nikolaos** (☎ 24 953), on Akti Koundourou, has interesting displays of fish and information about diving (including PADI courses) and snorkelling throughout Crete. It is open 10 am to 9 pm Monday to Saturday. Admission is 1300 dr.

Voulismeni Lake (Λίμνη Βουλισμένη) is the subject of many stories about its depth and origins. The locals have given it various names, including Xepatomeni (bottomless), Voulismeni (sunken) and Vromolimni (dirty). The lake isn't bottomless – it is 64m deep. The 'dirty' tag came about because the lake used to be stagnant and gave off quite a pong in summer. This was rectified in 1867 when a canal was built linking it to the sea.

Beaches

The popularity of Agios Nikolaos has nothing to do with its beaches. The town beach, south of the bus station, and Kritoplatia Beach, have more people than pebbles. Ammoudi Beach, on the road to Elounda, is equally uninspiring.

The sandy beach at Almiros about 1km south of town is the best of the lot and tends to be less crowded than the others. There's little shade but you can rent umbrellas for 500 dr a day.

Organised Tours

Travel agencies in Agios Nikolaos offer coach outings to all Crete's top attractions. Nostos Tours (☎ 22 819), Koundourou 30, has boat trips to Spinalonga (4000 dr) as well as guided tours of Phaestos and Matala (7500 dr), the Samaria Gorge (12,500 dr) and the Lassithi Plateau (7000 dr).

Places to Stay – Budget

The nearest camp site to Agios Nikolaos is *Gournia Moon Camping (☎ 0842-93 243)*, near the Minoan site of Gournia. It has a swimming pool, restaurant, snack bar and minimarket. Buses to Sitia can drop you off outside.

Green House (☎ 22 025, Modatsou 15) is a backpacker favourite. It is ramshackle but clean, with a lush garden. Singles/doubles are 3000/4000 dr. Breakfast is an additional 500 dr per person. Walk up Tavla (a continuation of Modatsou) from the bus station, and you'll find it on the right.

Hotel Pergola (☎ 28 152), on Akti Themistokleous, has comfortable rooms with bathroom for 5000/7000 dr. *Aphrodite Rooms (☎ 28 058, Koritsas 27)* has rooms for 3000/4000 dr and a tiny communal kitchen. At *Mary Pension (☎ 23 760, Evans 13)*, rooms with bathroom cost 5000/6000 dr.

One of the few places to stay open all year is the charming *Hotel Doxa (☎ 24 614, Idomeneos 7)* which has rooms for 8000/10,000 dr and a comfortable lounge filled with plants and flowers.

CRETE

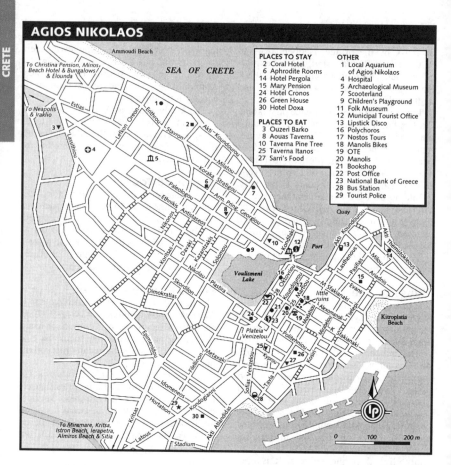

AGIOS NIKOLAOS

To Christina Pension, Minos
Beach Hotel & Bungalows
& Elounda

Ammoudi Beach

SEA OF CRETE

To Neapolis
& Iraklio

Voulismeni
Lake

Port

Quay

Kitroplatia
Beach

Plateia
Venizelou

To Miramare, Kritsa,
Istron Beach, Ierapetra,
Almiros Beach & Sitia

Stadium

0   100   200 m

PLACES TO STAY	OTHER
2 Coral Hotel	1 Local Aquarium
6 Aphrodite Rooms	of Agios Nikolaos
14 Hotel Pergola	4 Hospital
15 Mary Pension	5 Archaeological Museum
24 Hotel Cronos	7 Scooterland
26 Green House	9 Children's Playground
30 Hotel Doxa	11 Folk Museum
	12 Municipal Tourist Office
PLACES TO EAT	13 Lipstick Disco
3 Ouzeri Barko	16 Polychoros
8 Aouas Taverna	17 Nostos Tours
10 Taverna Pine Tree	18 Manolis Bikes
25 Taverna Itanos	19 OTE
27 Sarri's Food	20 Manolis
	21 Bookshop
	22 Post Office
	23 National Bank of Greece
	28 Bus Station
	29 Tourist Police

Places to Stay – Mid-Range & Top End

The opulent B class *Coral Hotel* (☎ 28 363/ 367) on the northern waterfront is about as upmarket as places get in town. It has rooms for 15,250/19,500 dr. There is a swimming pool.

Most luxury hotels are north of town on the road to Elounda but at *Miramare* (☎ 23 875, fax 24 164) you're less than 1 km out of town near Almiros Beach. Rooms with air-conditioning, private balcony and panoramic views are 21,000/28,000 dr. The most luxurious hotel is the deluxe *Minos Beach Hotel & Bungalows* (☎ 22 345/349, fax 22 548), north of town with seaside bungalows for 46,400/61,800 dr. Both places have a swimming pool and tennis courts.

Places to Eat

Agios Nikolaos' waterfront tavernas are expensive – head inland for better value. *Taverna Itanos (Kyprou 1)* is a lively traditional taverna, with a stuffed eggplant speciality for 1000 dr and *stifado* (beef stew) for 1800 dr.

Ouzeri Barko (Lassithiou 23) is a bit out of the way but well worth the effort. It has an excellent selection of mezedes priced from 500 dr to 900 dr. It opens only in the evenings.

Taverna Pine Tree, next to the lake, specialises in charcoal-grilled food, such as a plate of prawns for 1700 dr. *Aouas Taverna (Paleologou 50)* has traditional decor and a lovely garden. A large plate of mezedes (enough for four people) is 2700 dr. The tiny *Sarri's Food (Kyprou 15)* has tasty main courses for between 900 dr and 1400 dr.

Entertainment
Bars are everywhere in Agios Nikolaos. The only operating disco is *Lipstick Disco* on Akti Koundourou.

Getting There & Away
Bus Buses leave the Agios Nikolaos bus station for Elounda (230 dr, 20 daily), Kritsa (230 dr, 12 daily), Ierapetra (750 dr, eight daily), Iraklio (1400 dr, half-hourly), Istron (280 dr, 11 daily), Lassithi Plateau (1900 dr, one daily) and Sitia (1500 dr, six daily).

Ferry Agios Nikolaos has the same ferry schedule as Sitia (see Getting There & Away in the Sitia section later). Ferry tickets can be bought from Nostos Tours, among others. The port police (☎ 22 312) are in the same building as the tourist office.

Getting Around
You will find many car and motorcycle rental outlets on the northern waterfront. Scooterland (☎ 26 340), Akti Koundourou 10, has a huge range of scooters and motorcycles beginning at 4000 dr a day for a scooter, to 15,000 dr a day for a Kawasaki EN.

You can rent mountain bikes from Manolis (☎ 24 940) down the street from the OTE office on 25 Martiou. Prices begin at 2000 dr a day.

GOURNIA Γουρνιά
The important Minoan site of Gournia (goor-**nyah**) lies just off the coast road, 19km

south-east of Agios Nikolaos. The ruins, which date from 1550 to 1450 BC, consist of a town overlooked by a small palace. The palace was far less ostentatious than the ones at Knossos and Phaestos because it was the residence of an overlord rather than a king. The town is a network of streets and stairways flanked by houses with walls up to 2m in height. Trade, domestic and agricultural implements found on the site indicate Gournia was a thriving little community.

The site (☎ 0841-24 943) is open 8.30 am to 3 pm Tuesday to Sunday. Admission is 500 dr. Gournia is on the Sitia and Ierapetra bus routes from Agios Nikolaos and buses can drop you at the site.

MONI FANEROMENIS
Μονή Φανερωμένης
There are stunning views down to the coast from this late-Byzantine monastery, 5km south of the Agios Nikolaos-Sitia road. The turn-off to Moni Faneromenis is 2km west of Gournia.

KRITSA Κριτσά
The village of Kritsa (krit-**sah**), perched 600m up the mountainside 11km from Agios Nikolaos, is on every package itinerary. Tourists come in bus loads to the village every day in summer. The villagers exploit these invasions to the full, and craft shops of every description line the main streets.

The tiny triple-aisled **Church of Panagia Kera** is on the right 1km before Kritsa on the Agios Nikolaos road. The frescoes that cover its interior walls are considered the most outstanding examples of Byzantine art on Crete. Unfortunately the church is usually packed with tourists. It's open 8.30 am to 3 pm Monday to Friday, and 8.30 am to 2 pm Saturday. Admission is 500 dr.

Kritsa doesn't have any hotels, but there are several *domatia* – look for the signs.

There are 12 buses daily from Agios Nikolaos to Kritsa (15 minutes, 230 dr).

ANCIENT LATO Λατώ
The ancient city of Lato (lah-**to**), 4km north of Kritsa, is one of Crete's few non-Minoan

ancient sites. Lato was founded in the 7th century BC by the Dorians and at its height was one of the most powerful cities on Crete. It sprawls over the slopes of two acropolises in a lonely mountain setting, commanding stunning views down to the Gulf of Mirabello.

The city's name derived from the goddess Leto whose union with Zeus produced Artemis and Apollo, both of whom were worshipped here. Lato is far less visited than Crete's Minoan sites. It's open 8.30 am to 3 pm Tuesday to Sunday. Admission is free.

In the centre of the site is a deep well which is cordoned off. As you face the Gulf of Mirabello, to the left of the well are some steps which are the remains of a **theatre**.

Above the theatre was the **prytaneion**, where the city's governing body met. The circle of stones behind the well was a threshing floor. The columns next to it are the remains of a stoa which stood in the *agora* (commercial area). There are remains of a pebble mosaic nearby. A path to the right leads up to the **Temple of Apollo**.

There are no buses to Lato. The road to the site is signposted to the right on the approach to Kritsa. If you don't have your own transport, it's a pleasant walk through olive groves along this road.

SPINALONGA PENINSULA

Χερσόνησος Σπιναλόγκας

Just before Elounda (coming from Agios Nikolaos), a sign points right to **ancient Olous**, once the port of Lato. The city stood on and around the narrow isthmus (now a causeway) which joined the southern end of the Spinalonga Peninsula to the mainland. Most of the ruins lie beneath the water, and if you go snorkelling near the causeway you will see outlines of buildings and the tops of columns. The water around here appears to be paradise for sea urchins. The peninsula is a pleasant place to stroll and there is an early Christian mosaic near the causeway.

SPINALONGA ISLAND

Νήσος Σπιναλόγκα

Spinalonga Island lies just north of the Spinalonga Peninsula. The island's massive fortress was built by the Venetians in 1579 to protect Elounda Bay and the Gulf of Mirabello. It withstood Turkish sieges for longer than any other Cretan stronghold, finally surrendering in 1715, some 30 years after the rest of Crete. The Turks used the island as a base for smuggling. Following the reunion of Crete with Greece, Spinalonga Island became a leper colony. The last leper died there in 1953 and the island has been uninhabited ever since. It is still known among locals as 'the island of the living dead'.

The island is a fascinating place to explore. It has an aura that is both macabre and poignant. The **cemetery**, with its open graves, is an especially strange place. Dead lepers came in three classes: those who saved up money from their government pension for a place in a concrete box; those whose funeral was paid for by relations and who therefore got a proper grave; and the destitute, whose remains were thrown into a charnel house.

Getting There & Away

There are regular excursion boats to Spinalonga Island from Agios Nikolaos and a boat every half-hour from the port in Elounda (2000 dr). Alternatively, you can negotiate with the fishermen in Elounda and Plaka (a fishing village 5km farther north) to take you across. The boats from Agios Nikolaos pass Bird Island and Kri-Kri Island, one of the last habitats of the *kri-kri*, Crete's wild goat. Both these islands are uninhabited and designated wildlife sanctuaries.

ELOUNDA Ελούντα

☎ 0841 • postcode 720 53 • pop 1800

There are magnificent mountain and sea views along the 11km road from Agios Nikolaos to Elounda. Although formerly a quiet fishing village, Elounda is now bristling with tourists and is only marginally calmer than Agios Nikolaos. But the harbour is attractive, and there's a sheltered lagoon-like stretch of water formed by the Spinalonga Peninsula.

Orientation & Information

Elounda's post office is opposite the bus

stop. From the bus stop walk straight ahead to the clock tower and church which are on the central square. There is a small OTE office next to the church. Elounda doesn't have tourist police but a tourist office (☎ 42 464) has recently opened opposite the church.

Places to Stay

There's some good accommodation around, but nothing particularly cheap. *Hotel Aristea* *(☎ 41 300)*, in the town centre, has doubles/triples with a sea view for 7000/10,000 dr. *Hotel Sofia (☎ 41 482)*, on the seafront 100m from the town centre, has pleasantly furnished two-room apartments with kitchen for 12,000 dr among its range of options.

Getting There & Away

There are 20 buses daily from Agios Nikolaos to Elounda (20 minutes, 230 dr).

LASSITHI PLATEAU

Οροπέδιο Λασιθίου
☎ 0844 • postcode 720 52
The first view of the mountain-fringed Lassithi Plateau, laid out like an immense patchwork quilt, is stunning. The plateau, 900m above sea level, is a vast expanse of pear and apple orchards, almond trees and fields of crops, dotted by some 7000 windmills. These are not conventional stone windmills, but slender metal constructions with white canvas sails. They were built in the 17th century to irrigate the rich farmland but few of the original windmills are in service. Most have been replaced by less-attractive mechanical pumps. There are 20 villages dotted around the periphery of the plateau, the largest of which is **Tzermiado**, with 1300 inhabitants, a bank, post office and OTE.

The plateau's rich soil has been cultivated since Minoan times. The inaccessibility of the region made it a hotbed of insurrection during Venetian and Turkish rule. Following an uprising in the 13th century, the Venetians drove out the inhabitants of Lassithi and destroyed their orchards. The plateau lay abandoned for 200 years.

Most people come to Lassithi on coach trips, but it deserves an overnight stay. Once the package tourists have departed clutching their plastic windmill souvenirs, the villages return to pastoral serenity.

Dikteon Cave Δίκταιον Αντρον

Lassithi's major sight is Dikteon Cave, just outside the village of **Psyhro**. Here, according to mythology, Rhea hid the newborn Zeus from Cronos, his offspring-gobbling father. The cave, which has both stalactites and stalagmites, was excavated in 1900 by British archaeologist David Hogarth. He found numerous votive offerings, indicating the cave was a place of cult worship. These finds are housed in the archaeological museum in Iraklio.

The moment you reach the parking area beneath the site, representatives from the Association of Cave Guides & Donkey Owners will be upon you. The cave guides want 2000 dr for a lantern-guided tour, while the donkey owners want the same to save you the 15 minute walk up to the cave. A guide is not essential, but a torch is. So are sensible shoes. The path to the cave is pretty rough, and the cave itself is slippery. Opening times are 8 am to 4 pm daily. Admission is 800 dr.

Walk from Tzermiado to Psyhro

The 90 minute walk from Tzermiado to Psyhro goes through the heart of the plateau. From Tzermiado's central square take the street with the Agricultural Bank and OTE. At the end, turn right, and then take the first left onto a road which becomes a dirt track. Continue ahead for 1km. At the T-junction turn right, and then veer right onto the surfaced road. At the crossroads, turn left onto a rough dirt track. Turn right at the second crossroads and you will see Psyhro in the distance to the left. Continue straight ahead for 1km, and at the T-junction turn left. At the road, turn left to reach Psyhro's central square, or continue straight ahead to reach Dikteon Cave.

Places to Stay & Eat

Psyhro, the village nearest the cave, has only one place to stay – the D class *Zeus*

CRETE

Hotel (☎ *31 284*) where singles/doubles with bathroom cost 6000/8000 dr. On the main street, *Stavros* and *Platanos* tavernas serve similar fare at similar prices.

Agios Georgios, 5km away, has three accommodation options. At *Hotel Rea* (☎ *31 209*), opposite the school on the main street, there are cosy rooms for 2500/5000 dr. *Rent Rooms Maria* nearby has spacious stucco rooms decorated with weavings for 6000/8500/10,800 dr with bathroom. *Hotel Dias* (☎ *31 207*), also on the main street, has pleasant rooms for 3000/4000 dr. Both hotels have restaurants.

In Tzermiado, the well signposted *Hotel Kourites* (☎ *22 194*) is the only accommodation. Its comfortable rooms cost 6000/8000 dr with bathroom, breakfast included. There is free use of the hotel's bicycles.

Restaurant Kronio, on Tzermiado's main square, has a pleasant, folksy decor. The food is excellent, but avoid the place when the tour buses call, as the waiters go into frenzy mode. Nearby *Taverna Kri-Kri* is a good place to meet locals. The menu is limited but the food is good.

Getting There & Away
Public transport to the Dikteon Cave is problematic if you don't have your own wheels. From Agios Nikolaos there's an afternoon bus to Lassithi on Monday, Wednesday and Friday (1900 dr, 2½ hrs) and a morning bus from Lassithi to Agios Nikolaos also on Monday, Wednesday and Friday. From Iraklio there are two buses on weekdays to Lassithi (two hours, 1400 dr), and three on weekdays returning to Iraklio.

All buses go through Tzermiado and Agios Georgios before terminating at Psyhro at the foot of the road leading to Dikteon Cave.

SITIA Σητεία
☎ 0843 • postcode 723 00 • pop 8000
Back on the north coast road, Sitia (sih-**tee**-ah) is a good deal quieter than Agios Nikolaos. A sandy beach skirts a wide bay to the east of town. The main part of the town is terraced up a hillside, overlooking the port.

The buildings are a pleasing mixture of new and fading Venetian architecture.

Orientation & Information
The bus station is at the eastern end of Karamanli, which runs behind the bay. The town's main square, Plateia El Venizelou – recognisable by its palm trees and statue of a dying soldier – is at the western end of Karamanli.

There's no tourist office but Tzortzakis Travel (☎ 25 080), Kornalou 150, is a good source of information. There are plenty of ATMs and places to change money. The National Bank of Greece on the main square has a 24 hour exchange machine.

The harbour near the square is for small boats. Ferries use the large quay farther out, about 500m from Plateia Agnostou.

The post office is on Democritou. To get there from the main square, follow El Venizelou inland and take the first left. The OTE is on Kapetan Sifis, which runs uphill directly off Plateia El Venizelou.

Things to See & Do
Sitia's **archaeological museum** (☎ 23 917) houses a well displayed collection of local finds spanning from Neolithic to Roman times, with emphasis on the Minoan. The museum is on the left side of the road to Ierapetra. It is open 8.30 am to 3 pm Tuesday to Sunday. Admission is 500 dr.

Sitia produces superior sultanas and a **sultana festival** is held in the town in the last week of August, during which wine flows freely and there are performances of Cretan dances.

Places to Stay
Sitia's *youth hostel* (☎ *22 693, Therissou 4*) is on the road to Iraklio. It's a well run hostel with hot showers and a communal kitchen and dining room. Dorm beds cost 1500 dr and double rooms are 3000 dr. Camping in the grounds costs 1000 per person.

The D class *Hotel Arhontiko* (☎ *28 172, 22 993, Kondylaki 16*) is beautifully maintained and spotless. Singles/doubles are 5000/6000 dr. On summer evenings, the friendly owner enjoys sharing a bottle of *raki* with guests on the communal terrace. Kondylaki is two streets uphill from the port. The best way to get there is to walk out towards the ferry dock along El Venizelou, turn left up Filellinon and then right into Kondylaki. The co-owned **Rooms to Let Apostolis** *(Kazantzaki 27)*, an upmarket domatio, has doubles with fridge for 7500 dr. Kazantzaki runs uphill from the waterfront, one street north of the OTE.

Another attractive place is **Kazarma Rooms to Rent** *(☎ 23 211, Ionias 10)* where doubles with bathroom cost 8000 dr. There is a communal lounge and a well equipped kitchen. The rooms are signposted from Patriarch Metahaki. The well signposted **El Greco Hotel** *(☎ 23 133, Arkadou 13)* has more character than the town's other C class hotels. Comfortable rooms with bathroom cost 7000/10,000 dr. The B class **Itanos Hotel** *(☎ 22 900, fax 22 915)*, along the harbour, has air-conditioned rooms with balconies for 9000/12,000 dr. Add another 1500 dr per person for breakfast at the hotel but there are plenty of cafes nearby.

Places to Eat

There is a string of tavernas along the quay side on El Venizelou that offer an array of mezedes and fish dishes at comparable prices. Inland, there's **Mixos Taverna** *(Kornarou 117)*, which has excellent charcoal-grilled souvlaki. Walk up Patriarch Metahaki from the waterfront, take the first left and the taverna is on the right.

Kali Kardia Taverna *(Foundalidhou 20)* is excellent value and popular with locals. Mezedes cost from 400 dr to 800 dr and main dishes from 1250 dr to 1800 dr. Walk up Kazantzaki from the waterfront, take the second right and the taverna is on the right. **The Balcony**, on the corner of Kazantzaki and Foundalidou, provides the finest dining in Sitia with an extraordinarily creative menu that combines Greek, Italian and Mexican food. A meal for two with wine will cost about 12,000 dr.

The **galaktopoleio** *(Kornarou 33)* specialises in fine sheep's-milk products,

including fresh milk, curdled milk, delicious yogurt and cheese.

Getting There & Away

Air Sitia's tiny airport has flights to Athens once weekly for 23,100 dr. The agent for Olympic Airways is Tzortzakis Travel *(☎ 25 080/090)* at Kornarou 150.

Bus There are buses to Ierapetra (1½ hours, 1200 dr, six daily); Iraklio (3½ hours, 2850 dr, five daily) via Agios Nikolaos (1½ hours, 1500 dr); Vaï (one hour, 600 dr, five daily); and Kato Zakros (one hour, two daily) via Paleokastro and Zakros (one hour, 1000 dr). Buses to Vaï and Kato Zakros run during May to October only. During the rest of the year, the Vaï service terminates at Paleokastro and the Kato Zakros service at Zakros.

Ferry Ferries depart Sitia Tuesday, Thursday and Sunday afternoons for Piraeus (14½ hours, 7600 dr) via Agios Nikolaos. Ferries also leave Sitia on Thursday and Saturday morning for Karpathos (four hours, 3400 dr) and Kassos (six hours, 2600 dr), and Saturday morning for Rhodes (6000 dr). Ferry tickets can be bought at Tzortzakis Travel *(☎ 22 631, 28 900)*, Kor-narou 150.

Getting Around

The airport (signposted) is 1km out of town. There is no airport bus; a taxi costs about 1000 dr. Car and motorcycle rental outlets are mostly on Papandreou on the way to the archaeological museum.

AROUND SITIA
Moni Toplou Μονή Τοπλού

The imposing Moni Toplou, 18km from Sitia on the back road to Vaï, looks more like a fortress than a monastery. It was often treated as such, being ravaged by both the Knights of St John and the Turks. It holds an 18th century icon by Ioannis Kornaros, one of Crete's most celebrated icon painters. The monastery is open 9 am to 1 pm and 2 to 6 pm daily.

It is a 3km walk from the road from Sitia to Paleokastro. Buses can drop you off at the junction.

Vaï Βάι

The beach at Vaï, on Crete's east coast 24km from Sitia, is famous for its palm forest.

There are many stories about the origin of these palms, including the theory that they sprouted from date pits spread by Roman legionaries relaxing on their way back from conquering Egypt. While these palms are closely related to the date, they are a separate species unique to Crete.

You'll need to arrive early to appreciate the setting, because the place gets packed in July and August. It's possible to escape the worst of the ballyhoo – jet skis and all – by clambering over a rocky outcrop (to the right, facing the sea) to a small secluded beach. Alternatively, you can go over the hill in the other direction to a quiet beach frequented by nudists.

There are two tavernas at Vaï but no accommodation. If you're after more secluded beaches, head north for another 3km to the ancient Minoan site of **Itanos**. Below the site are several good swimming spots. There are buses to Vaï from Sitia (one hour, 600 dr, five daily).

ZAKROS & KATO ZAKROS
☎ 0843   • postcode 72 300

The village of Zakros (Ζάκρος), 37km southeast of Sitia, is the nearest permanent settlement to the Minoan site of Zakros, a further 7km away (see Ancient Zakros following).

Kato Zakros, next to the site, is a beautiful little seaside settlement that springs to life between March and October. If the weather is dry, there is a lovely two hour walk from Zakros to Kato Zakros through a gorge known as the Valley of the Dead because of the cave tombs dotted along the cliffs. The gorge emerges close to the Minoan site.

Places to Stay
Zakros has *domatia* and one hotel, the bleak C class *Hotel Zakros* (☎ 93 379), where doubles with bathroom are 5000 dr.

It's much better to stay at Kato Zakros, where there are three places to choose from. *Athena Rooms* (☎ 93 458/377) has doubles with bathroom for 8000 dr, and is jointly

owned with *Poseidon Rooms*, which has singles/doubles for 5000/6000 dr with shared bathroom. All these places are at the far end of the beach road.

George's Villas (☎ 93 201/207) has spotless, beautifully furnished rooms with bathroom and terrace. Rates are 6000/7000 dr. The villas are in a verdant setting 500m along the old road to Zakros.

Getting There & Away
There are buses to Zakros via Paleokastro from Sitia (one hour, 1000 dr, two daily). They leave Sitia at 11 am and 2.30 pm and return at 12.30 and 4 pm. From June through August, the buses continue to Kato Zakros. Hotel Zakros offers guests free transport to Kato Zakros.

ANCIENT ZAKROS
The smallest of Crete's four palatial complexes, ancient Zakros was a major port in Minoan times, maintaining trade links with Egypt, Syria, Anatolia and Cyprus. The palace comprised royal apartments, storerooms and workshops flanking a central courtyard.

The town occupied a low plain close to the shore. Water levels have risen over the years so that some parts of the palace complex are submerged. The ruins are not well preserved, but a visit to the site is worthwhile for its wild and remote setting. The site is open 8.30 am to 3 pm Tuesday to Sunday. Admission is 500 dr.

XEROKAMBOS Ξερόκαμπος
The tiny village of Xerokambos, on the next bay south of Kato Zakros, is an unspoilt haven near several coves of inviting pale sand. Unlike most domatia in Xerokambos, *Villa Petrina Rent Rooms* (☎ 0843-31 115, fax 31 693) is open all year. Its beautiful apartments cost 8000 dr per day.

There are no buses to Xerokambos. To get there from Zakros take the Kato Zakros road, and on the outskirts of Zakros turn left at the signpost for Liviko View Restaurant. This 10km dirt road to Xerokambos is only suitable for 4WDs. Otherwise there is a good paved road from Ziros.

IERAPETRA Ιεράπετρα
☎ 0842 • postcode 722 00 • pop 11,000
Ierapetra (yeh-**rah**-pet-rah) is Crete's most
southerly major town. It was a major port of
call for the Romans in their conquest of
Egypt. After the tourist hype of Agios Nikolaos, the unpretentiousness of Ierapetra is
refreshing, and the main business continues
to be agriculture, not tourism.

Orientation & Information
The bus station is on the eastern side of
town on Lasthenous, one street back from
the beachfront. From the ticket office, turn
right and after about 50m you'll come to a
six-road intersection. There are signposts to
the beach via Patriarhou Metaxaki, and to
the city centre via the pedestrian mall section of Lasthenous.

The mall emerges onto the central square
of Plateia Eleftherias. On the left of the
square is the National Bank of Greece. Turn
right opposite the bank to get to the OTE,
one block inland on Koraka.

If you continue straight ahead from
Plateia Eleftherias you will come to Plateia
Emmanual Kothri, where you'll find the
post office at Stylianou Houta 3.

There is no tourist office, but South
Crete Tours (☎ 22 892), opposite the bus
station, might have maps of Ierapetra. To
reach it, turn right from Plateia Emmanual
Kothri.

Things to See
The one-room **archaeological museum** is
perfect for those with a short concentration
span. Pride of place is given to an exquisite
statue of Demeter. The museum is open
8.30 am to 3 pm Tuesday to Sunday (free).

If you walk south along the waterfront
from the central square you will come to the
fortress, built in the early years of Venetian
rule and strengthened by Francesco Morosini in 1626. It's in a pretty fragile state
but you can visit it 8.30 am to 3 pm Tuesday to Sunday. Admission is free.

Inland from the fortress is the
labyrinthine old quarter, a delightful place
to lose yourself for a while.

Beaches
Ierapetra has two beaches. The main town
beach is near the harbour and the other beach
stretches east from the bottom of Patriarhou
Metaxaki. Both have coarse, grey sand.

The beaches to the east of Ierapetra tend
to get crowded. For greater tranquillity, head
for **Hrysi Islet**, where there are good, uncrowded sandy beaches. From June through
August an excursion boat (5500 dr) leaves
for the islet every morning and returns in the
afternoon. The islet has three tavernas.

Places to Stay
The nearest camp site is *Koutsounari
Camping* (☎ 61 213), 7km east of Ierapetra
at Koutsounari. It has a restaurant, snack
bar and minimarket. Ierapetra-Sitia buses
pass the site.

Most places to stay in Ierapetra are either
near the bus station or in the old quarter. An
exception is *Katerina Hotel* (☎ 28 345) on
the seafront where pleasant doubles with
bathroom are 7000 dr. To reach the hotel
from the bus station, follow Patriarhou
Metaxaki to the waterfront, turn right and
you'll see the hotel on the right.

Hotel Coral (☎ 22 846) has well kept
singles/doubles for 3000/5000 dr with bathroom. The owner also has some rooms for
3000/4000 dr with shared bathroom, and
comfortable apartments for 6000 dr. The
hotel is signposted just south of the port
police building on the waterfront.

Cretan Villa Hotel (☎ 28 522, Lakerda
16) is a lovely, well maintained 18th century house with traditionally furnished
rooms and a peaceful courtyard. Rooms are
7000/9000 dr with bathroom. From the bus
station walk towards the town centre and
take the first right from where the hotel is
signposted.

The best hotel in town is the B class
Astron Hotel (☎ 25 114, fax 25 917) at the
beach end of Patriarhou Metaxaki. Rates
are 13,000/17,500 dr, including breakfast.

Places to Eat
There are many souvlaki outlets on Kyrba.
Restaurant Castello is one of the better

tavernas along the waterfront in the old quarter. When the locals celebrate a special occasion they often head to *Lambrakis* about 1km east of the town centre along the beach road. The grilled chicken (1100 dr) is tender and juicy and it would be hard to find better stuffed tomatoes (1000 dr).

Getting There & Away

From June through August, there are buses to Iraklio (2½ hours, 2100 dr, six daily) via Agios Nikolaos (one hour, 750 dr), Gournia and Istron. There are also buses to Makrigialos (30 minutes, 600 dr, eight daily); Sitia (1½ hours, 1200 dr, six daily) via Koutsounari; Mirtos (30 minutes, 320 dr, six daily); and Ano Viannos (one hour, 800 dr, two weekly).

MIRTOS Μυρτός

☎ 0842   • postcode 722 00   • pop 600

Mirtos, on the coast 17km west of Ierapetra, is a sparkling village of whitewashed houses with flower-filled balconies. Mirtos has preserved its charm, despite having become popular with independent travellers. It has a decent dark sand and pebble beach.

You'll soon find your way around Mirtos which is built on a grid system. To get to the waterfront from the bus stop, facing south, take the road to the right passing Mertiza Studios on the right.

There is no post office, bank or OTE, but Aris Travel Agency (☎ 51 017/300) on the main street has currency exchange.

Places to Stay & Eat

Despina Rent Rooms (☎ 51 343) has pleasant but noisy doubles/triples with bathroom for 5000/6500 dr. At *Pandora Domatia (☎ 51 589)*, on the main street, there are prettily furnished singles/doubles for 3500/4000 dr. *Hotel Panorama (☎ 51 362)*, uphill from the town centre, has studios with bathrooms, kitchenettes and spectacular views for 5000/7000 dr. The superior C class *Hotel Mirtos (☎ 51 227)* has large, well kept rooms for 5000/7000 dr with bathroom.

Big Blue (☎ 51 094), on the western edge of town, has rooms for 6000/7000 dr with bathroom, and two-room apartments with two bathrooms and a kitchenette for 12,000 dr.

Mirtos Hotel Restaurant is popular with both locals and tourists. The no-frills *Kostos Taverna* nearby has good *dolmades* for 800 dr and stifado for 1500 dr. The waterfront *Karavoslasi Restaurant* is more stylish, with vegetarian dishes for 1000 dr and meat dishes for 1500 dr to 1800 dr.

Lost Wax

The *cire perdue* (lost wax) method of casting bronze statues was pioneered by the Cretans in preclassical times. A wax original was made, with iron ducts placed at strategic points. These ducts were sufficiently long to stick out of the clay mould which was subsequently put around the wax. A pouring funnel was fitted into the mould at a suitable place. The cast was then heated so that the wax melted and ran out through the ducts. When all the wax had escaped, the ducts were removed and the holes were plugged. Molten bronze was then poured through the funnel. When the bronze had cooled the mould was carefully chipped away.

Advantages of the cire perdue method of casting include the high degree of detail that can be achieved, and the absence of joining lines on the bronze cast. The process is still used today for high-precision work.

The cire perdue method may have given rise to various legends including one which tells of Talos, a man made of bronze, who had one vein running from his neck to his leg. He was a servant of King Minos, and it was his duty to help defend Crete. When the Argonauts arrived, he tried to repel them, but Medea, who had accompanied them, unplugged a pin in his ankle. He was drained of his colourless life-blood and died.

Traditional Cretan dress of breeches tucked into knee-high leather boots, and a black-fringed kerchief on the head, can still be seen.

Getting There & Away

Six buses daily go from Ierapetra to Mirtos (30 minutes, 320 dr). The Ano Viannos-Ierapetra bus passes through Mirtos.

MIRTOS TO ANO VIANNOS

Ano Viannos, 16km west of Mirtos, is a delightful village built on the southern flanks of Mt Dikti. The flower-decked **folklore museum** presents colourful costumes and traditional implements such as an olive press and key-making tools. It is open 10 am to 2 pm daily. Admission is 500 dr.

The village's 14th century **Church of Agios Pelagia** has fine frescoes by Nikoforos Fokas. Follow signs from the main street but first ask in a *kafeneio* for the whereabouts of the key.

From Ano Viannos it's 13km south to the unspoilt village of **Keratokambos**, where there's a pleasant tree-lined beach.

The turn-off for **Arvi** (population 300) is 3km east of Ano Viannos. Arvi is bigger than Keratokambos, but only gets crowded during July and August. Hemmed in by cliffs, Arvi is a sun trap where bananas grow in abundance. The main street skirts a long sand and pebble beach. It's a 15 minute walk inland to Moni Agios Andronios.

Places to Stay & Eat

Ano Viannos has one domatia. *Taverna & Rooms Lefkas* (☎ 0895-22 719), opposite the large church, has singles/doubles for 3000/4000 dr with bathroom.

In Keratokambos, a left turn at the coast will lead to *Taverna & Rooms Thoinikas* (☎ 0895-51 401), where singles/doubles with bathroom cost 4000/6000 dr. *Komis Studios* (☎ 0895-51 390) offers stunningly decorated three-level apartments on the sea built from stone, wood and stucco and outfitted with air-conditioning among other amenities. They cost 25,000 dr and are worth every bit of it.

Morning Star Taverna is the best bet for vegetarians with tasty artichoke stew for 1000 dr. *Taverna Kriti* offers excellent fish dishes and *Taverna Thoinikas* specialises in grilled food.

Arvi's *Pension Kolibi* (☎ 0895-71 250), in a quiet setting 1km west of the town, has immaculate doubles/triples with bathroom costing 6000/7000 dr. *Pension Gorgona* (☎ 0895-71 353), on Arvi's main street, has pleasant doubles for 7500 dr with bathroom. *Hotel Ariadne* (☎ 0895-71 300), farther west, has well kept singles/doubles for 7000/8000 dr with bathroom. At *Apartments Kyma* (☎ 0895-71 344) at the eastern end of the village luxurious apartments cost 8000 dr.

Kima Restaurant, on the main street, serves hearty Greek fare, and *Taverna Diktina* features vegetarian food.

Getting There & Away

Public transport is poor. From Ano Viannos there are two buses weekly to Iraklio (2½

CRETE

hours, 1900 dr) and Ierapetra (one hour, 800 dr) via Mirtos. There is no bus service to Keratokambos or Arvi, but in term-time it may be possible to use the school buses from Ano Viannos.

With 4WD you can use the 10km coastal dirt road between Keratokambos and Arvi.

Western Crete

The western part of Crete comprises the prefectures of Hania and Rethymno, which take their names from the old Venetian cities which are their capitals. The two towns rank as two of the region's main attractions, although the most famous is the spectacular Samaria Gorge. The south coast towns of Paleohora and Plakias are popular resorts.

RETHYMNO Ρέθυμνο
☎ 0831   • postcode 741 00   • pop 24,000
Rethymno (**reh**-thim-no) is Crete's third-largest town. The main attraction is the old Venetian-Ottoman quarter that occupies the headland beneath the massive Venetian *fortezza* (fortress). The place is a maze of narrow streets, graceful wood-balconied houses and ornate Venetian monuments; several minarets add a touch of the Orient. The architectural similarities invite comparison with Hania, but Rethymno has a character of its own. An added attraction is a beach right in town.

The approaches to the town couldn't be less inviting. The modern town has sprawled out along the coast, dotted with big package hotels attracted by a reasonable beach.

History
The site of modern Rethymno has been occupied since Late Minoan times – the evidence can be found in the city's archaeological museum. In the 3rd and 4th centuries BC, the town was known as Rithymna, an autonomous state of sufficient stature to issue its own coinage. A scarcity of references to the city in Roman and Byzantine periods suggest it was of minor importance at that time.

The town prospered once more under the Venetians, who ruled from 1210 until 1645, when the Turks took over. Turkish forces held the town until 1897, when it was taken by Russia as part of the occupation of Crete by the Great Powers.

Rethymno became an artistic and intellectual centre after the arrival of a large number of refugees from Constantinople in 1923. The city has a campus of the University of Crete, bringing a student population that keeps the town alive outside the tourist season.

Orientation
The city's old quarter occupies the headland north of Dimakopoulou, which runs from Plateia Vardinogianni on the west coast to Plateia Iroön on the east (becoming Gerakari en route).

Most of the good places to eat and sleep are to be found here, while banks and government services are just to the south on the edge of the new three-quarters of town. The beach is on the eastern side of town, curving around from the delightful old Venetian Harbour in the north. El Venizelou is the beachfront street. Curving parallel one block back is Arkadiou, the main commercial street.

A maze of twisting and curving streets make the old quarter an easy place to get lost in, especially since street signs are a rarity. Coming from the south, the best approach is through the Porto Guora (Great Gate) onto Ethnikis Antistaseos. This busy shopping street leads to the Rimondi fountain, the old quarter's best known landmark. The area around here is thick with cafes, restaurants and souvenir shops.

If you arrive in Rethymno by bus, you will be dropped at the new terminal at the western end of Igoumenou Gavriil, about 600m from the Porto Guora. To get there, follow Igoum Gavriil back into the town centre. A left turn at the far end of the park will leave you facing the gate. If you arrive by ferry, the old quarter is as far away as the end of the quay.

If you are driving into town from the expressway, your final approach to the city centre is along Dimitrikaki. The car park opposite the municipal park is a convenient spot to stop and check things out.

Information

Tourist Offices Rethymno's municipal tourist office (☎ 29 148) is on the beach side of El Venizelou, opposite the junction with Varga Kallergi. It's open 8 am to 8 pm Monday to Friday in summer, and 8 am to 3 pm in winter. The tourist police (☎ 28 156) occupy the same building and are open 7 am to 10 pm daily.

Money Banks are concentrated around the junction of Dimokratias and Pavlou Kountouriotou. The National Bank of Greece is on Dimokratias, on the far side of the square opposite the town hall. The Credit Bank, Pavlou Kountouriotou 29, and the National Mortgage Bank, next to the town hall, have 24 hour automatic exchange machines.

Post & Communications The OTE is at Kountouriotou 28, and the post office is a block south at Moatsou 21. From June through August there is a mobile post office about 200m south-east of the tourist office on El Venizelou. You can check your email at Net C@fe (☎ 55 133), Venieri 2, open 10 am to 10 pm daily. Take Papandreou from El Venizelou east of Plateia Iroön and you'll find it behind Elina Hotel.

Bookshops The International Press Bookshop, located at El Venizelou 81, stocks English-language novels, travel guides and history books. The bookshop at Souliou 43 stocks novels in English, books about Greece and tapes of Greek music, and has a small second-hand section.

Laundry The Laundry Mat laundrette at Tombazi 45, next door to the youth hostel, charges 2500 dr for a wash and dry.

Things to See

Rethymno's 16th century **fortress** stands on Paleokastro Hill, the site of the city's ancient acropolis. Within its massive walls once stood a great number of buildings, of which only a church and a mosque survive intact. The ramparts offer good views, while the site has lots of ruins to explore. The fortress is open 8 am to 8 pm daily. Admission is 800 dr.

The **archaeological museum** (☎ 29 975) is opposite the entrance to the fortress. The finds displayed here include an important coin collection. The museum is open 8.30 am to 3 pm Tuesday to Sunday. Admission is 500 dr. Rethymno's excellent **historical & folk art museum**, Vernardou 30, is open 10 am to 2 pm Monday to Saturday. Admission is 500 dr.

Pride of place among the many vestiges of Venetian rule in the old quarter goes to the **Rimondi fountain** with its spouting lion heads, and the 16th century **loggia**.

At the southern end of Ethnikis Antistaseos is the well preserved **Porto Guora**, a remnant of the Venetian defensive wall. Turkish legacies in the old quarter include the **Kara Musa Pasa mosque** near Plateia Iroön and the **Neradjes Mosque**, which was converted from a Franciscan church.

Activities

The Happy Walker (☎ 52 920), Tombazi 56, runs a varied program of mountain walks in the region. Most walks start in the early morning and finish with lunch. Prices start at 6500 dr per person. The EOS (☎ 57 766) is at Dimokratias 12.

Paradise Dive Centre (☎ 53 258), El Venizelou 76, offers activities and a PADI course for all grades of divers.

Special Events

Rethymno's main cultural event is the annual Renaissance Festival that runs during July and August. It features dance, drama and films as well as art exhibitions.

Some years there's a Wine Festival in mid-July held in the municipal park. Ask the tourist office for details.

Places to Stay – Budget

The nearest camp site is *Elizabeth Camping* (☎ 28 694), near Myssiria Beach, 3km

RETHYMNO

PLACES TO STAY
1 Lefteris Papadakis Rooms
4 Pension Anna
6 Hotel Fortezza
8 Rooms to Rent Barbara Dolomaki
19 Olga's Pension
24 Rent Rooms Garden
25 Rent Rooms Sea Front
29 Youth Hostel
31 Park Hotel

PLACES TO EAT
5 Taverna Pontios
11 Taverna Kyria Maria
18 Stella's Kitchen
20 Old Town Taverna
21 Gounakis Restaurant & Bar

OTHER
2 Entrance to Fortress
3 Archaeological Museum
7 Baja Club
9 Cretan Lines
10 Fortezza Disco
12 Rimondi Fountain
13 Motor Stavros
14 Loggia
15 International Press Bookshop
16 Paradise Dive Centre
17 Bookshop
22 Historical & Folk Art Museum
23 Neradjes Mosque
26 Municipal Tourist Office; Tourist Police
27 Happy Walker
28 Laundry Mat
30 Porto Guora
32 Bus Station
33 Car Park
34 OTE
35 Credit Bank
36 Town Hall
37 National Mortgage Bank
38 Kara Musa Pasa Mosque
39 National Bank of Greece
40 Hospital
41 Olympic Airways
42 Post Office
43 EOS

east of Rethymno. The site has a taverna, snack bar and minimarket. An Iraklio-bound bus can drop you at the site.

The **youth hostel** (☎ 22 848, Tombazi 41) is friendly and well run with beds for 1500 dr and free hot showers. Breakfast is available and there's a bar in the evening. There is no curfew and the place is open all year.

An excellent budget choice is **Olga's Pension** (☎ 28 665, Souliou 57), right in the heart of town. There's a wide choice of

rooms which are spread about in clusters off a network of terraces – all bursting with greenery. Prices range from basic singles for 6000 dr, to studio rooms with kitchen for 10,000 dr. In between comes a comfortable double with shower for 9000 dr. Owners George and Stella Mihalaki speak good English and run a very friendly show.

At **Rooms to Rent Barbara Dolomaki** (☎ 24 581, Thambergi 14), there are comfortable doubles with bathroom for 10,000 dr. Double studios with a fridge and small stove cost 11,000 dr.

If you're after sea views *Lefteris Papadakis Rooms* (☎ 23 803, Plastira 26) has clean singles/doubles with bathroom for 6500/7500 dr. Alternatively, try *Rent Rooms Sea Front* (☎ 51 062/981, El Venizelou 45) which has light, airy rooms with bathroom for 5000/7000 dr.

Rooms for Rent Anda (☎ 23 479, Nikiforou Foka 33) is on a quiet street and has prettily furnished doubles/triples for 9000/11,000 dr with bathroom.

Places to Stay – Mid-Range
An outstanding domatia is *Rent Rooms Garden* (☎ 26 274, 28 586, Nikiforou Foka 82) in the heart of the old town. It's an impeccably maintained 600-year-old Venetian house with many original features and a gorgeous grape-arboured garden. Double/triple rooms are 10,000/15,000 dr with bathroom.

Park Hotel (☎ 29 958, Igoum Gavriil 9) is good value, offering air-conditioned rooms with TV for 11,000/14,000 dr. *Astali* (☎ 24 721, fax 24 723, Papandreou 1) is a new hotel that offers spiffy air-conditioned rooms for 11,500/16,000 dr.

The smartest hotel in town is the B class *Hotel Fortezza* (☎ 55 551/552, 23 828, fax 54 073, Melissinou 16). It has a snack bar, restaurant and swimming pool. Singles/doubles/triples are 15,000/19,000/23,000 dr.

Places to Eat
The waterfront along El Venizelou is lined with amazingly similar tourist restaurants staffed by fast-talking waiters desperately cajoling passers-by into eating at their establishments. The situation is much the same around the Venetian Harbour, except the setting is better and the prices higher.

To find cheaper food and a more authentic atmosphere, wander inland down the little side streets. *Taverna Kyria Maria (Diog Mesologiou 20)*, behind the Rimondi fountain, is a cosy, traditional taverna that has outdoor seating under a leafy trellis with twittering birds. They serve a hearty vegetar-

ian plate for 1800 dr and all meals end with a complementary dessert and shot of raki.

Another reasonably priced place is *Old Town Taverna (Vernardou 31)*. Set menus for two with wine are 4000 dr. *Taverna Pontios (Melissinou 34)*, near the archaeological museum, is a popular hang-out with locals. The cheese-stuffed calamari at 1400 dr is commendable.

Gounakis Restaurant & Bar (Koroneou 6) is worth visiting for its food as much as for its music (see Entertainment). *Stella's Kitchen (Souliou 55)* serves tasty low-priced snacks and full meals.

If you have your own wheels, head to *Taverna Zisi*, about 2km out of town on the old road to Iraklio. This is where local families go for an evening out. The speciality is a platter of meaty mezedes for 3000 dr.

Entertainment
If your interests include drinking cheap wine and listening to live Cretan folk music, *Gounakis Restaurant & Bar (Koroneou 6)* is the place to go. There's music and impromptu dancing most nights.

Rethymno has no shortage of discos, most of them in the streets behind the old harbour. The current favourite is *Baja Club* on Salaminos which plays international and Greek music nightly from midnight on. *Fortezza Disco*, close to the waterfront, plays disco music.

Shopping
Zaharias Theodorakis turns out onyx bowls and goblets on the lathe in his small workshop opposite Pension Anna on Katehaki. Prices start at 5000 dr for a small bowl.

Getting There & Away
Bus There are numerous services to both Hania (one hour, 1350 dr) and Iraklio (1½ hours, 1550 dr) from Rethymno. There's a bus in each direction every half-hour during June to August, every hour during December to February. During June to August there are also buses to Plakias (one hour, 950 dr, four daily), Agia Galini (1½ hours, 1300 dr, four daily), Moni Arkadiou (30 minutes, 500

CRETE

dr, three daily), Preveli (950 dr, two daily) and Omalos (two hours, 2750 dr, one daily). The morning bus to Plakias continues to Hora Sfakion (two hours, 1450 dr).

Services to these destinations are greatly reduced from December through February.

Ferry Cretan Lines (☎ 29 221) operates a daily ferry between Rethymno and Piraeus (7000 dr) leaving both Rethymno and Piraeus at 7.30 pm.

Tickets are available from the Cretan Lines office at Arkadiou 250.

Getting Around
Most of the car rental firms are near Plateia Iroön. Motor Stavros (☎ 22 858), Paleologou 14, has a wide range of motorcycles and also rents bicycles.

AROUND RETHYMNO
Moni Arkadiou Μονή Αρκαδίου
This 16th century monastery, 23km south-east of Rethymno, is surrounded by attractive hill country. The most impressive of the buildings is the Venetian baroque church. Its striking facade, which features on the 100 dr note, has eight slender Corinthian columns and an ornate triple-belled tower.

In November 1866 the Turks sent massive forces to quell insurrections which were gathering momentum throughout the island. Hundreds of men, women and children who had fled their villages used the monastery as a safe haven. When 2000 Turkish soldiers attacked the building, rather than surrender, the Cretans set light to a store of gunpowder. The explosion killed everyone, Turks included, except one small girl, who lived to a ripe old age in a village nearby. Busts of the woman, and the abbot who lit the gun powder, stand outside the monastery.

The monastery is open 8 am to 1 pm and 3.30 to 8 pm daily. Admission is free. The small **museum** has an admission charge of 700 dr.

There are buses from Rethymno to the monastery (30 minutes, 500 dr) at 6 am,

10.30 am and 2.30 pm, returning at 7 am, noon and 4 pm.

Amari Valley Κοιλάδα Αμαρίου
If you have your own transport you can explore the enchanting Amari Valley, south-east of Rethymno, between Mts Ida and Kedros. The region harbours around 40 well watered, unspoilt villages set amid olive groves and almond and cherry trees.

The valley begins at the picturesque village of **Apostoli**, 25km south-east of Rethymno. The turn-off for Apostoli is on the coast 3km east of Rethymno. The road forks at Apostoli and then joins up again 38km to the south, making it possible to do a circular drive around the valley. Alternatively, you can continue south to Agia Galini.

There is an EOS refuge on **Mt Ida**, a 10km walk from the small village of **Kouroutes**, 5km south of Fourfouras. For information contact the Rethymno EOS (see Activities in the Rethymno section).

RETHYMNO TO SPILI
Heading south from Rethymno, there is a turn-off to the right to the Late Minoan cemetery of **Armeni** 2km before the modern village of Armeni. The main road south continues through woodland, which gradually gives way to a bare and dramatic land-scape. After 18km there is a turn-off to the right for **Selia** and **Frangokastello** and, a little beyond, another turn-off for Plakias (this turn-off is referred to on timetables as the Koxare junction or Bale). The main road continues for 9km to Spili.

SPILI ΣΠΗΛΙ
☎ 0832 • postcode 740 53 • pop 700
Spili is a gorgeous mountain town with cobbled streets, rustic houses and plane trees. Its centre piece is a unique Venetian fountain which spurts water from 19 lion heads. Tourist buses hurtle through but Spili deserves an overnight stay.

The post office and bank are on the main street. The huge building at the northern end of town is an ecclesiastic conference centre. The OTE is up a side street, north of the central square. The bus stop is just south of the square. Spili is on the Rethymno-Agia Galini bus route.

Places to Stay & Eat
Green Hotel (☎ 22 225), opposite the police station on the main street, is a homy place practically buried under plants and vines that also fill the interior. Attractive singles/doubles with bathroom are 5000/6000 dr. Behind it is *Heracles Rooms (☎ 22 111, fax 22 411)* where sparkling, beautifully furnished rooms with bathroom cost 5000/8000 dr.

Farther along on the left *Costos Inn (☎ 22 040/750)* has well kept, ornate rooms which are something of a minimalist's nightmare with TV, radio, even bathrobes – in case you forgot to pack yours. Doubles/triples with bathroom cost 8000/9000 dr. Another good choice is *Sunset Rooms (☎ 22 3060)*, which has doubles for 5000 dr with bathroom.

Taverna Stratidakis, opposite Costos Inn, serves excellent traditional Greek dishes. The specials of the day are in pots at the back of the room.

AROUND SPILI
Most people come to the alluring little village of **Patsos** to visit the nearby **Church of Agios Antonios** in a cave above a picturesque gorge. You can drive here from Rethymno, or you can walk from Spili along a scenic 10km dirt track.

To reach the track, walk along 28 Oktovriou, passing the lion fountain on your right. Turn right onto Vermopilan and ascend to the Spili-Gerakari road. Turn right here and eventually you will come to a sign for Gerakari. Take the dirt track to the left, and at the fork bear right. At the crossroads turn right, and continue on the main track for about one hour to a T-junction on the outskirts of Patsos. Turn left to get to the cave.

West of Spili, past the village of Koxare on the Plakias road, the road enters the dramatic **Kourtaliotis Gorge**. After the village of Astomatis there is a turn-off for Moni Preveli (see the Around Plakias section later

in the chapter). The road continues through Lefkogia, then passes the turn-off for Myrthios (2km) and enters Plakias.

PLAKIAS Πλακιάς
☎ 0832 • postcode 740 60 • pop 100
The south coast town of Plakias was once a tranquil retreat for adventurous backpackers – until the package tour operators discovered the fine beaches and dramatic mountain backdrop. It's still not a bad place to visit outside peak season and there are some good walks. A booklet of walks around Plakias is on sale at the minimarket by the bus stop (1200 dr).

Orientation & Information
It's easy to find your way around Plakias. One street skirts the beach and another runs parallel to it one block back. The bus stop is at the middle of the waterfront. The 30 minute path to Mythos begins just before the youth hostel.

Plakias doesn't have a bank, but Monza Tours (☎ 41 433, 31 923), near the bus stop, offers currency exchange. From June to August a mobile post office is on the waterfront.

Places to Stay
Camping Apollonia (☎ 31 318), on the right of the main approach road to Plakias, has a restaurant, minimarket, bar and swimming pool. Rates are 900 dr per person and 600 dr per tent.

The excellent *youth hostel* is tucked away in the olive trees behind the town, 10 minutes walk from the bus stop – follow the yellow signs from the waterfront. Dorm beds are 1200 dr and hot showers are free. The hostel is open from April until the end of October.

Morpheas Rent Rooms (☎ 31 583), next to the bus stop, has light, airy and attractively furnished rooms. Singles/doubles are 7000/10,000 dr with bathroom.

There are some agreeable pensions among the olive trees behind the town. *Pension Afrodite (☎ 31 266)* has spotless doubles/triples for 10,000/13,000 dr with bathroom. Head inland at Monza Tours, turn left at the T-junction and then take the first right and after 100m the pension is on the left. A right turn at the T-junction leads to *Studio Emilia* (☎ 31 302), set back in the trees to the left after 100m. It charges 6000/7000 dr for large rooms with bathroom and access to a well equipped communal kitchen. Studios cost 8000 dr.

Pension Paligremnos (☎ 31 003) has a great position at the southern end of Plakias Beach. Pleasant doubles with bathroom cost 6000 dr, and studio doubles are 7000 dr.

Plakias Bay (☎ 31 315) is a C class hotel also on the beach. Sparsely outfitted singles/doubles cost 12,000/15,000 dr with breakfast.

Places to Eat

Restaurant Ariadne, on the street opposite the mobile post office, is popular and reasonably priced. One of the best waterfront tavernas is *Taverna Christos* with a romantic terrace overlooking the sea. It has a good choice of main dishes for around 1450 dr.

Nikos Souvlaki, just inland from Monza Tours, is a good souvlaki place where a monster mixed grill of *gyros*, souvlaki, sausage, hamburger and chips costs 1500 dr.

Getting There & Away

Plakias has good bus connections during June to August, but virtually none from December through February. A timetable is displayed at the bus stop.

Services from June through August include four buses daily to Rethymno (one hour, 950 dr), and one to Hora Sfakion.

From December through February there are three buses daily to Rethymno, two at weekends. It's possible to get to Agia Galini from Plakias by catching a Rethymno bus to the Koxare junction (referred to on timetables as Bale) and waiting for a bus to Agia Galini. This works best with the 11.30 am bus from Plakias, linking with the 12.45 pm service from Rethymno to Agia Galini.

Getting Around

Cars Allianthos (☎ 31 851) is a reliable car rental outlet. Odyssia (☎ 31 596), on the waterfront, has a large range of motorcycles and mountain bikes available for hire.

AROUND PLAKIAS
Myrthios Μύρθιος

This pleasant village is perched on a hillside overlooking Plakias and the surrounding coast. Apart from taking in the views, the main activity is walking, which you'll be doing a lot of unless you have your own transport.

There are a few domatia in the village, including the comfortable *Niki's Studios & Rooms* (☎ 0832-31 593). Singles/doubles with bathroom cost 3500/6000 dr, and a studio costs 8000 dr for two.

Just above, *Restaurant Panorama* lives up to its name – it has great views. It also does good food, including vegetarian dishes and delicious desserts.

Moni Preveli Μονή Πρέβελη

The well maintained Moni Preveli, 14km east of Plakias, stands in splendid isolation high above the Libyan Sea. Like most of Crete's monasteries, it played a significant role in the islanders' rebellion against Turkish rule. It became a centre of resistance during 1866, causing the Turks to set fire to it and destroy surrounding crops. After the Battle of Crete in 1941, many Allied soldiers were sheltered here by Abbot Agathangelos before their evacuation to Egypt. In retaliation the Germans plundered the monastery. The monastery's **museum** contains a candelabra presented by grateful British soldiers after the war. It's open daily 8 am to 7 pm mid-March through May, and 8 am to 1.30 pm and 3.30 to 8 pm June to October (mornings only, in winter). Admission to the monastery and museum is 700 dr.

The road to Moni Preveli leads past the ruins of the old monastery, a fascinating place to explore. It was a hippie hang-out in the 1970s, and they left a large marijuana leaf on one wall and a few other cosmic decorations. It is now fenced off.

Lefkogia Village has *domatia* and *tavernas*, and is a pleasant base from which to explore the area.

In the 60's, hippies turned the caves at Matala, Crete, into a modern troglodyte city.

Ruins of a Turkish farmhouse near Galatas village, Crete

Cape Tigani and the rocky islet of Gramvousa, Crete

Outdoor cafe, Lassithi Plateau, Crete

Hikers trek through the narrows of Samaria Gorge, Crete.

CRETE

From June through August there are two buses daily from Rethymno to Moni Preveli.

Beaches

Preveli Beach, at the mouth of the Kourtaliotis Gorge, is one of Crete's most photographed beaches. The River Megalopotamos cuts the beach in half on its way into the Libyan Sea. It's fringed with oleander bushes and palm trees and is popular with freelance campers.

A steep path leads down to it from the road to Moni Preveli. You can get to Preveli Beach from Plakias by boat from June through August for 2500 dr return, or by taxi boat from Agia Galini for 5000 dr return.

Between Plakias and Preveli Beach there are several secluded **coves** popular with freelance campers and nudists. Some are within walking distance of Plakias, via **Damnoni Beach**. To reach them ascend the path behind Plakias Bay Hotel. Just before the track starts to descend turn right into an olive grove. At the first T-junction turn left and at the second turn right. Where six tracks meet, take the one signposted to the beach. Walk to the end of Damnoni Beach and take the track to the right, which passes above the coves. Damnoni Beach itself is pleasant out of high season, despite being dominated by the giant Hapimag tourist complex.

AGIA GALINI Αγία Γαλήνη
☎ 0832 • postcode 740 56 • pop 600

Agia Galini (ah-**yee**-ah gah-**lee**-nih) is another picturesque little town which has gone down the tubes due to an overdose of tourism. Still, it does boast 340 days of sunshine a year, and some places remain open out of season. It's a convenient base from which to visit Phaestos and Agia Triada, and although the town beach is mediocre, there are boats to better beaches.

Orientation & Information

The bus station is at the top of Eleftheriou Venizelou, which is a continuation of the approach road. The central square, overlooking the harbour, is downhill from the bus station. You'll walk past the post office

on the way and the OTE is on the square. There is no bank but there are lots of travel agencies with currency exchange.

Places to Stay

Agia Galini Camping (☎ 91 386/239) is next to the beach, 2.5km east of the town. It is signposted from the Iraklio-Agia Galini road. The site is well shaded and has a restaurant, snack bar and minimarket.

On the road to town *Areti* (☎ 91 240) has pleasant singles/doubles with bathroom and balcony for 6000/10,000 dr. In the centre of town *Angelika* (☎ 91 304) is over a newspaper kiosk and has rooms with bathroom and a balcony for 5000/6000 dr.

The D class *Hotel Selena* (☎ 91 273) has pleasant rooms for 10,000/12,000 dr with bathroom. It's open all year. To reach the hotel walk downhill from the bus station, turn left after the post office, take the second right and turn left at the steps.

The only accommodation on the beach is *Stochos Rooms* (☎ 91 433), where studios for two or three people cost 12,000/13,000 dr.

Places to Eat

Restaurant Megalonissis, near the bus stop, is one of the town's cheapest restaurants if not the friendliest. *Medousa Taverna* in the town centre is owned by a German-Greek couple and presents a menu of specialities from both countries. The upmarket *Acropol Taverna*, on Vasileos Ioannis, has an extensive menu of both Greek and international dishes. A meal for two with wine costs around 6000 dr.

Getting There & Away

Bus The story is the same here as at the other beach resorts – heaps of buses in summer, skeletal services in winter.

In peak season there are buses to Iraklio (2½ hours, 1500 dr, eight daily), Rethymno (1½ hours, 1300 dr, four daily), Matala (45 minutes, 600 dr, six daily) and Phaestos (40 minutes, 420 dr, six daily). You can get to Plakias by taking a Rethymno-bound bus and changing at Koxare (Bale).

Taxi Boat From June through August there are daily taxi boats from the harbour to the beaches of Agios Giorgios and Agios Pavlos. These beaches, west of Agia Galini, are difficult to get to by land, but are less crowded than, and far superior to, Agia Galini Beach.

AROUND AGIA GALINI

The outstanding **Museum of Cretan Ethnology** (☎ 0892-91 394) is in the pleasant, unspoilt village of Vori, 14km from Agia Galini, just north of the main Agia Galini-Iraklio road. It's open 9 am to 3 pm Monday to Friday, from November to March. From June through August it opens 10 am to 6 pm daily. Admission is 500 dr.

HANIA Χανιά

☎ 0821 • postcode 731 00 • pop 65,000
Hania (hahn-**yah**) is Crete's second city and former capital. The beautiful, crumbling Venetian quarter of Hania that surrounds the Old Harbour is one of Crete's best attractions. A lot of money has been spent on restoring the old buildings. Some of them have been converted into very fine accommodation while others now house chic restaurants, bars and shops.

The Hania district gets a lot of package tourists, but most of them stick to the beach developments that stretch out endlessly to the west. Even in a town this size many hotels and restaurants are closed from November to April.

Hania is a main transit point for trekkers going to the Samaria Gorge.

History

Hania is the site of the Minoan settlement of Kydonia, which was centred on the hill to the east of the harbour. Little excavation work has been done, but the finding of clay tablets with Linear B script has led archaeologists to believe that Kydonia was both a palace site and an important town.

Kydonia met the same fiery fate as most other Minoan settlements in 1450 BC, but soon re-emerged as a force. It was a flourishing city-state during Hellenistic times and continued to prosper under Roman and Byzantine rule.

The city became Venetian at the beginning of the 13th century, and the name was changed to La Canea. The Venetians spent a lot of time constructing massive fortifications to protect their city from marauding pirates and invading Turks. This did not prove very effective against the latter, who took Hania in 1645 after a siege lasting two months.

The Great Powers made Hania the island capital in 1898 and it remained so until 1971, when the administration was transferred to Iraklio.

Hania was heavily bombed during WWII, but enough of the old town survives for it to be regarded as Crete's most beautiful city.

Orientation

The town's bus station is on Kydonias, two blocks south-west of Plateia 1866, one of the city's main squares. From Plateia 1866 to the Old Harbour is a short walk north down Halidon.

The main hotel area is to the left as you face the harbour, where Akti Kountourioti leads around to the old fortress on the headland. The headland separates the Venetian port from the crowded town beach in the quarter called Nea Hora.

Zambeliou, which dissects Halidon just before the harbour, was once the town's main thoroughfare. It's a narrow, winding street, lined with craft shops, hotels and tavernas.

Information

Tourist Offices Hania's EOT (☎ 92 943, fax 92 624) is at Kriari 40, close to Plateia 1866. It is well organised and considerably more helpful than most. Opening hours are 7.30 am to 2.30 pm weekdays. The tourist police (☎ 53 333) are on Irakliou 23 and are open 7.30 am to 2.30 pm Monday to Friday. To get there, follow Apokoronou about 500m out of town when it becomes Irakliou.

Money The National Bank of Greece on the corner of Tzanakaki and Gianari and the Credit Bank at the junction of Halidon and

Skalidi have 24 hour automatic exchange machines. There are numerous places to change money outside banking hours. Most are willing to negotiate the amount of commission, so check around.

Post & Communications The central post office is at Tzanakaki 3, open 7.30 am to 8 pm Monday to Friday, and 7.30 am to 2 pm Saturday. The OTE is next door at Tzanakaki 5, open 7.30 am to 10 pm daily. Internet access is available at Vranas Studios (☎ 58 618), on Ag Deka.

Bookshops The George Chaicalis Bookshop, on Plateia Venizelou, sells English-language newspapers, books and maps.

Laundry Both Laundry Fidias, at Sarpaki 6, and the other laundry at Ag Deka 18 charge 1800 dr for a wash and dry.

Left Luggage Luggage can be stored at the bus station for 400 dr per day.

Museums
The **archaeological museum** (☎ 90 334) in Hania, at Halidon 21, is housed in the 16th century Venetian Church of San Francisco. The Turkish fountain in the grounds is a relic from the building's days as a mosque.

The museum houses a well displayed collection of finds from western Crete dating from the Neolithic to the Roman era. Exhibits include statues, pottery, coins, jewellery, three splendid floor mosaics and some impressive painted sarcophagi from the Late Minoan cemetery of Armeni. The museum is open 8 am to 4.30 pm Tuesday to Sunday. Admission is 500 dr.

The **naval museum** (☎ 44 156) has an interesting collection of model ships, naval instruments, paintings and photographs. It is open 10 am to 4 pm daily. Admission is 500 dr. The museum is housed in the fortress on the headland overlooking the Venetian port.

Hania's interesting **folklore museum** (☎ 90 816) is at Halidon 46B. It is open 9 am to 3 pm and 6 pm to 9 pm Monday to Friday. Admission is 500 dr. The new **war museum of Chania**, on Tzanakaki, is open 9 am to 1 pm Tuesday to Saturday. Admission is free.

Other Attractions
The area to the east of the Old Harbour, between Akti Tombazi and Karaoli Dimitriou, is the site of **ancient Kydonia**.

The search for Minoan remains began in the early 1960s and excavation work continues sporadically. The site can be seen at the junction of Kanevaro and Kandanoleu, and many of the finds are on display in the archaeological museum.

Kydonia has been remodelled by a succession of occupiers. After ejecting the Arabs, the Byzantines set about building their *kastelli* (castle) on the same site, on top of the old walls in some places and using the same materials. It was here, too, that the Venetians first settled. Modern Kanevaro was the Corso of their city. It was this part of town that bore the brunt of the bombing in WWII.

The massive **fortifications** built by the Venetians to protect their city remain impressive today. The best preserved section is the western wall, running from the fortezza to **Promahonas Hill**. It was part of a defensive system begun in 1538 by engineer Michele Sanmichele, who also designed Iraklio's defences.

The **lighthouse** at the entrance to the harbour is the most visible of the Venetian monuments. It looks in need of tender loving care these days, but the 30 minute walk around the sea wall to get there is worth it.

You can escape the crowds of the Venetian quarter by taking a stroll around the **Splantzia quarter** – a delightful tangle of narrow streets and little plateias.

Whether you are self-catering or not you should at least feast your eyes on Hania's magnificent covered **food market**. It makes all other food markets look like stalls at a church bazaar. Unfortunately, the central bastion of the city wall had to be demolished to make way for this fine cruciform creation, built in 1911.

CRETE

HANIA

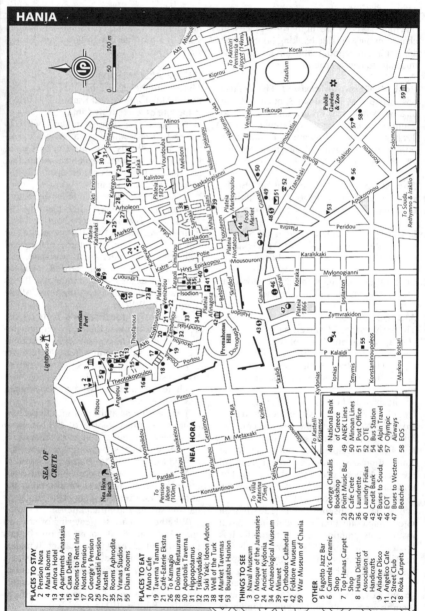

SEA OF CRETE

Lighthouse

Venetian Port

Nea Hora Beach

NEA HORA

SPLANTZIA

Promahonas Hill

Public Garden & Zoo

Stadium

Food Market

To Akrotiri Peninsula & Airport (14km)

To Souda, Rethymno & Iraklio

To Kastelli-Kissamos

To Villa Katerina (75m)

To Pension Ideon (700m)

PLACES TO STAY
2 Pension Nora
4 Maria Rooms
13 Amfora Hotel
14 Apartments Anastasia
15 Casa Delfino
16 Rooms to Rent Irini
17 Nostos Pension
20 George's Pension
25 Monastiri Pension
27 Kasteli
35 Rooms Aphrodite
37 Vranas Studios
55 Diana Rooms

PLACES TO EAT
19 Mano Cafe
21 Taverna Tamam
26 Café-Eaterie Ekstra
28 To Karnagio
30 Doloma Restaurant
31 Apostolis Taverna
32 Hippopotamus
33 Tsikoudadiko
34 Suki Yaki; Ideon Adron
38 Well of the Turk
44 Market Tavernas
53 Bougatsa Hanion

THINGS TO SEE
3 Naval Museum
10 Mosque of the Janissaries
24 Ancient Kydonia
34 Archaeological Museum
39 Minaret
41 Orthodox Cathedral
42 Folklore Museum
59 War Museum of Chania

OTHER
5 Fagotto Jazz Bar
6 Carmela's Ceramic Shop
7 Top Hanas Carpet Shop
8 Hania District Association of Handicrafts
9 Ariadne Disco
11 Angelico Cafe
12 Street Club
18 Roka Carpets
22 George Chaicalis Bookshop
23 Point Music Bar
29 Cafe Crete
36 Laundrette
40 Laundry Fidias
43 Credit Bank
45 Buses to Souda
46 EOT
47 Buses to Western Beaches
48 National Bank of Greece
49 ANEK Lines
50 Minoan Lines
51 Post Office
52 OTE
54 Bus Station
56 Alpin Travel
57 Olympic Airways
58 EOS

Activities

Alpin Travel (☎ 53 309), in the complex at Bonaili 11-19, offers many trekking programs. The owner, George Antonakakis, helps run the EOS (☎ 44 647), Tzanakaki 90, and is the guy to talk to about serious climbing in the Lefka Ori. George can provide information on Greece's mountain refuges, the E4 trail, and climbing and trekking in Crete in general. Alpin Travel is open 9 am to 2 pm (and sometimes in the evening after 7 pm) weekdays.

Trekking Plan (☎ 60 861), in Agia Marina on the main road next to Santa Marina Hotel, offers treks to the Agia Irini Gorge and climbs of Mt Gingilosamong and other destinations for about 7000 dr.

It also offers a full program of mountain bike tours at varying levels of difficulty. Prices begin at 8000 dr.

Children's Activities

If your five-year-old has lost interest in Venetian architecture before the end of the first street, head for the public garden between Tzanakaki and Dimokratias. There's plenty to occupy children here, including a playground, a small zoo with a resident krikri (the Cretan wild goat) and a children's resource centre that has a small selection of books in English.

Places to Stay – Budget

The nearest camp site is **Hania Camping** (☎ 31 138), 3km west of town on the beach. The site is shaded and has a restaurant, bar and minimarket. Take a Kalamaki Beach bus (every 20 minutes) from the south-east corner of Plateia 1866 and ask to be let off at the camp site.

The most interesting accommodation is around the Venetian port, but bear in mind it's a noisy area with numerous music bars. If you get a room in the back you'll have a better shot at a good night's sleep but you may swelter in the summer heat without the harbour breeze.

If it's character you're after, you can't do better than **George's Pension** (☎ 88 715, Zambeliou 30), in a 600-year-old house dot-

ted with antique furniture. Singles/doubles cost 3500/ 6000 dr.

Rooms to Rent Irini (☎ 93 909, Theotokopoulou 9) has clean, simply furnished doubles with bathroom for 7000 dr.

Monastiri Pension (☎ 54 776, Ag Markou 18) has a great setting next to the ruins of the Santa Maria de Miracolioco monastery in the heart of the old kastelli. Double rooms are fair value at 6000 dr, and there's a communal kitchen.

Vranas Studios (☎/fax 58 618, Ag Deka 10) is on a lively pedestrian street and has spacious studios with polished wood floors, balconies, TV and air-conditioning for 11,000 dr, except in August when the price climbs to 17,000 dr. Equally attractive rooms without air-conditioning are 1000 dr less.

If you want to hop straight out of bed and onto an early morning bus, the best rooms in the vicinity of the bus station are at **Diana Rooms** (☎ 97 888, P Kalaïdi 33). The light, airy and clean rooms are 5000/7000 dr with bathroom.

Apartments Anastasia (☎ 46 582, Theotokopoulou 21) has stylish, well equipped studios for 10,000 dr. **Rooms Aphrodite** (☎ 57 602, Ag Deka 10) has two-person apartments for 8000 dr, and double rooms with shared facilities for 5000 dr.

The Nea Hora quarter to the west of the old town has some accommodation bargains. The area lacks the charm of the old town but is considerably quieter. **Villa Katerina** (☎ 95 183, 98 940, Selinou 78) has a range of rooms starting with attractively furnished doubles for 8000 dr.

The well kept, friendly **Pension Ideon** (☎ 70 132/133) on Patriarhou Ioanikeiou charges 6000/10,000 dr for singles/doubles. Both these places are very near Nea Hora Beach.

Farther out of town, at Kalamaki Beach, **Akasti Hotel** (☎ 31 352) offers roomy singles/doubles across the street from a small cove for 5000/8000 dr except in August when prices increase 50%. The Kalamaki bus will let you off in front of the hotel.

Places to Stay – Mid-Range

Most places in this category are renovated Venetian houses, and there are some very stylish ones about. One of the best is *Nostos Pension* (☎ 94 740, Zambeliou 42-46), a mixture of Venetian style and modern fixtures. The 600-year-old building has been modelled into some very stylish split-level rooms/units, all with kitchen and bathroom. Rates for singles/doubles are 12,000/18,500 dr.

Pension Nora (☎/fax 72 265, Theotokopoulou 60) has large rooms attractively outfitted with Cretan rugs, iron lamps and wooden furniture. The composer Mikis Theodorikas reputedly lodged in one of them when he was a soldier. Rooms are 6500/10,000 dr with bathroom.

At *Kasteli* (☎ 57 057, fax 45 314, Kanevaro 39), immaculate rooms with high ceilings and white walls cost 8000/9000 dr, and very comfortable renovated apartments cost from 16,000 dr to 20,000 dr depending on size.

Places to Stay – Top End

In the A class category is *Amfora Hotel* (☎/fax 93 224/226, Parados Theotokopolou 2), an immaculately restored mansion with rooms around a courtyard. Rooms are 16,000/20,000 dr. Although beautifully furnished, front rooms can be noisy in the summer and there's no air-conditioning, only small fans.

Nearby is the old city's smartest accommodation, *Casa Delfino* (☎ 93 098, fax 96 500, Theofanous 7), the modernised former mansion of a wealthy merchant. The courtyard at the entrance features patterned cobblestones and the elegant rooms combine traditional furnishings with modern features such as air-conditioning. Doubles are 35,000 dr and a huge palatial split-level apartment, which sleeps up to four people, costs 66,000 dr including breakfast.

Places to Eat – Budget

The two *restaurants* in the food market are good places to seek out traditional food.

Their prices are almost identical. You can get a solid chunk of swordfish with chips for 1200 dr. More adventurous eaters can tuck into a bowl of garlic-laden snail and potato casserole for 1100 dr.

You'll find very similar fare at *Doloma Restaurant* (Kalergon 8). The place is a great favourite with students from the nearby Polytehnio.

For a treat try the excellent *bougatsa tyri* (filo pastry filled with local *myzithra* cheese) at *Bougatsa Hanion* (Apokoronou 37). A slice costs 500 dr and comes sprinkled with a little sugar. *Mano Cafe*, on Theotokopoulou, is a convenient place for juice, breakfast, or a light snack.

Places to Eat – Mid-Range

The port is the place to go for seafood. The prices are not cheap especially considering most of the seafood is frozen, but the setting is great. A favourite with locals is *Apostolis Taverna* on Akti Enosis, where swordfish is 1800 dr. Next door, *Hippopotamus* provides a change of pace with a menu of Mexican dishes.

There are some more chic places in the streets behind the port. An old Turkish *hammam* has been converted into the *Taverna Tamam* (Zambeliou 51), where you'll find tasty soups for about 800 dr and a good range of well prepared main dishes from 1700 dr. *Cafe-Eaterie Ekstra* (Zambeliou 8) offers a choice of Greek and international dishes. There are set menus for 2300 dr and many vegetarian dishes.

Tsikoydadiko (Zambeliou 31) offers a good mixed plate of mezedes for 2000 dr in a splendid old plant-filled courtyard. *Well of the Turk* (Sarpaki 1) is in the heart of the old Turkish residential district of Splantzia and has a wide range of Middle Eastern dishes, as well as occasional live music. *Suki Yaki* (Halidon 26), through the archway, is a Chinese restaurant run by a Thai family. The result is a large Chinese menu supported by a small selection of Thai favourites.

The best place in Hania for Cretan specialities is *To Karnagio* (Katehaki 8). Its specialties are outstanding, especially the zucchini-cheese pies known as *bourekia*.

Entertainment

Cafe Crete (Kalergon 22) is the best place in Hania to hear live Cretan music. It's a rough-and-ready joint with cheap mezedes and bulk wine, plus a lot of locals who like to reach for the instruments that line the walls once they've had a couple of drinks.

Ideon Adron (Halidon 26), next to Suki Yaki, promotes a more sophisticated atmosphere with discreet music and garden seating. *Fagotto Jazz Bar (Angelou 16)* has photographs of jazz greats lining the walls and an excellent selection of CDs. *Point Music Bar* on Plateia Venizelou has great sea views from its 1st floor vantage point.

Angelico Cafe, on the waterfront, plays rock music at a volume that renders conversation possible for lip readers only. For soul and Latin sounds try *Street Club* nearby. Angelico Cafe and Street Club charge very similar prices: beer is 800 dr, spirits are 1200 dr and cocktails start at 1300 dr. *Ariadne Disco*, on Akti Tombazi, is the most central disco.

Shopping

Good quality handmade leather goods are available from shoemakers on Skridlof, off Halidon, where shoes cost from 8500 dr. The old town has many craft shops. Top Hanas carpet shop, Angelou 3, specialises in Cretan kilims that were traditional dowry gifts; prices start at 30,000 dr. Carmela's Ceramic Shop nearby sells beautiful jewellery and ceramics handcrafted by young Cretans. At Roka Carpets, Zambeliou 61, you can watch Mihalis weave his wondrous rugs using methods that have remained essentially unchanged since Minoan times. Prices begin at 8000 dr for a small rug.

The Hania District Association of Handicrafts showroom, on Akti Tombazi, has ceramics, jewellery and embroidery for sale.

Getting There & Away

Air Olympic Airways has flights to Athens (19,900 dr, four daily) and Thessaloniki (29,900 dr, two weekly). The Olympic Airways office (☎ 57 701) is at Tzanakaki 88. Aegean Airlines, Air Greece, Air Manos and Cronus Airlines all offer cheaper competition on the Athens route, while Aegean also offers a daily flight to Thessaloniki (28,100 dr). Aegean's office (☎ 63 366) is at the airport.

The airport is on the Akrotiri Peninsula, 14km from Hania.

Bus Buses depart from the bus station for the following destinations:

Destination	Duration	Price	Frequency
Hora Sfakion	2 hours	1400 dr	3 daily
Iraklio	2½ hours	2900 dr	half-hourly
Kastelli-Kissamos	1 hour	900 dr	15 daily
Lakki	1 hour	600 dr	4 daily
Moni Agias Triadas	30 mins	400 dr	3 daily
Omalos (for Samaria Gorge)	1 hour	1250 dr	4 daily
Paleohora	2 hours	1450 dr	3 daily
Rethymno	1 hour	1500 dr	half-hourly
Sougia	2 hours	1400 dr	1 daily
Stavros	30 mins	300 dr	6 daily

Ferry Ferries for Hania dock at Souda, about 7km east of town. There is at least one ferry daily for the 10 hour trip to and from Piraeus. ANEK Lines has a boat leaving for Piraeus every night at 8.30 pm which costs 5900 dr for deck class. The ANEK Lines office (☎ 27 500) is opposite the food market. Souda's port police can be contacted on ☎ 89 240.

Getting Around

There is no airport bus. A taxi to the airport costs about 3000 dr.

Local buses (blue) for the port of Souda leave from outside the food market. Buses for the western beaches leave from Plateia 1866.

Car rental outlets include Avis (☎ 50 510), Tzanakaki 58; Budget (☎ 92 778), Karïskaki 39; and Europrent (☎ 40 810, 27 810), Halidon 87. Most motorcycle rental outlets are on Halidon.

CRETE

The Good Oil

DIANA MAYFIELD

The olive has been part of life in the eastern Mediterranean since the beginnings of civilisation. Olive cultivation can be traced back about 6000 years. It was the farmers of the Levant (modern Syria and Lebanon) who first spotted the potential of the wild European olive *(Olea europaea)* – a sparse, thorny tree that was common in the region. These farmers began the process of selection that led to the more compact, thornless, oil-rich varieties that now dominate the Mediterranean.

Whereas most westerners think of olive oil as being just a cooking oil, to the people of the ancient Mediterranean civilisations it was very much more. It was almost inseparable from civilised life itself. As well as being an important foodstuff, it was burned in lamps to provide light, it could be used as a lubricant and it was blended with essences to produce fragrant oils.

The Minoans were among the first to grow wealthy on the olive, and western Crete remains an important olive-growing area, specialising in high-quality salad oils. The region's show piece, Kolymvari cooperative, markets its extra-virgin oil in both the USA (*Athena* brand) and Britain (*Kydonia* brand).

Locals will tell you that the finest oil is produced from trees grown on the rocky soils of the Akrotiri Peninsula, west of Hania. The oil that is prized above all others, however, is *agourelaio*, meaning unripe, which is pressed from green olives.

Few trees outlive the olive. Some of the fantastically gnarled and twisted olive trees that dot the countryside of western Crete are more than 1000 years old. The tree known as *dekaoktoura*, in the mountain village of Anisaraki – near Kandanos on the road from Hania to Paleohora – is claimed to be more than 1500 years old.

Many of these older trees are being cut down to make way for improved varieties. The wood is burnt in potters' kilns and provides woodturners with the raw material to produce the ultimate salad bowl for connoisseurs. The dense yellow-brown timber has a beautiful swirling grain.

AKROTIRI PENINSULA

Χερσόνησος Ακρωτήρι

The Akrotiri (ahk-ro-**tee**-rih) Peninsula, to the east of Hania, has a few places of fairly minor interest, as well as being the site of Hania's airport, port and a military base. There is an immaculate **military cemetery** at Souda, where about 1500 British, Australian and New Zealand soldiers who lost their lives in the Battle of Crete are buried. The buses to Souda port from outside the Hania food market can drop you at the cemetery.

If you haven't yet had your fill of Cretan monasteries, there are three on the Akrotiri Peninsula. The impressive 17th century **Moni Agias Triada** was founded by the Venetian monks Jeremiah and Laurentio Giancarolo. The brothers were converts to the Orthodox faith. The monastery is open 6 am to 2 pm and from 5 to 7 pm daily. Admission is 300 dr.

The 16th century **Moni Gourvernetou** (Our Lady of the Angels) is 4km north of Moni Agias Triada. The church inside the monastery has an ornate sculptured Venetian facade. It's open 8 am to 12.30 pm and 4.30 to 7.30 pm daily. Both Moni Agias Triadas and Moni Gourvernetou are still in use.

From Moni Gourvernetou, it's a 15 minute walk on the path leading down to the coast to the ruins of **Moni Katholiko**. The monastery is dedicated to St John the Hermit who lived in the cave behind the ruins. It takes another 30 minutes to reach the sea.

There are three buses daily (except Sunday) to Moni Agias Triadas from Hania bus station (400 dr).

HANIA TO XYLOSKALO

The road from Hania to the beginning of the Samaria Gorge is one of the most spectacular routes on Crete. It heads through orange groves to the village of **Fournes** where a left fork leads to **Meskla**. The main road continues to the village of **Lakki**, 24km from Hania. This unspoilt village in the Lefka Ori Mountains affords stunning views wherever you look. The village was a cen-tre of resistance during the uprising against the Turks, and during WWII.

In Lakki *Kri-Kri Restaurant & Rooms* (☎ *0821-67 316*) has comfortable singles/doubles for 3000/5000 dr. The restaurant serves good-value meals.

From Lakki, the road continues to the Omalos Plateau and **Xyloskalo**, the start of the Samaria Gorge. *Kallergi Refuge* (☎ *0821-74 560*), a one hour walk along a signposted track from the Omalos-Xyloskalo road, is a good base for trekking and climbing in the surrounding mountains. Make a reservation either through the EOS in Hania (☎ 0821-44 647), or by telephoning the refuge.

SAMARIA GORGE

Φαράγγι της Σαμαριάς

It's a wonder the stones and rocks underfoot haven't worn away completely, given the number of people who tramp through the Samaria (sah-mah-rih-**ah**) Gorge. Despite the crowds, a trek through this stupendous gorge is still an experience to remember.

At 18km, the gorge is supposedly the longest in Europe. It begins just below the Omalos Plateau, carved out by the river that flows between the Lefka Ori and Mt Volikas. Its width varies from 150m to 3m and its vertical walls reach 500m at their highest points. The gorge has an incredible number of wildflowers, which are at their best in April and May.

It is also home to a large number of endangered species. They include the Cretan wild goat, the kri-kri, which survives in the wild only here and on the islet of Kri-Kri, off the coast of Agios Nikolaos. The gorge was made a national park in 1962 to save the kri-kri from extinction. You are unlikely to see too many of these shy animals, which show a marked aversion to trekkers.

An early start helps to avoid the worst of the crowds, but during July and August even the early bus from Hania to the top of the gorge can be packed.

The trek from Xyloskalo, the name of the steep wooden staircase that gives access to the gorge, to Agia Roumeli takes around six

CRETE

hours. Early in the season it's sometimes necessary to wade through the stream. Later, as the flow drops, it's possible to use rocks as stepping stones.

The gorge is wide and open for the first 6km, until you reach the abandoned village of Samaria. The inhabitants were relocated when the gorge became a national park. Just south of the village is a small church dedicated to Saint Maria of Egypt, after whom the gorge is named.

The gorge then narrows and becomes more dramatic until, at the 12km mark, the walls are only 3.5m apart – the famous **Iron Gates**.

The gorge ends just north of the almost abandoned village of Old Agia Roumeli. From here the path continues to the small, messy and crowded resort of Agia Roumeli, with a much-appreciated pebble beach and sparkling sea.

The Samaria gorge is open most years from May until mid-October. The opening date depends on the amount of water in the gorge. Visiting hours are 6 am to 4 pm daily, and there's an admission fee of 1200 dr. Spending the night in the gorge is forbidden.

What to Bring

Sensible footwear is essential for walking on the uneven ground covered by sharp stones. Trainers will do but hiking shoes are better. You'll also need a hat and sunscreen. There's no need to take water; while it's inadvisable to drink water from the main stream, there are plenty of springs along the way spurting delicious cool water straight from the rock. There is nowhere to buy food, so bring something to snack on.

Getting There & Away

There are excursions to the Samaria Gorge from every sizable town and resort on Crete. Most travel agents have two excursions: 'Samaria Gorge Long Way' and 'Samaria Gorge Easy Way'. The first comprises the regular trek from the Omalos Plateau to Agia Roumeli; the second starts at Agia Roumeli and takes you as far as the Iron Gates.

Obviously it's cheaper to trek the Samaria Gorge under your own steam, and Hania is the most convenient base. There are buses to Xyloskalo (one hour, 1250 dr) at 6.15, 7.30 and 8.30 am and 1.45 pm. If you intend to stay on the south coast ask for a one way ticket (750 dr), otherwise you'll automatically be sold a return. There's also a direct bus to Xyloskalo from Paleohora (1½ hours, 1400 dr) at 6 am.

AGIA ROUMELI TO HORA SFAKION

Agia Roumeli (Αγία Ρούμελη) has little going for it, but if you have just trekked through the Samaria Gorge and are too exhausted to face a further journey, there is one hotel here, the B class *Hotel Agia Roumeli* (☎ 0825-91 232), where singles/doubles are 6000/8000 dr with bathroom. There are also a number of *domatia* where you'll pay around 6000 dr for a double.

The small but rapidly expanding fishing village of **Loutro** (Λουτρό) lies between Agia Roumeli and Hora Sfakion. Loutro doesn't have a beach but there are rocks from which you can swim. There is one pension, the comfortable *Porto Loutro* (☎ 0825-91 433), which has doubles with bathroom for 9000 dr. There are plenty of *domatia* and *tavernas*.

An extremely steep path leads up from Loutro to the village of **Anopolis**, where there are also *domatia*. Alternatively, you can save yourself the walk by taking the Hania-Skaloti bus which runs via Anopolis. The bus leaves Hania at 2 pm and returns the following morning, calling in at Anopolis at 7 am.

From Loutro it's a moderate 2½ hour walk along a coastal path to Hora Sfakion. On the way you will pass the celebrated **Sweet Water Beach**, named after freshwater springs which seep from the rocks. Freelance campers spend months at a time here. Even if you don't feel inclined to join them, you won't be able to resist a swim in the translucent sea.

There are three boats daily from Agia Roumeli to Hora Sfakion (one hour, 1500 dr) via Loutro (30 minutes, 850 dr). It connects with the bus back to Hania, leaving you in Hora Sfakion just long enough to spend a few drachma. There's also a boat from Agia Roumeli to Paleohora (2100 dr) at 4.45 pm, calling at Sougia (950 dr).

HORA SFAKION Χώρα Σφακίων
☎ 0825 • postcode 730 01 • pop 340
Hora Sfakion (**ho**-rah sfah-**kee**-on) is a small coastal port where hordes of walkers from the Samaria Gorge spill off the boat and onto the bus. As such, in high season it can seem like Piccadilly Circus at rush hour. Most people pause only long enough to catch the next bus out.

Hora Sfakion played a prominent role during WWII when thousands of Allied troops were evacuated by sea from the town after the Battle of Crete.

Orientation & Information
The ferry quay is at the western side of the harbour. Buses leave from the square on the eastern side. The post office and OTE are on the square, and the police station overlooks it. There is no tourist office or tourist police.

Places to Stay & Eat
If you do end up staying, the options aren't so exciting. The D class **Hotel Stavros** **(☎ 91 220)**, up the steps at the western end of the port, has clean singles/doubles with bathroom for 5000/5500 dr. Don't expect a warm welcome though. **Hotel Samaria** **(☎ 91 261)**, on the waterfront, has rooms with bathroom for 4000/6000 dr. It also has a good restaurant which turns out a tasty plate of seafood pilaf for 1400 dr.

Hotel Xenia (☎ 91 202/206), close to the ferry dock, has the best rooms around. Hora Sfakion is one of the few places where this government-run chain has come up with the goods. It has spacious rooms overlooking the sea from 9000/12,000 dr including breakfast.

Getting There & Away
Bus There are four buses daily from Hora Sfakion to Hania (two hours, 1400 dr). From June through August there are two daily buses to Plakias (1¼ hours, 1150 dr)

via Frangokastello, leaving at 11.30 am and 5.30 pm, and one to Rethymno (two hours, 1700 dr) at 7.30 pm.

Boat From June through August there are daily boats from Hora Sfakion to Paleohora (three hours, 3500 dr) via Loutro, Agia Roumeli and Sougia. The boat leaves at 12.30 pm. There are also three or four boats daily to Agia Roumeli (one hour, 1500 dr) via Loutro (30 minutes, 500 dr).

From June there are boats to Gavdos Island on Saturday and Sunday leaving at 9.30 am and returning at 4 pm (2650 dr).

AROUND HORA SFAKION
The road from Vrises to Hora Sfakion cuts through the heart of the Sfakia region in the eastern Lefka Ori. The inhabitants of this region have long had a reputation for fearlessness and independence – characteristics they retain to this day. Cretans are regarded by other Greeks as being immensely proud and there is none more so than the Sfakiot.

One of Crete's most celebrated heroes, Ioannis Daskalogiannis, was from Sfakia. In 1770, Daskalogiannis led the first Cretan insurrection against Ottoman rule. When help promised by Russia failed to materialise, he gave himself up to the Turks to save his followers. As punishment the Turks skinned him alive in Iraklio. Witnesses related that Daskalogiannis suffered this excruciating death in dignified silence.

The Turks never succeeded in controlling the Sfakiots, and this rugged mountainous region was the scene of fierce fighting. The story of their resistance lives on in the form of folk tales and *rizitika* (local folk songs).

The village of **Imbros**, 23km from Vrises, is at the head of the beautiful 10km Imbros Gorge, which is far less visited than the Samaria Gorge. To get there, take any bus bound for Hora Sfakion from the north coast and get off at Imbros. Walk out of the village towards Hora Sfakion and a path to the left leads down to the gorge. The gorge path ends at the village of **Komitades**, from where it is an easy walk by road to Hora Sfakion. You can of course do the trek in reverse, beginning at Komitades. The Happy Walker organises treks through this gorge (see Organised Tours in the Rethymno section).

Frangokastello Φραγγοκάστελλο

Frangokastello is a magnificent fortress on the coast 15km east of Hora Sfakion. It was built by the Venetians in 1371 as a defence against pirates and rebel Sfakiots, who resented the Venetian occupation as much as they did the Turkish.

It was here in 1770 that Ioannis Daskalogiannis surrendered to the Turks. On 17 May 1828 many Cretan rebels, led by Hadzi Mihalis Dalanis, were killed here by the Turks. Legend has it that at dawn each anniversary the ghosts of Hadzi Mihalis Dalanis and his followers can be seen riding along the beach.

The castle overlooks a gently sloping, sandy beach. Domatia and tavernas are springing up rapidly here, but it's still relatively unspoilt.

Buses between Hora Sfakion and Plakias go via Frangokastello.

SOUGIA Σούγια

☎ 0823   • postcode 730 01   • pop 50

It's surprising that Sougia (**soo**-yiah) hasn't yet been commandeered by the package tour crowd. With a wide curve of sand and pebble beach and a shady, tree-lined coastal road, Sougia's tranquillity has been preserved only because it lies at the foot of a narrow, twisting road that would deter most tour buses.

If you arrive by boat, walk about 150m along the coast to the town centre. If you arrive by bus, the bus will drop you on the coastal road in front of Santa Irene hotel. The only other road intersects the coastal road by Santa Irene Hotel and runs north to the Agia Irini Gorge and Hania.

Sougia doesn't have a post office, OTE or bank, but you can change money at several places, including Polifimos Travel (☎ 51 022) and Roxana's Office (☎ 51 362). Both are just off the coastal road on the road to Hania.

Places to Stay

There's no camp site, but the eastern end of the long pebbled beach is popular with free-lance campers.

It seems almost every building in Sougia is a domatia or pension. *Rooms Maria* (☎ 51 337) has clean, white singles/doubles with bathroom for 5000/7000 dr in August, 1000 dr less during the rest of high season. Next door is the equally attractive *Rooms Ririka* (☎ 51 167) also with rooms overlooking the sea for about the same price. The smartest accommodation is *Santa Irene Hotel* (☎ 51 342, fax 51 181), which has studios for 8000/12,000 dr. Air-conditioning costs 2000 dr extra.

Inland, on the road to Hania, *Aretouca Rooms to Rent* (☎ 51 178) has lovely rooms with wood-panelled ceilings and balconies for 7000/8000 dr. Next door, *Pension Galini* (☎/fax 51 488) has beautiful rooms with bathroom for 5000/6000/7000 dr and studios for 8000 dr.

Places to Eat

Restaurants line the waterfront and there are more on the main street. *Kyma*, on the seafront as you enter town, has a good selection of ready-made food. *Taverna Rebetiko*, on the road to Hania, has an extensive menu including such Cretan dishes as *boureki* and stuffed zucchini flowers.

Getting There & Away

There's a daily bus from Hania to Sougia (2½ hours, 1400 dr) at 1.30 pm. Buses from Sougia to Hania leave at 7 am. Sougia is on the Paleohora-Hora Sfakion boat route.

AROUND SOUGIA

Sougia is at the mouth of the pretty **Agia Irini Gorge** which may not be as fashionable as the Samaria Gorge but is less crowded and less gruelling to walk. Paleohora travel agents offer guided walks through the gorge for 4500 dr. It's easy enough to organise independently – just catch the Omalos bus from Paleohora or the Hania bus from Sougia, and get off at Agia Irini. There are a couple of beautiful **Byzantine churches** tucked away in the olive groves at the start of the gorge.

The ruins of ancient **Lissos**, once a sanctuary to Asclepius, are 1½ hours away on the coastal path to Paleohora. The path heads inland at the western end of the beach.

PALEOHORA Παλαιοχώρα
☎ 0823 • postcode 730 01 • pop 2150

Paleohora was discovered by hippies back in the 1960s and from then on its days as a tranquil fishing village were numbered. However, the resort operators have not gone way over the top – yet. The place retains a certain laid-back feel. It is also the only beach resort on Crete which does not go into total hibernation in winter.

The little town is set on a narrow peninsula with a long, curving sandy beach exposed to the wind on one side and a sheltered pebbly beach on the other. On summer evenings the main street is closed to traffic and the tavernas move onto the road.

It's worth clambering up the ruins of the 13th century **Venetian castle** for the splendid view of the sea and mountains. The most picturesque part of Paleohora is the narrow streets huddled around the castle.

From Paleohora, a six hour walk along a scenic coastal path leads to Sougia, passing the ancient site of Lissos.

Orientation & Information
Paleohora's main street, El Venizelou, runs north to south, with several streets leading off east to the pebble beach. Boats leave from the old harbour at the southern end of this beach. At the southern end of El Venizelou, a west turn onto Kontekaki leads to the tamarisk-shaded sandy beach.

The municipal tourist office (☎ 41 507) is in the town hall on El Venizelou. It is open 10 am to 1 pm and 6 to 9 pm Wednesday to Monday between May and October.

The post office is on the road that skirts the sandy beach. On El Venizelou are the National Bank of Greece, with ATM, the OTE (on the west side, just north of Kontekaki) and PC Corner (☎ 42 422), where Internet access is available.

Organised Tours
Travel agents around town offer excursions to ancient Lissos (6500 dr) and dolphin-watching trips (3500 dr).

Places to Stay
Camping Paleohora *(☎ 41 225/120)* is 1.5km north-east of town, near the pebble beach. The camp site has a taverna but no minimarket.

Homestay Anonymous *(☎ 41 509, 42 098)* is a great place for backpackers, with clean, simply furnished rooms set around a small, beautiful garden. Singles/ doubles/ triples cost 3500/4500/5000 dr, and there is a communal kitchen. The owner, Manolis, is an amiable young guy who speaks good English and is full of useful information for travellers. To get there, walk south along El Venizelou from the bus stop and turn right at the town hall. Follow the road as it veers right, and the rooms are on the left.

Oriental Bay Rooms *(☎ 41 076)* occupies the large modern building at the northern end of the pebble beach. The owner, Thalia, is a very cheerful woman and the immaculate singles/doubles with bathroom and ceiling fans are good value at 5000/7000 dr. There's also a shaded terrace restaurant overlooking the sea, that serves decent meals.

Dream Rooms *(☎ 41 112)*, nearer the old quarter, is aptly named for the large, excellently maintained rooms with balconies overlooking the sea. Rooms with bathroom cost 6000/8000 dr. ***Spamandos Rooms*** *(☎ 41 197)*, in the old quarter, has spotless, nicely furnished doubles/triples with bathroom for 7000/8000 dr. To get there, walk south along Einai Yrela, take the first left after Pelican Taverna and then the first right. After 60m turn left and the rooms are on the right.

Nearby ***Kostas Rooms*** *(☎/fax 41 248)* offers simple, attractive rooms with ceiling fans, bathroom, fridge and sea views for 3500/5000 dr.

Out of season, try looking for a deal at one of the places offering self-catering apartments along the sandy beach on the other side of town. ***Poseidon Pension***

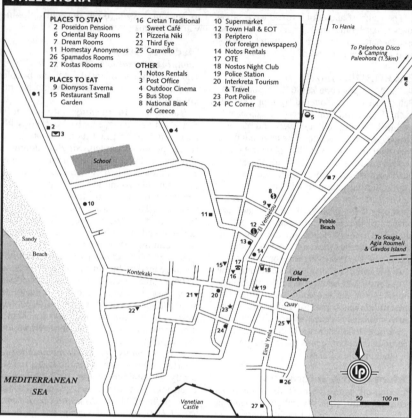

PALEOHORA

PLACES TO STAY	16 Cretan Traditional	10 Supermarket
2 Poseidon Pension	Sweet Café	12 Town Hall & EOT
6 Oriental Bay Rooms	21 Pizzeria Niki	13 Periptero
7 Dream Rooms	22 Third Eye	(for foreign newspapers)
11 Homestay Anonymous	25 Caravello	14 Notos Rentals
26 Spamados Rooms		17 OTE
27 Kostas Rooms	**OTHER**	18 Nostos Night Club
	1 Notos Rentals	19 Police Station
PLACES TO EAT	3 Post Office	20 Interkreta Tourism
9 Dionysos Taverna	4 Outdoor Cinema	& Travel
15 Restaurant Small	5 Bus Stop	23 Port Police
Garden	8 National Bank	24 PC Corner
	of Greece	

(☎ 41 374/115) has cosy rooms for 5000/6000 dr with bathroom, and studios for 7000/9000 dr.

Places to Eat

You'll find some good eateries in Paleohora. **Restaurant Small Garden**, behind the OTE, is a fine little taverna and does a good job of old favourites like fried aubergine (800 dr).

The very popular **Dionysos Taverna**, on El Venizelou, is a bit more expensive but also serves tasty food. **Pizzeria Niki**, just off

Kontekaki, serves superior pizzas cooked in a wood-fired oven.

Vegetarians have a treat in store at the **Third Eye**, near the sandy beach. The menu includes curries and a range of Asian dishes, all at very reasonable prices. You can eat well and enjoy a beer for less than 2000 dr. Unfortunately the place is closed from December through February.

Caravello Restaurant has a prime position overlooking the old harbour and offers a full array of fresh seafood.

Wherever you dine, round your meal off with a delicious dessert from the *Cretan Traditional Sweet Cafe* almost opposite Restaurant Small Garden.

Entertainment

Most visitors to Paleohora spend at least one evening at the well signposted *outdoor cinema*. Another option for a night out is the *Paleohora Disco*, next to Camping Paleohora north-east of town. If you've seen the movie and don't fancy the trek to the disco, try *Nostos Night Club* right in town, between El Venizelou and the old harbour.

Getting There & Away

Bus From June through August there are three buses daily to Hania (two hours, 1450 dr), going via Omalos (1½ hours, 1250 dr) to cash in on the Samaria Gorge trade. From December through February there are two, direct to Hania.

Ferry From June through August there are daily ferries from Paleohora to Hora Sfakion (three hours, 3700 dr) via Sougia (one hour, 950 dr), Agia Roumeli (two hours, 2100 dr) and Loutro (2½ hours, 2850 dr). The ferry leaves Paleohora at 9.30 am, and returns from Hora Sfakion at 12.30 pm. There's also a boat three times weekly from June through August to Gavdos (four hours, 3000 dr) that leaves Paleohora at 8.30 am.

Tickets for all of these boats can be bought at Interkreta Tourism & Travel (☎ 41 393/888, fax 41 050), Kontekaki 4.

Excursion Boat The excursion boat M/B *Elafonisos* gets cranked into action in mid-April ferrying people to the west coast beach of Elafonisi (one hour, 1300 dr). The service builds up from three times weekly to daily in June through September.

Getting Around

If you'd like to hire a car, motorcycle or bicycle, they are available at Notos Rentals (☎ 42 110), on El Venizelou and by the sandy beach.

AROUND PALEOHORA
Gavdos Island Νήσος Γαύδος

Gavdos Island (population 50), in the Libyan Sea, 65km from Paleohora, is the most southerly place in Europe. It is an excellent choice for those craving isolation and peace. The island has three small villages and pleasant beaches. There is a post office, OTE, police officer and doctor. The best source of information about the island is Interkreta Tourism & Travel in Paleohora.

There are no hotels but several of the locals have *domatia*, and there are *tavernas*. There is no official camp site but camping freelance is tolerated. Fishermen from Gavdos can take tourists to the remote, uninhabited island of Gavdopoula.

Getting There & Away A small post boat operates between Paleohora and Gavdos on Monday and Thursday all year, weather permitting. It leaves Paleohora at 8.30 am and takes about four hours (3000 dr). From June through August there's also a Tuesday boat. The boats turn around in Gavdos almost immediately.

There are also two boats weekly from Hora Sfakion to Gavdos (2650 dr) and a weekly boat from Sougia (2300 dr).

Elafonisi Ελαφονήσι

As one of the loveliest sand beaches in Crete it's easy to understand why people enthuse so much about Elafonisi, at the southern extremity of Crete's west coast. The beach is long and wide and is separated from Elafonisi Islet by about 50m of knee-deep water on its northern side. The islet is marked by low dunes and a string of semisecluded coves that attract a sprinkling of naturists.

The beaches are popular with day-trippers but there are two small hotels and a pension on a bluff overlooking the main beach for those who want to luxuriate in the late afternoon quiet that descends on the area: *Rooms Elafonissi* (☎ 0822-61 274), *Rooms Elafonissos* (☎ 0822-61 294) or *Inahorion* (☎ 0822-61 111). All three have singles/doubles for 5000/7000 dr with bathroom.

CRETE

Getting There & Away There are two boats daily from Paleohora to Elafonisi (one hour, 1140 dr) from June through August, as well as daily buses from Hania (2½ hours, 1500 dr) and Kastelli-Kissamos (1½ hours, 900 dr). The buses leave Hania at 7.30 am and Kastelli-Kissamos at 8.30 am, and both depart from Elafonisi at 4 pm. The final section of road from Hrysoskalitissas to the beach is very rugged.

Moni Hrysoskalitissas

Μονή Χρυσοσκαλίτισσας
Moni Hrysoskalitissas (mo-**nee** hris-o-skah-**lee**-tis-as), 5km north of Elafonisi, is inhabited by two nuns. It's a beautiful monastery perched on a rock high above the sea. Hrysoskalitissas means 'golden staircase', from a legend claiming that one of the 90 steps leading from the sea up to the monastery is made of gold. There are *tavernas* and *domatia* in the vicinity. Buses to Elafonisi drop passengers here.

KASTELLI-KISSAMOS

Καστέλλι-Κίσσαμος
☎ 0822 • postcode 734 00 • pop 3000
If you find yourself in the north coast town of Kastelli-Kissamos, you've probably arrived by ferry from the Peloponnese or Kythira. The most remarkable part of Kastelli-Kissamos is its unremarkableness. It's simply a quiet town of mostly elderly residents that neither expects nor attracts much tourism.

In antiquity, its name was Kissamos; it was the main town of the province of the same name. When the Venetians came along and built a castle here, the place became known as Kastelli. The name persisted until 1966 when authorities decided that too many people were confusing this Kastelli with Crete's other Kastelli, 40km south-east of Iraklio. The official name reverted to Kissamos, and that's what appears on bus and shipping schedules. Local people still prefer Kastelli, and many books and maps agree with them. An alternative that is emerging is to combine the two into

Kastelli-Kissamos, which leaves no room for misunderstanding.

Orientation & Information

The port is 3km west of town. From June through August a bus meets the boats; otherwise a taxi costs 800 dr. The bus station is just below the square, Plateia Kissamos, and the main street, Skalidi, runs east from Plateia Kissamos.

Kastelli-Kissamos has no tourist office. The post office is on the main road. Signs from the bus station direct you through an alley on the right of Skalidi which takes you to the post office. Turn right at the post office and you'll come to the National Bank of Greece which is on the central square. Turn left at the post office and the OTE office is opposite you about 50m along the main road. There is also a string of pensions and tavernas along the sea below the bus station.

Places to Stay

There are three camp sites to choose from. *Camping Kissamos* (☎ 23 444/322), close to the city centre, is convenient for the huge supermarket next door and for the bus station, but not much else. It's got great views of the olive-processing plant next door.

A much better choice is *Camping Mithimna* (☎ 31 444/445), 6km west of town. It's an excellent, shady site near the best stretch of beach. Facilities include a restaurant, bar and shop. It charges 900 dr per person and 600 dr per tent. It also has rooms to rent nearby. Getting there involves either a 4km walk along the beach, or a bus trip to the village of Drapanias – from where it's a pleasant 15 minute walk through olive groves to the site.

Camping Nopigia (☎ 31 111) is another good site, 2km west of Camping Mithimna. While the beach is no good for swimming, the swimming pool here makes up for that.

Back in town, one of the best deals is *Koutsounakis Rooms* (☎ 23 753, 22 064), adjacent to the bus station. Spotless singles/doubles are 4000/5500 dr with bathroom.

The C class *Hotel Castell* (☎ *22 140*) opposite has similar prices.

Argo Rooms for Rent (☎ *23 563/322*) on Plateia Teloniou has spacious rooms for 5000/7000 dr with bathroom. From the central square, walk down to the seafront, turn left, and you will come to the rooms on the left.

The C class *Hotel Kissamos* (☎ *22 086*), west of the bus station on the north side of the main road, is in an uninspiring location but has rooms with bathroom for 5500/7700 dr, including breakfast.

Places to Eat

Papadakis Taverna, opposite Argo Rooms for Rent, has a good setting overlooking the beach and serves well prepared food. For a meal with local colour go to the no-frills *Restaurant Macedonas* just west of Plateia Kissamos where an excellent meal of crispy fried whitebait and Greek salad costs 1800 dr.

Getting There & Away

Bus There are 13 buses daily to Hania (one hour, 900 dr), where you can change for Rethymno and Iraklio. There are also two buses daily for Falasarna (600 dr) at 10 am and 5.30 pm.

Ferry Golden Ferries Maritime operates the F/B *Maria* on a route that takes in Antikythira (two hours, 2100 dr), Kythira (four hours, 4200 dr) and Gythio (seven hours, 5100 dr). It leaves Kastelli-Kissamos at 2.30 pm Monday and Thursday.

Both the Miras agent Horeftakis Tours (☎ 23 250), and the ANEK Lines office (☎ 22 009, 24 030) are on the right side of Skalidi, east of Plateia Kissamos.

Getting Around

Cars can be hired from Hermes (☎ 22 980) on Skalidi, and motorcycles from Motor Fun (☎ 23 400) on Plateia Kissamos.

AROUND KASTELLI-KISSAMOS
Falasarna Φαλασαρνά

Falasarna, 16km west of Kastelli-Kissamos, was a Cretan city-state in the 4th century

BC. There's not much to see, and most people are here for the superb beach, which is long, sandy and interspersed with boulders. There are several *domatia* at the beach.

From June through August there are two buses daily from Kastelli-Kissamos to Falasarna (600 dr) as well as buses from Hania (1500 dr).

Gramvousa Peninsula
Χερσόνησος Γραμβούσα

North of Falasarna is the wild and remote Gramvousa Peninsula. There is a wide track, which eventually degenerates into a path, along the east coast side to the sandy beach of **Tigani**, on the west side of the peninsula's narrow tip. The beach is overlooked by the two islets of Agria (wild) and Imeri (tame) Gramvousa. To reach the track, take a west-bound bus from Kastelli-Kissamos and ask to be let off at the turnoff for the village of Kalyviani (5km from Kastelli-Kissamos). Walk the 2km to Kalyviani, then take the path that begins at the far end of the main street. The shadeless walk takes around three hours – wear a hat and take plenty of water.

You don't have to inflict this punishment upon yourself to see the beautiful peninsula. From June through August there are daily cruises around the peninsula in the *Gramvousa Express* (5000 dr). The boat leaves Kastelli-Kissamos at 9 am and returns at 6 pm.

Ennia Horia Εννιά Χωριά

Ennia Horia (nine villages) is the name given to the highly scenic mountainous region south of Kastelli-Kissamos, renowned for its chestnut trees. If you have your own transport you can drive through the region en route to Moni Hrysoskalitissas and Elafonisi or, with a little backtracking, to Paleohora. Alternatively, you can take a circular route, returning via the coast road. The village of **Elos** stages a chestnut festival on the third Sunday of October when sweets made from chestnuts are eaten. The road to the region heads inland 5km east of Kastelli-Kissamos.

CRETE

Polyrrinia Πολυρρηνία

The ruins of the ancient city of Polyrrinia (po-lih-reh-**nee**-ah) lie 7km south of Kastelli-Kissamos, above the village of Ano Paleokastro (sometimes called Polyrrinia). It's a steep climb to the ruins but the views are stunning.

The city was founded by the Dorians and was continuously inhabited until Venetian times. There are remains of city walls, and an aqueduct built by Hadrian. It's a scenic walk from Kastelli-Kissamos to Polyrrinia, otherwise there is a very infrequent bus service – ask at the Kastelli-Kissamos bus station.

To reach the Polyrrinia road, walk east along Kastelli-Kissamos' main road, and turn right after the OTE.

Ano Paleokastro has one taverna, *Taverna Odysseos*, but no accommodation.

Dodecanese Δωδεκάνησα

Strung along the coast of western Turkey, the Dodecanese archipelago is much closer to Asia Minor than to mainland Greece. Because of their strategic and vulnerable position, these islands have encountered an even greater catalogue of invasions and occupations than the rest of Greece.

The name means 'Twelve Islands', but a glance at the map confirms that the group includes quite a few more. The name originated in 1908 when 12 of the islands united against the newly formed Young Turk-led Ottoman parliament which had retracted the liberties the Dodecanese had been granted under the sultans. The Dodecanese islanders enjoyed greater autonomy than did the rest of Greece under the sultans, and they paid fewer taxes.

The 12 islands were Rhodes, Kos, Kalymnos, Karpathos, Patmos, Tilos, Symi, Leros, Astypalea, Nisyros, Kassos and Halki. The islands' vicissitudinous history has endowed them with a wealth of diverse archaeological remains, but these are not the islands' only attractions. The highly developed resorts of Rhodes and Kos have beaches and bars galore, while Lipsi and Tilos have appealing beaches, but without the crowds. The far-flung islands of Agathonisi, Arki, Kassos and Kastellorizo await Greek-island aficionados in pursuit of traditional island life, while everyone boggles at the extraordinary landscape that geological turbulence has created on Nisyros.

History
The Dodecanese islands have been inhabited since pre-Minoan times; by the Archaic period Rhodes and Kos had emerged as the dominant islands of the group. Distance from Athens gave the Dodecanese considerable autonomy and they were, for the most part, free to prosper unencumbered by subjugation to imperial Athens. Following Alexander the Great's death, Ptolemy I of Egypt ruled the Dodecanese.

HIGHLIGHTS

- The fascinating medieval city of Rhodes
- Enjoying the nightlife on Kos
- Nisyros' moon-like volcanic craters
- Trekking around picturesque Tilos

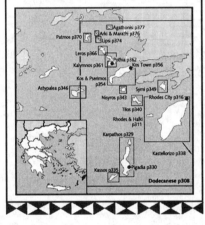

The Dodecanese islanders were the first Greeks to become Christians. This was through the tireless efforts of St Paul, who made two journeys to the archipelago, and through St John, who was banished to Patmos – where he had his revelation.

The early Byzantine era saw the islands prosper, but by the 7th century AD they were plundered by a string of invaders. By the early 14th century it was the turn of the crusaders – the Knights of St John of Jerusalem, or Knights Hospitallers. The Knights eventually became rulers of almost all the Dodecanese, building mighty fortifications, but not mighty enough to keep out the Turks in 1522.

The Turks were ousted by the Italians in 1912 during a tussle over possession of Libya. Inspired by Mussolini's vision of a

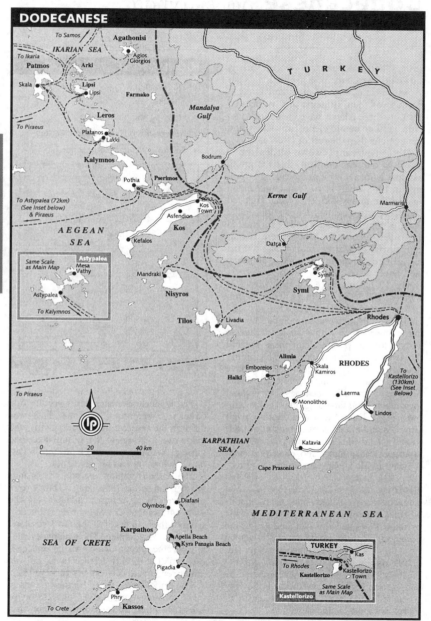

DODECANESE

vast Mediterranean empire, Italian was made the official language and the practice of Orthodoxy was prohibited. The Italians constructed grandiose public buildings in the Fascist style, which was the antithesis of archetypal Greek architecture. More beneficially, they excavated and restored many archaeological monuments.

After the Italian surrender of 1943, the islands became battle grounds for British and German forces, with much suffering inflicted upon the population. The Dodecanese were formally returned to Greece in 1947.

Getting There & Away

Air Astypalea, Karpathos, Kassos, Kos, Leros and Rhodes have flights to Athens. In addition, Rhodes has flights to Iraklio and Hania on Crete, Thessaloniki, and in summer to Mykonos and Santorini (Thira) in the Cyclades.

Ferry – Domestic Ferry schedules to the Dodecanese are incredibly complicated, mainly because of the distance from the mainland. The shortest round trip from Piraeus to the main port, Rhodes, takes about 28 hours, therefore it is impossible for the ferry companies to operate a simple daily timetable. Departure times in both directions tend to be geared to an early morning arrival at both Piraeus and Rhodes. This means that island-hopping in between can involve some antisocial hours.

The following table gives an overall view of ferry connections to the Dodecanese from the mainland and Crete in high season.

Connecting from the Dodecanese to the Cyclades can be difficult. It is possible to reach Astypalea from the Dodecanese and connect with ferries serving the Cyclades from there, but this is more by luck than by design.

Ferry Connections to the Dodecanese

Origin	Destination	Duration	Price	Frequency
Alexandroupolis	Kos	26 hours	10,800 dr	1 weekly
Alexandroupolis	Rhodes	30 hours	11,500 dr	1 weekly
Iraklio	Karpathos	7¾ hours	3800 dr	3 weekly
Iraklio	Rhodes	11 hours	6400 dr	3 weekly
Piraeus	Astypalea	10½ hours	7000 dr	3 weekly
Piraeus	Halki	25 hours	9700 dr	1 weekly
Piraeus	Kalymnos	12¾ hours	7200 dr	1 daily
Piraeus	Karpathos	21¼ hours	8000 dr	2 weekly
Piraeus	Kassos	17½ hours	7800 dr	2 weekly
Piraeus	Kos	11½ hours	7700 dr	1 daily
Piraeus	Leros	11¾ hours	6500 dr	1 daily
Piraeus	Lipsi	14 hours	7800 dr	1 weekly
Piraeus	Nisyros	19½ hours	7600 dr	1 weekly
Piraeus	Patmos	9½ hours	7200 dr	1 daily
Piraeus	Rhodes	14½ hours	9000 dr	1 daily
Piraeus	Symi	22½ hours	8800 dr	1 weekly
Piraeus	Tilos	20½ hours	8800 dr	1 weekly
Sitia	Karpathos	4 hours	3400 dr	1 weekly
Sitia	Kassos	2½ hours	2600 dr	1 weekly
Sitia	Rhodes	11 hours	6000 dr	1 weekly
Thessaloniki	Kos	18 hours	12,500 dr	1 weekly
Thessaloniki	Rhodes	21 hours	14,800 dr	1 weekly

DODECANESE

Ferry – International There are ferries to the Turkish ports of Marmaris and Bodrum from Rhodes and Kos respectively, and day trips to Turkey from Kastellorizo and Symi. Boats en route from Piraeus to Cyprus and Israel call at Rhodes.

Hydrofoil Samos Hydrofoils operates daily services from the North-East Aegean island of Samos to the northern Dodecanese, and occasional services from Ikaria.

Getting Around

Air There are flights between Rhodes and Kastellorizo, Karpathos and Kassos.

Ferry Island-hopping within the Dodecanese is fairly easy as the principal islands in the group have daily connections by either ferries or excursion boats. The more remote islands do not have daily boats and some depend on the F/B *Nissos Kalymnos*, which operates out of Kalymnos and plies up and down the chain, calling in at most of the islands at least twice weekly. Karpathos and Kassos are not included on its route. For more information, see the relevant sections under entries on individual islands.

Hydrofoil The Dodecanese Hydrofoil Company operates hydrofoils from Rhodes to most islands in the group. Samos Hydrofoils provides additional services on its routes from the North-East Aegean to Kos.

Rhodes Ρόδος

Rhodes (ro-dos in Greek), the largest by far of the Dodecanese, with a total population of 98,181, is the number one package tour destination of the group. With 300 days of sunshine a year, and an east coast of virtually uninterrupted sandy beaches, it fulfils the two prerequisites of the sun-starved British, Scandinavians and Germans who flock there.

But beaches and sunshine are not its only attributes. Rhodes is a beautiful island with unspoilt villages nestling in the foothills of its mountains. The landscape varies from arid and rocky around the coast to lush and forested in the interior.

The World Heritage-listed old town of Rhodes is the largest inhabited medieval town in Europe, and its mighty fortifications are the finest surviving example of defensive architecture of the time.

History & Mythology

As is the case elsewhere in Greece, the early history of Rhodes is interwoven with mythology. The sun god Helios chose Rhodes as his bride and bestowed upon her light, warmth and vegetation. Their son, Cercafos, had three sons, Camiros, Ialyssos and Lindos, who each founded the cities that were named after them.

The Minoans and Mycenaeans had outposts on the islands, but it was not until the Dorians arrived in 1100 BC that Rhodes began to exert power and influence. The Dorians settled in the cities of Kamiros, Ialyssos and Lindos and made each an autonomous state. They utilised trade routes to the east which had been established during Minoan and Mycenaean times, and the island flourished as an important centre of commerce.

Rhodes continued to prosper until Roman times. It was allied to Athens in the Battle of Marathon (490 BC), in which the Persians were defeated, but had shifted to the Persian side by the time of the Battle of Salamis (480 BC). After the unexpected Athenian victory at Salamis, Rhodes hastily became an ally of Athens again, joining the Delian League in 478 BC. After the disastrous Sicilian Expedition (416-412 BC), Rhodes revolted against Athens and formed an alliance with Sparta, which it aided in the Peloponnesian Wars.

In 408 BC, the cities of Kamiros, Ialyssos and Lindos consolidated their powers for mutual protection and expansion by co-founding the city of Rhodes. The architect Hippodamos, who came to be regarded as the father of town planning, planned the city. The result was one of the most harmonious cities of antiquity, with wide, straight

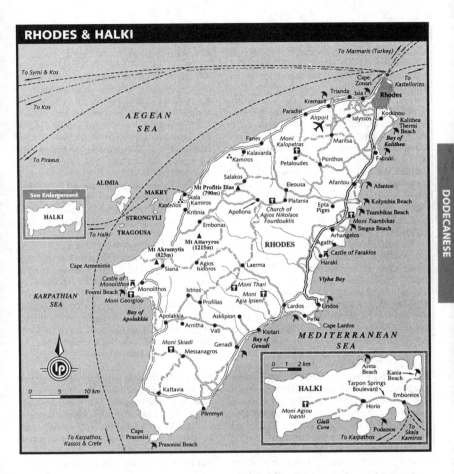

RHODES & HALKI

To Marmaris (Turkey)

To Symi & Kos

To Kos

*AEGEAN
SEA*

To Piraeus

ALIMIA

See Enlargement

HALKI

MAKRY

STRONGYLI

To Halki   TRAGOUSA

Cape Zonari

Trianda   Ixia   **Rhodes**
Kremasti   To
Paradisi   Kastellorizo
            Airport   Ialyssos   Koskinou
                                  Kalithea
Fanes   *Moni   Maritsa   Thermi
         Kalopetras*   Beach
    Kalavarda   *Bay of
    Kamiros   Petaloudes Psinthos   Kalithea*
                                        Faliraki
    Salakos   Eleousa   Afantou
Mt Profitis Ilias   Afantou
  (790m)   Platania   Kolymbia Beach
Skala Kamiros   *Church of   Epta
Kastellos Kritinia Agios Nikolaos Piges Tsambikas Beach
      Apollona   Fountouklis   *Moni Tsambikas*
   Embonas   Stegna Beach
                                    Arhangelos
  Mt Akramytis Mt Attavyros   Agathi
   (825m)   (1215m)   **RHODES**   Castle of Faraklos
Cape Armenistis   Agios   Haraki
         Siana   Isidoros Laerma
KARPATHIAN   Castle of   *Vlyha Bay*
   SEA   Monolithos   Istrios *Moni Thari*
Fourni Beach Monolithos   *Moni   Lardos
   Moni Georgiou   Profilias Agia Ipseni*   Lindos
                                  Pefki
Bay of   Apolakkia   Asklipion Cape Lardos
Apolakkia   Arnitha Vati
               Moni Skiadi Kiotari *MEDITERRANEAN
                  Messanagros Genadi *Bay of   SEA*
                              Genadi*
       Kattavia

       0   5   10 km

       Plimmyri

To Karpathos,   Cape
Kassos & Crete Prasonisi
                Prasonisi Beach

0   1   2 km

HALKI
                    Areta   Kania
                    Beach   Beach
        Tarpon Springs
        Boulevard   Emboreios
*Moni Agiou
Ioanni*   Horio
        *Giali   To
        Cove*   Podamos   Skala
To Karpathos   Kamiros

DODECANESE

streets connecting its four distinct parts: the acropolis, agora, harbour and residential quarter.

Rhodes now became Athens' ally again, and together they defeated Sparta at the battle of Knidos, in 394 BC. Rhodes then joined forces with Persia in a battle against Alexander the Great. However, when Alexander proved invincible, Rhodes hastily allied itself with him. In the skirmishes following Alexander's death, Rhodes sided with Ptolemy.

In 305 BC, Antigonus, one of Ptolemy's rivals, sent his son, the formidable Demetrius Poliorketes (the Besieger of Cities), to conquer the city. Rhodes managed to repel Demetrius after a long siege. To celebrate this victory, the 32m-high bronze statue of Helios Apollo (Colossus of Rhodes), one of the Seven Wonders of the Ancient World, was built. The statue was traditionally thought to have straddled Mandraki Harbour but this has now been refuted. It only stood for 65 years though, before collapsing during an earthquake. It lay abandoned until 653 AD when it was chopped up by the Saracens, who sold it to a merchant in Edessa (in modern-day Turkey). The story goes that after being shipped to Syria, it took almost 1000 camels to convey it to its final destination.

After the defeat of Demetrius, Rhodes knew no bounds. It built the biggest navy in the Aegean and its port became a principal Mediterranean trading centre. The arts also flourished, and the Rhodian school of sculpture supplanted that of Athens as the foremost in Greece. Its most esteemed sculptor was Pythocretes, whose works included the Victory of Samothrace, and the relief of the trireme (warship) at Lindos.

When Greece became the battleground upon which Roman generals fought for leadership of the empire, Rhodes allied itself with Julius Caesar. After Caesar's assassination in 44 BC, Cassius besieged Rhodes, destroying its ships and stripping the city of its artworks, which were then taken to Rome. This marked the beginning of Rhodes' decline. In 70 AD, Rhodes became part of the Roman Empire.

In 155 AD, Rhodes City was badly damaged by an earthquake, and in 269 the Goths invaded, rendering further damage. When the Roman Empire split, Rhodes became part of the Byzantine province of the Dodecanese. Raid upon raid followed; first the Persians in 620, then the Saracens in 653; the Turks followed. When the crusaders seized Constantinople, Rhodes was given independence. Later the Genoese gained control. The Knights of St John arrived in Rhodes in 1309 and ruled for 213 years until they were ousted by the Ottomans. Rhodes suffered several earthquakes during the 19th century, but greater damage was rendered to the city in 1856 by an explosion of gunpowder which had been stored and forgotten – almost 1000 people were killed and many buildings were wrecked. In 1947, after 35 years of Italian occupation, Rhodes became part of Greece along with the other Dodecanese islands.

Getting There & Away

All the addresses listed in this section are in Rhodes City (area code 0241).

Air Olympic Airways has at least five flights daily to Athens (24,900 dr), two daily to Karpathos (12,800 dr), one daily to Kastellorizo (10,900 dr), five weekly to Santorini (22,900 dr), four weekly to Iraklio (21,900 dr), three weekly to Kassos (13,400 dr) and two weekly to Thessaloniki (31,900 dr) and Mykonos (22,900 dr). The Olympic Airways office (☎ 24 571) is at Ierou Lohou 9.

Air Greece and Cronus offer cheaper options. Air Greece has two flights daily to Athens, four weekly to Thessaloniki and three weekly to Iraklio. Cronus has daily flights to Athens.

Triton Holidays (☎ 21 690, fax 31 625), Plastira 9, is the agent for Air Greece, while Cronus (☎ 25 444) is at 25 Martiou 5. The airport is 16km south-west of Rhodes City, near Paradisi.

Castellania Travel Service (☎ 75 860, fax 75 861, email castell@otenet.gr), on Plateia Hippocrates, specialises in youth and student fares, and is one of the best places for low-cost air tickets.

Ferry – Domestic Rhodes is the main port of the Dodecanese. The following table lists scheduled domestic ferries from Rhodes to other islands in the group in high season.

The EOT and the municipal tourist office in Rhodes City can provide you with schedules. Further details and inter-island links can be found under each island entry.

Destination	Duration	Price	Frequency
Astypalea	10 hours	4940 dr	2 weekly
Halki	1½ hours	2000 dr	1 weekly
Kalymnos	5½ hours	4300 dr	1 daily
Karpathos	3½ hours	4400 dr	2 weekly
Kassos	5 hours	4100 dr	2 weekly
Kastellorizo	3½ hours	4100 dr	2 weekly
Kos	3½ hours	3500 dr	1 daily
Leros	7½ hours	4700 dr	1 daily
Lipsi	9½ hours	5100 dr	1 weekly
Nisyros	3¾ hours	2800 dr	3 weekly
Patmos	8½ hours	5500dr	1 daily

Symi	2 hours	1600 dr	1 daily
Tilos	2½ hours	2800 dr	3 weekly

Ferry – International Poseidon Lines and Salamis Lines both stop at Rhodes en route from Piraeus to Cyprus (Lemesos/Limassol) and Israel (Haifa). From Rhodes to Cyprus takes 15 hours (22,000 dr), with a further 11 hours to Haifa (36,000 dr). The boats leave Rhodes on Tuesday and Friday. See the introductory Getting There & Away chapter and the Piraeus section of the Athens chapter for more information. You can buy tickets from Kydon Agency (☎ 23 000, 75 268) on Ethelondon Dodekanision, between Amerikis and Makariou in the new town, or Kouros Travel (☎ 24 377, 22 400), Karpathou 34.

There are two ferry services daily between Rhodes and Marmaris in Turkey. They leave Rhodes at 8 am and 3 pm, and leave Marmaris at 10 am and 4 pm. The crossing takes one hour. In addition, small Turkish car ferries run between Rhodes and Marmaris daily (except Sunday) between April and October; less frequently in winter. Prices vary, so shop around.

Immigration and customs are on the quay.

Hydrofoil – Domestic The Dodecanese Hydrofoil Company (☎ 24 000), on the quay at Plateia Neoriou 6, operates the following services from Rhodes in high season:

Destination	Duration	Price	Frequency
Astypalea	5½ hours	9880 dr	1 weekly
Kalymnos	3½ hours	8530 dr	1 weekly
Kos	2 hours	6790 dr	2 daily
Leros	3½ hours	9320 dr	3 weekly
Nysiros	2¼ hours	5550 dr	1 weekly
Patmos	3½ hours	10,730 dr	3 weekly
Symi	1 hour	3100 dr	2 weekly
Tilos	1¼ hours	5550 dr	2 weekly

Hydrofoil – International There are daily hydrofoils to Marmaris (weather permitting) from April to October. Fares are currently cheaper than ferries at 10,000/14,000 dr one way/return (plus 3500 dr Turkish port tax). You can buy tickets from Triton Holidays (☎ 21 657, fax 31 625), Plastira 9, to whom you must submit your passport on the day before your journey.

Caïque See the Getting There & Away section for Halki for information about caïques between Rhodes and Halki.

Excursion Boat There are excursion boats to Symi (4000 dr return) every day in summer, leaving Mandraki Harbour at 9 am and returning at 6 pm. You can buy tickets at most travel agencies, but it is better to buy them at the harbour, where you can check out the boats, and bargain. Look for shade and the size and condition of the boat, as these vary greatly. You can buy an open return if you want to stay on Symi.

Getting Around

To/From the Airport Each day 21 buses travel between the airport and Rhodes City's west side bus station (400 dr). The first leaves Rhodes City at 6 am and the last at 11 pm; from the airport, the first leaves at 5.55 am and the last at 11.45 pm.

Bus Rhodes City has two bus stations. From the east side bus station on Plateia Rimini there are 18 buses daily to Faliraki (400 dr), 10 to Lindos (1000 dr), eight to Kolymbia (600 dr), five to Genadi (1200 dr) via Lardos, and three to Psinthos (500 dr).

From the west side station next to the New Market there are 16 buses daily to Kalithea Thermi (400 dr), 11 to Koskinou (400 dr), five to Salakos (800 dr), and one to ancient Kamiros (1000 dr), Monolithos (1400 dr) via Skala Kamiros, and Embonas (1150 dr). The EOT and municipal tourist office give out schedules.

Car & Motorcycle There are numerous car and motorcycle rental outlets in Rhodes City's new town. Shop around and bargain because the competition is fierce.

Taxi Rhodes City's main taxi rank is east of Plateia Rimini. There are two zones on the island for taxi meters: zone one is Rhodes City and zone two (slightly higher) is everywhere else. Rates are a little higher between midnight and 6 am. Sample fares are: the airport (2500 dr), Filerimos (2200 dr), Petaloudes (4000 dr), ancient Kamiros (5500 dr), Lindos (7000 dr) and Monolithos (9000 dr). Taxi company phone numbers include ☎ 64 712, 64 734 and 64 778.

Rip-offs are rare but if you think you have been ripped off take the taxi number and go to the tourist police.

Bicycle The Bicycle Centre (☎ 28 315), Griva 39, Rhodes City, has three-speed bikes for 800 dr and mountain bikes for 1200 dr.

Excursion Boat There are excursion boats to Lindos (4000 dr return) every day in summer, leaving Mandraki Harbour at 9 am and returning at 6 pm. You might like to buy a one way ticket and return by bus or taxi.

RHODES CITY
☎ 0241 • postcode 851 00   • pop 43,500
The heart of Rhodes City is the old town, enclosed within massive walls. Avoid the worst of the tourist hordes by beginning your exploration early in the morning. But at any time of the day, away from the main thoroughfares and squares, you will find many deserted labyrinthine alleyways. Much of the new town to the north is a monument to package tourism, but it does have several places of interest to visitors.

Orientation
The old town is a mesh of Byzantine, Turkish and Latin architecture with quiet, twisting alleyways punctuated by lively squares. Sokratous, which runs east to west, and its easterly continuation Aristotelous, are the old town's bustling main commercial thoroughfares. The old town's two main squares are also along here: Plateia Martyron Evreon, with an attractive fountain, at the eastern end of Aristotelous; and Plateia Hippocrates, with the distinctive Castellania fountain, at the eastern end of Sokratous. Acquainting yourself with these two

squares will help with orientation, but getting lost is almost inevitable and part of the fun of exploring the place. Farther north, parallel to Sokratous, is Ippoton (Avenue of the Knights), which was the main medieval thoroughfare.

The commercial harbour, for international ferries and large inter-island ferries, is east of the old town. Excursion boats, small ferries, hydrofoils and private yachts use Mandraki Harbour, farther north. When you buy a ticket check where the ferry is leaving from.

In Mandraki, two bronze deer on stone pillars mark the supposed site of the Colossus of Rhodes. Mandraki's grandiose public buildings are relics of Mussolini's era. The main square of the new town is Plateia Rimini, just north of the old town. The tourist offices, bus stations and main taxi rank are on or near this square.

Most of the old town is off limits to motorists, but there are car parks on the periphery.

Information
Tourist Offices The EOT (☎ 23 255/655, fax 26 955, email eot~rodos@otenet.gr), on the corner of Makariou and Papagou, supplies brochures and maps of the city, and will help in finding accommodation. Opening times are 7.30 am to 3 pm Monday to Friday. In summer the same service is provided by Rhodes' municipal tourist office (☎ 35 945), Plateia Rimini. Opening times are 8 am to 8 pm Monday to Saturday and 8 am to noon on Sunday; closed in winter.

From either of these you can pick up the *Rodos News*, a free English-language newspaper.

The tourist police (☎ 27 423) are next door to the EOT and are open 24 hours daily.

Money The main National Bank of Greece and the Alpha Credit Bank are on Plateia Kyprou. In the old town there is a National Bank of Greece on Plateia Moussiou, and a Commercial Bank of Greece nearby. All have ATMs. Opening times are 8 am to 2 pm Monday to Thursday, 8 am to 1.30 pm Friday.

American Express (☎ 21 010) is represented by Rhodos Tours, Ammohostou 18.

Post & Communications The main post office is on Mandraki. Opening times are 7.30 am to 8 pm Monday to Friday. The old town sub post office is open seven days. The OTE at Amerikis 91 is open 7 am to 11 pm daily.

Rhodes has two Internet cafes: Rock Style, Dimokratias 7, just south of the old town, and Mango Cafe Bar, Plateia Dorieos 3, in the old town.

Bookshops Kostas Tomaras Bookstore, Venizelou Sofi 5, stocks some English-language books including Lonely Planet guides. Second Story Books, Amarantou 24, has a wide selection of second-hand foreign-language books.

Laundry Rhodes has two self-service laundrettes: Lavomatique, 28 Oktovriou 32, and Express Servis, Dilberaki 97 (off Orfanidou). Both charge around 1400 dr a load. Express Laundry, Kosta Palama 5, does service washes for 1000 dr.

Luggage Storage You can store luggage at Planet Holidays (☎ 35 722), Galias 6, for 500 dr for two hours and 1200 dr for up to two days. You can negotiate a price for a longer period.

Emergency Rhodes' general hospital (☎ 25 580) is at Papalouka, just north-west of the old town. For emergency first aid and the ambulance service, call ☎ 25 555 or ☎ 22 222.

Old Town
The town is divided into two parts. In medieval times, the Knights of St John lived in the Knights' Quarter and the other inhabitants lived in the Hora. The 12m-thick city walls are closed to the public, but at 2.45 pm on Tuesday and Saturday you can take a guided walk along them starting at the courtyard of the Palace of the Grand Masters (1200 dr).

Knights' Quarter An appropriate place to begin an exploration of the old town is the imposing cobblestone **Avenue of the Knights** (Ippoton), where the knights lived. The knights were divided into seven 'tongues' or languages, according to their place of origin – England, France, Germany, Italy, Aragon, Auvergne and Provence – each responsible for protecting a section of the bastion. The Grand Master, who was in charge, lived in the palace, and each tongue was under the auspices of a

---

The Knights of St John

The Knights of St John were a religious order of the church of Rome founded in Amalfi in the 11th century. They went to Jerusalem initially to minister to the pilgrims who arrived there, but soon extended their duties to tending the poor and sick of the Holy Land. Over the years they became increasingly militant, joining forces with the Knights Templars and the Teutonic Knights of St Mary in battles against infidels.

The Knights of St John were expelled from the Holy Land with the fall of Jerusalem. They went first to Cyprus and then, in 1309, to Rhodes. Through some wheeling and dealing with the island's ruling Genoese admiral, Viguolo de Viguoli, they became the possessors of Rhodes, transforming it into a mighty bulwark that stood at the easternmost point of the Christian west, safeguarding it from the Muslim infidels of the east. The knights withstood Muslim offensives in 1444 and 1480, but in 1522 Sultan Süleyman the Magnificent staged a massive attack with 200,000 troops. After a long siege the 600 knights, with 1000 mercenaries and 6000 Rhodians, surrendered – hunger, disease and death having taken their toll.

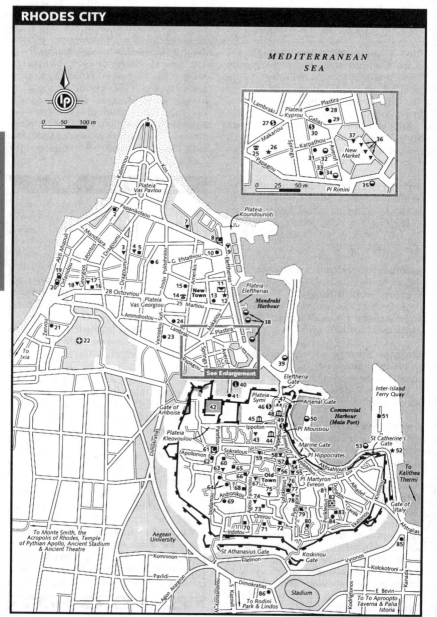

RHODES CITY

DODECANESE

MEDITERRANEAN SEA

0   50   100 m

Plateia Vas Pavlou

Plateia Koundourioti

Plateia Eleftherias

Mandraki Harbour

New Town

Plateia Vas Georgiou

25 Martiou

28 Octovriou

Plateia Vas Pavlou

To Ixia

See Enlargement

Eleftheria Gate

Plateia Symi

Arsenal Gate

Ippoton

Plateia Kleovoulou

Apollonion

Sokratous

Pl Hippocrates

Marine Gate

Commercial Harbour (Main Port)

Inter-Island Ferry Quay

Pl Moussiou

St Catherine's Gate

Pl Martyron Evreon

Old Town

Gate of Amboise

Gate of Italy

To Kalithea Thermi

To Monte Smith, the Acropolis of Rhodes, Temple of Pythian Apollo, Ancient Stadium & Ancient Theatre

Aegean University

St Athanasius Gate

Koskinou Gate

Komninon

Filelinon

Vyronos

Kolokotroni

Pavlidi

Dimokratias

Stadium

E Bevin

Kanada

To Rodini Park & Lindos

To To Aproopto Taverna & Palia Istoria

New Market

Plateia Kyprou

Lambraki

Plastira

Makariou

Spring

Galias

Avrof

Karpathou

Papagou

Pl Rimini

0   25   50 m

Aegean

RHODES CITY

DODECANESE

bailiff. The knights were divided into soldiers, chaplains and ministers to the sick.

To this day the street exudes a noble and forbidding aura, despite modern offices now occupying most of the inns. Its lofty buildings stretch in a 600m-long unbroken wall of honey-coloured stone blocks, and its flat facade is punctuated by huge doorways and arched windows. The inns reflect the Gothic styles of architecture of the knights' countries of origin. They form a harmonious whole in their bastion-like structure, but on closer inspection each possesses graceful and individual embellishments.

First on the right, at the eastern end of the Avenue of the Knights, is the **Inn of the Order of the Tongue of Italy** (1519); next to it is the **Palace of Villiers de l'Île Adam**. After Sultan Süleyman had taken the city, it was Villiers de l'Île who had the humiliating task of arranging the knights' departure from the island. Next along is the **Inn of France**, the most ornate and distinctive of all the inns. On the opposite side of the street is a wrought-iron gate in front of a Turkish garden.

Back on the right side is the **Chapelle Française** (Chapel of the Tongue of France), embellished with a statue of the Virgin and Child. Next door is the residence of the Chaplain of the Tongue of France. Across the alleyway is the **Inn of Provence**, with four coats of arms forming the shape of a cross, and opposite is the **Inn of Spain**.

On the right is the magnificent 14th century **Palace of the Grand Masters** (☎ 23 359). It was destroyed in the gunpowder explosion of 1856 and the Italians rebuilt it in a grandiose manner, with a lavish interior, intending it as a holiday home for Mussolini and King Emmanuel III. It is now a museum, containing sculpture, mosaics taken from Kos by the Italians, and antique furniture. The palace is open 8.30 am to 3 pm Tuesday to Sunday, and admission is 1200 dr.

The **archaeological museum** (☎ 27 657), Plateia Moussiou, is housed in the 15th century knights' hospital. Its most famous exhibit is the exquisite Parian marble statuette, the *Aphrodite of Rhodes*, a 1st century BC adaptation of a Hellenistic statue.

Less charming, to most people, is the 4th century BC *Aphrodite of Thalassia* in the next room. However, writer Lawrence Durrell was so enamoured of this statue that he named his book *Reflections on a Marine Venus* after it. Also in this room is the 2nd century BC marble *Head of Helios*, found near the Palace of the Grand Masters where a Temple of Helios once stood. The museum is open 8.30 am to 3 pm Tuesday to Sunday. Admission is 800 dr.

Across the square is the 11th century Church of the Virgin of the Castle. It was enlarged by the knights and became their cathedral. It is now the **Byzantine Museum**, with Christian artworks. It is open 8.30 am to 3 pm Tuesday to Sunday. Admission is 500 dr.

Farther north, on the opposite side, the **Museum of the Decorative Arts** houses a collection of artefacts from around the Dodecanese. Opening times are 8.30 am to 3 pm Tuesday to Sunday. Admission is 600 dr.

On Plateia Simi, there are the remains of a 3rd century BC **Temple of**

Aphrodite, one of the few ancient ruins in the old town.

Hora The Hora has many Ottoman legacies. During Turkish times, churches were converted to mosques, and many more were built from scratch. Most are now dilapidated. The most important one is the newly renovated, pink-domed **Mosque of Süleyman**, at the top of Sokratous. It was built in

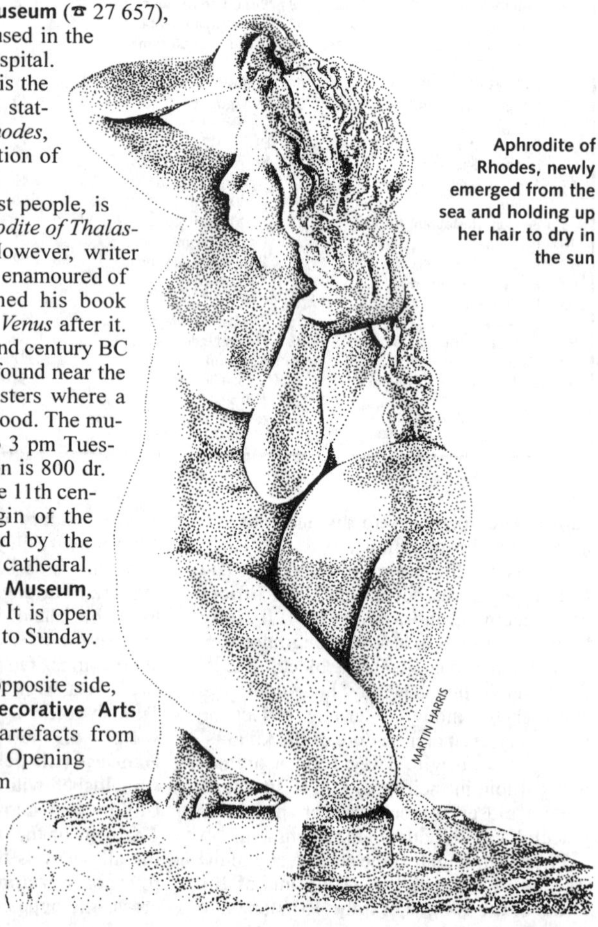

Aphrodite of Rhodes, newly emerged from the sea and holding up her hair to dry in the sun

MARTIN HARRIS

DODECANESE

1522 to commemorate the Ottoman victory against the knights, then rebuilt in 1808.

Opposite is the 18th century **Turkish library** where many Islamic manuscripts are kept. It is sometimes open to the public – check the times on the notice outside.

The 18th century **Turkish bath**, on Plateia Arionos, offers a rare opportunity to have a Turkish bath in Greece. It is open 1 pm to 7 pm Tuesday, 11 am to 7 pm on Wednesday, Thursday and Friday and 8 am to 6 pm Saturday. Entry is 500 dr.

The **synagogue** on Dosiadou has a commemorative plaque to the many members of Hora's large Jewish population who were sent to Auschwitz during the Nazi occupation. Jews still worship here and it is usually open in the morning. Close by is Plateia Martyron Evreon (Square of the Jewish Martyrs).

New Town

The **Acropolis of Rhodes**, south-west of the old town on Monte Smith, was the site of the ancient Hellenistic city of Rhodes. The hill is named after the English admiral Sir Sydney Smith, who watched for Napoleon's fleet from here in 1802. It has superb views.

The site's restored 2nd century **stadium** once staged competitions in preparation for the Olympic Games. The adjacent **theatre** is a reconstruction of one used for lectures by the Rhodes School of Rhetoric. Steps above here lead to the **Temple of Pythian Apollo**, with four re-erected columns. The unenclosed site can be reached on city bus No 5.

North of Mandraki, at the eastern end of G Papanikolaou, is the graceful **Mosque of Murad Reis**. In its grounds are a Turkish cemetery and the Villa Cleobolus, where Lawrence Durrell lived in the 1940s, writing *Reflections on a Marine Venus*.

The **aquarium** is housed in a red and cream Italianate building at the island's northernmost point. Opening times are 9 am to 9 pm daily. Admission is 600 dr.

The town **beach** begins north of Mandraki and continues around the island's northernmost point and down the west side of the new town. The best spot is on the northernmost point, where it's not quite as crowded.

Rodini Park, 3km south of the town, is a pleasant shady park with deer and peacocks. It's believed to have been the site of the School of Rhetoric. City bus No 3 goes there.

Activities

Scuba Diving Two diving schools operate out of Mandraki: the Waterhoppers Diving Centre (☎/fax 38 146), Perikleous 29, and Dive Med Centre (☎ 33 654). Both offer a range of courses including a One Day Try Dive for 13,500 dr. You can get information from the Waterhoppers boat MV *Kouros*, and Dive Med Centre's boats *Pheonix* and *Free Spirit* at Mandraki. Kalithea Thermi is the only site around Rhodes where diving is permitted.

Yachting You can hire yachts at the YAR Maritime Centre (☎ 22 927, fax 23 393), Vyronos 1. For more yachting information, contact the Rodos Yacht Club (☎ 23 287).

Windsurfing Pro Horizon (☎ 95 819), just west of town at Ialysos Beach, Ixia, rents boards. There are many other rental outlets around the coast. The Fun & Action Windsurfing School at Faliraki offers expert tuition.

Tennis Many of the large hotels have tennis courts open to nonguests. Rhodes Tennis Club (☎ 25 705) is on the waterfront north of Mandraki.

Greek Dancing Lessons The Nelly Dimoglou Dance Company (☎ 20 157, 29 085), at the Folk Dance Theatre on Andronikou, gives lessons.

Organised Tours

Triton Holidays (☎ 21 690, fax 31 625), Plastira 9, Mandraki, has a wide range of tours, and provides specialist advice on any of the islands and Turkey.

Places to Stay – Budget

The old town of Rhodes has lots of cheap accommodation. The unofficial *Rodos Youth Hostel (☎ 30 491, Ergiou 12)* charges

1500 dr per person. There is a kitchen for self-caterers. The more comfortable *Mike and Mama's Pension* (☎ 25 359, Menekleous 28) has singles/doubles/triples for 4000/5000/6000 dr. At *Mango Rooms* (☎/fax 24 877, Plateia Dorieos 3) clean, nicely furnished rooms with bathroom and refrigerator go for 7000/11,000/13,000 dr.

Hotel Via Via (☎ 27 895, Lisipou 2), just off Pythagora, has pristine, tastefully furnished doubles/triples for 7000/9500 dr, or with bathroom for 11,000/11,600 dr.

Pension Minos (☎ 31 813, Omirou 5) has spotless, spacious rooms for 8000/ 10,000 dr and a roof garden with views of the old town.

The exceptionally friendly *Pension Andreas* (☎ 34 156, fax 74 285, email andrea sch@otenet.gr, Omirou 28D) has clean, pleasant doubles for 8000 dr, triples with bathroom for 12,000 dr, and a terrace bar with terrific views. *Kamiros Rooms to Let* (☎ 33 545, Tavriscou 27 and Ikarou 26) is a characterful place (in two separate buildings) with immaculate doubles/triples for 9000/11,000 dr with bathrooms.

Maria's Rooms (☎ 20 730, Menekleous 147), just off Sokratous, has nicely furnished doubles for 8000/9000 dr with shared/private bathroom. *Hotel Spot* (☎ 34 737, Perikleous 21) has exceptionally clean, pleasant singles/doubles/triples for 9000/ 11,000/12,000 dr with bathroom. This long-established hotel was run until recently by a charming elderly couple. It is now run by their English-speaking son who plans to renovate. *Pink Elephant* (☎/fax 22 469, Irodotou 42) has doubles with bathroom for 9000 dr, doubles/triples for 7000/9000 dr without. Despite the name, the hotel's attractive decor is blue and white.

Pension Olympos (☎/fax 33 567), on Agiou Fanouriou, has pleasant singles/doubles for 8000/14,000 dr with bathroom and television. It has an attractive little courtyard.

Most of the new town's hotels are modern and characterless, but there are some exceptions. *Hotel Anastasia* (☎ 21 815, 28 Octovriou 46), in a former Italian mansion, is set back from the road, and is reasonably quiet.

The high-ceilinged rooms, with tiled floors, are spotless; singles/doubles are 7000/ 13,000 dr with breakfast. The hotel has a lovely, shady, flower and tree-filled garden – home to two large tortoises and five cats. The English-speaking owners enjoy helping guests to plan their itineraries.

New Village Inn (☎ 34 937, Konstantopedos 10) has tastefully furnished rooms with refrigerator and fan, and a traditional stone-walled courtyard, festooned with plants. Singles/doubles/triples cost 6000/ 10,000/12,000 dr. The Greek-American owned inn is on a quiet street.

Places to Stay – Top End
The pricey *Grand Hotel Astir Palace* (☎ 26 284) on Akti Miaouli has a bar, restaurant and swimming pools. Singles/doubles are 25,000/ 35,300 dr, and suites are 62,000 dr.

At Ixis, the A class *Cosmopolitan Hotel* (☎ 35 373) has singles/doubles/triples for 15,500/25,000/34,375 dr.

The deluxe *Rodos Palace* (☎ 25 222, fax 25 350), also at Ixia, is a vast place with loads of amenities. Singles/doubles cost 32,250/44,150 dr.

You can get discounts of up to 30% on the more expensive hotels if you book through Triton Holidays (see Organised Tours).

Places to Eat – Budget
Enthusiastic touting and displays of tacky photographs of food seem to be the order of the day at many restaurants in Rhodes, with the enthusiasm of the touts not reflected in the quality of the food. But if you hunt around you will find good-value places.

Fisherman's Ouzeria on Sofokleous is one of the best-value seafood places around. A huge plateful of *gavros* (small fish) is only 1200 dr. *Taverna Kostas* (Pythagora 62) is also good value with souvlaki for 1800 dr and swordfish for 2500 dr.

The unpretentious, low-priced *Neohora Psistaria*, on the corner of Kathopouli and Kazouli in the new town, features tender grilled liver among its well prepared dishes.

Thomas & Charlotte's Taverna, on Georgios Leontos, serves a selection of

PATRICK HORTON

Icon decorated church interior, Lindos, Rhodes, Dodecanese

D I HALL

Old Town, Rhodes, Dodecanese

JEANNE OLIVER

Elafonisi Beach at the southern extremity of Crete's west coast.

DIANA MAYFIELD

Byzantine church, Crete

JON DAVISON

Rethymno's delightful old Venetian harbour, Crete

Rhodes, Dodecanese

Lycian tomb, Kastellorizo, Dodecanese

Lively Plateia Ippokratus, Old Town, Rhodes

The superb, sandy Gadeu Beach near Lefkos, Karpathos, Dodecanese

Greek and Scandinavian dishes. One tasty dish is *Kleftiko* ('the thieves' dish'), which was originally prepared by *klepht* sheep thieves who skinned their prey, wrapped the meat in the skins with herbs and vegetables, buried it and lit fires above, so hiding all evidence of their crime. The meat, over a couple of days, cooked into a very tasty meal. Thomas' version is served wrapped in greaseproof paper.

Ipiros is the best of the *psistarias* in the New Market. A huge helping of succulent spit-roast lamb, Greek salad and soft drink costs 3000 dr.

To Aproopto Taverna (Kanada 95), half an hour's walk from the old town, serves well prepared, generous portions of ready-made food and grills. The chickpea patties are a delicious starter.

Back in the old town, *Diafani Garden Restaurant*, opposite the Turkish bath, serves gratifying, reasonably priced dishes, 'cooked from the heart', as the German owner says. The atmospheric *Paradosiako Kafeneio Araliki (Aristofanois 45)* serves creative dishes which reflect its Italian ownership.

Entos Ton Teeohon (Lahitos 13) is a welcome antidote to Rhodes' tacky tourist restaurants. 'Tourists are welcome here, but we do nothing to attract them' says the owner. Nothing, that is, except serve some of the most imaginative and reasonably priced dishes in town. They include chicken stuffed with cheese, cuttlefish stuffed with feta and spicy pork.

If you crave something other than Greek food, *Le Bistrot de L'Auberge (Praxitelous 21)* serves terrific French dishes, while the Italian chef at *Pizza da Spillo (Apellou 41)* conjures up a variety of mouthwatering pizzas. In the new town, *India Restaurant (☎ 38 395, Konstantopedos 16)* has a fantastic selection of Indian food. It's directly opposite the Kringlans Swedish Bakery on I Dragoumi.

If your feet are killing you after hours of walking the old town's pebbled thoroughfares, two pleasant options for a break are *Petite Cafe (Evripidou 13-15)*, near the Castellania fountain, with a tranquil walled garden, and *Walk-in Beer Garden*, just off Plateia Dhorias. Both serve coffee and snacks. For the best Greek coffee in town and a game of backgammon or chess, head for the fantastically funky old *cafe (Sokratous 76)*.

In the new town, *Kringlans Swedish Bakery (I Dragoumi 14)* serves sandwiches and pastries that are out of this world.

If you're self-catering, there is a small *supermarket* on Evripidou. There are many supermarkets in the new town, and fruit and vegetable stalls in the New Market.

Places to Eat – Mid-Range & Top End

Alexis Restaurant, on Sokratous, is a first-rate seafood restaurant. *Belgium Restaurant Rhobel (George Leontos 13-15)* specialises in steaks but, for something a bit different, the 'rabbit cooked in the traditional way' (with dried fruit) is commendable. *Restaurant Ellinikon (Papanikolaou 6)* excels in traditional Greek fare. The *stifado* is highly recommended, but leave room for the luscious iced caramel, which often features as dessert of the day. Three-course meals with wine at these places will cost around 9000 dr.

Cleo's Italian Restaurant (Agiou Fanouriou 17) is a sophisticated place with a cool, elegant interior and a quiet courtyard. Set menus cost around 4000 dr.

Feverish touting reaches its acme at the people-watching patisseries bordering the New Market. Nevertheless, they're convivial meeting places. Coffee and cake costs around 2000 dr.

Palia Istoria (☎ 32 421, 108 Mitropoleos), south of the old town, is popular with well heeled locals. Its large, imaginative menu includes delicious and unusual *mezedes* such as scallops with mushrooms, and artichokes in nutmeg sauce. Expect to pay 10,000 dr to 12,000 dr for a meal with wine. Reservations are recommended.

Entertainment

The *son et lumière (☎ 21 922)*, staged in the grounds of the Palace of the Grand Masters, depicts the Turkish siege of Rhodes and is

DODECANESE

superior to most such efforts. The entrance is on Plateia Rimini and admission is 1200 dr. A noticeboard outside gives the times for performances.

The Nelly Dimoglou Dance Company gives first-rate performances at the *Folk Dance Theatre* (☎ 29 085, 20 157) on Andronikou. Performances are nightly except Saturday from May to October and begin at 9.20 pm. Admission is 3500 dr. There are classical music recitals at the *National Theatre* (☎ 29 678).

Kafe Besara (*Sofokleous 11-12*) is Aussie owned, and one of the old town's liveliest bars. Live music is played three evenings a week. *Mango Cafe Bar* (*Dorieos 3*) claims to have the cheapest drinks in the old town as well as Internet access.

The new town has a plethora of discos and bars – over 600 at last count and rising. The two main areas are called Top Street and the Street of Bars. Top Street is Alexandrou Diakou and the Street of Bars is Orfanidou, where a cacophony of western music blares from every establishment. For a wild night of dancing on the bar top, make for *Down Under Bar* (*Orfanidou 35*). If you prefer somewhere more subdued, try *Red Lion* (*Orfanidou 9*), with the relaxed atmosphere of a British pub. Proprietors Ron and Vasilis will gladly answer questions about Rhodes for the price of a drink.

The most amazing of the theme music bars is *Blue Lagoon* (*25 Martiou 2*), where you can indulge your tropical island fantasies amid a shipwreck and lagoon, watched over by a live parrot, three turtles and a waxwork pirate who must have escaped from the adjoining *Dracula's Palace* – Rhodes' answer to Madame Tussaud's Chamber of Horrors. Above the bar is *Mega Club Gas Disco*.

For live rock and roll, try *Sticky Fingers* (*Zervou 6*).

Shopping

Good buys in Rhodes' old town are gold and silver jewellery, leather goods and ceramics. However, leather goods are cheaper in Turkey. Look around and be discriminating – it's quite acceptable to haggle.

Getting Around

Local buses leave from Mandraki. Bus No 2 goes to Analipsi, No 3 to Rodini, No 4 to Agios Dimitrios and No 5 to Monte Smith. You can buy tickets at the kiosk on Mandraki.

EASTERN RHODES

Rhodes' best beaches are on the east coast. There are frequent buses as far as Lindos, but some of the beaches are a bit of a trek from the road. With a bit of leg work, it's possible to find uncrowded stretches of coast even in high season.

Kalithea Thermi, 10km from Rhodes City, is a derelict Italian-built spa. Within the complex are crumbling colonnades, domed ceilings and mosaic floors. Buses from Rhodes City stop opposite the turn-off to the spa. The small beach is used by Rhodes' diving schools (see Activities in the Rhodes City section). To the right there's a small sandy beach (with a snack bar); take the track which veers right from the turn-off to the spa. Kalithea is currently being restored.

Faliraki Beach, 5km farther south, is the island's premier resort and comes complete with high-rise hotels, fast-food joints and bars. Although the main stretch of beach is crowded, the bay at the extreme southern end is uncrowded and popular with nude bathers.

Most accommodation is monopolised by package tour companies, but a pleasant option for independent travellers is the Greek-American owned *Cannon Bar Pension* (☎ 0241-85 596) where doubles/triples with bathrooms cost 9000/10,000 dr. *Falaraki Camping* (☎ 0241-85 358) has a restaurant, bar, minimarket and swimming pool. The bus stop is close to the beach.

Afantou, 6km farther on, has a long pebble beach and is the home of the island's only 18 hole golf course (☎ 0241-51 256, 51 451).

At Kolymbia, 4km south of Afantou, a right turn leads in over 4km of pine-fringed road to the **Epta Piges** (Seven Springs), a beautiful spot where a lake fed by springs can be reached either along a path or through a tunnel. There are no buses here, so take a Lindos bus and get off at the turnoff. With your own transport you can continue another 9km to **Eleousa** on the slopes of Profitis Ilias, and then another 3km to the **Church of Agios Nikolaos Fountouklis,** which has fine Byzantine frescoes.

Back on the coast, **Kolymbia** and **Tsambikas** are good but crowded beaches. A steep road (signposted) leads in 1.5km to **Moni Tsambikas**, from where there are terrific views. It is a place of pilgrimage for childless women. On 18 September, the monastery's festival day, they climb up to it on their knees and pray to conceive.

Arhangelos, 4km farther on and inland, is a large agricultural village with a tradition of carpet weaving and handmade goatskin boots production, both of which are being overtaken by tourism as the major money-earner. Just before Arhangelos there is a turn-off to **Stegna Beach**, and just after to the lovely sandy cove of **Agathi**; both are reasonably quiet. The **Castle of Faraklos** above Agathi was a prison for recalcitrant knights and the island's last stronghold to fall to the Turks. The fishing port of **Haraki**, just south of the castle, has a pebbled beach. There are more beaches between here and Vlyha Bay, 2km from Lindos.

Lindos Λίνδος
☎ 0244 • postcode 851 07 • pop 900

Lindos village, 47km from Rhodes, lies below the Acropolis and is a showpiece of dazzling-white 17th century houses, many with courtyards with black and white *hohlakia* (pebble mosaics) floors. Once the dwellings of wealthy admirals, many have been bought and restored by foreign celebrities. The main thoroughfares are lined with tourist shops and cafes, so you need to explore the labyrinthine alleyways to fully appreciate the place.

The 15th century **Church of Agia Panagia** on Acropolis is festooned with 18th century frescoes.

Orientation & Information The town is pedestrianised. All vehicular traffic terminates on the central square of Plateia Eleftherias, from where the main drag, Acropolis, begins. The donkey terminus is a little way along here.

The municipal tourist information office (☎ 31 900/288/227) is on Plateia Eleftherias, open 7.30 am to 10 pm daily. Pallas Travel (☎ 31 494, fax 31 595) and Lindos Sun Tours (☎ 31 333), both on Acropolis, have room-letting services. The latter also rents cars and motorcycles.

The Commercial Bank of Greece, with ATM, is by the donkey terminus. The National Bank of Greece is on the street opposite the Church of Agia Panagia. Turn right at the donkey terminus for the post office. There is no OTE, but there are cardphones on Plateia Eleftherias and the Acropolis. Lindos' Internet cafe is near the post office.

The privately owned Lindos Lending Library, on Acropolis, is well stocked with English books. It also has a laundrette (2500 dr per load).

The Acropolis of Lindos Lindos is the most famous of the Dodecanese's ancient cities, receiving 500,000 visitors a year. It was an important Doric settlement because of its excellent vantage point and good harbour. It was first established around 2000 BC and is overlaid with a conglomeration of Byzantine, Frankish and Turkish remains.

After the founding of the city of Rhodes, Lindos declined in commercial importance, but remained an important place of worship. The ubiquitous St Paul landed here en route to Rome. The Byzantine fortress was strengthened by the knights, and also used by the Turks.

The Acropolis of Lindos is spectacularly perched atop a 116m-high rock. It's about a 10 minute climb to the well signposted entrance gate. Once inside, a flight of steps leads to a large square. On the left (facing the next flight of steps) is a trireme (warship) hewn out of the rock by the sculptor Pythocretes. A statue of Hagesandros, priest of Poseidon, originally stood on the deck of the ship. At the top of the steps ahead, you enter the acropolis by a vaulted corridor. At the other end, turn sharp left through an enclosed room to reach a row of storerooms on the right. The stairway on the right leads to the remains of a 20-columned **Hellenistic stoa** (200 BC). The Byzantine **Church of Agios Ioannis** is to the right of this stairway. The wide stairway behind the stoa leads to a 5th century BC propylaeum, beyond which is the 4th century **Temple to Athena**, the site's most important ancient ruin. Athena was worshipped on Lindos as early as the 10th century BC, so this temple has replaced earlier ones on the site. From its far side there are splendid views of Lindos village and its beach.

Donkey rides to the acropolis cost 1200 dr one way. The site is open 8 am to 6.30 pm Tuesday to Sunday and 12.30 pm to 6.30 pm Monday. Admission is 1200 dr.

Places to Stay & Eat Accommodation is expensive and reservations are essential in summer.

Fedra Rooms to Rent (☎ 31 286), along the street opposite the Church of Agia Panagia, has doubles/triples for 8000/10,000 dr with bathroom.

Pension Electra (☎ 31 266) has a roof terrace with superb views and a beautiful shady garden; doubles with shared bathroom cost 9000 dr, and double/triple studios cost 14,000/16,000 dr. *Pension Katholiki (☎ 31 445)*, next door, has doubles with shared bathroom for 10,000 dr. To get there, follow the signs to the Acropolis but don't turn right at Restaurant Aphrodite – carry on towards the beach.

WESTERN RHODES

Western Rhodes is more green and forested than the east coast, but it's more exposed to winds so the sea tends to be rough, and the beaches are mostly of pebbles or stones. Nevertheless, tourist development is rampant, and consists of the suburb resorts of Ixia, Trianda and Kremasti. Paradisi, despite being next to the airport, has retained some of the feel of a traditional village. If you are on Rhodes between flights or have an early morning flight you may consider staying here. There are several *domatia* and restaurants.

Ialyssos Ιαλυσσός
Like Lindos, Ialyssos, 10km from Rhodes, is a hotchpotch of Doric, Byzantine and medieval remains. The Doric city was built on Filerimos Hill, which was an excellent vantage point, attracting successive invaders. The only ancient remains are the foundations of a 3rd century BC temple and a restored 4th century BC fountain. Also at the site are the restored **Monastery of Our Lady** and the **Chapel of Agios Georgios**.

The ruined fortress was used by Süleyman the Magnificent during his siege of Rhodes City. The site is open 8 am to 5 pm Tuesday to Sunday. Admission is 800 dr.

No buses go to ancient Ialyssos. The airport bus stops at Trianda, on the coast. Ialyssos is 5km inland from here.

Kamiros Κάμειρος
The extensive ruins of the Doric city of Kamiros stand on a hillside above the west coast, 34km from Rhodes City. The ancient city, known for its figs, oil and wine, reached the height of its powers in the 6th century BC. By the 4th century BC, it had been superseded by Rhodes. Most of the city was destroyed by earthquakes in 226 and 142 BC, but the layout is easily discernible.

From the entrance, walk straight ahead and down the steps. The semicircular rostrum on the right is where officials made speeches to the public. Opposite are the remains of a **Doric temple** with one standing column. The area next to it, with a row of intact columns, was probably where the public watched priests performing rites in the temple. Ascend the wide stairway to the ancient city's main street. Opposite the top of the stairs is one of the best preserved of the **Hellenistic houses** which lined the street. Walk along the street, ascend three flights of steps, and continue straight ahead to the ruins of the 3rd century **great stoa**, which had a 206m portico supported by two rows of Doric columns. It was built on top of a huge 6th century cistern which supplied the houses with rainwater through an advanced drainage system. Behind the stoa, at the city's highest point, stood the **Temple to Athena**, with terrific views inland.

The site is open 8 am to 5 pm Tuesday to Sunday. Admission is 800 dr. Buses from Rhodes City to Kamiros stop on the coast road, 1km from the site.

Kamiros to Monolithos Μονόλιθος
Skala Kamiros, 16km south of Kamiros, is touted as an 'authentic fishing village' so it's very much on the tour-bus circuit and only worth a visit to get a caïque to Halki (see the Halki section). The road south from here to Monolithos has some of the island's most impressive scenery. From Skala Kamiros the road winds uphill with great views across to Halki. This is just a taste of what's to come at the ruined 16th century **Castle of Kastellos,** reached along a rough road from the main road, 2km beyond Skala Kamiros. There is a left fork to Embonas (see The Interior, later in this section) 8km farther along. The main road continues for another 9km to **Siana**, a picturesque village below Mt Akramytis (825m), famed for its honey and *souma*, a local firewater.

The village of Monolithos, 5km beyond Siana, has the spectacularly sited **Castle of Monolithos** perched on a sheer 240m rock and reached along a dirt track. Continuing along this track, at the fork bear right for **Moni Georgiou** and left for the very pleasant shingled **Fourni Beach**.

Hotel Thomas (☎ 0246-61 291) at Monolithos has doubles for 10,000 dr.

SOUTHERN RHODES
South of Lindos, Rhodes becomes progressively less developed. Although **Pefki**, 2km south of Lindos, does get package tourists, it's still possible to get out of earshot of other tourists, away from the main beach.

Lardos is a pleasant village 6km west of Lindos and 2km inland from Lardos Beach.

From the far side of Lardos a turn right leads in 4km to **Moni Agia Ipseni** (Monastery of Our Lady) through hilly, green countryside.

The well watered village of **Laerma** is 12km north-west of Lardos. From here it's another 5km (signposted) to the beautifully sited 9th century **Moni Thari**, which was the island's first monastery and has recently been re-established as a monastic community. It contains some fine 13th century frescoes.

Asklipion, 8km north of Genadi, is an unspoilt village with the ruins of yet another castle and the 11th century **Church of Kimisis Theotokou**.

Genadi Γεννάδι
☎ 0244 • postcode 851 09 • pop 400
Genadi, 13km south of Lardos, is another burgeoning resort. Inland from the main street, however, it's an unspoilt agricultural village, with narrow, winding streets of whitewashed houses, an **olive press museum** and a stone fountain by a huge mulberry tree. At the crossroads turn left to reach the long pebble and sand beach, and right to reach the village. Genadi's main street is to the right (facing inland) of the central square.

Places to Stay & Eat *Tina's Studios (☎ 43 204)*, off the main street, has modern double studios for 10,000 dr. *Effie's Dreams Apartments (☎/fax 43 437, email dreams@srh.forthnet.gr)*, right by the mulberry tree, has modern, spotlessly clean studios with lovely rural and sea vistas from the communal balcony. Doubles/triples cost 9200/11,000 dr. The friendly Greek-Australian owners will meet you if you call ahead. The spacious *Betty Studios & Apartments (☎ 43 020)*, on the main street, has double/triple studios for 8600/10,000 dr and four-person apartments for 11,800 dr.

The nicest restaurant is *Restaurant Antonis* at the beach. The new *Effie's Dream Cafe Bar*, below the apartments, serves drinks and tasty snacks in a tranquil setting.

Greek Weddings

Greek weddings are lavish affairs and if you have ever been lucky enough to attend one and its ensuing lively wedding feast, you have indeed been privileged. While civil weddings in Greece have been legal for over fifteen years, most Greek couples still prefer the ritualistic ceremony of an orthodox church service followed by an afternoon and evening, or even weekend of eating, drinking and dancing.

The church ceremony is redolent of incense and ceremony. The participation of the bride and bridegroom is mainly passive since the main action is conducted by the priest and the *koumbaros* (best man) or *koumbara* (best woman) who literally 'crowns' the couple with a pair of interlinked garlands. The real excitement starts with the 'dance' during which the newly wed couple are led around in a circle by the priest while church participants shower them with rice.

After the ceremony it is customary for everyone in the church to line up and congratulate the couple, their family, the best man or woman and the bridesmaids with wishes such as *na zisete* (may you enjoy long life) to the couple and *na sas zisoun* (may they live for many years) to the parents. If the bridesmaids are single they are greeted with *kai sta dika sou* (your turn next).

Those invited to the wedding feast, which in rural areas often means the whole village, will retire to an evening of revelry and entertainment, part of which sees the bride and groom take the first dance and then literally get covered with money that is pinned to their clothes by guests. The party will often carry on all night and into the next day.

Genadi to Prasonisi Πρασονήσι
From Genadi an almost uninterrupted beach of pebbles, shingle and sand dunes extends down to **Plimmyri**, 11km south. It's easy to find deserted stretches.

From Plimmyri the main road continues to **Kattavia**, Rhodes' most southerly village. The 11km dirt road north to Messanagros winds through terrific scenery. From Kattavia a 10km road leads south to the remote **Prasonisi** (Green Island), the island's southernmost point, joined to Rhodes by a narrow sandy isthmus with rough sea on one side and calm water on the other. It's a popular spot for windsurfing. *The Lighthouse Taverna (☎ 0244-91 030)*, one of two tavernas on the access road, has double rooms for 10,000 dr. Many people simply pitch a tent on the surrounding land.

South of Monolithos
On the west coast the beaches south of Monolithos are prone to strong winds. From

Apolakkia, 10km south of Monolithos, a road crosses the island to Genadi, passing through the unspoilt villages of Arnitha, Istrios, Profilias and Vati. A turn-off to the left 7km south of Apolakkia leads to the 18th century **Moni Skiadi**. It's a serene place with terrific views down to the coast, and there is free basic accommodation for visitors.

The coast road beyond this turn-off is unsurfaced and runs close to the sea before veering inland for Kattavia.

THE INTERIOR
The east-west roads that cross the island have great scenery and very little traffic. If you have transport they're well worth exploring.

Petaloudes Πεταλούδες
Petaloudes (Valley of the Butterflies), one of the 'must sees' on the package tour itinerary, is reached along a 6km turn-off from the west coast road, 2.5km south of Paradisi.

The butterflies *(Callimorpha quadri-punctarea)* are lured to this gorge of rustic footbridges, streams and pools by the scent of the resin exuded by the styrax trees. Regardless of what you may see other tourists doing, do not make any noises to disturb the butterflies; their numbers are declining rapidly, largely due to noise disturbance. Petaloudes is open 8 am to 6 pm daily from 1 May to 30 September. Admission is 600 dr. There are buses to Petaloudes from Rhodes City.

Around Petaloudes
From Petaloudes a 2km dirt track leads to the 18th century **Moni Kalopetras** built by Alexander Ypsilantas, the grandfather of the Greek freedom-fighter. A small snack bar here sells soft drinks and *loukoumades*.

Also from Petaloudes, a 5km road leads to **Psinthos**, a pleasant village where *Artemidis Restaurant & Rooms (☎ 0246-51 735)* serves tasty traditional Greek fare and has a swimming pool. Double rooms above the restaurant cost 10,000 dr. Psinthos can also be reached from the east coast.

Salakos & Mt Profitis Ilias
Σάλακος & Ορος Προφήτης Ηλίας
Salakos is an attractive village below Mt Profitis Ilias (790m) reached along an 8km turn-off, 30km from Rhodes City along the west coast road. *Hotel Nimfi (☎ 0246-22 206/346)* has doubles for 10,000 dr.

From the village, a path leads almost to Mt Profitis Ilias' summit. Walk along the main road towards the mountains; at the curve, 60m beyond Hotel Nimfi, turn left, and after 50m take a path to the right signposted 'Profitis Ilias'. It ends near an asphalt road and the defunct Elafos Hotel. The *cafe* opposite is often open.

Beyond Salakos
The road forks 6km beyond Salakos. The left fork leads to Elafos Hotel from where a dirt road continues to the Byzantine **Church of Agios Nikolaos Fountouklis**, and Eleousa (see the Eastern Rhodes section).

The right fork leads to **Embonas** on the slopes of Mt Attavyros (1215m), the island's highest mountain. Embonas is, unfortunately, touted as a 'traditional mountain village' and visited by many tourist buses. It's also renowned for its wine and is surrounded by vineyards that produce the dry white 'Villare'. It costs around 1800 dr a bottle and is produced at the **Emery Winery** (☎ 0246-29 111), where you can enjoy free wine tasting on weekdays until 3 pm.

Agios Isidoros, 14km south of Embona, is a lovely unspoilt village to which you can detour en route to Siana.

Halki Χάλκη

☎ 0241 • postcode 851 10 • pop 281
Halki is a small island 16km off the west coast of Rhodes (refer to the map at the start of the Rhodes section). It has escaped the tourist development of its large neighbour; but much of the accommodation is monopolised by package tourists who want a holi-day on an untouristy island. It's a barren, rocky island with a severe water shortage. The population has been greatly reduced by emigration. Many islanders moved to Tarpon Springs, Florida, where they have established a sponge-fishing community.

Getting There & Away
Ferry Ferries call at Halki once weekly in summer on the Piraeus-Rhodes run.

Caïque A caïque operates between Halki and Skala Kamiros on Rhodes. From Monday to Saturday, it leaves Halki at 5.30 am (to connect with the 7.30 am bus from Skala Kamiros to Rhodes); the return trip departs Skala Kamiros at 2.30 pm. On Sunday, it leaves Halki at 9 am and Skala Kamiros at 4 pm. The fare is 2000 dr.

To get to Skala Kamiros from Rhodes City, take the 1.15 pm Monolithos bus from the west side bus station. There are no connecting buses on Sunday morning.

Getting Around
Halki has no cars, buses or taxis. There are excursion boats to the island's beaches and to the nearby uninhabited islet of Alimia which has good beaches.

EMBOREIOS Εμπορειός
Halki has only one settlement, the attractive little port town of Emboreios. Many of its imposing mansions are now derelict. The Church of Agios Nikolaos has the tallest belfry in the Dodecanese.

Orientation & Information
The quay is in the middle of the harbour. There is one road out of Emboreios, incongruously named Tarpon Springs Boulevard for the ex-Halkiots in Florida, who financed its construction. It passes Podamos, the island's only sandy beach.

There is a small tourist information kiosk between the post office (opposite the quay) and the war memorial. The staff will help you to find accommodation. There is no OTE, but there are cardphones.

Places to Stay & Eat
The nicest place to stay is *Captain's House* (☎ *45 201)*, a beautiful 19th century mansion with period furniture and a tranquil tree-shaded garden. It is owned by a retired Greek sea captain and his British wife, Christine. Doubles with bathroom are 10,000 dr. *Pension Cleanthi (☎ 45 334)*, on the road to Podamos Beach, has modern doubles with bathroom for 10,000 dr.

Several *tavernas* line the waterfront and there is a good taverna on Podamos Beach.

AROUND HALKI
Horio, a 30 minute walk along Tarpon Springs Boulevard from Emboreios, was the 'pirate-proof' inland town. Once a thriving community of 3000 people, it's now derelict and uninhabited. A path leads from Horio's churchyard to a Knights of St John castle.

Moni Agiou Ioanni is a two hour walk from Horio. There are no monks here now, but the shepherd-cum-caretaker, Dimitris, lives here with his family. Free beds are available for tourists, but you must take your own food and water. Take the right fork of Tarpon Springs Boulevard. There are fine views of many Dodecanese islands and Turkey.

Karpathos Κάρπαθος

☎ 0245   • postcode 857 00   • pop 5323
The elongated island of Karpathos (**kar**-pahthos), midway between Crete and Rhodes, is traversed by a north-south mountain range. For hundreds of years the north and south parts of the island were isolated from one another and so they developed independently. It is even thought that the northerners and southerners have different ethnic origins. The northern village of Olymbos is of endless fascination to ethnologists for the age-old customs of its inhabitants. Karpathos has rugged mountains, numerous beaches and unspoilt villages, and despite having charter flights from northern Europe, it has not, so far, succumbed to the worst excesses of mass tourism.

Karpathos has a relatively uneventful history. Unlike almost all other Dodecanese islands, it was never under the auspices of the Knights of St John. It is a wealthy island, receiving more money from emigrants living abroad (mostly in the USA) than any other Greek island.

A culinary speciality is *makarounes* (handmade macaroni cooked with onions and cheese).

Getting There & Away
Air There are three flights weekly to Athens (26,000 dr) and two daily to Rhodes (12,800 dr). The Olympic Airways office (☎ 22 150/057) is on the central square in Pigadia. The airport is 18km south-west of Pigadia.

Ferry Karpathos has two ports: Pigadia (Karpathos Port) and Diafani. At 3.45 pm on Wednesday the F/B *Daliana* arrives at Pigadia from Piraeus, Syros, Paros, Naxos, Ios, Santorini, Iraklio and Kassos, and then departs for Diafani and Rhodes. At 7.30 am

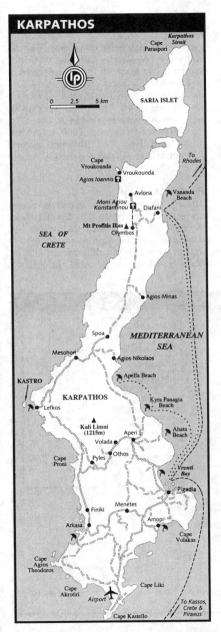

KARPATHOS

Cape Parospori

Karpathos Strait

0   2.5   5 km

SARIA ISLET

Cape Vroukounda

Vroukounda

Agios Ioannis

To Rhodes

Avlona

Vananda Beach

Moni Agiou Konstantinou

Diafani

Mt Profitis Ilias

Olymbos

SEA OF CRETE

Agios Minas

Spoa

MEDITERRANEAN SEA

Mesohori

Agios Nikolaos

KASTRO

Apella Beach

Lefkos

KARPATHOS

Kyra Panagia Beach

Kali Limni (1215m)

Aperi

Ahata Beach

Volada

Pyles

Othos

Cape Proni

Vronti Bay

Pigadia

Menetes

Finiki

Amopi

Arkasa

Cape Volakas

Cape Agios Theodoros

Cape Akrotiri

Airport

Cape Liki

To Kassos, Crete & Piraeus

Cape Kastello

on Wednesday it arrives back at Diafani from Rhodes, and takes the same route back to Piraeus.

At 2.10 pm on Saturday the F/B *Vitsentsos Kornaros* arrives at Pigadia from Piraeus, Milos, Crete and Kassos. From Pigadia it continues to Diafani, Halki and Rhodes. At 8.50 am on Sunday it leaves Pigadia for Piraeus via the same route.

Getting Around

To/From the Airport There was no airport bus at the time of research, but check with the Olympic Airways office.

Bus Pigadia is the transport hub of the island. A schedule is posted at the bus terminal. There are four buses daily to Amopi (300 dr), Pyles (380 dr) via Aperi (300 dr), Volada (300 dr) and Othos (300 dr); two daily to Finiki (380 dr) via Menetes (300 dr) and Arkasa (380 dr); and buses to Lefkos on Monday and Thursday. There is no bus between Pigadia and Olymbos or Diafani.

Car, Motorcycle & Bicycle Gatoulis Car Hire (☎ 22 747, fax 22 814), on the east side of the road to Aperi, hires cars, motorcycles and bicycles.

The 21km stretch of road from Spoa to Olymbos is unsurfaced but driveable. Check on its current condition with the tourist police before setting off, though, and make sure you know where the petrol stations are – they're few and far between.

Taxi Pigadia's taxi rank (☎ 22 705) is on Dimokratias, just around the corner from Apodimon Karpathou. A price list is supposed to be displayed. If this is not the case check the price with the tourist police or a travel agent, as rip-offs do occur. A taxi from Pigadia to Diafani is a steep 25,000 dr.

Excursion Boat In summer there are daily excursion boats from Pigadia to Diafani for 5000 dr return. There are also frequent boats to the beaches of Kyra Panagia and Apella for 3000 dr. Tickets can be bought from Karpathos Travel in Pigadia.

PIGADIA Πηγάδια
* **pop 1300**

Pigadia is the island's capital and main port. It's a modern town, pleasant enough, but without any eminent buildings or sites. The town is built on the edge of Vronti Bay, a 4km-long sandy beach where you can rent water sports equipment. On the beach are the remains of the early Christian basilica of Agia Fotini.

Orientation & Information

From the quay, turn right and take the left fork onto Apodimon Karpathou, Pigadia's main thoroughfare, which leads to the central square of Plateia 5 Oktovriou.

Pigadia has no EOT. The tourist police (☎ 22 218) are on Ethnikis Anastasis. Also on this street are the post office and OTE. The most helpful of the travel agencies is Karpathos Travel (☎ 22 148/754), on Dimo-

kratias; its guided walks around the island cost around 5000 dr.

The National Bank of Greece, with an ATM, is on Apodimon Karpathou. The bus station is one block up from the waterfront on Dimokratias. There's a laundrette, Laundro Express, on Mitr Apostolou. Carol's Corner Shop, on Apodimon Karpathou, sells new and second-hand books.

Caffe Galileo Internet 2000, on Apodimon Karpathou, has Internet access. Karpathos has several supermarkets and bakeries.

Places to Stay

There's plenty of accommodation and owners meet the boats. The E class *Hotel Avra* (☎ 23 468), on 28 Oktovriou, has comfortable doubles/triples for 6000/7000 dr, and doubles with bathroom for 8000 dr. *Harry's Rooms* (☎ 22 188), just off 28

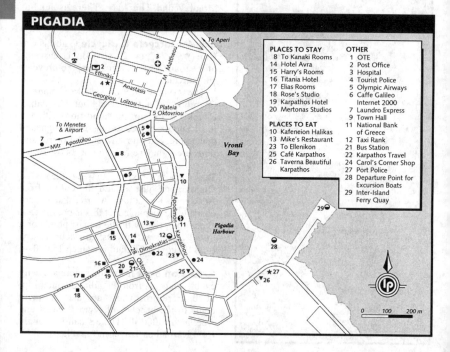

PIGADIA

To Aperi

PLACES TO STAY
8 To Kanaki Rooms
14 Hotel Avra
15 Harry's Rooms
16 Titania Hotel
17 Elias Rooms
18 Rose's Studio
19 Karpathos Hotel
20 Mertonas Studios

PLACES TO EAT
10 Kafeneion Halikas
13 Mike's Restaurant
23 To Ellenikon
25 Café Karpathos
26 Taverna Beautiful
      Karpathos

OTHER
1 OTE
2 Post Office
3 Hospital
4 Tourist Police
5 Olympic Airways
6 Caffe Galileo
      Internet 2000
7 Laundro Express
9 Town Hall
11 National Bank
      of Greece
12 Taxi Rank
21 Bus Station
22 Karpathos Travel
24 Carol's Corner Shop
27 Port Police
28 Departure Point for
      Excursion Boats
29 Inter-Island
      Ferry Quay

To Menetes & Airport

Mitr Apostolou

Vronti Bay

Pigadia Harbour

Ap. Dimokratias

Pigadia Harbour

0   100   200 m

DODECANESE

Oktovriou, has spotless singles/doubles for 3500/6000 dr. Farther along 28 Oktovriou, *To Kanaki Rooms* (☎ 22 908) has very pleasant doubles for 7000 dr with bathroom.

The immaculate, cosy *Elias Rooms* (☎ 22 446) is in a quiet part of town with great views. Singles/doubles/triples with bathroom are 4000/6000/8000 dr. The owner, Elias Hatzigorgiou, is friendly and helpful. Ascend the steps by the Karpathos Hotel to reach the rooms. Farther up the steps, *Rose's Studios* (☎/fax 22 284), has well kept double studios with bathroom and kitchen for 6000 dr. Doubles with large well equipped communal kitchen and bathrooms cost 4000 dr.

The C class *Karpathos Hotel* (☎ 22 347) has light, airy rooms for 6000/6500 dr with bathroom. Opposite, the C class *Titania Hotel* (☎ 22 144, fax 23 307) has spacious, pleasant rooms for 8000/10,000/13,000 dr. *Mertonas Studios* (☎ 22 622, 31 396) has lovely, tastefully furnished studios, managed by the warm and friendly Eva Angelos. Rates for doubles/triples are 8000/9000 dr, and four-person studios are 10,000 dr. Take the first left after Cafe Karpathos, turn right at the T-junction, take the first left, and the studios are on the right.

Places to Eat
Pigadia is well supplied with good restaurants. *Mike's Restaurant*, just off Apodimon Karpathou, is excellent. A meal of lamb stew, Greek salad and retsina costs 3000 dr.

The popular *Kafeneion Halikas* is open all day for drinks, but only serves meals in the evenings. The menu is limited but the food is tasty and live music is played. It's a crumbling white building, just beyond the National Bank of Greece.

Taverna Beautiful Karpathos, near the quay, serves a wide range of traditional Karpathian dishes and reputedly the best makarounes in Pigadia. *To Ellenikon*, on Apodimou Karpathou, has a pleasant outdoor terrace and a tasteful interior. The Karpathian *stifado* is particularly commendable.

Cafe Karpathos, at the beginning of Apodimou Karpathou, is a great place to meet locals, expats and tourists. If you speak Greek or Italian, Ilias, the owner, can fill you in on some interesting walks on the island. The cafe serves good coffee and tasty sandwiches.

SOUTHERN KARPATHOS
Amopi Αμόπι
The island's premier holiday resort, Amopi, is 8km from Pigadia. It's not especially attractive but has two bays of golden sand, translucent sea and pebbled coves. There are four buses daily from Pigadia.

Places to Stay & Eat Amopi is a scattered place without any centre or easily identifiable landmarks, so ask the bus or taxi driver to drop you off at whichever establishment you decide to check. The cheapest place is *Amopi Beach Rooms* (☎ 22 723) where spotless, simply furnished doubles cost 3500 dr. The rooms are at the far end of Amopi.

Farther back along the main road, *Hotel Sophia* (☎ 22 078), behind the Blue Sea Hotel, has doubles/triples for 9000/15,000 dr. Nearby, *Votsalakia Rooms & Restaurant* (☎ 22 204), has attractively furnished doubles for 8000 dr. *Four Seasons Studios* (☎ 22 116), farther back along the road, has equally commendable doubles with bathroom for 8000 dr.

Kastelia Bay Hotel (☎ 22 678) has light, airy singles/doubles for 12,000/14,000 dr. A little way along the approach road to Amopi a sign points to the hotel.

Four Seasons Restaurant serves delicious Greek dishes and freshly baked brown bread.

Menetes Μενετές
Menetes is perched on a sheer cliff 8km above Pigadia. It's a picturesque, unspoilt village with pastel-coloured neoclassical houses lining its main street. Behind the main street are narrow, stepped alleyways that wind between more modest white-washed dwellings. The village has a little **museum** on the right as you come from

Pigadia. The owner of Taverna Manolis will open it up for you.

Places to Stay & Eat Menetes has only one place to stay: the *domatia* of friendly Greek-American Mike Rigas (☎ *81 269/255*), in a traditional Karpathian house with a garden brimming with trees and flowers. Doubles/triples with bathroom are 4700/5500 dr. As you approach from Pigadia, the rooms are 150m down a cement road (signposted 'Lai') veering off to the right. *Taverna Manolis* dishes up generous helpings of grilled meat. *Fiesta Dionysos* specialises in local dishes, including omelette made with artichokes and Karpathian sausages.

Arkasa & Finiki Αρκάσα & Φοινίκι

Arkasa, 9km farther on, straddles a ravine. It is metamorphosing from traditional village to holiday resort. Turn right at the T-junction to reach the authentic village square.

A turn-off left, just before the ravine, leads after 500m to the remains of the 5th century Basilica of Agia Sophia. Two chapels stand amid mosaic fragments and columns.

The serene fishing village of Finiki is 2km north of Arkasa. The little sculpture at the harbour commemorates the heroism of seven local fishers during WWII – locals will tell you the story.

Places to Stay & Eat *Pension Philoxenia* (☎ *61 341*), on the left before the T-junction, has clean doubles for 6500 dr. *Elini Rooms* (☎ *61 248*), on the left along the road to Finiki, has attractive double apartments for 10,000 dr.

Fay's Paradise (☎ *61 308*), near Finiki's harbour, has lovely double studios for 10,000 dr. *Finiki View Hotel* (☎ *61 309/400*), on the right as you come from Arkasa, has spacious doubles for 12,000 dr and a swimming pool and bar.

There is a good taverna on Arkasa's main square and locals come from all over the island to eat the fresh fish at *Dimitrios Fisherman's Taverna* in Finiki.

Lefkos Λεύκος

Lefkos, 13km north of Finiki, and 2km from the coast road, is a burgeoning resort centred around a little fishing quay. It is a beach-lover's paradise with five superb sandy beaches. In summer Lefkos gets crowded, but at other times it still has a rugged, off-the-beaten-track feel about it.

Local boat owners sometimes take visitors to the islet of Sokastro where there is a ruined castle. Another diversion from the beaches is the ancient catacombs, reached by walking inland and turning left at Imeri Rooms.

Places to Stay & Eat *Imeri Rooms* (☎ *71 375*), owned by a friendly elderly couple, is in a peaceful rural setting halfway between the coast road and the beaches. Sparkling doubles/triples cost 7000/8000 dr with bathroom. Inquire at *Small Paradise Taverna & Rooms* (☎ *71 171/184*), farther down the road, about its Sunset Studios which overlook Golden Beach. Immaculate doubles/triples cost 8000/9000 dr. *Golden Sands Studios* (☎ *71 175, fax 71 219*), almost on Golden Beach, are bright, new double/triple studios with well equipped kitchens, for 9000/12,000 dr. *Zorba's Rooms*, near the quay, are equally nice with double studios for 11,000 dr.

Small Paradise Taverna serves tasty local dishes and fresh seafood on a vine-shaded terrace.

Getting There & Around There are two buses weekly to Lefkos and a taxi costs 8000 dr, but telephone the rooms' proprietors and they may be able to arrange a lift from Pigadia, providing you intend staying with them, of course! Hitching is dicey as there is not much traffic.

Lefkos Rent A Car (☎/fax 71 057) is a reliable outlet with very competitive prices. The English-speaking owner will deliver vehicles free of charge to anywhere in southern Karpathos.

East Coast Beaches

The fine beaches of **Ahata**, **Kyra Panagia** and **Apella** can be reached along dirt roads off the east coast road, but are most easily reached by excursion boat from Pigadia. Only Kyra Panagia has accommodation and tavernas.

Mesohori & Spoa Μεσοχώρι & Σπόα
Mesohori, 4km beyond the turn-off for Lefkos, is a pretty village of whitewashed houses and stepped streets. Spoa village, 5km farther on along a dirt road, is at the beginning of the 21km dirt road to Olymbos. It overlooks the east coast and has a track down to **Agios Nikolaos Beach**.

Mountain Villages
Aperi, **Volada**, **Othos** and **Pyles**, the well watered mountain villages to the north of Pigadia, are largely unaffected by tourism. None has any accommodation, but all have tavernas and kafeneia. Aperi was the island's capital from 1700 until 1892. Its ostentatious houses were built by wealthy returning emigrants from the USA. Like Aperi, Volada has an air of prosperity.

Othos (altitude 510m) is the island's highest village. It has a small ethnographic museum. From Othos the road winds downhill to Pyles, a gorgeous village of twisting, stepped streets, pastel houses and citrus groves. It clings to the slopes of Mt Kali Limni (1215m), the Dodecanese's second-highest peak.

NORTHERN KARPATHOS
Diafani & Olymbos
Διαφάνι & Ολυμπος
Diafani is Karpathos' small northern port. There's no post office or bank, but Orfanos Travel Holidays (☎ 51 410), owned by helpful English-speaking Nikos, has currency exchange. There's no OTE but there are cardphones.

Clinging to the ridge of barren Mt Profitis Ilias, 4km above Diafani, Olymbos is a living museum (population 340). Women wear bright, embroidered skirts, waistcoats and headscarves, and goatskin boots. The interiors of the houses are decorated with embroidered cloth and their facades feature brightly painted, ornate plaster reliefs. The

inhabitants speak in a vernacular which contains some Doric words, and the houses have wooden locks of a kind described by Homer. Olymbos is a matrilineal society – a family's property passes down from the mother to the first-born daughter. The women still grind corn in windmills and bake bread in outdoor communal ovens.

Olymbos, alas, is no longer a pristine backwater caught in a time warp. Nowadays hordes of tourists come to gape, and tourist shops are appearing everywhere. However, Olymbos is still a fascinating place, and accommodation and food are inexpensive.

Avlona & Vroukounda
Until early this century the inhabitants of Olymbos spent the summer in Avlona, a village lying in a fertile valley to the north of Olymbos. It's an attractive place of pastel coloured *stavlos* (farmhouses) and neat terraces. Nowadays, due to migration and, more recently, the locals' preference for involvement in the tourist industry, Avlona has only a small population of farmers in summer.

Avlona is reached along a dirt road from the Diafani-Olymbos road, or in a two hour walk along a path which begins at the bottom of the steps to the right of the row of windmills in Olymbos. The **Church of Agios Ioannis** at Vroukounda, a deserted village to the north of Avlona, is the scene of a lively four day festival which begins on 29 August.

Places to Stay & Eat There's an unofficial *camp site* at Vananda Beach, 30 minutes walk (signposted) north of Diafani. *Golden Beach Hotel* (☎ *51 315*), opposite the quay in Diafani, has doubles with bathroom for 8000 dr. *Nikos Hotel* (☎ *51 289*), just back from the waterfront, has comfortable singles/doubles/triples for 5000/7000/85000 dr with bathroom and breakfast included. The hotel is owned by Nikos of Orfanos Travel. The new *Balaskas Hotel*, close by, has pleasant doubles for 8000 dr with bathroom.

Just off the main street in Olymbos, the clean, simply furnished rooms at *Pension Olymbos* (☎ *51 252*) cost 3000/6000 dr. Just beyond the bus turnaround, *Mike's Rooms* (☎ *51 304*) cost 6000 dr a double.

Hotel Aphrodite (☎ *51 307/454*), near the central square, has immaculate doubles/triples for 7000/9000 dr with bathroom.

In Diafani the *Golden Beach Taverna* and *Taverna Anatoli* are good.

Makarounes are served at all the restaurants in Olymbos. You'll eat well at *Olymbos Taverna*, below Pension Olymbos, at *Mike's Taverna*, directly below his rooms, and also at *Parthenonas Restaurant*, on the central square.

Getting Around A bus meets the excursion boats from Pigadia at Diafani and transports people up to Olymbos.

From Diafani, excursion boats go to nearby beaches and occasionally to the uninhabited islet of Saria where there are some Byzantine remains.

Kassos Κάσσος

☎ 0245 • postcode 858 00 • pop 1088
Kassos, 11km south of Karpathos, is a rocky little island with prickly pear trees, sparse olive and fig trees, drystone walls, and sheep and goats. One of the least-visited of the Dodecanese, it's the perfect island to see something of traditional Greek life, and is also great for walks.

History
Despite being diminutive and remote, Kassos has an eventful and tragic history. During Turkish rule it flourished, and by 1820 it had 11,000 inhabitants and a large mercantile fleet. Mohammad Ali, the Turkish governor of Egypt, regarded this fleet as an impediment to his plan to establish a base on Crete from which to attack the Peloponnese and quell the uprising there. So, on 7 June 1824, Ali's men landed on Kassos and killed around 7000 inhabitants. This massacre is commemorated annually on the anniversary of the slaughter and Kassiots return from around the world to participate.

During the late 19th century, many Kassiots emigrated to Egypt and around 5000 of them helped build the Suez Canal. In this century many have emigrated to the USA.

Getting There & Away
Air There are three flights weekly to Rhodes (13,400 dr), and one weekly from Athens (24,700 dr). The Olympic Airways office (☎ 41 444) is on Kritis.

Ferry Kassos has the same ferry schedule as Karpathos.

Excursion Boat In summer there are excursion boats from Phry to the uninhabited Armathia Islet (2000 dr return) where there are sandy beaches.

Getting Around
At the time of writing there was no island bus. The airport is only 600m along the coast road from Phry.

There are just two taxis on Kassos. For further details ask Kassos Maritime and Travel Agency (see Information). Motorbikes can be rented from Frangiscos Moto Rentals (☎ 41 746).

PHRY Φρυ
Phry is the island's capital and port. The town's focal point is the picturesque old fishing harbour of Bouka. The suburb of Emboreios is 1km east of Phry.

Orientation & Information
Turn left at the quay to reach Bouka. Veer left, and then right, and continue along the waterfront to the central square of Plateia Iroön Kassou. Turn right here to reach Kritis, Phry's main street. To reach Emboreios, continue along the waterfront passing the turn-off (signposted 'Agia Mamas') for Panagia, Poli and Agia Mamas.

Kassos does not have an EOT or tourist police, but Emmanuel Manousos, at Kassos Maritime and Travel Agency (☎ 41 495,

KASSOS

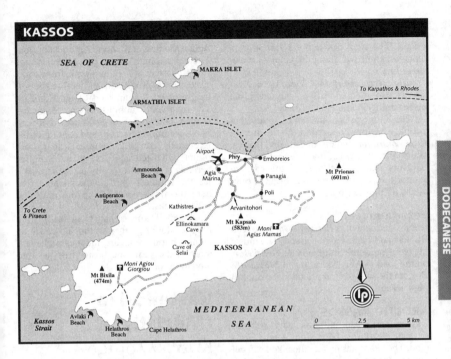

SEA OF CRETE

MAKRA ISLET

To Karpathos & Rhodes

ARMATHIA ISLET

Airport

Phry ● Emboreios

Ammounda
Beach

Agia
Marina

● Panagia

Mt Prionas
(601m)

Antiperatos
Beach

● Poli

To Crete
& Piraeus

Kathistres

Arvanitohori

Ellinokamara
Cave

Mt Kapsalo
(583m)

Moni
Agias Mamas

Cave of
Selai

KASSOS

Moni Agiou
Giorgiou

Mt Bixila
(474m)

MEDITERRANEAN

SEA

0   2.5   5 km

Kassos
Strait

Avlaki
Beach

Helathros
Beach   Cape Helathros

DODECANESE

41 323), Plateia Iroön Kassou, is helpful and speaks English.

The National Bank of Greece is represented by the supermarket on Kritis. At the time of writing there was a rumour that Kassos would soon have a bank. From the waterfront, take the first turn left along Kritis to reach the post office. The OTE is behind Plateia Dimokratias – you'll see the huge satellite dishes.

The port police (☎ 41 288) are behind the Church of Agios Spyridon. The police (☎ 41 222) are just beyond the post office, on the opposite side.

Places to Stay

All of the island's accommodation (and there's not that much) is in Phry, except for the rooms at Moni Agiou Giorgiou (see Monasteries in the Around Kassos section). *Ketty Markous* (☎ 41 613/ 498) rents doubles

for 5000 dr, including kitchen. They're on the south side of the road to Emboreios. Farther along this road, on the opposite side, *Elias Koutlakis Rooms* (☎ 41 363) costs 8000 dr a double with bathroom.

Anessis Hotel (☎ 41 234/201), above the supermarket on Kritis, has singles/doubles for 6000/8000 dr with bathroom. *Anagennisis Hotel* (☎ 41 495, fax 41 036), on Plateia Iroön Kassou, has clean and comfortable rooms for 5500/7000 dr, or with bathroom for 7000/9500 dr.

The owner of the Anagennisis Hotel, Emmanuel Manousos, also has well equipped double/triple *apartments* for 15,000/18,000 dr. Emmanuel's brother, Georgios Manousos, has apartments for the same price.

Places to Eat

Phry has two restaurants and several snack bars. *Kassos Restaurant* on Plateia

Dimokratias is run by a women's cooperative. The food is well prepared and low-priced. The mezedes include *kritamos*, a plant which grows along the island's rocky shore line.

Milos Restaurant, on Plateia Iroön Kassou, is also good and offers tasty casserole dishes and grilled meat and fish.

There are several kafeneia in Phry, but young Kassiots congregate at the trendy *Cafe Zananta* which overlooks Bouka. Giorgious, the owner, makes excellent cappuccino. *Ouzeri Meltimi*, on the road to Emborious, is also commendable, but only opens in high season.

Entertainment
Kassos' night club is *Perigaili Bar*, between Bouka and Plateia Iroön Kassou. The music played is predominantly Greek. *Alenti Bar*, on the road to Agia Marina, and *Marianthi Bar*, on the way to Emboreios, open only in high season.

AROUND KASSOS
Kassos' best beach is the isolated, pebbled cove of **Helathros**, near Moni Agiou Giorgiou. The beach has no facilities. You can get there either along a dirt track which bears left (downhill) from the road to the monastery, or along a slightly longer track from the monastery. Avlaki is another decent beach reached along a path from the monastery.

The mediocre **Ammounda Beach**, beyond the airport, near the blue-domed Church of Agios Konstantinos, is the nearest to Phry. There are slightly better beaches farther along this stretch of coast.

Agia Marina, 1km south-west of Phry, is a pretty village with a gleaming white and blue church. On 17 July the Festival of Agia Marina is celebrated here. From Agia Marina the road continues to verdant **Arvanitohori**, with fig and pomegranate trees.

Poli, 3km south-east of Phry, is the former capital, built on the ancient acropolis. **Panagia**, between Phry and Poli, has fewer than 50 inhabitants. Its once-grand sea captains' and ship owners' mansions are now derelict.

Monasteries
The island has two monasteries: **Moni Agias Mamas** and **Moni Agiou Giorgiou**. The uninhabited Moni Agias Mamas on the south coast is a 1½ hour walk from Phry. Take the Poli road and just before the village turn left (signposted 'Agia Mamas'). The road winds uphill through a dramatic, eroded landscape of rock-strewn mountains, crumbling terraces and soaring cliffs. Eventually you will come to a sharp turn right (signposted again). Hold onto your hat here, as it's known locally as *aeras* (air) – it's the windiest spot on the island. From here the track descends to the blue and white monastery.

A new 11km asphalt road leads from Phry to Moni Agiou Giorgiou. There are no monks, but there is a resident caretaker for most of the year, and basic (free) accommodation for visitors.

Kastellorizo (Megisti)
Καστελλόριζο

☎ 0241 • postcode 851 11 • pop 275

Tiny, rocky Kastellorizo (kah-stel-o-rih-zo), a mere speck on the map, is 118km east of Rhodes, its nearest Greek neighbour, and only 2.5km from the southern coast of Turkey. Its official name is Megisti (the biggest), for it is the largest of a group of 14 islets. The island's remoteness has so far ensured that its tourism is low-key. There are no beaches, but there are rocky inlets from where you can swim and snorkel in a crystal-clear sea.

The island featured in the Oscar-winning Italian film *Mediterraneo* (1991) which was based on a book by an Italian army sergeant. The little book *Capture Kastellorizo* by Marina Pitsonis is available on the island. The author is a Greek/Australian whose father came from Kastellorizo. The book features eight island walks.

History

The ghost town you see today is made all the more poignant by an awareness of the island's past greatness. Due to its strategic position, Dorians, Romans, crusaders, Egyptians, Turks, Venetians and pirates have all landed on its shores. The 20th century has been no less traumatic, with French, British and Italian occupiers.

In 1552, Kastellorizo surrendered peacefully to the Turks and so was granted special privileges. It was allowed to preserve its language, religion and traditions. Its cargo fleet became the largest in the Dodecanese and the islanders achieved a high degree of culture and education.

Kastellorizo lost all strategic and economic importance after the 1923 population exchange. In 1928 it was ceded to the Italians, who severely oppressed the islanders; in contrast, Turkish rule must have seemed like the good old days. Many islanders emigrated to Perth, Australia, where today some 10,000 of them live.

During WWII, Kastellorizo suffered severe bombardment, and English commanders ordered the few remaining inhabitants to abandon their island. They fled to Cyprus, Palestine and Egypt, with no belongings. In October 1945, 300 islanders boarded the Australian ship *Empire Control* to return to Kastellorizo. Tragically, the ship caught fire and 35 people lost their lives. Two months later the remaining refugees returned to their island to find that most of their houses had been destroyed by bombing and the remainder ransacked by the occupying troops. Not surprisingly, more islanders emigrated. Most of the houses that escaped the bombing in WWII stand empty. Despite this gloomy picture, Kastellorizo's waterfront is very lively.

Getting There & Away

Air In July and August there are daily flights to and from Rhodes (10,900 dr), dropping to three weekly at other times. You can buy tickets from Dizi Tours & Travel (☎/fax 49 240) in Kastellorizo Town.

The Woman of Ro

The islet of Ro, one of Kastellorizo's 13 satellites, has been immortalised along with its last inhabitant, Despina Achladioti, alias the Woman of Ro, who died in 1982. Despina and her shepherd husband were the only inhabitants of Ro. When her husband died, Despina remained alone on the island, staunchly hoisting the Greek flag every morning, and lowering it in the evening, in full view of the Turkish coast. The Woman of Ro has become a symbol of the Greek spirit of indomitability in the face of adversity. There are excursion boats to the islet; look for signs along the waterfront at Kastellorizo Town. There is a bust of the Woman of Ro on Plateia Horafia.

Ferry The F/B *Nissos Kalymnos* leaves Rhodes at 4 pm on Monday and Friday, arriving in Kastellorizo at 10 pm. At 10.15 pm it heads back for Rhodes. In addition, a ferry on a long indirect route to Piraeus, via the Cyclades and Crete or the northern Dodecanese, calls once a week, but this schedule is subject to frequent changes.

Excursion Boat to Turkey Islanders go on frequent shopping trips to Turkey and day trips (5000 dr) are also offered to tourists. Look for the signs along the waterfront.

Getting Around

There is one bus on the island, which is used solely to transport people to and from the airport (500 dr).

Excursion boats go to the islets of **Ro**, **Agios Georgios** and **Strogyli** and the spectacular **Blue Cave** (Parasta), named for its brilliant blue water, due to refracted sunlight. All of these trips cost around 5000 dr.

KASTELLORIZO TOWN

Kastellorizo Town is the only settlement. Built around a U-shaped bay, its waterfront is skirted with imposing, spruced-up three

DODECANESE

DODECANESE

KASTELLORIZO

To Ro
To Rhodes
Moni Agiou Stefanou
To Turkey
Knights of St John Castle
Kastellorizo
To Strogyli
Moni Agias Triadas
Mandraki
Paleokastro
Vikla (273m)
Horafia
Airport
KASTELLORIZO
Moni Agiou Georgiou
Blue Cave
MEDITERRANEAN SEA

0 0.5 1 km

storey mansions with wooden balconies and red-tiled roofs. However, this alluring facade contrasts with backstreets of abandoned houses overgrown with ivy, crumbling stairways and stony pathways winding between them.

Orientation & Information

The quay is at the eastern side of the bay. The central square, Plateia Ethelonton Kastellorizou, abuts the waterfront almost halfway round the bay, next to the yachting jetty. The suburbs of Horafia and Mandraki are reached by ascending the wide steps at the east side of the bay.

On the bay's western side are the post office and police station (☎ 49 333). There is no OTE but there are cardphones. The National Bank of Greece is in the middle of the waterfront, next to the ferry ticket agency (☎ 49 356). The port police (☎ 49 333) are at the eastern tip of the bay.

Things to See

The **Knights of St John Castle** stands above the quay. A metal staircase leads to the top

from where there are splendid views of Turkey. The **museum** within the castle houses a well displayed collection. Opening times, in theory, are 7.30 am to 2.30 pm Tuesday to Sunday; entry is free. Beyond the museum, steps lead down to a coastal pathway, from where more steps go up the cliff to a **Lycian tomb** with a Doric facade. There are several along the Anatolian coast, but this is the only known one in Greece.

Moni Agiou Georgiou is the largest of the monasteries which dot the island. Within its church is the subterranean Chapel of Agios Haralambous reached by steep stone steps. Here Greek children were given religious instruction during Turkish times. The church is kept locked; ask around the waterfront for the whereabouts of the caretaker. To reach the monastery ascend the conspicuous zigzag white stone steps behind the town and at the top take the path straight ahead.

Moni Agiou Stefanou, on the north coast, is the setting for one of the island's most important celebrations, Agiou Stefanou Day on 1 August. The path to the little white monastery begins behind the post office. From the monastery a path leads to a bay where you can swim.

Paleokastro was the island's ancient capital. Within its Hellenistic walls are an ancient tower, a water cistern and three churches. Concrete steps, just beyond a soldier's sentry box on the airport road, are the beginning of the steep path to Paleokastro.

Places to Stay – Budget

Accommodation is of a high standard. Most *domatia* do not display signs but it's not difficult to find the owners – that is, if they don't find you first when you disembark.

Villa Kaserma (☎ 49 370, fax 49 365) is the red and white building standing above the western waterfront. The very pleasant doubles/triples with bathrooms cost 9000/ 11,000 dr. Inquire about a room here at Lazarakis Restaurant (see Places to Eat).

Pension Palameria (☎ 49 282) is a newly converted building on the small square at the north-west corner of the waterfront. Spotless doubles cost 10,000 dr with bathroom and kitchen/dining area. Inquire about these rooms at Little Paris Taverna. *Sydney Rooms* (☎ 49 302), above the Sydney Restaurant, has rates of 4000/7000 dr for singles/doubles. The owner, Angelo, also has some lovely double rooms with bathroom for 10,000 dr.

Karreta Apartments (☎/fax 49 028), just off Plateia Ethelonton Kastellorizou, are lovely light and airy rooms with blue and white decor. Doubles with bathrooms are 11,000 dr and a family room is 15,000 dr. Inquire about these rooms at the Karreta Art and Crafts shop behind the agora, or at Restaurant Oraia Megisti.

Places to Stay – Mid-Range
Farther around, the island's only hotel, the B class *Hotel Megisti* (☎ 49 272), has attractive singles/doubles/triples for 14,500/19,000/26,500 dr. The friendly English-speaking manager, Nektarios Karavelatzis, owns *Karnayo Apartments* (☎/fax 49 266), housed in a beautifully restored red and ochre mansion near the top of the harbour's west side. These traditionally furnished double/triple apartments cost 15,000 dr and a five-person apartment is 20,000 dr.

Krystalls Apartments (☎ 49 363, fax 49 368), just beyond the central square, has comfortable, spotless doubles/triples for 16,000/19,000 dr with TV and well equipped kitchen.

Places to Eat
As with the accommodation, restaurants are of a high standard on Kastellorizo. *Restaurant Oraia Megisti*, on Plateia Ethelonton Kastellorizou, serves a range of well prepared casserole dishes and also spit-roast goat and lamb, both of which are superlative, especially when accompanied with rice cooked with herbs – a local speciality. *Little Paris Taverna* farther along the waterfront has been going strong for 30 years. It serves generous helpings of grilled fish and meat. *Sydney Restaurant*, a little farther around, is also highly commendable and serves similar fare. Beyond the square, *Lazarakis Restaurant* on the

waterfront opposite the jetty, excels in seafood.

Restaurant Platania, on Plateia Horafian, is a nice unpretentious place which appeared in the film *Mediterraneo*, a fact it proudly proclaims in huge lettering on the outside wall.

There are several traditional kafeniea on the waterfront. The younger set hang out at *Poseidon Coffee Bar* next to the old agora. At the time of writing, the finishing touches were being put to *Kaz Bar*, close by.

Tilos Τήλος

☎ 0241   • postcode 850 02   • pop 279

Tilos lies 65km west of Rhodes. With good, uncrowded beaches, two abandoned, evocative villages, a well kept monastery at the end of a spectacularly scenic road, and its authentic Greek-island image intact, Tilos is still remarkably little visited. It's a terrific island for walkers, with vistas of high cliffs, rocky inlets and sea, valleys of cypress, walnut and almond trees, and bucolic meadows with well fed cattle.

Tilos' agricultural potential is not utilised, since, rather than work the land for a pittance, young Tiliots prefer to leave for the mainland or emigrate to Australia or the USA.

There are two settlements: the port of Livadia, and Megalo Horio, 8km north.

History
Bones of mastodons – midget elephants that became extinct around 4600 BC – were found in a cave on the island in 1974. The cave, named **Cherkadio**, is signposted from the Livadia-Megala Horio road, but is kept locked. Irini, one of the greatest of ancient Greece's female poets, lived on Tilos in the 4th century BC.

Elephants and poetry apart, Tilos' history shares the same catalogue of invasions and occupations as the rest of the archipelago.

Getting There & Away
Ferry The F/B *Nissos Kalymnos* calls at Tilos on Tuesday and Saturday. Tilos is also

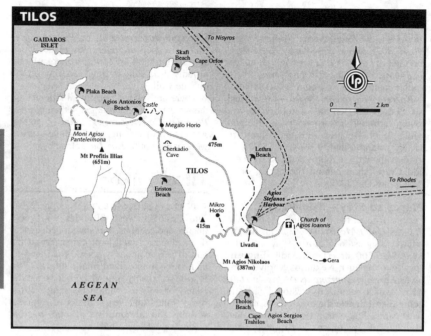

TILOS

GAIDAROS ISLET

To Nisyros

Skafi Beach   Cape Orfos

Plaka Beach

Agios Antonios Beach   Castle

Moni Agiou Panteleimona

Megalo Horio

Mt Profitis Illias (651m)

Cherkadio Cave

475m

TILOS

Lethra Beach

To Rhodes

Eristos Beach

Mikro Horio

Agios Stefanos Harbour

415m

Church of Agios Ioannis

Livadia

Mt Agios Nikolaos (387m)

Gera

AEGEAN SEA

Tholos Beach

Cape Trahilos   Agios Sergios Beach

0   1   2 km

---

included in the weekly connection between the Dodecanese and Mykonos and Syros.

Hydrofoil On Wednesday a hydrofoil from Kalymnos via Kos and Nisyros arrives at Tilos at 9.40 am and then continues to Rhodes. It follows the same route back, arriving at Tilos at 7.30 pm and continuing to Nisyros and Kos. On Sunday there is a morning hydrofoil from Kos via Rhodes to Tilos, returning late afternoon through Rhodes and Kos to Kalymnos.

Excursion Boat A high-speed inflatable boat goes to numerous small beaches around the island, but it costs a pricey 7500 dr per person. Make inquiries at Taverna Blue Sky.

Getting Around

Tilos' public transport consists of two buses, a minibus and a full-sized bus. They go frequently in summer from Livadia to Megalo Horio (300 dr), Eristos Beach and Agios Antonios Beach (350 dr). There are three motorcycle rental outlets in Livadia.

Tilos has two taxis (☎ 44 066/169).

LIVADIA Λιβάδια

Livadia skirts a large bay with a long pebble beach on the island's east coast. All the tourist facilities, and most of the accommodation, are here.

Orientation & Information

From the quay, turn left, ascend the steps beside Stefanakis Travel, and continue ahead to the central square. If you continue straight ahead, the road curves and turns right, passing the Church of Agios Nikolaos, to skirt the beach.

Tilos has no EOT but the staff at both Stefanakis Travel (☎ 44 310) and Tilos

DODECANESE

Travel Agency (☎ 44 259), opposite the quay, are helpful. The post office and OTE are on the central square. The port police (☎ 44 322) share the white Italianate building at the quay with the regular police (☎ 44 222).

Walks

Lethra Beach is a long pebble beach an hour's walk along a path going south from Livadia. Before WWII, Tilos had two villages, Megalo Horio and **Mikro Horio**. No-one lived at the port because it was vulnerable to pirates. After WWII people began to leave Mikro Horio, although one elderly woman remained there alone until her death in 1974. The village, signposted 3km from Livadia, on the Livadia-Megala Horio road, is a lonely, evocative place. Hawks circle overhead and lizards run for cover as you wander along the overgrown pathways.

High above Tilos' east coast, **Gera** was the summer settlement of Mikro Horio. Its wooden-roofed houses are now derelict. You can walk there in about one hour, along a scenic path which begins by Faros Rooms (see Places to Stay).

Two Scottish expatriates, Iain and Lynne, organise group walks around the island. Inquire at Joanna's Cafe Bar.

Places to Stay

The information kiosk at the harbour is open whenever a ferry arrives and has photographs and prices of Livadia's accommodation. Freelance *camping* is permitted on the beaches – Plaka Beach is good if you have your own transport, but there are no facilities or drinking water. Eristos Beach is better and has a small facilities block, but charges 500 dr per tent.

Paraskevi Rooms (☎ 44 280), the best of the three domatia on the beach has clean, nicely furnished doubles with bathrooms and well equipped kitchens for 10,000 dr. To get there, walk between the sea and the Italianate building, and continue ahead.

The E class *Hotel Livadia (☎ 44 202/131),* behind the central square, has doubles

with bathrooms for 7000 dr. *Casa Italiana Rooms (☎ 44 253/259),* overlooking the quay, has well kept doubles with bathrooms and refrigerators for 8000 dr, and a four-person apartment for 15,000 dr. *Stefanakis Studios (☎ 44 310/384)* above Stefanakis Travel is equally commendable and has the same rates for doubles.

Manos Hagifundas Studios (☎ 44 259), past Sophia's Taverna on the beach road, has nice doubles for 12,000 dr. Telephone in advance and Manos will meet the boat; alternatively, you'll find him in Taverna Blue Sky.

Hotel Eleni (☎ 44 062, fax 44 063), 400m along the beach road, has beautiful, tastefully furnished double rooms with bathrooms, refrigerator and telephone. The rate for singles/doubles/triples is 9000/12,000/14,000 dr, including breakfast.

Marina Beach Rooms (☎/fax 44 169) on the bay's eastern side, 1km from the quay, has immaculate but small rooms with seaview balconies. Doubles are 12,000 dr. A little farther along, the new *Faros Rooms (☎ 44 029)* has spotless, tastefully furnished doubles/triples for 12,000/14,500 dr.

Places to Eat

Sophia's Taverna, 20m along the beach road, serves delicious, low-priced food. *Taverna Blue Sky,* on the harbour, is good for grilled fish and *Taverna Michalas,* beyond the central square, and *Zorba's Taverna,* beyond the Ereni Hotel, serve tasty grilled meat. The zany owner of Zorbas may break into a song and dance routine while taking your order.

Kafeneion Omonoias, next to the post office, is a favourite place for breakfast. The newer *Joanna's Cafe Bar* is equally popular, serving good cappuccino, yogurt and muesli, pizza made by Joanna's Italian husband, Andrea, and delicious home-made cakes.

Beyond the central square there is a *bakery* and three *supermarkets*.

Entertainment

La Luna at the quay and a new place, still unnamed, next to Zorba's Taverna on the

DODECANESE

waterfront, are the local hot spots. In summer the *Mikro Horio Music Bar* belts out music till 4 am.

MEGALO HORIO Μεγάλο Χωριό

Megalo Horio is a serene whitewashed village, crowned by a ruined knights' castle which has an intact gateway, and a small chapel with frescoes. Follow the signpost for Kastro at the beginning of the village to reach the castle.

The little museum on the main street houses finds from the Cherkadio Cave. It's kept locked, but if you ask at the town hall on the first floor someone will show you around.

Places to Stay & Eat

Megalo Horio has three places to stay. *Pension Sevasti (☎ 44 237)*, just beyond the Eristos Beach turn-off, has singles/doubles for 3000/4500 dr. *Milou Rooms and Apartments (☎ 44 204)* and *Elefantakia Studios (☎ 44 242/213)*, next to one another on the main street, have doubles for 8000 dr. *Kali Kardia*, next to Pension Sevasti, is Megalo Horio's nicest taverna.

Entertainment

Megalo Horio has two atmospheric bars. *Ilakati*, on the steep road signposted Kastro, plays rock and blues, and *Anemona*, at the top of the steps by the Castle Restaurant, plays Greek music.

AROUND MEGALO HORIO

Just before Megalo Horio, a turn-off to the left leads after 2.5km to the pleasant, tamarisk-shaded Eristos Beach – a mixture of gritty sand and shingle. A signposted turn-off to the right from this road leads to Agios Antonios Beach. Plaka Beach, 3km farther west, is dotted with trees.

The 18th century Moni Agiou Panteleimona is 5km beyond here along a scenic road. It is uninhabited but well maintained, with fine 18th century frescoes. The island's minibus driver takes groups of visitors here on Sunday. A three day festival takes place at the monastery, beginning on 25 July.

Places to Stay

Tropicana Taverna & Rooms (☎ 44 223/ 020), on the Eristos road, has doubles/ triples for 5000/6500 dr, and *Nausika Taverna & Rooms*, to the left of Eristos Beach (signposted), has similar rates. The new *Eristos Beach Hotel (☎ 44 024)*, right on the beach, has attractive doubles for 10,000 dr.

The immaculate D class *Hotel Australia (☎ 44 296)* overlooks Agios Antonios Beach. Doubles/triples with bathroom are 7000/ 8000 dr.

Nisyros Νίσυρος

☎ 0242 • postcode 853 03 • pop 913

Nisyros (nee-sih-ros) is one of the strangest and most beautiful of all Greek islands – an unusual mixture of lush vegetation and dramatic, barren moonscapes.

The nucleus of the island is a dormant volcano. This creates a curious anomaly whereby the island, although waterless, is fertile. The mineral-rich earth holds moisture and yields olives, vines, figs, citrus fruit and almonds. Another unusual feature of Nisyros is that it is completely free of mosquitoes.

The island's settlements are Mandraki, the capital; the fishing village of Pali; and the crater-top villages of Emboreios and Nikea.

The island's population has not suffered the drastic depletion of other small islands because some of its men earn a living quarrying pumice.

The island attracts a lot of day-trippers from Kos, but few stop overnight.

Getting There & Away

Nisyros has the same ferry schedule as Tilos. The island is serviced by a weekly hydrofoil from Rhodes. In summer there are daily excursion boats from Kardamena, Kefalos and Kos Town on Kos (3000-5500 dr).

Getting Around

Bus There are at least two buses every day to the volcano (2000 dr), and at least four daily to Pali, Nikea and Emboreios. The bus terminal is at the quay.

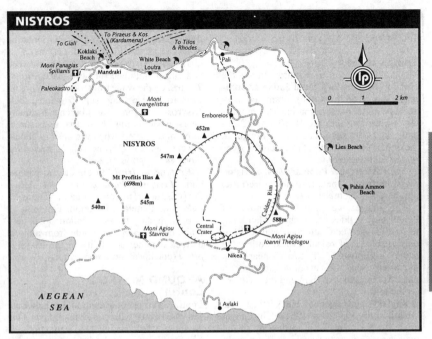

NISYROS

To Giali · Koklaki Beach · To Piraeus & Kos (Kardamena) · To Tilos & Rhodes

Moni Panagias Spilianis · Mandraki · White Beach · Loutra · Pali

Paleokastro

Moni Evangelistras

Emboreios

452m

NISYROS

547m

Lies Beach

Mt Profitis Ilias (698m)

540m · 545m

Pahia Ammos Beach

Caldera Rim

588m

Moni Agiou Stavrou · Central Crater · Moni Agiou Ioanni Theologou

Nikea

AEGEAN SEA

Avlaki

0 · 1 · 2 km

DODECANESE

Motorcycle There are three motorcycle-rental outlets on Mandraki's main street.

Taxi There are two taxi companies on Nisyros: Bobby's Taxi (☎ 31 460) and Irene's Taxi (☎ 31 474). A sample of tariffs are: the volcano (5000 dr), Emboreios (4000 dr), Nikea (5000 dr) and Pali (5000 dr).

Excursion Boat From June to September there are excursion boats (2500 dr return) to the pumice-stone islet of **Giali** where there is a good sandy beach.

MANDRAKI Μανδράκι

Mandraki is the attractive port and capital of Nisyros. Its two-storey houses have brightly painted wooden balconies. Some are whitewashed but many are painted in bright colours, predominantly ochre and turquoise. The web of streets huddled below

the monastery and the central square are especially charming.

Orientation & Information

To reach Mandraki's centre, walk straight ahead from the quay. At the fork bear right; the left fork leads to Hotel Porfyris. Beyond here a large square adjoins the main street, which proceeds to Plateia Aristotelous Fotiadou, then continues diagonally opposite, passing the town hall. Turn left at the T-junction for the central square of Plateia Elikiomini.

There is a tourist information office (☎ 31 204) at the quay, open 10 am to 1 pm and 6 to 8 pm daily. The staff here, and at Enetikon Travel (☎ 31 180, fax 31 168), on the main street, are helpful. The latter has a good library of used books.

The post office, port police (☎ 31 222) and the regular police share premises opposite the quay. The National Bank of Greece is represented by Diakomihalis Tours (☎ 31 457/527) on the main street.

Things to See
Mandraki's greatest tourist attraction is the cliff-top 14th century **Moni Panagias Spilianis** (Virgin of the Cave), crammed with ecclesiastical paraphernalia. The monastery's opening times are 10.30 am to 3 pm daily, and admission is free. Turn right at the end of the main street to reach the steps up to the monastery.

The **Historical & Popular Museum** is on the waterfront. Opening times are erratic, but there's no admission fee.

The impressive ancient acropolis of **Paleokastro** (Old Kastro), above Mandraki, has well preserved Cyclopean walls built of massive blocks of volcanic rock. Follow the route signposted 'kastro', near the monastery steps. This eventually becomes a path. At the road turn right and the *kastro* is on the left.

Koklaki is a beach of black stones. Its 'Heath Robinson' house was built by a local artist. To get there, walk to the end of the waterfront, go up the steps and turn right onto a path.

Places to Stay & Eat
Mandraki has a fair amount of accommodation but, unusually, owners do not meet the ferries. There is no camp site.

If you turn left from the quay, you will come to *Hotel Romantzo* (☎/fax 31 340) with clean, well kept singles/doubles/triples for 5000/7000/10,000 dr with bathroom. The rooms are above a snack bar and there is a large communal terrace with a refrigerator, tables and chairs. *Three Brothers Hotel* (☎ 31 344), opposite, is another pleasant option, with single/double rooms with bathooms for 5000/8000 dr. Almost next door, *Xenon Hotel* (☎ 31 012) has rooms for 6500/9000/10,000 dr. Beyond here on the right, *Mire Mare Apartments* (☎ 31 100) has modern, well equipped rooms for 6000/10,000/14,000 dr. There is a communal washing machine and iron.

The C class *Hotel Porfyris* (☎/fax 31 376), with a swimming pool, has singles/doubles for 8000/14,000 dr (see Orientation & Information, earlier, for directions).

Taverna Nisyros, just off the main street, is a cheap and cheerful little place. *Tony's Tavern*, on the waterfront, does great breakfasts for 800 dr, and superb meat dishes. Nisyros-born Tony was a butcher for many years in Melbourne, Australia, so is something of an expert when it comes to choosing cuts of meat. Beyond Tony's, *Klearithis Taverna* has good mezedes.

Restaurant Irini, on the central square, and *Taverna Panorama*, near Hotel Porfyris, are also commendable. There's a *bakery* on Plateia Aristotelous Fotiadou.

Be sure to try the nonalcoholic local beverage called *soumada*, made from almond extract. Another speciality of the island is *pittia* (chickpea and onion patties).

AROUND NISYROS
Loutra Λουτρά
Loutra, 2km east of Mandraki, has a thermal spa (☎ 31 284), with two spa buildings. One is derelict, but the other still functions. If you fancy a curative dip you'll need a quick health check at the clinic (☎ 31 217) near Hotel Porfyris first. The spa's well worn *Loutra Restaurant* is surprisingly good.

The Volcano
Nisyros is on a volcanic line which passes through the islands of Aegina, Paros, Milos, Santorini, Nisyros, Giali and Kos. The island originally culminated in a mountain of 850m, but the centre collapsed 30,000-40,000 years ago after three violent eruptions. Their legacy is the white and orange pumice stones which can still be seen on the northern, eastern and southern flanks of the island, and the large lava flow which covers the whole south-west of the island around Nikea village. The first eruption partially blew off the top of the ancestral cone, but the majority of the sinking of the central part of the island came about as a result of the removal of magma from within the reservoir underground.

Another violent eruption occurred in 1422 on the western side of the caldera depression (called Lakki), but this, like all others since, emitted steam, gases and mud, but no lava. The islanders call the volcano Polyvotis, because the Polyvotis crater on the western side of the caldera floor was the site of the eruptions in 1873, 1874 and 1888, and remains the most active of the craters.

There are five craters in the caldera. A path descends into the largest one, Stefanos, where you can examine the multicoloured fumaroles, listen to their hissing and smell their sulphurous vapours. The surface is soft and hot, making sturdy footwear essential.

If you arrive by bus you'll be with hordes of day-trippers, which detracts from the extraordinary sight. Also, the bus does not allow you long enough to wander around and savour a glass of soumada from the cafe. It's a good idea to walk either to or from the crater from Nikea.

Emboreios & Nikea
Εμπορειός & Νίκαια
Emboreios and Nikea perch on the volcano's rim. From each, there are stunning views down into the caldera. Only 20 inhabitants linger on in Emboreios. You may encounter a few elderly women sitting on their doorsteps crocheting, and their husbands at the kafeneio. However, generally, the winding, stepped streets are empty, the silence broken only by the occasional braying of a donkey or the grunting of pigs.

In contrast to Emboreios, picturesque Nikea, with 50 inhabitants, buzzes with life. It has dazzling white houses with vibrant gardens and a central square with a lovely pebble mosaic. The bus terminates on Plateia Nikolaou Hartofili. Nikea's main street links the two squares.

The steep path down to the volcano begins from Plateia Nikolaou Hartofili. It takes about 40 minutes to walk it one way. Near the beginning you can detour to **Moni Agiou Ioanni Theologou**.

Places to Stay & Eat Emboreios has no accommodation for tourists and no taver-nas, but the owner of its *kafeneio* can rustle up a tasty meal.

Nikea's only accommodation is a *Community Hostel*, on Plateia Nikolaou Hartofili, managed by Panayiotis Mastro-mihalis (☎ 31 285), the owner of Nikea's only taverna. Doubles cost 5000 dr.

Pali Πάλοι
The island's best beaches are at Pali, 4km east of Mandraki, and Lies, 5km farther on. Pali's C class *Hotel Hellenis* (☎ 31 453) has comfortable doubles for 8000 dr with bathroom. Paraskevi, the owner, serves up delectable dishes in the adjoining restaurant. Her shepherd husband, the charismatic Manolis, sometimes plays the lyre in the restaurant.

Astypalea
Αστυπάλαια

☎ 0243   • postcode 859 00   • pop 1073
Astypalea (ah-stih-**pah**-lia), the most westerly island of the archipelago, is geographically and architecturally more akin to the Cyclades. The island's two land masses are joined by a narrow isthmus.

With a wonderfully picturesque hilltop Hora, and bare, gently contoured hills, high mountains, green valleys and sheltered coves, it's surprising Astypalea does not get more foreign tourists. It is, however, popular with urban Greeks.

Getting There & Away
Air There are four flights weekly from Astypalea to Athens (20,100 dr). Astypalea Tours, in Astypalea Town, is the agent for Olympic Airways.

Ferry Lying between the Cyclades and the Dodecanese, Astypalea is the most easterly destination of some Cyclades services, and the most westerly of the Dodecanese services.

The F/B *Nissos Kalymnos* does a round trip to Astypalea from Kalymnos on Tuesday and Saturday.

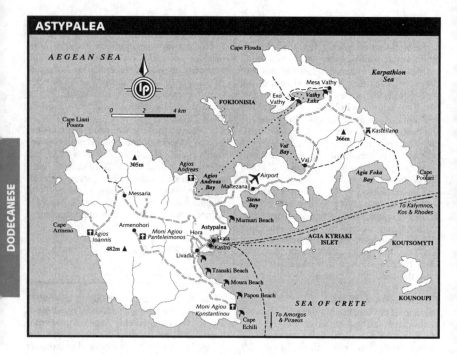

ASTYPALEA

Ferries sail twice weekly to and from Piraeus via the Cyclades Islands (16 hours). One ferry goes via Syros, Paros, Naxos, Donousa, Katapola (Amorgos) and Aegiali (Amorgos) to Astypalea; the other sails via Paros, Naxos, Iraklia, Shinousa, Koufonisia, Donousa, as well as both ports on Amorgos.

Two ferries weekly make a through-connection from Piraeus to the Dodecanese and Rhodes via Astypalea.

Hydrofoil Between June and September there is one hydrofoil a week plying its way on a round trip from Rhodes (5½ hours, 9880 dr) to Astypalea via Symi, Kos and Kalymnos.

Getting Around

Bus From Skala a bus travels fairly frequently to Hora and Livadia (200 dr), and from Hora and Skala to Maltezana (300 dr) via Marmari.

Excursion Boat In summer there are daily excursion boats to the island's less accessible beaches and to Agia Kyriaki Islet (2000 dr). Tickets can be bought from the stalls by the boats.

ASTYPALEA TOWN

Astypalea Town, the capital, consists of the port of Skala and the hilltop district of Hora, crowned by a fortress.

Skala has a friendly pelican, who blew in one windy day. He landed on his feet, it seems, for the local fishers throw him lots of tasty titbits. Hora has narrow streets of dazzling-white cubic houses with brightly painted wooden balconies, doors and banisters. A line of windmills completes the picture.

Orientation & Information

From Skala's quay, turn right to reach the waterfront. The steep road to Hora begins beyond the white Italianate building. In Skala the waterfront road skirts the beach and then veers right to continue along the coast to Marmari and beyond.

A municipal tourist office adjoins the quayside cafe. The owner of Astypalea Tours (☎ 61 571/572, fax 61 328), below Vivamare Apartments, is helpful and is the agent for Olympic Airways and ferry lines.

The post office is at the top of the Skala-Hora road. The OTE is close to the waterfront's Hotel Paradissos. The Commercial Bank, with an ATM, is on the waterfront.

The police (☎ 61 207) and port police (☎ 61 208) are in the Italianate building.

Castle

During the time of the Knights of St John, Astypalea was occupied by the Venetian Quirini family, who built the imposing castle. In the Middle Ages the population lived within its walls, but gradually the settlement outgrew them. The last inhabitants left in 1948 and the stone houses are now in ruins. Above the entrance is the Church of Our Lady of the Castle and within the walls is the Church of Agios Giorgios.

Places to Stay

Camping Astypalea (☎ 61 338) is 3km east of Skala.

Hotel and domatia owners meet incoming boats. *Hotel Australia* (☎ 61 338), on the waterfront, has well kept doubles/triples for 7500/9000 dr, and a friendly Greek-Australian owner. At the time of writing, some co-owned luxury studios were near completion.

Farther along, *Karlos Rooms* (☎ 61 330) has rates of 9000/10,000 dr. *Akth Rooms* (☎ 61 281/168, email astrooms@otenet.gr), beyond Karlos Rooms, has attractive singles/doubles/triples for 6000/10,000/12,000 dr and good sea views from the communal terrace.

Hotel Aegeon (☎ 61 236), on the Skala-Hora road, has singles/doubles for 5000/8000 dr. The ageing but well maintained *Hotel Paradissos* (☎ 61 224/256) has comfortable singles/doubles/triples with bathroom for 8000/9500/10,000 dr. *Vivamare Apartments* (☎ 61 571/572), a little way up the Skala-Hora road, has double/triple/quad studios for 10,000/12,000/14,500 dr.

Aphrodite Studios (☎ 61 478/086, fax 61 087), between Skala and Hora, has beautiful, well equipped double/triple studios for 12,000/14,000 dr. Take the Hora road, turn left after the shoe shop and it's on the left.

Places to Eat

Restaurant Australia, below Hotel Australia, serves delicious fish; the speciality is lobster and macaroni. *Restaurant Astropalia* is also commendable and has wonderful views down to Skala from its terrace. *Vicki's* near the quay offers decent, low-priced fare. *Aitherio Restaurant* is a trendy place serving a range of imaginative mezedes and main courses.

Up in Hora, *Kafeneio Apaskoi* and *Ouzeri Meltimi*, opposite the windmills, are popular hang-outs with Astypalea's young crowd.

There is a *supermarket* on the waterfront and two in Hora, near the post office.

LIVADIA Λιβάδια

The little resort of Livadia lies in a fertile valley 2km from Hora. Its beach is the best on the island, but also the most crowded.

Quieter beaches can be found farther south at Tzanaki, the island's unofficial nudist beach, and at Agios Konstantinos below the monastery of the same name. You can drive to Moni Agiou Konstantinou, or walk there in about 40 minutes.

Places to Stay & Eat

There's plenty of accommodation in Livadia. Pleasant budget options are *Gerani Rooms* (☎ 61 484/337), where doubles/triples go for 9000/9500 dr with bathrooms and refrigerators, and *Kaloudis Domatia* (☎ 61 318/336), with doubles for 9000 dr and a communal kitchen. Both are on the dirt road (a dried-up riverbed) that runs inland from the waterfront.

A sign at the end of the beach road points to *Jim Venetos Studios & Apartments* (☎ 61 490/150), where attractive double studios cost 12,000 dr and four-person apartments are 17,000 dr. *H Kalamia*, the first taverna on the waterfront, serves good food. Its speciality is rice-stuffed goat.

OTHER BEACHES

Marmari, 2km north-east of Skala, has three bays with pebble and sand beaches. **Maltezana** is 7km beyond Marmari in a fertile valley on the isthmus. Maltezana is a scattered, pleasantly laid-back settlement, but its two beaches are grubby. There are some remains of Roman baths with mosaics on the settlement's outskirts.

The road from Maltezana is reasonable as far as **Vaï**, but it's atrocious beyond here. **Mesa Vathy** is a fishing hamlet with a beach at the end of a narrow inlet. It takes about 1½ hours to walk here from Vaï. From Mesa Vathy a footpath leads to **Exo Vathy**, another hamlet with a beach.

Places to Stay & Eat

There are plenty of accommodation options in Maltazena but many only operate during the summer. *Maltezana Rooms* (☎ 61 446), to the left of the quay, has doubles for 8000 dr.

Hotel Castillo (☎/fax 61 552/553), a complex of self-contained units on both sides of the main road, has beautifully furnished, immaculate studios with a well equipped kitchen area, television and telephone. Doubles cost 10,000 dr and four-person apartments are 13,000 dr. *Oveli Taverna* and *Armera Restaurant* are recommended; their fish dishes are especially good.

There is a *domatia* at Exo Vathy, but check with Astypalea Tours in Astypalea town whether it's operating.

Symi Σύμη

☎ 0241   • postcode 856 00   • pop 2332
Symi lies in the straits of Marmara, 24km north of Rhodes, its nearest Greek neigh-

bour, and only 10km from the Turkish peninsula of Dorakis. The island has a scenic rocky interior, dotted with pine and cypress woods. It has a deeply indented coast with precipitous cliffs, and numerous small bays with pebbled beaches.

The island suffers from a severe water shortage.

Symi gets an inordinate number of day-trippers from Rhodes. Most of them don't venture any farther than the restaurants, bars and tourist shops on the waterfront in Gialos.

History

Symi has a long tradition of both sponge diving and shipbuilding. During Ottoman times it was granted the right to fish for sponges in Turkish waters. In return Symi supplied the sultan with first-class boat builders and top-quality sponges.

These factors, and a lucrative shipbuilding industry, brought prosperity to the island. Gracious mansions were built and culture and education flourished. By the beginning of the 20th century the population was 22,500 and the island was launching some 500 ships a year. But the Italian occupation, the introduction of the steamship and Kalymnos' rise as the Aegean's principal sponge producer put an end to Symi's prosperity.

The treaty surrendering the Dodecanese islands to the Allies was signed on Symi on 8 May 1945.

Getting There & Away

Ferry & Hydrofoil Symi has a similar ferry schedule to Tilos and Nisyros. Every Saturday a hydrofoil departs Rhodes at 8 am, arriving on Symi at 8.50 am before leaving for Kos, Kalymnos and Astypalea. It returns to Symi at 7.30 pm and heads back for Rhodes.

Excursion Boat There are daily excursion boats running between Symi and Rhodes' Mandraki Harbour. The Symi-based *Symi I* and *Symi II* are the cheapest. They are owned cooperatively by the people of Symi, and operate as excursion boats as well as

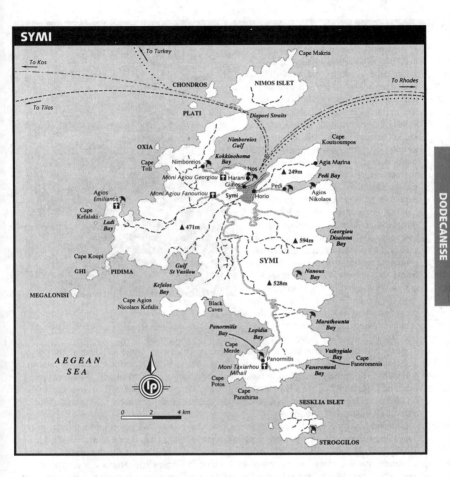

SYMI

To Kos
To Turkey
Cape Makria
CHONDROS
NIMOS ISLET
To Rhodes
To Tilos
PLATI
Diapori Straits
Nimboreios Gulf
Cape Koutsoumpos
OXIA
Cape Toli
Nimboreios
Kokkinohoma Bay
Nos
Agia Marina
▲ 249m
Moni Agiou Georgiou
Harani
Gialos
Pedi
Pedi Bay
Moni Agiou Fanouriou
Symi
Horio
Agios Nikolaos
Agios Emilianos
Cape Kefalaki
Ladi Bay
▲ 471m
Georgiou Disalona Bay
Cape Koupi
▲ 594m
GHI
PIDIMA
Gulf St Vasilou
SYMI
Nanous Bay
MEGALONISI
Kefalos Bay
▲ 528m
Cape Agios Nicolaos Kefalis
Black Caves
Panormitis Bay
Lopidia Bay
Marathounta Bay
Cape Merde
Panormitis
Vathygialo Bay
Cape Faneromenis
AEGEAN SEA
Moni Taxiarhou Mihail
Faneromeni Bay
Cape Potos
Cape Parathiras
SESKLIA ISLET
0   2   4 km
STROGGILOS

DODECANESE

regular passenger boats. Tickets cost 3200 dr return and can be bought on board.

Symi Tours has excursion trips to the town of Datça in Turkey on Saturday, which is market day. The cost is 10,000 dr return (including 4000 dr Turkish port tax). You must hand in your passport the day before.

Getting Around

Bus & Taxi A minibus makes frequent runs between Gialos and Pedi Beach (via Horio).

Check the current schedule with Symi Tours. The bus stop and taxi rank (☎ 72 666) are on the east side of the harbour. Sample taxi tariffs are Horio (600 dr), Pedi (700 dr) and Nimboreios (1200 dr).

Excursion Boat Several excursion boats do trips to Moni Taxiarhou Mihail and Sesklia Islet where there's a shady beach. Check the boards for the best value tickets. Symi Tours also has trips to the monastery (10,000 dr).

DODECANESE

As Long as It's Black

A bent old lady clad from head to foot in black, silhouetted against sparkling, sugar cube buildings, makes a striking, evocative image – so much so that you will see it reproduced on 'arty postcards' throughout Greece. But it is not only elderly women who dress in black, the colour of mourning; many younger people do, too. Traditionally, Greek women marry men much older than themselves, so are often widowed in middle age. Until recently a widow was expected to wear black for the rest of her life, or until she remarried, something she could not do during the first five years after her husband's death. She was also expected to wear a black kerchief that completely covered her hair, forehead and neck. You will still see elderly women wearing this headdress.

LIZ THOMPSON

In the Greek Orthodox faith, the five years following death is known as the liminal period. It is believed that during this time the soul of the deceased journeys to heaven. Throughout the liminal period a widow makes daily visits to her husband's grave, lighting candles and leaving food there.

At the end of the liminal period the body is exhumed and the bones are cleaned and placed in a casket. This symbolises the final purification of the soul and its readiness to enter heaven. Nowadays widows are expected to wear black only during the liminal period following their husband's death. After this the care of the grave is carried out collectively. Five times a year, on All Souls' Days, neighbouring widows exchange plates of food, which are then blessed by a priest and placed on the graves.

Likewise, if a child dies, the mother wears black for at least five years, and tends the grave daily. Upon the death of a parent or sibling the mourning time is one to five years, for an in-law it is one year, and for a more distant relation it is 40 days. If the deceased is a child, a relation she was close to, or someone who died in tragic circumstances, a woman is expected to wear black for longer. After the period of mourning, a woman is expected to dress in a subdued manner, replacing black with dark blue, then with brown and then gradually adding brighter colours. During the time of mourning a woman is not expected to socialise or entertain.

In comparison, men get off lightly. The only requirement expected of a man is that he wears a black armband and refrains from socialising for the 40 days following a death.

. In keeping with the rest of the western world's hip, young Greek women have come to hold the maxim 'any colour as long as it's black' with regard to clothes. However, it is not difficult to spot the difference between a woman wearing black to make a fashion statement and one wearing black because she is in mourning!

Excursion boats also go to some of the island's more remote beaches.

Taxi boats These small boats do trips to many of the island's beaches.

SYMI TOWN
Symi Town is a Greek treasure. Neoclassical mansions in a harmonious medley of colours are heaped up the steep hills which flank its U-shaped harbour. Behind their strikingly beautiful facades, however, many of the buildings are derelict. The town is divided into two parts: Gialos, the harbour, and Horio, above, crowned by the kastro (castle).

Symi Town's beach is the crowded, minuscule Nos Beach. Turn left at the quay's clock tower to get there.

The **Symi Maritime Museum**, behind the central square, is open 10 am to 2 pm Tuesday to Sunday. Admission is 500 dr.

Orientation & Information
Facing inland, the quay front skirts the right side of the harbour. Inter-island ferries dock at the tip of the quay, and excursion boats from Rhodes dock farther in. Excursion boats to Symi's beaches leave from the top of the opposite side. The central square is behind the top of the harbour's right side. The smaller Plateia tis Skalas is near the top of the left side. Kali Strata, a broad stairway, leads from here to Horio.

There is no EOT in Symi Town, but the staff at Symi Tours (☎ 71 307, fax 72 292) are helpful.

The post office, police (☎ 71 111) and port police (☎ 71 205) share the large white building beside the clock tower. The OTE is signposted from the eastern side of the central square. The National Bank of Greece is at the top of the harbour. The Ionian Bank on the waterfront has an ATM.

Symi's Internet cafe is the Vapori Bar, near the beginning of Kali Strata.

Things to See & Do
Horio consists of narrow, labyrinthine streets crossed by crumbling archways. As you approach the kastro, the once-grand 19th century neoclassical mansions give way to small, modest stone dwellings of the 18th century.

The **Museum of Symi**, on the way to the castle, has archaeological and folklore exhibits. Opening times are 10 am to 2 pm Tuesday to Sunday. Admission is 500 dr. The castle incorporates blocks from the ancient acropolis, and the **Church of Megali Panagia** is within its walls.

Symi Tours has multilingual guides who lead **walks** around the island. The publication *Walking on Symi* by Francis Noble (3000 dr) is on sale at Kalodoukas Holidays at the beginning of Kali Strata.

Places to Stay – Budget
There is very little budget accommodation. The cheapest doubles cost around 12,000 dr. Some accommodation owners meet the boats.

Rooms to Let Titika, located behind the Nautical Museum, has clean, nicely furnished air-con double/triple rooms for 12,000/14,000 dr with bathrooms. Make inquiries at Kostos Tourist Shop at the top of the harbour.

Hotel Kokona (☎ 71 549/451, fax 72 620) has comfortable rooms with bathroom for 12,000/14,000 dr. The hotel is on the street to the left of the large church.

Nikolitsi Fotini Studios (☎ 71 780), near Nos Beach, are clean, comfortable studios with well equipped kitchen areas. Doubles are 12,000 dr. If you call ahead the owner will pick you up from the harbour.

Pension Katerinettes (☎/fax 72 698, email marina~epe@rho.forthnet.gre) is housed in the former town hall where the treaty granting the Dodecanese to the Allies was signed. Some of its rooms have magnificent painted ceilings. Doubles with a sea view are 15,000 dr, and those without are 9500 dr.

Hotel Fiona (☎/fax 72 088), in Horio, has lovely rooms with wood-panelled ceilings. Doubles/triples are 14,000/16,500 dr with bathroom. To reach the hotel turn left at Taverna Georgios.

DODECANESE

Places to Stay – Mid-Range

Opera House Hotel (☎ *72 034, fax 72 035)*, well signposted from the harbour, is an impressive cluster of buildings in a peaceful garden. Spacious double/triple studios are 20,000/25,000 dr.

Hotel Nireus (☎ *72 400/403, fax 72 404)* has elegant, traditional double/triple rooms for 20,000/30,000 dr and double/triple suites for 29,000/30,200 dr. Turn left at the clock tower (facing the sea) and the hotel is on the left. Farther along, the A class *Hotel Aliki* (☎/*fax 71 665)* is another traditional-style hotel. Singles/doubles are 20,000/30,000 dr.

Places to Eat

Many of Gialos' restaurants are mediocre, catering for day-trippers. Some exceptions are *Vigla Restaurant* and *Vassilis Restaurant*, both at the top of the harbour; *O Meraklis Taverna*, two blocks back; and the excellent, low-priced *Taverna Neraida*, beyond Hotel Glafkos.

Restaurant Les Katerinettes, below the pension, offers an extensive range of well prepared dishes; the mixed mezedes plate costs 2500 dr.

Taverna Tholos, just before Nos Beach, is excellent. The imaginative dishes include chicken in orange sauce, lamb in egg and lemon sauce, and green beans with feta.

In Horio, there are three good restaurants in a row on Kali Strata. *To Kima* and *Georgios* serve well prepared traditional Greek dishes, and *Restaurant Sillogos* offers imaginative fare such as chicken with prunes and pork with leek.

O'Hylios, at the top of the harbour, is a good vegetarian restaurant serving snacks during the day and three-course meals in the evening. *White House Cafe*, nearby, serves great coffee and a range of snacks. *Vapori Bar* serves good breakfasts and snacks and has free newspapers and magazines as well as Internet access.

Hellenikon, in Gialos, has a cellar of 140 different Greek wines, and is known as the wine restaurant of Symi. The food offered is equally impressive. Unusual mezedes include sea urchin roe, snails with pesto and goat's cheese with mulberries. Desserts include a luscious concoction of ice cream, cream, dried fruits, red wine and rum. Expect to pay around 12,000 dr for a three course meal with wine.

Entertainment

There are several lively bars in the streets behind the south side of the harbour. *White House Cafe* and *Vapori Bar* are also lively in the evenings, and sometimes feature live music. The expat-owned *Jean & Tonic* in Horio is a popular late night bar.

AROUND SYMI

Pedi is a little fishing village and burgeoning holiday resort in a fertile valley 2km downhill from Horio. It has some sandy stretches on its narrow beach. There are domatia, hotels and tavernas.

Nimboreios is a long pebbled beach 2km west of Gialos. It has some natural shade as well as sun-beds and umbrellas. You can walk there from Gialos along a scenic Byzantine path. Take the road by the east side of the central square, and continue straight ahead. At the fork, bear right and go uphill, passing a cemetery and a monastery on either side. When the road curves right, take the narrower cement road to its left, which becomes a paved path passing between stone walls. Continue ahead through two gates. After passing Moni Agiou Georgiou the path drops down to **Kokkinohoma Bay**. Turn left to reach Nimboreios.

Taxi boats go to **Georgiou Disalona Bay** and the more developed **Nanous Beach**, which has sun-beds, umbrellas and a taverna, and **Agia Marina**, which also has a taverna. These are all shingle beaches. Symi's only sandy beach is the tamarisk-shaded **Agios Nikolaos**.

The more remote **Marathounta** and **Agios Emilianos** beaches are best reached by excursion boat.

Moni Taxiarhou Mihail

Μονή Ταξιάρχου Μιχαήλ

Symi's principal sight is the large Moni Taxiarhou Mihail (Monastery of Michael of

Panormitis) in Panormitis Bay, and it's the stopping-off point for many of the day-trippers from Rhodes. A monastery was first built here in the 5th or 6th century, but the present building dates from the 18th century. The katholikon contains an intricately carved wooden iconostasis, frescoes, and an icon of St Michael which supposedly appeared miraculously where the monastery now stands. St Michael is the patron saint of Symi, and protector of sailors.

The monastery complex comprises a museum, restaurant and basic guest rooms. Beds cost 3000 dr; reservations are necessary in July and August.

Kos Κως

☎ 0242   • postcode 853 00
(Psalidi 852 00)   • pop 26,379

Kos is the third-largest island of the Dodecanese and one of its most fertile and well watered. It lies only 5km from the Turkish peninsula of Bodrum. It is second only to Rhodes in both its wealth of archaeological remains and its tourist development, with most of its beautiful beaches wall-to-wall with sun beds and parasols. It's a long, narrow island with a mountainous spine.

Pserimos is a small island between Kos and Kalymnos. It has a good sandy beach, but unfortunately becomes overrun with day-trippers from both of its larger neighbours.

History

Kos' fertile land attracted settlers from the earliest times. So many people lived here by Mycenaean times that it was able to send 30 ships to the Trojan War. During the 7th and 6th centuries BC, Kos flourished as an ally of the powerful Rhodian cities of Ialyssos, Kamiros and Lindos. In 477 BC, after suffering an earthquake and subjugation to the Persians, it joined the Delian League and flourished once more.

Hippocrates (460-377 BC), the father of medicine, was born and lived on the island. After Hippocrates' death, the Sanctuary of Asclepius and a medical school were built, which perpetuated his teachings and made Kos famous throughout the Greek world.

Ptolemy II of Egypt was born on Kos, thus securing it the protection of Egypt, under which it became a prosperous trading centre. In 130 BC, Kos came under Roman domination, and in the 1st century AD it was put under the administration of Rhodes, with which it came to share the same vicissitudes, right up to the tourist deluge of the present day.

Getting There & Away

Air There are three flights daily to Athens (21,400 dr). The Olympic Airways office (☎ 28 330) is at Vasileos Pavlou 22, in Kos Town.

Ferry – Domestic Kos has daily connections to Rhodes and Piraeus. It is also included in the route linking the Dodecanese with Mykonos and Syros and has a link with Thessaloniki via Samos.

Ferry – International There are daily ferries in summer from Kos Town to Bodrum (ancient Halicarnassus) in Turkey (one hour, 13,000 dr return, including Turkish port tax). Boats leave at 8.30 am and return at 4 pm. Many travel agents around Kos Town sell tickets.

Hydrofoil Kos is served by both the Dodecanese Hydrofoil Company and Samos Hydrofoils. In high season there are daily shuttles, morning and evening, to and from Rhodes, (two hours, 6670 dr), with good connections to all the major islands in the group, as well as Samos, Ikaria and Fourni in the North-Eastern Aegean. From Samos you can easily connect with the Cyclades.

Information and tickets are readily available from the many travel agents.

Excursion Boat From Kos Town there are many boat excursions, both around the island and to other islands. Some examples of return fares include: Kalymnos (3000 dr); Pserimos, Kalymnos and Plati (6000 dr);

DODECANESE

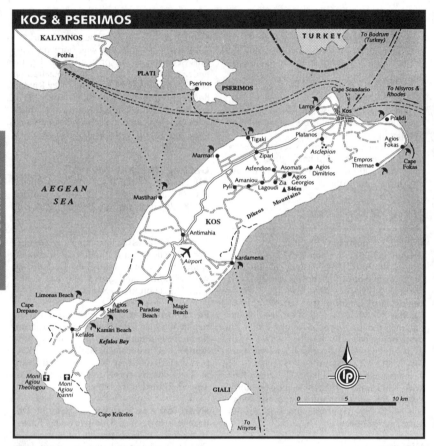

KOS & PSERIMOS

KALYMNOS

Pothia

PLATI

Pserimos   **PSERIMOS**

TURKEY   To Bodrum
(Turkey)

Cape Scandario   To Nisyros &
Rhodes

Lamp.   Kos   Psalidi

Tigaki   Platanos   Agios
Fokas

Marmari   Zipari   Asclepion   Empros
Thermae   Cape
Fokas

Asfendion   Asomati   Agios
Dimitrios

*AEGEAN
SEA*   Amaniou   Agios
Pyli   Zia   Georgios
Mastihari   Lagoudi   ▲ 846m

Dikeos Mountains

KOS

Antimahia

✈ *Airport*   Kardamena

Limonas Beach
Cape
Drepano   Agios
Stefanos   Paradise   Magic
Beach   Beach

Kamari Beach
Kefalos
Kefalos Bay

Moni
Agiou
Theologou   Moni
Agiou
Ioanni

GIALI

Cape Krikelos   To
Nisyros

0   5   10 km

and Nisyros and Giali (5500 dr). There is also a daily excursion boat from Kardamena to Nisyros (3000 dr return) and from Mastihari to Pserimos and Kalymnos.

Getting Around
To/From the Airport An Olympic Airways bus (1000 dr) leaves the airline's office two hours before each flight. The airport is 26km south-west of Kos Town, near the village of Antimahia, and is poorly served by public transport, though buses to

and from Kardamena and Kefalos stop at the roundabout nearby.

Many travellers choose to share a taxi into town (4000 dr).

Bus The bus station (☎ 22 292, fax 20 263) is at Kleopatras 7, just west of the Olympic Airways office. There are 10 buses daily to Tigaki (350 dr), five to Mastihari (550 dr), six to Kardamena (600 dr), five to Pyli (350 dr), six to Kefalos (800 dr) via Paradise, Agios Stefanos and Kamari beaches, and three to Zia (350 dr). There are frequent local buses to the Asclepion, Lampi and Agios Fokas from the bus stop on Akti Kountouriotou.

Car, Motorcycle & Bicycle There are numerous car, motorcycle and moped rental outlets.

You'll be tripping over bikes to rent. Prices range from 1000 dr for an old bone-shaker to 3000 dr for a top-notch mountain bike.

Excursion Boat These boats line the southern side of Akti Kountouriotou in Kos Town and make trips around the island.

KOS TOWN

Kos Town, on the north-east coast, is the island's capital and main port. The old town of Kos was destroyed by an earthquake in 1933. The new town, although modern, is picturesque and lush, with palms, pines, oleander and hibiscus everywhere. The Castle of the Knights dominates the port, and Hellenistic and Roman ruins are strewn everywhere.

Orientation

The ferry quay is north of the castle. Excursion boats dock on Akti Kountouriotou to the south-west of the castle. The central square of Plateia Eleftherias is south of Akti Kountouriotou along Vasileos Pavlou. Kos' so-called Old Town is on Ifestou. Its souvenir shops, jewellers and boutiques denude it of any old-world charm, though.

South-east of the castle, the waterfront is called Akti Miaouli. It continues as Vasileos Georgiou and then G Papandreou, which leads to the beaches of Psalidi, Agios Fokas and Empros Thermae.

Information

Kos Town's municipal tourist office (☎ 24 460, fax 21 111) is on Vasileos Georgiou. The staff are efficient and helpful. From May to October the office is open 8 am to 8 pm Monday to Friday and 8 am to 3 pm on weekends. The tourist police

(☎ 22 444) and regular police (☎ 22 222) share the yellow building opposite the quay.

The post office is on Vasileos Pavlou and the OTE is at Vyronos 6. Kos Town has two Internet cafes, Del Mare at Megalou Alexandrou 4 and Status at Navarinou 55.

Both the National Bank of Greece, on Antinavarhou Ioannidi, and the Ionian Bank, on El Venizelou, have ATMs. The Alpha Credit Bank on Akti Kountouriotou has a 24 hour automatic exchange machine.

To get to the bus station walk up Vasileos Pavlou and turn right at the Olympic Airways office.

The hospital (☎ 22 300) is at Ippokratous 32. The Happy Wash laundrette is at Mitropolis 20 and the Laundromat Center is at Alikarnassou 124.

The port police (☎ 28 507) are at the corner of Akti Kountouriotou and Megalou Alexandrou.

Archaeological Museum

The archaeological museum (☎ 28 326), on Plateia Eleftherias, has a fine 3rd century AD mosaic in the vestibule and many statues from various periods. The most renowned is the statue of Hippocrates. The museum is open 8.30 am to 3 pm Tuesday to Sunday. Admission is 800 dr.

Archaeological Sites

The **ancient agora** is an open site south of the castle. A massive 3rd century BC stoa, with some reconstructed columns, stands on its western side. On the north side are the ruins of a **Shrine of Aphrodite**, **Temple of Hercules** and a 5th century **Christian basilica**. There is no admission charge.

North of the agora is the lovely cobblestone Plateia Platanou where you can pay your respects to the **Hippocrates Plane Tree**. Under this tree, according to the EOT brochure, Hippocrates taught his pupils. Plane trees don't usually live for more than 200 years – so much for the power of the Hippocratic oath – though in all fairness it is certainly one of Europe's oldest. This once-magnificent tree is held up with scaffolding, and looks to be in its death throes. Beneath it is an old sarcophagus which the Turks converted into a fountain. Opposite the tree is the well preserved 18th century **Mosque of Gazi Hassan Pasha**, its ground floor loggia now converted into souvenir shops.

From Plateia Platanou a bridge leads across Finikon (called the Avenue of Palms) to the **Castle of the Knights**. Along with the castles of Rhodes City and Bodrum, this impregnable fortress was the knights' most stalwart defence against the encroaching Ottomans. The castle, which had massive

outer walls and an inner keep, was built in the 14th century. Damaged by an earthquake in 1495, it was restored by the Grand Masters d'Aubusson and d'Amboise (each a master of a 'tongue' of knights) in the 16th century. The keep was originally separated from the town by a moat (now Finikon). Opening times are 8.30 am to 3 pm Tuesday to Sunday. Admission is 800 dr.

The other ruins are mostly in the southern part of the town. Walk along Vasileos Pavlou to Grigoriou and cross over to the

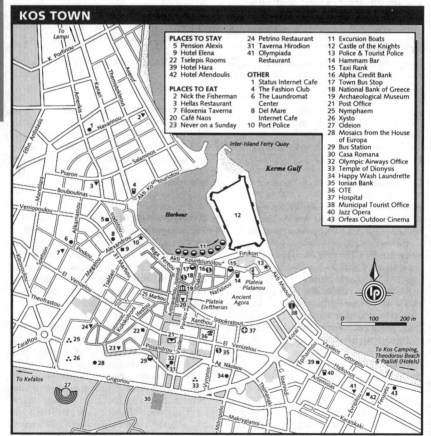

KOS TOWN

PLACES TO STAY
5 Pension Alexis
9 Hotel Elena
22 Tselepis Rooms
39 Hotel Hara
42 Hotel Afendoulis

PLACES TO EAT
2 Nick the Fisherman
3 Hellas Restaurant
7 Filoxenia Taverna
20 Café Naos
23 Never on a Sunday
24 Petrino Restaurant
31 Taverna Hirodion
41 Olympiada Restaurant

OTHER
1 Status Internet Cafe
4 The Fashion Club
6 The Laundromat Center
8 Del Mare Internet Cafe
10 Port Police
11 Excursion Boats
12 Castle of the Knights
13 Police & Tourist Police
14 Hammam Bar
15 Taxi Rank
16 Alpha Credit Bank
17 Town Bus Stop
18 National Bank of Greece
19 Archaeological Museum
21 Post Office
25 Nymphaem
26 Xysto
27 Odeion
28 Mosaics from the House of Europa
29 Bus Station
30 Casa Romana
32 Olympic Airways Office
33 Temple of Dionysis
34 Happy Wash Laundrette
35 Ionian Bank
36 OTE
37 Hospital
38 Municipal Tourist Office
40 Jazz Opera
43 Orfeas Outdoor Cinema

Inter-Island Ferry Quay

Kerme Gulf

Harbour

To Kos Camping, Theodorou Beach & Psalidi (Hotels)

To Kefalos

0   100   200 m

restored **Casa Romana**, an opulent 3rd century Roman villa which was built on the site of a larger 1st century Hellenistic house. It is open 8.30 am to 3 pm Tuesday to Sunday. Admission is 800 dr. Opposite here are the scant ruins of the 3rd century **Temple of Dionysos**.

Facing Grigoriou, turn right to reach the **western excavation** site. Two wooden shelters at the back of the site protect the 3rd century mosaics of the **House of Europa**. The best preserved mosaic depicts Europa's abduction by Zeus in the guise of a bull. In front of here an exposed section of the Dekumanus Maximus (the Roman city's main thoroughfare) runs parallel to the modern road, then turns right towards the **nymphaeum**, which consisted of once-lavish public latrines, and the **xysto**, a large Hellenistic gymnasium, with some restored columns. On the opposite side of Grigoriou is the restored 3rd century **odeion**.

Places to Stay – Budget
Kos' one camp site is *Kos Camping* (☎ 23 910/275), 3km along the eastern waterfront. It's a well kept, shaded site with a taverna, snack bar, minimarket, kitchen and laundry. Rates are 1400 dr per person and 700 dr per tent.

The convivial *Pension Alexis* (☎ 28 798, 25 594, Irodotou 9) is highly recommended. Clean singles/doubles/triples cost 4500/7000/8500 dr. The friendly English-speaking Alexis promises never to turn anyone away, and he's a mine of information. A little farther east, his other hotel, *Hotel Afendoulis* (☎/fax 25 797, Evripilou 1), has tastefully furnished rooms with bathroom for 7000/10,000/12,000 dr. Laundry for guests costs 1000 dr a load.

Other commendable budget options include the D class *Hotel Elena* (☎ 22 740, Megalou Alexandrou 7) with doubles/triples with bathroom for 7000/8000 dr, and *Tselepis Rooms* (☎ 28 896, Metsovou 8) where rooms cost 10,000/12,000 dr with bathroom.

At the other end of town the D class *Hotel Hara* (☎ 22 500, Halkonos 6) is a clean, well maintained hotel, with singles/ doubles/triples with bathroom for 6000/8500/10,000 dr.

Places to Stay – Mid-Range & Top End
The B class *Theodorou Beach* (☎ 23 363), on G Papandreou, has a cool, spacious interior and nicely furnished rooms. Singles/doubles/triples cost 12,500/16,000/18,800 dr with bathroom.

Most of Kos' top end hotels are on the beaches to either side of town. The luxurious *Kipriotis Village* (☎ 27 640) at Psalidi, 4km east of town, has singles/doubles for 45,000/55,000 dr and apartments for up to three people for 60,000 dr. The A class *Platanista Hotel* (23 749), also at Psalidi, is an architecturally interesting, crenellated building. Singles/doubles are 22,000/27,800 dr.

Places to Eat
The restaurants lining the central waterfront are generally expensive and poor value. *Taverna Hirodion* (Artemisias 27) serves good food and has a highly entertaining menu, featuring dishes such as Godfish (1700 dr), Humbergers (1400 dr), Gordon Blu (1800 dr) and Jack potato (750 dr). *Olympiada Restaurant*, behind the Olympic Airways office is an unpretentious place serving reasonably priced, tasty food.

Filoxenia Taverna, on the corner of Pindou and Alikarnassou, has a good reputation for traditional home-cooked food. *Hellas Restaurant*, on Amerikis, and *Never on a Sunday*, on Pissandrou, are also highly commendable.

Cafe Aenaos, in a former mosque opposite the market at Plateia Eleftherias, and *Central Cafe (Vasileos Pavlou 17)* are popular meeting places for locals and tourists alike.

Restaurant Ambavros, on the outskirts of town, serves a delicious array of mezedes. Walk inland along Grigoriou, turn left after the Casa Romana and the taverna is 800m along on the left.

Petrino Restaurant (Theologou 1) is a stylish place in a stone mansion, with outdoor eating in a romantic garden setting. It offers a wide range of well prepared food. For a fishy feast head for *Nick the Fisherman* on Averof.

Entertainment

Kos Town has two streets of bars, Diakon and Nafklirou, that positively pulsate in high season. Most belt out techno, but *Hammam Bar (Akti Kountourioti 1)* plays Greek music. *Jazz Opera (Arseniou 5)* is popular with locals and tourists.

Kos Town has three discos. *Heaven (Zouroudi 5)* plays mostly house. At *Calua* next door the music is more mixed and includes R&B. Both are outdoor and have swimming pools. The indoor *Fashion Club (Kanari 2)* has three air-con bars. *Orfeus* outdoor cinema is on Vasileos Georgiou (open summer only).

AROUND KOS TOWN

Asclepion Ασκληπιείον

The Asclepion (☎ 28 763), built on a pine-covered hill 4km south-west of Kos Town, is the island's most important ancient site. From the top there is a wonderful view of Kos Town and Turkey. The Asclepion consisted of a religious sanctuary to Asclepius, the god of healing, a healing centre, and a school of medicine, where the training followed the teachings of Hippocrates.

Hippocrates was the first doctor to have a rational approach to diagnosing and treating illnesses. Until 554 AD people came from far and wide to be treated here, as well as for medical training.

The ruins occupy three levels. The **propylaea**, the Roman-era public **baths** and the remains of guest rooms are on the first level. On the next level is a 4th century BC **altar of Kyparissios Apollo**. West of this is the **first Temple of Asclepius**, built in the 4th century BC. To the east is the 1st century BC **Temple to Apollo**; seven of its graceful columns have been re-erected. On the third level are the remains of the once-magnificent 2nd century BC **Temple of Asclepius**. The site is open 8.30 am to 3 pm Tuesday to Sunday. Admission is 800 dr.

Frequent buses go to the site, but it is pleasant to cycle or walk there.

Platanos

The village of Platanos, on the way to the Asclepion, has many Turkish inhabitants. The village has a mosque and Turkish and Jewish cemeteries. *Arup Taverna*, on the central square, serves well prepared traditional Greek/Turkish fare.

AROUND KOS

Kos' main road runs south-west from Kos Town with turn-offs for the mountain villages and the resorts of Tigaki and Marmari. Between the main road and the coast, a quiet road, ideal for cycling, winds through flat agricultural land as far as Marmari.

The nearest decent beach to Kos Town is the crowded **Lampi Beach**, 4km to the north. Farther round the coast, **Tigaki**, 11km from Kos Town, has an excellent, long, pale sand beach. **Marmari Beach**, 4km west of Tigaki, is slightly less crowded.

G Papandreou in Kos Town leads to the three crowded beaches of **Psalidi**, 3km from Kos Town; **Agios Fokas**, 7km away; and **Empros Thermae**, 11km away. The latter has hot mineral springs which warm the sea.

Antimahia (near the airport) is a major crossroads with two large roundabouts. A worthwhile detour is to the **Castle of Antimahia** along a turn-off to the left, 1km before Antimahia. There's a ruined settlement within its well preserved walls.

Kardamena, 27km from Kos Town, and 5km south-east of Antimahia, is an over-developed, tacky resort best avoided, unless you want to take an excursion boat to Nisyros (see the Getting There & Away section for Kos).

Mastihari Μαστιχάρι

Mastihari, north of Antimahia and 30km from Kos Town, retains some charm, despite recent development. It has a good sandy beach and secluded spots can be found at its extreme western end. From here there are excursion boats to Kalymnos and the small island of **Pserimos**. The road from

Antimahia terminates at the central square at Mastihari's waterfront.

There's loads of accommodation in Mastihari. *Fessaras Rooms to Rent (☎ 59 005)* has doubles for 5000 dr. Walk up the road by Kali Kardia Restaurant, take the third turn to the right and the rooms are on the left. Make inquiries at Thomas minimarket. Walk inland along the main road to *Rooms to Rent Anna (☎ 59 041)*, on the left, where doubles are 6000 dr. Farther up on the right, *Pension Elena (☎ 59 010)* has doubles for 5500 dr. Next door, *Rooms to Let David (☎ 59 122)* has doubles for 7000 dr.

Kali Kardia Restaurant, on the central square, is commendable and the fish is particularly good.

Kamari & Kefalos
Καμάρι & Κέφαλος

From Antimahia the main road continues south-west to the huge Kefalos Bay, fringed by a 5km stretch of sand and pebble beaches which, although not isolated, are less crowded than most on Kos. The first is the sandy **Paradise Beach** reached down a track from the main road. The next, **Agios Stefanos**, is taken up by a vast Club Med complex. But the beach, reached along a short turn-off from the main road, is still worth a visit to see the island of Agios Stefanos (named after its church), which is within swimming distance, and the ruins of two 5th century basilicas to the left of the beach as you face the sea. The beach continues to Kamari.

Kefalos, 43km south of Kos Town, is the sprawling village perched high above Kamari Beach. It's a pleasant place with few concessions to tourism. The central square, where the bus terminates, is at the top of the 2km road from the coast.

Between Antimahia and Kefalos a dirt road leads down to the undeveloped **Magic Beach**. Along the same road a turn off leads to **Plaka**, a pleasant forested valley with a network of paths.

Places to Stay Most of the accommodation in Kefalos Bay is monopolised by tour groups. A good option is *Petros and Maria Rooms (☎ 71 306)*, on the main road 50m from the Agios Stefanos bus stop. It has a beautiful garden and doubles/triples with bathroom cost 6000/7000 dr. *Studios Dionisia (☎ 71 276/176)*, farther south near the Kamari fishing quay, has double studios for 7000 dr.

Around Kefalos
The southern peninsula has the island's most wild and rugged scenery. **Moni Agiou Theologou** is on the east coast, 4km away, just beyond a sand and pebble beach. Sunsets here are spectacular. **Moni Agiou Ioanni** is at the end of the road, 7km south of Kefalos.

Restaurant Agiou Theologou, near the beach, serves good main dishes and delicious home-made traditional cakes. The sea is quite rough here and the taverna rents out body boards for 2000 dr.

Limonas, 10km north of Kefalos, is a little fishing harbour. Its two small sandy beaches rarely get crowded. There are two tavernas.

Mountain Villages
Several attractive villages are scattered on the northern slopes of the green and wooded, alpine-like Dikeos mountain range. At **Zipari**, 10km from the capital, a road to the south-east leads to **Asfendion**. From Asfendion, a turn-off to the left leads to the pristine hamlets of **Agios Georgios** and **Agios Dimitrios**. The road straight ahead leads to the village of **Zia**, which is touristy but worth a visit for the surrounding countryside and some great sunsets. *Taverna Olympia*, 70m uphill from the central square, is the best taverna.

Lagoudi is a small, unspoilt village to the west of Zia. From here you can continue to **Amaniou** (just before modern Pyli) where there is a left turn to the ruins of the medieval village of **Pyli**, overlooked by a ruined castle. Just off the central square at modern Pyli, the little *Taverna Old Pygi*, overlooking a lion-headed fountain, serves tasty, low-priced fare.

Kalymnos Κάλυμνος

☎ 0243 • postcode 852 00 • pop 18,200

Kalymnos (**kah**-lim-nos), only 2.5km south of Leros, is a mountainous, arid island, speckled with fertile valleys. Kalymnos is renowned as the 'sponge-fishing island', but with the demise of this industry it has begun to exploit its tourist potential. However, out of high season its coast is still relatively uncrowded.

Kalymnos hit the Greek headlines in 1995 when local fisherman Antonis Hatziantoniou looked into his net on New Year's Eve and saw a beautiful 2m-high bronze statue of a woman. No, he hadn't been over-indulging in New Year celebrations. Archaeologists think his priceless 'catch' may be the work of the renowned 4th century BC sculptor Praxiteles. The statue is presently in Athens for evaluation. Theoretically a museum is to be built on Kalymnos to house it; needless to say it hasn't happened yet, but at least Antonis was suitably rewarded.

Getting There & Away

Air At the time of writing, Kalymnos' airport was due to open at the end of 1999 – but they've been saying that since 1995, so don't hold your breath.

Ferry The F/B *Nissos Kalymnos* is based on Kalymnos and runs an important service connecting most of the major islands in the chain, as well as the more outlying islands such as Astypalea and Kastellorizo, and Samos in the North-Eastern Aegean. It operates five different daytime routes six days a week, setting out each morning from either Kalymnos or Rhodes. You can check schedules at the company office (☎ 29 612) on 25 Martiou in Pothia.

The following table shows the F/B *Nissos Kalymnos* schedule from Kalymnos in high season.

Destination	Duration	Price	Frequency
Agathonisi	6½ hours	2700 dr	2 weekly
Arki	5¼ hours	2600 dr	2 weekly
Astypalea	3½ hours	2600 dr	2 weekly
Leros	2 hours	1800 dr	2 weekly
Lipsi	3 hours	1800 dr	2 weekly
Patmos	4 hours	2400 dr	2 weekly
Samos	7½ hours	3200 dr	2 weekly

Hydrofoil Kalymnos is served by both the Dodecanese Hydrofoil Company and Samos Hydrofoils. In high season there is a morning service daily to Kos (35 minutes, 2620 dr), with a connection to Rhodes, (three hours, 8055 dr), returning every evening. There are good connections to all the major islands in the group, as well as Samos, Ikaria and Fourni in the North-Eastern Aegean. From Samos you can easily connect with the Cyclades. Buy tickets for Samos hydrofoils at GA Ferries office. The Hydrofoil Agency (☎ 29 886, 28 502) is near the quay.

Excursion Boat In summer there are three excursion boats daily from Pothia to Mastihari on Kos, and one to Pserimos (2000 dr return). There are also weekly excursions to Turkey for 11,000 dr (including Turkish port tax).

There are daily excursions from Myrties to Xirokambos on Leros (3000 dr return).

Getting Around

Bus In summer there is a bus on the hour to Masouri (250 dr) via Myrties; to Emboreios (300 dr) at 9 am and 3.15 pm on Monday, Wednesday and Friday; to Vathy (300 dr) at 6.30 am, 1.30 and 5 pm from Monday to Saturday, and at 7.30 am, 1.30 and 5 pm on Sunday. Buy tickets from Themis Minimarket.

Motorcycle There are several motorcycle rental outlets along Pothia's waterfront.

Taxi Shared taxis are an unusual feature of Kalymnos that cost just a little more than buses. They go from Pothia to Masouri and leave from the taxi rank on Plateia Kyprou (☎ 50 300). These taxis can also be flagged down en route. A taxi to Emboreios costs 3000 dr and to Vathy 2000 dr.

DODECANESE

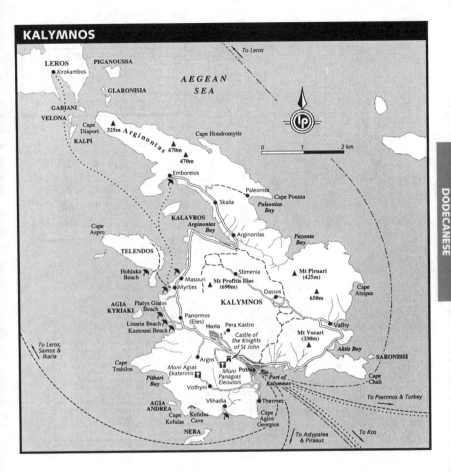

KALYMNOS

AEGEAN SEA

DODECANESE

Excursion Boat From Myrties there are daily excursion boats to Emboreios (15,000 dr). Day trips to the Kefalas Cave (6000 dr), impressive for its stalactites and stalagmites, run from both Pothia and Myrties.

POTHIA Πόθια

Pothia, the port and capital of Kalymnos, is where the majority of the island's inhabitants live. Although it's considerably bigger and noisier than most island capitals, it's not without charm. However, a word of warning!

Pothia is short in the pavement department and has more than its fair share of kamikaze motorcyclists – keep your wits about you.

Orientation & Information

Pothia's ferry quay is at the southern side of the bay. To reach the town centre, turn right at the end of the quay. Follow the waterfront around and you will pass a tourist information kiosk (☎ 23 140, open summer only) behind the statue of Poseidon, 100m north of the start of the quay.

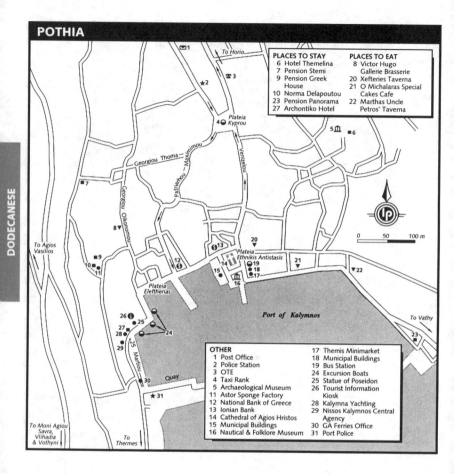

POTHIA

To Horio

PLACES TO STAY
6 Hotel Themelina
7 Pension Stemi
9 Pension Greek
   House
10 Norma Delapoutou
23 Pension Panorama
27 Archontiko Hotel

PLACES TO EAT
8 Victor Hugo
   Gallerie Brasserie
20 Xefteries Taverna
21 O Michalaras Special
   Cakes Cafe
22 Marthas Uncle
   Petros' Taverna

Plateia
Kyprou

Georgiou Thoma — Maximimou

Patriarhou — Maximimou

Venizelou

Georgiou Oikonomou

To Agios
Vasilios

Plateia
Eleftherias

Plateia
Ethnikis Antistasis

Port of Kalymnos

To Vathy

OTHER
1 Post Office
2 Police Station
3 OTE
4 Taxi Rank
5 Archaeological Museum
11 Astor Sponge Factory
12 National Bank of Greece
13 Ionian Bank
14 Cathedral of Agios Hristos
15 Municipal Buildings
16 Nautical & Folklore Museum

17 Themis Minimarket
18 Municipal Buildings
19 Bus Station
24 Excursion Boats
25 Statue of Poseidon
26 Tourist Information
   Kiosk
28 Kalymna Yachting
29 Nissos Kalymnos Central
   Agency
30 GA Ferries Office
31 Port Police

25 Martiou

Quay

To Moni Agiou
Savra,
Vlihadia
& Vothyni

To
Thermes

0   50   100 m

Continue around the waterfront and you will see the two matching municipal buildings flanking the Nautical & Folklore Museum. The Cathedral of Agios Hristos is behind, and the bus station is just to the east of the cathedral. The main thoroughfare of Venizelou runs north from here to Plateia Kyprou, the town's central square. Another busy street, Patriarhou Maximimou, also runs from the waterfront to this square. North of the square are the OTE, on Venizelou, and the post office and police

(☎ 29 301), on Patriarhou Maximimou. The settlement of Horio, 3km inland, is the island's former capital.

The National Bank of Greece, at the bottom of Patriarhou Maximimou, and the Ionian Bank, 100m farther east along the waterfront, both have ATMs. The port police (☎ 29 304) are at the start of the quay.

Things to See & Do

The **Archaeological Museum** (☎ 23 113), housed in a neoclassical mansion which once belonged to a wealthy sponge merchant, Mr Vouvalis, is east of Plateia Kyprou. In one room there are some Neolithic and Bronze Age objects. Other rooms are reconstructed as they were when the Vouvalis family lived here. The museum is open 10 am to 2 pm Tuesday to Sunday. Admission is 500 dr. The **Nautical & Folklore Museum** is in the centre of the waterfront. It is open 8 am to 2 pm daily. Admission is 500 dr.

You can hire **yachts** from Kalymna Yachting (☎ 24 083/084, fax 29 125), 50m north of the quay.

Places to Stay

Domatia owners meet the ferries. A pleasant budget option is *Pension Greek House* (☎ 29 559, 23 752), inland from the port near the Astor Sponge Factory. It has cosy wood-panelled singles/doubles/triples with bathroom and kitchen facilities for 4500/6000/7200 dr. Norma Delapoutou rents well kept *domatia* (☎ 24 054, 48 145) behind the Astor Sponge Factory, which is owned by her brother. Doubles with kitchen and verandah are 5000 dr.

Farther inland, *Pension Stemi* (☎ 28 361) has clean, modern rooms with balconies. Doubles/triples cost 6000/7000 dr. *Pension Panorama* (☎ 29 249), 400m along the road to Vathy, has pleasant singles/doubles/triples for 5000/6500/8000 dr.

Archontiko Hotel (☎/fax 24 149), at the top of the quay, is a new hotel in a renovated century-old mansion. Immaculate rooms go for a reasonable 7000/9000/ 10,000 dr.

Hotel Themelina (☎ 22 682), by the well signposted archaeological museum, is a 19th century mansion with swimming pool. Spacious, traditionally furnished doubles/triples cost 16,000/19,500 dr with bathroom. In summer the mansion is booked by tour operators, but there are 30 modern rooms around the pool for the same price.

Places to Eat

The century-old *Xefteries Taverna*, just off Venizelou, serves delicious, inexpensive food; you'll be taken into the kitchen to choose from the pots. Of the fish tavernas on the eastern waterfront, *Marthas Uncle Petros' Taverna* is the best; the crab salad is a delicious and filling starter. *O Michalaras Special Cakes Cafe* serves *galaktoboureko*, a speciality of Kalymnos. A generous slice of this gooey confection is 550 dr.

The owners of *Victor Hugo Gallerie Brasserie*, on Georgiou Oikonomou, Soletatis Coulouritis, a professional photographer, and Vaughelis Kassos, a philosophy graduate, have travelled widely but returned to their island to 'do something for its young people'. Here, young locals are given the opportunity to exhibit their art work and stage live music performances. Coffees, soft and alcoholic drinks and snacks are served, and visitors are warmly welcomed.

AROUND POTHIA

The ruined **Castle of the Knights of St John** (or Castle Hrysoherias) looms to the left of the Pothia-Horio road.

Pera Kastro was a pirate-proof village inhabited until the 18th century. Within the crumbling walls are the ruins of stone houses and six tiny, well kept churches. Steps lead up to Pera Kastro from Horio. It's a strenuous climb but the splendid views make it worthwhile.

A tree-lined road continues from Horio to **Panormos** (also called Elies), a pretty village 5km from Pothia. Its pre-war name of Elies (olives) derived from its abundant olive groves, which were destroyed in WWII. An enterprising post-war mayor planted abundant trees and flowers to create beautiful panoramas wherever one looked – hence its present name, meaning 'panorama'. The sandy beaches of **Kantouni**, **Linaria** and **Platys Gialos** are all within walking distance.

Pension Graziella (☎ 47 314/346), signposted from the main road in Panormos, has comfortable doubles for 5000 dr, double studios for 7000 dr and five-person apartments for 14,000 dr. The owner, the dynamic English-speaking Menelaos, enjoys informing guests of the delights of Kalymnos. Just outside Panormos, on the road to Myrties, ***Hotel Kamari*** *(☎ 47 278)* has great views and well kept singles/doubles/triples for 5000/6000/7000 dr.

The monastery **Moni Agiou Savra** is reached along a turn-off left from the Vothyni and Vlihadia road. You can enter the monastery but a strict dress code is enforced, so wear long sleeves and long trousers or skirts.

MYRTIES & TELENDOS ISLET
Μυρτιές & Νήσος Τέλενδος

From Panormos the road continues to the west coast with stunning views of Telendos

---

Sponge Fishing

Sponge fishing has occupied Kalymniots since ancient times and was, until recently, their major industry. Kalymnos is now the only Greek island with a sponge-diving fleet, comprising 300 divers.

As well as the obvious one, sponges have had many uses throughout history – everything from padding in armour to tampons. For hundreds of years the sponges were fished from the waters around Kalymnos, but as the industry grew, fishermen were forced to venture farther away. By the 19th century, divers sailed such great distances that they had to spend months at a time away from home, departing shortly after Easter and returning at the end of October. These two events were celebrated in religious and secular festivals.

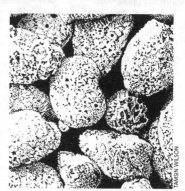

Until the first diving suit was invented in the late 19th century, sponge divers were weighed down with stones and had to hold their breath under water. The early diving suits were made of rubber and canvas and were worn with a huge bronze helmet joined to an air pump by a long hose. This contraption enabled divers to stay under the water for much longer. Sponge diving was perilous work and those who didn't die young were often paralysed by the bends.

For many years fishing fleets dived for sponges off the Libyan coast, but Muammar Gadaffi proved an unwelcoming host, exacting an exorbitant tax from the divers. Nowadays, the few remaining sponge-gatherers wear oxygen tanks and work much closer to home, in the North-Eastern Aegean and around Crete. The demise of the sponge industry has been caused by overfishing in the Aegean and the availability of low-priced synthetic sponges.

Greeks are not ones to decline an excuse for feasting and celebration, even if the reasons for so doing have largely disappeared, so the festivals have been preserved. For the week following Easter, the Iprogros (Sponge Festival) occurs, with traditional dancing, music, feasting and drinking, ending with church bell ringing. The fleet then sails out of Pothia Harbour.

At the Astor Sponge Factory, behind Plateia Eleftherias in Pothia, you can watch the process which transforms a disgusting black object into a nice pale-yellow sponge. It goes without saying that Kalymnos is one of the best places in Greece to buy sponges, but if people realised what they were actually buying they might think again. The black objects retrieved from the sea are colonies of micro-organisms living in their fibrous waste products, which are then boiled alive and bleached in acid. Anyone for a bath?

Islet opposite the package resorts of Myrties. From Myrties there's a daily caïque to Xirokambos on Leros (3000 dr return) and frequent caïques for Telendos between 8 am and 11 pm (600 dr return).

The lovely, tranquil and traffic-free islet of Telendos, with a little quayside hamlet, was part of Kalymnos until separated by an earthquake in 554 AD.

If you turn right from the Telendos quay you will pass the ruins of a basilica. Farther on, beyond On the Rocks Cafe, there are several pebble and sand beaches. To reach **Hohlaka Beach**, turn left from the quay and then right at Zorba's Restaurant.

Places to Stay & Eat
Telendos has several domatia. All have pleasant, clean rooms with bathroom. Opposite the quay, *Pension & Restaurant Uncle George* (☎ 47 502, 23 855) has singles/doubles for 4000/6000 dr. Next door at *Pension Rita* (☎ 47 914, fax 47 927) the rates are the same, and there are also double studios for 7000 dr. To the right of the quay, *Nicky Rooms* (☎ 47 584) has doubles for 5000 dr and *Galanommatis Fotini Rooms* (☎ 47 401) has rooms for 7000 dr.

Port Potha Hotel (☎ 47 321, fax 48 108), beyond On the Rocks Cafe, has well kept singles/doubles/triples for 6000/8000/9000 dr. The new *apartments* adjoining On the Rocks Cafe (☎ 48 260, fax 48 261, email OTE@greece2000.freeserve.co.uk) cost 10,000 dr for two people.

Restaurant Uncle George serves excellent seafood. *On the Rocks Cafe* serves well prepared meat and fish dishes. In the evening it's a lively music bar and if you can't drag yourself away from the fun to catch the last caïque back to Myrties, then George, the friendly Greek-Australian owner, will take you back in his boat free of charge.

EMBOREIOS Εμπορειός
The scenic west-coast road continues to Emboreios, where there's a pleasant tree-shaded pebble beach. One of the nicest places to stay is *Harry's Apartments* (☎ 47 434/922) where modern double/triple apartments cost 9000/10,800 dr. The adjoining *Paradise Restaurant* has a good reputation around the island. *Taverna Kastril* on the beach is also commendable.

VATHY Βαθύ
Vathy, 8km north-east of Pothia, is one of the most beautiful and peaceful parts of the island. Vathy means 'deep' in Greek and refers to the slender fjord which cuts through high cliffs into a fertile valley, where narrow roads wind between citrus orchards. There is no beach at Vathy's harbour, Rena, but excursion boats take tourists to quiet coves nearby.

Places to Stay & Eat
Vathy has two places to stay, both at Rena. The C class *Hotel Galini* has well kept doubles for 7000 dr with bathroom and balcony, breakfast included. *Pension Manolis* (☎ 31 300), above the right side of the harbour, has beautiful singles/doubles/triples for 5000/6000/7200 dr with bathroom. There is a communal kitchen and terraces surrounded by an attractive garden. The English-speaking Manolis is a tour guide and very knowledgeable about the area.

Poppy's Taverna serves reasonably priced, well prepared food and, according to one customer, the best dolmades he's ever tasted.

Leros Λέρος

☎ 0247　• postcode 854 00　• pop 8059

An infamous psychiatric institution, shabby Mussolini-inspired public buildings, a heavy military presence and, during the junta years, a prison for political dissidents, have saddled Leros with an almighty image problem. However, offsetting these flaws is the island's gentle, hilly countryside dotted with small holdings and huge, impressive, almost-landlocked bays, which look more like lakes than open sea.

Lakki is the main port of Leros, but smaller ferries and some excursion boats

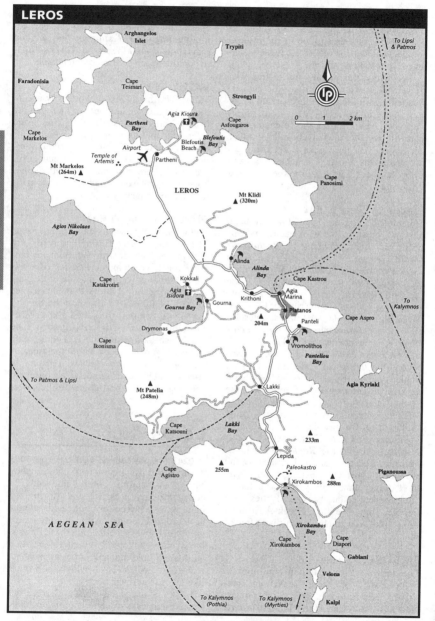

LEROS

Arghangelos Islet

Trypiti

Faradonisia

Cape Tesmari

Strongyli

Partheni Bay

Agia Kioura

Cape Asfougaros

Cape Markelos

Temple of Artemis

Airport

Blefoutis Beach

Blefoutis Bay

Mt Markelos (264m)

Partheni

To Lipsi & Patmos

0   1   2 km

LEROS

Mt Klidi (320m)

Cape Panosimi

Agios Nikolaos Bay

Cape Katakrotiri

Kokkali

Agia Isidora

Gourna Bay

Gourna

Alinda

Alinda Bay

Krithoni

Cape Kastrou

Agia Marina

Platanos

Panteli

Cape Aspro

204m

Vromolithos

To Kalymnos

Drymonas

Cape Ikonisma

Panteliou Bay

Agia Kyriaki

To Patmos & Lipsi

Mt Patelia (248m)

Lakki

Lakki Bay

233m

Cape Katsouni

Lepida

Paleokastro

255m

Xirokambos

288m

Piganoussa

Cape Agistro

AEGEAN SEA

Xirokambos Bay

Cape Xirokambos

Cape Diapori

Gabiani

Velona

To Kalymnos (Pothia)

To Kalymnos (Myrties)

Kalpi

DODECANESE

use the Agia Marina port, and the caïque from Myrties on Kalymnos docks at Xirokambos. Platanos is the capital of Leros. Lakki is one of the best natural harbours in the Aegean; during their occupation of the Dodecanese the Italians chose it as their principal naval base in the eastern Mediterranean.

Getting There & Away
Air There is one flight daily to Athens (21,200 dr). The Olympic Airways office (☎ 22 844, 24 144) is in Platanos, just before the turn-off for Panteli. The airport is in the north of the island at Partheni.

Ferry Leros has the same ferry connections as Kalymnos.

Hydrofoil In summer there are hydrofoils every day to Patmos (45 minutes, 3045 dr), Lipsi (30 minutes, 2650 dr), Samos (two hours, 5000 dr), Kos (one hour, 4100 dr) and Rhodes (3¼ hours, 9300 dr); and almost every day to Agathonisi (1½ hours, 4460 dr) via Patmos and Fourni (4600 dr). Hydrofoils leave from Agia Marina.

Excursion Boat The caïque leaves Xirokambos every day at 7.30 am for Myrties on Kalymnos (1500 dr one way). In summer the Lipsi-based *Anna Express* makes daily trips between Agia Marina and Lipsi, and the *Captain Makis* runs on Tuesday and Thursday. Both cost 5000 dr return.

Getting Around
The hub for Leros' buses is Platanos. There are four buses daily to Partheni via Alinda and six buses to Xirokambos via Lakki.

There is no shortage of car, motorcycle and bicycle rental outlets around the island.

LAKKI Λακκί
If you arrive on one of the large inter-island ferries, you'll disembark at Lakki. The grandiose buildings and wide tree-lined boulevards dotted around the Dodecanese reach their apogee here, for Lakki was built as a Fascist showpiece during the Italian occupation. But the buildings are now shabby and most visitors head straight for Platanos or one of the seaside resorts. Taxis meet all the boats.

PLATANOS Πλάτανος
Platanos, the capital of Leros, is 3km north of Lakki. It's a picturesque little place which spills over a narrow hill pouring down to the port of Agia Marina to the north, and Panteli to the south, both within walking distance. On the east side of Platanos, houses are stacked up a hillside topped by a massive castle. To reach the castle you can either climb up 370 steps, or walk or drive 2km along an asphalt road. It is usually – but not necessarily – open 8 am to noon; entry is 200 dr.

Orientation & Information
The focal point of Platanos is the lively central square, Plateia N Poussou. Xarami links this square with Agia Marina.

There is a tourist information kiosk at the quay. Laskarina Tours (☎ 24 550, fax 24 551), at the Elefteria Hotel, and Kastis Travel & Tourist Agency (☎ 22 140), near the quay in Agia Marina, are very helpful. Laskarina Tours organises trips around the island (3500 dr to 5500 dr).

The post office and OTE share premises on the right side of Xarami. The National Bank of Greece is on the central square. There is a freestanding Commercial Bank ATM on the quay in Agia Marina. The police station (☎ 22 222) is in Agia Marina; turn left from Xarami and it's on the right. The bus station and taxi rank are both on the Lakki-Platanos road, just before the central square.

Places to Stay & Eat
The C class *Elefteria Hotel (☎ 23 550/145)*, near the taxi rank, has pleasant, well kept rooms for 5000/6000/7500 dr with bathroom. The *cafe* on the main square does great coffee and sandwiches.

AROUND PLATANOS
The port of **Agia Marina** has a more authentic ambience than the resort of Alinda

DODECANESE

to the north. Walking in the other direction from Platanos, you'll arrive at **Panteli**, a little fishing village-cum-resort with a sand and shingle beach. Just outside of Platanos, beyond the turn-off for Panteli, a road winds steeply down to **Vromolithos** where there's a good shingle beach.

Places to Stay & Eat

In Panteli, the waterfront *Pension Roza* (☎ *22 798*) has doubles/triples for 4000/6000 dr. A bit farther along, *Rooms to Rent Kavos* (☎ *23 247, 25 020*) has rates of 8000/9000 dr. *Pension Happiness* (☎ *23 498*), on the left of the road down from Platanos, has modern, sunny rooms with bathroom for 9000/10,000 dr.

Dimitris Taverna is probably Leros' best taverna. Its delicious mezedes include cheese courgettes, stuffed calamari, and onion and cheese pies; main courses include chicken in retsina and pork in red sauce. Take the road to Vromolithos, a little way down turn left at a shop, and the taverna's on the right. There are also several tavernas at Agia Marina.

In Panteli, *Zorbas* and *Psarapoula* are popular tavernas, but the unpretentious little *Taverna Drossia* is just as good.

Entertainment

Agia Marina is the heart of the island's nightlife, with several late night music bars.

In Panteli, head for *Savana Bar*, run by two English guys, Simon and Peter. It is open from mid-afternoon till late and has a great music policy: you can choose what you want.

KRITHONI & ALINDA
Κριθώνι & Αλίνδα

Krithoni and Alinda are contiguous resorts on the wide Alinda Bay, 3km north-west of Agia Marina. On Krithoni's waterfront there is a poignant, well kept **war cemetery**. After the Italian surrender in WWII, Leros saw fierce fighting between German and British forces. The cemetery contains the graves of 179 British, two Canadian and two South African soldiers.

Alinda, the island's biggest resort, has a long, tree-shaded sand and gravel beach. If you walk beyond the development you'll find some quiet coves.

Places to Stay & Eat

Hotel Kostantinos (☎ *22 337/904*), on the right coming from Agia Marina, has comfortable doubles with bathrooms for 6000 dr. A bit farther along, the B class *Crithoni Paradise Hotel* (☎ *25 120, fax 24 680*) complete with bars, restaurant and swimming pool, has singles/doubles/triples for 21,000/28,000/33,500 dr and suites for 45,000 dr. Just beyond the war cemetery, a road veers left to *Hotel Gianna* (☎/*fax 24 135*) which has nicely furnished rooms for 4000/8000/9600 dr. The sparkling, pine-furnished *Studios & Apartments Diamantis* (☎ *22 378, 23 213*), behind the cemetery, has rates of 7000/10,000/12,000 dr.

Alinda's waterfront *Finikas Taverna* has an extensive menu of well prepared Greek specialities; mezedes are 600 dr to 1200 dr and souvlaki is 1800 dr.

GOURNA Γούρνα

The wide bay of Gourna, on the west coast, has a similar beach to Alinda but is less developed. At the northern side, the chapel of **Agia Isidora** is on a tranquil islet reached by a causeway.

NORTHERN LEROS

Partheni is a scattered settlement north of the airport. Despite having a large army camp, it's an attractive area of hills, olive groves, fields of beehives and two large bays.

Artemis, the goddess of the hunt, was worshipped on Leros in ancient times. Just before the airport there's a signposted turn to the left that leads to the **Temple of Artemis**. A dirt track turns right 300m along it. Where the track peters out, clamber up to the left. You will see the little derelict **Chapel of Agia Irini**. There's little in the way of ancient ruins but it's a strangely evocative, slightly eerie place.

Farther along the main road there is a turn-off to the right to **Blefoutis Bay**, which has a shaded sand and pebble beach and a good taverna. Beyond this turn-off, the main road skirts **Partheni Bay** and its poor beach. But if you continue straight ahead, turn right at the T-junction, go through a gate to pass the **Chapel of Agia Kioura**, then through another gate and bear right, you'll come to a lovely secluded pebbled cove.

XIROKAMBOS Ξερόκαμπος

Xirokambos Bay, in the south of the island, is a low-key resort with a gravel and sand beach and some good spots for snorkelling. Just before the camp site, on the opposite side, a signposted path leads up to the ruined fortress of **Paleokastro**.

Leros' Diving Club (☎ 23 372) is based in Xirokambos. Seven-day diving courses cost around 85,000 dr (all-inclusive).

There are several *domatia* and the island's only camp site, *Camping Leros (☎ 23 372)*, on the right coming from Lakki. It's pleasant and shaded, with a restaurant and bar.

Patmos Πάτμος

☎ 0247   • postcode 855 00   • pop 2663
Patmos is a place of pilgrimage for both Orthodox and western Christians, for it was here that St John wrote his divinely inspired revelation (the Apocalypse). Once a favourite venue for the pious and hippies wishing to tune into its spiritual vibes, Patmos is now just as popular with sun and sea worshippers. The only remaining vestiges of the island's former isolation are the many signs (often ignored) that forbid topless and nude bathing.

History

In 95 AD, St John the Divine was banished to Patmos from Ephesus by the pagan Roman Emperor Domitian. While residing in a cave on the island, St John wrote the *Book of Revelations*. In 1088 the Blessed Christodoulos, an abbot who came from Asia Minor to Patmos, obtained permission from the Byzantine Emperor Alexis I Comnenus to build a monastery to commemorate

St John. Pirate raids necessitated powerful fortifications, so the monastery looks like a mighty castle.

Under the Duke of Naxos, Patmos became a semiautonomous monastic state, and achieved such wealth and influence that it was able to resist Turkish oppression. In the early 18th century, a school of theology and philosophy was founded by Makarios Kalogheras and it flourished until the 19th century.

Gradually the island's wealth polarised into secular and monastic entities. The secular wealth was acquired through shipbuilding, an industry which diminished with the arrival of the steam ship.

Getting There & Away

Ferry Patmos has the same ferry connections as Kalymnos and Leros.

Church belltower on Patmos

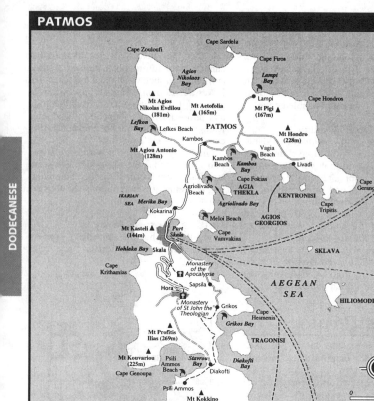

PATMOS

Cape Zouloufi
Cape Sardela
Cape Firos

Agios Nikolaos Bay

Lampi Bay

Mt Agios Nikolas Evdilou (181m)
Mt Aetofolia (165m)
Lampi
Cape Hondros
Mt Pigi (167m)

Lefkon Bay
Lefkes Beach
PATMOS
Kambos
Mt Hondro (228m)

Mt Agiou Antonio (128m)
Vagia Beach

Kambos Beach
Kambos Bay
Livadi

Cape Fokias
AGIA THEKLA
Cape Geranou
To Arki, Agathonisi, Ikaria & Samos

IKARIAN SEA *Merika Bay*
Agriolivado Beach
Agriolivado Bay
KENTRONISI
Cape Tripitis

Kokarina
Meloi Beach
AGIOS GEORGIOS

Mt Kasteli (144m)
Port Skala
Cape Vamvakias

Hohlaka Bay Skala
SKLAVA

Cape Krithamias
Monastery of the Apocalypse
To Lipsi

AEGEAN SEA

Hora
Sapsila
HILIOMODI

Monastery of St John the Theologian
Grikos
Cape Hesmenis

Mt Profitis Ilias (269m)
Grikos Bay

TRAGONISI

Mt Kouvariou (225m)
Psili Ammos Beach
Stavrou Bay
Diakofti Bay
Cape Genoupa
Diakofti

Psili Ammos
Mt Kokkino (194m)

Cape Kalana
Cape Vitsilia
To Piraeus
To Leros & Rhodes

0   1   2 km

Hydrofoil There are daily hydrofoils to Rhodes (10,280 dr), via Kalymnos (4620 dr) and Kos (5560 dr), and to Fourni, Ikaria and Samos in the North-Eastern Aegean. Every Saturday, a hydrofoil runs to and from Agathonisi.

Excursion Boat In summer the Lipsi-based *Anna Express* and *Captain Makis* sail to Patmos every day (see also the Getting There & Away section for Lipsi). The cost is 3800 dr return.

Daily Patmos-based excursion boats go to Marathi, and the caïque *Delfini* goes to Arki almost every day in high season – Monday and Thursday at other times. If you can't see the *Delfini* at Skala's quay, call ☎ 31 995/371 for information.

Getting Around

Bus From Skala there are seven buses daily to Hora (210 dr), five to Grikos (230 dr) and four to Kambos (230 dr). There is no bus service to Lampi.

Motorcycle There are lots of motorcycle and car rental outlets in Skala. Competition is fierce, so shop around.

Taxi From Skala's taxi rank, examples of tariffs are: Meloi Beach (800 dr), Lampi (1500 dr), Grigos (1200 dr) and Hora (1000 dr).

Excursion Boat Boats go to all the island's beaches from Skala, leaving about 11 am and returning about 4 pm.

SKALA Σκάλα
All boats dock at the island's port and capital of Skala. The town sprawls around a large curving bay. It's quite a glitzy place, pandering to the passengers of the many visiting cruise ships.

Although it's very busy and not especially attractive, it's a convenient transport hub and has all the tourist facilities and plenty of accommodation. There are great views from the site of the island's ancient acropolis, behind Skala.

Orientation & Information
Facing inland from the quay, turn right to reach the main stretch of waterfront where excursion boats and yachts dock. The right side of the large, white Italianate building opposite the quay overlooks the central square. For the road to Hora, turn left at the quay and right at Taverna Grigoris.

The municipal tourist office (☎ 31 666), open summer only, shares the Italianate building with the post office and police station. Astoria Travel (☎ 31 205, fax 31 975), on the waterfront near the quay, and Travel Point (☎ 32 801, fax 32 802, email info@travelpoint.gr), just inland from the central square, are helpful. The latter has a room-finding service.

The National Bank of Greece on the central square has an ATM. Inland from the central square is another smaller square; the OTE is on the left side of the road heading inland from here. The hospital (☎ 31 211) is 2km along the road to Hora.

Just Like Home Laundry is at the western end of the waterfront.

Patmos' port police (☎ 31 231) are behind the large quay's passenger-transit building. The bus terminal and taxi rank (☎ 31 225) are at the large quay.

Places to Stay – Budget
Domatia owners meet the boat. If you are not scooped up by one, there are several budget places along the Hora road. *Pension Sofia's* (☎ 31 876), 250m up on the left, has doubles/triples with bathroom and balcony for 6000/7000 dr. Farther up, *Pension Maria Paskeledi* (☎ 32 152) has singles/doubles/triples for 4000/7000/8500 dr.

The D class *Hotel Rex* (☎ 31 242) has rooms for 6000/7500/8500 dr with bathroom. It's on a narrow street opposite the cafeteria/passenger-transit building.

Pension Sydney (☎ 32 118) has rooms for 4000/7000/10,000 dr with bathroom. The nearby *Pension Avgerinos* (☎ 32 118), run by the same family, has doubles with superb views and bathroom for 7000 dr. Turn left 100m past the cemetery to reach these places.

Villa Knossos (☎ 32 189, fax 32 284), in a lovely garden, has immaculate rooms with bathroom and balcony. Doubles/triples are 10,000/12,000 dr. A sign points left 50m beyond the cemetery. Farther along the coast road, the C class *Hotel Hellinos* (☎ 31 275) has attractive rooms for 12,000/13,000 dr with bathroom. Co-owned with the hotel are some well kept *domatia* for 7500/8000 dr with shared bathroom.

Yvonne Studios (☎ 32 466, 33 066) has beautifully furnished apartments overlooking Hohlaka Bay for 10,000/12,000 dr. Inquire about them at Yvonne's Tourist Shop, near O Pantelis Taverna.

Places to Stay – Mid-Range
Hotel Chris (☎ 31 403) has singles/doubles/triples for 6600/11,000/13,200 dr. Turn right at the quay and it's on the waterfront.

The C class *Hotel Delfina* (☎ 32 060, fax 32 061), to the left of the quay, has well kept rooms for 10,000/13,000/15,000 dr. Next door, *Captain's House* (☎ 31 793, fax 34 077) has rates of 7000/14,000/15,000 dr. Around

DODECANESE

the corner, *Hotel Byzance* (☎ *31 052/663*) charges 11,000/16,000/19,000 dr.

Hotel Blue Bay (☎ *31 165, fax 32 303*) has very clean, nicely furnished rooms for 13,500/17,000/20,000 dr. The owner lived in Australia for many years, and now offers Aussie guests Vegemite at breakfast. Turn left at the quay and the hotel is 150m along on the right.

Skala's best hotel is the B class *Hotel Skala* (☎ *31 343, fax 31 747*), on the waterfront. Rates are 18,000/25,000/30,500 dr, including breakfast, and there's a swimming pool. (For Patmos' most luxurious hotel see the North of Skala section.)

Places to Eat
For excellent seafood try *Hiliomodi Ouzeri*, 50m up the Hora road on the left. The tasty 'variety of appetisers plate' is excellent value at 2000 dr. *Grigoris Taverna*, on the corner of the Hora road, is also highly commendable. There are two excellent *bakeries* on the square. The waterfront *Cafe Bar Arion* is great for people-watching, and is a popular evening haunt for young locals.

Restaurant Benetou, a little way along the Grikou road, is Skala's best restaurant, favoured by Prince Michael of Greece during his annual sojourn on Patmos. The menu features a wide range of imaginative dishes.

Entertainment
For nightlife, try *Music Club 2000*, just past the Argo petrol station on the far side of the bay. You can dance until 5 am and it has an outdoor swimming pool. Other 'in' places are *Consolatos Dancing Bar* and *Aman*, next to one another left of the quay.

MONASTERIES & HORA
The immense **Monastery of St John the Theologian**, with its buttressed grey walls, crowns the island of Patmos. A 4km asphalt road leads in from Skala, but many people prefer to walk up the Byzantine path. To do this, walk up the Skala-Hora road and take the steps to the right 100m beyond the far side of the football field. The path begins opposite the top of these steps.

A little way along, a dirt path to the left leads through pine trees to the **Monastery of the Apocalypse**, built around the cave where St John received his divine revelation. In the cave you can see the rock which the saint used as a pillow, and the triple fissure in the roof, from which the voice of God issued, and which supposedly symbolises the Holy Trinity. Opening times are 8 am to 1 pm Monday to Saturday, 8 am to noon Sunday and 4 to 6 pm on Tuesday, Thursday and Sunday.

To rejoin the Byzantine path, walk across the monastery's car park and bear left onto the (uphill) asphalt road. After 60m, turn sharp left onto an asphalt road, and almost immediately the path veers off to the right. Soon you will reach the main road again. Cross straight over and continue ahead to reach Hora and the Monastery of St John the Theologian.

The finest frescoes of this monastery are those in the outer narthex. The priceless contents in the monastery's treasury include icons, ecclesiastical ornaments, embroideries and pendants made of precious stones. Opening times are the same as for the Monastery of the Apocalypse. Admission to the treasury is 1000 dr.

Huddled around the monastery are the immaculate whitewashed houses of **Hora**. The houses are a legacy of the island's great wealth of the 17th and 18th centuries. Some of them have been bought and renovated by wealthy Greeks and foreigners.

Places to Stay & Eat
There are no hotel or domatia signs in Hora. There is accommodation but it is expensive and the best places are pre-booked months in advance. If you wish to stay in Hora, contact Travel Point in Skala.

Vagelis Taverna, on the central square, with a garden at the back, is deservedly popular.

The elegant *Patmian House* (☎ *31 180*) in a restored mansion, is the island's restaurant par excellence. There's a large choice of superb mezedes; the little spinach and cheese pies are especially good. The fillet steak is also commendable. Expect to pay around 10,000 dr for a three-course meal with wine. Reservations are recommended.

NORTH OF SKALA

The pleasant, tree-shaded **Meloi Beach** is just 2km north-east of Skala, along a turn-off from the main road.

Two kilometres farther along the main road there's a turn-off right to the relatively quiet **Agriolivado Beach**. The main road continues to the inland village of **Kambos** and then descends to the shingle beach from where you can walk to the secluded pebbled **Vagia Beach**. The main road ends at **Lampi**, 9km from Skala, where there is a beautiful beach of multicoloured stones.

Places to Stay & Eat

Stefanos Camping (☎ 31 821), at Meloi, is a good camp site, with bamboo-shaded sites, a minimarket, cafe bar and motorcycle rental facilities. The rates are 1300 dr for an adult and 600 dr for a tent. The rainbow-coloured minibus meets most boats.

Next to the well signposted Taverna Meloi there is a basic **domatia** (☎ 31 213, 31 247) where doubles are 5000 dr. The family also owns some newer rooms nearby, where doubles with bathroom are 8000 dr.

At Kambos, the owners of George's Place Snack Bar (see Places to Eat) offer an unofficial room-letting service.

Patmos has two luxury hotels. **Porto Scoutari** (☎ 33 124/125, fax 33 175), at Meloi, has double/triple studios for 26,000/30,000 dr. In Kambos, **Patmos Paradise** (☎ 32 624) has singles/doubles for 22,000/27,000.

The excellent **Taverna Meloi** serves traditional Greek dishes. **Glaros Taverna** on Agriolivado Beach is also commendable. **George's Place Snack Bar**, on Kambos Beach, is a good place to hang out. It's home-made fare includes irresistible apple pie. **Cafe Vagia**, overlooking Vagia Beach, has great food and views.

Lampi's **Taverna Leonidas** specialises in fish dishes but the saganaki is also very good.

SOUTH OF SKALA

Grikos, 4km south-east of Skala, is a rather lifeless resort with a sandy beach. Farther south, the long, sandy, tree-shaded **Psili Ammos**, reached by excursion boat, is the island's best beach. Most of the accommodation in Grikos is monopolised by tour groups. But try the **Restaurant O Stamatis and Rooms** (☎ 31 302), by the beach, which has comfortable doubles with bathroom for 8000 dr. Psili Ammos has a seasonal **taverna**, but no accommodation.

Lipsi Λειψοί

☎ 0247   • postcode 850 01   • pop 606

Lipsi (lip-see), 12km east of Patmos and 11km north of Leros, is an idyllic little island with good beaches. The cheery inhabitants busy themselves with fishing and farming and keeping happy the relatively small number of tourists who venture here. The picturesque port town of Lipsi is the only settlement. Lipsi produces a potent wine known as Lipsi Black.

Getting There & Away

Ferry The F/B Nissos Kalymnos calls at Lipsi on Wednesday and Saturday. It is also included in the route which links the Dodecanese to Mykonos and Syros.

Hydrofoil In summer, hydrofoils call at Lipsi at least twice daily (except Monday) on their routes north and south between Samos, in the North-Eastern Aegean, and Kos.

Excursion Boat The Captain Makis and Anna Express do daily trips in summer to Agia Marina on Leros and to Skala on Patmos (both 4200 dr return). Black Beauty and Margarita do excursion trips including Arki and Marathi for around 4000 dr return.

Getting Around

Lipsi has two minibuses which go to Platys Gialos (300 dr), Katsadia and Kohlakoura (both 250 dr). There are several motorcycle rental outlets.

DODECANESE

LIPSI TOWN
Orientation & Information
All boats dock at Lipsi Town, where there are two quays. The Lipsi-based *Anna Express* and *Captain Makis* dock at the small quay opposite Hotel Calypso. All other boats and ferries dock at the large quay.

From the large quay, facing inland, turn right. Continue along the waterfront to the large Plateia Nikiforias, which is just beyond Hotel Calypso. Ascend the wide steps at the far side of Plateia Nikiforias and bear right to reach the central square. The left fork leads to a second, smaller square.

The municipal tourist office (☎ 41 288) is on the central square, but you may find Paradisos Travel (☎ 41 120, fax 41 110), at the base of the wide steps, more helpful. The post office and OTE are on the central square. There is a freestanding Commercial Bank ATM near the wide steps. Paradisos Travel changes money and cashes Eurocheques. The police (☎ 41 222) are in the large white building opposite Paradisos Travel. The port police (☎ 41 133) are in the long white building to the right of the wide steps.

Things to See & Do
Lipsi's **museum** is on the central square. Its underwhelming exhibits include pebbles and plastic bottles of holy water from around the world. Admission is free, but opening times are erratic. There is a **carpet factory** in the same building as the port police. The hand-woven carpets are not for sale here but you can see them being made.

The town beach of **Liendos** is a short walk from the waterfront.

Places to Stay
The D class ***Hotel Calypso*** (☎ 41 242) has comfortable doubles/triples for 8000/9000 dr

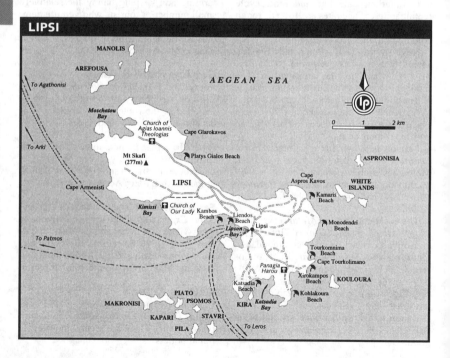

with bathroom. *Rena's Rooms (☎ 41 363)*, owned by Greek-Americans John and Rena Paradisos (of Paradisos Travel), are spotless, beautifully furnished and spacious. Rooms are 9000/10,000 dr with bathroom. There is a communal refrigerator and electric hot plates, and a terrace overlooking Liendos Beach. Turn right from the large quay (left from the small quay) and take the signposted road to Liendos. The rooms are on the left.

Rooms Galini (☎ 41 212), opposite the large quay, has lovely, light rooms with bathroom, refrigerator, gas ring and balcony for 9000/10,000 dr. Nearby, above Cafeteria Fotina, *Panorama Studios (☎ 41 235)* are equally agreeable and the rates are the same.

Flisvos Pension (☎ 41 261), just beyond the carpet factory, has singles/doubles/ triples for 5500/7500/9500 dr.

Barbarosa Studios (☎ 41 092/312), near the central square, has spacious, well equipped studios from 12,500 dr.

The A class *Aphrodite Hotel (☎ 41 394)*, overlooking Liendos Beach, has luxurious double studios for 20,000 dr and four-person apartments for 28,000 dr.

Places to Eat

Restaurant Barbarosa, near Rena's Rooms, serves reasonably priced, decent food. There's a string of restaurants and cafes on the waterfront between the two quays. They include the highly recommended *Giannis Restaurant*, *Fish Restaurant*, which serves (surprise, surprise) only fish, *Rock Coffee Bar & Ouzeri*, which offers some unusual mezedes, and *Cafe Stratos* which serves ice cream, pastries and good coffee. *Calypso Restaurant*, adjoining the hotel, serves very tasty, low-priced food.

Lipsi's shady, traffic-free square, with two inexpensive *kafeneia*, is a lovely spot for breakfast.

Entertainment

Lipsi's hot spots are *Aphrodite Music Bar* and *Scorpion Night Club*. At the latter, evenings begin with international music but Greek music gradually takes over, with locals giving tourists impromptu lessons in Greek dancing.

BEACHES

Away from Lipsi Town the beaches are the island's main attractions. They make pleasant walks, passing through countryside dotted with small holdings, olive groves and cypresses but buses also go to most of them.

Beyond Liendos Beach the road forks; if you take the right fork, after about 40 minutes you will arrive at **Platys Gialos**, a lovely sandy beach with a decent taverna.

Another good beach is the sand and pebble **Katsadia**, shaded with tamarisk trees. Its small, rustic *Gamricris Taverna*, above the beach, is owned by an elderly couple, who serve simple, low-priced meat and fish dishes. Nearer the beach, the modern *Dilaila Cafe Restaurant* is owned by their son, Christodoules, who has travelled widely and speaks good English. Good, reasonably priced food is served, and music from Christodoules' eclectic collection is played.

The pebble **Kohlakoura Beach**, to the east of Katsadia, is near the **Church of Panagia Harou** (The Virgin of Death), where, according to tradition, dried flowers are resurrected on 24 August, the church's festival day. Also nearby, is **Dimitris Makris' vineyard** where you can buy Lipsi Black wine (bring a container).

Farther north, **Monodendri** (One Tree) is the island's unofficial nudist beach. It stands on a rocky peninsula, the neck of which is pebbled. There are no facilities. It takes about one hour to walk there. To do so, turn left after Pension Flisvos and continue straight ahead passing the high school on the left. The road becomes a cobbled track, then climbs steadily and levels out to a dirt track. Continue ahead at the intersection by a church. Keep on this main track which eventually ends after curving sharply to the left. From here a network of paths lead down to Monodendri, recognisable by its one tree.

KIMISSI Κοίμηση

Kimissi is a little bay on the south-west coast. A hermit monk lives here beside the

DODECANESE

DODECANESE

little **Church of Our Lady**. If you visit, behave appropriately with respect for his peace and holiness. In Ottoman times monks hid in a cave here, choosing death from starvation rather than capture by the Turks. A casket in the church contains their bones.

To walk there, take the Platys Gialos road, and veer left onto the uphill track by a stone wall, opposite the asphalt road to the right. Go through a gap in a stone wall, continue ahead and you will eventually come to the **Church of the Virgin of the Cross**, from where an asphalt road leads down to Kimissi.

Arki & Marathi

ARKI Αρκοί
☎ 0247 • 850 01 • pop 50

Tiny Arki, 5km north of Lipsi, is hilly, with shrubs but few trees. Its only settlement, the little port on the west coast, is also called Arki. Islanders make a meagre living from fishing.

There is no post office, OTE or police on the island, but there is a cardphone. Away from its little settlement, the island seems almost mystical in its peace and stillness.

Getting There & Away
The F/B *Nissos Kalymnos* calls on Wednesday or Sunday. In summer the Lipsi-based excursion boats visit Arki and Marathi, and the Patmos-based caïque *Delfini* does frequent trips (4000 dr return) also.

Things to See & Do
The **Church of Metamorphosis** stands on a hill behind the settlement. From its terrace there are superb views of Arki and its surrounding islets. The cement road between Taverna Tripas and Taverna Nikolaos leads to the path up to the church. The church is kept locked but ask a local if it's possible to look inside.

Several secluded sandy coves can be reached along a path skirting the right side of the bay. To reach the path, walk around the last house at the far right of the bay, go through a little wooden gate in the stone wall, near the sea, and continue ahead.

Tiganakia Bay on the south-east coast has a good sandy beach. To walk there from Arki village, take the cement road which skirts the left side of the bay. Continue along the dirt track passing the blue-domed church. At the end of the track, take the path ahead and go through a gate at the seaward end of a stone wall. Tiganakia Bay, reached by a network of goat tracks, lies at the far side of the headland. You will recognise it by the incredibly bright turquoise water and the offshore islets.

Places to Stay & Eat
Arki has three tavernas, two of which have double rooms for 8000 dr with bathroom. *O Tripas Taverna & Rooms* (☎ 32 230) is to the right of the quay, as you face inland. The owner, Manolis, speaks good English. *Taverna Nikolaos Rooms* (☎ 32 477) is adjacent to it. Both tavernas are good. The black eye beans and onions served at O Tripas Taverna make a tasty starter.

The third taverna, *Taverna Manolis*, opposite the quay, is also highly commendable. Nektaria, the delightful owner, doesn't speak English, but enjoys giving customers impromptu Greek lessons.

MARATHI Μαράθι

Marathi is the largest of Arki's satellite islets. Before WWII it had a dozen or so inhabitants, but now has only one family. The old settlement, with an immaculate little church, stands on a hill above the harbour. The island has a superb sandy beach.

Marathi has two tavernas, both of which rent rooms. *Taverna Pantelis* (☎ 32 609/759) and *Taverna Mihalis* (☎ 31 580), owned by the island's only permanent inhabitants, have comfortable doubles for 8000 dr. Both owners speak English.

Agathonisi Αγαθονήσι

☎ 0247 • postcode 850 01 • pop 112

Agathonisi is the most northerly island of the archipelago. It's a little gem, still only visited by adventurous backpackers and yachties. There are three villages: the port of Agios Giorgios, Megalo Horio and Mikro Horio, all less than 1km apart. The island is hilly and covered with thorn bushes.

Getting There & Away

The F/B *Nissos Kalymnos* calls on Wednesday and Sunday. The twice-weekly supply boat from Samos also takes passengers, but its schedule is subject to change – check with the police officer or locals. A hydrofoil running to and from Samos, Patmos, Lipsi, Leros, Kalymnos and Kos calls in every day in summer except Sunday.

Getting Around

There is no public transport, but it takes less than 15 minutes to walk from Mikro Horio to Megalo Horio or Agios Giorgios.

AGIOS GIORGIOS Αγιος Γεώργιος

The village of Agios Giorgios is a delightful little place with just enough waterfront

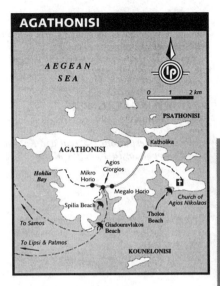

activity to stop you sinking into a state of inertia. It has a pebbled beach and **Spilia Beach**, also pebbled, is close by, reached along the track around the far side of the bay.

Orientation & Information

Boats dock at Agios Giorgios from where cement roads ascend right (facing inland) to Megalo Horio and left to Mikro Horio. There is no tourist information, post office, bank or OTE, but there are cardphones.

The one police officer, who is also the port police officer, has an office in the white building at the beginning of the Megalo Horio road.

Places to Stay & Eat

Agios Giorgios has three pensions: *Pension Maria Commits* (☎ 29 003), *Theologies Rooms* (☎ 29 005) next door and *George's Pension* (☎/fax 29 064) behind them. All charge 7000 dr for doubles with bathroom.

There are three restaurants. *George's Taverna* is nearest the quay. George and his German wife speak English. *Restaurant*

Seagull is farther around the bay. The owners, Ovule and Lianas, also speak English. Both restaurants are excellent.

Restaurant Lamina, between the two, is the locals' favourite, serving well prepared grilled fish.

AROUND AGATHONISI

Megalo Horio is Agathonisi's biggest village. It does not have any accommodation for tourists. *Restaurant I Eireni* and *Kafeneio/Pantopoleio Ta Badelfia M Kanelli*, both on the central square, serve cheap meals.

Tholos Beach, and **Katholika**, an abandoned fishing hamlet, are reached by taking the cement road from Megalo Horio. At the T-junction turn left to reach Tholos Beach, near a fish farm. You can also visit the little **Church of Agios Nikolaos**; ask a local if it's possible to look inside.

Katholika is reached by turning left at the T-junction. There's not much to see but the walk is worth it for the views.

North-Eastern Aegean Islands
Τα Νησιά του Βορειοανατολικού Αιγαίου

The North-Eastern Aegean Islands are grouped together more for convenience than for any historical, geographical or administrative reason. Apart from Thasos and Samothraki, they are, like the Dodecanese, much closer to Turkey than to the Greek mainland, but, unlike the Dodecanese, they are not close to one another. This means island-hopping is not the easy matter it is within the Dodecanese and Cyclades, although, with the exception of Thasos and Samothraki, it is possible.

These islands are less visited than either the Dodecanese or the Cyclades. Scenically, they also differ from these groups. Mountainous, green and mantled with forests, they are ideal for hiking but most are also blessed with long stretches of delightful beaches.

Although historically diverse, a list of the islands' inhabitants from classical times reads like a who's who of the ancient world. Some of the North-Eastern Aegean Islands also boast important ancient sites. All of them became part of the Ottoman Empire and were then reunited with Greece after the Balkan Wars in 1912.

There are seven major islands in the group: Chios, Ikaria, Lesvos (Mytilini), Limnos, Samos, Samothraki and Thasos. Fourni near Ikaria, Psara and Inousses near Chios, and Agios Efstratios near Limnos are small, little-visited islands in the group.

Accommodation throughout the island chain tends to be a little more expensive than on some of the more touristed islands, but bear in mind that the high season (July to August) prices quoted in this chapter are 30 to 50% cheaper out of season.

Getting There & Away
Air Samos, Chios, Lesvos, Limnos and Ikaria have air links with Athens. In addition, Samos, Chios, Lesvos and Limnos have flights to Thessaloniki.

HIGHLIGHTS

- Lush, sub-tropical Samos – a paradise for lovers of nature
- The abundant migratory bird life of Lesvos
- The mystical Sanctuary of the Great Gods on remote Samothraki
- Volcanic Limnos – offering space, solitude and sandy beaches
- Mesahti Beach near Armenistis, Ikaria, where you can believe you're in the Caribbean
- Ikaria's quirky and laid-back villages
- Medieval Mesta, the most atmospheric of Chios' mastic villages

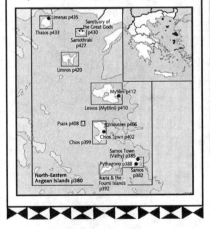

Ferry – Domestic The following table gives an overview of scheduled domestic ferries to this island group from mainland ports during high season. Further details and inter-island links can be found under individual island entries.

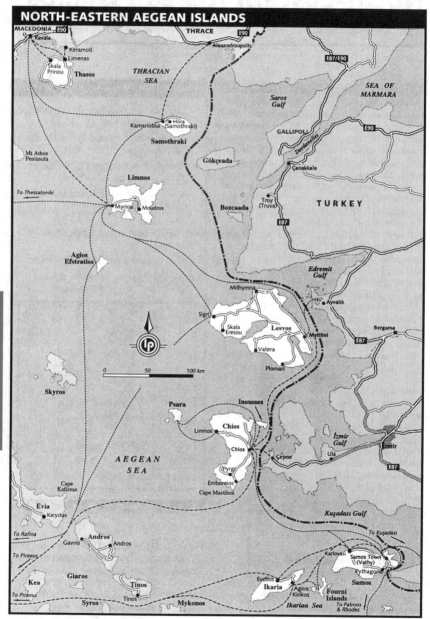

NORTH-EASTERN AEGEAN ISLANDS

Ferry Connections to the North-Eastern Aegean Islands

Origin	Destination	Duration	Price	Frequency
Alexandroupolis	Agios Efstratios	7¼ hours	3790 dr	1 weekly
Alexandroupolis	Chios	16 hours	6800 dr	1 weekly
Alexandroupolis	Lesvos (Mytilini)	10 hours	5000 dr	1 weekly
Alexandroupolis	Limnos	5 hours	3300 dr	2 weekly
Alexandroupolis	Samothraki	2 hours	2300 dr	2 daily
Kavala	Agios Efstratios	6 hours	6700 dr	1 weekly
Kavala	Chios	16 hours	6800 dr	1 weekly
Kavala	Lesvos (Mytilini)	11 hours	5700 dr	3 weekly
Kavala	Limnos	5 hours	3700 dr	4 weekly
Kavala	Samothraki	4 hours	3000 dr	2 weekly
Kavala	Thasos (Skala Prinou)	1¼ hours	850 dr	hourly
Keramoti	Thasos (Limenas)	35 mins	330 dr	hourly
Piraeus	Chios	8 hours	5800 dr	1 daily
Piraeus	Ikaria	9 hours	5300 dr	1 daily
Piraeus	Lesvos (Mytilini)	12 hours	6700 dr	1 daily
Piraeus	Limnos	13 hours	7000 dr	1 weekly
Piraeus	Samos	13 hours	6700 dr	2 daily
Rafina	Agios Efstratios	8½ hours	4550 dr	1 weekly
Rafina	Lesvos (Sigri)	8½ hours	4460 dr	1 weekly
Rafina	Limnos	10 hours	5500 dr	4 weekly
Thessaloniki	Chios	18 hours	8400 dr	1 weekly
Thessaloniki	Lesvos	13 hours	8300 dr	2 weekly
Thessaloniki	Limnos	7 hours	3300 dr	2 weekly

Ferry – International In summer there are daily ferries from Samos to Kuşadası (for Ephesus) and from Chios to Çeşme. Ferries from Lesvos to Ayvalık run five times weekly.

Hydrofoil In summer there are regular hydrofoil links between Kavala and Thasos and some hydrofoils between Alexandroupolis, Samothraki and Limnos. Hydrofoils also operate out of Samos west towards Ikaria and south towards the Dodecanese.

Getting Around
Air Lesvos is connected to both Limnos and Chios by local flights. Samos is connected to Mykonos and Santorini by local flights.

Ferry There are ferries daily between Ikaria and Samos, Chios and Lesvos; three times weekly between Lesvos and Limnos; and twice weekly between Chios and Samos. See also the entries at the beginning of sections on individual islands.

Samos Σάμος

☎ 0273   • pop 32,000
Samos, the most southerly island of the group, is the closest of all the Greek islands to Turkey, from which it is separated by the 3km-wide Mykale Straits. The island is the most visited of the North-Eastern Aegean group. Charter flights of tourists descend on the island from many northern European countries. Samos is a popular transit point for travellers heading from the Cyclades to Turkey or vice versa. Most barely pause in Samos, which is a pity because the island has a lot to offer.

Despite the package tourists, Samos is still worth a visit. Forays into its hinterland are rewarded with unspoilt villages and mountain vistas. In summer the humid air is permeated with heavy floral scents, especially jasmine. This, and the prolific greenery of the landscape, lends Samos an exotic and tropical air. Orchids are grown here for export and an excellent table wine is made from the local muscat grapes.

Samos has three ports: Samos Town (Vathy) and Karlovasi on the north coast, and Pythagorio on the south coast.

History

The first inhabitants of Samos, the Pelasgian tribes, worshipped Hera, whose birthplace was Samos. Pythagoras was born on Samos in the 6th century BC. Unfortunately, his life coincided with that of the tyrant Polycrates, who in 550 BC deposed the Samian oligarchy. As the two did not see eye to eye, Pythagoras spent much of his time in exile in Italy. Despite this, Samos became a mighty naval power under Polycrates, and the arts and sciences also flourished. 'Big is beautiful' seems to have been Polycrates' maxim – almost every construction and artwork he commissioned appears to have been ancient Greece's biggest. The historian Herodotus wrote glowingly of the tyrant's achievements, stating that the Samians had accomplished the three greatest projects in Greece at that time: the Sanctuary of Hera (one of the Seven Wonders of the Ancient World), the Evpalinos Tunnel and a huge jetty.

After the decisive Battle of Plataea (479 BC), in which Athens had been aided by the Samians, Samos allied itself to Athens and returned to democracy. In the Battle of Mykale, which took place on the same day as the Battle of Plataea, the Greek navy (with many Samian sailors) defeated the Persian fleet. However, during the Peloponnesian Wars, Samos was taken by Sparta.

Under Roman rule Samos enjoyed many privileges, but after successive occupations by the Venetians and Genoese it was conquered by the Turks in 1453. Samos played a major role in the uprising against the Turks in the early 19th century, much to the

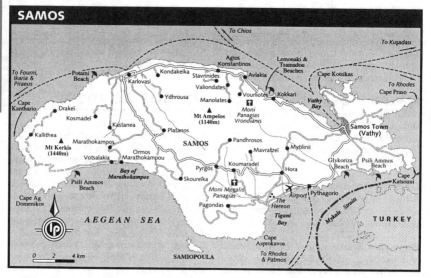

detriment of its neighbour, Chios (see the Chios section later in this chapter).

Trekking

Samos is a popular place for rambling, or more demanding mountain treks. Its natural fecundity and appealing combination of mountains and sea make it a popular destination for walkers from all over Europe. Should you be planning a hike on Samos, Brian and Eileen Anderson's *Landscapes of Samos*, a pocket guide to walks on the island, contains descriptions of over 20 walks. The book is available in most decent bookshops and can also be found in Samos.

Getting There & Away

Air There are at least four flights daily from Samos to Athens (17,400 dr) and two flights weekly to Thessaloniki (25,400 dr). The Olympic Airways office (☎ 27 237) is on the corner of Kanari and Smyrnis in Samos Town. There is also an Olympic Airways office (☎ 61 213) on Lykourgou Logotheti in Pythagorio.

Air Manos flies daily to Athens (12,000 dr) and twice weekly to Thessaloniki (18,400 dr), Mykonos (14,300 dr) and Santorini (16,400 dr). The airport is 4km west of Pythagorio.

Ferry – Domestic Samos is the transport hub of the North-Eastern Aegean, with ferries to the Dodecanese and Cyclades as well as to the other North-Eastern Aegean Islands. Schedules are subject to seasonal changes, so consult any of the ticket offices for the latest versions. ITSA Travel (☎ 23 605, fax 27 955, email itsa@gemini .diavlos.gr) is the closest agency to the ferry terminal in Samos Town and covers most destinations. Your luggage can also be stored for free whether you buy a ticket or not. Ask for Dimitris Sarlas. The following summary will give you some idea of the ferry options from Samos during summer.

Services to other North-Eastern Aegean Islands include two to three ferries daily to Ikaria (2½ hours, 2200 dr) and one to Fourni (two hours, 1800 dr); three weekly to Chios (four hours, 2690 dr); and one weekly to Lesvos (seven hours, 4000 dr), Limnos (11 hours, 6500 dr), Alexandroupolis (20 hours, 8300 dr) and Kavala (20 hours, 8400 dr).

To Piraeus there are one to two ferries daily (13 hours, 6700 dr) which usually call in at Ikaria and sometimes Fourni.

Cyclades services include daily ferries to Naxos and/or Paros (6½ hours, 4900 dr) with connections to Mykonos, Ios, Santorini (Thira) and Syros.

Dodecanese connections include about five ferries per week to Patmos (2½ hours, 2200 dr) and one per week to Leros (3½ hours, 2400 dr), Kalymnos (four hours, 3400 dr), Kos (5½ hours, 3800 dr) and Rhodes (nine hours, 6000 dr).

Ferry – International In summer two ferries go daily from Samos Town to Kuşadası (for Ephesus) in Turkey. From November to March there are one to two ferries weekly. Tickets cost around 8000/11,000 dr one way/return (plus 3000 dr Greek port tax and US$10 Turkish port tax, payable upon arrival). Daily excursions are also available from 1 April to 31 October and for an additional 6500 dr you can visit Ephesus. Tickets are available from many outlets but the main agent is ITSA Travel.

Bear in mind that the ticket office will require your passport in advance for port formalities. Turkish visas, where required, are issued upon arrival in Turkey for US$45. Check with the Turkish diplomatic mission in your home country for your own particular requirements since these change frequently.

Hydrofoil In summer hydrofoils link Pythagorio twice daily with Patmos (one hour, 5500 dr), Leros (two hours, 6600 dr) and Kos (3½ hours, 7800 dr). There are also two services weekly from Samos Town to Fourni (1¾ hours, 3450 dr) and Ikaria (2¼ hours, 4180 dr). Schedules are subject to frequent changes, so contact the tourist office in Pythagorio or the port police (☎ 61 225) for up-to-date information. Tickets are available from By Ship Travel (☎/fax 61 914) in Pythagorio or ITSA Travel in Samos Town.

Excursion Boat In summer there are excursion boats once weekly on Thursday between Pythagorio and Patmos (8000/11,000 dr one way/return) leaving at 8.30 am. Daily excursion boats also go to the little island of Samiopoula for 8000 dr, including lunch.

Getting Around

To/From the Airport There are no Olympic Airways buses to the airport. A taxi from Samos Town should cost about 2600 dr. Alternatively, you can take a local bus to Pythagorio and a taxi to the airport from there for about 1100 dr.

Bus Samos has an adequate bus service which continues till about 8 pm in summer. There are 13 buses daily from Samos Town bus station (☎ 27 262) to both Kokkari (20 minutes, 270 dr) and Pythagorio (25 minutes, 320 dr), eight to Agios Konstantinos (40 minutes, 450 dr), seven to Karlovasi (via the north coast, one hour, 750 dr), six to the Hereon (25 minutes, 450 dr), five to Mytilinii (20 minutes, 280 dr), three to Psili Ammos Beach on the east coast (20 minutes, 280 dr), and two to Ormos Marathokampou and Votsalakia (two hours, 1070 dr).

In addition to frequent buses to Samos Town there are six buses from Pythagorio to the Hereon and two to both Mytilinii and Karlovasi. Pay for your tickets on the bus.

Car & Motorcycle Samos has many car rental outlets, including Hertz (☎ 61 730), Lykourgou Logotheti 77, and Europcar (☎ 61 522), Lykourgou Logotheti 65, both in Pythagorio.

There are also many motorcycle rental outlets on Lykourgou Logotheti. Many of the larger hotels can arrange motorcycle or car rental for you.

Taxi From the taxi rank (☎ 28 404) on Plateia Pythagora in Samos Town, tariffs are: Kokkari 200 dr, Pythagorio 2200 dr, Psili Ammos 1900 dr, Avlakia 2300 dr, the airport 2600 dr, and the Hereon 2900 dr.

SAMOS TOWN (VATHY) Βαθύ
• postcode 831 00   • pop 5790

The island's capital is the large and bustling Samos Town, also called Vathy, on the north-east coast. The waterfront is crowded with tourists who rarely venture to the older and extremely attractive upper town of Ano Vathy where 19th century red-tiled houses perch on a hillside. The lower and newer town is strung out along Vathy Bay and it is quite a walk from one end to the other.

Orientation

From the ferry terminal (facing inland) turn right to reach the central square of Plateia Pythagora on the waterfront. It's recognisable by its four palm trees and statue of a lion. A little farther along and one block inland are the shady municipal gardens with a pleasant outdoor cafe. The waterfront road is called Themistokleous Sofouli.

Information

The municipal tourist office (☎ 28 530) is just north of Plateia Pythagora in a little side street, but it only operates during the summer season. The staff will assist in finding accommodation.

The tourist police (☎ 27 980) and the regular police are at Themistokleous Sofouli 129 on the south side of the waterfront.

The National Bank of Greece is on the waterfront just south of Plateia Pythagora and the Commercial Bank is on the east side of the square. Both sport ATMs.

The post office is on Smyrnis, four blocks from the waterfront. The OTE is on Plateia Iroön, behind the municipal gardens.

There is an Internet Cafe (☎ 28 521) at Emmanouil Sofouli 15, one block south-west of the museum. Access is fast and costs 1000 dr per hour.

The island's bus station (KTEL) is just back from the waterfront on Ioannou Lekati. The taxi rank (☎ 28 404) is on Plateia Pythagora. Samos' general hospital (☎ 27 407) is on the waterfront, north of the ferry quay.

The port police (☎ 27 318) are just north of the quay, one block back from the waterfront.

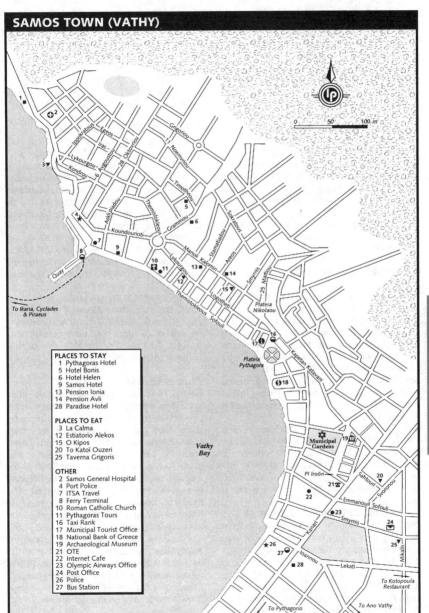

SAMOS TOWN (VATHY)

0   50   100 m

To Ikaria, Cyclades
& Piraeus

Quay

Vathy
Bay

Plateia
Nikolaou

Plateia
Pythagora

Kapetan Katavani

Municipal
Gardens

Pl Iroón

Emmanouil Sofouli

Smyrnis

Kanari

Ioannou

Lekati

To Kotopoula
Restaurant

To Pythagorio

To Ano Vathy

PLACES TO STAY
1   Pythagoras Hotel
5   Hotel Bonis
6   Hotel Helen
9   Samos Hotel
13 Pension Ionia
14 Pension Avli
28 Paradise Hotel

PLACES TO EAT
3   La Calma
12 Estiatorio Alekos
15 O Kipos
20 To Katoï Ouzeri
25 Taverna Grigoris

OTHER
2   Samos General Hospital
4   Port Police
7   ITSA Travel
8   Ferry Terminal
10 Roman Catholic Church
11 Pythagoras Tours
16 Taxi Rank
17 Municipal Tourist Office
18 National Bank of Greece
19 Archaeological Museum
21 OTE
22 Internet Cafe
23 Olympic Airways Office
24 Post Office
26 Police
27 Bus Station

Things to See

Apart from the charming old quarter of Ano Vathy, which is a peaceful place to stroll, and the municipal gardens, which are a pleasant place to sit, the main attraction of Samos Town is the **archaeological museum** (☎ 27 469).

Many of the fine exhibits in this well laid out museum are a legacy of Polycrates' time. They include a gargantuan (4.5m) *kouros* statue which was found in the Hereon (Sanctuary of Hera). In true Polycrates fashion, it was the largest standing kouros ever produced. The collection also includes many more statues, mostly from the Hereon, bronze sculptures, stelae and pottery.

The museum is east of the municipal gardens. Opening times are 8.30 am to 3 pm Tuesday to Sunday. Admission is 800 dr, 400 dr for students.

Places to Stay – Budget

Samos does not have a camp site. Be wary of touts who may approach you as you disembark and tell you that places listed in this guide are closed – it's usually a scam.

The cheapest and perhaps homeliest places to stay are the *domatia* of **Pension Ionia** (☎ 28 782, Manoli Kalomiri 5). Its clean and pretty rooms cost 3000/4000 dr for singles/doubles. To get there from the quay, turn right onto the waterfront, left at Stamatiadou, then left into Manoli Kalomiri.

Close by, the traditional **Pension Avli** (☎ 22 939) is a former Roman Catholic convent, built around a lovely courtyard. The rooms are spacious and tastefully furnished. Rates are between 5000 dr and 7000 dr for doubles with bathroom, depending on the season.

The C class **Pythagoras Hotel** (☎ 28 422, fax 27 955), 800m to the left from the ferry arrival point, is an excellent budget option. Clean and simply furnished rooms go for 4000/6000 dr. Ask for a room with a sea view.

The C class **Hotel Helen** (☎ 28 215, fax 22 866, Grammou 2) has cosy rooms with fitted carpets and attractive furniture. Air-conditioned doubles are 10,000 dr with

bathroom, fridge and TV. Turn right from the quay, and left just before the Roman Catholic church, veer right at the intersection and the hotel is on the right.

Close by is the C class **Hotel Bonis** (☎ 28 790, fax 22 501) with large singles/doubles with TV for 8000/10,000 dr including breakfast. This place is open all year.

Places to Stay – Mid-Range

The nearest hotel to the quay is the grand-looking C class **Samos Hotel** (☎ 28 377, fax 23 771, email hotsamos@otenet.gr). It is well kept with a spacious and elegant cafeteria, bar, snack bar, restaurant, breakfast room, TV room and billiard room. The comfortable rooms have fitted carpets, balcony, telephone and bathroom. Rates fluctuate from 5900 dr to 8000 dr for singles and 7400 dr to 9200 dr for doubles, depending on the season. On leaving the quay turn right and you'll come to the hotel on the left.

Very handy for the bus station is the modern C class **Paradise Hotel** (☎ 23 911, fax 28 754, email paradise@gemini.diavlos.gr) with a snack bar, pool and comfortable doubles for 15,000 dr. In the high season it is likely to be booked out by tour groups.

Places to Eat

Samos Town has a good selection of eateries. When dining out on Samos don't forget to sample the Samian wine, extolled by Byron. Just one street back from the waterfront, **Estiatorio Alekos** (Lykourgou Logotheti 49) serves ready-made staples and made-to-order dishes at around 2000 dr for a decent meal. The food at **To Katoï Ouzeri** is superlative and moderately priced. The modern, tastefully decorated *ouzeri* is tucked away on a little side street behind the municipal gardens.

Greeks escape the tourists and head for **Kotopoula** restaurant, hidden away in the backstreets. Follow Ioannou Lekati inland for about 800m until you find it on your left. Chicken is the speciality, but the scrumptious *mezedes* can be had for around 750 dr a pop.

Another commendable place is *Taverna Grigoris* on Smyrnis, near the post office. If you are here between 8.30 and 9.30 pm your table number may be drawn out of a hat, in which case you'll eat free. This is a reasonably priced restaurant and is open all day.

For live *neo kyma* (1960s new wave) music and maybe some dancing, seek out *O Kipos*, just off Lykourgou Logotheti (entry is from the next street up to the north) in a garden setting. The food is commendable; try a splendid Samena Golden white wine with it. For a romantic evening ambience, try *La Calma* which overlooks the sea. The seductive views and tasty food complement each other perfectly. Prices at these last two places are somewhat more upmarket.

PYTHAGORIO Πυθαγόρειο
• postcode 831 03   • pop 1400

Pythagorio, on the south east coast of the island, is 14km from Samos Town. Today, it's a crowded and rather twee tourist resort, but it's a convenient base from which to visit the ancient sites of Samos.

Pythagorio stands on the site of the ancient city of Samos. Although the settlement dates from the Neolithic era, most of the remains are from Polycrates' time (around 550 BC). The mighty jetty of Samos projected almost 450m into the sea, protecting the city and its powerful fleet from the vagaries of the Aegean. Remains of this jetty lie below and beyond the smaller modern jetty, which is on the opposite side of the harbour to the quay. The town beach begins just beyond the jetty. All boats coming from Patmos, and other points south of Samos, dock at Pythagorio.

Orientation
From the ferry quay, turn right and follow the waterfront to the main thoroughfare of Lykourgou Logotheti, a turn-off to the left. Here there are supermarkets, greengrocers, bakers, travel agents and numerous car, motorcycle and bicycle rental outlets. The central square of Plateia Irinis is farther along the waterfront.

Information
The tourist office (☎ 62 274, fax 61 022) is on the south side of Lykourgou Logetheti. The English-speaking staff are particularly friendly and helpful and give out a town map, bus timetable and information about ferry schedules. They also exchange currency, and are open 8 am to 10 pm daily.

The tourist police (☎ 61 100) are also on Lykourgou Logetheti, to the left of the tourist office.

The post office and the National Bank of Greece are both on Lykourgou Logetheti. The OTE is on the waterfront near the quay.

The bus station (actually a bus stop) is on the south side of Lykourgou Logetheti. There is a taxi rank (☎ 61 450) on the corner of the waterfront and Lykourgou Logetheti.

Things to See
Walking north-east on Polykratous from the town centre, a path off to the left passes traces of an ancient theatre. The **Evpalinos Tunnel** can also be reached along this path: take the left fork after the theatre. The right fork leads up to **Moni Panagias Spilianis** (Monastery of the Virgin of the Grotto). The ancient city walls extend from here to the Evpalinos Tunnel.

Back in town, the remains of the **Castle of Lykourgos Logothetis** are at the southern end of Metamorfosis. The castle was built in 1824 and became a stronghold of Greek resistance during the War of Independence.

The **Pythagorio Museum** (☎ 61 400) in the town hall at the back of Plateia Irinis has some finds from the Hereon. It is open 9 am to 2 pm Sunday, Tuesday, Wednesday and Thursday, and noon to 2 pm on Friday and Saturday. Admission is free.

Evpalinos Tunnel The 1034m-long Evpalinos Tunnel (Ευπαλίνειο Ορυγμα), completed in 524 BC, is named after its architect. It penetrated through a mountainside to channel gushing mountain water to the city. The tunnel is, in effect, two tunnels: a service tunnel and a lower water tunnel which you can see at various points along the narrow walkway. The diggers began at

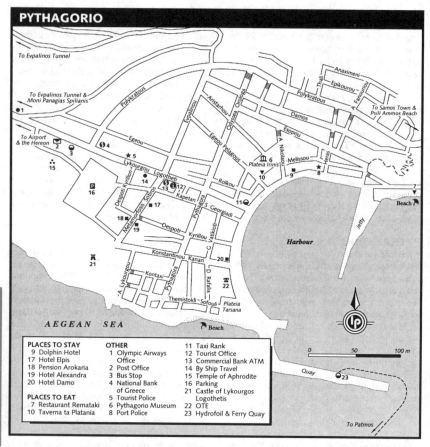

PYTHAGORIO

PLACES TO STAY
9 Dolphin Hotel
17 Hotel Elpis
18 Pension Arokaria
19 Hotel Alexandra
20 Hotel Damo

PLACES TO EAT
7 Restaurant Remataki
10 Taverna ta Platania

OTHER
1 Olympic Airways
   Office
2 Post Office
3 Bus Stop
4 National Bank
   of Greece
5 Tourist Police
6 Pythagorio Museum
8 Port Police

11 Taxi Rank
12 Tourist Office
13 Commercial Bank ATM
14 By Ship Travel
15 Temple of Aphrodite
16 Parking
21 Castle of Lykourgos
    Logothetis
22 OTE
23 Hydrofoil & Ferry Quay

each end and managed to meet in the middle, an achievement of precision engineering that is still considered remarkable.

In the Middle Ages the inhabitants of Pythagorio used the tunnel as a hide-out during pirate raids. The tunnel is fun to explore, though access to it is via a very constricted stairway. If you are tall, portly, or suffer from claustrophobia, give it a miss!

The tunnel is most easily reached from the western end of Lykourgou Logotheti, from where it is signposted. If you arrive by road, a sign points you to the tunnel's southern mouth as you enter Pythagorio from Samos. Opening times are 8.15 am to 2 pm daily except Monday. Admission is 500 dr; 300 dr for students.

Places to Stay

Many of Pythagorio's places to stay are block-booked by tour companies. Two pleasant and quiet places for independent travellers are opposite one another on Metamorfosis. ***Pension Arokaria*** (☎ *61 287)* has a cool and leafy garden. The lovely owner charges 8000/10,500 dr for doubles/triples. The D class *Hotel Alexandra* (☎ 61 429), just opposite, charges 8000 dr for a double with bathroom. In the same street is the neat and clean D class *Hotel Elpis* (☎/fax 61 144) with singles/doubles with a fridge for 7000/8000 dr.

At the northern end of the waterfront, beyond the main intersection, is the C class *Dolphin Hotel* (☎ 61 205, fax 61 842) with spotless and cosy wood-panelled rooms for 8650/11,350 dr with bathroom, fridge, TV, room safe and air-conditioning. At the other end of the waterfront is the C class *Hotel Damo* (☎ 61 303, fax 61 745), which is near the OTE. The agreeable self-contained studios here are 16,000 dr for two or three people.

Places to Eat

The waterfront is packed with restaurants all offering much the same fare. Walk 100m east of Dolphin Hotel to find *Restaurant Remataki* at the beginning of the town beach. This place has an imaginative menu of carefully prepared, delicious food. Try a meal of various mezedes for a change: *revithokeftedes* (chickpea patties), *piperies Florinis* (Florina peppers) and *gigantes* (lima beans) make a good combination. Main courses start from around 1000 dr. A block inland is *Taverna ta Platania* on Plateia Irinis opposite the museum, and away from the more expensive waterfront eateries.

AROUND PYTHAGORIO

Hereon Ηραίον

The Sacred Way, once flanked by thousands of statues, led from the city to the Hereon. The Hereon was a sanctuary to Hera, built at the legendary place of her birth, on swampy land where the River Imbrasos enters the sea.

There had been a temple on the site since Mycenaean times, but the one built in the time of Polycrates was the most extraordinary: it was four times the size of the Parthenon. As a result of plunderings and

earthquakes only one column remains standing, although the extent of the temple can be gleaned from the foundations. Other remains on the site include a *stoa*, more temples and a 5th century basilica.

The Hereon is now listed as a World Heritage Site. It is on the coast 8km west of Pythagorio. The site (☎ 95 277) is open 8.30 am to 2.30 pm Tuesday to Sunday. Admission is 800 dr; 400 dr for students. It's free on Sunday.

Mytilinii Μυτιληνιοί

The fascinating **paleontology museum** (☎ 52 055), on the main thoroughfare of the inland village of Mytilinii, between Pythagorio and Samos Town, houses bones and skeletons of prehistoric animals. Included in the collection are remains of animals that were the antecedents of the giraffe and elephant. The museum is open 9 am to 2 pm and 5 to 7 pm Monday to Saturday, and 10.30 am to 2.30 pm Sunday. Admission is 500 dr; free on Sunday.

Beaches

Back on the coast, sandy **Psili Ammos** (not to be confused with a beach of the same name near Votsalakia) is the finest beach near Pythagorio. This gently sloping beach is ideal for families and is popular, so be there early to grab your spot. The beach can be reached by car or scooter from the Vathy-Pythagorio road (signposted), or by excursion boat (3000 dr) from Pythagorio, leaving each morning at 9 am and returning at 4 pm. There are also buses from Samos Town. **Glykoriza Beach** nearer Pythagorio (also signposted) is dominated by a few hotels nearby, but is a clean, public beach of pebbles and sand and is a good alternative to the sometimes very busy Psili Ammos Beach. It's easily reached by scooter or car.

There are a couple of places to stay at Psili Ammos. *Elena Apartments* (☎ 23 645, fax 28 959), right on the beach, has rather cramped self-contained double apartments for 10,000 dr for bookings of at least a few days. Nearby, *Apartments Psili Ammos* (☎ 25 140) has self-contained rooms for two to three people for between 9000 dr and 11,000 dr. There are four eating places, of which **Restaurant Psili Ammos** and the more intimate **Sunrise** – commendable for its classy choice of ambient music – are both favourably located overlooking the beach.

SOUTH-WEST SAMOS

The south west coast of Samos remained unspoilt for longer than the north coast, but in recent years a series of resorts have sprung up alongside the best beaches. **Ormos Marathokampou**, 50km from Samos Town, has a pebble beach. From here a road leads 6km to the inland village of **Marathokampos**, which is worth a visit for the stunning view down to the immense Bay of Marathokampos. **Votsalakia**, 4km west of Ormos Marathokampou and known officially as Kampos, and **Psili Ammos** (not to be confused with the Psili Ammos Beach near Pythagorio), 2km beyond, have long, sandy beaches. There are many domatia and tavernas on this stretch of coast though this stretch has a rather scrappy feel to it and lacks the intimacy of smaller coastal resorts. The best taverna of an otherwise uninspiring bunch is **Ta Votsalakia**, with tables overlooking the beach.

With your own transport you may like to continue on the dirt road from Psili Ammos which skirts Mt Kerkis, above the totally undeveloped and isolated west coast. The road passes through the village of **Kallithea**, and continues to **Drakeï** where it terminates.

WEST OF SAMOS TOWN

The road which skirts the north coast passes many beaches and resorts. The fishing village of **Kokkari**, 10km from Samos Town, is also a holiday resort with a pebble beach. The place is fairly popular with tourists, but it is exposed to the frequent summer winds and for that reason is popular with windsurfers. Rooms, studios and tavernas abound, all offering much the same quality.

Beaches extend from here to **Avlakia**, with **Lemonaki** and **Tsamadou** beaches being the most accessible for walkers staying in Kokkari. Clothing is optional at these two pebbly, secluded beaches. Continuing west, beyond Avlakia, the road is flanked by trees, a foretaste of the alluring scenery encountered on the roads leading inland from the coast. A turn-off south along this stretch leads to the delightful mountain village of **Vourliotes**, from where you can walk another 3km to **Moni Panagias Vrondianis**. Built in the 1550s, it is the island's oldest extant monastery; a sign in the village points the way.

Continuing along the coast, a 5km road winds its way up the lower slopes of Mt Ampelos through thick, well watered woodlands of pine and deciduous trees, to the gorgeous village of **Manolates**. The area is rich in bird life, with a proliferation of nightingales, warblers and thrushes. There are no buses to Manolates so you'll have to find your own way (Agios Konstantinos is the nearest bus stop). In the village there are many old houses built of stone with projecting balconies. The surfaces of the narrow streets and idyllic little squares are decorated with whitewashed floral designs. There is also a sizable community of well fed and slightly aristocratic cats. The Samians say that if you have not visited either Vourliotes or Manolates, then you have not seen Samos.

Back on the coast, the road continues to the quiet resort of **Agios Konstantinos**. Beyond here it winds through rugged coastal and mountain scenery to the town of **Karlovasi**, Samos' second port. The town consists of three contiguous settlements: Paleo (old), Meson (middle) and Neo (new). It once boasted a thriving tanning industry, but now it's a lacklustre town with little of interest for visitors. The nearest beach is the sand and pebble **Potami**, 2km west of town.

Places to Stay

Despite the onset of package tourism, Kokkari still has many accommodation options for independent travellers. In the high season an EOT (☎ 92 217) operates in the village and will assist in finding accommodation. The bus stops on the main road at a large stone church, and the EOT is a little way down the street opposite the church.

Pension Eleni (☎ 92 317, fax 92 620) has immaculate, tastefully furnished rooms for 8000 dr a double with bathroom. From the large stone church, continue along the main road; at the T-junction veer left and, 50m along on the left, next to the Dionyssos Garden restaurant, you will see a sign pointing to the pension. There are many more domatia, apartments and small hotels along this stretch of road, which is just one block back from the waterfront.

Farther west along the coast road, close to a beach, are *Calypso Rooms to Rent (☎ 94 124)*, named after their friendly and kind owner. The rooms are well kept and surrounded by a gorgeous garden. Doubles are 7000 dr with bathroom and use of a communal kitchen. Coming from Kokkari, turn right opposite the turn-off for Manolates (signposted) and after 50m you will come to a sign pointing right to the rooms. There are quite a few more domatia in this area. The bus stop is just before the Manolates turn-off. In Manolates itself try *Studio Angella (☎ 94 478)* or call ☎ 94 331 for a little unnamed house to rent in the village.

If you get stuck in Karlovasi there are several budget hotels and *domatia (☎ 32 133)* with doubles for 7500 dr. This accommodation is signposted from the central square where the bus terminates.

Places to Eat

There are many reasonably priced restaurants in Kokkari all offering 'English menus' and the usual range of bland tourist fare. One reader recommends *Brothers Restaurant,* the last restaurant at the eastern end of Kokkari, past the headland and the little harbour.

Paradisos Restaurant, at the turn-off to Manolates, serves delectable dishes; a full meal with wine or beer will cost around 2500 dr. In Manolates, head for *Loukas Taverna* for the best and cheapest food around and great views. Try the stuffed courgette flowers, or *bekri mezes* (tasty

oven-cooked pork in sauce) and the special home-made *moschato* wines. Follow the prominent signs to the back end of the village to find this place.

Ikaria & the Fourni Islands

☎ 0275 • pop 9000

Ikaria (Ικαρία; ih-kah-**ree**-ah) is a rocky and mountainous island west of Samos. Like Samos it is also fertile, with an abundance of cypress trees, pine forests, olive and fruit trees – Ikarian apricots are especially luscious. At present the island's tourism is low-key, but Ikaria is slowly being 'discovered' by Germans and Austrians seeking a quiet alternative. Ikaria's beaches at Livadia and Mesahti, near Armenistis on the north coast, have to be rated as among the best in Greece.

Ailing Greeks have visited Ikaria since ancient times because of its therapeutic radioactive springs which they believe to be the most efficacious in Europe. One spring is so highly radioactive that it was deemed unsafe and forced to close.

The name Ikaria originates from the mythical Icarus (see 'The Myth of the Minotaur' boxed text in the Crete chapter). Another myth ascribes the island as the birthplace of Dionysos.

Ikaria has two ports, Agios Kirykos on the south coast, and Evdilos on the north coast. The island's best beaches are on the north coast, west of Evdilos.

Ikaria is a bit of an oddity as a tourist destination. Long neglected by mainland Greece and used as a dumping ground for left-wing political dissidents by various right-wing governments, Ikaria and Ikarians have a rather devil-may-care approach to things, including tourism. The islanders, while welcoming tourists, are taking a slow approach to cultivating the tourist dollar. The result is that Ikaria is an island that may take a bit of getting used to at first, but will surely remain long in your memory.

NORTH-EASTERN AEGEAN

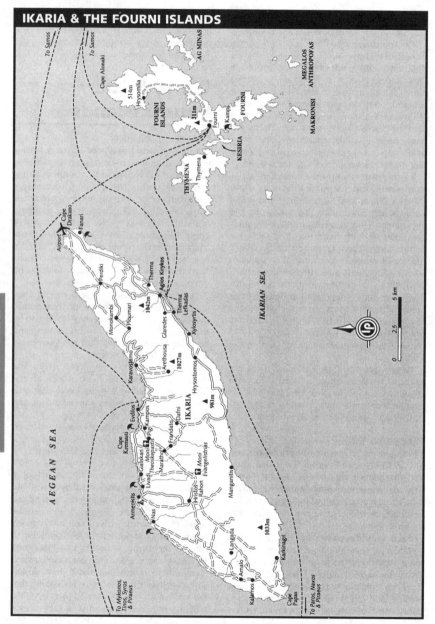

IKARIA & THE FOURNI ISLANDS

To Samos
To Samos

AG MINAS

Cape Alonaki

514m
Hrysomilia

FOURNI ISLANDS

311m
Fourni

Kamp

FOURNI

KESIRIA

MEGALOS
ANTHROPOFAS

MAKRONISI

THYMENA
Thymena

Cape
Drakano
Fanari

Airport

Perdiki

Therma

Agios Kirykos

IKARIAN SEA

Monokambi

Ploumari

1042m

Therma
Lefkadas

Therma

Xylosyrtis

Karavostamo

Arethousa

1027m

Glaredes

Hrysostomos

IKARIA

981m

Cape
Kremasti

Evdilos

Kampos
Pigi
Moni
Theoskepasti

Frandato

Dafni

AEGEAN SEA

Gialiskari
Livadi
Moni

Maratho

Moni
Evangelistrias

Armenistis

Nas

Hristos
Rahon

Manganitis

1033m

Langada

Amalo

Kalamos

Cape
Papas

To Mykonos,
Tinos, Syros
& Piraeus

Karkinagri

To Paros, Naxos
& Piraeus

0   2.5   5 km

Getting There & Away

Air In summer there are four flights weekly to Athens (17,100 dr) which usually depart in the early afternoon. The Olympic Airways office (☎ 22 214) is in Agios Kirykos, though tickets can also be bought from Blue Nice Agency (☎ 31 990, fax 31 752) in Evdilos. There is no bus to the airport and a taxi will cost around 3000 dr.

Ferry Nearly all ferries which call at Ikaria's two ports of Evdilos and Agios Kirykos are on the Piraeus-Samos route. In general there are departures every day from Agios Kirykos and three to four times weekly from Evdilos. Sample fares are Piraeus (nine hours, 5300 dr), Samos (three hours, 2100 dr), Mykonos (three hours, 3100 dr) and Tinos (four hours, 3200 dr). Tickets can be bought at Roustas Travel (☎ 22 441, fax 31 428) in Agios Kirykos or from Roustas Travel (☎ 22 441, fax 31 428) and Blue Nice Agency in Evdilos.

Chios-based Miniotis Lines also runs a couple of small boats leaving twice weekly up to Chios (8½ hours, 4800 dr) from Agios Kirykos via Fourni and Samos.

Hydrofoil Ikaria and the Fourni Islands are linked with Samos by fairly frequent summer services and twice weekly connections to Patmos and further connections to Kos. Sample fares are Patmos (one hour, 3520 dr), Samos (2¼ hours, 4280 dr), Kos (2½ hours, 7230 dr). Check with Dolihi Tours (☎ 23 230, fax 22 346) for the latest information.

Caïque A caïque leaves Agios Kirykos on Monday, Wednesday and Friday at 1 pm for Fourni, the largest island in the miniature Fourni archipelago. The caïque calls at the main settlement, where there are domatia and tavernas. Tickets cost 1000 dr one way. Day excursion boats to Fourni from Agios Kirykos cost around 4000 dr and 6000 dr from Armenistis on the north coast.

Getting Around

Bus Ikaria's bus services are almost as mythical as Icarus, but they do occasionally exist. In summer a bus is supposed leave Evdilos for Agios Kirykos daily at 8 am and return to Evdilos at noon, or thereabouts. However, it is best not to count on there being a service since the buses (where they do operate) exist mainly to service the schools during term time.

Buses to the villages of Hristos Rahon (near Moni Evangelistrias), Xylosyrtis and Hrysostomos from Agios Kirykos are more elusive and depend mainly on the whims of the local drivers. It is usually preferable to share a taxi with locals or other travellers for long-distance runs.

Car & Motorcycle Cars can be rented from Dolihi Tours Travel Agency (☎ 23 230, fax 22 346), Rent Cars & Motorcycles DHM (☎ 22 426) in Agios Kirykos, Marabou Travel (☎ 71 460, fax 71 325) in Armenistis, and from Aventura Car Rental (☎ 31 140, fax 71 400) in Evdilos.

Taxi Boat In summer there are daily taxi boats from Agios Kirykos to Therma and to the sandy beach at Fanari on the northern tip of the island. A return trip costs 2000 dr.

AGIOS KIRYKOS Αγιος Κήρυκος
• postcode 833 00   • pop 1800

Agios Kirykos is Ikaria's capital and main port. It's a pleasant, relaxed little town with a tree-shaded waterfront flanked by several *kafeneia*. Beaches in Agios Kirykos are stony; the pebbled beach at Xylosyrtis, 7km to the south-west, is the best of a mediocre bunch of beaches near town.

Orientation & Information

To reach the central square from the quay, turn right and walk along the main road. As you walk away from the quay, turn left on the central square and you will come to the post office and OTE on the left. The bus stop is just west of the square.

Ikaria does not have an EOT or tourist police. A good unofficial source of information is Vasilis Dionysos, a charismatic fellow who owns the village store in the

NORTH-EASTERN AEGEAN

north coast village of Kampos (see the Kampos section).

At the bottom of the steps which lead to Agios Kirykos' police building you will find Dolihi Tours Travel Agency. The staff here have information about hydrofoil schedules and can also arrange accommodation.

The National Bank of Greece is on the central square, and the Ionian Bank is next to Dolihi Tours; both have ATMs. The police (☎ 22 222) and port police (☎ 22 207) share a building in the eastern part of town. Continue along the waterfront from the central square and go up the six steps; continue up the next flight of steps and at the top you will see the police building on the right.

Things to See & Do
The **radioactive springs** are between Hotel Akti and the police building. A dip costs 800 dr and supposedly cures a multitude of afflictions including arthritis, rheumatism, skin diseases and infertility. There are more hot springs at Therma, 3km north-east of Agios Kirykos. This thriving spa resort has many visitors in summer.

Agios Kirykos' small **archaeological museum** houses many local finds. Pride of place is given to a large, well preserved stele (500 BC) depicting in low relief a mother (seated) with her husband and four children. The stele was discovered some years ago during the building of a school in a nearby village. It took a court case to prize the stele from the clutches of the school.

The museum is west of the quay and is well signposted. Opening times are generally 10 am to 1 pm, but don't bet on it. Admission is free.

Places to Stay
One of the cheapest places to stay in Agios Kirykos is the E class *Hotel Akti (☎ 22 694, fax 22 346)*. The tidy rooms cost 6500/8500 dr for singles/doubles with bathroom. The pension has great sea views from its appealing garden. To reach it, turn right facing Dolihi Tours, go up the steps to the left and follow the signs.

Pension Maria-Elena (☎ 22 835, fax 71 331) has impeccable rooms. Rates are 12,000/14,000 dr for doubles/triples with bathroom. From the quay turn left at the main road, take the first right, and then first left into Artemidos – the pension is along here on the right.

Agios Kirykos' best-appointed hotel is the C class *Hotel Kastro (☎ 23 480, fax 23 700)*. The rooms are beautifully furnished and have a telephone, three-channel music system, bathroom and balcony. Rates are 12,650/15,950 dr for singles/doubles, including breakfast. On a clear day you can see the islands of Amorgos, Naxos, Fourni, Patmos, Samos, Arki and Lipsi from the communal terraces. The hotel is opposite the police building.

Places to Eat
Agios Kirykos has a number of restaurants, snack bars, ouzeria and kafeneia. *Taverna Klimataria (☎ 22 686)* serves good grilled meats in a neat little courtyard hidden away in the backstreets and is open all year. A decent-sized pork chop should be about 1300 dr and it will taste even better with a small bottle of Samaina Sec from Samos. On the main square is *Restaurant Dedalos (☎ 22 473)* which offers delicious fresh fish. Its draught wine is highly recommended.

Filoti Pizzeria Restaurant is one of the town's best regarded restaurants. Apart from excellent pizza and pasta, there are good souvlaki and chicken dishes. The restaurant can be found at the top of the cobbled street that leads from the butcher's shop.

If you feel like a brisk walk and fancy a change of scenery, try the nifty little taverna *To Tzaki (☎ 22 113)* in the village of Glaredes, about 4km west of Agios Kirykos.

AGIOS KIRYKOS TO THE NORTH COAST
The island's main north-south asphalt road begins a little west of Agios Kirykos and links the capital with the north coast. As the road climbs up to the island's mountainous spine there are dramatic mountain, coastal and sea vistas. The road winds through

several villages, some with traditional stone houses topped with rough-hewn slate roofs. It then descends to the island's second port of Evdilos, 41km by road from Agios Kirykos. Look out for the island's only **cork tree** on the west side of the village of Monokambi. A returned migrant to America planted it many years ago. Look out for the white-painted steps leading up to it.

This journey is worth taking for the views, but if you are based in Agios Kirykos and want to travel by bus you will more than likely have to stay overnight in Evdilos or Armenistis. A taxi back to Agios Kirykos will cost 7000 dr. Hitching is usually OK, but there is not much traffic.

EVDILOS Εύδηλος
• postcode 833 00   • pop 440

Evdilos, the island's second port, is a small, dusty fishing village. Like Agios Kirykos it's a pleasant and relaxing place, but you may prefer to head further west to the island's best beaches. There is, nonetheless, a reasonable beach to the east of Evdilos. Walk 100m up the hill from the square and take the path down past the last house on the left. If you are heading to Ikaria by boat and intend to base yourself on the north coast, take a boat direct to Evdilos rather than Agios Kyrikos.

Places to Stay
For a quiet stay upon arrival in Evdilos you might consider making the 3km (40 minute) walk to Kampos (see West of Evdilos) where there are domatia, a couple of excellent beaches and a couple of restaurants. The nearest and cheapest accommodation option in Evdilos is the *pension* of Ioannis Spanos *(☎ 31 220)*. The rooms are centrally located just back from the main square. Reasonable singles/doubles are 6000/7000 dr. On the road to Kampos are the neat *Stenos Domatia (☎ 31 365)*, which go for around 7000 dr.

Facing the sea from the middle of the waterfront, the plush-looking building on the far right with black wrought-iron balconies is the *domatia* belonging to Spyros

Rossos *(☎ 31 518)*. Rates are 7000 dr for a double with bathroom.

Evdilos has two good quality hotels. The B class *Hotel Atheras (☎ 31 434, fax 31 926)* is a breezy, friendly place with modern rooms with balconies. There is also a small pool and bar. Rooms go for 13,000/15,000 dr in high season. At the top of the hill is the small B class *Hotel Evdoxia (☎ 31 502, fax 31 571)* with doubles for 13,000 dr, if you don't mind the petty house rules. There is a minimarket with basic provisions, a laundry service, money exchange and restaurant (see Places to Eat), and it's open all year.

Places to Eat
In season, there are a number of eateries to choose from, including the fairly obvious *Souvlarhio* with its blue cane chairs. Try their tasty Ikarian specialities *soufiko* or *mayirio* – pan-simmered concoctions of the season's first vegetables. *Kavos Restaurant* on the east side of the little harbour is open all day for lunch and dinner.

Cuckoo Ouzeri, also on the harbour, serves tasty mezedes and has a comprehensive selection of bottled Ikarian wine. For home-cooked food with a view, *Hotel Evdoxia Restaurant* is a good meeting place for travellers. You can even order your favourite dish if you are staying at the hotel. Prices at all places are mid-range.

WEST OF EVDILOS
Kampos Κάμπος
• postcode 833 01   • pop 127

Kampos, 3km west of Evdilos, is an unspoilt little village with few concessions to tourism. Although it takes some believing, sleepy little Kampos was the island's ancient capital of Oinoe (etymologically derived from the Greek word for wine). The name comes from the myth that the Ikarians were the first people to make wine. In ancient times Ikarian wine was considered the best in Greece, but a phylloxera outbreak in the mid-60s put paid to many of the vines. Production is now low-key and mainly for local consumption. Ancient coins found in

NORTH-EASTERN AEGEAN

Ancient coin depicting Dionysos, the god of wine and revelry

the vicinity of Kampos have a picture of Dionysos, the wine god, on them. Kampos' sandy beach is excellent and easily accessible.

Information The irrepressible Vasilis Dionysos, who speaks English, is a fount of information on Ikarian history and walking in the mountains. You will often find him in his gloomy but well stocked village store – on the right as you come from Evdilos. The village's post box is outside this shop and inside there is a metered telephone. There is also a cardphone nearby.

Things to See & Do As you enter Kampos from Evdilos, the ruins of a **Byzantine palace** (strictly speaking a *kyvernio*, or governor's house) can be seen up on the right. In the centre of the village there is a small **museum** housing Neolithic tools, geometric vases, fragments of classical sculpture, small figurines and a very fine 'horse head' knife sheath carved from ivory. The museum is open 8 am to 2 pm.

Next to the museum is the 12th century **Agia Irini**, the island's oldest church. It is built on the site of a 4th century basilica, and columns standing in the grounds are from this original church. Agia Irini's supposedly fine frescoes are currently covered with whitewash because of insufficient funds to pay for its removal. Vasilis Dionysos has the keys to both the museum and church.

The village is also a good base for mountain walking. A one day circular walk along dirt roads can be made, taking in the village of **Dafni**, the remains of the 10th century Byzantine **Castle of Koskinas**, and the villages of **Frandato** and **Maratho** and a cave at **Mikropouli** which can be difficult to find – ask Vasilis Dionysos if you get stuck. Take a torch if you plan to enter it. The trek up to the little granite-roofed Byzantine **Chapel of Theoskepasti** is worth the effort for this unusual and photogenic sight. Inside you will be shown the skulls of a couple of macabre internees. To get to the chapel and the neighbouring **Theoktisti Church** look for the signs at the village of Pigi on the road to Frandato.

Places to Stay & Eat There are a couple of *domatia* in Kampos, the best of which is owned by – you guessed it – Vasilis Dionysos (☎ *31 300, fax 31 688*) and his brother Yiannis, who create a wonderful family atmosphere for their guests. The very pleasant rooms are between 5000 dr and 8000 dr for doubles with bathroom. The optional enormous breakfasts are something to be experienced and are accompanied by tasteful Greek music. From Evdilos, take the dirt road to the right from near the cardphone and follow it round to the blue and white building on your left. Alternatively, make your presence known at the village store.

Vasilis often cooks delicious fish or lobster dishes for his guests and his original pitta recipe is exquisite. Otherwise, there is a moderately priced taverna in the village, *Klimataria*, and a summer taverna, *Pashalia*, on Partheni Beach about 400m past Vasilis Dionysos' place.

Armenistis Αρμενιστής
• postcode 833 01   • pop 70

Armenistis, 15km west of Evdilos, is the island's largest resort with two beautiful long beaches of pale golden sand, separated by a narrow headland. Places to stay are springing up quickly here, but it's still visited predominantly by independent travellers. Marabou Travel (☎ 71 460, fax 71 325), on the road which skirts the sea, organises walking tours and jeep safaris on the island. Just east of Armenistis a road leads inland to **Moni Evangelistrias**.

From Armenistis a 3.5km dirt road continues west to the small and secluded pebbled beach of **Nas** at the mouth of a stream. This is Ikaria's unofficial nudist beach. Behind the beach are some scant remains of a **temple of Artemis**. Nas has in recent times begun to witness a mini-boom with no less than 45 beds available and a choice of five tavernas to eat at.

Places to Stay – Budget Ikaria's only camp site is the rather scrawny *Armenistis Camping (☎ 71 250)*, on the beach at Armenistis. Facilities are fairly minimal though the owners are planning expansions and renovations. It opens about mid-June and costs 1600 dr for two persons with a tent.

One of the cheapest places to stay in Armenistis is *Rooms Ikaros (☎ 71 238)*. Doubles are 4000/5000 dr without/with bathroom. The elderly owner, Dimitris Hroussis, speaks a little English and is kind and friendly. The place is signposted as you enter the village. Above the Pashalia restaurant are the *domatia (☎ 71 302)* belonging to the restaurant. Clean and modern doubles with bathroom and most with sea-view balconies go for between 4000 dr and 7000 dr according to season.

At the approach to the village, before the road forks, you will see *Rooms Fotinos (☎ 71 235)* on the left. The rooms are light, airy and beautifully furnished. Rates are 7000/8400 dr for doubles/triples with bathroom.

Artemis Taverna (☎ 71 485) at Nas serves as a pension with small but neat double rooms with bathroom for 6000 dr. *Pension Thea (☎ 71 491)*, also at Nas, is newer, but the rooms are more exposed to the sun. Still, they have a fridge, a sea view and go for between 5000 dr and 8000 dr for two persons.

Places to Stay – Mid-Range One of Armenistis' better hotels is around to the west of the village. The C class *Hotel Dedalos (☎ 71 390, fax 71 393)* has a cool and inviting interior. The stucco-walled rooms open out onto a large private terrace overlooking a rocky seascape. The hotel has a large restaurant and bar and a sea water swimming pool built into the rocks. Singles/doubles cost 15,000/16,500 dr, breakfast included.

The most exquisite accommodation on the island, however, is the Cycladic-inspired *pension (☎/fax 71 310)* belonging to Dimitris Ioannidopoulos, known as *o yermanos* (the German) because of his many years of residence in that country. The individual studios and apartments, 800m west of Armenistis, spill down a hillside which overlooks the sea amid a riotous profusion of flowers and plants. A small studio for two people with private patio goes for 10,000 dr while a fully equipped two to three person apartment complete with music system and enormous patio goes for a very reasonable 12,000 dr. Bookings are absolutely essential and must be for a minimum of one week. Phone or fax ☎ 089-690 1097 in Germany during the winter months.

Places to Eat There are three restaurants along the Armenistis harbourside: *To Symposio*, *Kafestiatorio o Ilios* and *To Mouragio* – take your pick, though the Symposio is probably more popular.

Farther up the hill, *Pashalia Taverna* offers prompt service and a variety of ready-made dishes. Try the filling pasta and veal in a clay pot for about 1400 dr.

Directly opposite and below the Pashalia Taverna is the folksy *Delfini* restaurant offering great grilled souvlaki to complement the view over the water. Wherever you eat, see if you can get to taste some of the locally made light but potent wine.

Handy for the camp site and the beach is *Atsahas* taverna, 2km east of Armenistis. The views are great and the food is pretty reasonable and moderately priced – though service is very slow.

NORTH-EASTERN AEGEAN

Nas now has six tavernas of which *Astra* (☎ *71 255*) is probably the best. All dishes are wood-oven cooked. Try the potato salad – almost a meal in itself – or ask to sample the oven-cooked kid and wash it down with the mean draught red wine.

FOURNI ISLANDS Οι Φούρνοι
• postcode 834 00 • pop 1030

The Fourni Islands are a miniature archipelago lying between Ikaria and Samos. Two of the islands are inhabited: Fourni and Thymena. The capital of the group is **Fourni Town** (also called Kampos), which is the port of Fourni Island. Fourni has one other village, tiny Hrysomilia, 10km north of the port; the island's only road connects the two. The islands are mountainous and a good number of beaches are dotted around the coast.

The telephone number of Fourni's port police is ☎ 51 207. The local police number is ☎ 51 222 and the local doctor's number is ☎ 51 202.

Fourni is the only island with accommodation for tourists and is ideal for those seeking a quiet retreat. Other than the settlement of Fourni itself and a beach over the headland to the south at **Kampi**, the island offers little else besides eating, sleeping and swimming. Most of the islanders make a living from fishing, sending their catch to the Athens fish market.

For accommodation try the rooms and studios of *Nikolas Kondylas* (☎ *51 364, fax 51 209*) which range in price from 7000 dr to 12,000 dr depending on facilities. Some are in Fourni Town itself; others are on Kampi Beach, a 15 minute walk away. Alternatively, try the *Pension* (☎ *51 148*) of Maria and Kostas Makrakis in Fourni Town.

For eating out *Taverna Nikos* (☎ *51 253*) or *Miltos* (☎ *51 407*) on the waterfront will keep you amply supplied with fresh fish and other grilled dishes.

Various services connect Fourni with Ikaria and other Aegean islands. See the Ikaria Getting There & Away section for information about how to get to Fourni.

Chios Χίος

☎ 0271 • pop 54,000

Chios (**hee**-os) does not feature prominently on the travel circuit. Situated rather awkwardly on the ferry routes and without a tangible international profile, the island attracts curious travellers and expat Greeks rather than hordes of package tourists, though those that do come find the island subtly rewarding in its own distinct way. Like its neighbours Samos and Lesvos, Chios is a large island covering 859 sq km. It is separated from the Turkish Karaburun Peninsula by the 8km-wide Chios Straits. It is a verdant island, although in recent years fires have destroyed many of its forests giving it a dry and scrawny appearance at first glance.

A large number of highly successful ship owners come from Chios and its dependencies, Inousses and Psara. This, and its mastic production, have meant that Chios has not needed to develop a large tourist industry. In recent years, however, package tourism has begun to make inroads, though it's limited to a fairly small coastal stretch south of Chios Town. The mastic villages of the south and its role as a stepping stone to Turkey is what primarily brings travellers to Chios.

History

In ancient times, Chios, like Samos, excelled in the arts, which reached their peak in the 7th century BC when the Chios school of sculpture produced some of Greece's most eminent sculptors of the time. The technique of soldering iron was invented in this school. During the Persian Wars, Chios was allied to Athens, but after the Battle of Plataea it became independent, and prospered because it didn't have to pay the annual tribute to Athens.

In Roman times Chios was invaded by Constantine, who helped himself to its fine sculptures. After the fall of Byzantium, the island fell prey to attacks by pirates, Venetians, Catalans and Turks. It revived somewhat under the Genoese, who took control in the 14th century. However, it was recaptured

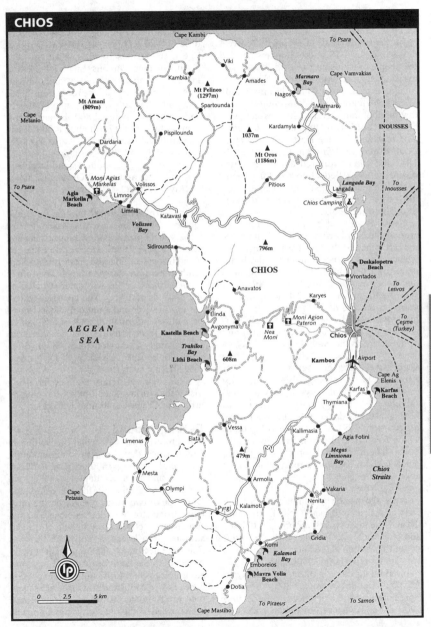

CHIOS

Cape Kambi

To Psara

Viki

Kambia

Marmaro Bay

Cape Vamvakias

Amades

Mt Pelineo (1297m)

Nagos

Marmaro

Spartounda

INOUSSES

Mt Amani (809m)

Cape Melanio

Kardamyla

1037m

Pispilounda

Dardaria

Mt Oros (1186m)

Pitious

Langada Bay

Langada

Moni Agias Markelas

Volissos

To Inousses

Agia Markella Beach

Limnos

Chios Camping

To Psara

Limnia

Katavasi

796m

Volissos Bay

Sidirounda

Deskalopetra Beach

Vrontados

To Lesvos

CHIOS

Anavatos

Karyes

Karyes

Moni Agion Pateron

Elinda

To Çeşme (Turkey)

Avgonyma

Nea Moni

Chios

Kastella Beach

Kambos

AEGEAN SEA

Trahilos Bay
Lithi Beach

608m

Airport

Cape Ag Elenis

Karfas

Karfas Beach

Thymiana

Vessa

Kallimasia

Agia Fotini

Limenas

Elata

Megas Limnionas Bay

Chios Straits

479m

Mesta

Armolia

Vakaria

Cape Petasas

Olympi

Nenita

Pyrgi

Kalamoti

Gridia

Komi

Kalamoti Bay

Emboreios
Mavra Volia Beach

Dotia

Cape Mastiho

To Piraeus

To Samos

0   2.5   5 km

NORTH-EASTERN AEGEAN

by the Turks in 1566 and became part of the Ottoman Empire.

In the 19th century, Chios suffered two devastations. In 1822 the Samians cajoled the people of Chios into assisting them in an uprising against Ottoman rule. The Turks retaliated by sacking Chios, killing 25,000 of its inhabitants and taking almost twice that number into slavery. The massacre was the subject of Victor Hugo's poem *L'Enfant de Chios* and Eugène Delacroix's painting *Le Massacre de Chios* (in the Louvre). In 1881 the island suffered a violent earthquake which killed almost 6000 people, destroyed many of the buildings in the capital and caused considerable damage throughout the island.

Chios is one of a number of places around the Mediterranean that claim to be the birthplace of the epic bard, Homer. The island is also in the running for the birthplace of Christopher Columbus. Ruth G Durlacher-Wolper, director of the New World Museum in San Salvador, has researched the life of the great seafarer, and has hypothesised that he was born on Chios and that the island may have been his point of departure to the New World.

Getting There & Away

Air Chios has on average five flights daily to Athens (15,800 dr), two weekly to Thessaloniki (22,400 dr) and two weekly to Lesvos (10,900 dr). The Olympic Airways office (☎ 20 359) is on Leoforos Egeou in Chios Town. The airport is 4km from Chios Town. There is no Olympic Airways bus, but a taxi to/from the airport should cost about 800 dr.

Ferry – Domestic In summer at least one ferry goes daily to Piraeus (eight hours, 5800 dr) and one to Lesvos (three hours, 3300 dr), and one weekly to Kavala (16 hours, 7400 dr) and Thessaloniki (18 hours, 8400 dr) both via Limnos (five hours, 5300 dr).

In addition, there is one ferry weekly to Alexandroupolis (16 hours, 6800 dr), Samos (three hours, 3000 dr), Kos (nine hours, 4900 dr) and Rhodes (15 hours, 7000 dr).

Tickets for these routes can be bought from the Maritime Company of Lesvos (NEL) office (☎ 23 971, fax 41 319) at Leoforos Egeou 16 in Chios Town.

The smaller Miniotis Lines (☎ 24 670, fax 25 371, email miniotis@compulink.gr) at Neorion 23 in Chios Town runs three small boats to Karlovasi (3½ hours, 2400 dr) and Vathy (4½ hours, 2800 dr) on Samos, then on to Fourni (7½ hours, 4400 dr) and Ikaria (8½ hours, 4800 dr). It also has three boats weekly to Psara (3½ hours, 2250 dr). The *Oinoussai II* is another small local boat that runs to and from Oinousses twice weekly (1¼ hours, 1100 dr).

Ferry – International During April and October there are usually three ferries weekly to Çeşme, leaving Chios at 8 am and returning at 6.30 pm. During May there is an additional sailing and from July to September there are daily sailings. The fare is 15,000/20,000 dr one way/return (including the 3000 dr port tax). The cost for a small car is 23,000 dr and a motorcycle is 14,000 dr. Further information and tickets can be obtained from Miniotis Tours. There are special daily excursion rates which often work out cheaper. Check with local agencies offering such trips.

Bear in mind that travellers requiring visas for Turkey can obtain them upon arrival in Çeşme for around US$45.

Getting Around

Bus From the long-distance bus station in Chios Town there are, in summer, eight buses daily to Pyrgi (600 dr), five to Mesta (800 dr) and six to Kardamyla (700 dr) via Langada; take this bus for the camp site. Only one or two buses weekly do the journey to Anavatos (470 dr) via Nea Moni and Avgonyma – check the schedule at the bus station, or ask for a copy of the bus timetable in English. There are fairly regular buses to the main beaches of Emborios, Komi, Nagos and Lithi and extra excursion buses to Nea Moni and Anavatos are scheduled on Tuesdays. Buses to Karfas Beach are serviced by the blue (city) bus company.

Bus timetables are available from the municipal tourist office.

Car & Motorcycle The numerous car rental outlets in Chios Town include Budget (☎ 41 361), on Psyhari, near the post office and Europcar (☎ 41 031, mobile 094 517 141) on Leoforos Egeou 56. Chios' ELPA representative is K Mihalakis (☎ 22 445), Rodokanaki 19. There are many moped and motorcycle hire outlets on and near the waterfront.

CHIOS TOWN
• postcode 821 00   • pop 22,900

Chios Town, on the east coast, is the island's port and capital. It's a large town, home to almost half of the island's inhabitants. Its waterfront, flanked by concrete modern buildings and trendy coffee shops, is noisy in the extreme with an inordinate amount of cars and motorcycles careering up and down. However, things improve considerably once you begin exploring the backstreets. The atmospheric old quarter, with many Turkish houses built around a Genoese castle, and the lively market area, are both worth a stroll. Chios Town doesn't have a beach; the nearest is the sandy beach at Karfas, 6km south.

Orientation

Most ferries dock at the northern end of the waterfront at the western end of Neorion. Bear in mind that ferries from Piraeus (to Mytilini) arrive at the very inconvenient time of 4 am – worth remembering if you are planning to find a room. The old Turkish quarter (called Kastro) is to the north of the ferry quay. To reach the town centre from here, follow the waterfront round to the left and walk along Leoforos Egeou. Turn right onto Kanari to reach the central square of Plateia Vounakiou. To the northwest of the square are the public gardens, and to the south-east is the market area. As you face inland, the bus station for local buses (blue) is on the right side of the public gardens and the station for long-distance buses (green) is on the left.

Information

The municipal tourist office (☎ 44 389, fax 44 343, email tourismos@chi.forthnet.gr) is at Kanari 18. The helpful staff give information on accommodation, bus and boat schedules. The magazine *Chios Summertime* is available here. Opening hours are 7 am to 2.30 pm and 7.30 to 10 pm on weekdays, 10 am to 1 pm on Saturday and 7 to 10 pm on Sunday.

The post office and OTE are both one block back from the waterfront while most banks are between Kanari and Plateia Vounakiou. There is an ATM halfway along Aplotarias.

The Enter Internet Cafe (☎ 41 058) is at Egeou 48 (upstairs) on the southern waterfront and charges 1000 dr an hour.

The tourist police (☎ 44 427) and the port police (☎ 44 432) are at the eastern end of Neorion.

Museums

Chios Town's most interesting museum is the **Philip Argenti Museum** (☎ 23 463), in the same building as the **Koraïs Library**, one of the country's largest libraries. The museum, which is on Koraïs near the cathedral, contains exquisite embroideries, traditional costumes and portraits of the wealthy Argenti family. The museum and the library are open 8.30 am to 2 pm Monday to Thursday, 5 to 7 pm Friday and 8 am to 12.30 pm Saturday. Admission is free.

The town's other museums are not so compelling. The **archaeological museum** (☎ 44 239), on Polemidi, contains sculptures, pottery and coins and is open 10 am to 1 pm Tuesday to Sunday. No admission fee had been announced at the time of writing. The **Byzantine Museum** (☎ 26 866) is housed in a former mosque, the Medjitie Djami, on Plateia Vounakiou. Opening times are 10 am to 3 pm Tuesday to Sunday. Admission is 500 dr, 300 dr for students.

Places to Stay – Budget

With over 30 domatia to choose from, budget accommodation is fairly plentiful in Chios Town. Call into the municipal tourist office for a full listing. Be aware, though,

NORTH-EASTERN AEGEAN

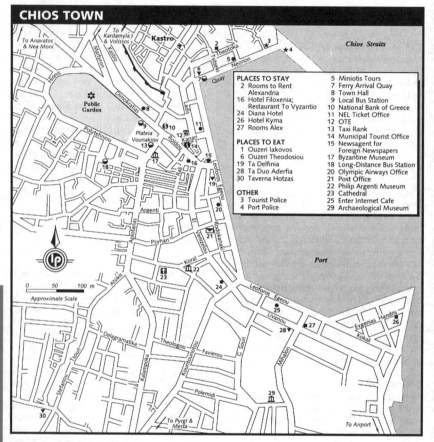

CHIOS TOWN

PLACES TO STAY
2 Rooms to Rent Alexandria
16 Hotel Filoxenia; Restaurant To Vyzantio
24 Diana Hotel
26 Hotel Kyma
27 Rooms Alex

PLACES TO EAT
1 Ouzeri Iakovos
6 Ouzeri Theodosiou
19 Ta Delfinia
28 Ta Duo Aderfia
30 Taverna Hotzas

OTHER
3 Tourist Police
4 Port Police
5 Miniotis Tours
7 Ferry Arrival Quay
8 Town Hall
9 Local Bus Station
10 National Bank of Greece
11 NEL Ticket Office
12 OTE
13 Taxi Rank
14 Municipal Tourist Office
15 Newsagent for Foreign Newspapers
17 Byzantine Museum
18 Long-Distance Bus Station
20 Olympic Airways Office
21 Post Office
22 Philip Argenti Museum
23 Cathedral
25 Enter Internet Cafe
29 Archaeological Museum

that accommodation in central Chios Town can be very noisy –choose carefully.

Chios has one camp site, ***Chios Camping*** (☎ 74 111), on the beach at Agios Isidoros, between Sykiada and Langada, 14km north of Chios Town. The site has good facilities, a bar and restaurant. To reach it take a Kardamyla or Langada bus.

The most welcoming domatia option is ***Rooms Alex*** (☎ 26 054, Livanou 29). Alex has six doubles which go for 7500/8000 dr without/with bathroom. There is a relaxing

roof garden festooned with flags, and Alex will pick you up at your boat if you call him. He will also help with car or bike rentals and give general information on Chios.

The D class ***Hotel Filoxenia*** (☎ 26 559) is signposted from the waterfront and is above Restaurant To Vyzantio. The unadorned but clean singles/doubles cost 4500/6000 dr, or 6000/8500 dr with bathroom.

In the old quarter, ***Rooms to Rent Alexandria*** (☎ 41 815), on Theotoka, has agreeable doubles for 6500 dr; a few rooms have private bathrooms.

Places to Stay – Mid-Range

The C class *Diana Hotel* (☎ 44 180, fax 26 748, El Venizelou 92) is a good hotel aimed primarily at the Greek business market. Single/double rates here are 10,500/15,000 dr including breakfast. The C class *Hotel Kyma* (☎ 44 500, fax 44 600, email kyma@chi.forthnet.gr, Evgenias Handris 1) occupies a century-old mansion and has lots of character. Rates for air-con rooms are 14,000/18,000 dr with breakfast.

Places to Eat

Restaurant To Vyzantio, on the corner of Ralli and Roïdou, is a bright, cheerful and unpretentious place which serves traditional Greek fare at low prices. Right opposite the ferry disembarkation point on Neorion is *Ouzeri Theodosiou*, an old-style and very popular establishment. Tucked away in the old town is the relocated *Ouzeri Iakovos* *(Agiou Georgiou Frouriou 20)* specialising in tasty fish mezedes.

Ta Delfinia, on the waterfront, is a bit touristy (with photo menus), but the food and service are good and it's the best place to watch street life. Main dishes start at around 1300 dr. Opposite Rooms Alex is *Ta Duo Aderfia (Livanou 38)* with a pleasant walled garden. Try the special spare ribs in barbecue sauce for around 1500 dr.

Open evenings only, at the southern end of town is *Taverna Hotzas* (☎ 42 787) – a bit of an institution, with cats, hens and ducks wandering around the garden. To get there, walk up Aplotarias and turn right at the fork along Stefanou Tsouri; follow it until you come across the restaurant.

CENTRAL CHIOS

North of Chios Town is an elongated beachside suburb leading to **Vrontados** where you can sit on the supposed stone chair of Homer, the Daskalopetra, though it is quietly accepted that it is unlikely to have been used by Homer himself. It is a serene spot though, and it would not be hard to

imagine Homer and his acolytes reciting epic verses to their admiring followers.

Immediately south of Chios Town is a warren of walled mansions, some restored, others crumbling, called the **Kampos**. This was the preferred place of abode of wealthy Genoese and Greek merchant families from the 14th century onwards. It's easy to get lost here so keep your wits about you – the free Chios map from the EOT is helpful. You are also better off touring the area by bicycle or moped, since it is fairly extensive. Chios' main beach resort **Karfas** is here too, 7km south of Chios Town. The beach is sandy though comparatively small with some moderate development and some A class hotels; if you like your beaches quiet, look elsewhere.

In the centre of the island is the 11th century **Nea Moni**. This large monastery, now World Heritage-listed, stands in a beautiful mountain setting, 14km from Chios Town. Like many monasteries in Greece it was built to house an icon of the Virgin Mary before the eyes of three shepherds. In its heyday the monastery was one of the richest in Greece with the most pre-eminent artists of Byzantium commissioned to create the mosaics in its *katholikon*.

During the 1822 atrocities the buildings were set on fire and all the resident monks were massacred. There is a macabre display of their skulls in the ossuary of the monastery's little chapel. In the earthquake of 1881 the katholikon's dome caved in, causing quite a lot of damage to the mosaics. Nonetheless, the mosaics, esteemed for the striking contrasts of their vivid colours and the fluidity and juxtapositions of the figures, still rank among the most outstanding examples of Byzantine art in Greece. A few nuns live at the monastery. Opening times are 8 am until 1 pm and 4 to 8 pm daily. Admission is free. The bus service to the monastery is poor, but travel agents in Chios Town have excursions here and to the village of Anavatos.

Ten kilometres from Nea Moni, at the end of a road that leads to nowhere, stands the forlorn ghost village of **Anavatos**. Its abandoned grey-stone houses stand as lonely sentinels to one of Chios' great tragedies. Nearly all the inhabitants of the village perished in 1822 and today only a small number of elderly people live there, mostly in houses at the base of the village.

Anavatos is a striking village, built on a precipitous cliff which the villagers chose to hurl themselves over, rather than be taken captive by the Turks. Narrow, stepped pathways wind between the houses to the summit of the village. **Avgonyma**, farther back along the road, is only slightly more populated than Anavatos, but lacks the drama of its neighbour.

The beaches on the mid-west coast are not spectacular, but they are quiet and generally undeveloped. **Lithi Beach**, the southernmost, is popular with weekenders and can get busy.

SOUTHERN CHIOS

Southern Chios is dominated by medieval villages that look as though they were transplanted from the Levant rather than built by Genoese colonisers in the 14th century. The rolling, scrubby hills are covered in low mastic trees that for many years were the main source of income for these scattered settlements (see the boxed text 'Gum Mastic').

There are some 20 *Mastihohoria* (mastic villages); the two best preserved are Pyrgi and Mesta. As mastic was a highly lucrative commodity in the Middle Ages, many an invader cast an acquisitive eye upon the villages, necessitating sturdy fortifications. The archways spanning the streets were to prevent the houses from collapsing during earthquakes. However, because of the sultan's fondness for mastic chewing gum, the inhabitants of the Mastihohoria were spared in the 1822 massacre.

Pyrgi Πυργί
• pop 1300

The largest of the Mastihohoria, and one of the most extraordinary villages in the whole of Greece, is the fortified village of Pyrgi, 24km south-west of Chios Town. The vaulted streets of the fortified village are narrow and labyrinthine, but what makes Pyrgi unique are the building facades, decorated with intricate grey and white designs. Some of the patterns are geometric and others are based on flowers, leaves and animals. The technique used, called *xysta*, is achieved by coating the walls with a mixture of cement and black volcanic sand, painting over this with white lime, and then scraping off parts of the lime with the bent prong of a fork, to reveal the matt grey beneath.

From the main road, a fork to the right (coming from Chios Town) leads to the heart of the village and the central square. The little 12th century **Church of Agios Apostolos**, just off the square, is profusely decorated with well preserved 17th century frescoes. Ask at the taverna or kafeneio for the church's caretaker, who will open it up for you. The facade of the larger church, on the opposite side of the square, has the most impressive xysta of all the buildings here.

Places to Stay & Eat The *Women's Agricultural Cooperative of Chios* (☎ 72 496) rents a number of traditionally furnished rooms in private houses throughout Pyrgi. Rates are around 5000 dr to 7000 dr for doubles, depending on the season. The co-operative's office is near the central square of Pyrgi and is signposted. On the edge of the village are the very pleasant *Rooms to Let Nikos* (☎ 72 425), with doubles for 7500 dr, including the use of a kitchen and fridge.

The little taverna *I Manoula* on the central square (on the left as you face the large church) is the main eating option, or the upstairs *Snack Bar* on the square can probably rustle up a few mezedes or a snack. Either way, the choice is sadly limited.

Emboreios Εμπορειός

Six kilometres to the south of Pyrgi, Emboreios was the port of Pyrgi in the days when mastic production was big business. These days Emboreios is a quiet holiday resort for people who like to relax. As you come from Chios Town, a signpost points left to Emboreios, just before you arrive at Pyrgi.

Gum Mastic

Gum mastic comes from the lentisk bush, and conditions in southern Chios are ideal for its growth. Many ancient Greeks, including Hippocrates, proclaimed the pharmaceutical benefits of mastic. Ailments it was claimed to cure included stomach upsets, chronic coughs and diseases of the liver, intestines and bladder. It was also used as an antidote for snake bites. During Turkish rule Chios received preferential treatment from the sultans who, along with the ladies of the harem, were hooked on chewing gum made from mastic – try the stuff and you will no doubt wonder why.

Until recently, mastic was widely used in the pharmaceutical industry, as well as in the manufacture of chewing gum and certain alcoholic drinks, particularly arak, a Middle Eastern liqueur. In most cases mastic has now been replaced by other products. But mastic production may yet have a future. Some adherents of alternative medicine claim that it stimulates the immune system and reduces blood pressure and cholesterol levels. Chewing gum made from mastic can be bought on Chios, under the brand name Elma.

There are three tavernas, *Neptune* with the most prominent position, and to the side *Ifestio* and *Porto Emborios*, the former with a marginally better ambience. If you want to stay in Emboreios, call *Studio Apartments Vasiliki* (☎ 71 422), or *Themis Studios* (☎ 71 810).

Mavra Volia Beach is at the end of the road and has unusual black volcanic pebbles as its main attraction. There is another more secluded beach, just over the headland along a paved track.

Mesta Μεστά

Continuing on the main road from Pyrgi, after 5km you will reach the mastic village of **Olympi**. It's less immediately attractive than its two neighbours but still worth a brief stop.

Mesta, 5km farther on, has a very different atmosphere from that created by the striking visuals of Pyrgi and should be on any visitor's itinerary. The village is exquisite and is completely enclosed within massive fortified walls. Entrance to the maze of streets is via one of four gates. This method of limiting entry to the settlement and its disorienting maze of streets and tunnels is a prime example of 14th century defence architecture, as protection against pirates and marauders. The labyrinthine cobbled streets of bare stone houses and arches have a melancholy aura.

The village has two churches of the Taxiarhes (archangels). The older one dates from Byzantine times and has a magnificent 17th century iconostasis. The second one, built in the 19th century, has very fine frescoes.

Orientation Buses stop on Plateia Nikolaou Poumpaki, on the main road outside Mesta. To reach the central square of Plateia Taxiarhon, with your back to the bus shelter, turn right, and then immediately left, and you will see a sign pointing to the centre of the village.

Places to Stay & Eat Many of the rooms in Mesta belong to the Pyrgi Women's Co-operative, and prices are similar. One place to start is *Anna Floradis Rooms* (☎ 28 891) next to the church. Her five rooms are very comfortable and go for around 6500 dr a double. Otherwise look for the blue and yellow EOT signs on the walls and take pot luck.

Alternatively, Dionysios Karambelas, the affable owner of *O Morias Sta Mesta* (☎ 76 400) – one of the two restaurants on Plateia Taxiarhon in romantic courtyard settings – may be able to organise accommodation for you. Originally from the Peloponnese (hence the name of the restaurant: Morias is the old name for the Peloponnese), Dionysios will provide you with superb country cooking. Ask to try the *hortokeftedes* (vegetable patties) and an unusual wild green, *kritamos* (rock samphire), that grows by the sea. You may be given a glass of *souma*, an ouzo made from figs.

NORTHERN CHIOS
Northern Chios is characterised by its craggy peaks (Mt Pelineo, Mt Oros and Mt Amani), deserted villages and scrawny hillsides once blanketed in rich pine forests. The area is mainly for the adventurous and those not fazed by tortuous roads. Public transport up here is poor; you will need a reasonably powered motorcycle to get around.

Volissos is the main focus for the villages of the north-western quarter. Reputedly Homer's place of birth, it is today a somewhat crumbling settlement, capped with an impressive Genoese fort. Volissos' port is **Limnia**, a workaday fishing harbour. It's not especially appealing, but has a welcoming *taverna*. You can continue to **Limnos**, 1km away, where caïques sometimes leave for Psara. The road onwards round the north end is very winding and passes some isolated villages.

On the eastern side a picturesque road leads out of **Vrontados** through a landscape that is somewhat more visitor-friendly than the western side. Pretty **Langada** is the first village, wedged at the end of a bay looking out towards Inousses. Next are **Kardamyla** and **Marmaro**, the two main settlements, though coastal Marmaro is not geared for tourism and is mercilessly exposed to the summer *meltemi* wind that howls through its narrow bay. If you choose to stay up here, try the comfortable *Hotel Kardamyla* (☎ *0272-23 353*) run by the same management as Hotel Kyma in Chios Town.

Most people go no further than the beach at **Nagos**, which is not bad, though still exposed to the vagaries of the winds – as is all the north coast. The road onwards winds upwards, skirting craggy Mt Pelineo. The scenery is green enough, but settlements are fewer and more remote. **Amades** and **Viki** are two villages you will traverse before hitting the last village, **Kambia**, perched high up on a ridge overlooking bare hillsides and the sea far below. From here a mostly sealed road

leads you round Mt Pelineo, past a futuristic phalanx of 10 huge wind-driven generators on the opposite side of the valley, and back to the trans-island route near Volissos.

Inousses Οινούσσες

Off the north-eastern coast of Chios lie nine tiny islets, collectively called Inousses. Only one of these, also called Inousses, is inhabited. Those that live here permanently make their living from fishing and sheep farming. The island has three fish farms and exports small amounts of fish to Italy and France. Inousses is hilly and covered in scrub and has good beaches.

However, these facts apart, this is no ordinary Greek island. Inousses may be small, but it is the ancestral home of around 30% of Greece's ship owners. Most of these exceedingly wealthy maritime barons conduct their businesses from Athens, London and New York, but in summer return with their families to Inousses where they own luxurious mansions.

There is a rumour that these ship owners offer financial incentives to discourage people from opening tavernas or domatia on the island, because they don't want to attract foreign tourists. It may not be possible to vouch for the truth of this but certainly tourism is not encouraged on the island: no domatia owners come to meet the boat, there are no domatia signs and

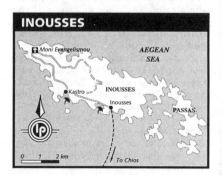

wandering around the streets fails to bring offers of accommodation. The place has a curiously barren and sterile air since there are few tourist facilities and even fewer visitors. Several islanders have stated that Inousses has a few domatia, but they are vague as to their whereabouts.

On a more positive note – and if these quirks have not discouraged you from going to Inousses – the island has a picturesque town of neoclassical mansions and abandoned houses; good beaches – **Kastro Beach** is the usual swimming stop for day-trippers; lots of opportunities for walking; stunning vistas and no package tourists. In Inousses Town there is a large naval boarding school. If you visit during term time you may well encounter the pupils parading around town to bellowed marching orders.

Getting There & Away
The island is served only by the local ferry boat *Oinoussai II*, which plies daily between the island and Chios Town. It leaves Chios Town at 2 pm and Inousses at 9 am, so is of no use for day trips. Purchase tickets on board for 1100 dr (one way). The trip takes about one hour. In summer there are sometimes excursion boats from Chios Town to the island. The little caïque *Smaragdi* does return excursions with a beach barbecue lunch thrown in for around 6000 dr. Call ☎ 0271-22 931 for details.

Getting Around
Inousses has no public transport, but there is one taxi.

INOUSSES TOWN
☎ 0271 • postcode 821 01 • pop 640
The island has one settlement, the little village called Inousses. To reach the centre of the village from the boat quay, facing inland turn left and follow the waterfront to Plateia Antoniou P Lemou; veer slightly right here, and you will immediately come to the tiny Plateia tis Naftisynis; veer right once again and you will see ahead Restaurant & Kafeneio Pateroniso. Facing this establishment turn right and ascend the steps.

There are no EOT or tourist police on the island. If you turn left at Restaurant Pateroniso and then take the first right into Konstantinou Antonopoulou you will come to the National Bank of Greece which, one can surmise, is kept very busy. Next door to the bank is a combined post office and OTE.

The police (☎ 55 222) are at the top of the steps which lead to the town centre.

Maritime Museum
This museum (☎ 55 182) is between the Restaurant Pateroniso and the National Bank of Greece. It opened in 1990 and the benefactors were wealthy ship owners from the island. Many island families donated nautical memorabilia, which includes *objets d'art*, photographs, models of early ships, cannons and nautical instruments.

The museum opens 10 am to 1.30 pm daily. Admission is 400 dr.

Places to Stay & Eat
There is no camp site on the island and camping freelance would definitely be frowned upon. For domatia, ask at one of the restaurants or kafeneia. Good luck!

Inousses' one hotel is the comfortable, but rather bland-looking C class *Hotel Thalassoporos* (☎ 55 475), at the top of the steps which lead to the village centre. Rates are 7000/10,000 dr for singles/doubles with bathroom. These prices drop to 5500/8500 dr in low season. It's unlikely ever to be full, but just in case, phone ahead in July and August.

Of Inousses' two restaurants, *Restaurant Pateroniso* (☎ 55 586) has been established the longest. The food is reasonably priced and well prepared. Alternatively at the far western end of the harbour is the little *Zepagas* fish restaurant. *Remezzo* is a small bar on the waterfront while *Trigono* bar is up in the village and mainly patronised by the few local young people left on the island.

The town has three grocery stores: one is near Restaurant Pateroniso and the other two are in the centre of the village on the road which leads up to the prominent Agios Nikolaos church.

NORTH-EASTERN AEGEAN

ISLAND WALK

Although most of this three hour circular walk is along a narrow cement road, you are unlikely to meet much traffic. Take plenty of water and a snack with you as there are no refreshments available along the way. Also take your swimming gear as you will pass many of the island's beaches and coves.

Just beyond the maritime museum you will see a signpost to **Moni Evangelismou**. This will take you along the cement road which skirts the west coast. Along the way you will pass several inviting beaches and coves. Only **Apiganos Beach** is signposted, but there are others which are easily accessible from the road. After about one hour the road loops inland, and a little farther along is the entrance to the palatial Moni Evangelismou, surrounded by extensive grounds.

Within the convent is the mummified body of Irini Pateras, daughter of the late Panagos Pateras, a multimillionaire ship owner. Irini became a nun in her late teens and died in the early 1960s when she was 20. Her distraught mother decided to build the convent in memory of her daughter. In the Greek Orthodox religion, three years after burial the body is exhumed and the bones cleaned and reburied in a casket. When Irini's body was exhumed it was found to have mummified rather than decomposed; this phenomenon is regarded in Greece as evidence of sainthood. Irini's mother is now abbess of the convent, which houses around 20 nuns. Only women may visit the convent and of course they must be appropriately (modestly) dressed.

Continuing along the cement road, beyond the entrance to the convent, you will come to two stone pillars on the left. The wide path between the pillars leads in 10 minutes to an enormous white cross which is a **memorial** to St Irini. This is the highest point of the island and commands stunning views over to northern Chios and the Karaburun Peninsula in Turkey. About 20 minutes farther along, the cement road gives way to a dirt track. Continue straight ahead to reach Inousses Town.

Psara Ψαρά

☎ 0274   • postcode 821 04   • pop 500

Psara (psah-**rah**) lies off the north-west coast of Chios. The island is 9km long and 5km wide and is rocky with little vegetation. During Ottoman times Greeks settled on the remote island to escape Turkish oppression. By the 19th century, many of these inhabitants, like those of Chios and Inousses, had become successful ship owners. When the rallying cry for self-determination reverberated through the country, the Psariots zealously took up arms and contributed a large number of ships to the Greek cause. In retaliation the Turks stormed the island and killed all but 3000 of the 20,000 inhabitants. The island never regained its former glory and today all of the inhabitants live in the island's one settlement, also called Psara.

Like Inousses, Psara sees few tourists. The old parliament building has been converted into an *EOT Guesthouse* (☎ *61 293*). Doubles without/with bathroom are 6500/7500 dr. Information may be obtained by either telephoning the guesthouse or ringing ☎ 0251-27 908 in Lesvos. There are also *domatia* in Psara.

There are a small number of eating places on the island.

Getting There & Away

Ferries leave Chios Town for Psara at 7 am three times weekly. Check with a local

agent for current departure days since these may change from year to year. Local caïques also run from Limnos on the west coast, but departure times are unpredictable and often depend on the prevailing weather conditions.

Lesvos (Mytilini)
Λέσβος (Μυτιλήνη)

• pop 88,800

Lesvos is the third-largest island in Greece, after Crete and Evia. It lies north of Chios and south-east of Limnos. The island is mountainous with two bottleneck gulfs penetrating its south coast. The south and east of the island are fertile, with numerous olive groves. Lesvos produces the best olive oil in Greece and has many olive oil refineries. In contrast to the south and east, the west has rocky and barren mountains, creating a dramatic moonscape.

Lesvos is becoming a popular package-holiday destination, but is large enough to absorb tourists without seeming to be overrun. Most Greeks call the island Mytilini, which is also the name of the capital.

History

In the 6th century BC, Lesvos was unified under the rule of the tyrant Pittakos, one of ancient Greece's Seven Sages. Pittakos succeeded in resolving the long-standing animosity between the island's two cities of Mytilini and Mithymna. This new-found peace generated an atmosphere conducive to creativity, and Lesvos became a centre of artistic and philosophical achievement.

Terpander, the musical composer, and Arion, the poet, were both born on Lesvos in the 7th century BC. Arion's works influenced the tragedians of the 5th century BC such as Sophocles and Euripides. In the 4th century BC, Aristotle and Epicurus taught at an exceptional school of philosophy which flourished on Lesvos.

Sappho, one of the greatest poets of ancient Greece, was born on Lesvos around 630 BC. Unfortunately little of her poetry is extant, but what remains reveals a genius for combining passion with simplicity and detachment, in verses of great beauty and power.

On a more prosaic level, Lesvos suffered at the hands of invaders and occupiers to the same extent as all other Greek islands. In 527 BC the Persians conquered the island,

Sappho

Sappho is renowned chiefly for her poems that speak out in favour of lesbian relationships, though her range of lyric poetry extends beyond works of an erotic nature. She was born in 630 BC in the town of Eresos on the western side of Lesvos. Little is known about her private life other than that she was married, had a daughter and was exiled to Sicily in about 600 BC. Only fragments remain of her nine books of poems, the most famous of which are the marriage songs. Among her works were hymns, mythological poems and personal love songs. Most of these seem to have been addressed to a close inner-circle of female companions. Sappho uses sensuous images of nature to create her own special brand of erotic lyric poetry. It is a simple yet melodious style, later copied by the Roman poet Catullus.

Lesvos, and Eresos in particular, is today visited by many lesbians paying homage to Sappho.

MARTIN HARRIS

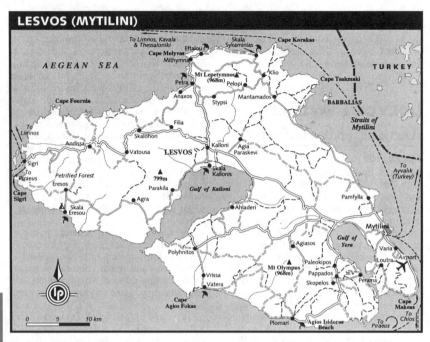

LESVOS (MYTILINI)

but in 479 BC it was captured by Athens and became a member of the Delian League. In the following centuries the island suffered numerous invasions, and in 88 BC it was conquered by Julius Caesar. Byzantines, Venetians, Genoese and Turks followed.

However, through all these vicissitudes the arts retained a high degree of importance. The primitive painter Theophilos (1866-1934) and the Nobel Prize-winning poet Odysseus Elytis were both born on Lesvos. The island is to this day a spawning ground for innovative ideas in the arts and politics, and is the headquarters of the University of the Aegean.

Trekking

Lesvos has an admirably well organised and well publicised set of trekking trails in the north and south of the island. These are marked with colour coded, easily spotted signs and cover a wide variety of landscapes. Get a copy of the booklet *Trekking Trails on Lesvos* from the Tourism Directorate of the North Aegean (☎ 0251-42 511), PO Box 37, Mytilini GR-811 00, or from any good EOT office. These walks can be taken in sections, or over a few days, stopping off along the way wherever appropriate. They are a mixture of dirt vehicle tracks and walking-only trails. The four trails are:

Vatera to Gera – This is a longish trail that leads from the beach enclave of Vatera over some of Lesvos' finest forest and mountain scenery to Gera on the gulf of the same name. This trail is marked by a sign with a yellow circle.

Petra to Lapsarna – This route takes you along the north coast of Lesvos from the resort of Petra to Lapsarna in the far west mainly along walking-only trails. This is a beautiful walk for beachcombers. The trail is marked by a sign with a yellow square.

Kapi to Sykamia – This route circles Mt Lepetymnos in northern Lesvos and traverses ravines covered with olive groves, poplar and oak trees and passes through a number of villages. This route is marked by a sign with a yellow triangle.

Sigri to Eresos – This route crosses the barren landscape of south western Lesvos between the two villages of Sigri and Eresos and follows the old road all the way, skirting the forest of petrified trees. This is an easy day trek. This route is marked by a sign with a yellow oblong.

Bird-Watching

Bird-watching – or 'birding', as the experts call it – is big business in Lesvos. The island is the transit point and home to over 279 species of birds ranging from raptors to waders. As a result, Lesvos is attracting an ever-increasing number of visitors – both human and feathered – particularly in spring. There are four main observation areas centred on Eresos, Petra, Skala Kallonis and Agiasos.

The major aim of birders seems to be spotting the elusive Cinereous bunting and Kruper's nuthatch. At any rate it is a growing and popular activity – birders seem to be more numerous than birds at times.

A folksy and detailed handbook to the hobby is Richard Brooks' *Birding in Lesbos*, which retails for a fairly steep 7500 dr on Lesvos, but is probably the most authoritative, and entertaining, book on the topic. Fax 44-1328-878 632 for further distribution details.

Getting There & Away

Air There are five flights daily from Lesvos to Athens (17,100 dr) and one daily to Thessaloniki (20,900 dr), as well as two flights weekly to Chios (10,900 dr) and weekly flights to Limnos (13,400 dr). Note that Lesvos is always referred to as Mytilini on air schedules. The Olympic Airways office (☎ 0251-28 659) in Mytilini is at Kavetsou 44 (Kavetsou is a southerly continuation

of Ermou). The airport is 8km south of Mytilini. A taxi to/from the airport will cost about 1000 dr.

Ferry – Domestic In summer there is at least one ferry daily to Piraeus (12 hours, 6700 dr) via Chios and some direct services (10 hours), three weekly to Kavala (11 hours, 5700 dr) via Limnos, and two weekly to Thessaloniki (13 hours, 8300 dr) via Limnos. Ferry ticket offices line the eastern side of Pavlou Kountouriotou, in Mytilini. Get tickets for the above destinations from the Maritime Company of Lesvos (NEL) (☎ 0251-28 480, fax 28 601), Pavlou Kountouriotou 67.

The port police (☎ 0251-28 827) are next to Picolo Travel on the east side of Pavlou Kountouriotou.

Ferry – International Ferries to Ayvalık in Turkey run roughly five times weekly in season. There is a Turkish boat, *Yeni Istanbul*, plus two or three boats owned by Miniotis Lines from Chios. One-way tickets cost 16,000 dr (including port taxes) and return tickets cost 21,000 dr. A small car costs 18,000/23,000 dr one way/return. Tickets are available from Aeolic Cruises (☎ 0251-23 266, fax 34 694) at Kountouriotou 47.

Getting Around

Bus Lesvos' transport hub is the capital, Mytilini. In summer, from the long-distance bus station (☎ 0251-28 873) there are three buses daily to Skala Eresou (2½ hours, 1950 dr) via Eresos. There are five buses daily to Mithymna (1¾ hours, 1350 dr) via Petra, and two buses to Sigri (2½ hours, 2000 dr). There are no direct buses between Eresos, Sigri and Mithymna. If you wish to travel from one of these villages to another, change buses in the town of Kalloni, which is 48km from Eresos and 22km from Mithymna. There are five buses daily to the south coast resort of Plomari (1¼ hours, 900 dr).

Car & Motorcycle The many car hire outlets in Mytilini include Troho Kinisi (☎ 0251-41 160, mobile 0932-237 900), which operates from the Erato Hotel just south of the Olympic Airways office, and Lesvos Car (☎ 0251-28 242), Pavlou Kountouriotou 47.

Many motorcycle rental firms are located along the same stretch of waterfront. You will, however, be better off hiring a motorcycle or scooter in Mithymna or Skala Eresou, since Lesvos is a large island and an underpowered two-wheeler is not really a practical mode of transport for getting around.

MYTILINI Μυτιλήνη
☎ 0251 • postcode 811 00 • pop 23,970
Mytilini, the capital and port of Lesvos, is a large workaday town. If you are enthralled by pretty and sparkling towns like Mykonos and Paros then you won't necessarily find the same ambience in Mytilini. However, this town has its own attractions including a lively harbour and nightlife, its once-grand 19th century mansions (which are gradually being renovated), and its jumbled streets.

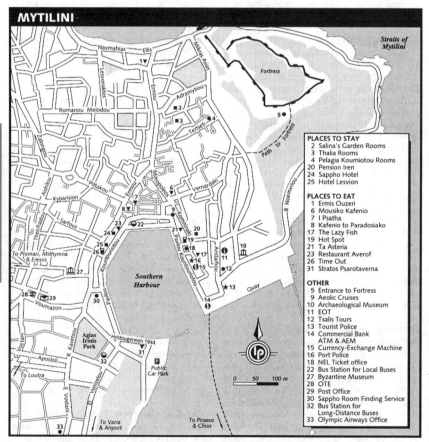

MYTILINI

PLACES TO STAY
2 Salina's Garden Rooms
3 Thalia Rooms
4 Pelagia Koumiotou Rooms
20 Pension Iren
24 Sappho Hotel
25 Hotel Lesvion

PLACES TO EAT
1 Ermis Ouzeri
6 Mousiko Kafenio
7 I Psatha
8 Kafenio to Paradosiako
17 The Lazy Fish
19 Hot Spot
21 Ta Asteria
23 Restaurant Averof
26 Time Out
31 Stratos Psarotaverna

OTHER
5 Entrance to Fortress
9 Aeolic Cruises
10 Archaeological Museum
11 EOT
12 Tsalis Tours
13 Tourist Police
14 Commercial Bank ATM & AEM
15 Currency-Exchange Machine
16 Port Police
18 NEL Ticket office
22 Bus Station for Local Buses
27 Byzantine Museum
28 OTE
29 Post Office
30 Sappho Room Finding Service
32 Bus Station for Long-Distance Buses
33 Olympic Airways Office

NORTH-EASTERN AEGEAN

Mytilini won't enthral sun, sea and sand lovers. The town beach is mediocre, crowded and you have to pay to use it (adults 200 dr, children 100 dr). However, you will appreciate Mytilini if you enjoy seeking out traditional kafeneia and little backstreet ouzeria, or if you simply take pleasure in wandering through unfamiliar towns.

The northern end of Ermou, the town's main commercial thoroughfare, is a wonderful ramshackle street full of character. It has old-fashioned *zaharoplasteia*, grocers, fruit and vegetable stores, bakers, and antique, embroidery, ceramic and jewellery shops.

Orientation

Mytilini is built around two harbours (north and south) which occupy both sides of a promontory and are linked by the main thoroughfare of Ermou. East of the harbours is a large fortress surrounded by a pine forest. All passenger ferries dock at the southern harbour. The waterfront here is called Pavlou Kountouriotou and the ferry quay is at its southern end. The northern harbour's waterfront is called Navmahias Ellis.

Information

The EOT has an office close to the quay at Aristarhou 6. The tourist police (☎ 22 776) have an office at the entrance to the quay.

Tsalis Tours (☎ 42 174, fax 21 481, email tsalis@otenet.gr) is an independent travel agency which is very helpful to travellers seeking accommodation, car hire or tour bookings. It is a few doors away from the EOT at Aristarhou 2. Further information on Lesvos can be found on the Web at www.greeknet.com.

Banks, including the National Bank of Greece with an ATM, can be found on Pavlou Kountouriotou. There is also an ATM and an exchange machine at the Commercial Bank booth on this street, near the ferry terminal. The post office is on Vournazon, west of the southern harbour. The OTE is on the same street just west of the post office.

Things to See

Mytilini's imposing **castle** with its well preserved walls was built in early Byzantine times, renovated in the 14th century by Fragistco Gatelouzo, and subsequently enlarged by the Turks. The surrounding pine forest is a pleasant place for a picnic. The castle is open 8.30 am to 3 pm daily. Admission is 500 dr, 300 dr for students.

The **archaeological museum** (☎ 22 087) is housed in a neoclassical mansion one block north of the quay and has impressive finds from Neolithic to Roman times. Opening times are 8.30 am to 3 pm Tuesday to Sunday. Admission is 500 dr.

The dome of the **Church of Agios Therapon** can be spotted from almost anywhere on the southern waterfront. The church has a highly ornate interior with a huge chandelier, an intricately carved iconostasis and priest's throne, and a frescoed dome. The **Byzantine Museum** (☎ 28 916) in the church's courtyard houses some fine icons. The museum is open 10 am to 1 pm Monday to Saturday. Admission is 300 dr.

Whatever you do, don't miss the **Theophilos Museum** (☎ 41 644), which houses the works of the prolific primitive painter Theophilos, who was born on Lesvos. Several prestigious museums and galleries around the country now proudly display his works. However, he lived in abject poverty, painting the walls of kafeneia and tavernas in return for sustenance. The museum is open 8.30 am to 1.30 pm and 5.30 to 8 pm Tuesday to Sunday. Admission is 500 dr.

The **Teriade Museum** (☎ 23 372), next door, commemorates the artist and critic Stratis Eleftheriadis (he Gallicised his name to Teriade) who was born on Lesvos but lived and worked in Paris. It was largely due to Teriade's efforts that Theophilos' work gained international renown. On display are reproductions of Teriade's own illustrations and his collection of works by 20th century artists, including such greats as Picasso, Chagall and Matisse. The museum is open 8.30 am to 1.30 pm and 5.30 to 8 pm Tuesday to Sunday. Admission is 500 dr.

NORTH-EASTERN AEGEAN

STELLA HELLANDER

The dome of the Church of Agios Therapon is a feature of Mytilini's charming waterfront

These museums are 4km from Mytilini in the village of **Varia** where Theophilos was born. Take a local bus from the bus station at the northernmost section of Pavlou Kountouriotou.

Places to Stay – Budget

In Mytilini, domatia owners belong to a cooperative called Sappho Room Finding Service. There are 28 establishments; if any of the ones recommended are full or don't suit, the owner will direct you to another. Most of these domatia are in little side streets off Ermou, near the northern harbour. The nearest to the quay is *Iren* (☎ 22 787, Komninaki 41). The clean and simply furnished doubles/triples cost 8000/10,000 dr with breakfast. Komninaki is one block behind the eastern section of Pavlou Kountouriotou. *Salina's Garden Rooms* (☎ 42 073, Fokeas 7) are cosy and clean with a delightful garden. Doubles are 7000/7500 dr without/with bathroom. The

rooms are signposted from the corner of Ermou and Adramytiou.

Coming from Ermou, if you turn right opposite Salina's rooms you will reach *Thalia Rooms* (☎ 24 640, Kinikiou 1). The pleasant doubles/triples in this large family house are 7000/8000 dr with bathroom. *Pelagia Koumiotou Rooms* (☎ 20 643, Tertseti 6), in an old family house near the castle, are lovely. Rates are 6500/8000 dr for doubles/triples. Walk along Mikras Asias and turn left into Tertseti; the rooms are on the right.

Places to Stay – Mid-Range

There are several hotels on the southern waterfront, but you will pay more at these than in the domatia. The C class *Sappho Hotel* (☎ 22 888, fax 24 522, Kountouriotou 31), on the west side of the harbour, has singles/doubles for 9500/14,000 dr with bathroom. The more luxurious B class *Hotel Lesvion* (☎ 22 037, fax 42 493,

Kountouriotou 27a), just two doors away, has rooms for 10,000/17,500 dr which can usually be negotiated for a better deal.

Places to Eat
You will eat well on Lesvos whether you enjoy fish dishes, traditional Greek food, international cuisine or vegetarian meals. You might wish to avoid the restaurants on the western section of the southern waterfront where the waiters tout for customers. These restaurants are atypical of Mytilini as they pander to tourists and serve bland, overpriced food.

The small, mildly ramshackle but delightfully atmospheric *Ermis Ouzeri (☎ 26 232, Kornarou 2)* has yet to be discovered by the mass tourist crowd. It is at the north end of Ermou on the corner with Kornarou. Its interior is decorated with scattered antiques, old watercolour paintings and old black and white photos of previous clients. A mezedes style meal with beer will cost around 2300 dr. Closer to the main harbour, locals congregate at *Kafenio to Paradosiako (Thasou 3)*, a little ouzeri with tables that spill out into the street.

Restaurant Averof, in the middle of the southern waterfront, is a no-nonsense traditional restaurant serving hearty Greek staples like *patsas* (tripe soup), while *Ta Asteria* on the opposite side of the harbour is slightly more upmarket and serves similar food for slightly higher prices.

If you want some good value meat dishes, check out *I Psatha* (winter only) on Methodiou, off Ermou. There is an old jukebox that actually works. For top quality fish dishes, go to *Stratos Psarotaverna (☎ 21 739)*, on Hristougennon 1944, at the bottom end of the main harbour. It is more upmarket in price. Tables from all the surrounding restaurants take over the road in summer.

For a good beer and a decent meal try *The Lazy Fish (☎ 44 831, Imvrou 5)*. The restaurant is set back from the southern end of Komninaki and is a bit difficult to find – look for a stone building with black wrought-iron wall lamps at the entrance.

Entertainment
Mousiko Kafenio, on the corner of Mitropoleos and Vernardaki, is a hip place – arty without being pretentious. Drinks are in the mid-price range rather than cheap, but worth it for the terrific atmosphere. Tapes of jazz, blues and classical music are played, and there is live music on Wednesday evenings (winter only) – usually jazz. The cafe is open 7.30 am to 2 am. Another couple of 'in' places are *Time Out* on the west side of the harbour and *Hot Spot* on the east side. Both are popular with students and at the latter you can borrow board games.

Getting There & Away
Mytilini has two bus stations: the one for long-distance buses is just beyond the south-western end of Pavlou Kountouriotou; the bus station for buses to local villages is on the northernmost section of Pavlou Kountouriotou. For motorists, there is a large free parking area just south of the main harbour.

NORTHERN LESVOS
Northern Lesvos is dominated both economically and physically by the exquisitely preserved traditional town of Mithymna, a town of historical, and modern, importance in Lesvos' commercial life. The neighbouring beach resort of Petra, 6km south, receives low-key package tourism and the villages surrounding Mt Lepetymnos are authentic, picturesque and worth a day or two of exploration.

Mithymna Μήθυμνα
☎ 0253 • postcode 811 08 • pop 1333
Although this town has officially reverted to its ancient name of Mithymna (Methymna), most locals still refer to it as **Molyvos**. It is 62km from Mytilini and is the principal town of northern Lesvos. The one-time rival to Mytilini, picturesque Mithymna is nowadays the antithesis of the island capital. Its impeccable stone houses with brightly coloured shutters reach down to the harbour from a castle-crowned hill. Its two main thoroughfares of Kastrou and 17 Noemvriou

are winding, cobbled and shaded by vines. In contrast to Mytilini, Mithymna's pretty streets are lined with souvenir shops.

Orientation & Information From the bus stop, walk straight ahead towards the town. Where the road forks, take the right fork into 17 Noemvriou. At the top of the hill, the road forks again; the right fork is Kastrou and the post office is along here on the left. The left fork is a continuation of 17 Noemvriou.

There is a small municipal tourist office (☎ 71 347) on the left, between the bus stop and the fork in the road. The National Bank of Greece is on the left, next to the tourist office and sports an ATM. There is also a Commercial Bank booth with an ATM directly opposite.

Things to See & Do One of the most pleasant things to do in Mithymna is to stroll along its gorgeous streets. If you have the energy, the ruined 14th century **Genoese castle** is worth clambering up to for fine views of the coastline and over the sea to Turkey. From this castle in the 15th century, Onetta d'Oria, wife of the Genoese governor, repulsed an onslaught by the Turks by putting on her husband's armour and leading the people of Mithymna into battle. In summer the castle is the venue for a drama festival; ask for details at the tourist office. The castle is open 8.30 am to 5 pm daily. Admission is 500 dr.

The beach at Mithymna is pebbled and crowded, but in summer excursion boats leave daily at 10 am for the superior beaches of Eftalou, Skala Sykaminias, Petra and Anaxos.

Places to Stay – Budget The excellent and refreshingly shady camp site, *Camping Mithymna* (☎ 71 169), is 1.5km from town and signposted from near the tourist office. It opens in early June, though you can usually camp if you arrive a bit earlier than that. For one person with a tent it costs 1550 dr.

There are over 50 official domatia in Mithymna; most consist of only one or two rooms. All display domatia signs and most

are of a high standard. The municipal tourist office will help you if you can't be bothered looking; otherwise, the best street to start at is 17 Noemvriou. Among the first signposted rooms you will come to are those of *Nassos Guest House* (☎ 71 022) on Arionos, which leads off to the right. The rooms are simply furnished and most have a panoramic view. The cost is 6000 dr.

A beautifully restored stone building on Myrasillou houses the *domatia* of Myrsina Baliaka (☎ 71 414). From the bus stop walk towards the town and take the second right by the cardphone. The domatia are 50m on your right. Look out for the prominent green shutters. A double room will cost around 7500 dr.

Places to Stay – Mid-Range A pleasant C class hotel is *Hotel Eftalou* (☎ 71 584, fax 71 669, email parmakel@otenet.gr), among the cluster of small, low-key resort hotels on the road out to Eftalou. A comfortable double goes for 12,000 dr in the low season and 17,000 dr in the high season. There's a swimming pool and restaurant to boot.

Nearby are the secluded *Eftalou Villas* (☎ 22 662, fax 26 535, email dimopulu@ otenet.gr), each with a different name and sleeping from four to eight people. A villa for four ranges in price from 16,000 dr to 20,000 dr, depending on the season.

An older but superior hotel is *Hotel Delfinia* (☎ 71 315, fax 71 524, email delfinia@otenet.gr). It caters mainly to packages, but is very accommodating to independent travellers. Single/double room rates in high season are 14,900/19,650 dr. It is 1km out of Mithymna on the road to Petra.

Places to Eat The streets 17 Noemvriou and Kastrou have a wide choice of restaurants serving typical Greek fare. Look out for *Nassos, Gatos, Asteria tis Molyvou* and *To Hani*, most of which have fine views over the sea. For more of a fishing-village ambience, head down to the far end of the little harbour where there is a clutch of eating places, the best of which is the Australian-Greek *Captain's Table* (☎ 71 241).

Sandy beach of Platys Gialos, Lipsi, Dodecanese

Waterfront of Kastellorizo Town, Dodecanese

Karlovasi Cathedral, Samos, NE Aegean

The long pale golden beaches of Arministis, Ikaria, NE Aegean, are some of Greece's finest.

Grocer's, Zakynthos, Ionian Islands

Chapel, Ithaka, Ionian Islands

Papandreou Rock, Ikaria, NE Aegean

Traditional house, Hora, Kythira, Ionian Islands

The mezedes are exquisite: try *adjuka* – a Ukrainian-inspired spicy aubergine dish – or the unique spinach salad. There is live bouzouki music once a week and Melinda and her husband Theodoros will make you more than welcome.

Petra Πέτρα
☎ 0253 • postcode 811 09 • pop 1150
Petra, 5km south of Mithymna, is a popular coastal resort with a long sandy beach shaded by tamarisk trees. Despite tourist development it remains an attractive village retaining some traditional houses. Petra means 'rock' and looming over the village is an enormous, almost perpendicular rock which looks as if it's been lifted from Meteora in Thessaly. The rock is crowned by the 18th century Panagia Glykophilousa (Church of the Sweet Kissing Virgin). You can reach it by climbing up the 114 rock-hewn steps – worth it for the view. Petra, like many settlements on Lesvos, is a 'preserved' village. It has not and will not make any concessions to the concrete monstrosities that characterise tourist development elsewhere in Greece.

Petra has a post office, OTE, bank, medical facilities and bus connections.

Places to Stay There are around 120 private rooms available in Petra, but your best bet for accommodation is to head straight for Greece's First Women's Agricultural Tourism Collective (☎ 41 238, fax 41 309). The women can arrange for you to stay with a family in the village where you will pay around 5000/7000 dr for a single/double room. The office is on the central square – signposted from the waterfront.

Of the cluster of small pensions at the western end of Petra's waterfront, *Studio Niki* (☎ 41 601) is a good bet. Neat double/triple rooms with kitchenette go for around 8500 dr. Bookings are recommended in peak season.

Places to Eat *Syneterismos* (☎ 41 238), belonging to the Women's Agricultural Tourism Collective, has mouth-watering

moussaka and Greek salad for about 2000 dr. There's a gamut of eateries along the waterfront, all pandering to the tourist and Greek palate alike.

The most outstanding restaurant both in service and food quality is *Pittakos*, housed in an old building at the western end of the waterfront. Fresh fish, while always on the expensive side, is cooked to perfection here. Romantic tables for two are perched at the water's edge.

To Tyhero Petalo towards the eastern end, has attractive decor and sells ready-made food for around 1300 dr for a main course dish. For a change of scenery and a meal with a view, head up to *Taverna tou Ilia* (☎ 71 536) at Vafios, 8km inland from Mithymna. The food is top-notch.

WESTERN LESVOS
Western Lesvos is quite different from the rest of the island and this becomes apparent almost immediately as you wind westward out of Kalloni. The landscape becomes drier and barer and there are fewer settlements, though when they do appear they look very tidy and their red-tiled roofs add vital colour to an otherwise mottled green-brown landscape. The far western end is almost devoid of trees other than the petrified kind. Here you will find Lesvos' 'petrified forest' on a windswept and barren hillside. One resort, a remote fishing village, and the birthplace of Sappho are what attract people to western Lesvos.

Eresos & Skala Eresou
Ερεσός & Σκάλα Ερεσού
☎ 0253 • postcode 881 05 • pop 1560
Eresos, 90km from Mytilini, is a traditional inland village. It is reached via the road junction just after the hillside village of Andissa. The road leading down to Eresos, through what looks like a moonscape, belies what is ahead. Beyond the village of Eresos a riotously fertile agricultural plain leads to Eresos' beach annexe, Skala Eresou, which is 4km beyond on the west coast. It is a popular resort linked to Eresos by an attractive, very straight tree-lined

road. A new sealed road links Eresos with Kalloni via Parakila and Agra.

Skala Eresou is built over ancient Eresos where Sappho (628-568 BC) was born. Although it gets crowded in summer it has a good, laid-back atmosphere. It is also a popular destination for lesbians who come on a kind of pilgrimage in honour of the poet. If you're a beach-lover you should certainly visit – there is almost 2km of coarse silvery-brown sand. Nudists congregate beyond the river, while lesbians tend to hang out near the river mouth.

Orientation & Information From the bus turnaround at Skala Eresou, walk towards the sea to reach the central square of Plateia Anthis & Evristhenous abutting the waterfront. The beach stretches to the left and right of this square. Turn right at the square onto Gyrinnis and just under 50m along you will come to a sign pointing left to the post office; the OTE is next door.

There is no EOT or tourist police, but Philippos at Krinellos Travel (☎ 53 246, 53 982, email krinellos@otenet.gr), close to the main square, is very helpful. He can arrange accommodation, car, motorcycle and bicycle hire and treks on foot or on horses and donkeys. Neither Skala Eresou nor Eresos has a bank but there is a prominent exchange machine and ATM.

Things to See Eresos' **archaeological museum** houses Archaic, classical Greek and Roman finds including statues, coins and grave stelae. The museum, in the centre of Skala Eresou, stands near the remains of the early Christian Basilica of Agios Andreas. Opening times are 8.30 am to 3 pm Tuesday to Sunday. Admission is free.

The **petrified forest**, as the EOT hyperbolically refers to this scattering of ancient tree stumps, is near the village of Sigri, on the west coast north of Skala Eresou. Experts reckon the petrified wood is at least 500,000, but possibly 20 million, years old. If you're intrigued, the forest is easiest reached as an excursion from Skala

Eresou; inquire at Exeresis Travel. If you're making your own way, the turn-off to the forest is signposted 7km before the village of Sigri.

Places to Stay There are a few domatia in Eresos but most people head for Skala Eresou, where there are a number of domatia, pensions and hotels. *Rooms to Let Katia (☎ 53 148)*, at the eastern end of the waterfront, has comfortable singles/doubles with a view for 7000/10,000 dr.

The C class *Sappho Hotel (☎ 53 233, fax 53 174)* is a small women-only hotel on the waterfront with rooms for 7000/12,000 dr. It can be noisy here, though.

Skala Eresou's best hotel is the C class *Hotel Galini (☎ 53 137, fax 53 155)*. Its light and airy rooms cost 8000/10,000 dr for rooms with bathroom. The hotel has a comfortable TV room-cum-bar and an outside terrace under a bamboo shade. It is clearly signposted.

Places to Eat The shady promenade offers many eating options, most with beach and sea views across to Chios and Psara. *Gorgona (☎ 53 320)* with its stone-clad facade is as good a place to start as any. Sample its tasty, stuffed courgettes in lemon sauce. Excellent Greek home cooking can be found at *Egeo (☎ 53 608)* in the middle of the waterfront. Try its stuffed tomatoes or moussaka. Prices at both establishments are mid-range to budget.

Yamas (☎ 53 693) is a pancake and snack joint run by Canadians Nick and Linda. Here you can get home-made North American cooking and chocolate cake. You can also listen to 70s music, and the occasional jam takes place when the mood takes over. Chill out with a cold beer on their comfy, shaded sofas overlooking the beach.

Bennett's Restaurant (☎ 53 624) is an English-run establishment owned by Max and Jackie and offers a good menu selection, including vegetarian and Asian, at the eastern end of the waterfront. Prices are mid-range.

Tenth Muse on the square is the current favourite gay bar, though in practice it attracts a mixed clientele. *Mariannas* on the promenade is another popular watering hole.

SOUTHERN LESVOS

Southern Lesvos is dominated by Mt Olympus (968m). Pine forests decorate its flanks, though in recent years fires have ravaged large sections – particularly the steep slopes north of the resort town of Plomari.

The large village of **Agiasos** on the northern flank of Mt Olympus features prominently in most local tourist publications and is a popular day-trip destination. Agiasos is very picturesque but not tacky, with artisan workshops making anything from handcrafted furniture to pottery. Its winding, cobbled streets will eventually lead you to the church of the Panagia Vrefokratousa with its Byzantine Museum and Popular Museum in the courtyard.

A couple of restaurants near the bus stop are perhaps your best bet for eating in Agiasos. One of these is *Anatoli* and the other is a nameless *psistaria* owned by Grigoris Douladellis.

Plomari on the south coast is a cramped and crumbling resort. A large, traditional village, it also has a laid-back beach settlement. It is not too exciting, but is very popular with Scandinavian tourists who are lured by cheap accommodation, but end up paying for it with expensive food. Most people stay at **Agios Isidoros**, 3km to the east where there is a narrow, overcrowded beach.

A far superior option is the low-key family resort of **Vatera** over to the east and reached via the inland town of **Polyhnitos**. This relaxing oasis has a very good, clean 9km-long beach and widely scattered hotels, domatia and restaurants.

There is one camp site here: *Camping Dionysos (☎ 0252-61 151, fax 61 155)*. It's quite good, if somewhat small, but has a pool, minimarket, restaurant and cooking facilities. It is set back about 100m from the beach. Open 1 June to 30 September, it charges about 1700 dr per person with tent.

Your best eating and accommodation option by far is the modern C class *Hotel Vatera Beach (☎ 0252-61 212, fax 61 164,*

Fascinating Fossil Find

Lesvos is hardly the kind of place that you would associate with great excitement in the musty and dusty world of palaeontology. Nonetheless, the island has been thrust onto centre stage recently with the extraordinary discovery of fossils of animals, fish and plants at Vatera, a sleepy beach resort on the south coast of Lesvos, hitherto more associated with sun and sand than fossilised fish.

Among the fossils found in the Vatera region are elephants, mastodons, giraffes, bones of rhinoceros and hippopotamus, deer, tortoises, snails, fish, and pieces of a gigantic prehistoric horse. Dated up to 5.5 million years old, the fossils are being temporarily displayed at the newly established Museum of Natural History in the neighbouring village of Vrissa, just 2km from the excavation sites.

Dr Michael Dermitzakis, Athens University Professor of Palaeontology, formally announced his findings recently. He considers the collection of fossilised mammals found at Vatera to be unique to the entire Mediterranean area. During the continuing excavations, hundreds of important finds have been noted. Geological scientists maintain that the site was originally a large lake surrounded by forests in which many varieties of prehistoric animals lived.

The rarity and importance of these finds cannot be overemphasised. They have created enormous interest within the international scientific community, and for visitors who have the opportunity to view these unusual finds in their natural setting at Vatera.

email hovatera@otenet.gr). American-Greek owners George and Barbara Ballis provide a relaxed environment and offer chronic stress relief for burned-out members of the rat race. Excellent Greek home cooking tops it all off. A double room ranges in price from 11,200 dr to 15,500 dr depending on the season.

Limnos Λήμνος

☎ 0254 • pop 16,000

There is a saying on Limnos that when people come to the island they cry twice: once when they arrive and once when they leave. Limnos' appeal is not immediate; its charm slowly but surely captivates.

The deeply penetrating Moudros Bay almost severs the island in two. The landscape of Limnos lacks the imposing grandeur of the forested and mountainous islands and the stark beauty of the barren and rocky ones. Gently undulating, with little farms, Limnos has a unique and understated appeal. In spring vibrant wild flowers dot the landscape, and in autumn purple crocuses sprout forth in profusion. Large numbers of flamingoes grace the lakes of eastern Limnos and the coastline boasts some of the best beaches in the North-Eastern Aegean group. The island is sufficiently off the beaten track to have escaped the adverse effects of mass tourism.

History

Limnos' position near the Straits of the Dardanelles, midway between the Mt Athos Peninsula and Turkey, has given it a traumatic history. To this day it maintains a large garrison, and jets from the huge air base loudly punctuate the daily routine.

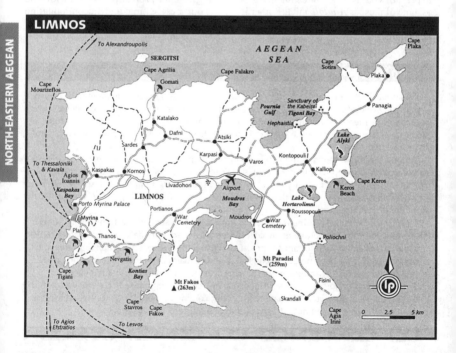

Limnos had advanced Neolithic and Bronze Age civilisations, and during these times had contact with peoples in western Anatolia, including the Trojans. In classical times the twin sea gods, the Kabeiroi, were worshipped at a sanctuary on the island, but later the Sanctuary of the Great Gods on Samothraki became the centre of this cult.

During the Peloponnesian Wars, Limnos sided with Athens and suffered many Persian attacks. After the split of the Roman Empire in 395 AD it became an important outpost of Byzantium. In 1462 it came under the domination of the Genoese who ruled Lesvos. The Turks succeeded in conquering the island in 1478 and Limnos remained under Turkish rule until 1912. Moudros Bay was the Allies' base for the disastrous Gallipoli campaign in WWI.

Getting There & Away
Air In summer there are two flights daily to Limnos from Athens (15,000 dr), five weekly from Thessaloniki (15,200 dr) and a weekly flight from Lesvos (13,400 dr). The Olympic Airways office (☎ 22 214) is on Nikolaou Garoufallidou, opposite Hotel Paris, in Myrina.

The airport is 22km east of Myrina. An Olympic Airways bus from Myrina to the airport (1000 dr) connects with all flights.

Ferry In summer four ferries go weekly from Limnos to Kavala (five hours, 3700 dr), and to Rafina (10 hours, 5500 dr) via Agios Efstratios (1½ hours, 1600 dr), and one via Sigri in Lesvos (six hours, 3200 dr). There are also three boats weekly to Chios (11 hours, 5300 dr), three to Piraeus via Lesvos and Chios, and one to Piraeus directly (13 hours, 7000 dr). There are two boats weekly to Thessaloniki (seven hours, 5300 dr) and Kavala (4½ hours, 3100 dr), and two to Alexandroupolis (five hours, 3300 dr) via Samothraki (three hours, 1600 dr).

Aiolis, a small local ferry, does the run to Agios Efstratios (2½ hours, 1600 dr) three times weekly on Monday, Wednesday and Friday. Tickets can be bought at Myrina Tourist & Travel Agency (☎ 22 460, fax 23 560, email root@mirina.lim.forthnet.gr) on the harbourfront in Myrina.

Hydrofoil In July and August there are two hydrofoils weekly to and from Alexandroupolis (three hours, 6600 dr) via Samothraki (1½ hours, 5000 dr). Purchase tickets from Myrina Tourist & Travel Agency.

Excursion Boat In July and August the *Aiolis* does a couple of extra day returns per week to the small island of Agios Efstratios (see Agios Efstratios, later in the chapter, for details). The boat usually leaves at about 8 am and returns from Agios Efstratios at 5 pm. The excursion fare is around 5000 dr.

Getting Around
Bus Bus services on Limnos are poor. In summer there are two buses daily from Myrina to most of the villages. Check the schedule (only in Greek) at the bus station (☎ 22 464) on Plateia Eleftheriou Venizelou.

Car & Motorcycle In Myrina, cars and jeeps can be rented from Myrina Rent a Car (☎ 24 476, fax 22 484) on Kyda near the waterfront. Prices range from 10,000 dr to 15,000 dr for a small car or jeep, depending on the season. There are several motorcycle hire outlets on Kyda.

MYRINA Μύρινα
• postcode 814 00   • pop 4340
Myrina is the capital and port of Limnos. Surrounded by massive hunks of volcanic rock, it is not immediately perceived as a picturesque town, but it is animated, full of character and unfettered by establishments pandering to tourism.

The main thoroughfare of Kyda is a charming paved street with clothing stores, traditional shops selling nuts and honey, old-fashioned kafeneia and barber shops – the latter are testimony to the island's military presence. Down the side streets you'll see (interspersed with modern buildings) little whitewashed stone dwellings, decaying neoclassical mansions and 19th century wattle-and-daub houses with overhanging

NORTH-EASTERN AEGEAN

wooden balconies. A Genoese castle looms dramatically over the town.

Orientation & Information

From the end of the quay turn right onto Plateia Ilia Iliou. Continue along the waterfront passing the Hotel Lemnos and the town hall. A little farther along you will see the Hotel Aktaion, set back from the waterfront. Turn left here, then immediately veer half-left onto Kyda. Proceeding up here you will reach the central square where the National Bank of Greece and the OTE are located. The taxi rank (☎ 23 033) is also on this square. Continue up Kyda and take the next turn right onto Nikolaou Garoufallidou. The post office is here on the right. Back on Kyda, continue for another 100m and you will come to Plateia Eleftheriou Venizelou where you will see the bus station.

There is a small tourist information kiosk on the quay. A laundrette (☎ 24 392) is on Nikolaou Garoufallidou, opposite the Olympic Airways office. The police station (☎ 22 201) is at the far end of Nikolaou Garoufallidou – on the right coming from Kyda. The port police (☎ 22 225) are on the waterfront near the quay.

Things to See & Do

As with any Greek island **castle**, the one towering over Myrina is worth climbing up to. From its vantage point there are magnificent views over the sea to Mt Athos. As you walk from the harbour, take the first side street to the left by an old Turkish fountain. An inconspicuous sign here points you to the castle.

Myrina has a lovely long sandy **beach** right in town. It stretches north from the castle and can be reached by walking along Kyda from the harbour, and taking any of the streets off to the left. The first part of the beach is known as Romeïkos Gialos, and the northern end, just before Akti Marina Hotel resort, is known as Riha Nera (shallow water), so named because of its gently shelving beach which is ideal for children.

The **archaeological museum** in Myrina, housed in a neoclassical mansion, is worth a visit. It contains finds from all the three sites on Limnos, and also from an unusual archaeological dig in the grounds of the Porto Myrina Palace. The museum overlooks the beach, next to the Hotel Castor. It's open 8 am to 2.30 pm Monday to Saturday and 9 am to 2.30 pm on Sunday and public holidays. Admission is 500 dr.

Organised Tours

In the absence of a decent bus service, daily bus excursions around the island can be organised with Theodoros Petridis Travel Agency (☎ 22 039, fax 22 129). These include a visit to ancient Poliochni, Hephaistia and the Sanctuary of the Kabeiroi. There is also a swimming stop and lunch break at Moudros. The cost is 6000 dr.

The agency also organises round-the-island boat trips which again include stops for swimming and lunch. The all-up cost is 10,000 dr.

Places to Stay – Budget

Limnos doesn't have any official camp sites. There is an information board with a map of the island and the names and telephone numbers of all domatia and hotels in Limnos on the harbourfront square. Budget accommodation is thin on the ground in Myrina.

On the harbourfront, *Hotel Lemnos* (☎ 22 153, fax 23 329) is about the cheapest hotel accommodation you will find, with singles/doubles for 8000/12,000 dr. But the staff are neither particularly friendly nor over-accommodating to backpackers.

The neoclassical *Apollo Pavillion* (☎/fax 23 712, email apollo47@otenet.gr) on Frynis, with friendly English-speaking owners, has spacious and clean rooms with a variety of accommodation options. Backpacker basement rooms cost 4500 dr per person. Studios with bathroom and kitchen cost 13,000/16,750 dr for doubles/triples. Walk along Nikolaou Garoufallidou from Kyda and you will see the sign 150m along on the right.

Places to Stay – Mid-Range
Blue Waters Hotel (☎ 24 403, fax 25 004, email bwkon@otenet.gr) on Romeïkos Gialos is a small discerning place on the beachfront, north of the Kastro, with tastefully decorated airy rooms with air-con and fridge. Singles/doubles go for a reasonable 12,000/14,000 dr.

Afroditi Apartments (☎ 23 489, fax 25 031), set back 200m from Riha Nera Beach, provides tastefully furnished, self-contained doubles/triples, all with air-con, for 16,000/19,200 dr. The breezy, well appointed rooms of *Poseidon Domatia (☎ 23 982, fax 24 856)* are close to the beach near the museum. Each room has a TV and bathroom and there is a small bar and breakfast room for guests. Rooms go for 17,500/19,500 dr in high season.

One of the island's best is the A class *Diamantidis Hotel (☎ 22 397, fax 23 187)*. Spacious, airy single/doubles go for 18,000/20,000 dr. The hotel is located inland from Myrina town on the main road.

Places to Eat
Restaurants are of a high standard on Limnos. Several fish restaurants line the waterfront. Locals give top marks to *Taverna Glaros*, which probably has the best harbourside location, but somewhat expensive prices. By the ferry quay is *Avra* restaurant; handy if you are waiting for a boat to leave.

Halfway along Kyda is the small, unassuming but very pleasant *O Platanos Taverna*, on the left as you walk from the waterfront. It is on a small square under a couple of huge plane trees and makes an attractive alternative to the waterfront establishments. Moussaka, salad, chips and local retsina should cost around 2500 dr.

Finally, the posh *Filoktetes* restaurant, 200m inland from Riha Nera Beach has – unusually for Greece – an access ramp and toilet for disabled diners. The food is excellent and marginally cheaper than the harbourside joints. Open for lunch and dinner, it offers a range of ready-made dishes.

Given the large number of off-duty soldiers at any given moment, there are plenty of watering holes around town. *Jolly Caffe*, overlooking the northern end of Romeïkos Gialos Beach, seemed to be the most popular spot among Greeks at the time of writing.

WESTERN LIMNOS
North of Myrina is the five-star mega resort *Porto Myrina Palace* on the south side of pristine Kaspakas Bay. Turn left just past the little village of **Kaspakas** and a narrow road will lead you down to **Agios Ioannis Beach**. The beach is pleasant enough, but Agios Ioannis consists of a few desultory fishing shacks, scattered beach houses and a couple of tavernas, one of which has its tables set out in the embrace of a large volcanic rock.

Inland from Kaspakas, the barren hilly landscape dotted with sheep and rocks (particularly on the road to Katalako via Sardes and Dafni) reminds you more of the English Peak District than an Aegean island. The villages themselves have little to cause you to pause and you will certainly be an object of curiosity if you do. There is a remote and completely undeveloped beach at Gomati on the north coast and it can be reached by a good dirt road from Katalako.

Heading 3km south from Myrina you will reach one of Limnos' best beaches, below the village of **Platy**. To get to Platy Beach follow the signs out of Myrina for Platy and Thanos, but turn right just before the cemetery. Look out for the signs to the resorts of Villa Afroditi and Lemnos Village.

As well as the clubby, exclusive and English-owned Lemnos Village Resort Hotel, Platy Beach has a few reasonably priced budget places to stay. In Platy village are *Filoxenia Domatia (☎ 24 211, fax 23 545)* owned by Greek-Australians Andreas and Konstantina Sarmonikas. The large, airy rooms with kitchenette have a great view and there is a guest common room downstairs. Doubles/triples go for 10,000/12,000 dr.

On the beach itself, the owner of Jimmy's Taverna has some somewhat cramped *domatia (☎ 24 142)* as well as some newer studios (with fridges) back on the road.

They go for between 8000 dr and 10,000 dr. There are also other unofficial domatia in the village.

Apart from *Jimmy's Taverna* on the beach which specialises in fish, the best food to be had is in Platy Village itself, where *Zimbabwe* restaurant and the striking blue and white *Kalouditsa* taverna vie for clientele by spilling out across two squares next to each other.

Back on the beach road, if you continue along the dirt road, past the Lemnos Village Resort Hotel, you will come to a sheltered sandy cove with an islet in the bay. The beach here will probably be less crowded than Platy. **Thanos Beach** is the next bay around from Platy; it is also less crowded, and long and sandy. To get there, continue on the main road from Platy Village to Thanos Village, where a sign points to the beach.

CENTRAL LIMNOS

Central Limnos is flat and agricultural with wheat fields, small vineyards, and cattle and sheep farms. The island's huge air-force base is ominously surrounded by endless barbed-wire fences. The muddy and bleak Moudros Bay cuts deep into the interior, with **Moudros**, the second-largest town, positioned on the eastern side of the bay. Moudros does not offer much for the tourist other than a couple of small hotels with tavernas on the waterfront. The harbour has none of Myrina's picturesque qualities.

One kilometre out of Moudros on the road to Roussopouli, you will come across the **East Moudros Military Cemetery** where Commonwealth soldiers from the Gallipoli campaign are buried. Limnos, with its large protected anchorage, was occupied by a force of Royal Marines on 23 February 1915 and became the principal base for this ill-fated campaign. A metal plaque, just inside the gates, gives a short history of the Gallipoli campaign. A second Commonwealth cemetery, the **Portianos Military Cemetery**, is at Portianos, about 6km south of the village of Livadohori on the trans-island highway. The cemetery is not as obvious as the Australian-style blue and white street

sign sporting the name Anzac St. Follow Anzac St to the church and you will find the cemetery off a little lane behind the church.

EASTERN LIMNOS

Eastern Limnos has three archaeological sites. The Italian School of Archaeologists has uncovered four ancient settlements at **Poliochni**, on the island's east coast. The most interesting was a sophisticated pre-Mycenaean city, which predated Troy VI (1800-1275 BC). The site is well laid-out with colour-coded maps to show the so-called Blue, Green, Red and Yellow periods of settlement and there are good descriptions in Greek, Italian and English. However, there is nothing too exciting to be seen; the site is probably of greater interest to archaeological buffs than casual visitors.

The second site is that of the **Sanctuary of the Kabeiroi** (Ta Kaviria) in north-eastern Limnos on the shores of remote Tigani Bay. This was originally a site for the worship of Kabeiroi gods predating those of Samothraki (see Sanctuary of the Great Gods, under Samothraki, later in this chapter). There is little of the Sanctuary of Samothraki's splendour, but the layout of the site is obvious and excavations are still being carried out.

The major site, which has 11 columns, is that of a Hellenistic sanctuary. The older site is farther back and is still being excavated. Of additional interest is the cave of Philoctetes, the hero of the Trojan War, who was abandoned here while a gangrenous leg (a result of snakebite) healed. The sea cave can be reached by a path that leads down from the site. The cave can actually be entered by a hidden, narrow entrance (unmarked) to the left of the main entrance.

You can reach the sanctuary easily, if you have your own transport, via a fast new road that was built for the multimillion-drachma (and now white elephant) tourist enclave, Kaviria Palace. The turn-off is about 5km to the left, after the village of **Kontopouli**. From Kontopouli itself you can make a detour to the third site, along a rough dirt track to **Hephaistia** (Ta Ifestia), once the most important city on the island. Hephaestus was the god of fire and metallurgy and, according to mythology, was thrown here from Mt Olympus by Zeus. The site is widely scattered over a scrub-covered, but otherwise desolate, small peninsula. There is not much to see of the ancient city other than some low walls and a partially excavated theatre. Excavations are still under way. All three sites are open 8 am to 2.30 pm daily and admission is, so far, free.

The road to the northern tip of the island is worth exploring. There are some typical Limnian villages in the area and the often deserted beach at **Keros** is popular with windsurfers. From the cape at the north eastern tip of Limnos you can see the islands of Samothraki and Imvros (Gökçeada) in Turkey.

Agios Efstratios
Αγιος Ευστράτιος

☎ 0254 • postcode 815 00 • pop 290

The little-known island of Agios Efstratios, called locally Aï-Stratis, deservedly merits the title of perhaps the most isolated island in the Aegean. Stuck more or less plumb centre in the North Aegean some distance from its nearest neighbour Limnos, it has few cars and fewer roads, but a steady trickle of curious foreign island-hoppers seeking to find some peace and quiet.

Large numbers of political exiles were sent here for enforced peace and quiet before and after WWII. Among the exiled guests were such luminaries as composer Mikis Theodorakis and poets Kostas Varnalis and Giannis Ritsos.

The little village of Aï-Stratis was once picturesque, but in the early hours of the morning of 21 February 1968 a violent earthquake, with its epicentre in the seas between Limnos and Aï-Stratis, virtually destroyed the vibrant village in one fell swoop. Many people emigrated as a result and there are now large numbers of islanders living in Australia and elsewhere.

Ham-fisted intervention by the then ruling junta saw the demolition of most of the remaining traditional homes and in their place, cheaply built concrete boxes were erected to house the islanders. Needless to say, the islanders are still pretty miffed over 30 years after the event, and the remaining hillside ruins stand silent sentinel over a rather lacklustre village today.

Still, if you yearn for serenity and traffic-free bliss, and enjoy walking, Aï-Stratis is a great place to visit. It has some great beaches – though most are only accessible by caïque – ample accommodation, simple island food and a surprisingly busy nightlife.

There is a post office, one cardphone and one metered phone for the public.

Getting There & Away

Agios Efstratios is on the Kavala-Rafina ferry route, which includes Limnos. There are four services weekly to Rafina (8½ hours, 4500 dr) and another four in the other direction to Limnos (1½ hours, 1600 dr) and Kavala (6½ hours, 4500 dr).

In addition, the small local ferry *Aiolis* putters to and from Limnos three times weekly on Monday, Wednesday and Friday. On the off-days, during summer, *Aiolis* does a more or less daily excursion run from Limnos for around 5000 dr. But the harbour is exposed to the west winds, causing ferry services to often be cancelled or delayed.

Beaches

Apart from the reasonable village beach of dark volcanic sand, the nearest beach worth making the effort to visit is **Alonitsi Beach** on the north-east side of the island. It is a long, totally undeveloped, pristine strand and it can be all yours if you are prepared to walk the 90 minutes to reach it. To get there take the little track from the north-east side of the village, starting by a small bridge, and follow it up towards the power pylons. Halfway along the track splits; take the right track for Alonitsi, or the left track for the **military lookout** for great views. **Lidario Beach** on the west side can be reached – with difficulty – on foot, but is better approached by sea, if you can get someone to take you there.

Places to Stay & Eat

Accommodation options in Agios Efstratios are now pretty good. There is no hotel on the island but there are currently about 100 beds available and you will always find somewhere to stay unless you turn up at the height of the summer season without a reservation.

The spotless and airy *Xenonas Aï-Strati* (☎ *93 329)*, run by Julia and Odysseas Galanakis, has doubles/triples ranging in price from 5000 dr to 10,000 dr, depending on facilities and the season. The rooms are in one of the few buildings that survived the earthquake on the north-eastern side of the village.

The *domatia* of Malama Panera (☎ *93 209)*, on the south side of the village, are equally well appointed with similar prices. There are also other unofficial domatia available. Ask at the little convenience store, if you get stuck. You can fax the community fax machine (93 210) if you want to make a booking.

For eating you have the choice of the fairly obvious community-run *Thanasis Taverna* which overlooks the harbour, or *Tasos Ouzeri* diagonally opposite. At the far south end of the waterfront is *Taverna tou Antoni* which opens in the summer, when Antonis feels like it. All places are fairly inexpensive, though fish still tends to be a bit on the steep side.

Samothraki
Σαμοθράκη

☎ 0551   • pop 2800

The egg-shaped island of Samothraki is 32km south-west of Alexandroupolis. Scenically it is one of the most awe-inspiring of all Greek islands. It is a small island, but a great deal of diverse landscape is packed into its 176 sq km. Its natural attributes are dramatic, big and untamed, culminating in the mighty peak of Mt Fengari (1611m), the highest mountain in the Aegean. Homer

related that Poseidon watched the Trojan War from Mt Fengari's summit.

The jagged, boulder-strewn Mt Fengari looms over valleys of massive gnarled oak and plane trees, thick forests of olive trees, dense shrubbery and damp, dark glades where waterfalls plunge into deep, icy pools. On the gentler, western slopes of the island there are corn fields studded with wild flowers. Samothraki is also rich in fauna Its springs are the habitat of a large number of frogs, toads and turtles; in its meadows you will see swarms of butterflies and may come across the occasional lumbering tortoise. On the mountain slopes there are an inordinate number of bell-clanking goats. The island's beaches, with one exception, are stony or pebbly.

Samothraki's ancient site, the Sanctuary of the Great Gods, at Paleopolis, is one of Greece's most evocative ancient sites. Historians are unable to ascertain the nature of the rites performed here, and its aura of potent mysticism prevails over the whole island.

Samothraki is relatively difficult to reach and does not have any package tourism. It does, however, attract a fair number of Greek holiday-makers in July and August, so you may have some difficulty finding a room then. With the exception of Xenia Hotel, all of Samothraki's hotels were built in the 1980s and were designed to a high standard with sensitive regard to the environment. All are very pleasant places to stay but none fall into the budget category. This doesn't mean budget travellers are not welcome or catered for as there are a fair number of domatia and two camp sites.

History

Samothraki was first settled around 1000 BC by Thracians who worshipped the Great Gods, a cult of Anatolian origin. In 700 BC the island was colonised by people from Lesvos, who absorbed the Thracian cult into the worship of the Olympian gods.

This marriage of two cults was highly successful and by the 5th century BC Samothraki had become one of Greece's major religious centres, attracting prospective initiates from far and wide to its Sanctuary of the Great Gods. Among the luminaries initiated into the cult were King Lysander of Sparta, Philip II of Macedon and Cornelius Piso, Julius Caesar's father-in-law. One famous visitor who did not come to be initiated was St Paul, who dropped in en route to Philippi.

The cult survived until paganism was outlawed in the 4th century AD. After this the island became insignificant. Falling to the Turks in 1457, it united with Greece, along with the other North-Eastern Aegean Islands, in 1912. During WWII Samothraki was occupied by the Bulgarians.

Getting There & Away

Ferry Samothraki has ferry connections with Alexandroupolis (two hours, 2300 dr), Kavala (four hours, 3000 dr), and Limnos (three hours, 1600 dr). The sailing times vary from year to year, but in summer there are usually five departures weekly to Kavala, two weekly to Limnos and two daily to Alexandroupolis. Tickets can be bought at Niki Tours (☎ 41 465, fax 41 304,

mobile 093-534 648) or Saos Travel (☎ 41 505), in Kamariotissa.

Hydrofoil Hydrofoil services operate from Samothraki from 1 May to 31 October. Currently there are services linking Samothraki with Limnos, Thasos, Halkidiki (Stavros), Kavala, Maronia, Porto Lagos and Alexandroupolis. For departure details contact Niki Tours in Kamariotissa or the office for the *Thraki III* hydrofoil (☎ 41 100, fax 230 200) which is near Budget car rentals. Ticket prices are roughly twice as much as the equivalent ferry ticket.

Getting Around

Bus In summer there are at least nine buses daily from Kamariotissa to Hora and Loutra (Therma), via Paleopolis. Some of the Loutra buses continue to the nearby camp sites. There are four buses daily to Profitis Ilias (via Lakoma). A bus schedule is displayed in the window of Saos Travel, in Kamariotissa.

Car & Motorcycle Cars and small jeeps can be rented from Niki Tours (☎ 41 465,

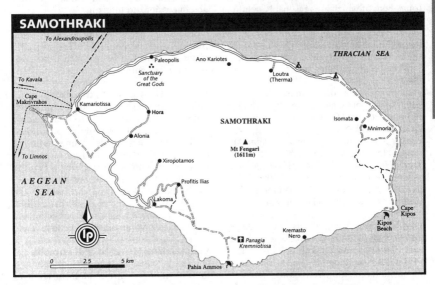

fax 41 304) and Budget (☎ 41 100). A 4WD jeep, recommended for Samothraki, costs about 18,000 dr per day, whereas a small car will cost about 12,000 dr. Motorcycles can be rented from Rent A Motor Bike, opposite the ferry quay

Excursion Boat Depending on demand, caïques do trips from the Kamariotissa jetty to Pahia Ammos and Kipos beaches.

KAMARIOTISSA Καμαριώτισσα
• postcode 680 02   • pop 826

Kamariotissa, on the north-west coast, is Samothraki's port. Hora (also called Samothraki), the island's capital, is 5km inland from here. Kamariotissa is the transport hub of the island, so you may wish to use it as a base. It has a fairly lively nightlife and a few decent restaurants.

Orientation & Information
The bus station is on the waterfront just east of the quay (turn left when you disembark). There is no EOT or tourist police and the regular police are in Hora. Opposite the bus station you will find Saos Travel and Niki Tours, both of which are reasonably helpful. There is a National Bank of Greece on the waterfront, but no post office or OTE; these are in Hora. The port police (☎ 41 305) are on the eastern waterfront at Kamariotissa.

Places to Stay
Domatia owners often meet ferries in Kamariotissa, but *domatia* are easy to find in the compact port. *Hotel Kyma* (☎ 41 263), at the eastern end of the waterfront, has comfortable doubles for 11,000 dr with bathroom. Farther along the waterfront, the C class *Niki Beach Hotel* (☎ 41 545, 41 461) is airy and spacious. Room rates here are 9,000/12,000 dr for singles/doubles with bathroom. The hotel is at the eastern end of the waterfront.

Behind the Niki Beach is Samothraki's most luxurious hotel, the B class *Aeolos Hotel* (☎ 41 595, fax 41 810), where rooms cost 10,000/15,000 dr with breakfast. The hotel has a swimming pool and a commanding position on a hill overlooking the sea.

Places to Eat
Samothraki's culinary offerings have improved considerably. *Horizon* is one of Kamariotissa's better restaurants. Main courses include chicken casserole for 1000 dr; meatballs, moussaka and souvlaki are all 1200 dr. The restaurant is just back from the waterfront on the left side of the road which leads up to Hora.

At the eastern end of the waterfront *Klimitaria Restaurant* (☎ 41 535) serves an unusual speciality called *gianiotiko* for 1800 dr. This is an oven-baked dish of diced pork, potatoes, egg and other goodies.

HORA Χώρα
Hora, concealed in a fold of the mountains above Kamariotissa, is one of the most striking of Greek-island villages. The crumbling red-tiled houses – some of grey stone, others whitewashed – are stacked up two steep adjacent mountainsides.

The twisting cobbled streets resound with cockerels crowing, dogs barking and donkeys braying, rather than the ubiquitous roar of motorcycles and honking of car horns. The village is totally authentic with no concessions to tourism.

The ruined castle at the top of the main thoroughfare is fascinating to explore and from its vantage point there are sweeping vistas down to Kamariotissa. It is an open site with free entrance.

Orientation & Information
To get to Hora's narrow winding main street, follow the signs for the kastro from the central square where the bus turns around. Here on the main street, which is nameless (as are all of Hora's streets; houses are distinguished by numbers), are the OTE, the Agricultural Bank and the post office. The police (☎ 41 203) are next to the ruined castle at the top of Hora's main street. Further up on the main street, on the right, a fountain gushes refreshing mountain water.

Walk from Hora to Paleopolis
It takes between 45 minutes and one hour to walk along a dirt road from Hora to

Paleopolis (Sanctuary of the Great Gods). On this walk there are tremendous views of Fengari to the right and rolling hills, corn fields and the sea to the left. To get to the road, walk up to the castle ruins in Hora and take the dirt road which leads down to the right. Alternatively, you can start the walk from the road just below the bus stop.

Follow the main track all the way down and around and look out for the Kastro Hotel to your left as you come over the rise. Bear right along a smaller track as you come down the hill and you will eventually come across the museum and ancient site. You can negotiate this road in a car (4WD recommended, though). Keep going straight down the hill until you hit the main road.

Places to Stay & Eat

There are no hotels in Hora. There are two reasonably priced *pensions* just off the central square, but the best places to stay in Hora are *domatia* in private houses. Almost all of these are unofficial and do not display signs. If you ask in one of the kafeneia you will be put in touch with a room owner.

There is a *psistaria* on the square where the bus stops, and *Taverna Kastro* on the central square. Both places serve food catering for local tastes rather than for tourists. Ask for fish, if they have it. Bear in mind that these places may well be closed out of season.

SANCTUARY OF THE GREAT GODS

Το Ιερό των Μεγάλων Θεών
The Sanctuary of the Great Gods, next to the little village of Paleopolis, is 6km north-east of Kamariotissa. The extensive site, lying in a valley of luxuriant vegetation between Mt Fengari and the sea, is one of the most magical in the whole of Greece. The Great Gods were of greater antiquity than the Olympian gods worshipped in the official religion of ancient Greece. The principal deity, the Great Mother (Alceros Cybele), was worshipped as a fertility goddess.

When the original Thracian religion became integrated with the state religion, the Great Mother was merged with the Olympian female deities Demeter, Aphrodite and Hecate. The last of these was a mysterious goddess, associated with darkness, the underworld and witchcraft. Other deities worshipped here were the Great Mother's consort, the virile young Kadmilos (god of the phallus), who was later integrated with the Olympian god Hermes; as well as the demonic Kabeiroi twins, Dardanos and Aeton, who were integrated with Castor and Pollux (The Dioscuri), the twin sons of Zeus and Leda. These twins were invoked by mariners to protect them against the perils of the sea. The formidable deities of Samothraki were venerated for their immense power. In comparison, the Olympian gods were a frivolous and fickle lot.

Initiates were sworn on punishment of death not to reveal what went on at the sanctuary; so there is only very flimsy knowledge of what these initiations involved. All that the archaeological evidence reveals is that there were two initiations, a lower and a higher. In the first initiation, gods were invoked to bring about a spiritual rebirth within the candidate. In the second initiation the candidate was absolved of transgressions. There was no prerequisite for initiation – it was available to anyone.

The site's most celebrated relic, the Winged Victory of Samothrace (now in the Louvre in Paris), was found by Champoiseau, the French consul, at Adrianople (present-day Edirne in Turkey) in 1863. Sporadic excavations followed in the late 19th and early 20th centuries, but did not begin in earnest until just before WWII, when the Institute of Fine Arts, New York University, under the direction of Karl Lehmann and Phyllis Williams Lehmann, began digging.

The site is open 8.30 am to 3 pm Tuesday to Sunday. Admission is 500 dr, but is free on Sunday and public holidays.

Exploring the Site

The site is labelled in both Greek and English. If you take the path which leads south from the entrance you will arrive at the rectangular **anaktoron**, on the left. At the southern end was a **sacristy**, an antechamber where candidates put on white gowns ready for their first (lower) initiation. The initiation ceremony took place in the main body of the anaktoron. Then one at a time each initiate entered the holy of holies, a small inner temple at the northern end of the building, where a priest instructed them in the meanings of the symbols used in the ceremony. Afterwards the initiates returned to the sacristy to receive their initiation certificate.

The **arsinoein**, which was used for sacrifices, to the south-west of the anaktoron, was built in 289 BC and was then the largest cylindrical structure in Greece. It was a gift to the Great Gods from the Egyptian queen Arsinou. To the south-east of here you will see the **sacred rock**, the site's earliest altar, which was used by the Thracians.

The initiations were followed by a celebratory feast which probably took place in the **temenos**, to the south of the arsinoein. This building was a gift from Philip II. The next building is the prominent Doric **hieron**, which is the most photographed ruin on the

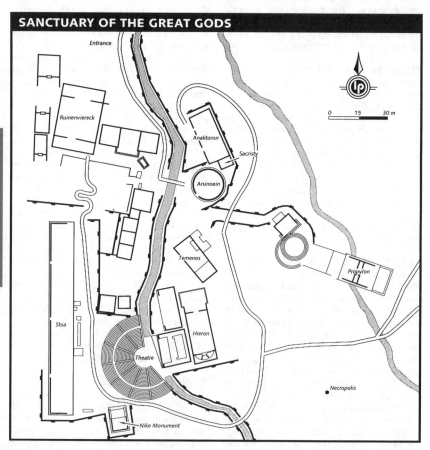

SANCTUARY OF THE GREAT GODS

Entrance

Ruinenviereck

Anaktoron

Sacristy

Arsinoein

0   15   30 m

Temenos

Propylon

Stoa

Hieron

Theatre

Necropolis

Nike Monument

NORTH-EASTERN AEGEAN

site; five of its columns have been reassembled. It was in this temple that candidates received the second initiation.

On the west side of the main path (opposite the hieron) are a few remnants of a **theatre**. Nearby, a path ascends to the **Nike monument** where the magnificent Winged Victory of Samothrace once stood. The statue was a gift from Demetrius Poliorketes (the 'besieger of cities') to the Kabeiroi for helping him defeat Ptolemy II in battle. To the north-west of here are the remains of a massive **stoa**, which was a two-aisled portico where pilgrims to the sanctuary sheltered. Names of initiates were recorded on its walls. North of the stoa are the ruins of the **ruinenviereck**, a medieval fortress.

Retrace your steps to the Nike monument and walk along the path leading east; on the left is a good plan of the site. The path continues to the southern **necropolis** which is the most important ancient cemetery so far found on the island. It was used from the Bronze Age to early Roman times. North of the cemetery was the **propylon**, an elaborate Ionic entrance to the sanctuary; it was a gift from Ptolemy II.

Museum The site's museum is well laid out, with English labels. Exhibits include terracotta figurines, vases, jewellery and a plaster cast of the Winged Victory. It's open 9 am to 3 pm Tuesday to Sunday. Admission is 500 dr, but is free on Sunday and public holidays.

Places to Stay & Eat

There are several *domatia* at Paleopolis, all of which are signposted from near the museum. The B class *Xenia Hotel (☎ 41 230, fax 41 166)* near the museum was built in 1952 to provide accommodation for archaeologists. Although clean, cool and comfortable, it lacks the sophistication of Samothraki's newer hotels. Doubles cost 10,800 dr with bathroom.

Just west of Paleopolis, above the coast road, is the C class *Kastro Hotel (☎ 41 001, fax 41 000)*, the island's newest hotel. The rooms are simply and tastefully furnished

and rates are 13,000/17,000 dr for singles/doubles, including breakfast. The hotel has a swimming pool.

There is at least one taverna at Paleopolis but both hotels have a restaurant and bar. If you have your own transport there are some other eating places to choose from along the road towards Loutra (Therma).

AROUND SAMOTHRAKI
Loutra (Therma) Λουτρά (Θερμά)

Loutra, also called Therma, is 14km east of Kamariotissa and a short walk inland from the coast. It's in an attractive setting with a profusion of plane and horse-chestnut trees, dense greenery and gurgling creeks. While not an authentic village, it is the nearest Samothraki comes to having a holiday resort. Many of its buildings are purpose-built domatia, and most visitors to the island seem to stay here.

The village takes both its names from its therapeutic, sulphurous, mineral springs. Whether or not you are arthritic you may like to take a thermal bath here. The baths are in the large white building on the right as you walk to the central square from the bus stop. Opening times are 6 to 11 am, and 5 to 7 pm. Admission is 450 dr.

Places to Stay Samothraki has two official camp sites; both are near Loutra, and both are signposted 'Multilary Campings'. Rest assured, the authorities mean municipal camp sites and not military camp sites. The first *Multilary Camping (☎ 41 784)* is to the left of the main road, 2km beyond the turn-off for Loutra, coming from Kamariotissa. The site is very spartan, with toilets and cold showers but no other amenities. It charges 500 dr per person and 400 dr per tent. The second *Multilary Camping (☎ 41 491)* is 2km farther along the road. It has a minimarket, restaurant and hot showers, but is still a rather scrappy and dry camp site. It charges 800 dr per person, and 600 dr per tent. Both sites are open only from June through August.

Domatia owners meet the buses at Loutra. There are also two lovely hotels in Loutra.

The C class *Mariva Bungalows* (☎ 98 230, fax 98 374) are set on a hillside in a secluded part of the island, near a waterfall. The spacious doubles cost 12,000 dr with bathroom. To reach the hotel take the first turn left along the road which leads from the coast up to Loutra. Follow the signs to the hotel which is 600m along this road.

The B class *Kaviros Hotel* (☎ 98 277, fax 98 278) is bang in the middle of Loutra, just beyond the central square. It is a very pleasant family-run hotel with singles/doubles for 10,000/11,000 dr. The hotel is surrounded by a pretty garden.

Places to Eat In Loutra there are a number of restaurants and tavernas scattered throughout the upper and lower village. There is not a lot to choose between them, but chopping and changing may be part of the fun. In the upper village try *Paradisos Restaurant* which plies its trade under a huge plane tree with its welcome shade on a hot day. Take the road to the right from the bus stop to find it. *Fengari Restaurant*, signposted from near the bus stop, cooks its food in traditional Samothraki ovens and is hidden away on a backstreet.

Fonias River

Visitors to the north coast should not miss the walk along the Fonias River to the **Vathres** rock pools. The walk starts at the bridge over the river 4.7km east of Loutra – the track being over-optimistically signposted as a vehicular road. After an easy 40 minute walk along a fairly well marked track you will come to a large rock pool fed by a dramatic 12m waterfall. The water is pretty cold but very welcome on a hot day. Locals call the river the 'Murderer' – winter rains can transform the waters into a raging torrent.

Beaches

The gods did not over-endow Samothraki with good beaches. However, its one sandy beach, **Pahia Ammos**, on the south coast, is superb. You can reach this 800m stretch of sand by walking along an 8km winding dirt road from Lakoma. In summer there are

caïques from Kamariotissa to the beach. Around the headland is the equally superb **Vatos Beach**, used mainly by nudists.

Opposite Pahia Ammos, on a good day, you can see the mass of the former Greek island of Imvros (Gökçeada), ceded to the Turks under the Treaty of Lausanne in 1923.

There is now a restaurant, *Taverna Pahia Ammos*, and *domatia* at Pahia Ammos, but bookings are recommended for July and August, since there are only six rooms, which go for 8000 dr each. Write to Nikolaos Kapelas, Profitis Ilias, Samothraki.

Samothraki's other decent beach is the pebbled **Kipos Beach** on the south-east coast. It can be reached on the unsealed road which is the easterly continuation of the road skirting the north coast. However, there are no facilities here other than a shower and a freshwater fountain, and there is no shade. It pales in comparison to Pahia Ammos Beach.

Kipos Beach can also be reached by caïque from Kamariotissa.

Other Villages

The small villages of **Profitis Ilias**, **Lakoma** and **Xiropotamos** in the south-west, and **Alonia** near Hora, are serene unspoilt villages all worth a visit. The hillside Profitis Ilias, with many trees and springs, is particularly delightful and has several tavernas of which *Vrahos* is famous for its delicious roast kid. Asphalt roads lead to all of these villages.

Thasos Θάσος

☎ 0593 • pop 13,300

Thasos lies 10km south-east of Kavala. It is almost circular in shape and although its scenery is not as awesome as Samothraki's it has some pleasing mountain vistas. The EOT brochures tout it as the 'emerald isle', but like so many other Greek islands it has suffered bad fires which have destroyed much of its forest. The main attractions of Thasos are its excellent beaches and the many archaeological remains in and around the capital of Limenas. A good asphalt road goes around the island so all the beaches are easily accessible.

There are still enough rooms for everyone even in the high season and Thasos has no less than six camp sites dotted around its coast. A notice opposite the bus station in Limenas lists the town's hotels, and also, very helpfully, indicates which hotels remain open in the winter.

History

Thasos has been continuously inhabited since the Stone Age. Its ancient city was founded in 700 BC by Parians, led there by a message from the Delphic oracle. The oracle told them to 'Find a city in the Isle of Mists'. From Thasos, the Parians established settlements in Thrace where they mined for gold in Mt Pangaion.

Gold was also mined on Thasos, and the islanders were able to develop a lucrative export trade based on ore, marble, timber and wine, as well as gold. As a result Thasos built a powerful navy, and culture flourished. Famous ancient Thassiots included the painters Polygnotos, Aglafon Aristofon and the sculptors Polyclitos and Sosicles. The merchants of Thasos traded with Asia Minor, Egypt and Italy.

After the Battle of Plataea, Thasos became an ally of Athens, but war broke out between the two cities when Athens attempted to curtail Thasos' trade with Egypt and Asia Minor. The islanders were defeated and forced into becoming part of the Delian League; the heavy tax imposed crippled its economy. Thasos' decline continued through Macedonian and Roman times. Heavy taxes were imposed by the Turks, many inhabitants left the island and during the 18th century the population dropped from 8000 to 2500.

Thasos was revived in the 19th century when Mohammed Ali Pasha of Egypt became governor of Kavala and Thasos. Ali allowed the islanders to govern themselves and exempted them from paying taxes. The revival was, however, short-lived. The Egyptian governors who superseded Ali

Pasha usurped the island's natural resources and imposed heavy taxes. In 1912, along with the other islands of the group, Thasos was united with Greece. Like Samothraki, Thasos was occupied by Bulgaria in WWII.

In recent years Thasos has once again struck 'gold'. This time it's 'black gold', in the form of oil which has been found in the sea around the island. Oil derricks can now be spotted at sea at various locations around Thasos.

Getting There & Away

Ferry There are ferries every hour between Kavala, on the mainland, and Skala Prinou (1½ hours, 850 dr, 4400 dr for a car). There is only one ferry daily between Kavala and Limenas. Ferries direct to Limenas leave every hour or so in summer (40 minutes, 330 dr) from Keramoti, 46km south-east of Kavala.

Hydrofoil There are six hydrofoils every day between Limenas and Kavala (30 minutes, 1600 dr).

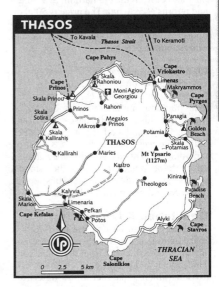

Getting Around

Bus Limenas is the transport hub of the island. There are many buses daily to Limenaria (via the west coast villages) and to Golden Beach via Panagia and Potamia. There are six buses to Theologos and three to Alyki. Six buses daily journey in a clockwise direction all the way around the island. The cost of a complete two hour circuit of the island by bus is 2000 dr.

Car & Motorcycle Cars can be hired from Avis Rent a Car (☎ 22 535) on the central square in Limenas or in Skala Prinou (☎ 71 202) and Potamia (☎ 61 506). You can hire motorcycles and mopeds from Billy's Bikes (☎ 22 490), opposite the foreign-language newspaper agency.

Bicycle Bicycles can be hired from Babi's Bikes (☎ 22 129), on a side street between 18 Oktovriou and the central square in Limenas.

Excursion Boat The *Eros 2* excursion boat makes daily trips around the island, with stops for swimming and a barbecue. The boat leaves from the old harbour at 9.30 am and returns at 5.30 pm. The price is 5000 dr. There are also a couple of water taxis running regularly to Hrysi Ammoudia and Makryammos beaches.

LIMENAS Λιμένας
• postcode 640 04   • pop 2600

Limenas, on the north-east coast, is the main port and capital of the island. Confusingly, it is also called Thasos Town and Limin. The island's other port is Skala Prinou on the west coast. Limenas is built on top of the ancient city, so ruins are scattered all over the place. It is also the island's transport hub, with a reasonable bus service to the coastal resorts and villages.

Orientation & Information

The quay for both ferries and hydrofoils is at the centre of the waterfront. The central square is straight ahead from the waterfront. The towns main thoroughfare is 18 Oktovriou, which is parallel to the waterfront

and north of the central square. Turn left into 18 Oktovriou from the quay to reach the OTE on the right. Take the next turn right into Theogenous and the second turn right to reach the post office, which is on the left.

There is no EOT on Thasos, but the helpful tourist police (☎ 22 500) are on the waterfront near the bus station. They will assist in finding accommodation if necessary.

The National Bank of Greece is on the waterfront opposite the quay and has both an exchange machine and ATM. The newsagent on Theogenous sells English-language newspapers.

The bus station is on the waterfront; to reach it turn left from the quay. To reach the town's picturesque small harbour turn left from the quay and walk along the waterfront. The crowded town beach begins at the end of the western waterfront.

Street name signs are a bit of a novelty in Limenas, so don't be surprised if you can't find one.

Things to See

Thasos' **archaeological museum** is next to the ancient agora at the small harbour. The most striking exhibit is a very elongated 6th century BC *kouros* statue which stands in the foyer. It was found on the acropolis of the ancient city of Thasos. Other exhibits include pottery and terracotta figurines and a large well preserved head of a rather effeminate Dionysos. The ancient city of Thasos was excavated by the French School of Archaeology, so the museum's labelling is in French and Greek.

The **ancient agora** next to the museum was the bustling marketplace of ancient and Roman Thasos – the centre of its civic, social and business life. It's a pleasant, verdant site with the foundations of stoas, shops and dwellings. Entrance is free.

The **ancient theatre**, in a lovely wooded setting, has been fitted with wooden seats (now a bit dilapidated), and performances of ancient dramas are staged here annually, though the theatre is currently undergoing renovation. The theatre is signposted from the small harbour.

NORTH-EASTERN AEGEAN

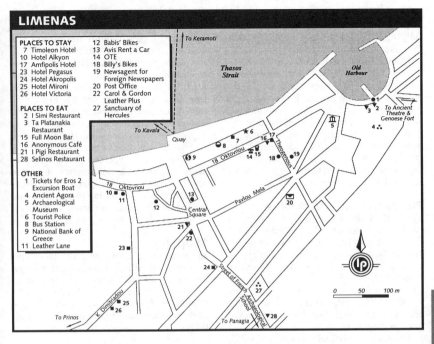

LIMENAS

PLACES TO STAY
7 Timoleon Hotel
10 Hotel Alkyon
17 Amfipolis Hotel
23 Hotel Pegasus
24 Hotel Akropolis
25 Hotel Mironi
26 Hotel Victoria

PLACES TO EAT
2 I Simi Restaurant
3 Ta Platanakia Restaurant
15 Full Moon Bar
16 Anonymous Café
21 I Pigi Restaurant
28 Selinos Restaurant

OTHER
1 Tickets for Eros 2 Excursion Boat
4 Ancient Agora
5 Archaeological Museum
6 Tourist Police
8 Bus Station
9 National Bank of Greece
11 Leather Lane

12 Babis' Bikes
13 Avis Rent a Car
14 OTE
18 Billy's Bikes
19 Newsagent for Foreign Newspapers
20 Post Office
22 Carol & Gordon Leather Plus
27 Sanctuary of Hercules

To Keramoti

Thasos Strait

Old Harbour

To Kavala

Quay

To Ancient Theatre & Genoese Fort

Theogenous

18 Oktovriou

18 Oktovriou

Pavlou Mela

Central Square

K. Dimitriadou

To Prinos

Street of French Archaeological School

To Panagia

0   50   100 m

From the theatre a path leads up to the **acropolis** of ancient Thasos where there are substantial remains of a medieval fortress built on the foundations of the ancient walls which encompassed the entire city. From the topmost point of the acropolis there are magnificent views. From the far side of the acropolis, steps carved into the rock (with a dodgy-looking metal handrail) lead down to the foundations of the ancient wall. From here it's a short walk to the Limenas-Panagia road at the southern edge of town.

Special Events

In July and August, performances of ancient plays are held at Limenas' ancient theatre, as part of the Kavala Festival of Drama. Information and tickets can be obtained from the EOT in Kavala or the tourist police on Thasos. The theatre has been undergoing renovations; check whether performances have recommenced.

Places to Stay – Budget

The nearest camp site to Limenas is *Nysteri Camping* (☎ 23 327), just west of the town. With the exception of the camp site on Golden Beach, all of Thasos' other camp sites are on the west and south-west coasts.

Limenas has many reasonably priced *domatia*. If you are not offered anything when you arrive, then look for signs around the small harbour and the road to Prinos.

Close to the waterfront is the very pleasant and clean C class *Hotel Alkyon* (☎ 22 148). Singles/doubles will cost about 7000/10,000 dr. Take a back room if you prefer less noise from street life. The hotel also has a snack bar where tea is the speciality; the co-owner is English. *Hotel Akropolis* (☎ 22 488), one block south of the central square, is a very well maintained century-old mansion with a lovely garden. The beautifully furnished rooms cost 9000/11,800 dr for doubles/triples with bathroom.

Hotel Mironi (☎ *23 256, fax 22 132*) is modern and spacious with lots of cool marble. Rates are 12,000 dr for both singles and doubles with bathroom. From the ferry quay walk to 18 Oktovriou and turn right and then left on the road signposted to Prinos. The hotel is along here on the left. Next door, *Hotel Victoria* (☎ *22 556, fax 22 132*) is a lovely, traditional place with doubles/triples for 8000 dr. Both establishments are run by the same owner.

Places to Stay – Mid-Range

The B class *Hotel Pegasus* (☎ *22 061, fax 22 373*) is a pleasant choice. It has a pool, restaurant and bar. Its quality rooms are 10,000/14,000 dr for singles/doubles, including breakfast. The B class *Timoleon Hotel* (☎ *22 177, fax 23 277*) has clean spacious rooms with balcony. Rates are 12,000/15,000 dr with bathroom, including breakfast. The hotel is on the waterfront just beyond the bus station.

The A class *Amfipolis Hotel* (☎ *23 101, fax 22 110*), on the corner of 18 Oktovriou and Theogenous, is an attractive mock castle complete with turrets. Rates are 15,500/19,700 dr, including a buffet breakfast. The hotel has a swimming pool.

Places to Eat

Limenas has a good selection of restaurants serving well prepared food. *I Pigi Restaurant*, on the central square, is an inviting, unpretentious restaurant next to a spring. The food is good and the service friendly and attentive. Try *stifado* (stew in tomato sauce), mussel *saganaki* or swordfish.

The old harbour, and the area just beyond it along the beach, boasts no less than eight restaurants. They all cater primarily to the tourist trade and feature multilingual menu cards. The first two, *Ta Platanakia* and *I Simi*, are convenient and slightly more downmarket than the other establishments. The food is good at both restaurants and the

prices aren't too bad. Reckon on about 2600 dr for a meal with beer or wine.

The very good *Selinos Restaurant* is a little out of town, but is worth a visit. Check out a couple of the specialities: *kolokythokeftedes* (zucchini rissoles), *ohtapodi krasato* (octopus in wine) or *mydia saganaki* (mussels in sauce). Prices are mid-range. Walk inland from the central square and the restaurant is a little way beyond the Sanctuary of Hercules. The taverna is only open in the evening.

Anonymous Cafe, on 18 Oktovriou, serves English-style snacks and Guinness in a can (and many other beers) to a background of eclectic music. Two doors along is another popular watering hole, *Full Moon*, which has an Australian owner.

Shopping

Limenas has two excellent leather shops, both of which sell high-quality leather bags. They are Carol & Gordon Leather Plus on the central square, and Leather Lane on 18 Oktovriou. The latter also has a used-book exchange (with mostly English and German titles).

EAST COAST

The neighbouring hillside villages of **Panagia** and **Potamia** are quite touristy but picturesque. Both are 4km west of Golden Beach. The Greek-American artist Polygnotos Vagis was born in Potamia in 1894 and some of his work can be seen in the **Polygnotos Vagis Museum** in the village next to the main church. It is open 9 am to 1 pm and 6 to 9 pm Tuesday to Saturday and 10 am to 2 pm on Sunday and holidays. (The municipal museum in Kavala also has a collection of Vagis' work.)

The long and sandy **Golden Beach** is the island's best beach and roads from both Panagia and Potamia lead down to it. These roads are very pleasant to walk along, but if you prefer, the bus from Limenas calls at both villages before continuing to the southern end of the beach.

The next beach south is at the village of **Kinira**, and just south of here is the very pleasant **Paradise Beach**. The little islet just off the coast here is also called Kinira. **Alyki**, on the south-east coast, consists of two quiet beaches back to back on a headland. The southernmost beach is the better of the two. There is a small archaeological site near the beach and a marble quarry. The road linking the east side with the west side runs high across the cliffs, providing some great views of the bays at the bottom of the island. With only a few breaks, the island circuit (110km) can be completed by motorcycle in about 3½ hours.

Places to Stay & Eat
Hrysi Ammoudia (☎ 61 472), on Golden Beach, is the only camp site on this side of the island and is only a stone's throw from the inviting water. Facilities are good and include a minimarket. On Golden Beach, *Hotel Emerald (☎ 61 979, fax 61 451)* has self-contained studios for two to four people for around 15,000 dr.

In Panagia, *Hotel Elvetia (☎ 61 231, fax 61 451)* has pleasant doubles costing 12,000 dr. With your back to the fountain in the central square of Panagia (where the bus stops), turn left and take the first main road to the left and the hotel is on the left. Just beyond here on the right, *Hotel Hrysafis (☎/fax 61 451)* has singles and doubles for 11,000 dr with bathroom. There are *domatia* at both Kinira and Alyki.

There are reasonably priced restaurants in Panagia. *Restaurant Vigli (☎ 61 506)*, overlooking the northern end of Golden Beach, has superb views and food and offers live music on Thursday evenings. There are tavernas on the beach at Kinira and Alyki.

WEST COAST
The west coast consists of a series of seaside villages with Skala (literally 'step' or 'ladder', but in essence meaning 'by the sea') before their names. Roads lead from each of these to inland villages with the same name (minus the 'skala'). Beaches along the west coast are uniformly pebbly

and exposed. Travelling from north to south the first village is **Skala Rahoniou**. This is Thasos' latest development, having recently been discovered by the package-tour companies. It has an excellent camp site and the inland village of Rahoni remains unspoilt. Just before Rahoni there is a turn-off left to Moni Agiou Georgiou.

Skala Prinou, the next coastal village, and Thasos' second port, is crowded and unattractive. **Skala Sotira** and **Skala Kallirahis** are more pleasant and both have small beaches. Kallirahi, 2km inland from Skala Kallirahis, is a peaceful village with steep narrow streets and old stone houses. It has a large population of skinny, anxious-looking cats and, judging by the graffiti and posters, a lot of communists.

Skala Marion is a delightful fishing village and one of the least touristy places around the coast. It was from here, early in the 20th century, that the German Speidel Metal Company exported iron ore from Thasos to Europe. There are beaches at both sides of the village, and between here and Limenaria there are stretches of uncrowded beach.

Limenaria (42km from Limenas) is Thasos' second-largest town and a very crowded resort with a narrow sandy beach. The town was built in 1903 by the Speidel Metal Company. There are slightly less crowded beaches around the coast at **Pefkari** and **Potos**.

From Potos a scenic 10km road leads inland to **Theologos**, which was the capital of the island in medieval and Turkish times. This is the island's most beautiful village and the only mountain settlement served by public transport. The village houses are of whitewashed stone with slate roofs. It's a serene place, still unblemished by mass tourism.

Places to Stay
Camping Perseus (☎ 81 242), at Skala Rahoniou, is an excellent, grassy camp site in a pretty setting of flowers and olive and willow trees. The cook at the site's taverna will prepare any Greek dish you wish if you

place your order a day in advance. The EOT-owned *Camping Prinos* (☎ *71 171)*, at Skala Prinou, is well maintained with lots of greenery and shade and is about 1km or so south of the ferry quay.

The next camp site, *Camping Daedalos* (☎ *71 365)*, is just north of Skala Sotira right on the beach. It has a minimarket, restaurant and bar. The next site, *Pefkari Camping* (☎ *51 190)*, at Pefkari Beach, is a nifty site south of Limenaria but requires a minimum three night stay. Look carefully for the sign; it is not so obvious.

All sites charge around 850 dr per person and 650 dr per tent.

All of the seaside villages have hotels and domatia and the inland villages have rooms in private houses. For information about these inquire at kafeneia or look for signs.

Places to Eat
All of the coastal villages have tavernas. *Taverna Drosia*, in Rahoni, features live bouzouki music on Friday and Saturday evenings. *Taverna Orizontes* (☎ *31 389)*, first on the left as you enter Theologos, features *rembetika* nights. *Taverna Kleoniki*, on the main street in Theologos, has an outdoor terrace with wonderful views of the surrounding mountains.

Ionian Islands Τα Επτάνησα

The Ionian group consists of seven main islands anchored in the Ionian Sea: Corfu, Paxi, Kefallonia, Zakynthos, Ithaki, Lefkada and Kythira. The last is more accessible from the Peloponnese. The islands differ from other island groups and, geographically, are less quintessentially Greek. More reminiscent of Corfu's neighbour Italy, not least in light, their colours are mellow and green compared with the stark, dazzling brightness of the Aegean.

These islands receive a great amount of rain and consequently, the vegetation, with the exception of the more exposed Kythira, is more luxuriant. Corfu has the nation's highest rainfall. Overall, vegetation combines elements of the tropical with forests that could be northern European: exotic orchids as well as wild flowers emerge below spring snowlines, and eucalypts and acacias share soil with plane, oak and maple trees. The islands do not experience the *meltemi*, and as a result they can be extremely hot in summer.

The culture and cuisine of each Ionian island is unique and differs from the Aegean islands and Crete. Influences from Mediterranean Europe and Britain have also been stronger yet have developed with special individuality on each island.

Accommodation prices in this chapter are for the high season (July and August).

History & Mythology

The origin of the name Ionian is obscure but is thought to derive from the goddess Io. Yet another of Zeus' countless paramours, Io, while fleeing the wrath of a jealous Hera (in the shape of a heifer), happened to pass through the waters now known as the Ionian Sea.

If we are to believe Homer, the islands were important during Mycenaean times; however, no magnificent palaces or even modest villages from that period have been revealed, although Mycenaean tombs have

HIGHLIGHTS

- The fine Venetian buildings and narrow streets of Corfu's old town

- The traditional, unspoilt villages and fine pebble beaches of Meganisi

- Cruising around Skorpios Islet near Lefkada, once home to Jackie and Aristotle Onassis

- Relaxing on the white sand beach of Myrtos with a bottle of the unique Robola white wine of Kefallonia

- The picturesque fishing villages of Frikes and Kioni on Ithaki, Odysseus' homeland

- The ancient olive groves of Paxi, and Antipaxi's exquisite wine

- The magically haunting inland villages of Kythira, and some of the Aegean's cleanest beaches

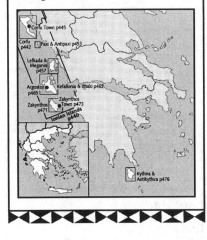

been unearthed. Ancient history lies buried beneath tonnes of earthquake rubble – seismic activity has been constant on all Ionian Islands, including Kythira.

IONIAN ISLANDS

Othoni Erikousa
Diapondia
Islands
To Brindisi
& Bari
(Italy)
Mathraki
Agios Stefanos
Sidari
Corfu
ALBANIA
Paleokastritsa
Pelekas
Corfu
Sagiada
To Ioannina
& Thessaloniki
Igoumenitsa
E92
Lefkimmi
GREECE
South
Kerkyra
Straits
Lakka
Parga
Paxi
Gaïos
EPIROS
Antipaxi
E55
To Athens
0   15   30 km
Preveza
Lefkada
Lefkada
STEREA
ELLADA
Nydri
Vasiliki
Meganisi
Mytikas
Kalamos
Fiskardo
Frikes
Kastos
Kefallonia
Myrtos
Piso
Aetos
Agia
Evfymia
Ithaki
Ithaki
To
Astakos
Lixouri
Sami
Argostoli
Pesada
Poros
To Patras
IONIAN
SEA
Skinari
Zakynthos
Strait
To
Patras
Kyllini
Zakynthos
Zakynthos
PELOPONNESE
Bay of
Laganas
To Kythira
E55

According to Homer, Odysseus' kingdom consisted not only of Ithaca (Ithaki) but also encompassed Kefallonia, Zakynthos and Lefkada. Ithaca has long been controversial. Classicists and archaeologists in the 19th century concluded that Homer's Ithaca was modern Ithaki, his Sami was Sami on Kefallonia, and his Zakynthos was today's Zakynthos, which sounded credible. But in the early 20th century German archaeologist Wilhelm Dorpfeld put a spanner in the works by claiming that Lefkada was ancient Ithaca, modern Ithaki was ancient Sami and Kefallonia was ancient Doulichion. His theories have now fallen from favour with everyone except the people of Lefkada.

By the 8th century BC, the Ionian Islands were in the clutches of the mighty city-state of Corinth, which regarded them of value as stepping stones on the route to Sicily and Italy. A century later, Corfu staged a successful revolt against Corinth, which was allied to Sparta, and became an ally of Sparta's archenemy, Athens. This alliance provoked Sparta into challenging Athens, thus precipitating the Peloponnesian Wars, which raged from 431 to 404 BC. The wars left Corfu depleted as they did all participants and Corfu became little more than a staging post for whoever happened to be holding sway in Greece. By the end of the 3rd century BC, Corfu, along with the other Ionian Islands, had become Roman. Following the decline of the Roman Empire, the islands saw the usual waves of invaders that Greece suffered. After the fall of Constantinople, the islands became Venetian.

Corfu was never part of the Ottoman Empire. Paxi, Kefallonia, Zakynthos, Ithaki and Kythira were variously occupied by the Turks, but the Venetians held them longest. The exception was Lefkada, which was Turkish for 200 years. The Ionian Islands fared better under the Venetians than their counterparts in the Cyclades.

Venice fell to Napoleon in 1797. Two years later, under the Treaty of Campo Formio, the Ionian Islands were allotted to France. In 1799 Russian forces wrested the islands from Napoleon, but by 1807 they were his again. By then, the all-powerful British couldn't resist meddling. As a result, in 1815, after Napoleon's downfall, the islands became a British protectorate under the jurisdiction of a series of Lord High Commissioners.

British rule was oppressive but, on a more positive note, the British constructed roads, bridges, schools and hospitals, established trade links and developed agriculture and industry. However, the nationalistic fervour in the rest of Greece soon reached the Ionian Islands.

A call for *enosis* (political union with Greece) was realised in 1862 when Britain relinquished the islands to Greece. In WWII the Italians invaded Corfu as part of Mussolini's plan to resurrect the mighty Roman Empire. Italy surrendered to the Allies in September 1943 and, in revenge, the Germans massacred thousands of Italians who had occupied the island. The Germans also sent some 5000 Corfiot Jews to Auschwitz.

A severe earthquake shook the Ionian Islands in 1953. It did considerable damage, particularly on Zakynthos and Kefallonia.

Getting There & Away

Air Corfu, Kefallonia, Zakynthos and Kythira have airports. Many charter flights to Corfu come from northern Europe and the UK. Kefallonia and Zakynthos also receive flights. These islands have frequent flights to Athens.

Bus Buses go from Athens and Thessaloniki to Corfu and from Athens to Kefallonia and Zakynthos. Lefkada is joined to the mainland by a causeway and can be reached by bus from Athens as well as Patras. There is a direct daily bus to Paxi from Athens.

Ferry – Domestic The Peloponnese has several ports of departure for the Ionian Islands: Patras for ferries to Kefallonia, Ithaki, Paxi and Corfu; Kyllini for ferries to Kefallonia and Zakynthos, and Piraeus, Monemvasia, Neapoli and Gythio for Kythira which is also served from Crete. Epiros has one port, Igoumenitsa, for Corfu and Paxi; and Sterea Ellada has one, Astakos, for Ithaki and Kefallonia.

The following table gives an overall view of the available scheduled domestic ferries to this island group from mainland ports in high season. Further details and inter-island links can be found under each island entry.

Ferry – International From Corfu, ferries depart for Brindisi, Bari, Ancona, Trieste and Venice in Italy. At least three times weekly, a ferry goes from Kefallonia to Brindisi via Igoumenitsa and Corfu. In July and August this ferry also calls at Zakynthos and Paxi.

Ferry Connections to the Ionian Islands

Origin	Destination	Duration	Price	Frequency
Astakos	Piso Aetos (Ithaki)	3 hours	1300 dr	1 daily
Gythio	Agia Pelagia (Kythira)	2½ hours	1700 dr	2 daily
Igoumenitsa	Corfu	1¼ hours	1400 dr	14 daily
Igoumenitsa	Paxi	2 hours	1600 dr	3 weekly
Kyllini	Zakynthos	1½ hours	1160 dr	5 daily
Kyllini	Argostoli (Kefallonia)	2¼ hours	2310 dr	2 daily
Kyllini	Poros (Kefallonia)	1¼ hours	1620 dr	4 daily
Neapoli	Agia Pelagia (Kythira)	45 mins	1500 dr	2 daily
Patras	Sami (Kefallonia)	2½ hours	2630 dr	2 daily
Patras	Vathy (Ithaki)	3¾ hours	2900 dr	2 daily
Sagiada	Corfu	45 mins	1100 dr	1 weekly

IONIAN ISLANDS

Corfu & the Diapondia Islands

☎ 0661 (Corfu Town) • postcode 491 00

Corfu (Κέρκυρα) is the second-largest and greenest Ionian island. It is also the best known. In Greek, the island's name is Kerkyra (**ker**-kih-rah). It was Homer's 'beautiful and rich land', and Odysseus' last stop on his journey home to Ithaca. Shakespeare reputedly used it as a background for *The Tempest*. In the 20th century, the Durrell brothers, among others, have extolled its virtues.

With its beguiling landscape of vibrant wild flowers and slender cypress trees rising out of shimmering olive groves, Corfu is considered by many as Greece's most beautiful island. With the highest rainfall, it's also the nation's major vegetable garden and produces scores of herbs. The mountain air is heavily scented. In autumn, the night sky over the sea is a spectacular sight.

CORFU

Getting There & Away

Air Corfu has at least three flights to Athens every day (20,700 dr). There are flights to Thessaloniki on Monday, Thursday and Saturday (20,900 dr). The Olympic Airways office (☎ 38 694, fax 36 634) is at Polyla 11, Corfu Town.

Bus There are two buses daily to Athens (11 hours, 8150 dr including ferry), at 9 am and 6.30 pm, and one to Thessaloniki (8000 dr), at 7 am. Tickets must be bought in advance.

Ferry – Domestic From Corfu, hourly ferries go to Igoumenitsa (1¼ hours, 1400 dr). Every Friday a ferry goes to Sagiada on the mainland (45 minutes, 1100 dr). Car ferries go to Paxi (four hours, 1900 dr) four times weekly, via Igoumenitsa. In summer, a fast passenger boat, the Pegasus, goes direct to Paxi (1½ hours, 3300 dr). This boat leaves from the old port. For details on ferries to Patras, see the following section. Corfu's port police can be contacted on ☎ 32 655.

Ferry – International Corfu is on the Patras-Igoumenitsa ferry route to Italy (Brindisi, Bari, Ancona, Trieste, Venice), though some ferries originate in Igoumenitsa. About six ferries daily go to Brindisi (9½ hours). At least one ferry daily goes to Bari and Ancona, and one goes to Venice (27 hours) in summer.

A fast daily catamaran service links Corfu with Brindisi from 1 July to 19 September with reduced services between April and June. The price of a one way ticket is 27,000 dr. The Corfu agents are Italian Ferries.

Brindisi-bound ferries tend to leave Corfu's new port between 8.30 and 9.30 am.

Prices to Italy from Corfu are the same as those from Igoumenitsa on the mainland. For comparative ticket prices see the Igoumenitsa Getting There & Away section in the Northern Greece chapter.

Agencies selling tickets are mostly on Xenofondos Stratigou. Shop around for the best deal. You can take one of the frequent international ferries to Patras (10 hours, 5800 dr), daily in summer.

The main ferry offices are:

Adriatica (☎ 38 089, fax 35 416)
   Ilios Holidays Ltd, Xenofondos Stratigou 46
ANEK Lines (☎ 24 503, fax 36 935,
   email book ing@anek.cha.forthnet.gr)
   Mancan Travel, Eleftheriou Venizelou 38
Fragline (☎ 24 912, fax 37 967)
   Ahilleas Avramidis, Eleftheriou Venizelou 46
   Hellenic Mediterranean (☎ 39 747, fax 32 047
   email hml@otenet.gr)
   Eleftheriou Venizelou 46
Italian Ferries (☎ 36 439, fax 45 153)
   3rd Parodos, Eleftheriou Venizelou 4
Minoan Lines (☎ 25 000, fax 46 555,
   email ver gis@minoan.ker.forthnet.gr)
   Ethnikis Antistasis 58a
Strintzis Lines (☎ 25 232, fax 46 945,
   email sales@strintzis.gr)
   Ferry Travel, Ethnikis Antistasis 2
Ventouris Ferries (☎ 32 664, fax 36 935,
   email info@ventouris.gr)
   Mancan Travel, Eleftheriou Venizelou 38

Getting Around

To/From the Airport There is no Olympic Airways shuttle bus between Corfu Town and the airport. Bus No 3 from Plateia San Rocco stops on the main road 500m from the airport.

Bus Destinations of KTEL buses (green-and-cream) from Corfu Town's long distance bus station (☎ 30 627) are as follows:

Destination	Duration	Frequency	Via
Agios Gordios	40 mins	4 daily	Sinarades
Agios Stefanos	1½ hours	5 daily	Sidari
Aharavi	1¼ hours	4 daily	Roda
Glyfada	45 mins	6 daily	Vatos
Kavos	1½ hours	10 daily	Lefkimmi
Loutses	1¼ hours	4 daily	Kassiopi
Messongi	45 mins	7 daily	
Paleokastritsa	45 mins	7 daily	
Pyrgi	30 mins	9 daily	Ypsos

Fares range from 300 dr to 800 dr. Sunday and holiday services are reduced considerably, often by as much as 70%.

IONIAN ISLANDS

The numbers and destinations of local buses (dark blue) from the bus station at Plateia San Rocco, Corfu Town, are:

Destination	Bus No	Duration	Frequency	Via
Afra	8	30 mins	8 daily	
Agios Ioannis	11	30 mins	9 daily	Pelekas
Ahillion	10	20 mins	6 daily	Gastouri
Kastellani	5	25 mins	14 daily	Kourmades
Kontokali	7	30 mins	hourly	Gouvia & Dassia
Perama	6	30 mins	12 daily	Benitses
Potamos	4	45 mins	12 daily	Evroupoli & Tembloni

The flat rate is 200 dr. Tickets can be bought on board or on Plateia San Rocco.

Car, Motorcycle & Bicycle Car hire companies in Corfu Town include Autorent (☎ 44 623/624/625), Xenofondos Stratigou 34; Avis (☎ 24 042), Ethnikis Antistasis 42; Budget (☎ 22 062), Donzelot 5; and Europcar (☎ 46 931/932/933), Xenofondos Stratigou 32.

Motorcycle hire outlets are on Xenofondos Stratigou and Avramiou. For mountain bikes try Charitos Travel Agency (☎ 44 611/620, fax 36 825), Arseniou 35.

CORFU TOWN
☎ 0661 • pop 36,000

The island's capital is Corfu Town (Kerkyra), built on a promontory. It's a gracious medley of numerous occupying influences, which never included the Turks. The Spianada (esplanade) is green, gardened and boasts Greece's only cricket ground, a legacy of the British. After a match, spectators may join players in drinking ginger beer made to an old Victorian recipe or, typically, tea or gin and tonic.

The Liston, a row of arcaded buildings flanking the north-western side of the Spianada, was built during the French occupation and modelled on Paris' Rue de Rivoli. The buildings function as upmarket cafes, lamplit by night. Georgian mansions and Byzantine churches complete the picture.

The Venetian influence prevails, particularly in the enchanting old town, wedged between two fortresses. Narrow alleyways of 18th century shuttered tenements in muted ochres and pinks are more reminiscent of Venice or Naples than Greece.

Orientation
The town is separated into northern and southern sections. The old town is in the northern section between the Spianada and the New Fortress. The Palaio Frourio (Old Fortress) is east of here and projects out to sea, cut off from the town by a moat. The Neo Frourio (New Fortress) is west. The Spianada separates the Old Fortress from the town. The southern section is the new town.

The old port is north of the old town. The new port is west. Between them is the hulking New Fortress. The long distance bus station is on Avramiou, inland from the new port. The local bus station is on Plateia San Rocco. Local buses serve the town and nearby villages.

Information
Tourist Offices The EOT (☎ 37 520, fax 30 298) is on Rizospaston Voulefton. The tourist police (☎ 30 265) are at Samartzi 4, near Plateia Solomou.

Money The National Bank of Greece is at the junction of Voulgareos and G Theotoki. It has a 24 hour cash exchange machine as does the Commercial Bank opposite the new port, and many others. There is a handy Bureau de Change booth at the southern corner of the cricket ground. American Express is represented by Greek Skies Tours (☎ 32 469) at Kapodistria 20a.

Post & Communications The post office is on Alexandras. It is open 7.30 am to 8 pm Monday to Friday, 7.30 am to 2 pm Saturday, and 9 am to 1.30 pm Sunday. The OTE phone office at Mantzarou 9 is open 6 am to midnight daily.

Bookshops The Xenoglosso Bookshop, Markora 45, stocks English-language books

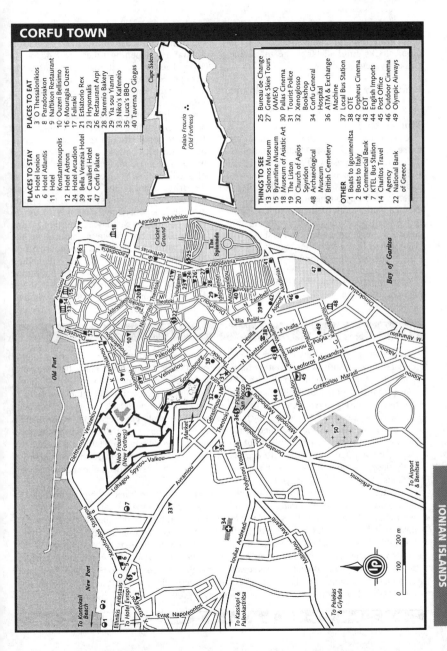

CORFU TOWN

PLACES TO EAT
3 O Thessalonikios
8 Paradosiakon
9 Naftikon Restaurant
10 Ouzeri Bellisimo
16 Mouragia Ouzeri
17 Faliraki
21 Estiatorio Rex
23 Hrysomalis
26 Restaurant Arpi
28 Starenio Bakery
29 Yia sou Yianni
33 Niko's Kafeneio
35 Luca's BBQ
40 Taverna O Giogas

PLACES TO STAY
5 Hotel Ionion
6 Hotel Atlantis
11 Hotel Konstantinoupolis
12 Hotel Astron
24 Hotel Arcadion
39 Bella Venezia Hotel
41 Cavalieri Hotel
47 Corfu Palace

THINGS TO SEE
13 Solomos Museum
15 Byzantine Museum
18 Museum of Asiatic Art
19 The Liston
20 Church of Agios Spyridon
48 Archaeological Museum
50 British Cemetery

OTHER
1 Boats to Igoumenitsa
2 Boats to Italy
4 Commercial Bank
7 KTEL Bus Station
14 Charitos Travel Agency
22 National Bank of Greece
25 Bureau de Change
27 Greek Skies Tours (AMEX)
30 Pallas Cinema
31 Tourist Police
32 Xenoglosso Bookshop
34 Corfu General Hospital
36 ATM & Exchange Machine
37 Local Bus Station
38 OTE
42 Orpheus Cinema
43 EOT
44 English Imports
45 Post Office
46 Outdoor Cinema
49 Olympic Airways

IONIAN ISLANDS

including novels and a few travel guides. English Imports, in a side street off Methodiou, stocks English-language magazines and daily newspapers.

Emergency The Corfu General Hospital (☎ 45 811) is on I Andreadi.

Things to See
The star exhibit of the **archaeological museum** is the Gorgon Medusa sculpture, one of the best-preserved pieces of Archaic sculpture in Greece. It was part of the west pediment of the 6th century Temple of Artemis at Corcyra (the ancient capital), on the peninsula south of the town. The petrifying Medusa is depicted in the instant before she was beheaded by Perseus. This precipitated the birth of her sons, Chrysaor and Pegasus (the winged horse), who emerged from her headless body.

Also impressive is the 7th century crouching lion, found near the Tomb of Menecrates.

Archaeologists ascertained that it stood on top of the tomb. The museum (☎ 30 680) is at Vraïla 5. Opening times are 8.45 am to 3 pm Tuesday to Saturday and 9.30 am to 2.30 pm Sunday. Admission is 800 dr.

The **museum of Asiatic art** houses the impressive collection, bequeathed by the Greek diplomats Grigoris Manos and Nikolaos Hatzivasiliou. It includes Chinese and Japanese porcelain, bronzes, screens, sculptures, theatrical masks, armour, books and prints. The museum is housed in the Palace of St Michael & St George, built in 1819 as the British Lord High Commissioner's residence. The palace is just north of the cricket ground. The museum is open 8.30 am to 3 pm Tuesday to Sunday. Admission is free.

The **Byzantine museum**, housed in the Church of Our Lady of Antivouniotissa on Arseniou (☎ 38 313), has an outstanding collection of Byzantine and post-Byzantine icons. Opening times are 8.30 am to 2.30 pm Tuesday to Sunday. Admission is 500 dr.

Is it Cricket?

Newcomers to Corfu's Liston promenade cafe scene may be puzzled by the sight of men dressed in white surrounding another man dressed in white attempting to hit a hard leather ball out of the rather scruffy park with a long willow bat. This is cricket – Greek-style. Travellers from the former British Empire will recognise and delight at this eccentric and quintessentially British game replete with its sixes, fours, LBWs and owzats!

The game was imported to Corfu by the British during their 49 year hegemony of the island from 1815 to 1864. It has remained firmly entrenched in Corfu ever since. The few teams around the island gather to battle it out on sunny Sundays. While the pitch has seen better days and the distance from the batting crease to the tables of the Liston cafes can seem alarmingly close, the game is played with unusual verve and enthusiasm. This is also the only place in Greece where cricket is played.

The basic aim, for those unfamiliar with the game, is to score 'runs' by hitting the ball as far as possible and then running to and fro between the wooden wickets before the ball is returned by the fielders. Batters are considered 'out' when the ball hits their wickets, when a fielder catches the ball, when the ball hits the leg when it could have hit the wicket, or when the fielder hits the wickets before the batter has returned to the crease after running.

It's a complex game and spectators enjoy its subtleties as well as its seemingly slow pace as much as the players do. Good cricket watching is always accompanied by copious amounts of beer, the occasional shouts of encouragement from the sidelines and the odd comment on the weather. It wouldn't be cricket any other way – even in Greece.

The **Solomos museum** occupies the building that was once the home of the poet Dionysios Solomos who lived in Corfu for 30 years. Look for the sign at the western end of Arseniou. It is open 9.30 am to 2 pm Monday to Friday (200 dr).

Apart from the pleasure of wandering the narrow streets of the old town and the gardens of the Spianada, you can explore the two fortresses, Corfu Town's most dominant landmarks. The promontory on which the **Neo Frourio** stands was first fortified in the 12th century. The existing remains date from 1588. Entrance is 400 dr. The ruins of **Palaio Frourio** date from the mid-12th century. Entrance is 800 dr. Both are open all day.

In Corfu, many males are christened Spyros after the island's miracle-working patron St Spyridon. His mummified body lies in a silver glass-fronted coffin in the 16th century **Church of Agios Spyridon** on Agiou Spyridonos. It is paraded on Palm Sunday, Easter Sunday, 11 August and the first Sunday in November.

Activities

Go yachting with a crew or bareboat in fabled waters. Corfu's biggest charterer is Corfu Yachting Centre, Theotokou 120, near the new port. Or buy a copy of *Corfu Walks* by Hilary Whitton Piapeti, at Xenoglosso (see Bookshops earlier in this section), and take to the hills. The book also contains mountain bike tour details.

Cricket is played on Greece's only cricket ground on a rather scruffy pitch abutting the Liston. The actual wicket is made of artificial turf and resounds, during the summer months, to the rather incongruous sound of leather balls on willow bats as white-clad players of the few Corfu cricket clubs attempt to score sixes by dropping the balls into the coffee cups of the spectators watching from the Liston (see the 'Is it Cricket?' boxed text).

Organised Tours

Charitos Travel Agency (☎ 44 611, fax 36 825), Arseniou 35, has coach, mountainbike and walking tours.

Places to Stay – Budget

Most of the D class hotels have closed, resulting in a shortage of low-priced accommodation. There are no EOT-approved *domatia* but locals who unofficially let rooms often meet the boats.

Hotel Evropi (☎ 39 304), near the new harbour, is the town's only D class hotel. It has little to recommend it other than being near the new port. Singles/doubles cost 5500/6000 dr, and doubles with bathroom are 7000 dr. It's signposted from the western end of Xenofondos Stratigou.

Hotel Ionion (☎ 30 628, fax 44 690, Xenofondos Stratigou 46) is the cheapest C class, with reasonable rooms for 8500/10,600 dr.

Places to Stay – Mid-Range

Hotel Arcadion (☎ 37 670, fax 45 087, Kapodistria 44) has small, comfortable rooms for 13,000/17,000 dr, including breakfast. *Hotel Atlantis* (☎ 35 560, fax 46 480, email atlanker@mail.otenet.gr, Xenofondos Stratigou 48) has pleasant rooms for 13,750/16,500 dr.

The refurbished C class *Hotel Konstantinoupolis* (☎ 48 716, fax 48 718, Zavitsianou 1), reincarnated from a shabby backpacker's favourite into a splendid art-nouveau hostelry, has rates of 14,000/19,000 dr with breakfast. Nearby, the B class *Hotel Astron* (☎ 39 505, 33 708, Donzelot 15) has a neoclassical ambience but somewhat timeworn room rates of 19,500/28,000 dr.

Places to Stay – Top End

The A class *Cavelieri Hotel* (☎ 39 041, fax 39 283, Kapodistria 4) occupies a 300-year-old building and has an interior of classical elegance. Rates are 30,000/35,000 dr and family suites cost 40,000 dr.

Corfu Palace (☎ 39 485, fax 31 749, email cfupalace@hol.gr) on Dimokratias is the town centre's only deluxe hotel, the choice of Prince Rainier and the late Princess Grace. It has two bars, two restaurants and pools. Rates are a healthy 54,000/74,000 dr.

Places to Eat – Budget

As it was not conquered by the Turks, Corfu maintains a distinctive cuisine influenced by other parts of Europe, including Russia.

There are several low-priced eateries near the new port. Both the tiny *O Thessalonikios* on Xenofondos Stratigou and *Luca's BBQ* on Avramiou serve low-priced, succulent spit-roast chicken.

There's a cluster of atmospheric restaurants at the southern end of the old town. *Taverna O Giogas (Guilford 16)* serves reasonably priced *mezedes* and main courses at outdoor tables under a grapevine. The cosy *Yia sou Yianni (Idromenon 19)* has similar food and prices.

Nearby, *Restaurant Arpi (Giotopoulou 20)* is a classy little place with *pastitsada* for 1900 dr and *sofrito* for 1700 dr.

One of Corfu's oldest restaurants is *Hrysomalis (Nik. Theotoki 6)*, just behind the expensive Liston cafe strip. Lawrence and Gerald Durrell used to dine here. The food is cheap and tasty and the local rosé wine is superb.

Farther north, most eateries are touristy and downmarket, but there are exceptions. *Paradosiakon (Solomou 20)* serves delicious food and *Naftikon Restaurant (Nik. Theotoki 150)* has fair prices and Corfiot food. At *Ouzeri Bellisimo (N Theotoki)*, a tasty mezedes plate costs 1900 dr.

Places to Eat – Mid-Range

Indulge in a little people-watching at one of the cafes on the Liston. You will pay around 1250 dr for coffee and croissant.

Mouragia Ouzeri (Arseniou 15) has a large range of mezedes. The small mixed fish plate (2250 dr) or the grilled beef patties *soudzoukakia* make an enjoyable meal overlooking the sea.

Behind the Liston is another established eatery which has operated since 1932, *Estiatorio Rex (Kapodistria 66)*. Claiming to be the oldest restaurant in town, it is now a quietly modern, tasteful eating place, with main courses averaging around 2200 dr.

Faliraki (☎ 21 118), on the corner of Arseniou and Kapodistria, is a refurbishment of a popular Victorian bathing spot. It's a great waterside spot for a meal in the shadow of the old Kastro.

Entertainment

Having fun in Corfu is comprised mainly of strolling around, sitting at the cafes on the Liston or being cool at the multitude of little bars and pubs that dot the old and new town. Young and old have their spots and you can tell at a glance.

That said, perhaps the most entertaining spot to spend an idle hour or two is at one of the cafes bordering the cricket ground, watching cricket on a Sunday afternoon.

If it's visual entertainment you want, Corfu Town has two indoor cinemas: the *Pallas (Theotoki)* and the *Orpheus (Aspioti)*. A little farther south of the latter, there's an outdoor cinema that is supposed to operate in summer.

Corfu's disco strip lies 1 to 2km northwest of the new harbour. Here, high-tech palaces of hype jostle cheek by jowl for the tourist buck. The *Hippodrome* is the biggest and flashiest – it's even got a pool. *Apokalypsis* and *Coco Club* are garish and expensive and there's a pseudo *Hard Rock Cafe* to complete the scene.

The more sedate at heart may enjoy horse and carriage rides around the old town – great for taking photos or making a quick home video memento.

NORTH OF CORFU TOWN

Most of the coast of northern Corfu is package-tourist saturated, and thoroughly de-Greeked, though once you venture beyond the main package resorts ending at Pyrgi you enter some of Corfu's most privileged scenery. Writers Lawrence and Gerald Durrell knew this well too and spent much of their creative years along this coastline which, in parts, is little more than a short boat hop to the Albanian coastline opposite.

Ipsos is a brash tourist strip full of bars, restaurants and cafes. The beach is rather narrow and a very busy road separates the sea from the fun and entertainment. You

Whitewashed houses of picturesque Skyros Town, Skyros, Sporades

Moni Vlahernas, Kanoni, Corfu, Ionian Islands

View from the New Citadel, Corfu, Ionian Islands

Port of Linaria, Skyros, Sporades

An old windmill, Skyros, Sporades

Strike a pose...Rupert Brooke, Skyros, Sporades

will probably not want to linger long in Ipsos if you are seeking solitude.

More or less extending out of Ipsos is **Pyrgi**, 16km north of Corfu Town, where a road continues east around the base of **Mt Pantokrator** (906m), the island's highest peak. From Pyrgi, another road snakes north and inland over the western flank of the mountain to the north coast. A detour can be made to the picturesque village of **Strinylas** from where a now surfaced road leads through stark terrain to the summit, Moni Pantokratora and stupendous views. There is a small taverna near the summit.

Heading westwards around the winding coastal road you will first hit **Nisaki**, little more than a small cove with a pebble beach, a couple of tavernas and some domatia. Still, it's prettier than Ipsos.

The next village of interest is **Kalami** where the **White House** was the home of the Durrell brothers. The building is perched right on the water's edge and must have been idyllic during the writers' sojourn here. It is now a restaurant.

Just round the next headland west is the little harbour of **Kouloura**, where many daily excursion boats from farther north bring visitors. There is a pleasant restaurant overlooking the harbour here. From both Kalami and Kouloura the houses and buildings of Butrint in neighbouring Albania can be seen quite clearly.

Kassiopi is the next major port of call. It is a sizable little resort village around a circular harbour where its more sedate package-tour visitors opt for fishing and strolling. There is a reasonable beach just west of Kassiopi round the headland.

The coast road continues to the resort of **Roda**, a rather dull and uninspiring place after the arresting scenery of the east coast opposite Albania and the beach scene is not all that brilliant. Better to move on to **Sidhari**, where you can walk south along a footpath by the River Tyflos, a habitat for terrapins,

The Brothers Durrell

The name Durrell is synonymous with Corfu, though it is perhaps surprising that of the two brothers Lawrence (1912-90) and Gerald (1925-95) it is the naturalist Gerald rather than the poet and novelist Lawrence who has so inextricably linked the name of this famous duo with the island of Corfu and the little village of Kalami on Corfu's north-east coast.

Gerald Durrell was born in India and gained considerable repute among conservationists for his role in breeding endangered animal species for eventual release in the wild. He was also a prolific author, producing more than 35 informative yet amusing books about animals. Durrell's love of animals started when living in Corfu in the 1930s. His best-known books were *The Overloaded Ark* (1953), *Three Singles to Adventure* (1953), *My Family and other Animals* (1956), *A Zoo in my Luggage* (1960) and *Birds, Beasts and Relatives* (1969).

Brother Lawrence, also born in India, was the dedicated writer in the family. He was at once a novelist, poet, writer of topographical books, verse plays and farcical short stories. He is best known for the Alexandria Quartet, a series of four interconnected novels. His Greek trilogy included *Prospero's Cell* (1945) in which he describes his life in Corfu during 1937 and 1938, *Reflections on a Marine Venus* (1953) for which he spent two years in Rhodes in 1945-46 as press officer for the Allied government and *Bitter Lemons of Cyprus* (1957) where he spent the 1952-56 years as a teacher and government official – latterly during the Cypriot insurgency.

Both brothers were well known around Corfu and some of the older restaurant owners near Corfu Town's Liston still remember their illustrious literary patrons. Their former house overlooking the sea at the village of Kalami is now a quaint fish restaurant.

herons and egrets. Sidhari is still a rather tacky package resort, but its shallow sandy beach is ideal for children. **Peroulades**, 3km west of Sidhari, is less developed and there's a track to beautiful Cape Drastis.

Agios Stefanos, farther around the coast, is still quite pleasant out of high season. It has a long sandy beach extending under the lee of high sand cliffs and is a good spot for windsurfing. Regular boats to the Diapondia Islands (see the Diapondia Islands section following) leave from the little harbour of Agios Stefanos 1.5km from the village centre.

Places to Stay & Eat
Camp sites along the north-east coast include: *Karda Beach* (☎ *0661-93 595)* and *Kormarie* (☎ *0661-93 587)* at Dassia; *Kerkira Camping* (☎ *0661-93 579)* and *Ipsos Ideal* (☎ *0661-93 243)* at Ipsos; and *Paradise Camping* (☎ *0661-93 557)* at Pyrgi. *San Stefanos Golden Beach Hotel* (☎ *0663-51 053/154)*, by the bus stop in Agios Stefanos, has comfortable single/ double rooms and studios for 7500/9000 dr.

Durrell fans can have a nostalgic meal at the *White House* in Kalami.

SOUTH OF CORFU TOWN
The Kanoni peninsula, 4km from Corfu Town, was the site of the ancient capital but little has been excavated. **Mon Repos Villa**, at its north-east tip was Prince Philip's birthplace. The beautiful wooded grounds are open 8 am to 8 pm daily. Opposite the entrance are two excavation sites, both closed to the public. One is the ruins of the 5th century **Basilica of Agia Kerkyra**, built on the site of a 5th century BC temple. You can walk to the **Kardaki Spring** from Analypsi nearby.

Just off the southern tip of Kanoni are two pretty islets. On one is **Moni Vlahernas**, reached by a causeway. On the other, **Mouse Island** (Poutikonisi), there is a 13th century church. Caïques ply back and forth from the top of the Kanoni peninsula.

The coast road continues south with a turn-off to the **Ahillion Palace** (☎ 0661-56 245), near the village of Gastouri. In the

1890s it was the summer palace of Austria's Empress Elizabeth (King Otho of Greece was her uncle). She dedicated the villa to Achilles. The beautifully landscaped garden is guarded by kitsch statues of the empress' other mythological heroes. The palace is open 9 am to 4 pm Monday to Sunday. Admission is 1000 dr.

The resort of **Benitses** used to be the playground of holiday hooligans, but in recent times has made strenuous efforts to get its act together. Still, the excesses of too much package tourism in the past have taken the sheen off the little fishing village, but the narrow winding streets of the old village still maintain an air of authenticity. If the beach scene is not to your liking, head inland for a splendid 30 minute walk along an almost tropical-looking valley to the scene of old waterworks, built during the time of the British protectorate.

The **Shell Museum** (☎ 0661-99 340) at Benitses reputedly contains the best private shell collection in Europe. It is open 9 am to 10 pm daily. Entrance is 500 dr.

Heading farther south from Corfu town you will next hit **Messonghi**, similar to Benitses but quieter. The beach scene while not ideal is certainly better than its neighbour farther north. The winding coastal road between Benitses and **Boukaris** is decidedly more appealing and is dotted with a few tavernas and small pebbly beaches.

Places to Stay & Eat
There is accommodation aplenty around Benitses and farther south along the coast. Try *Potamaki Hotel* (☎ *0661-71 140, fax 72 451)* in Benitses itself if you can't decide. Singles/doubles are 10,500/12,500 dr.

It's touristy, kitsch and a bit over the top, but it's popular, it's been around a long time and the food is unusual. *Tripa Tavern* (☎ *0661-56 333)* at the little village of Kinopiastes has hosted its fair share of illustrious patrons including Jane Fonda, Aristotle Onassis, Anthony Quinn and François Mitterand. For 6000 dr a head you get a sumptuous set banquet with a wide range of original Corfiot dishes.

THE WEST COAST

Corfu's best beaches are on the west coast. **Paleokastritsa**, 26km west of Corfu, is the coast's largest resort. Built around sandy and pebbled coves with a green mountain backdrop, it's incredibly beautiful. Once paradisal, it's been the victim of rampant development. While the water here looks enticing, it is generally considerably colder than on other parts of the island.

Moni Theotokou perches on the rocky promontory at Paleokastritsa, above the shimmering turquoise sea. The monastery was founded in the 13th century but the present building dates from the 18th century. A small museum contains icons. It is open 7 am to 1 pm and 3 to 8 pm daily. Admission is free, but a donation is expected.

From Paleokastritsa a path ascends to the unspoilt village of **Lakones**, 5km inland. Walk back along the approach road and you'll see a signposted footpath on the left.

There are superb views along the 6km road west to **Makrades** and **Krini**. The restaurants along the way extol the views from their terraces.

From Krini you can explore the ruins of the 13th century Byzantine fortress of **Angelokastro** where Paleokastritsa's inhabitants took refuge from attackers. A long distance bus goes twice daily to Krini from Corfu Town.

Farther south, the beach at **Ermones** is near **Corfu Golf Course**, the largest in Europe. Hilltop **Pelekas**, 4km away, is renowned for its spectacular sunsets. It's as busy as the coast, but with young independent travellers, rather than package tourists. Pelekas is close to three sandy beaches, **Glyfada**, **Pelekas** and **Myrtiotissa**, the last an unofficial nudist beach. There is a free bus from Pelekas to the first two. Don't miss the superb panoramic views over Corfu from the **Kaiser's Lookout** high up above Pelekas village. Just follow the main road upwards to the end.

Agios Gordios is a popular backpacker hang-out 8km south of Glyfada. The beach is reasonably pretty, but the village is rather overdeveloped with the usual conglomeration of shops, souvenir stalls, eateries and domatia accommodation. Overall it's a laid-back kind of place and will appeal to travellers interested primarily in the 'beach and bar' scene. There are three long distance buses daily from Corfu Town to Agios Gordios, via Sinarades.

At Sinarades, 4km from Agios Gordios, the **Folk Museum of Central Corfu** occupies a 19th century house. It is open 9.30 am to 3 pm Tuesday to Sunday. Admission is around 300 dr.

Freshwater **Lake Korission**, a little farther south, is a habitat for wading birds. The long stretch of inviting sand and dunes between the lake and sea continues to Issos. This is one of the least spoilt stretches of Corfu's coast, but it's back to rampant development at Agios Georgios.

Places to Stay

Paleokastritsa Camping (☎ *0663-41 204, fax 41 104)* is on the main approach road to the resort, shortly after the signposted turn-off to the village of Lakones. It's a reasonably well organised camp site, with a restaurant and minimarket on site, but is a fair way back from the beach scene. The bus will drop you at the entrance. Paleokastritsa also has many hotels, studios and domatia. *Vatos Camping* (☎ *0661-94 505)* near the village of Vatos is a quiet retreat but handier if you have some kind of transport of your own.

The Pink Palace (☎ *0661-53 103)* at Agios Gordios is a brash backpacker hostel designed for the under 25s who want fun and sun without the hassles of having to look for it. You'll pay between 5000 dr and 10,000 dr per person for average accommodation and that includes breakfast and dinner.

Alexandros Pension (☎ *0661-94 215, 94 833)*, at Pelekas, on the road signposted 'sunset', has pleasant doubles for 7000 dr with bathroom. A bit farther along, *Rooms to Let Thomas* (☎ *0661-94 491, fax 94 190)* has clean, comfortable singles/doubles with private bathroom for 9000/11,000 dr, and doubles with shared bathroom for 6000 dr. Back near the central square, the

IONIAN ISLANDS

bougainvillea-smothered *Pension Tellis & Brigitte (☎ 0661-94 326)* near the central square has pleasant doubles for 6500 dr with bathroom.

The stylish, neoclassical *Levant Hotel (☎ 0661-94 230, fax 94 115)*, higher up on the Pelekas road, has beautiful singles/doubles for 16,000/18,000 dr.

High up overlooking Paleokastritsa and just beyond Lakones village is *Golden Fox Apartments (☎/fax 0663-41 381)* with studios costing 13,000 dr. The swimming pool here must have the best view in the whole of Greece.

Places to Eat

Bella Vista perched high up above Paleokastritsa just past Lakones looks nothing special but the views are breathtaking. Reputedly the Kaiser, Tito and Nasser all dined here. Farther west from Lakones along the cliff-top road, *Golden Fox Restaurant (☎ 0663-41 381/409)* serves excellent charcoal-grilled dishes.

Alexandros Restaurant, of the pension of the same name in Pelekas, is as good as anywhere for an unfussy meal. In Paleokastritsa there is a fairly wide choice but little difference in quality between the eating places. Look out for *Astakos Taverna* or *Corner Grill* which serve up Greek and tourist favourites.

THE DIAPONDIA ISLANDS

Τα Διαπόντια Νησιά
☎ 0633

Scattered like forgotten stepping stones to Puglia in Italy, lie a cluster of little-known and even less visited satellite islands belonging administratively to Corfu. Of the five islands only Ereikousa, Mathraki and Othoni are inhabited, though many of their original residents have long since departed for the lure of New York city and only return in the summer months to renew their ties.

Often isolated by tricky seas, the islands are worth the extra effort to visit them and serious island collectors should place them high on their agenda. Development is proceeding slowly and cautiously and all offer

places to stay. Most people visit on day trips from Sidhari, though regular ferries do link the islands with both Agios Stefanos on the north-west tip of Corfu and Corfu Town.

Getting There & Away

The most reliable link is the thrice-weekly service from Corfu Town (1500-1800 dr) with the *Alexandros II* which leaves shortly after dawn for the long haul round Corfu to bring supplies and the odd vehicle. From Agios Stefanos a small passenger boat services Ereikousa and then Othoni and Mathraki alternatively at least twice weekly (1000-1200 dr). Schedules vary without warning so check beforehand (☎ 094-999 771 or 0663-95 248).

The easiest solution may be to jump on a day excursion out of Sidhari Harbour. Excursions are advertised widely around Sidhari's hotels and travel agencies.

Ereikousa Ερείκουσα

Ereikousa (eh-**ree**-koo-sah; population 334) is perhaps the most visited and popular of the three islands and the closest of the three to Corfu Town and Sidhari. Touted as a desert island getaway, Ereikousa does in fact have some decent beaches and if you can only manage to visit one of the Diapondia Islands, then consider Ereikousa. Not surprisingly it attracts more than its share of visitors and can get busy in high season.

If you want to stay, contact the one hotel, *Ereikousa Hotel (☎ 71 555),* for room availability. For eating you have *Anemomylos Taverna (☎ 71 647)*. It also has a few domatia.

Mathraki Μαθράκι

Wild and wooded Mathraki (population 143) is the least developed of the trio, but offers solitude, some fine walking, at least three seasonal tavernas and some domatia to stay at. There is a very long beach – which is also home to the loggerhead turtle, so discretion is necessary when beachcombing – a small scattered settlement inland and a tiny harbour with a cardphone. Excursion boats will inevitably drop you off at Piadini

Beach, which is a 30 minute walk east along a rough dirt track to the harbour.

Taverna o Yiannis (☎ 72 108) on Piadini beach will be open if you have come by excursion boat. By the harbour is the modern **Port Center Restaurant** owned by Spyridoula Kassimi and her husband and up in the village is the *kafeneio*/restaurant/store **Taverna o Geis** run by Spyros and his wife.

Accommodation is provided by the **domatia** of Christos Argyris (☎ 71 652) who has doubles for 6000 dr with breakfast, or newer **apartments** run by Anastasios Kassimis (☎ 71 700).

Othoni Οθονοί

The largest of the group is also the farthest out. Othoni (o-tho-**nee**; population 98) is popular with Italian yachties. The interior is wooded and the 35 minute walk up to the inland village of Horio is worth the effort for the views. Beach bums will find little comfort in the island's two pebbly beaches near the port.

Gourmets will find one decent Italian restaurant here, **La Locanda dei Sogni** (☎ 71 640), which also has rooms, but other eating options include **New York** and **Mikros**. Rooms can also be found courtesy of the owner of New York; ring ☎ 71 581 for availability.

Paxi & Antipaxi

PAXI Παξοί
☎ 0662   • postcode 490 82   • pop 2200
Paxi (pahx-**ee**), 10km long and 4km wide, is the smallest main Ionian island. It has a captivating landscape of dense, centuries-old olive groves, snaking dry stone walls, derelict farmhouses and abandoned stone olive presses. The olive trees have amazingly twisted, gnarled and hollowed trunks, which gives them the look of sinister, ancient monsters. Walking through the olive groves at dusk is quite eerie.

Paxi has escaped the mass tourism of Corfu and caters for small, discriminating tour companies. People come here because they have fallen in love with Paxi's inimitable cosy feel, or have heard about its friendly islanders and its captivating scenery.

There are only three coastal settlements – Gaïos, Longos and Lakka – and a few inland villages. The whole island is walkable, though good roads do cover the length of the island. Paxi is an absolute must for any serious island-hopper and is worth the extra effort needed to get there.

Getting There & Away
Bus Buses go directly to Athens (eight hours, 8150 dr) three times weekly. Tickets are available at Bouas Tours (☎ 32 401). Buses from Athens to Paxi depart from the Hotel Marina (☎ 01-522 9109), Voulgari 13 in Athens, at midnight.

Ferry – Domestic At least one regular passenger ferry, the *Pegasus*, connects Paxi and Corfu daily in summer (1½ hours, 3300 dr). Twice weekly the *Pegasus* also calls in at Lakka on the north coast. Other larger car

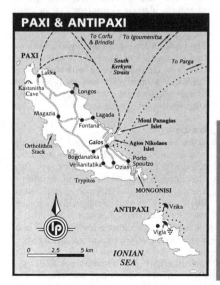

PAXI & ANTIPAXI

To Corfu & Brindisi
To Igoumenitsa
To Parga
PAXI
South Kerkyra Straits
Lakka
Kastanitha Cave
Longos
Magazia
Lagada
Fontana
Moni Panagias Islet
Ortholithos Stack
Gaïos
Agios Nikolaos Islet
Bogdanatika
Porto Spoutzo
Vellianitatika
Ozias
Trypitos
MONGONISI
ANTIPAXI
Vrika
Vigla
0   2.5   5 km
IONIAN SEA

IONIAN ISLANDS

ferries also run throughout the year from Corfu and Igoumenitsa (two hours, 1600 dr) on the mainland. Daily excursion boats also come from Corfu and Parga on the mainland. Ferries dock at Gaïos' port 1km east of the central square, though the *Pegasus* departs from the Gaïos waterfront. Excursion boats dock by the central square and along the quay towards the new port. Hydrofoils between Corfu and Paxi started in 1999 and should hopefully be running each summer.

Tickets for Corfu and Igoumenitsa can be obtained from Zefi Travel (☎ 32 114, fax 32 253) on the waterfront. Tickets for the *Pegasus* can be obtained from Gaios Travel (☎ 32 033, fax 32 175). Paxi's port police can be contacted on ☎ 31 222.

Ferry – International In July and August a ferry goes two or three times weekly from Paxi to Brindisi in Italy, via Igoumenitsa and Corfu. Ticket prices are the same as from Corfu. A catamaran service to Brindisi via Corfu also runs from 8 July to 5 September, making the trip in 5¼ hours. A one way ticket costs 33,000 dr.

Tickets can be obtained from Paxos Magic Holidays in Gaïos (see that section).

Getting Around
The island's bus links Gaïos and Lakka via Longos up to five times daily (300 dr). A taxi from Gaïos to Lakka will cost around 3000 dr. Motorcycles can be hired from Makris Motorcycles (☎ 32 031), on Gaïos' waterfront.

Gaïos Γάιος
Gaïos, on a wide, east coast bay, is the island's capital. It's a delightfully attractive place with crumbling 19th century red-tiled pink, cream and whitewashed buildings. The fortified Agios Nikolaos Islet almost fills its harbour. Moni Panagias Islet, named after its monastery, lies at the entrance to the bay. On 15 August, a lively festival ends with dancing in Gaïos' central square.

Orientation & Information The main square abuts the central waterfront. The main street of Panagioti Kanga runs inland from here to another square where you'll find the bus stop. The post office is just beyond here and the OTE is next door.

There is no tourist office, but the staff at Paxos Magic Holidays (☎ 32 269, fax 32 122, email paxoshld@hol.gr), on Panagioti Kanga, are very helpful. They also sell the *Bleasdale Walking Map of Paxos* (3000 dr), which comes with an explanatory booklet. The Road Editions 'Corfu and Paxi' map is currently the best map available for the island.

Things to See & Do The excellent **Cultural Museum of Paxi**, on the waterfront, has a well displayed eclectic collection. Don't miss the mind-boggling stirrups hanging from a four-poster bed – a 19th century sex aid. The museum is open 11 am to 1.30 pm and 7 to 10 pm daily. Admission is 500 dr.

The best way to get to know Paxi is to walk the island along its many pathways lined with dry stone walls through the countless olive groves that blanket the island.

Paxos Magic Holidays also organises horseback picnic rides (13,900 dr), an island discovery cruise (5400 dr) or a History and Traditions Evening which takes in olive oil making, feta cheese making, cooking and finally dining to Greek music (8,500 dr, all inclusive).

Places to Stay Accommodation tends to mostly consist of prebooked studios and apartments, though you can always find somewhere private to stay. The large *San Giorgio Rooms to Rent (☎ 32 223)* above the waterfront, 150m north of the central square, has well kept doubles for 6000 dr, studios for 8000 dr and apartments for 14,000 dr.

Up the hill opposite the bus stop are a few domatia. *Magda's Domatia (☎ 32 573)* has a few clean and basic doubles/triples for 6000/8000 dr. Next door up the hill is *Spiro's Domatia (☎ 31 172)*. His somewhat better serviced rooms go for around 8000 dr for a double.

The B class **Paxos Beach** (☎ 31 211, fax 31 166) is a bungalow complex, overlooking the sea, 1.5km south-east of Gaïos. The tastefully furnished doubles cost 35,000 dr (half-board) in high season. The complex has a tennis court, beach, bar and restaurant.

Places to Eat Gaïos has a glut of generally good eating places. Cheap and popular is **George's Place** on the main square. Go there for his great gyros or chicken. Off the south side of the square is **Taverna Andreas**. This cosy little eatery is the best place for fresh fish and home cooking. Close by is the homy **Kirki**, offering among other tasty fare a chicken dish done in mustard sauce. Kirki is open all year round.

A great evening's eating can be had at the tastefully furbished **Afthendiko** at the inland end of Gaïos. This tavern does superb home-cooked dishes – try octopus in tomato sauce or rooster with pastitsada. Both dishes are around 2000 dr.

If you fancy a walk, head uphill along the signposted Vellianitatika road and look for the rather laid-back but still popular **O Kakaletzos** (☎ 32 129), diagonally opposite the Paxos Club, just west of Gaïos. It serves a wide range of ready-cooked dishes and grilled food.

Around Paxi

Paxi's gentle east coast has small pebble beaches, while the west coast has awesome vistas of precipitous cliffs, punctuated by several grottoes only accessible by boat. You can walk to **Trypitos**, a high cliff from where there are stunning views of Antipaxi. From Gaïos, walk westwards along the Makratika road and turn right uphill at Villa Billy's, marked with a small sign on the wall. Stay on the main track and just before it ends turn left onto a narrow path which leads to Trypitos.

Longos A small fishing village-cum-resort, Longos is 5km north of Gaïos, and has several beaches nearby. It's much smaller than Gaïos and has a more intimate

feel. The village consists of little more than a cramped square and a winding waterfront with a couple roads leading in and out. It's a great base if you want a quieter stay on Paxi.

Most of the accommodation is monopolised by tour companies, but **Babis Dendias** (☎/fax 31 597) rents four-person studios for between 22,000 dr and 28,000 dr. Inquire at his *pantopoleio* (general store), 20m beyond the bus stop.

For eating, try **Kagarantzas** or **Taverna o Gios**. Coffees and cold drinks can be taken at **Ores** music cafe and wine bar in between the two. The best bread on the island can be found at the ramshackle **Loukas Bakery**, up a little alley off the square.

Lakka This is another pretty harbour and feels more like Gaïos. It lies at the end of a deep, narrow bay on the north coast and is another popular yachtie call. It's an ideal alternative base to Gaïos since you can also take the twice-weekly ferry to Corfu from here. There are a couple of decent beaches, Vigla and Mesorahi, around either side of the bay's headland and there are some great walks from here.

If you would like to stay, contact Routsis Holidays (☎ 31 807, fax 31 161) on the waterfront. The helpful owners are the agents for many rooms in and around Lakka. They also organise various activities like day trips to Antipaxi and Parga, and rent out boats for 10,000 dr a day.

Lakka also has a glut of good and tasteful tavernas, though **Souris** on the square and **Stasinos** in a little side street off the square are worth looking at first

ANTIPAXI Αντίπαξοι

Diminutive Antipaxi, 2km south of Paxi, is covered with grape vines from which excellent wine is produced. Caïques and tourist boats run daily out of Gaïos and usually pull in at couple of beaches. Vrika Beach at the north-eastern tip is sandy and gently sloping. Two restaurants, **Spiro's Taverna** and **Vrika Taverna**, serve the often busy tourist trade.

Vineyards are a common sight on the tiny
island of Antipaxi

A coastal path links Vrika Beach with
Voutoumi Beach, farther south round a
couple of headlands. Voutoumi Beach is
very pretty, but is made up of large pebbles. A *taverna* high up on the bluff serves
hungry bathers.

If you don't fancy just beach bumming,
take a walk up to the little scattered settlement of Vigla, stopping to admire the many
little vineyards along the way and dotted
throughout the village.

The cheapest way to get to Antipaxi is via
the Antipaxos Lines boat (1300 dr return)
from Gaïos that leaves at 10 am and returns
from Vrika Beach at 5 pm.

Lefkada, Meganisi & Kalamos

LEFKADA Λευκάδα
☎ 0645   • postcode 311 00   • pop 21,100
Lefkada is the fourth largest island in the
Ionian group. Joined to the mainland by a
narrow isthmus until the occupying
Corinthians dug a canal in the 8th century
BC, its 25m strait is spanned from the main-
land by a causeway.

Lefkada has 10 satellite islets: Meganisi,
Kalamos, Kastos, Madouri, Skorpidi, Skorpios, Sparti, Thilia, Petalou and Kythros.

Lefkada is mountainous with two peaks
over 1000m. It is also fertile, well watered
by underground streams, with cotton fields,
acres of dense olive groves, vineyards, fir
and pine forests.

Once a very poor island, Lefkada's
beauty is also in its people, who display in-
tense pride in their island. Many of the older
women wear traditional costume. An International Festival of Literature & Art is held
in the last two weeks of August.

Getting There & Away
Air Lefkada has no airport but Aktion air-
port, near Preveza on the mainland, is a 30
minute bus journey away. It has four flights
weekly to Athens (13,900 dr). Lefkada's
Olympic Airways office (☎ 22 881) is at
Dorpfeld 1; Preveza's (☎ 0682-28 343) is at
Spiliadou 5.

Bus From Lefkada Town's bus station
(☎ 22 364) there are buses to Athens (5½
hours, 6200 dr, four daily), Patra (three
hours, 2900 dr, two weekly) and Aktion airport (30 minutes, 360 dr, five daily).

Ferry From Vasiliki, at least two ferries
daily go to Fiskardo (1½ hours, 940 dr) on
Kefallonia and Frikes (1½ hours, 940 dr) on
Ithaki in high season. In summer one ferry
leaves daily from Nydri for Frikes on Ithaki
and then Fiskardo. Lefkada's port police
can be contacted on ☎ 22 322.

Getting Around
From Lefkada Town, frequent buses go to
Karya and Vlyho via Nydri. Four go daily
to Vasiliki and two daily go to Poros. Other
villages are served by one or two buses
daily.

Cars are available for hire from Europcar
(☎ 25 726), Stratigou Mela 7, among others,

TRUDI CANAVAN

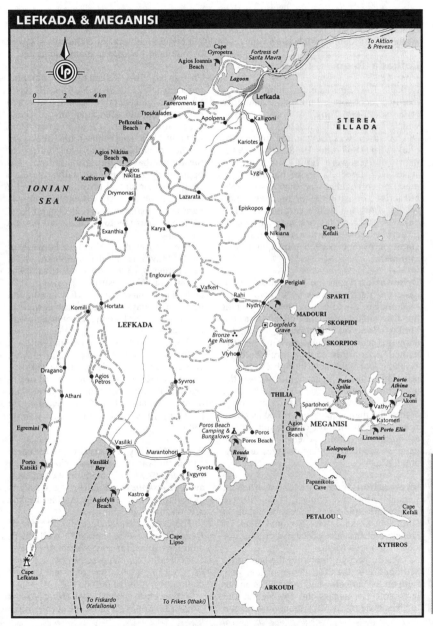

LEFKADA & MEGANISI

To Aktion & Preveza

Cape Gyropetra
Agios Ioannis Beach
Fortress of Santa Mavra
Lagoon

Moni Faneromenis
Lefkada
Tsoukalades
Apolpena
Kalligoni

STEREA ELLADA

Pefkoulia Beach
Kariotes

Agios Nikitas Beach
Agios Nikitas
Lygia

Kathisma

IONIAN SEA

Drymonas
Lazarata
Episkopos

Kalamitsi
Cape Kefali
Exanthia
Karya
Nikiana

Englouvi
Vafkeri
Perigiali
Rahi
SPARTI
Nydri
MADOURI

Komili
Hortata
SKORPIDI
LEFKADA
SKORPIOS
Bronze Age Ruins
Dorpfeld's Grave

Vlyho

Dragano
Porto Spilia
Porto Athina
Agios Petros
Syvros
Cape Akoni
Athani
THILIA
Spartohori
Vathy
Katomeri
MEGANISI
Egremini
Agios Giannis Beach
Porto Elia
Poros Beach Camping & Bungalows
Poros
Limenari
Vasiliki
Poros Beach
Marantohori
Rouda Bay
Kolopoulos Bay
Porto Katsiki
Vasiliki Bay
Syvota
Evgyros
Papanikolis Cave
Kastro
Agiofylli Beach
Cape Kefali
Cape Lipso
PETALOU

KYTHROS
Cape Lefkatas

To Fiskardo (Kefallonia)
To Frikes (Ithaki)
ARKOUDI

IONIAN ISLANDS

0   2   4 km

and motorcycles from Motorcycle Rental Santas (☎ 23 947), on Aristoteli Valaoriti. At the top of Ioannou Mela, turn right.

Lefkada Town
• pop 6800

Lefkada Town, the island's capital and primarily a yacht port, is built on a promontory at the south-east corner of a salty lagoon, which is used as a fish hatchery.

The town was devastated by earthquakes in 1867 and 1948. After 1948, many houses were rebuilt in a unique style, with upper floors of painted sheet metal or corrugated iron that is strangely attractive, constructed in the hope they would withstand future earthquakes. The belfries of churches are made of metal girders – another earthquake precaution. Damage from the 1953 earthquake was minimal.

Orientation From the bus station on the eastern waterfront, walk back towards the beginning of the causeway road, turn left at the first major road, and left again at the Nirikos Hotel on to Dorpfeld, the town's animated main thoroughfare. This street is named after 19th century archaeologist Wilhelm Dorpfeld, held in high esteem for postulating that Lefkada, not Ithaki, was the home of Odysseus.

Dorpfeld leads to Plateia Agiou Spyridonos, the main square where locals enjoy *soumadia* (an almond drink), during the evening *volta* (stroll). After the square, the name of the thoroughfare changes to Ioannou Mela.

Information There is no tourist office on Lefkada. The tourist police (☎ 26 450) are in the same building as the regular police on Dimitriou Golemi. The National Bank of Greece and the post office are on the east side of Ioannou Mela.

Take the second right after the bank onto Mitropolis for the OTE phone office. Veer right on to Zambelou and the OTE is on the left. You can access the Internet at the Internet Cafe (☎ 21 507), Ioannou Gazi 5, a five minute walk south (inland) from the bus station.

Lefkada's library, at Skiadaresis 1, has books about Lefkada in many languages.

Things to See Lefkada's **phonographic museum** (☎ 21 088) at Kalkani 10 has a collection of venerable gramophones and memorabilia and sells tapes of old Greek songs for 1000 dr. It's signposted from Ioannou Mela, and admission is free.

The art gallery in the ground floor of the library has changing exhibitions. It's open between 7 and 9 pm daily. There's a small **archaeological museum** (☎ 23 678) at Pefaneromenis 20 which runs almost parallel to Ioannou Mela. It is open 9 am to 1 pm Tuesday to Sunday; admission costs 300 dr.

The 14th century Venetian **Fortress of Santa Mavra** is on the mainland. **Moni Faneromenis**, 3km west of town, was founded in 1634, destroyed by fire in 1886 and rebuilt. Inhabited by a few monks and nuns, the monastery's church can be visited. The views of the lagoon and town are worth the ascent.

West of the lagoon, past windmills, is **Agios Ioannis Beach** where, at sunset, clouds are neon-lit islands in the sky. The nearest beaches to town are at the northern side of the lagoon, about a 2km walk away. The eastern coastal beaches are pebbled, while most on the west are white sand.

Places to Stay & Eat The nearest camp site to Lefkada Town is *Kariotes Beach Camping* (☎ 71 103), on the east coast, 5km away. *Episkopos Camping* (☎ 23 043) is 3km farther south. See the Around Lefkada section for other camp sites.

The D class *Hotel Byzantio* (☎ 21 315, Dorpfeld 4) has clean, well kept doubles/triples for 5500/8800 dr. The C class *Hotel Santa Maura* (☎ 21 308, fax 26 253) nearby has pleasant singles/ doubles for 9000/14,000 dr.

At the comfortable B class *Hotel Niricos* (☎ 24 132, fax 23 756), on the corner of the waterfront and Dorpfeld, rooms cost 14,000 dr (half-board) for singles and doubles alike. Close by, facing the port, the palatial B class *Hotel Lefkas (☎ 23 916, fax 24 579, Panagou 2)* has rates of 17,000/26,000 dr with breakfast.

Karaboulias Restaurant on the eastern waterfront offers traditional fare with flair. The intimate *Eftyhia Taverna (Stambogli 2)* has hearty, inexpensive food. The walls are graced by watercolours by Panagos. Facing inland, turn left at the fountain on Dorpfeld to find the taverna.

Regantos Taverna (Vergioti 17) is another atmospheric little place with good food. A meal of stuffed eggplant, Greek salad and wine costs around 2200 dr. To reach the taverna, turn right at the central square off Dorpfeld.

Around Lefkada

Nydri A sleepy fishing village not so long ago, Nydri, 16km south of Lefkada Town, fell hook, line and sinker to the lure of the tourist trade. Now it's a busy, commercialised but fun town from where you can cruise around the islets of **Madouri**, **Sparti**, **Skorpidi** and **Skorpios** for 3000 dr, or 7000 dr if a barbecue and unlimited drinks are included.

The privately owned Madouri islet, where the Greek poet Aristotelis Valaoritis (1824-79) spent his last 10 years, is off limits. It's not officially possible to land on Skorpios, where Ari, sister Artemis and children Alexander and Christina Onassis are buried in a cemetery visible from the sea, but you can swim off a sandy beach on the north side of the island.

If you would rather explore the islets independently, boats can be hired from Trident Travel Agency (☎/fax 92 037) on the main street. Motorboats cost around 10,000 dr a day (excluding fuel) and sailing dinghies are 8000 dr. The agency also has motorcycle and car hire and a room-finding service.

Windsurfing, water-skiing, parasailing and sailing (bareboating with licence or

Onassis

The most famous of all shipping magnates is undoubtedly the Turkish-born Greek Aristotle Socrates Onassis, who was born in Smyrna (now İzmir) in 1906, the son of a tobacco merchant. At the age of 16 his family fled from Turkish hostility to Athens. The following year he arrived in Buenos Aires with a total of $60 and worked as a telephone operator by night while building up his own tobacco business during the day.

At the age of 25 he was already a millionaire and the following year he began what became the world's largest independent shipping line, investing in six Canadian freighters in the midst of a serious recession and putting them into service as the market recovered. Onassis was one of the pioneers of supertankers in the 1950s, and he was awarded the contract to operate the Greek national airline, Olympic Airways, which started in 1957. At 62 he married President Kennedy's widow, Jacqueline. He died in 1975.

crewed yachts) out of Nydri can be organised by Nikos Thermes' Sport Boat Charter (☎ 92 431), Perigiali. Englishman Andy Fenna runs the island's only PADI School of Diving (☎ 92 286) from Nydri.

The quiet village of Vlyho is 3km south of Nydri. Beyond here, a road leads to a peninsula where Wilhelm Dorpfeld is buried. Just west of the Nydra-Vlyho road are the Bronze Age ruins which he excavated, leading him to believe Lefkada was Homer's Ithaca.

Places to Stay & Eat Desimi Beach Camping (☎ 95 223) is south of Nydri. It is signposted after the village of Vlyho.

There are a large number of rooms and studios in Nydri though a fair few get block-booked by tour companies. Samba Tours (see the Vasiliki section following) also has an accommodation office in Nydri.

IONIAN ISLANDS

Armeno Beach Hotel (☎ 92 112, fax 92 018), at the quieter northern end of Nydri, has some wonderful rooms overlooking the beach and the island of Skorpios. Doubles go for 18,000 dr in high season and 10,000 dr in low season.

Forget the touristy waterfront restaurants and walk 1km north to Perigiali. *Mangano* (☎ 93 188) is easily the best restaurant in Nydri and is much better value for money. The moussaka served here is mouthwatering and you can dine on the beach. You'll find the restaurant close to Armeno Beach Hotel.

Poros This little village overlooks Poros Bay, and makes a great alternative base to the often raucous Nydri. The beach is good and there are boats for hire.

There is a camp site, *Poros Beach Camping & Bungalows* (☎ 95 452), as well as the cosy and cool domatia of *Yiannoula* (☎ 95 507) at the eastern end of the bay. A double with kitchen will cost you 9000 dr. For meals, try the nearby *Zolithros* or *Molos*, both quaint and friendly tavernas.

Vasiliki Purported to be *the* best windsurfing location in Europe, Vasiliki is a pretty fishing village with both sand and pebbled beaches. It attracts a sizable crowd each season and you can hop over to Kefallonia from here if you are heading south.

You can rent surf boards from Club Vas (☎ 31 588) and instruction for all levels is available. It's crowded in summer so prepare to commute.

Wild Wind (☎/fax 31 610) rents out catamarans and offers instruction. You can take a cruise on a *felucca* (☎ 93 116) for between 10,000 dr and 12,000 dr, including food and drink.

Caïques take visitors from Vasiliki to swim at the best sand beaches on the west coast, which include **Porto Katsiki**, **Egremini** and **Kathisma**. All are signposted on the west coast off the road leading to the island's south-west promontory. A boat will also take you to the unspoilt **Agiofylli Beach**. A sanctuary of Apollo once stood at **Cape Lefkatas**.

Places to Stay & Eat The best bet for accommodation is to drop in to Samba Tours (☎ 92 658, fax 92 659) and see what's available. Rooms go for between 8000 dr and 11,000 dr in season. Studios cost from 15,000 dr to 20,000 dr.

The waterfront restaurants are all pretty similar and of good quality. Instead, try *To Steki ton Piraton*, set back from the waterfront on the main street. *Alexandros*, on the west end of the waterfront, offers a wide range of Chinese dishes if you hanker after something other than Greek food.

MEGANISI Μεγανήσι
☎ 0645 • postcode 310 83 • pop 1250

Meganisi has the largest population of Lefkada's three inhabited satellite islets, but like many small Greek islands it has suffered population depletion. It's easily visited on a day trip.

It's a tranquil islet with a lovely, verdant landscape and deep bays of turquoise water, fringed by pebbled beaches. It's visited primarily by yachties and is untouched by package tour operators. It has three settlements: the capital of Spartohori, the port of Vathy and the village of Katomeri.

Getting There & Away
There are about four ferries daily between Nydri and Meganisi. They usually call in first at Porto Spilia and then into Vathy before heading back to Nydri. In the past there have been services from Meganisi to Kefallonia and Ithaki; check to see if they are running again.

A minibus meets boats at both ports and takes passengers to Spartohori and Katomeri.

Spartohori Σπαρτοχώρι
Spartohori, with narrow, winding lanes and pretty, flower-bedecked houses, perches on a plateau above Porto Spilia.

Boats dock at Porto Spilia. No-one lives here, but there are several tavernas. A road ascends steeply to Spartohori or you can walk the 1km there up steps. To reach Spartohori's main street and central square turn right at Tropicana Pizzeria. The island's only post office is at Vathy.

One of the island's best beaches is Agios Giannis, a long stretch of small pebbles, 3km south-west of Spartohori.

Other good beaches are on the island's tapering southern tail. In summer, the owner of Taverna Lakis (see Places to Stay & Eat) takes visitors there in his boat.

Places to Stay & Eat There are no official camp sites but wild camping is tolerated.

The owner of *Chicken Billy's Psistaria* (*☎ 51 442*) has some low-priced *domatia*. Beyond the central square, just before the main street curves left, turn right, and Chicken Billy's is on the right.

Kostas Rooms (*☎ 51 372*) are clean and well kept with a communal kitchen. Double/triple rooms are 6000/8000 dr. Take the street signposted to Agios Giannis and the rooms are on the right.

The immaculate *Studios For Rent Argyri* (*☎ 51 502, fax 24 911*) has double/triple studios for 10,000/12,000 dr. Inquire at Oasi Bar, opposite Chicken Billy's.

Tropicana Pizzeria has pizzas for 1200 dr and stunning views of Skorpios.

Taverna Lakis offers tasty Greek fare and features Greek evenings. When things really get going, Mamma Lakis, who is no spring chicken, dances with a table on her head. *Chicken Billy's* serves delectably tender, low-priced chicken. In its heyday, it was visited by Christina Onassis – her photograph is on the wall to prove it.

Down on Agios Giannis Beach, *Paradiso* restaurant operates in season.

Vathy Βαθύ

This is the island's second port. The post office is on the waterfront near the quay. Farther round there's a children's playground. Beyond here, the road climbs to **Katomeri**, 700m away.

There are no EOT-approved domatia in Vathy or Katomeri, but locals let rooms unofficially – ask around. For dining try *Taverna Porto Vathy*, a small fish tavern right next to the ferry quay, or *Rose Garden*, a rose-covered restaurant-cum-cafe on the little square.

There are several beaches near Katomeri. At secluded Porto Elia beach, *Porto Elia Rooms* (*☎ 51 341*), owned by English-speaking Fotis Katopodis, are lovely studios costing 12,000 dr. The well signposted *Hotel Meganisi* (*☎ 51 240*) has spotless, modern singles/doubles for 9000/13,000 dr with bathroom. Its restaurant serves tasty traditional dishes.

Restaurant Niagas, at Porto Athina Beach, serves well prepared, freshly caught fish.

KALAMOS Κάλαμος
☎ 0646 • postcode 311 00 • pop 400
Beautiful, mountainous and wooded, Kalamos is the second largest of Lefkada's satellite islets. It has two settlements, the port of Kalamos, on the south-east coast, where most of the inhabitants live, and the north coast village of Episkopi, 8km away. Most of the houses in Episkopi are derelict and only 20 inhabitants remain. Kefali, 8km south-west of Kalamos, was abandoned after the 1953 earthquake, but its church is well kept.

A few adventurous yachties sail into Kalamos port, but it is extremely unusual for any other type of tourist to turn up.

Kalamos village is built on a steep hillside. Its narrow lanes wind between well kept little houses with pretty gardens. There's a post office in the village and a cardphone on the waterfront. The beautiful long, pebbled **Agra Pedia Beach** is a short walk away; locals will direct you.

There is only one place to stay, *Dionysis Lezentinos Rooms* (*☎ 91 238*), just back from the waterfront in Kalamos. Basic but clean doubles/triples are 5500/6500 dr. A reservation is essential in July and August. There are several restaurants on the waterfront. *Restaurant O Zefyros* is owned by a friendly couple. The food is delicious and reasonably priced.

Infrequent ferries serve Kalamos from Lefkada. A caïque leaves Mytikas on the mainland every morning around 11 am for Kalamos.

Kefallonia & Ithaki

KEFALLONIA Κεφαλλονιά
- pop 32,500

Kefallonia, the largest of the Ionian Islands, has rugged, towering mountains. The highest, Mt Enos (1520m), is the Mediterranean's only mountain with a unique fir forest species, *Abies kefallia*. While not as tropical as Corfu, Kefallonia has many species of wild flowers, includ-

ing orchids and, when you approach it by sea on a windy summer's day, the scents of thyme, oregano, bay leaves and flowers will reach you before you land. The island receives package tourists, but not on the same scale as Corfu and Zakynthos. The island has received unprecedented publicity in recent times thanks to Louis de Bernières novel *Captain Corelli's Mandolin*, which is set in Kefallonia. Most beach bums will have a dog-eared copy of the novel.

KEFALLONIA & ITHAKI

Monk seals may be seen on the north-west coasts of Kefallonia and Ithaki.

Kefallonia is also a nesting ground for loggerhead turtles, which lay their eggs on southern beaches in June. Turtle numbers ashore have remained stable, unlike on Zakynthos. See the boxed text 'Loggerhead Turtles' later in this chapter.

Kefallonia's capital is Argostoli but the main port is Sami. As the island is so big and mountainous, travelling between towns is time consuming. In summer there are art exhibitions in the major towns. In August and September an international choral festival is held in Argostoli and Lixouri.

Getting There & Away

Air There is at least one flight daily from Kefallonia to Athens (17,900 dr). The Olympic Airways office (☎ 0671-28 808) in Argostoli is at Rokou Vergoti 1.

Ferry Kefallonia has six ports – the telephone numbers of the port police are in

The Mediterranean Monk Seal

The Mediterranean monk seal is the rarest of all the seal species and one of the six most endangered mammals in the world. It belongs to the same genus as the Hawaiian and Caribbean monk seals. The latter is now believed to be extinct, since none has been sighted since the 1950s.

Monk seals (Monachus monachus) have been in existence for around 15 million years, and in ancient times were so abundant that Homer wrote of herds of them lying on beaches. There is also mention of them in the works of Plutarch, Pliny and Aristotle. It is estimated that in the 15th century around 5000 of the seals lived around the coasts of Spain, France, Portugal, Italy, Albania, Egypt, Israel, Turkey, Algeria and the Lebanon. Numbers have declined drastically in the last 100 years and the present population now stands at around 400 individuals, about half of which live in Greece. There are small numbers in Madeira and Italy, but the second-largest colony lives in the Atlantic, off the coast of north-west Africa, entirely cut off from the rest.

In the past the seals were hunted for their skin and oil, and were killed by fishers because they ate the fish caught in nets. Nowadays they are threatened by marine pollution, oil spills and the numerous pesticides that end up in the sea. But the greatest threat comes from disturbance by humans. Before the days of mass tourism the seals would haul themselves onto gently sloping sandy beaches to give birth, where they and their young were safe from rough waves. Then, as remote beaches became exploited by the tourist industry, the seals abandoned them and resorted to quiet coastal caves fronted by a patch of sand. However, these caves are now also becoming tourist attractions. Unfortunately, the births take place between May and November which coincides with the tourist season. A seal usually only has one pup at a time. The pup remains on land until it is weaned six to eight weeks later. If a female is frightened by the presence of tourists she may miscarry or abandon her helpless pup.

Tourism has driven the monk seal from Sardinia, Sicily and Corsica. To prevent the same happening in Greece it is imperative that tourists do not visit remote sea caves – the last safe refuge of the seal. If the necessary measures are not taken the species could become extinct within 25 years. If you are lucky enough to see a monk seal, keep a distance from it and keep quiet, to make your presence felt as little as possible.

The Hellenic Society for the Study & Protection of the Monk Seal (☎ 01-522 2888, fax 522 2450), Solomou 53, Athens 104 32, has a seal rescue centre on Alonnisos, and the WWF funds a seal watch led by Dimitris Panos (☎ 0671-31 114) at Fiskardo, Kefallonia.

brackets: Sami (☎ 0674-22 031), Argostoli (☎ 0671-22 224), Poros (☎ 0674-72 460), Lixouri (☎ 0671-94 100), Pesada, and Fiskardo (☎ 0674-41 400).

Domestic From Fiskardo, at least two ferries daily leave for Vasiliki (850 dr) on Lefkada. At least two daily go from Sami to Patras (2½ hours, 2630 dr). From Poros (90 minutes, 1620 dr), and Argostoli (2¾ hours, 2700 dr), at least two ferries ply daily to Kyllini in the Peloponnese. From Pesada, near Spartia, there are two high-season services daily (1¼ hours, 836 dr) to Skinari on Zakynthos. Daily ferries go from Fiskardo to Ithaki (Frikes) and Lefkada (Vasiliki).

In summer, small boats leave Sami at 6.30 am to go to Fiskardo via Piso Aetos on Ithaki. From Fiskardo they continue to Vasiliki to return to Kefallonia later in the day. Frequent ferries take 30 minutes to reach Lixouri from Argostoli. Tickets (350 dr) are sold on board.

International A daily ferry leaves Sami for Brindisi in Italy, via Igoumenitsa and Corfu. In high season two or three ferries weekly leave Sami for Ancona and Venice, via Igoumenitsa and Corfu.

Tickets can be obtained from either Vasilatos Shipping (☎ 0671-22 618, fax 24 992) on Metaxa 54, or Romanos Travel (☎ 0671-23 541, fax 25 451) at Antoni Tritsi 48, in Argostoli.

Getting Around

To/From the Airport The airport is 9km south of Argostoli. There is no airport bus. A taxi costs 2000 dr.

Bus From Argostoli (☎ 0671-22 276) frequent buses go to Platys Gialos and Sami (500 dr), three daily to Poros (850 dr), via Peratata, Vlahata and Markopoulo, two daily to Skala (800 dr) and two daily to Fiskardo (850 dr). In the off season, only one return service daily connects Fiskardo (1000 dr) with Argostoli. Four daily return buses leave Athens' A terminal for Argostoli (eight hours via ferry to Poros, 7500 dr).

Car & Motorcycle Cars can be hired from Ainos Travel (☎ 0671-22 333, fax 24 608), Georgiou Vergoti 14, and motorcycles from Sunbird Motor Rent (☎ 0671-23 723), on the waterfront in Argostoli. Vehicle hire is recommended during the off season because of the infrequency of buses.

Argostoli Αργοστόλι
☎ 0671 • postcode 281 00 • pop 7300

Argostoli, unlike Zakynthos Town, was not restored to its former Venetian splendour after the 1953 earthquake. It's a modern, lively port set on a peninsula. Its harbour is divided from Koutavos lagoon by a British-built causeway connecting it with the rest of Kefallonia. There is a colourful produce market on the waterfront on most mornings.

Orientation & Information The EOT (☎ 22 248) is on the waterfront, south of the quay. The post office is on Diad Konstantinou and the OTE phone office is on Georgiou Vergoti. Plateia Vallianou is the huge palm-treed central square up from the waterfront off 21 Maïou.

The modern and (for once) very user-friendly bus station is on the southern waterfront near the causeway. The ferry quay is at the waterfront's northern end.

The National Bank of Greece is one block back from the southern end of the waterfront. The National Mortgage Bank on the waterfront has a 24 hour cash exchange machine. There is also a Commercial Bank ATM on the corner of Vyronos and Vergoti.

The town's closest sandy beaches are **Makrys Gialos** and **Platys Gialos**, 5km south. The island's most expensive accommodation is here, although domatia can be found.

Things to See Argostoli's **archaeological museum** (☎ 28 300), on Rokou Vergoti, has a small collection of island relics including Mycenaean finds from tombs. Opening times are 8.30 am to 3 pm Tuesday to Sunday. Admission is 500 dr.

The **historical and cultural museum** (☎ 28 835), farther up Rokou Vergoti, has a collection of traditional costumes, furniture

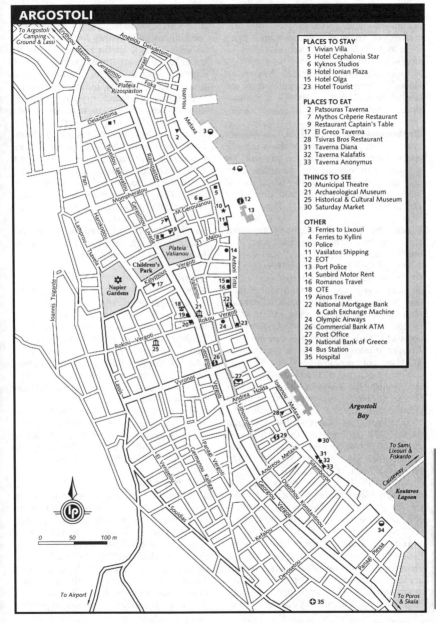

ARGOSTOLI

To Argostoli
Camping
Ground & Lassi

PLACES TO STAY
1 Vivian Villa
5 Hotel Cephalonia Star
6 Kyknos Studios
8 Hotel Ionian Plaza
15 Hotel Olga
23 Hotel Tourist

PLACES TO EAT
2 Patsouras Taverna
7 Mythos Crêperie Restaurant
9 Restaurant Captain's Table
17 El Greco Taverna
28 Tsivras Bros Restaurant
31 Taverna Diana
32 Taverna Kalafatis
33 Taverna Anonymus

THINGS TO SEE
20 Municipal Theatre
21 Archaeological Museum
25 Historical & Cultural Museum
30 Saturday Market

OTHER
3 Ferries to Lixouri
4 Ferries to Kyllini
10 Police
11 Vasilatos Shipping
12 EOT
13 Port Police
14 Sunbird Motor Rent
16 Romanos Travel
18 OTE
19 Ainos Travel
22 National Mortgage Bank
   & Cash Exchange Machine
24 Olympic Airways
26 Commercial Bank ATM
27 Post Office
29 National Bank of Greece
34 Bus Station
35 Hospital

Plateia
Rizospaston

Plateia
Valianou

Children's
Park

Napier
Gardens

Argostoli
Bay

To Sami,
Lixouri &
Fiskardo

Causeway

Koutavos
Lagoon

To Airport

To Poros
& Skala

0   50   100 m

IONIAN ISLANDS

and tools, items which belonged to British occupiers, and photographs of pre-earthquake Argostoli. The museum is open 9 am to 2 pm Monday to Saturday. Admission is 500 dr.

Argostoli's new **municipal theatre**, on Georgiou Vergoti, was inaugurated by the late Melina Merkouri. There's a ground-floor art gallery.

Organised Tours The KTEL organises tours to Drogarati Cave, Melissani Lake and Fiskardo for 5000 dr, and to Ithaki for 8000 dr. Inquire at the marked office at the bus station and pick up the handy island bus timetable and tour brochure while you're there.

Places to Stay The pleasant *Argostoli Camping* (☎ 23 487) is on the coast, 2km north of town.

One of the nicest places is *Vivian Villa* (☎ 23 396, fax 28 670, Deladetsima 9). The friendly owners offers beautiful, spotless double/triple rooms for 10,000/12,000 dr with bathroom. Studios cost 13,000/15,800 dr and a large, well equipped apartment costs 21,000 dr. Another pleasant option is *Kyknos Studios* (☎ 23 398, M Geroulanou 4), where doubles are 12,500 dr.

There's a string of C class hotels along the waterfront. *Hotel Cephalonia Star* (☎ 23 181, 23 180, Ioannou Metaxa 60) has comfortable air-con singles/doubles for 12,000/17,000 dr. Rates at *Hotel Tourist* (☎/fax 22 510, Antoni Tritsi 109) are 13,000/20,000 dr, and the beautifully refurbished *Hotel Olga* (☎ 24 981, fax 24 985), on Antoni Tristi, charges 14,400/21,050 dr.

Argostoli's best hotel is the marble-decorated *Hotel Ionian Plaza* (☎ 25 581, fax 25 585) on Plateia Vallianou. Comfortable air-con suites cost 11,900/16,400 dr.

Places to Eat The waterfront's neighbouring restaurants *Taverna Diana*, *Taverna Kalafatis* and *Taverna Anonymus* are all commendable, and the Kalafatis – around since 1945 – stays open all year. Kefallonia has a distinctive cuisine, repres-

ented by meat pies and *skordalia* (garlic dip) which accompanies fish. Greeks find these dishes at *Patsouras Taverna (Ioannou Metaxa 40)* opposite the ferry quay. Ask for the island's famed Robola wine, which is expensive but wonderful and comes from grapes grown in stony, mountainous soil.

El Greco Taverna (Kalypsous Vergoti 3), opposite the children's park, is also popular with locals. Well prepared cod with skordalia is 1700 dr. The old-fashioned *Tsivras Bros Restaurant* (☎ 24 259), just off the waterfront, serves filling goat broth for 1000 dr and many dishes under 1000 dr.

Off the central square, *Restaurant Captain's Table (Rizospaston 3)* serves pies, spaghetti and fish dishes at medium prices and has live guitar music each night. Nearby, *Mythos Crêperie Restaurant* has a similarly priced selection of crepes and Mexican and Chinese dishes.

Sami Σάμη
☎ 0674 • postcode 280 82 • pop 1000

Sami, 25km from Argostoli and the main port of Kefallonia, was also devastated by the 1953 earthquake. Now with undistinguished buildings, its setting is pretty, nestled in a bay, flanked by steep hills. Classical Greek and Roman ruins have been found. It's worth an overnight stay to visit the nearby caves. A post office, OTE and bank are in town.

Buses for Argostoli meet ferries. Many domatia owners meet the boats. The well kept *Karavomylos Beach Camping* (☎ 22 480) is 800m west of Sami. Turn right from the quay and follow the coast.

Around Sami
The **Mellisani Cave** is a subterranean sea-water lake. When the sun is overhead its rays shine through an opening in the cave ceiling, lighting the water's many shades of blue. The cave is 2.5km from Sami. To get there walk along the Argostoli road and turn right at the signpost for Agia Evfymia. There is a sign pointing left to the cave beyond the seaside village of Karavomylos. The large **Drogarati Cave** has impressive

stalactites. It's signposted from the Argostoli road, 4km from Sami. Both caves are open all day and charge 1000 dr.

The picturesque fishing village of **Agia Evfymia** with its pebbled beach is 10km north of Sami. It is another popular yachting stop, and while the beach is rather narrow the water is very clear and the swimming is good. There are one or two hotels and some domatia for travellers wishing to stay.

Spiros Restaurant (☎ 0674-61 739) on the south waterfront is a good place to stop and eat. The food is great; aim for the roast suckling pig on Saturday night. Phone ahead to book your plate.

Fiskardo Φισκάρδο

☎ 0674 • postcode 280 84 • pop 300

Fiskardo, 50km north of Argostoli, was the only village not devastated by the 1953 earthquake. Framed by cypress-mantled hills, and with fine Venetian buildings, it's a delightful place. A Roman cemetery and Mycenaean pottery have been found here. It's a popular place, especially with yachties, but it's pleasant outside high season.

The bus will drop you off on the road which bypasses Fiskardo. Walk across the car park, descend the steps to the left of the church and continue ahead to Fiskardo's central square and waterfront.

You can get to Fiskardo by ferry from Lefkada and Ithaki or by bus from Argostoli.

Places to Stay & Eat You're unlikely to find accommodation in high season. At others times it's OK, but prices are high.

At *Regina's Rooms* (☎ 41 125) doubles/triples are 10,000/11,000 dr, and new studios are 12,000/15,000 dr. *John Palikisianos Rooms* (☎ 41 304), opposite, has rates of 7000/8500 dr. To get to these from the bus stop, cross the car park, turn left at the church, turn left again, and look for the signs.

The tastefully furnished rooms at *Tselenti Domatia* (☎ 41 204), just back from and west of the central square, are a pricey 15,000/18,000 dr. The *Philoxenia Traditional Settlement* (☎ 41 410, fax 41 319) occupies a lovely 19th century house near the square. Room rates are 20,700/22,000 dr. Farther around the waterfront, *Nefeli Studios* has immaculate self-contained units and great sea views. Rates are 25,000 dr.

Gaïta traditional grill house on the west harbourfront and *Lagoudera* just back from the harbourfront are both worth seeking out for a good traditional Kefallonian meal.

Around Fiskardo

Assos Village is a gem of white-washed and pastel houses, straddling the isthmus of a peninsula on which stands a Venetian fortress. Assos was damaged in the 1953 earthquake but sensitively restored with the help of a donation from the city of Paris.

There's an outstanding white sandy beach at **Myrtos**, 3km south of Assos. If you explore by boat, you'll find nearby hidden coves between tall limestone cliffs.

Southern Kefallonia

Kastro, above the village of **Peratata**, 9km south-east of **Argostoli**, was the island's capital in the Middle Ages. Ruined houses stand beneath the 13th century castle of **Agios Georgios**, which affords magnificent views.

Peratata has *domatia*, as has **Vlahata**, a pleasant village east along the road which branches to **Lourdata Beach** where you can go horse riding. On a scenic 2½ hour circular walk from Lourdata, you pass thickets, orchards and olive groves with flowers and birds, and return along the coast. A free Lourdata trail walk guide is available from the EOT in Argostoli.

The superb two to four-person apartments of *Ionian Star* (☎ 0671-31 419, fax 31 019) at Lourdata Beach make a great base for this part of the island. Prices range between 10,000 dr and 20,000 dr depending on the season.

At **Markopoulo** an extraordinary event creeps up on 15 August (the Feast of the Assumption). The village church becomes infested with harmless snakes with crosses on their heads. They are said to bring good luck.

Poros is overdeveloped, but has a rather scruffy, pebbled beach. **Skala**, on the southern tip, is a preferable resort with a

IONIAN ISLANDS

large, fine sand beach backed by a cooling pine wood. There are domatia and hotels at both locations.

ITHAKI Ιθάκη
☎ 0674   • postcode 283 00   • pop 3100

Ithaki (ancient Ithaca) was Odysseus' long-lost home, the island where the stoical Penelope sat patiently, weaving a shroud for her father-in-law. She told her suitors, who believed Odysseus was dead, that she would choose one of them once she had completed the shroud. Cunningly, she unravelled it every night in order to keep her suitors at bay, as she awaited Odysseus' return.

Ithaki is separated from Kefallonia by a strait, only 2 to 4km wide. The unspoilt island has a harsh, precipitous east coast and a soft, green west coast. The interior is mountainous and rocky with pockets of pine forest, stands of cypresses, olive groves and vineyards.

Because of its general lack of good beaches, Ithaki doesn't attract large crowds, but it's a great place to spend a quiet holiday, perhaps walking or just relaxing.

Odysseus & Ithaki

Ithaki (Ithaca) has long been the symbolic image for the end of a long journey. For mythical hero Odysseus (Ulysses), Ithaki was the home he left to fight in the Trojan Wars. According to the often wild tales recounted in Homer's *Iliad*, though more specifically in the *Odyssey*, it took the wily hero Odysseus 10 long years to return home to Ithaki from Troy on the Asia Minor coast.

Tossed by tempestuous seas, attacked by sea monsters, delayed by a cunning siren yet helped on his way by friendly Phaeacians, Odysseus finally made landfall on Ithaki. Here, disguised as a beggar, he teamed up with his son Telemachus and his old swineherd Eumaeus, and slayed a castleful of conniving suitors who had been eating him out of home and fortune while trying unsuccessfully to woo the ever-patient and faithful Penelope, Odysseus' long-suffering wife who had waited 20 years for him to return.

Despite Ithaki owing its fame to such illustrious classical connections, no mention of the island appears in writings of the Middle Ages. As late as 1504 AD Ithaki was almost uninhabited following repeated depredations by pirates. The Venetians were obliged to induce settlers from neighbouring islands to repopulate Ithaki. Yet the island is described in considerable detail in the *Odyssey*, which match in many respects the physical nature of the island today. 'The Fountain of Arethousa' has been identified with a spring rising at the foot of a sea cliff in the south of the island and the 'Cave of the Naiads' with a fairly nondescript cave up from the Bay of Phorkys. However, many Homerists have been hard-pressed to ascribe other locales described in the *Odyssey* – particularly Odysseus' castle – to actual places on the islands since scant archaeological remains assist the researcher. Other Homerists conclude that Ithaki may well have been Lefkada, a theory espoused by German archaeologist Willem Dorpfeld, though this idea seems to have fallen on rocky ground in more recent times.

Odysseus as a mythical man is everyone's hero, a pre-classical Robin Hood or John Wayne, both villain and king bundled into one well marketed package. Classical Greek writers presented him sometimes as an unscrupulous politician, and sometimes as a wise and honourable statesman. Philosophers usually admired his intelligence and wisdom. To listeners of yore he was the hero underdog that everyone wanted to see win. Whether he actually existed or not is almost irrelevant since the universal human qualities that he embodied are those that most of us, whether we want to or not, admire and aspire to.

IONIAN ISLANDS

Getting There & Away

From Ithaki there are daily ferries to Patras, to Vasiliki on Lefkada via Fiskardo on Kefallonia, and to Sami and Agia Efthymia on Kefallonia. In high season, a daily ferry sails from Frikes (Ithaki) to Fiskardo, Meganisi and Nydri. The telephone number of Ithaki's port police is ☎ 32 909.

Getting Around

The island's one bus runs two or three times daily to Kioni (via Stavros and Frikes) from Vathy (550 dr).

Ithaki Town Ιθάκη Χώρα
• pop 1800

Ithaki Town (or Vathy; Βαθύ) is small with a few twisting streets, a central square, nice cafes and restaurants, and a few tourist shops, grocers and hardware stores. Old mansions rise up from the seafront.

Orientation & Information The ferry quay is on the west side of the bay. To reach the central square of Plateia Efstathiou Drakouli, turn left and follow the waterfront. The main thoroughfare, Kallinikou, is parallel to, and one block inland from, the waterfront.

Ithaki has no tourist office. The tourist police (☎ 32 205) are on Evmeou, which runs south from the middle of the waterfront.

The National Bank of Greece is just south-west of the central square. The post office is on the central square and the OTE is farther east along the waterfront.

Things to See The town's **archaeological museum** is on Kallinikou. It is open 8.30 am to 3 pm Tuesday to Sunday. Entrance is free. The **nautical and folklore museum** is housed in an old generating station. Ithaki was the first place in Greece to have electricity, thanks to the generosity of George Drakoulis, a wealthy Ithakan shipowner. The museum, behind the Agricultural Bank, is open 9.30 am to 1.30 pm and 6 to 9 pm Monday to Friday; admission is 300 dr.

A summer music and theatre festival is held in Ithaki Town.

Places to Stay *Andriana Kouloupi Domatia (☎ 32 387)*, just south of the quay, has agreeable single/double rooms for 5000/6600 dr with shared bathroom, and doubles/triples with private bathroom for 8000/10,000 dr. At *Vasiliki Vlasopoulou Domatia (☎ 32 119)* pleasant doubles with bathroom cost 8000 dr. Turn left from the quay and right at the town hall, take the steps ahead, and you will see the sign.

Just off the eastern waterfront, *Dimitrios Maroudas Rooms & Apartments (☎/fax 32 751)*, signposted 180m beyond the OTE, has clean doubles/triples for 7000/10,000 dr and four-person apartments for 14,000 dr.

On the western waterfront, *Hotel Odysseus (☎ 32 381, fax 32 587)* has pleasant doubles for 9000 dr. The B class *Hotel Mentor (☎ 32 433, fax 32 293)* near the OTE has a bar, restaurant and roof garden. Attractive singles/doubles cost 12,500/17,000 dr.

Places to Eat *Taverna Trehantiri*, a long-established place west of the central square, serves quality traditional Greek dishes. *O Nikos*, one block back from the square, does great fish dishes which you can wash down with fine Ithakan wine. The classy *Sirens Yacht Club Restaurant & Bar*, nearby, has old photos of Vathy on its walls. The imaginative menu includes shrimps with lemon and mushroom sauce. *Restaurant Kantouni*, on the waterfront, excels in reasonably priced fish dishes.

Young locals meet at the stylish *Drakoulis Cafe* in a waterfront mansion, which was the home of George Drakoulis. Try the sweet, gooey *rovani*, the local speciality, at one of the waterfront's *zaharoplasteia*.

Around Ithaki

Ithaki has a few sites associated with Homer's *Odyssey*. Though none is impressive, you may enjoy (or endure) the scenic walks to them. The most renowned is the **Fountain of Arethousa**, where Odysseus' swineherd, Eumaeus, brought his pigs to drink and where Odysseus, on his return to Ithaca, went to meet him disguised as a beggar after receiving directions from the goddess Athena. Lesser mortals have to deal with inadequate signposting. The walk takes 1½ to two hours. Take plenty of water as the spring shrinks in summer.

A shorter trek is to the **Cave of the Nymphs**, where Odysseus concealed the splendid gifts of gold, copper and fine fabrics that the Phaeacians had given him. The cave is signposted from the town. Below the cave is the **Bay of Dexa** (where there is decent swimming), thought to be ancient Phorkys where the Phaeacians disembarked and laid the sleeping Odysseus on the sand.

The location of Odysseus' palace has been much disputed and archaeologists have been unable to find conclusive evidence. Schliemann erroneously believed it was near Vathy, whereas present-day archaeologists speculate it was on a hill near Stavros.

Anogi Fourteen kilometres north of Vathy, Anogi was the old capital. Its church of Agia Panagia has beautiful frescoes. Ask for Gerasimos who has the key.

Stavros In this village, 17km north-west of Ithaki Town, there's a small **archaeological museum**. It's open 9.30 am to 2 pm Tuesday to Sunday. Admission is free. *Villa St Ilias (☎ 31 751)* near the museum has lovely rooms with bathroom for 12,500 dr. From Stavros it's 1km to the **Bay of Polis**, which has a stony beach.

Frikes This charming fishing village with wind-swept cliffs is 1.5km in the opposite direction. Kiki Travel Agency (☎ 31 726, fax 31 387), owned by helpful Angeliki Digaletou, has a range of services including moped hire.

Kiki Domatia (☎ 31 726) has tastefully furnished, spotless double rooms for 12,000 dr with bathroom. *Raftopoulos Rooms (☎ 31 733)*, 1km away in a quiet rural setting, has clean doubles/triples for 8000/9500 dr. Inquire about these at Restaurant Ulysses. The well kept C class *Hotel Nostos (☎ 31 644/716)*, in lovely verdant country-side behind the village, has spacious, modern singles/doubles for 13,000/17,000 dr and friendly, helpful owners.

Symposium Restaurant, owned by two friendly sisters, serves imaginative fare including local dishes from their grandmother's recipes. *Restaurant Ulysses* on the waterfront does fresh fish and lobster which you choose from a large tank.

Kioni Four kilometres south-east of Frikes, Kioni is perhaps one of Ithaki's better-kept secrets. It is a small village draped around a verdant hillside spilling down to a picturesque little harbour where yachties congregate. There are tavernas and a couple of bars, though it's not the best place to swim. Instead, seek out the little bays between Kioni and Frikes.

Kioni's cheapest accommodation is *Maroudas Apartments (☎ 31 691, fax 31 753)*, opposite the doctor's surgery. Immaculate double/triple studios are 12,000/16,000 dr. Farther back up the hill, the well maintained, beautifully furnished *Dellaportas Apartments (☎ 31 481, fax 31 090)* have spacious double studios with TV and phone for 12,000 dr and four-person apartments for 20,000 dr.

Zakynthos Ζάκυνθος

☎ 0695 • postcode 291 00 • pop 32,560

Zakynthos (**zahk**-in-thos) has inspired many superlatives. The Venetians called it Fior' di Levante (flower of the orient). The poet Dionysios Solomos wrote that 'Zakynthos could make one forget the Elysian Fields'. Indeed, it is an island of exceptional natural beauty and outstanding beaches.

Unfortunately, Zakynthos' coastline has been the victim of the most unacceptable manifestations of package tourism. The lack of general budget accommodation and a rapacious attitude to tourism on the part of islanders make Zakynthos the least attractive of the Ionian Islands as a destination for independent travellers. Even worse, tourism is endangering the loggerhead turtle,

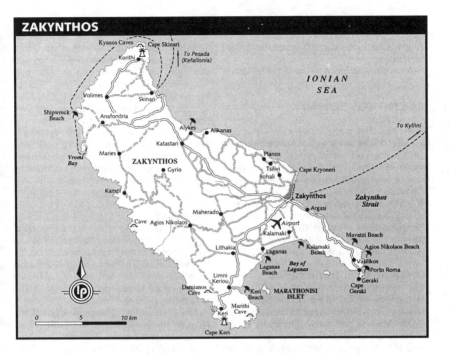

ZAKYNTHOS

Caretta caretta (see the boxed text later in this section), and the Mediterranean monk seal, *Monachus monachus* (see the boxed text earlier in this chapter).

Getting There & Away

Air There is one daily flight from Zakynthos to Athens (17,400 dr). The Olympic Airways office (☎ 28 611) in Zakynthos Town is at Alexandrou Roma 16. You can call the airport on ☎ 28 322.

Bus There are five or more buses daily from Zakynthos Town to Patras (3½ hours, 2860 dr). The same bus continues on to Athens (seven hours, 6310 dr). Ticket price includes the ferry fare.

Ferry Depending on the season, between three and seven ferries daily operate from Zakynthos Town to Kyllini, in the Peloponnese (1½ hours, 1400 dr). Tickets can be obtained from the Zakynthos Shipping Cooperative (☎ 41 500, fax 48 301) at Lombardou 40 in Zakynthos Town.

From Skinari the F/B *Ionion Pelagos* shuttles across to Pesada on Kefallonia from May to October (two hours, 1025 dr). There is inexplicably no bus from Pesada to anywhere else on Kefallonia. Check with the port police (☎ 42 417) for the times of the Skinari-Pesada ferries, though in general there are two departures daily from Skinari at 9.15 am and 7 pm.

Getting Around

There is no shuttle service between Zakynthos Town and the airport, 6km to the southwest. A taxi costs 1400 dr.

Frequent buses go from Zakynthos Town's modern bus station (☎ 22 255) to Alykes (320 dr), Tsilivi (230 dr), Argasi

(230 dr) and Laganas (230 dr). Bus services to other villages are poor (one or two daily). Check the current schedule at the bus station.

A motorcycle and car hire outlet is Moto Stakis, at Dimokratias 3, Zakynthos Town.

ZAKYNTHOS TOWN
• pop 10,250

Zakynthos Town is the capital and port of the island. The town was devastated by the 1953 earthquake but was reconstructed with its former layout preserved in wide arcaded streets, imposing squares and gracious neoclassical public buildings. It is hardly cosy, given its strung-out feel, but it is a reasonable place for an overnight stop and in comparison to many of the overtouristed parts of the island there is at least a semblance of Greekness left in the town.

Orientation & Information

The central Plateia Solomou is on the waterfront of Lombardou, opposite the ferry quay. Another large square, Plateia Agiou Markou, is nearby. The bus station is on Filita, one block back from the waterfront and south of the quay. The main thoroughfare is Alexandrou Roma, parallel to the waterfront and several blocks inland.

Zakynthos Town has no tourist office. The helpful tourist police (☎ 27 367) are at Lombardou 62.

The National Bank of Greece is just west of Plateia Solomou, while directly opposite is a Commercial Bank with an ATM. The post office is at Tertseti 27, one block west of Alexandrou Roma. The OTE phone office is on Plateia Solomou. Zakynthos' hospital (☎ 22 514) is west of town.

The Top's Internet Cafe (☎ 26 650) is at Filita 34, near the bus station.

Museums

The **Museum of Solomos**, on Plateia Agiou Markou, is dedicated to Dionysios Solomos (1798-1857), who was born on Zakynthos. His work *Hymn to Liberty* became the stirring Greek national anthem. Solomos is regarded as the father of modern Greek poetry, because he was the first to use Demotic Greek rather than Katharevousa. This museum houses memorabilia associated with his life, as well as displays pertaining to the poets Andreas Kalvos (1792-1869) and Ugo Foskolo (1778-1827), also born on Zakynthos. Opening times are 9 am to 2 pm daily. Entrance is free.

The **neo-Byzantine museum**, on Plateia Solomou, houses an impressive collection of ecclesiastical art which was rescued from churches razed in the earthquake. Opening times are 8 am to 2.30 pm Tuesday to Sunday; admission is 500 dr.

Churches

At the southern end of town, the **Church of Agios Dionysios** is named after the island's patron saint and contains the saint's relics in a silver coffer. This is paraded around the streets during the festivals held in his honour on 24 August and 17 December. The church has notable frescoes.

The 16th century **Church of Agios Nikolaos**, on Plateia Solomou, was built in Italian Renaissance style. Partially destroyed in the earthquake, it has been carefully reconstructed.

Organised Tours

The KTEL has a 'round Zakynthos Island' tour which costs 3000 dr. Inquire at the bus station. There are many round-island boat tours operating from the northern end of the waterfront, but boat tours which visit Langadas and the blue cave should be avoided as they disturb the loggerhead turtles and monk seals.

Places to Stay

The nearest camp site to Zakynthos Town is *Zante Camping* (☎ 61 710) at Tsilivi, 5km away while 8km south-west of the port is *Camping Laganas* (☎ 22 292) at Agios Sostis.

The clean *Rent Rooms* (☎ 26 012, *Alexandrou Roma 40*) are 6000/8000 dr for singles/doubles. Enter from Spyrou Gouskou. *Athina Rooms* (☎ 45 194, *Tzoulati 29*) are simply furnished, costing 5000/10,000 dr.

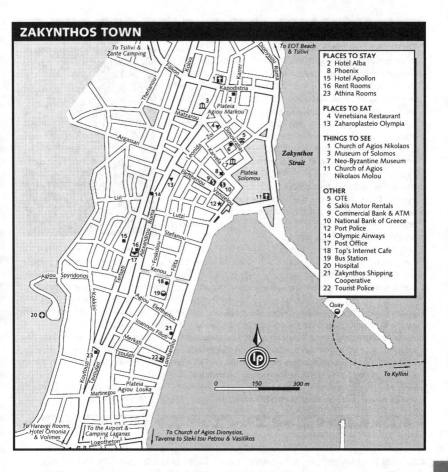

ZAKYNTHOS TOWN

PLACES TO STAY
2 Hotel Alba
8 Phoenix
15 Hotel Apollon
16 Rent Rooms
23 Athina Rooms

PLACES TO EAT
4 Venetsiana Restaurant
13 Zaharoplasteio Olympia

THINGS TO SEE
1 Church of Agios Nikolaos
3 Museum of Solomos
7 Neo-Byzantine Museum
11 Church of Agios
Nikolaos Molou

OTHER
5 OTE
6 Sakis Motor Rentals
9 Commercial Bank & ATM
10 National Bank of Greece
12 Port Police
14 Olympic Airways
17 Post Office
18 Top's Internet Cafe
19 Bus Station
20 Hospital
21 Zakynthos Shipping
Cooperative
22 Tourist Police

The pleasant *Haravgi Rooms* (☎ 23 629, *Xanthopoulou 4*) has doubles/triples with bathroom for 9000/10,000 dr. Opposite, *Hotel Omonia* (☎ 22 113, *Xanthopoulou 7*) has rates of 10,000/12,500 dr. Walk south along Alexandrou Roma, at the fork head right along Agiou Lazarou, and Xanthopoulou is 250m along on the left.

The small *Hotel Apollon* (☎ 42 838, *Tertseti 30*) with its unsmiling owner will do as an alternative resort. Its single/double rooms are 9000/13,000 dr.

The C class *Phoenix* (☎ 23 514, 45 083, *Plateia Solomou 2*), close to the ferry quay, has standard rooms for 10,000/15,000 dr. Farther back and just off Plateia Agiou Markou is the B class *Hotel Alba* (☎ 26 641, *fax 26 642, 1 Ziva 38*), which is good value with rates of 11,000/12,000 dr for small but adequate rooms.

Places to Eat

Cafes featuring *mandolato*, a local nougat sweet, are on Alexandrou Roma. Try the

Loggerhead Turtles

The loggerhead turtle *(Caretta caretta)* is one of Europe's most beautiful yet most endangered marine species. In Greece the loggerhead turtle nests on two of the Ionian Islands, on the Peloponnese coast and in Crete. It prefers large tracts of clean, flat and uninhabited sand. So too do basking tourists from northern Europe and it is this fateful convergence of interests that has led to the turtle being placed under the threat of extinction.

The female turtle lays about 120 eggs the size of ping-pong balls in the sand in preferred sites. After laying her eggs she returns to the sea and the eggs must lie undisturbed for up to 60 days before the hatchlings emerge. For at least 150 million years the turtle has survived geological and climatic changes but the change now placed on to its environment by modern mass tourism has rung alarm bells within the conservation world.

Zakynthos in the Ionian Islands hosts the largest congregation of nests. There are some 1300 nests along the Bay of Laganas on the island's south coast alone. In recent years this popular resort has come under repeated fire with conservation lobbies clashing with local authorities and businesses involved in the lucrative tourist trade. Operators who make handsome profits from renting out beach umbrellas and sun beds have attracted particular criticism. Umbrella poles indiscriminately destroy eggs and nests and the very coexistence of humans anywhere near the nesting sites is totally counterproductive to the turtles' survival.

As a visitor to Greece you can assist the deteriorating situation by completely avoiding beaches where loggerhead turtles nest. In Zakynthos this means Daphni, Sekania, Gerakas, Kalamaki and Laganas beaches as well as the islet of Marathonisi. In Kefallonia, where turtles are less common, Mounda Beach should be avoided at all costs.

For further information on the turtles get in touch with the conservation group MEDASSET (email medasset@hol.gr) at 24 Park Towers, 2 Brick St, London W1Y 7DF, UK.

traditional *Zaharoplasteio Olympia* for sheep's milk yogurt and rice pudding. *Venetsiana Restaurant (Plateia Agiou Markou 8)* is the best restaurant on the central square, with excellent pizzas featuring prominently. The untouristy *Taverna To Steki tou Petrou*, 150m south of Agios Dionysios on Lombardou, serves delicious, reasonably priced food.

AROUND ZAKYNTHOS

Loggerhead turtles come ashore to lay their eggs on the golden sand beaches of the huge Bay of Laganas, on Zakynthos' south coast.

Laganas is a highly developed, tacky resort and is a truly dreadful place to spend a holiday unless you like lager and loud discos and would rather be in the UK than Greece. Avoid it like the plague, or at least drop by to see how Mammon and mass tourism have met in the most abominable set of circumstances.

Kalamaki is not much quieter and even Geraki, where the highest number of turtles lay their eggs, has not been spared water sports. The turtles also nest on nearby Marathonisi Islet. You may decide to avoid these beaches for the turtles' sakes and to bypass the commercialism.

Vasilikos and **Porto Roma**, south of Zakynthos Town, both have crowded sand beaches but are less developed than those of Laganas. **Agios Nikolaos Beach** at the end of the peninsula has great (turtle-free) water sport facilities and a few domatia and studios, and is where the more discerning Greek youth hangs out in the summer.

The famous **Shipwreck Beach** (Navagio) is at the north-western tip of the island. It truly is a splendid beach with crystalline, aquamarine waters. But unless you have your own boat, it can only be visited by excursion boat, best undertaken from the little harbour of **Vromi Bay** which in turn is reachable by a decently powered motorbike or scooter from **Anafonitria**. Take a picnic since there are no facilities on the beach.

You can escape from the tourist hype by visiting inland farming villages. The village of **Maherado** has the impressive 14th century church of Agia Mavra. **Agios Nikolaos** is an attractive village. The drive north from here to **Maries** is through splendid hilly country. Make an effort to visit the little village of **Gyrio** in the centre of the island where there is a cosy *taverna* with live *arekia* (traditional Zakynthian ballads) music on weekends. It is patronised mainly by Greeks in the know.

Kythira & Antikythira

KYTHIRA Κύθηρα
☎ 0735 • pop 3100

The island of Kythira (kee-thih-rah) is to many Greeks the Holy Grail of island-hopping. The 'Road to Kythira', a well known 1973 song by Dimitris Mitropanos, epitomises what for most people is the end of the line that is never reached. Indeed Kythira can be a hard place to get to – mentally, if not physically – since you have to make a special effort just to get there.

Some 30km long and 18km wide, Kythira dangles off the Laconian Peninsula

of the Peloponnese between the often turbulent Ionian and Aegean seas. It is a curiously barren island in parts, with misty moors, winding lanes backed by low stone walls and hidden valleys that rent the dreamy landscape. More than forty villages are scattered evenly across the island, and ghosts are said to roam the inland villages. Kythira was part of the British Ionian Protectorate for many years, evidenced by the sprinkling of arched stone bridges around the island.

Kythira is the least 'Ionian' of the Ionian island group. Physically separated from its nearest neighbour Zakynthos by a long stretch of sea, it is administered from Piraeus and mostly resembles the Cyclades in appearance and architecture.

Mythology suggests that it is in Kythira that Aphrodite was born. She is supposed to have risen from the foam where Zeus had thrown Cronos' sex organ after castrating him. The goddess of love then re-emerged near Paphos in Cyprus, so both islands haggle over her birthplace.

The EOT has begun encouraging tourists to visit Kythira but it's still unspoilt. Its attractions are its relatively undeveloped and excellent beaches, its enduring feel as a special island and the fact that it is 'the end of the line'.

Kythira's main port is Agia Pelagia, though hydrofoils depart from and arrive at the custom-built port of Diakofti. Public transport on Kythira ranges from abysmal to nonexistent, so bringing your own wheels or renting them locally is advisable.

Getting There & Away

Air There are flights to Athens (45 minutes, 14,400 dr) every day except Thursday. The Olympic Airways office (**☎** 33 362) is on the central square in Potamos. Book also at Kythira Travel (**☎** 31 390) in Hora. The airport is 10km east of Potamos.

Ferry The modern car ferry F/B *Maria* of Golden Ferries sails from Agia Pelagia to Gythio in the Peloponnese twice daily during summer (two hours, 1600 dr), with

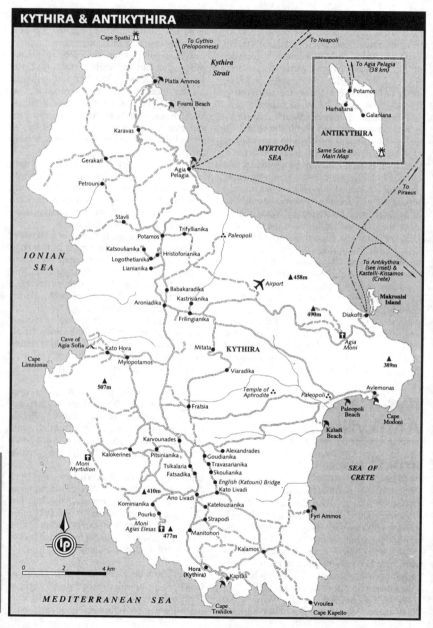

KYTHIRA & ANTIKYTHIRA

Cape Spathi

To Gythio (Peloponnese)

To Neapoli

Kythira Strait

Platia Ammos

Fourni Beach

To Agia Pelagia (38 km)

Potamos

Harhaliana

Galaniana

ANTIKYTHIRA

Same Scale as Main Map

Karavas

Gerakari

MYRTOÖN SEA

Agia Pelagia

Petrouni

To Piraeus

Stavli

IONIAN SEA

Potamos

Trifyllianika

Paleopoli

Katsoulianika

Hristoforianika

Logothetianika

Lianianika

To Antikythira (see inset) & Kastelli-Kissamos (Crete)

Babakaradika

Kastrisianika

▲458m

Airport

Makronisi Island

Aroniadika

▲490m

Diakofti

Frilingianika

Cave of Agia Sofia

Kato Hora

Mitata

KYTHIRA

Agia Moni

Cape Limnionas

Mylopotamos

Viaradika

▲389m

▲507m

Fratsia

Temple of Aphrodite

Paleopoli

Avlemonas

Paleopoli Beach

Cape Modoni

Kaladi Beach

Karvounades

Kalokerines

Alexandrades

Moni Myrtidion

Pitsinianika

Goudianika

Travasarianika

Tsikalaria

Skoulianika

Fatsadika

English (Katouni) Bridge

SEA OF CRETE

▲410m

Kato Livadi

Ano Livadi

Kominianika

Katelouzianika

Pourko

Moni Agias Elesas

Strapodi

Fyri Ammos

▲477m

Manitohori

Kalamos

Hora (Kythira)

Kapsali

0   2   4 km

MEDITERRANEAN SEA

Cape Trahilos

Vroulea

Cape Kapello

twice-weekly connections to Antikythira (two hours, 2000 dr) and Kasteli in Crete (4½ hours, 4000 dr). Schedules and times are often subject to delays so check at Agia Pelagia's Megalokonomou Shipping Agency (☎ 33 490, fax 33 890).

The older *Nisos Kythira* run by BOIAI Lines shuttles between Agia Pelagia, Neapoli (one hour, 1500 dr) and Gythio (two hours, 1600 dr). A newer ship may be in operation by the time you read this. Tickets are sold at the quay before departure, or at the BOIAI office in Potamos.

The port police (☎ 33 280) are at Agia Pelagia on the waterfront.

Hydrofoil In summer, there are five hydrofoils weekly from Diakofti on Kythira to Piraeus (five hours, 10,300 dr) via Monemvasia, Spetses and Hydra. Tickets are available from Kythira Travel in Hora, or Megalokonomou Shipping Agency in Agia Pelagia.

Getting Around

Bus Kythira's bus service is designed to ferry schoolchildren to and from school. Outside of term times it is nonexistent. During school terms a couple of services link Agia Pelagia with Kapsali twice daily – before school in the morning and in the early afternoon when school is out. There is no airport bus. Not surprisingly, Kythira has many taxis and a taxi from Agia Pelagia to Kapsali will cost around 4000 dr. Hitching is fairly easy.

Car & Motorcycle Panayiotis, at Moto Rent (☎ 31 600) on Kapsali's waterfront, rents cars, jeeps, mopeds and motorcycles. Easy Rider (☎ 33 486) rents motorbikes at Agia Pelagia.

Agia Pelagia Αγία Πελαγία
• pop 280
Kythira's northern port of Agia Pelagia is a simple, friendly waterfront village ideal for relaxing, swimming and finding peace of mind. A room-finding office (no telephone) is at the top of the quay, and operates in

high season. Lia at Megalokonomou Shipping Agency, opposite the quay, happily assists newcomers.

Mixed sand and pebble beaches are to either side of the quay.

Places to Stay – Budget Prebooking in high season is almost essential in Agia Pelagia. One of the friendliest and most pleasant places to stay is the domatia of *Georgos Kambouris* (☎ 33 480). His wife, Maria, maintains spotless, airy doubles/ triples for 12,000/14,000 dr. The building is just in front of Hotel Romantica.

Opposite the quay above Faros Taverna, *Alexandra Megalopoulou's Rooms* (☎ 33 282) are tidy, simply furnished and with bathroom for 12,500 dr a double.

The welcoming D class *Hotel Kytheria* (☎ 33 321, 33 825), owned by helpful Angelo from Australia, has very comfortable, tidy singles/doubles with bathroom for 13,000/17,000 dr. Considerable discounts to the above prices apply out of high season.

Places to Stay – Mid-Range & Top End *Filoxenia Apartments* (☎ 33 100, fax 33 610) each have a bedroom, lounge and kitchen. However, the interior layout is a little claustrophobic. An attached pool makes up for this. Rates for doubles/quads are 22,000/26,000 dr. Two-bedroom units for four/six people are 26,000 dr. Turn left then right from the quay.

Hotel Romantica (☎ 33 834, fax 33 915) has stunning, sparkling self-contained apartments for four (32,000 dr) and double air-con studios with TV and phone for 25,000 dr. There is also a swimming pool. Turn right from the quay and look for the sign after 600m.

Another good place is *Venardos Hotel* (☎ 34 205, fax 33 850, email venardos@ mail.otenet.gr), where airy singles/doubles are 18,000/22,000 dr. Australians get a special welcome and the hotel is open all year.

Kythira's sole A class hotel, *Hotel Marou* (☎ 33 466, fax 33 497), with the island's only tennis court, a bar, snack bar and laundry, is above the north-west end of the village. Doubles are between 18,000 dr and 24,000 dr.

Places to Eat The blue and white *Faros Taverna* close to the quay serves good, economical Greek staples. To the far right, *Ouzeri Moustakias*, next to the minimarket, offers food ranging from mezedes to seafood. *Kaleris*, in between the two, is a tasteful little eatery with old photographs and painted wooden signs on the wall. The speciality is roast wild goat.

For breakfast *Sempreviva Patisserie* close by serves wickedly delicious Greek cakes and jugs of freshly brewed coffee.

Bar life revolves around *En Plo*, *Oionos* and *Mouragio*, all neat little bars slotted in between the eateries.

Potamos Ποταμός
• pop 680

Potamos, 10km from Agia Pelagia, is the island's commercial hub. On Sunday it attracts almost every islander to market. The National Bank of Greece is on the central square. The post office and police are south of the central square, and the OTE is 150m north.

The only domatia are those of *Panayiotis Alevizopoulos* (☎ 33 245) whose neat doubles are 13,000 dr. The one hotel is *Hotel Porfyra* (☎ 33 329), where self-contained units surround an internal courtyard. Doubles/triples are 11,500/14,000 dr.

Taverna Panaretos (☎ 34 290) on the central square serves well prepared international and Greek dishes.

Mylopotamos Μυλοπόταμος
• pop 90

Mylopotamos is an alluring, verdant village. Its central square is flanked by a much-photographed church and kafeneio. Stroll to the **Neraïda** (water nymph) waterfall. From the square, continue along the road and take the right fork. After 100m, a path on the right leads to the waterfall. It's magical, with luxuriant greenery and mature, shady trees.

To reach the abandoned **kastro** of Mylopotamos, take the left fork after the church

and follow the sign for Kato Hora (lower village). The road leads to the centre of Kato Hora, from where a portal with the insignia of St Mark leads into the spooky kastro, with derelict houses and well preserved little churches (locked).

The **Cave of Agia Sofia** was first explored by the famous speleologists Ioannis and Anna Patrohilos, who also discovered the Diros Cave in the Peloponnese. In the 12th century, the cave was converted into a chapel and dedicated to Agia Sophia. Legend says she visited the cave with her daughters Pistis, Elpis and Haris (Faith, Hope and Charity). The cave is reached by a precipitous 2km road or a steep path from Mylopotamos. Irregular opening times are pinned on a signpost to the cave beyond Mylopotamos' square. Admission is 500 dr and includes a guided tour.

Hora Χώρα
• postcode 801 00 • pop 550

Hora (or Kythira; Κύθηρα), the pretty capital, with white, blue-shuttered houses, perches on a long, slender ridge 2km uphill from Kapsali. The central square, planted with hibiscus, bougainvillea and palms, is Plateia Dimitriou Staï. The main street runs south of it. The post office is on the left, at its southern end. The OTE is up the steps beside Kythira Travel on the central square.

The National Bank of Greece is on the central square. Next to it is the Agricultural Bank which sports an ATM. The police station (☎ 31 206) is near the kastro.

Hora has no tourist office or tourist police but English-speaking Panayiotis offers information to tourists at his Moto Rent office (☎ 31 600) on Kapsali's waterfront.

Things to See Hora's Venetian **kastro** is at the southern end of town. If you walk to its southern extremity, passing the Church of Panagia, you will come to a sheer cliff. From here there is a stunning view of Kapsali and on a good day of Antikythira.

The **museum** is north of the central square. It features gravestones of British soldiers and their infants who died on the island in the 19th century. (Hora was part of the British Ionian Protectorate from 1815 to 1864.) A large stone lion is exhibited and a sweet terracotta figurine of a woman and child. The museum is open 8.45 am to 3 pm Tuesday to Saturday and 8.30 am to 2.30 pm Sunday. Admission is free.

Places to Stay Hora's cheapest accommodation is to be found at *Georgiou Psi Rooms (☎ 31 070)*, where doubles are 8,000 dr. Walk south along the main street and look for the sign on the left.

Castello Rooms (☎/fax 31 069) are spacious, and have kitchens, bathrooms and terraces with breathtaking views. Rates are 9000 dr a double. There's a sign at the southern end of the main street. *Papadonicos Rooms (☎ 31 129)*, a bit farther south, has pleasant double studios for 9000 dr. *Belvedere Apartments (☎/fax 31 761)*, just beyond the turn-off for Kapsali, features attractive apartments for 12,000 dr. It has terrific views of Kapsali.

The B class *Hotel Margarita (☎ 31 711, fax 31 325)*, on the main street, is a renovated 19th century mansion. Rates are 15,200/19,300 dr for singles/doubles with breakfast. Air-con rooms have TV and telephone.

Places to Eat There are not a lot of restaurant choices in Hora, but 100m south of the square is *Zorba's Taverna (Spyridonos Staï 34)* which offers tasty grilled food. On the square itself, *La Frianderie* on Plateia Staï is a hip place serving savoury and sweet crepes and snacks. Also on the square, *Vengera Cafe* serves evening snacks in summer.

Kapsali Καψάλι
• postcode 801 00   • pop 70

Kapsali is a picturesque village located down a winding road from Hora. It looks particularly captivating from Hora's castle, with its twin sandy bays and curving waterfront. Restaurants and cafes line the beach, and safe sheltered swimming in aquamarine waters is Kapsali's trademark. Not surprisingly, this is a very popular place so

accommodation can be scarce unless you book well beforehand. It can also get pretty crowded so if you like your beach in solitude look elsewhere.

Offshore you can see the stark rock island known as the **Avgo** (Egg) rearing above the water. It is here that the Kytherians claim Aphrodite sprang from the sea.

Canoes, pedal boats, surf boards and water-skis can be hired from Panayiotis at Moto Rent, on the waterfront. Kapsali's port police (☎ 31 222) are next door.

Places to Stay & Eat Kythira's camp site, *Camping Kapsali (☎ 31 580)*, is pine-shaded and open in summer only. The site is 400m from Kapsali's quay and signposted from the inland road to Hora.

Irene Megaloudi's Rooms (☎ 31 340) has clean doubles/triples with bathroom for 10,000/12,000 dr. At *Poulmendis Rooms (☎ 31 451)* clean, pleasant rooms with bathroom cost 12,000/15,000 dr. Both are on the waterfront.

Rigas Apartments (☎ 31 365, fax 31 265) are more expensive. The accommodation, in a cluster of white terraced buildings back from the waterfront, ranges from beautifully furnished double studios for 22,000 dr to two-bedroom maisonettes for 38,000 dr.

There are three restaurants on the seafront road of Kytherias Afroditis. The first, heading towards Hora, is the *Artena*, noticeable for its striking blue chairs and tables. In operation since 1935, it has a wide range of ready-made and to-order fish dishes at mid-range prices. The *Venetsianiko* farther along serves a wide range of Greek dishes, pasta and fish, and the lively *Ydragogio* at the far end by the rocks specialises in fish and mezedes.

Around Kythira

If you have transport, a tour round the island is rewarding. The monasteries of **Agia Moni** and **Agia Elesa** are mountain refuges with superb views. **Moni Myrtidion** is a beautiful monastery surrounded by trees. From Hora, drive north-east to the picturesque village of **Avlemonas** via **Paleopoli** with its wide, pebbled beach. Here, archaeologists spent years searching for evidence of a temple at Aphrodite's birthplace.

Just north of the village of Kato Livadi make a detour to see the remarkable, and seemingly out of place, British-made **Katouni Bridge**, a legacy of Kythira's time as part of the British Protectorate in the 19th century. In the far north of the island the village of **Karavas** is verdant and very attractive and close to both Agia Pelagia and the reasonable beach at **Platia Ammos**. Beachcombers should seek out **Kaladi Beach**, near Paleopoli. Another good beach is **Fyri Ammos**, closer to Hora.

While heading out across the island, stop in at *Estiatorion Pierros (☎ 31 014)* in **Ano Livadi**. Here you will find no-nonsense traditional Greek staples in a great little roadside establishment. The *Karydies Taverna (☎ 33 664)* in **Logothetianika**, near Potamos, attracts a good crowd to its weekend music evenings. Bookings are recommended. When the mist is up and sweeping across the island stop by the little *Ouzeri-Kafeneio Grigoraki (☎ 33 971)* on the main road in

Aroniadika and partake of an ouzo and mezedes. It can get quite spooky in this little village around which ghosts are reported to roam on dark and windy winter's evenings.

ANTIKYTHIRA Αντικύθηρα
* pop 70

The tiny island of Antikythira, 38km southeast of Kythira, is the most remote island in the Ionian group. It has only one settlement, **Potamos**, one doctor, one police officer, one teacher (with five pupils), one metered telephone and a monastery. It has no post office or bank. The only accommodation for tourists is 10 basic *rooms* in two purpose-built blocks, open in summer only. Potamos has a *kafeneio* and *taverna*.

The F/B *Maria* calls at least twice weekly in the early hours on the way to Crete, returning the same day to Kythira and Gythio. If the sea is choppy, the ferry does not stop, so this is not an island for tourists on a tight schedule. Check conditions in Piraeus if you intend to come direct, or with Megalokonomou Shipping Agency in Kythira's Agia Pelagia.

Evia & the Sporades

Evia (Εύβοια), Greece's second-largest island, is so close to the mainland historically, physically and topographically that one tends not to regard it as an island at all. Athenians regard Evia as a convenient destination for a weekend break, so consequently it gets packed. Except for the resort of Eretria, however, it is not frequently visited by foreign tourists.

The Sporades (Οι Σποράδες) lie to the north and east of Evia and to the east and south-east of the Pelion Peninsula, to which they were joined in prehistoric times. With their dense vegetation and mountainous terrain, they seem like a continuation of this peninsula. There are 11 islands in the archipelago, four of which are inhabited: Skiathos, Skopelos, Alonnisos and Skyros. The first two have a highly developed tourist industry, whereas Alonnisos and Skyros, although by no means remote, are far less visited and retain more local character.

Getting There & Away

Air Skiathos airport receives charter flights from northern Europe and there are also domestic flights to Athens. Skyros airport has domestic flights to Athens and occasional charter flights from the Netherlands.

Bus From Athens' Terminal B bus station there are buses every half-hour to Halkida from 5.45 am to 9.45 pm (one hour, 1350 dr), three daily to Kymi from 6 am to 7 pm (3¼ hours, 2950 dr), and three daily to Loutra Edipsou (3½ hours, 2800 dr).

From the Mavromateon terminal in Athens, there are buses every 45 minutes to Rafina (for Karystos and Marmari; one hour, 460 dr).

Train There are hourly trains each day from Athens' Larisis station to Halkida (1½ hours, 700 dr).

HIGHLIGHTS

- The changing tides of the Evripous channel in Evia that so puzzled Aristotle

- Skiathos' golden beaches – among the best in Greece

- Getting delightfully lost in the labyrinthine streets of picturesque Skopelos Town

- Quirky Skyros and pretty Skyrian houses – Greece's hidden island treasure

- Nature walks, fine food and *rembetika* music on clean and green Skopelos

- Relaxing on Alonnisos, one of the Aegean's greenest and most underrated islands and mingling with artists and poets in restored Hora

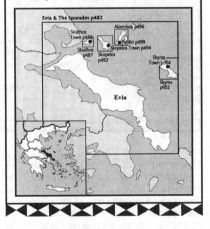

Ferry The table following gives an overall view of the available ferries to this island group from mainland ports in high season. Further details and inter-island links can be found under each island entry.

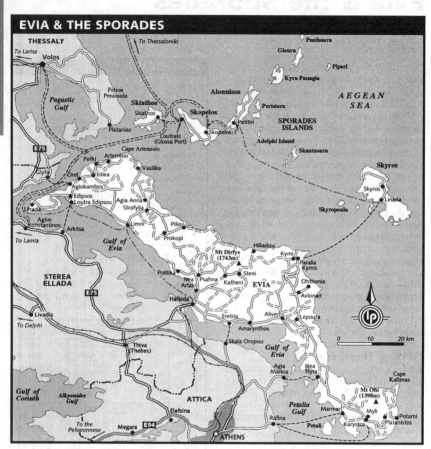

EVIA & THE SPORADES

Hydrofoil Hydrofoil links by and large follow similar routes as the ferries, except for the Evia (Kymi) to Skyros (Linaria) link. The table following gives an overall view of the hydrofoil connections in high season. Further details and inter-island links can be found under each island entry. The summer hydrofoil timetable is usually available in late April from Minoan Flying Dolphin (☎ 01-428 0001, fax 428 3526), Akti Themistokleous 8, Piraeus GR-185 36. The Athens office (☎ 01-324 4600) is at Filelli-

non 3. The timetable is also available from local hydrofoil booking offices.

Getting Around

Halkida is the transport hub of Evia. There are buses to the port of Kymi (2½ hours, 1650 dr, nine daily) via Eretria and Kymi town; to Steni (45 minutes, 650 dr, six daily); and to Karystos (3½ hours, 2250 dr, three daily) via Eretria. There are also buses to Limni (2½ hours, 1500 dr, four daily). Timetables are outside the ticket office.

Ferry & Hydrofoil Connections to Evia & the Sporades

Ferries

Origin	Destination	Duration	Price	Frequency
Agia Marina	Evia (Nea Styra)	40 mins	650 dr	5 daily
Agios Konstantinos	Alonnisos	5½ hours	4400 dr	1 daily
Agios Konstantinos	Skiathos	3½ hours	3220 dr	2 daily
Agios Konstantinos	Skopelos	4½ hours	4100 dr	4 daily
Arkitsa	Evia (Edipsos)	1 hour	690 dr	12 daily
Kymi	Skyros	2¼ hours	2300 dr	2 daily
Rafina	Evia (Karystos)	1¾ hours	1768 dr	2 daily
Rafina	Evia (Marmari)	1¼ hours	1239 dr	4 daily
Skala Oropou	Evia (Eretria)	30 mins	310 dr	half-hourly
Thessaloniki	Skiathos	6½ hours	4500 dr	3 weekly
Thessaloniki	Skopelos	6 hours	4600 dr	3 weekly
Volos	Alonnisos	5 hours	3700 dr	3 daily
Volos	Skiathos	3½ hours	2750 dr	4 daily
Volos	Skopelos	4½ hours	3380 dr	4 daily

Hydrofoils

Origin	Destination	Duration	Price	Frequency
Agios Konstantinos	Alonnisos	2½ hours	8800 dr	3 daily
Agios Konstantinos	Skiathos	1½ hours	6600 dr	3 daily
Agios Konstantinos	Skopelos	2¼ hours	8200 dr	3 daily
Thessaloniki	Alonnisos	4½ hours	11,700 dr	1 daily
Thessaloniki	Skiathos	3½ hours	8500 dr	6 weekly
Thessaloniki	Skopelos	4¾ hours	9300 dr	1 daily
Thessaloniki	Skyros	6¼ hours	13,400 dr	4 weekly
Volos	Alonnisos	2½ hours	7500 dr	5 daily
Volos	Skiathos	1¼ hours	5500 dr	4 daily
Volos	Skopelos	2¼ hours	6800 dr	5 daily
Volos	Skyros	4¼ hours	14,100 dr	5 weekly

Evia Εύβοια

The island of Evia (**eh**-vih-ah) will probably never be a prime destination for foreign tourists, but if you're based in Athens with a few days to spare, and (preferably) your own transport, a foray into Evia is well worthwhile for its scenic mountain roads, pristine inland villages, and a look at some resorts which cater for Greeks (including one for ailing Greeks), rather than for foreign tourists.

A mountainous spine runs north-south; the east coast consists of precipitous cliffs, whereas the gentler west coast has a string of beaches and resorts. The island is reached overland by a bridge over the Evripous channel to the island's capital, Halkida. At the mention of Evia, most Greeks will eagerly tell you that the current in this narrow channel changes direction around seven times daily, which it does, if you are prepared to hang around to watch it. The next bit of the story, that Aristotle became so perplexed at not finding an explanation for this mystifying occurrence that he threw himself into the channel and drowned, can almost certainly be taken with a grain of salt.

HALKIDA Χαλκίδα

☎ 0221 • postcode 341 00 • pop 45,000
Halkida was an important city-state in ancient times, with several colonies dotted around the Mediterranean. The name derives from the bronze manufactured here in antiquity (*halkos* means 'bronze' in Greek). Today it's a lively industrial and agricultural town, but with nothing of sufficient note to warrant an overnight stay.

However, if you have an hour or two to spare between buses then have a look at the **archaeological museum**, Leoforos Venizelou 13; it's worth a mosey around. It houses finds from Evia's three ancient cities of Halkida, Eretria and Karystos, including a chunk from the pediment of the Temple of Dafniforos Apollo at Eretria. The museum (☎ 25 131) is open 8.30 am to 3 pm Tuesday to Sunday; admission is 500 dr.

The Halkida train station is on the mainland side of the bridge. To reach central Halkida, turn right outside the train station, walk over the bridge, turn left and you will find Leoforos Venizelou, Halkida's main drag, off to the right.

The phone number of the Halkida tourist police is ☎ 87 000.

CENTRAL EVIA

Steni Στενή

☎ 0228 • postcode 340 03 • pop 1300
From Halkida it's 31km to the lovely mountain village of Steni, with gurgling springs and plane trees. The village has two hotels, both C class. *Hotel Dirfys* (☎ 51 217) has singles/doubles for 5000/9500 dr. *Hotel Steni* (☎ 51 221, fax 51 325) has rooms for 7000/10,000 dr with bathroom.

For a meal, look for *Sakaflias* (☎ 51 205) restaurant on the main square. Try *tiganopsomo*, a kind of pan-fried cheese pie, and the house rosé. It shouldn't cost you more than 1900 dr.

Steni is the starting point for the climb up **Mt Dirfys** (1743m), which is Evia's highest mountain. The EOS-owned *Dirfys Refuge* (☎ 51 285), at 1120m, can be reached along a 9km dirt road, or after a two hour walk along a forest footpath. From the refuge it's two hours to the summit. For further information contact the EOS (☎ 0221-25 230), Angeli Gyviou 22, Halkida.

A partially sealed road continues from Steni to **Hiliadou**, on the north coast, where there is a fine beach.

Kymi Κύμη

☎ 0222 • postcode 340 03 • pop 3850
Kymi is a picturesque town built on a cliff 250m above the sea. The port of Kymi (called Paralia Kymis), 4km downhill, is the only natural harbour on the precipitous east coast, and the departure point for ferries to Skyros.

The **folklore museum** (☎ 22 011), on the road to Paralia Kymis, has an impressive collection of local costumes and memorabilia, including a display commemorating Kymi-born Dr George Papanikolaou, who invented the Pap smear test. Opening times are 5 pm to 7.30 pm Wednesday and Saturday and 10 am to 1 pm Sunday.

Paralia Kymis has two hotels, both C class. *Hotel Beis* (☎/fax 22 604) has singles/doubles for 10,000/12,000 dr, and *Hotel Corali* (☎ 22 212, fax 23 353) has rooms for 8500/9900 dr. This hotel is set back from the main road up a steep hill on the south side of Paralia Kymis. There are some *domatia* (☎ 23 896) in Kymi itself, on the left along the main Halkida road. Neat, clean rooms with TV go for 8000 dr.

Back in Paralia Kymis, the best place to eat is *To Egeo* (☎ 22 641) where you can dine under an awning overlooking the sea. It specialises in lobsters and prawns and does tasty platters.

NORTHERN EVIA

From Halkida a road heads north to **Psahna**, the gateway to the highly scenic mountainous interior of northern Evia. The road climbs through pine forests to the beautiful agricultural village of **Prokopi**, 52km from Halkida. The inhabitants are descendants of refugees who, in 1923, came from Prokopion (present-day Ürgüp) in Turkey, bringing with them the relics of St John the Russian. On 27 May (St John's festival), hordes of pilgrims come to worship his relics in the Church of Agios Ioannis Rosses.

At Strofylia, 14km beyond Prokopi, a road heads south-west to **Limni**, a pretty (but crowded) fishing village with whitewashed houses and a beach. With your own transport or a penchant for walking, you can visit the 16th century **Convent of Galataki**, 8km south-east of Limni. Its *katholikon* (main church) has fine frescoes. Limni has two hotels and some domatia. There's one camp site, *Rovies Camping (☎ 71 120)*, on the coast, 13km north-west of Limni.

The road continues to the sedate spa resort of **Loutra Edipsou** (119km from Halkida) whose therapeutic sulphur waters have been celebrated since antiquity. Many luminaries, including Aristotle, Plutarch, Strabo and Plinius, sang the praises of these waters. The waters are reputed to cure many ills, mostly of a rheumatic, arthritic or gynaecological nature. Today the town has Greece's most up-to-date hydrotherapy-physiotherapy centre. If you're interested, contact any EOT or the EOT Hydrotherapy-Physiotherapy Centre (☎ 23 500), Loutra Edipsou. Even if you don't rank among the infirm you may enjoy a visit to this resort with its attractive setting, a beach, many domatia and hotels.

SOUTHERN EVIA

Eretria Ερέτρια
☎ 0211 • postcode 340 08 • pop 5000
As you head east from Halkida, Eretria is the first major place of interest. Ancient Eretria was a major maritime power and also had an eminent school of philosophy. The city was destroyed in 87 AD during the Mithridatic War, fought between Mithridates (king of Pontos) and the Roman commander Sulla. The modern town was founded in the 1820s by islanders from

Psara fleeing the Turkish. Once Evia's major archaeological site, it has metamorphosed into a tacky resort patronised by British package tourists.

Things to See From the top of the **ancient acropolis**, at the northern end of town, there are splendid views over to the mainland. West of the acropolis are the remains of a palace, temple, and a theatre with a subterranean passage once used by actors. Close by, the **Museum of Eretria** (☎ 62 206) contains well displayed finds from ancient Eretria. Opening times are 8.30 am to 3 pm Tuesday to Sunday; admission is 500 dr. In the centre of town are the remains of the **Temple of Dafniforos Apollo** and a mosaic from an ancient bath.

Places to Stay Eretria has loads of *hotels* and *domatia*, and *Eva Camping (☎ 61 081)* is at Malakonda, 5km west along the coast. *Milos Camping (☎ 60 360)* is 1km west of Eretria town.

Karystos Κάρυστος
☎ 0224 • postcode 340 01 • pop 4500
Continuing east from Eretria, the road branches at Lepoura: the left fork leads to Kymi, the right to Karystos (**kah**-ris-tos). Set on the wide Karystian Bay, below Mt Ohi (1398m), Karystos is the most attractive of southern Evia's resorts. The town was designed on a grid system by the Bavarian architect Bierbach, who was commissioned by King Otho. If you turn right from the quay you will come to the remains of a 14th century Venetian castle, the **Bourtzi**, which has marble from a temple dedicated to Apollo incorporated into its walls. Beyond this there is a sandy beach; there is another at the other end of the waterfront.

Places to Stay & Eat Look for *domatia* signs or the three easy-to-find hotels on the waterfront. Opposite the ferry quay, the C class *Hotel Als (☎ 22 202)* has single/double rooms for 5800/11,400 dr. The ageing *Hotel Galaxy (☎ 22 600, fax 22 463)* is at the west end of Kriezotou, on the corner with

Omirou, with rooms for 8500/12,300 dr including breakfast. The pleasant *Hotel Karystion (☎ 22 391, fax 22 727, Kriezotou 2)* is 200m south of the Bourtzi. It has rooms for 13,000/18,000 dr, including breakfast.

The best place to get a bite to eat is the *Cavo d'Oro (☎ 22 326)*, Parodos Sahtouri, in an alleyway just off the main square. It is a traditional restaurant serving cheap, oil-based dishes *(ladera)* from 700 dr, with meat dishes for 1350 dr. On the seafront opposite the harbour the pick of the bunch is *Marinos Restaurant (☎ 24 126)* with ladera from 1000 dr and tasty local fish at 2600 dr.

Around Karystos

The ruins of **Castello Rossa** (red castle), a 13th century Frankish fortress, are a short walk from **Myli**, a delightful, well watered village 4km inland from Karystos. The aqueduct behind the castle once carried water from the mountain springs and a tunnel led from this castle to the Bourtzi in Karystos. A little beyond Myli there is an **ancient quarry** scattered with fragments of the once-prized Karystian marble.

With your own transport you can explore the sleepy villages nestling in the southern foothills of Mt Ohi. The rough road winds through citrus groves and pine trees high above the south coast. From **Platanistos**, a charming village named for its plane trees, a 5km dirt road (driveable) leads to the coastal village of **Potami** with its sand and pebble beach.

Skiathos Σκιάθος

☎ 0427   • postcode 370 02   • pop 4100

The good news is that much of the pine-covered coast of Skiathos is blessed with exquisite beaches of golden sand. The bad news is that the island is overrun with package tourists – at least in August – and is very expensive. Despite the large presence of sun-starved northern Europeans, and the ensuing tourist excess, Skiathos is still a pretty island and not surprisingly one of Greece's premier resorts.

The island has only one settlement, the port and capital of Skiathos Town, on the south-east coast. The rest of the south coast is one long chain of holiday villas and hotels. The north coast is precipitous and less accessible. Most people come to the island for the beaches and nightlife, but the truly curious will discover some picturesque walks, hidden valleys and even quiet beaches.

Getting There & Away

Air As well as the numerous charter flights from northern Europe to Skiathos, during summer there are up to five flights daily to Athens (16,700 dr). The Olympic Airways office (☎ 22 200) is in Skiathos Town on the right side of Papadiamanti, the main thoroughfare, as you walk inland.

Ferry In summer, there are ferries from Skiathos to Volos (3½ hours, 2750 dr, three to four daily), to Agios Konstantinos (3½ hours, 3220 dr, two daily) and to Alonnisos (two hours, 1800 dr, four to six daily) via Glossa (Skopelos) and Skopelos Town (1½ hours, 1400 dr). There are also boats from Skiathos to Thessaloniki (5½ to seven hours, 4500 dr, three weekly) in July and August. Tickets can be most easily obtained from Alkyon Tourist Office (☎ 22 029). The port police can be contacted on ☎ 22 017.

Hydrofoil In summer, there is a bewildering array of hydrofoils from Skiathos and around the Sporades in general. Among the main services, there are hydrofoils from Skiathos to Volos (1¼ hours, 5500 dr, three or four daily), and to Alonnisos (one hour, 3600 dr, eight to 10 daily) via Glossa (Skopelos) and Skopelos Town (35 minutes, 2800 dr). There are also hydrofoils to Agios Konstantinos (1½ hours, 6600 dr, two or three daily). Three to five weekly go to Skyros (2¼ hours, 8400 dr) and Kymi (three hours, 10,055 dr), and five or six weekly go to Thessaloniki (3½ hours, 8500 dr). There are also services to the Pelion Peninsula, Halkidiki, various ports in northern Evia and to Stylida near Lamia. Hydrofoil tickets may be purchased from Skiathos Holidays

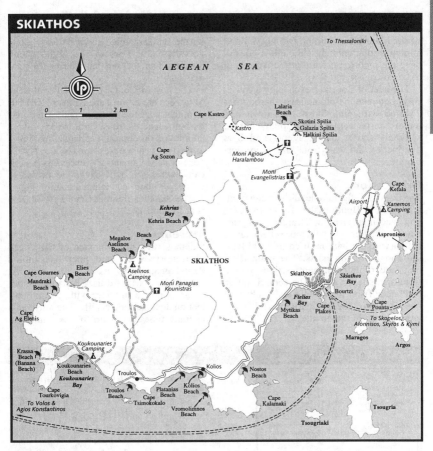

AEGEAN SEA

To Thessaloniki

0   1   2 km

Cape Kastro

Lalaria
Beach

Kastro

Skotini Spilia
Galazia Spilia
Halkini Spilia

Cape
Ag Sozon

Moni Agiou
Haralambou

Moni
Evangelistrias

Cape
Kefala

Airport

Xanemos
Camping

Kehrias
Bay
Kehria Beach

Aspronisos

Beach

Megalos
Aselinos
Beach

SKIATHOS

Skiathos

*Skiathos
Bay*

Elies
Beach

Aselinos
Camping

Cape Gournes

Mandraki
Beach

Moni Panagias
Kounistras

Bourtzi

Cape
Ag Elenis

*Ftelias
Bay*

Mytikas
Beach

Cape
Plakes

Cape
Pounta

To Skopelos,
Alonnisos, Skyfos & Kymi

Koukounaries
Camping

Maragos

Argos

Krassa
Beach
(Banana
Beach)

Koukounaries
Beach

*Koukounaries
Bay*

Troulos

Kolios

Nostos
Beach

Cape
Tourkovigia

Troulos
Beach

Platanias
Beach

Kolios
Beach

Cape
Tsimokokalo

Vromolimnos
Beach

Cape
Kalamaki

To Volos &
Agios Konstantinos

Tsougria

Tsougriaki

(☎ 22 018, fax 22 771) in the middle of Skiathos Town's new harbour waterfront.

Getting Around

Bus Crowded buses leave Skiathos Town for Koukounaries Beach (30 minutes, 350 dr) every half-hour between 7.30 am and 10.30 pm. The buses stop at all the access points to the beaches along the south coast. A couple of buses connect for passengers going to Megalos Aselinos Beach, on the north coast.

Car & Motorcycle Car hire outlets including Alamo (☎ 23 025) and Euronet (☎ 24 410), as well as heaps of motorcycle hire outlets, are along the town's waterfront.

Excursion Boat Excursion boats go to most of the south-coast beaches from the old harbour. Trips around the island cost about 3500 dr and include a visit to Kastro, Lalaria Beach, and the three caves of Halkini Spilia, Skotini Spilia and Galazia Spilia, which are only accessible by boat.

EVIA & THE SPORADES

SKIATHOS TOWN
Skiathos Town, with its red-roofed, white-washed houses, is built on two low hills. It is picturesque enough, although it doesn't have the picture postcard attractiveness of Skopelos or Skyros towns.

The islet of Bourtzi (reached by a causeway) between the old and new harbours is covered with pine forest. The town is a major tourist centre, with many hotels, souvenir shops, travel agents and bars dominating the waterfront and main thoroughfares.

Orientation
The quay is in the middle of the waterfront, just north of Bourtzi Islet. To the right (as you face inland) is the straight, new harbour; to the left, and with more character, is the curving old harbour used by local fishing and excursion boats. The main thoroughfare of Papadiamanti strikes inland from opposite the quay. The central square of Plateia Trion Ierarhon is just back from the middle of the old harbour and has a large church in the middle.

Information
The tourist police office (☎ 23 172), opposite the regular police about halfway along Papadiamanti, next to the high school, operates 8 am to 9 pm daily during the summer season.

The post office, OTE and National Bank of Greece are all on Papadiamanti. The bus terminus is at the northern end of the new harbour. There are several ATMs and a couple of automatic exchange machines around town. Mare Nostrum Holidays (☎ 21 463) at Papadiamanti 21 represents American Express. It will exchange travellers cheques without deducting a commission.

The Skiathos Internet Centre (☎ 22 021) is at Miaouli 12.

Museum
Skiathos was the birthplace of the Greek short-story writer and poet Alexandros Papadiamantis, as well as the novelist Alexandros Moraïtidis. Papadiamantis' house is now a museum with a small collection documenting his life. The museum's opening times are 9 am to 1 pm and 5 to

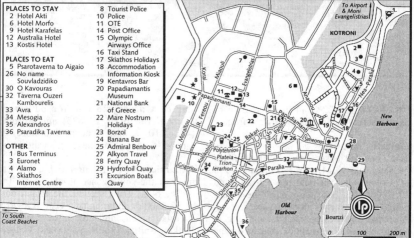

SKIATHOS TOWN

PLACES TO STAY
2 Hotel Akti
6 Hotel Morfo
9 Hotel Karafelas
12 Australia Hotel
13 Kostis Hotel

PLACES TO EAT
5 Psarotaverna to Aigaio
26 No name
   Souvladzidiko
30 O Kavouras
32 Taverna Ouzeri
   Kambourelis
33 Avra
34 Mesogia
35 Alexandros
36 Psaradika Taverna

OTHER
1 Bus Terminus
3 Euronet
4 Alamo
7 Skiathos
   Internet Centre

8 Tourist Police
10 Police
11 OTE
14 Post Office
15 Olympic
   Airways Office
16 Taxi Stand
17 Skiathos Holidays
18 Accommodation
   Information Kiosk
19 Kentavros Bar
20 Papadiamantis
   Museum
21 National Bank
   of Greece
22 Mare Nostrum
   Holidays
23 Borzoï
24 Banana Bar
25 Admiral Benbow
27 Alkyon Travel
28 Ferry Quay
29 Hydrofoil Quay
31 Excursion Boats
   Quay

8 pm; it's closed on Monday. It is just off the right side of Papadiamanti coming up from the harbour. Entry is 250 dr.

Organised Tours
Various local operators run excursion boat trips around the island. See the Getting Around section for Skiathos Island.

Places to Stay – Budget
Most accommodation is booked solid by package-tour operators from July to the end of August, when prices are often double those of low season. Prices quoted here are for high season. There is a kiosk on the harbourfront with information on room availability. If you're brave enough to arrive during the summer rush, then just about any travel agent will endeavour to fix you up with accommodation. Worth trying are Alkyon Travel (☎ 22 029), at the bottom of Papadiamanti; Meridian (☎ 21 309, Papadiamanti 8); or Mare Nostrum Holidays (☎ 21 463, Papadiamanti 21).

There is only one officially recognised camp site here, *Koukounaries Camping* (☎ 49 250), at the east end of the beach of the same name at the west end of the island. This is a well run setup and very close to the beach.

There are in principle two other sites: *Aselinos Camping* (☎ 49 312), on the north coast, at Megalos Aselinos Beach; and *Xanemos Camping*, close to the airport. In the first case, the site doesn't always open (it doesn't have a licence) and Xanemos Camping is far too close to the airport for comfort – hardly anyone uses it.

The E class *Hotel Karafelas* (☎ 21 235, *Papadiamanti 59)* is one of the town's best-value hotels. The comfortable singles/doubles are 8000/11,000 dr with bathroom. The hotel is at the far end of Papadiamanti, on the left. Also worth a try is the slightly more expensive E class *Australia Hotel* (☎ 22 488), which has tidy rooms for 12,500/15,100 dr with bathroom. Walk up Papadiamanti to the post office, turn right and take the first left.

Kostis Hostel (☎ 23 982, fax 22 909, *Evangelistrias 5)* has been given the thumbs up from some LP readers. Its neat rooms go for 12,000/14,000 dr.

Places to Stay – Mid-Range
The C class *Hotel Morfo* (☎ 21 737, fax 23 222, Ananiou 23) has smallish but quite adequate doubles for 13,000 dr with bathroom. From the waterfront take M Ananiou (parallel to, and to the right of, Papadiamanti), and the hotel is on the left.

For a very central location with a great waterfront view, try the C class *Hotel Akti* (☎ 22 024) overlooking the new harbour. Airy singles/doubles go for 14,000/18,000 dr. The roomy four-person penthouse apartment on the top floor goes for 30,000 dr. Book ahead if you can.

Places to Stay – Top End
Most of the island's top-end hotels are on the coast to the west of Skiathos Town. The A class *Hotel Paradise* (☎/fax 21 939), 3km west of town, is one of the newest and smallest of these hotels. It has tastefully furnished air-con rooms and a restaurant and bar. Doubles are 25,500 dr.

At Nostos Beach, the A class *Nostos Bungalows* (☎ 22 420, fax 22 525) is a well designed complex 5km west of town. The complex has bars, a restaurant, taverna, pool and tennis court. Bungalows sleeping up to four cost 27,000 dr.

For solitude and a blissful rural ambience in a hidden valley look no further than *Zorbades* (☎/fax 49 473, email info@ skiathos.info.com). Proprietor Geof Baldry owns two fully equipped stone houses that accommodate up to five people. He rents them out to discerning clients for between 28,000 dr and 40,000 dr daily.

Places to Eat
The good news is that there is a wide choice of eateries in Skiathos; the downside is that most of them tend to gear their cuisine to the tourist trade and are somewhat more expensive than elsewhere. Finding some decent Greek cuisine can be a matter of trial and error. For a quick, cheap bite, the no-name *souvladzidiko* in the back streets off

Papadiamanti seems to draw the Greek youth and is a clean, bright and cheery establishment.

There is a swathe of restaurants just down from Plateia Trion Ierarhon, overlooking the old harbour. Of these, *Avra*, though seemingly not as popular as its more bustling neighbour, has a better reputation for grills and chicken dishes. Right opposite the hydrofoil terminal, is *O Kavouras*. Service is surprisingly good for such a busy place and food is consistently tasty and reasonably priced.

Taverna Ouzeri Kambourelis on the waterfront of the old harbour also rates reasonably well and opens earlier in the season than other establishments. *Psarotaverna to Aigaio* has reasonable prices and ready-made dishes as well as fish, but is in a less attractive location on the new harbourfront. *Psaradika Ouzeri* at the far end of the old harbour near the fish market has, not surprisingly, fresh fish and also inventive *mezedes*. It's more expensive than other places. Reckon on around 5000 dr to 6000 dr for a meal for two with wine.

Two other restaurants close to each other and away from the main tourist traps are *Mesogia* and *Alexandros*. Both are signposted from Polytehniou. Prices are still in the 2700 dr range for a meal from a varied menu, but the tables spill out onto the narrow streets, making a change from the rush of the waterfront.

Entertainment

Scan Papadiamanti and Polytehniou and check out which disco or bar takes your fancy. *Banana Bar*, patronised by tourists from the UK, and *Borzoï*, playing both Greek and non-Greek music, are both on Polytehniou. *Admiral Benbow* also on Polytehniou caters to the British crowd by playing all the old favourites from the 1960s and 70s.

Kentavros Bar, one of Skiathos' more established joints, promises rock, funky soul, acid jazz and blues, and gets the thumbs up from local expats. It's in view of the Papadiamantis museum.

AROUND SKIATHOS
Beaches

With some 65 beaches to choose from, beach-hopping on Skiathos can become a full-time occupation. Many are only accessible by caïque and the ones that are more easily accessible tend to get crowded.

Buses ply the south coast stopping at the beach access points. The ones nearest town are extremely crowded; the first one worth getting off the bus for is the pine-fringed, long and sandy **Vromolimnos Beach**, which has been awarded an EU blue flag for cleanliness. Farther along, **Platanias** and **Troulos** beaches are also good but both, alas, are very popular. The bus continues to **Koukounaries Beach**, backed by pine trees and a lagoon and touted as the best beach in Greece. Nowadays it's best viewed at a distance from where the wide sweep of pale gold sand does indeed look beautiful.

Krassa Beach, at the other side of a narrow headland, is more commonly known as **Banana Beach**, because of its curving shape and soft yellow sand. It is nominally a nudist beach, though the skinny-dippers tend to abscond to **Little Banana Beach** around the corner if things get too crowded. It has two or three snack bars.

The north coast's beaches are less crowded but exposed to the strong summer *meltemi* winds. From Troulos a road heads north to the sandy, rather scruffy-looking **Megalos Aselinos Beach**. Turn left onto a dirt road to reach this beach. A right fork from this road leads to **Mikros Aselinos Beach** and farther on to **Kehria Beach**, also reachable by a dirt road from nearer Skiathos Town.

Lalaria, on the northern coast, is a striking beach of pale grey pebbles, much featured in tourist brochures. It is most easily reached by excursion boat from Skiathos Town.

Kastro Κάστρο

Kastro, perched dramatically on a rocky headland above the north coast, was the fortified pirate-proof capital of the island from 1540 to 1829. It consisted of some 300 houses and 20 churches and the only access was by a drawbridge. Except for two churches, it is now in ruins. Access is by steps, and the views from it are tremendous. Excursion boats come to the beach below Kastro, from where it's an easy clamber up to the ruins.

Moni Evangelistrias

Μονή Ευαγγελίστριας

The 18th century Moni Evangelistrias is the most appealing of the island's monasteries. It is in a delightful setting, poised above a gorge, 450m above sea level, and surrounded by pine and cypress trees. The monastery, like many in Greece, was a refuge for freedom fighters during the War of Independence, and the islanders claim the first Greek flag was raised here in 1807.

The monastery is an hour's walk from town or you can drive here. It's signposted off the Skiathos Town ring road, close to the turn-off to the airport.

Skopelos Σκόπελος

☎ 0424   • postcode 370 03   • pop 5000

Skopelos is less commercialised than Skiathos, but following hot on its trail. Like Skiathos, the north-west coast is exposed, with high cliffs. The sheltered south-east coast harbours many beaches but, unlike Skiathos, most are pebbled. The island is heavily pine-forested and has vineyards, olive groves and fruit orchards. There are two large settlements: the capital and main port of Skopelos Town on the east coast; and the lovely, unspoilt hill village of Glossa, the island's second port, 3km north of Loutraki on the west coast.

Skopelos has yielded an exciting archaeological find. In ancient times the island was an important Minoan outpost ruled by Staphylos, who, according to mythology, was the son of Ariadne and Dionysos. *Staphylos* means grape in Greek and the Minoan ruler is said to have introduced wine making to the island. In the 1930s a tomb containing gold treasures, and believed to be that of Staphylos, was unearthed at Staphylos, now a resort.

Getting There & Away

Ferry In summer there are three ferries daily to Alonnisos from Glossa (1¼ hours, 1300 dr) and Skopelos Town (30 minutes, 1100 dr). There are also ferries to Volos (4½ hours, 3380 dr, four daily), to Agios Konstantinos (4½ hours, 4100 dr, two daily) and to Skiathos (1½ hours, 1400 dr, four or five daily). In addition, there are boats to Thessaloniki (six hours, 4600 dr, three weekly).

The times given are for Skopelos Town; Glossa is one hour less. Boats from Glossa actually depart from Loutraki, on the coast. Tickets are available from Lemonis Agents (☎ 23 055, fax 22 363). The telephone number of Skopelos' port police is ☎ 22 180.

Hydrofoil Like Skiathos, Skopelos is linked to a large number of destinations by hydrofoil. The main services during summer include: to Alonnisos (20 minutes, 2200 dr, eight or nine daily), to Skiathos (one hour, 2800 dr, 10 to 12 daily), to Volos (2¼ hours, 6800 dr, five daily), to Agios Konstantinos (2¼ hours, 8200 dr, three daily), to Skyros (2¼ hours, 8000 dr, four to six weekly) and to Thessaloniki (4¾ hours, 9300 dr, one daily). Cheaper return fares apply on most of these services.

In addition, there are services to the Pelion Peninsula, Halkidiki, to various points in Evia and to Stylida, near Lamia. Tickets may be purchased from Madro Travel in Skopelos Town (☎ 22 145, fax 22 941).

Getting Around

Bus There are buses from Skopelos Town all the way to Glossa/Loutraki (one hour, 750 dr, eight daily), a further three that go only as far as Milia (35 minutes, 510 dr) and another two that go only as far as Agnontas (15 minutes, 225 dr).

Car & Motorcycle There are a fair number of car and motorcycle rental outlets, mostly at the eastern end of the waterfront. Among them is Motor Tours (☎ 22 986), on the waterfront near Hotel Eleni.

SKOPELOS TOWN

Skopelos Town is one of the most captivating of the island's towns. It skirts a semi-circular bay and clambers in tiers up a hillside, culminating in a ruined fortress. Dozens of churches are interspersed among tall, dazzlingly white houses with brightly shuttered windows and flower-adorned balconies. Traditionally, roofs in Skopelos Town were tiled with beautiful rough-hewn bluestone, but these are gradually being replaced with mass-produced red tiles.

Orientation

Skopelos Town's quay is on the west side of the bay. From the ferry, turn left to reach the bustling waterfront lined with cafes, souvenir shops and travel agencies. The bus station is to the left of the new quay, at the end of the excursion boat moorings.

Information

There is no tourist office or tourist police on Skopelos. The regular police station (☎ 22 235) is above the National Bank. Go up the steps to the right of the bank, turn left and the entrance is on the left.

The post office lurks in an obscure alleyway: walk up the road opposite the bus station, take the first left, the first right and the first left and it's on the right. To reach the OTE follow the road inland next to the Armoloï craft shop and you'll come to it on the left at the first crossroad.

The National Bank of Greece is on the waterfront near the old quay. It has an ATM and an automatic exchange machine. To reach Skopelos' self-service laundrette go up the street opposite the bus station, turn right at Platanos Taverna and it's on the left.

Museum
Strolling around town and sitting at the waterside cafes will probably be your chief occupations in Skopelos Town, but there is also a small **folk art museum**. Located on Hatzistamati, it is open 7 am to 10 pm daily and admission is free. Walk up the steps to the left of the pharmacy on the waterfront, take the first right, the first left, the first right and it's on the right.

Places to Stay – Budget
Skopelos Town is still a place where you have a good chance of renting a room in a family house, and people with rooms to offer meet the ferries and hydrofoils. The Rooms & Apartments Association of Skopelos (☎ 24 567) has an office on the waterfront and might be a better starting point.

There are a couple of places away from the town that are easy to find on your own. *Pension Soula* (☎ 22 930) is a lovely place owned by a hospitable elderly couple. Doubles/triples are 8000/10,000 dr with bathroom. Turn left at Hotel Amalia and, after about 200m, bear right. You will find the domatia on your right.

The domatia of *Marigoula Abelakia* (☎ 22 662) at Tria Platania are in a pleasant garden setting with a barbecue area, 10 minutes walk south from the waterfront. Rooms are 10,000/14,000 dr.

Skopelos has no official camp sites, but some people camp rough on Velanio Beach.

Places to Stay – Mid-Range
The wooden-floored rooms of the pension *Kyr Sotos* (☎ 22 549, fax 23 668), in a lovely old building in the middle of the waterfront, are delightful and very popular with visitors. There's a little courtyard, a communal kitchen and a fridge for guests' use, and each well appointed room is different. Doubles/ triples are 8,800/14,600 dr respectively.

In a prime location overlooking all the waterfront action is the C class *Hotel Adonis* (☎ 22 231). Its comfortable and homy rooms (a couple with large balconies overlooking the street) go for 15,000/20,000 dr.

Places to Stay – Top End
Ionia Hotel (☎ 22 568, fax 23 30) on Manolaki is an attractive hostelry located in the back streets. Comfy singles/doubles are 14,000/22,000 dr. The B class *Dolphin Hotel* (☎ 23 015, fax 23 016), south of the bus station, is a striking pastel-coloured building with an ultramodern, luxurious interior. Rooms are 17,500/23,000 dr.

Places to Eat
For DIY diners there is a well stocked *Alpha-Pi supermarket* on Doulidi, just inland from the bus station. There are also a lot of restaurants in Skopelos Town and the quality is somewhat better than that on Skiathos. The following are among the better ones. *O Platanos*, just back from the bus station, on a little open space known locally as Souvlaki Square, has tables beneath a large plane tree. It's cheap, basic and popular, and specialises in souvlaki (500 dr).

There are two reasonable Greek restaurants next to each other on the waterfront near the old ferry and hydrofoil quay. *Klimataria* and *Molos* serve a wide range of good food. A meal with retsina will cost around 2300 dr.

Two more expensive, but very pleasant restaurants are set back a little from the waterfront. *Taverna Finikas* (☎ 23 247), on Drosopoulou, has a varied cuisine and is set round an enormous palm tree. *Taverna Alexander* (☎ 22 324), on Anthypolohagou

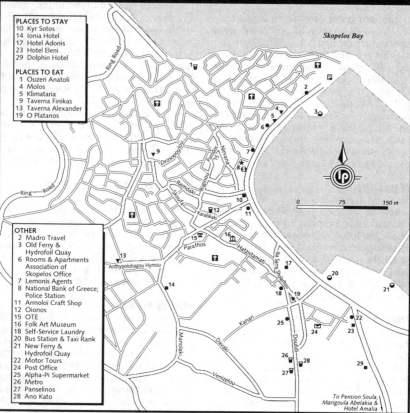

SKOPELOS TOWN

PLACES TO STAY
10 Kyr Sotos
14 Ionia Hotel
17 Hotel Adonis
23 Hotel Eleni
29 Dolphin Hotel

PLACES TO EAT
1 Ouzeri Anatoli
4 Molos
5 Klimataria
9 Taverna Finikas
13 Taverna Alexander
19 O Platanos

Skopelos Bay

Ring Road

Drosopouliou
Pandou
Nirvana
Rigiou
Remdaki
Skoufa
Karaïskaki
Parathos
Anthypolohagou Hymou
Hatzistamati
Ilia Sarra Skiarihou
Kanari
Davaki
Lvmanolaki
Doulidi
Venizelou

0   75   150 m

OTHER
2 Madro Travel
3 Old Ferry & Hydrofoil Quay
6 Rooms & Apartments Association of Skopelos Office
7 Lemonis Agents
8 National Bank of Greece; Police Station
11 Armoloï Craft Shop
12 Oionos
15 OTE
16 Folk Art Museum
18 Self-Service Laundry
20 Bus Station & Taxi Rank
21 New Ferry & Hydrofoil Quay
22 Motor Tours
24 Post Office
25 Alpha-Pi Supermarket
26 Metro
27 Panselinos
28 Ano Kato

To Pension Soula, Marigoula Abelakia & Hotel Amalia

Hymou, has excellent local specialities including the local cheese pie, *tyropitta*. You dine in a cosy walled garden which also sports a very deep well that is floodlit at night. Look for the signs to both these places from the OTE.

For mezedes and live music, in summer only, head to ***Ouzeri Anatoli*** high up above the town in the Kastro. Here from 11 pm onwards, you will hear *rembetika* music sung by Skopelos' own exponent of the Greek blues, Georgos Xindaris. The easiest though most strenuous way there is to follow the path up past the church at the northern end of the quay.

Entertainment

Oionos Karaïskaki is a cool little bar offering tasteful jazz and ethnic music. Follow the street to the OTE and you will find it off to your right. For more lively entertainment there is a strip of clubs along Doulidi, just off Souvlaki Square. Still a favourite is ***Ano Kato*** for disco music, though ***Panselinos*** and ***Metro***, opposite, give it a run for its money. Each attracts its own age group; poke your nose in to see if you fit in.

GLOSSA Γλώσσα

Glossa, Skopelos' other major settlement, is another whitewashed delight and considerably quieter than the capital. It has managed to retain the feel of a pristine Greek village while having most of the amenities that visitors require.

The bus stops in front of a large church at a T-junction. As you face the church, the left road winds down to Loutraki and the right to the main thoroughfare of Agiou Riginou. Along here you'll find a bank and a few small stores.

Skopelos' beaches are just as accessible by bus from Glossa as they are from Skopelos Town; Milia, the island's best beach, is actually closer to Glossa. There are also places to stay and tavernas at Loutraki, but there's not a lot to do other than hang around, eat, sleep and drink since the narrow pebble beach is not so inviting.

Places to Stay & Eat

In summer, if accommodation gets tight in Skopelos Town, you can try *Hotel Atlantes* (☎ *33 223)*, at the T-junction in Glossa. The clean, attractive single/double rooms are 7500/8500 dr. Just before you enter Glossa from Skopelos Town, you will see *Rooms Kerasia (☎ 33 373)* in a newish building set back from the road to the left. Rates here are around 8000 dr a double. Glossa also has a few other rooms in private houses – inquire at *kafeneia*.

Taverna Agnanti (☎ 33 076) serves well prepared, reasonably priced Greek fare. It's on the left side of Agiou Riginou as you walk from the T-junction. Just before you enter Glossa you'll find *Kali Kardia (☎ 33 716)* taverna, which has excellent views down to the sea.

AROUND SKOPELOS
Monasteries

Skopelos has many monasteries, several of which can be visited on a scenic, although quite strenuous, one day trek from Skopelos

Town. Facing inland from the waterfront, turn left and follow the road which skirts the bay and then climbs inland (signposted 'Hotel Aegeon'). Continue beyond the hotel and you will come to a fork. Take the left fork for the 18th century **Moni Evangelismou** (now a convent). From here there are breathtaking views of Skopelos Town, 4km away. The monastery's prize piece is a beautiful and ornately carved and gilded iconostasis in which there is an 11th century icon of the Virgin Mary.

The right fork leads to the uninhabited 16th century **Moni Metamorfosis**, the island's oldest monastery. From here the track continues to the 18th century **Moni Prodromou** (now a nunnery), 8km from Skopelos Town.

Walking Tours

There is a useful English-language walking guide to Skopelos called *Sotos Walking Guide* by Heather Parsons. It lists 21 different walking itineraries around Skopelos Town and Glossa. The hand-drawn sketches and maps are a bit rough, but the suggestions for walking tours of the island are excellent. It costs 2500 dr and is available in waterfront stores selling books.

Heather also runs guided walking tours. Her evening walk to Panormos Beach is very popular as you finish off the four hour hike with a swim and a meal. The all-in cost is 3500 dr. Call ☎ 24 022 for bookings.

Beaches

Skopelos' beaches are almost all on the sheltered south-west and west coasts. All the buses stop at the beginning of paths which lead down to them. The first beach along is the crowded sand and pebble **Staphylos Beach** (site of Staphylos' tomb), 4km south-east from Skopelos Town. There is a welcoming taverna, *Pefkos*, here with romantic views when there is a full moon.

From the eastern end of the beach a path leads over a small headland to the quieter **Velanio Beach**, the island's official nudist beach. **Agnontas**, 3km west of Staphylos, has a small pebble beach and from here caïques sail to the superior and sandy **Limnonari Beach**. There are three waterside tavernas at Agnontas; *Pavlos* is reputedly the best one and *Fotini* is next best. From Agnontas the road cuts inland through pine forests before re-emerging at sheltered **Panormos Beach**. The next beach along, **Milia**, is considered the island's best – a long swathe of tiny pebbles.

All of these beaches have tavernas or portable snack bars, and there are hotels and domatia at Staphylos, Limnonari, Panormos and Milia. However, the comfortable *domatia* at Limnonari (☎ 23 046) are a little more secluded and the beach is smaller and less likely to be crowded. Rooms here cost 14,000 dr for a double.

Alonnisos
Αλόννησος

☎ 0424 • postcode 370 05 • pop 3000

Alonnisos is still a serene island despite having been ferreted out by 'high-quality'

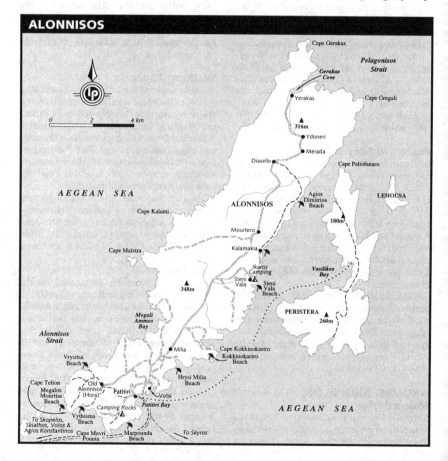

ALONNISOS

Cape Gerakas

Pelagonisos Strait

Gerakas Cove

Yerakas

Cape Gregali

0   2   4 km

▲ 316m
Ydoneri

Merada

Diasello

AEGEAN SEA

Agios Dimitrios Beach

Cape Paliofanaro

LEHOUSA

ALONNISOS

Cape Kalami

180m ▲

Mourtero

Cape Maïstra

Kalamakia

Vasilikos Bay

Ikaros Camping

Steni Vala ▲△

Steni Vala Beach

▲ 348m

Megali Ammos Bay

PERISTERA ▲ 260m

Alonnisos Strait

Vrysitsa Beach

Milia

Cape Kokkinokastro
Kokkinokastro Beach

Cape Telion
Megalos Mourtias Beach

Old Alonnisos (Hora)

Patitiri

Hrysi Milia Beach

Votsi

To Skopelos, Skiathos, Volos & Agios Konstantinos

Camping Rocks

Patitiri Bay

Vythisma Beach

Cape Mavri Pounta

Marpounda Beach

To Skyros

AEGEAN SEA

package-tour companies. Package tourism would no doubt have taken off in a bigger way had the airport (erroneously and optimistically shown on island maps) materialised. This project was begun in the mid-1980s, but the rocks of Alonnisos proved unyielding and the politics Byzantine, making the construction of a runway impossible.

Alonnisos once had a flourishing wine industry, but in 1950 the vines were struck with the disease phylloxera and, robbed of their livelihood, many islanders moved away. Fate struck another cruel blow in 1965 when a violent earthquake destroyed the hilltop capital of Alonnisos Town (now called Old Alonnisos, Hora or Palio Horio). The inhabitants abandoned their hilltop homes and were subsequently re-housed in hastily assembled concrete dwellings at Patitiri. In recent years many of the derelict houses in the capital have been bought for a song from the government and renovated by British and German settlers. There is now a flourishing expat artist community, several of whom reside here year-round.

Alonnisos is a green island with pine and oak trees, mastic and arbutus bushes, and fruit trees. The west coast is mostly precipitous cliffs but the east coast is speckled with pebbled beaches. The water around Alonnisos has been declared a marine park, and is the cleanest in the Aegean. Every house has a cesspit, so no sewage enters the sea.

Getting There & Away
Ferry There are ferries from Alonnisos to Volos (five hours, 3700 dr, two or three daily), four to five daily to both Skopelos Town (30 minutes, 1100 dr) and Skiathos (two hours, 1800 dr), and one daily to Agios Konstantinos (5½ hours, 4400 dr). In addition, there are one to three ferries weekly to Thessaloniki via Skiathos (6½ hours, 4500 dr). Tickets can be purchased from Alonnisos Travel (☎ 65 198, fax 65 511). The port police (☎ 65 595) are on Ikion Dolopon in Patitiri.

Hydrofoil As with Skiathos and Skopelos, there are a lot of connections in summer.

The more important ones include up to five daily to Volos (2½ hours, 7500 dr), eight or nine daily to both Skopelos Town (20 minutes, 2200 dr) and Skiathos (40 minutes, 3600 dr), two or three daily to Agios Konstantinos (2½ hours, 8800 dr), and one daily to both Skyros (1¼ hours, 8000 dr) and Thessaloniki (4½ hours, 11,700 dr).

Cheaper return fares apply on most of these services. In addition, there are also services to the Pelion Peninsula, Halkidiki, various ports in Evia and to Stylida near Lamia. Tickets may be purchased from Ikos Travel (☎ 65 320, fax 65 321) in Patitiri.

Getting Around
If you'd prefer to leave the travel arrangements up to someone else, Ikos Travel in Patitiri operates various excursions. See Organised Tours under the Patitiri entry.

Bus In summer, Alonnisos' one bus plies more or less hourly between Patitiri (from opposite the quay) and Old Alonnisos (250 dr one way). There is also an additional service to Steni Vala from Old Alonnisos via Patitiri (300 dr one way).

Motorcycle There are several motorcycle hire outlets on Pelasgon, in Patitiri. I'M Bike Rentals (☎ 65 010) on Pelasgon is worth checking out. Be wary when taking the tracks off the main trans-island road down to the beaches since some of these tracks are steep and slippery.

Taxi Boat The easiest way to get to the east coast beaches is by the taxi boats that leave from the quay in Patitiri every morning.

PATITIRI Πατητήρι
Patitiri sits between two high sandstone cliffs at the southern end of the east coast. Not surprisingly, considering its origins, it's not a traditionally picturesque place, but it nevertheless makes a convenient base and has a very relaxed atmosphere. Patitiri means 'wine press' and is where, in fact, grapes were processed prior to the demise of the wine industry.

Orientation

Finding your way around Patitiri is easy. The quay is in the centre of the waterfront and two roads lead inland. Facing away from the sea, turn left and then right for Pelasgon or right and then left for Ikion Dolopon.

Information

There is no tourist office or tourist police. The regular police (☎ 65 205) are at the southern end of Ikion Dolopon, as is the National Bank of Greece. The bank has an ATM that accepts most credit cards.

The post office is on Ikion Dolopon and the OTE is on the waterfront to the right of the quay. There is a laundrette called Gardenia (☎ 65 831) on Pelasgon.

Walk to Old Alonnisos

From Patitiri to Old Alonnisos a delightful path winds through shrubbery and orchards. Walk up Pelasgon and, 80m beyond Pension Galini, a now unmarked turn-off indicates the start of the path to Old Alonnisos. Take this path and after 10 minutes turn right at a water tap, which may not be functioning. After about 15 minutes the path is intersected by a dirt road. Continue straight ahead on the path and after about 25 minutes you will come to the main road. Walk straight along this road and you will see Old Alonnisos ahead.

If you are coming from Old Alonnisos the start of the track is fairly obvious though not yet marked with a sign. Walk down the main road to Patitiri for about 350m and look for a short, concrete OTE obelisk on the left. The stone-paved trail starts here on the opposite side of the road.

Organised Tours

Ikos Travel (☎ 65 320, fax 65 321), opposite the quay, offers several excursions. These include to Kyra Panagia, Psathoura and Peristera islets (10,000 dr, including a picnic on a beach, snacks and drinks), and a round-the-island excursion (6500 dr).

It also organises four guided walking tours along the back tracks of Alonnisos and then usually down to a beach for a picnic lunch and a swim. Stout walking shoes, trousers and a long-sleeved shirt are recommended. Ikos Travel, or your guides Chris and Julia, will provide you with a locally produced, but very detailed, walking map.

Places to Stay

Accommodation standards are good on Alonnisos (and cheaper than on Skiathos and Skopelos) and, except for the first two weeks of August, you shouldn't have any difficulty finding a room. The Rooms to Let service (☎ 65 577), opposite the quay, will help you find a room on any part of the island.

Places to Stay – Budget

The nearest camp site to the port is the semi-official *Camping Rocks* (☎ *65 410)*. Don't be put off by the name; it doesn't refer to the site's surface but to the nearest rocky beach (a nudist beach). Camping is under cool and shady pine trees but can suffer from noise from the site's disco. The site is a 700m uphill slog from the quay (turn left at Enigma Disco on Pelasgon.

Eleni Athanasiou rents lovely *domatia* (☎ *65 240, fax 65 598)* in a sparkling white, blue-shuttered building high above the harbour. Rates are 10,000 dr for a self-catering unit for two or three people with cooker and fridge, and 20,000 dr for five-person apartments. Take the first left off Ikion Dolopon and follow the path upwards until you see the rooms on your right.

The *domatia* of Eleni Alexiou (☎ *65 149)* are a pleasant place to stay. If you call ahead, you will be met at the quay. Rates are 8000/9400 dr for doubles/triples. The rooms, equipped with kitchens, are a little higher up from Eleni Athanasiou and even have car parking. Along Pelasgon, on the left at No 27, are the prettily furnished *Ilias Rent Rooms* (☎ *65 451)*. They cost 8000/9600 dr for rooms with bathroom.

Pension Galini (☎ *65 573, fax 65 094)* is beautifully furnished and has a fine flower-festooned terrace. Rooms cost 8500/10,500 dr with bathroom, and well equipped apartments for five/six people are 15,000/17,500 dr. The pension can be found on the left, 400m up Pelasgon.

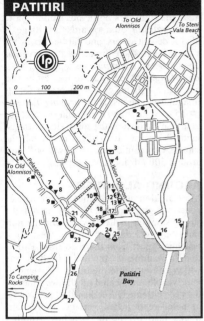

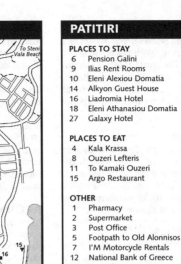

PATITIRI

PLACES TO STAY
6   Pension Galini
9   Ilias Rent Rooms
10 Eleni Alexiou Domatia
14 Alkyon Guest House
16 Liadromia Hotel
18 Eleni Athanasiou Domatia
27 Galaxy Hotel

PLACES TO EAT
4   Kala Krassa
8   Ouzeri Lefteris
11 To Kamaki Ouzeri
15 Argo Restaurant

OTHER
1   Pharmacy
2   Supermarket
3   Post Office
5   Footpath to Old Alonnisos
7   I'M Motorcycle Rentals
12 National Bank of Greece
13 Symvolo
17 Rooms to Let Service
19 Ikos Travel
20 Alonnisos Travel
21 Police Station
22 Gardenia Laundrette
23 Enigma Disco
24 Hydrofoil Quay
25 Ferry Quay
26 Ble Notes

Places to Stay – Mid-Range

On the waterfront, the C class *Alkyon Guest House* (☎ 65 220, fax 65 195) has comfortable singles/doubles for 10,300/13,500 dr with bathroom. The entrance is from Ikion Dolopon.

The attractive rooms in the C class *Liadromia Hotel* (☎ 65 521, fax 65 096) have stucco walls, stone floors, balcony and traditional carved-wood furniture. Walk inland up Ikion Dolopon and take the first turn right up the steps, follow the path around and the hotel is on the left. Rooms are 12,000/15,000 dr.

Alonnisos' classiest hotel is the C class *Galaxy Hotel* (☎ 65 251, fax 65 110), where luxurious rooms with balcony cost 12,500/16,500 dr. The hotel is built on a hill to the left of the bay as you face inland. Turn left at the port and beyond the waterfront tavernas take the steps up to the right; turn left at the top to reach the hotel.

Places to Eat

If you feel you can't stomach another moussaka, pastitsio or souvlaki, then Alonnisos will come as a revelation, for the island has some top-notch eateries. Most specialise in imaginatively prepared fish dishes. At *To Kamaki Ouzeri*, on Ikion Dolopon, try mussels in cream sauce or other delicious *saganaki* ('cooked in a small frying pan') dishes. This place also opens out of season.

Farther up Ikion Dolopon on the opposite side is newcomer *Kala Krassa*. It is yet another establishment specialising in tasty mezedes and manages to squeeze one or two tables onto its little streetside terrace.

Another superlative little ouzeri is *Ouzeri Lefteris*, on Pelasgon, which offers stuffed cuttlefish as well as lobster with tomatoes and peppers. *Argo Restaurant* (☎ 65 141) has wonderful sea views from its terrace and the food is good, with main meals for about 2500 dr. The restaurant is on the headland on the north side of the harbour.

The waterfront restaurants are all much of a muchness: take your pick and hope for the best.

Entertainment
At the time of research, *Symvolo Bar* on Ikion Dolopon was the 'in' bar, though *Ble Notes* at the south end of the beach restaurant strip was offering live Greek music. *Enigma Disco* on Pelasgon rocks to teenybopper tunes when the tourist season kicks in.

OLD ALONNISOS
Nowadays, Old Alonnisos (Hora or Palio Horio) has a strange appearance. The narrow streets of the upper village have a haunted, deserted feel, but the lower village is coming alive with renovated houses and newer villas. These dwellings are owned mainly by Brits and Germans hankering after the simple life or artists seeking inspiration.

Old Alonnisos is a tranquil, picturesque place with lovely views. From the main road just outside Old Alonnisos a path leads down to Megalos Mourtias Beach and other paths lead south to Vythisma and Marpounda beaches.

Places to Stay
There are no hotels in Old Alonnisos, but there is a steadily growing number of domatia. One agreeable place is the *Rooms & Studios* of John Tsoukanas (☎ 65 135), with rates of 6000/9000 dr for singles/doubles with bathroom. The triple rooms have a kitchen. It is on the central square of Plateia Hristou, which is named after its 17th century church. Nearby is the newer *Fadasia House* (☎ 65 186) with lovely rooms for 9000 dr and a studio with fridge and cooker for 13,000 dr. There is also a little snack bar and garden.

Places to Eat
Old Alonnisos has a couple of tavernas close to the bus stop. Both are good, but the one with the best view is *Taverna Aloni*. Take the right fork at the bus stop to get to it. *Bouboulina*, 50m towards the village, is also a decent eatery and farther up in the village itself, there are at least six tavernas open in season. *Nappo* does top-rate pizzas, *Astrofengia* (☎ 65 182), to the left as you enter the village, gets high praise for its imaginative menus, and *Paraport Taverna* (☎ 65 608) up in the main village street has great views towards the south side of the island. Prices at all of them are much the same. A romantic meal for two will cost around 5000 dr including drinks.

AROUND ALONNISOS
Most of Alonnisos' beaches are on the east coast which also means they avoid the strong summer meltemi winds and the flotsam that gets dumped on the west coast beaches. Apart from the road from Patitiri to Old Alonnisos, the only road is one which goes north to the tip of the island. It is driveable and sealed all the way though the last settlement, Yerakas (19 km), is a bit of a let-down when you get there. Dirt tracks lead off to the beaches. Another sealed road leads to the yacht port of Steni Vala and a little farther as far as Kalamakia.

The first beach is the gently shelving **Hrysi Milia Beach**, which is the best beach for children. The next beach up is **Kokkinokastro**, the site of the ancient city of Ikos (once the capital); there are remains of city walls and a necropolis under the sea.

Steni Vala is a small fishing village with a permanent population of 30 and a good beach. There are three tavernas and 30-odd rooms in *domatia*, as well as *Ikaros Camping* (☎ 65 258). This is a small camp site, but it is right on the beach and has reasonable shade from olive trees. Try *Taverna Steni Vala* (☎ 65 590) for both food and lodgings. Mind you don't trip over the posing yachties; they're thick on the ground.

Kalamakia, 3km farther north, has a good beach, rooms and tavernas. **Agios Dimitrios Beach**, farther up still, is an unofficial nudist beach.

ISLETS AROUND ALONNISOS

Alonnisos is surrounded by eight unin-habited islets, all of which have rich flora and fauna. The largest remaining popu-lation of the monk seal *(Monachus monachus)*, a Mediterranean sea mammal faced with extinction, lives in the waters around the Sporades. These factors were the incentive behind the formation of the **marine park** in 1983, which encompasses the sea and islets around Alonnisos. Its research sta-tion is on Alonnisos, near Gerakas Cove. See the boxed text 'Alonnisos Marine Park'.

Piperi, to the north-east of Alonnisos, is a refuge for the monk seal and it is forbid-den to set foot there without a licence to carry out research.

Also north-east of Alonnisos, **Gioura** has many rare plants and a rare species of wild goat. **Kyra Panagia** has good beaches and two abandoned monasteries. **Psathoura** has the submerged remains of an ancient city and the brightest lighthouse in the Aegean.

Peristera, just off Alonnisos' east coast, has several sandy beaches and the remains of a castle. **Lehousa** sits immediately north-west of here.

Skantzoura, to the south-east of Alon-nisos, is the habitat of falcons and the rare Aegean seagull. The eighth islet is tiny **Adelphi**, between Peristera and Skantzoura.

Skyros Σκύρος

☎ 0222   • postcode 340 07   • pop 2800

Skyros is some distance from the rest of the group and differs from them topographic-ally. Almost bisected, its northern half has rolling, cultivated hills and pine forests, but the largely uninhabited south is barren and rocky.

There are only two settlements of any worth on the island: the small port of Linaria, and Skyros Town, the capital, 10km away on the east coast. Skyros is visited by

Alonnisos Marine Park

The National Marine Park of Alonnisos – Northern Sporades is an ambitious but belatedly conceived project begun in May 1992. Its prime aim was the protection of the endangered Mediterranean monk seal (see the boxed text under Kefallonia in the Ionian Islands chapter), but also the preservation of other rare plant and animal species threatened with extinction.

The park is divided into two zones. Zone B, west of Alonnisos, is the less accessible of the two areas and comprises the islets of Kyra Panagia, Gioura, Psathoura, Skantzoura and Piperi. Restrictions on activities apply on all islands and in the case of Piperi, visitors are banned, since the island is home to around 33 species of bird, including 350 to 400 pairs of Eleanora's falcon. Other threatened sea birds found on Piperi include the shag and Audouin's gull. Visitors may approach other islands with private vessels or on day trips organised from Alonnisos.

Zone A comprises Alonnisos Island itself and the island of Peristera off Alonnisos' east coast. Most nautical visitors base themselves here at the yacht point of Steni Vala, though in theory the little harbour of Yerakas in the north of the island could serve as a base, though there are no facilities whatsoever. Restrictions on activities here are less stringent.

For the casual visitor the Alonnisos Marine Park is somewhat inaccessible since tours to the various islands are fairly limited and run during summer only. Bear in mind also that the park exists for the protection of marine animals and not for the entertainment of human visitors, so do not be surprised if you see very few animals at all. In a country not noted in its recent history for long-sightedness in the protection of its fauna, the Alonnisos Marine Park is a welcome and long-overdue innovation.

EVIA & THE SPORADES

poseurs rather than package tourists – and as many of these are wealthy young Athenians as foreigners. Skyros also has quite a different atmosphere from other islands in this region, reminding you more of the Cyclades than the Sporades, especially the stark, cubist architecture of Skyros Town.

Some visitors come to Skyros to attend courses at the Skyros Centre, a centre for holistic health and fitness. See the Skyros Town section for details. Solo women travellers are increasingly drawn to Skyros because of its reputation as a safe, hassle-free island.

Skyros' factual history was mundane in comparison to its mythological origins until Byzantine times, when rogues and criminals from the mainland were exiled on Skyros. Rather than driving away invading pirates, these opportunist exiles entered into a mutually lucrative collaboration with them.

The exiles became the elite of Skyrian society, furnishing and decorating their houses with elaborately hand-carved

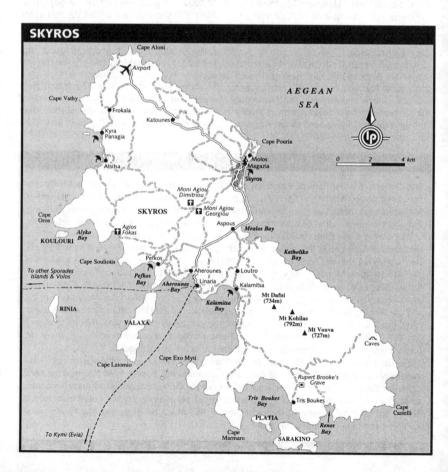

SKYROS

furniture, plates and copper ornaments from Europe, the Middle East and East Asia. Some of these items were brought by sea-farers and some were simply looted by pirates from merchant ships.

Those people on the island before the mainland exiles arrived soon began to emulate the elite in their choice of decor, so local artisans cashed in by making copies of the furniture and plates, a tradition which continues to this day. Almost every Skyrian house is festooned with plates, copperware and hand-carved furniture.

Other traditions also endure. Many elderly Skyrian males still dress in the traditional baggy pantaloons and *trohadia* (multi-thonged footwear unique to the island). The Skyros Lenten Carnival is Greece's weirdest and most wonderful festival, and is the subject of Joy Koulentianou's definitive book on the subject, *The Goat Dance of Skyros*. See the 'Skyros Carnival' in the boxed text.

Another special feature of Skyros which shouldn't go unmentioned, although it will probably go unseen, is the wild Skyrian pony, a breed unique to Skyros. The ponies used to roam freely but are now almost extinct. The only ones you are likely to see are tame ones kept as domestic pets.

Finally, Skyros was the last port of call for the English poet Rupert Brooke (1887-1915), who died of septicaemia at the age of 28 on a ship off the coast of Skyros in 1915, en route to Gallipoli.

Getting There & Away

Air In summer there are now only two flights weekly (Wednesday and Sunday) between Athens and Skyros (50 minutes, 14,200 dr). It is rumoured that a private air service will eventually supplement Olympic's severely reduced schedule. For tickets see Skyros Travel & Tourism Agency, in Skyros Town.

Ferry & Hydrofoil There are ferry services at least twice daily in summer, provided by F/B *Lykomidis,* between the port of Kymi (Evia) and Skyros (2¼ hours, 2300 dr). Five hydrofoils weekly go to Volos (4¼ hours, 14,100 dr) via Alonnisos (1¼ hours, 8000 dr), Skopelos Town (2¼ hours, 8000 dr), Glossa (Skopelos) and Skiathos (2¼ hours, 8400 dr). There are also hydrofoils to Thessaloniki (6¼ hours, 13,400 dr, four weekly).

You can buy ferry tickets from Lykomidis Ticket Office (☎ 91 789, fax 91 791), on Agoras in Skyros Town. Hydrofoil tickets can be bought at Skyros Travel & Tourism. There are also ferry and hydrofoil ticket offices at Linaria. The port police telephone number is ☎ 93 475.

Skyros Travel & Tourism also sells tickets for the Kymi-Athens bus (3¼ hours, 2950 dr) which meets the ferry on arrival at Kymi.

Skyros Carnival

In this pre-Lenten festival, which takes place on the last two Sundays before *Kathara Deftera* (Clean Monday – the first Monday in Lent), young men don goat masks, hairy jackets and dozens of copper goat bells. They then proceed to clank and dance around town, each with a partner (another man), dressed up as a Skyrian bride but also wearing a goat mask. Women and children also wear fancy dress. During these revelries there is singing and dancing, performances of plays, recitations of satirical poems and drinking and feasting. These riotous goings-on are overtly pagan, with elements of Dionysian festivals, goat worship (in ancient times Skyros was renowned for its excellent goat meat and milk), and the cult of Achilles, the principal deity worshipped here. The transvestism evident in the carnival may derive from the fact that Achilles hid on Skyros dressed as a girl to escape the oracle's prophecy that he would die in battle at Troy.

Getting Around

In addition to the options listed here, it is also possible to join a boat trip to sites around the island. See Organised Tours under the Skyros Town entry.

Bus There are five buses daily from Skyros Town to Linaria (250 dr), and Molos (via Magazia). Buses for both Skyros Town and Molos meet the boats and hydrofoils at Linaria. Bus services to Kalamitsa, Pefkos and Atsitsa are organised on an ad hoc basis during summer. Contact Skyros Travel & Tourism for full details.

Car & Motorcycle Cars and 4WD vehicles can be rented from Skyros Travel & Tourism. A car goes for between 12,000 dr and 14,000 dr and a 4WD from 17,000 dr to 19,000 dr. Motorcycles can be rented from Motorbikes (☎ 92 022). To find the outlet, walk north and take the second turn right past Skyros Travel & Tourism. Look for the prominent sign. Giannakakis Bikes (☎ 91 233) also rents out motorcycles. The office is on the left between the bus stop and the main square.

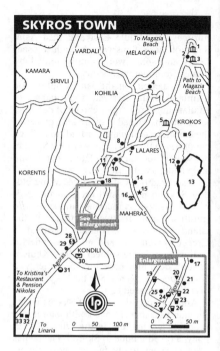

SKYROS TOWN

Skyros' capital is a striking, dazzlingly white town of flat-roofed Cycladic-style houses draped over a high rocky bluff, topped by a 13th century fortress and the monastery of Agios Georgios. It is a gem of a place and a wander around its labyrinthine, whitewashed streets will probably produce an invitation to admire a traditional Skyrian house by its proud and hospitable owner.

Orientation

The bus terminal is at the southern end of town on the main thoroughfare of Agoras, an animated street lined with tavernas, snack bars and grocery shops, and flanked by narrow winding alleyways. To reach the central square of Plateia Iroön walk straight ahead up the hill.

Beyond Plateia Iroön, Agoras forks, with the right fork leading up to the fortress and Moni Agiou Georgiou (with fine frescoes), from where there are breathtaking views. The left fork leads to Plateia Rupert Brooke, dominated by a disconcerting bronze statue of a nude Rupert Brooke. The frankness of the statue caused an outcry among the islanders when it was first installed in the 1930s. From this square a cobbled, stepped path leads in 15 minutes to Magazia Beach.

Information

Skyros does not have tourist police, but you can find most information from Skyros Travel & Tourism (☎ 91 600, fax 92 123) including room bookings. The regular police (☎ 91 274) are just beyond Motorbikes (see the previous Getting Around section).

The National Bank of Greece is on Agoras, a little way up from the bus terminal on the left, and sports an ATM. It is scheduled to move farther up into the village, so be alerted. Foreign-language newspapers and

SKYROS TOWN

PLACES TO STAY	3	Archaeological Museum	19	Apokalypsis
6 Elpida House	4	Skyros Centre	21	Foreign Language
32 Hotel Nefeli	5	Traditional Skyrian House		Newsagency
33 Skyriana Spitia	7	Skyros Shop	22	Iröon
	8	Traditional Greek Products	23	Kata Lathos
PLACES TO EAT		Shop	24	Taxi Rank
10 O Pappous kai Ego	9	Pharmacy	25	Plateia Iröon
11 Margeris	12	Moni Agiou Georgiou		(Main Square)
20 Trypa	13	The Fortress	26	Ares
27 Skyriani Gonia	14	Motorbikes	28	National Bank
	15	Police Station		of Greece
OTHER	16	OTE	29	Giannakakis Bikes
1 Faltaïts Museum	17	Lykomidis Ticket Office	30	Post Office
2 Plateia Rupert Brooke	18	Skyros Travel & Tourism	31	Bus Stop

magazines can be bought at an agency just opposite the main square.

To get to the post office, take the first turn right after the bus terminal and it's on the left. The OTE is opposite the police station, a little way back towards Linaria, on the right as you walk from the bus terminal.

Museums
Skyros Town has three museums. The **archaeological museum** (☎ 91 327) features an impressive collection of artefacts from Mycenaean to Roman times, as well as a traditional Skyrian house interior, transported in its entirety from the home of the benefactor. It is open 8.30 am to 3 pm Tuesday to Sunday. Admission is 500 dr.

The **Faltaïts Museum** is a private museum housing the outstanding collection of a Skyrian ethnologist, Manos Faltaïts. The collection includes costumes, furniture, books, ceramics and photographs. Daily opening times are 10 am to 1 pm, and 5.30 to 8 pm. Admission is free. Both museums are just off Plateia Rupert Brooke.

The little-known **Traditional Skyrian House** (Skyriano Spiti) is just what its name implies. It's difficult to find, but worth the effort. Take the steps which lead up to the fortress. When you come to a crossroad with house No 992 on your right, turn left and the museum is a little way along on the left. It's open 11 am to noon and 6 to 8 pm Monday to Saturday. Admission is 400 dr.

Courses
The Skyros Centre runs courses on a whole range of subjects, from yoga and dancing, to massage and windsurfing. The emphasis is on developing a holistic approach to life. There is a branch in Skyros Town, but the main 'outdoor' complex is at Atsitsa Beach, on the west coast. For detailed information on their fortnightly programs contact the Skyros Centre (☎ 020-7267 4424, fax 7284 3063, email skyros@easynet.co.uk), 92 Prince of Wales Rd, London NW5 3NE, UK.

In the off season, Australian and long-term Skyros resident Kristin Brooks-Tsalapatani of Kristina's Restaurant (see Places to Eat) runs Kristina's Cooking School. Her Greek cookery course runs over five mornings, teaching a maximum of eight nascent gastronomes all about cooking Greek-style. The course costs A$600 (109,000 dr). Bookings are essential.

Organised Tours
Skyros Travel & Tourism (☎ 91 600, fax 92 123), on the left, north of the central square, runs a boat excursion (5500 dr) to Sarakino Islet and the Pendekali and Gerania sea caves. Ask for manager Lefteris Trakos.

Places to Stay – Budget
Accommodation in Skyros Town itself is usually in the form of traditional rooms often decorated with traditional plates. Since these can be hard to find yourself, you

will often be met at the bus stop with offers of domatia from the women who run them. It's not a bad idea to take up one of these offers, at least for starters. Prices should be in the 8000 dr to 12,000 dr range, though as elsewhere there are seasonal fluctuations.

Failing that, head for Skyros Travel & Tourism (see Information) for references to suitable rooms. One of the better options is **Elpida House** where a room for two will work out at about 12,000 dr.

Pension Nikolas (☎ 91 778, fax 93 400) is a small complex of very comfortable, self-contained domatia at the back of Kristina's Restaurant. This is a better option for visitors wanting a quieter place to stay. Ask for the 'room with a view' if you can get it. Prices range from 13,000 dr to 18,000 dr for three people.

Places to Stay – Mid-Range
The C class **Hotel Nefeli** (☎ 91 964, fax 92 061) is the only decent hotel as such in Skyros Town. The lovely rooms have old photographs depicting traditional Skyrian life. It sports a large swimming pool. Rates are 17,500/21,500 dr for singles/doubles. The hotel is on the left just before you enter Skyros Town.

The same hotel can offer you an apartment in **Skyriana Spitia**, an adjoining complex made up of self-contained units in traditional Skyrian style. An apartment for three people costs 36,850 dr but prices may be 50% lower out of season.

Places to Eat
Restaurants in Skyros have proliferated like mushrooms in a dark cellar in recent times and things are definitely looking up on the culinary front. For the best and cheapest coffee in town as well as breakfast, pizzas and sandwiches, seek out **Trypa** on the main street. It's only a small place – blink and you've missed it.

Skyriani Gonia is easy to spot (though the sign is only in Greek) just south of the main square. It opens at 9 am for breakfast and does lunch and dinner. Prices are generally lower than elsewhere. Along the

main street is the very popular and tastefully decorated **O Pappous kai Ego** which serves traditional mezedes as well as dishes to order. It opens at 10 am and closes late. Prices are mid-range – around the 2200 dr mark for a good feed with local wine.

Margeris is the place to go for fresh fish. Other restaurants sell fish but Margeris specialises in it. It's only a small place, but easy enough to spot on the main street. Fish prices are somewhat higher, though still reasonable.

One of the more long-standing establishments is **Kristina's Restaurant** (☎ 91 778), set in a delightful walled garden. Kristina conjures up delectable local and international dishes. The *kaseri* and *sac* cheeses (local specialities), chicken fricassee and cheesecake are recommended. Prices are very reasonable. The restaurant is closed on Sunday. Look for the sign on the south side of town.

Entertainment
The popularity enjoyed by particular bars in Skyros is ephemeral, but flavours of the month at the time of research were the stylish **Kata Lathos**, **Apokalypsis**, **Ares** and **Iröon**, all on or just off Agoras. **Borio**, just south of Skyros Town, was an 'in' disco. There is always some place open all year due to the large transient population of young soldiers.

At Linaria **To Kastro** is another 'in' disco club, as is **O Kavos** for drinks and evening gossip. Try to be at the Kavos when the Lykomidis ferry comes in and witness the impressive sound reception when Richard Strauss' *Also Sprach Zarathustra*, as used in the movie *2001: A Space Odyssey*, is blasted out over the bay from huge speakers. Better still, listen out for it while on the ferry – the sound is better. Sparklers are also handed out to Kavos customers in summer.

MAGAZIA & MOLOS
Μαγαζιά & Μώλος

The resort of Magazia is at the southern end of a splendid, long sandy beach, a short distance north of Skyros Town; quieter Molos is at the northern end of the beach, although there is not much to physically distinguish the two communities these days.

Places to Stay – Budget & Mid-Range

Skyros has one camp site, *Skyros Camping* (☎ *92 458)*, at Magazia. It's a scruffy, run-down place with a few thirsty-looking olive trees offering shade.

Efrosyni Varsamou Rooms (☎ 91 142), above the family ceramics shop in Magazia, are spacious and beautifully furnished. Rates are 12,000/14,800 dr for doubles/triples. If you're walking, go down the cobbled path from Skyros Town, turn right at the bottom, and then right at the camp site (signposted to Magazia and Xenia Hotel) and the rooms are on the left. If you take the bus, get off at the camp site.

If you turn left at Xenia Hotel, in just under 150m you will come to *Alekos Domatia (☎ 91 828)*, on the right overlooking the beach. Pleasant and comfortable rooms are 12,000/14,000 dr with bathroom.

To Perigiali (☎ 91 889, fax 92 770) is a newcomer to the scene. It offers very pleasant rooms surrounding a beautiful garden. It is set back and signposted from Magazia Beach. Rates are 15,500/18,000 dr for singles/doubles.

At Molos, *Motel Hara (☎ 91 601)* has clean, pine-furnished doubles/triples for 11,000/13,200 dr, and some newer self-contained apartments. If you arrive by bus look for it on the right. *Angela's Bungalows (☎ 91 764, fax 92 030)*, set in a lovely garden, has clean, spacious rooms with bathroom, balcony and telephone for 17,000/ 18,000 dr, including breakfast. The bungalows are signposted from the Molos bus terminal. The C class *Hotel Paradise (☎ 91 220, fax 91 441)*, next to the bus terminal, is an attractive hotel with cream marble floors and white walls. Rates here are 18,000 dr for doubles.

Places to Stay – Top End

The island's most luxurious hotel is the A class *Skyros Palace (☎ 91 994, fax 92 070)*, a complex of attractive apartments, which stand in splendid isolation just north of Molos. The apartments have air-con, verandas and music channels. The complex has a cafe, bar, restaurant, TV lounge and swimming pool, and is 50m from a good beach. Mosquitoes can be a problem here: ask for a mosquito zapper. Singles/doubles go for 19,000/22,900 dr in high season.

Places to Eat

Due the more compact nature of the layout of the village, Magazia is probably the better of the two settlements to dine in, with *Stefanos* restaurant first in the stakes for location overlooking the beach. *Korfari* farther along gets good press for its mezedes, while *Tou Thoma to Magazi* on the beach at Molos specialises in lobster. Prices at all three are mid-range, though lobster is quite expensive.

Shopping

A good selection of ceramics is on sale at Efrosyni Varsamou's shop below the domatia of the same name at Magazia. It's hard to imagine any non-Skyrian wanting to wear the multi-thonged trohadia, except maybe a foot fetishist who is into bondage. They can be bought at the Skyros Shop, on the street which leads to Plateia Rupert Brooke.

The Traditional Greek Products Shop (☎ 93 191), on the left at the north end of the main street, stocks all kinds of natural products from royal jelly to retsina, from olive oil to cheese. Woodcarvings are a classy buy, though they can be expensive. There are at least three workshops scattered round town and they're easy to spot.

AROUND SKYROS
Beaches

At **Atsitsa**, on the west coast, there's a tranquil pebble beach shaded by pines. The beach attracts freelance campers, and there's the main outdoor centre of the Skyros Centre and a *taverna* with domatia here. Just to the north is the even less crowded beach of **Kyra Panagia** (also with freelance campers). At **Pefkos**, 10km south-east of Atsitsa, there is another good but small beach and a taverna. If you don't have transport take a Skyros Town-

Linaria bus and ask to be let off at the turn-off. It's a 3km walk from there to the beach. Farther east, the pebble and sand beach at **Kalamitsa** is reasonable but not really worth the extra effort to get there and there is not much shade.

Rupert Brooke's Grave

Rupert Brooke's well tended grave is in a quiet olive grove just inland from Tris Boukes Bay in the south of the island. The actual grave is poorly marked with a rough wooden sign in Greek on the roadside, but you can hardly miss it. The gravestone is inscribed with some verses of Brooke's among which is the following apt epitaph:

If I should die think only this of me:
That there's some corner of a foreign field
That is forever England.

No buses go to this corner of the island. However, you can take an excursion boat to Sarakino Islet, or drive or walk along a good, graded scenic road from Kalamitsa, built for the Greek navy, which now has a naval station on Tris Boukes Bay.

If you walk it will take about 1½ hours; take food and water. If you have come this far with the aim of getting to the sea, you will have to turn back since the area farther down the hill is restricted by the Greek navy and the road onwards is closed.

Language

The Greek language is probably the oldest European language, with an oral tradition of 4000 years and a written tradition of approximately 3000 years. Its evolution over the four millennia was characterised by its strength during the golden age of Athens and the Democracy (mid-5th century BC); its use as a lingua franca throughout the Middle Eastern world, spread by Alexander the Great and his successors as far as India during the Hellenistic period (330 BC to 100 AD); its adaptation as the language of the new religion, Christianity; its use as the official language of the Eastern Roman Empire; and its eventual proclamation as the language of the Byzantine Empire (380-1453).

Greek maintained its status and prestige during the rise of the European Renaissance and was employed as the linguistic perspective for all contemporary sciences and terminologies during the period of Enlightenment. Today, Greek constitutes a large part of the vocabulary of any Indo-European language, and much of the lexicon of any scientific repertoire.

The modern Greek language is a southern Greek dialect which is now used by most Greek speakers both in Greece and abroad. It is the result of an intralinguistic influence and synthesis of the ancient vocabulary combined with words from Greek regional dialects, namely Cretan, Cypriot and Macedonian.

Greek is spoken throughout Greece by a population of around 10 million, and by some five million Greeks who live abroad.

Pronunciation

All Greek words of two or more syllables have an acute accent which indicates where the stress falls. For instance, άγαλμα (statue) is pronounced **agh**alma, and αγάπη (love) is pronounced a**gha**pi. In the following transliterations, bold lettering indicates where stress falls. Note also that **dh** is pronounced as 'th' in 'then'; **gh** is a softer, slightly guttural version of 'g'.

Greetings & Civilities

Hello.
   yasas   Γειά σας.
   yasu (informal)   Γειά σου.
Goodbye.
   an**dio**   Αντίο.
Good morning.
   kali**me**ra   Καλημέρα.
Good afternoon.
   herete   Χαίρετε.
Good evening.
   kali**spe**ra   Καλησπέρα.
Good night.
   kali**nih**ta   Καληνύχτα.
Please.
   paraka**lo**   Παρακαλώ.
Thank you.
   efhari**sto**   Ευχαριστώ.
Yes.
   ne   Ναι.
No.
   ohi   Οχι.
Sorry. (excuse me, forgive me)
   sigh**nomi**   Συγγνώμη.
How are you?
   ti **ka**nete?   Τι κάνετε;
   ti **ka**nis?   Τι κάνεις;
   (informal)
I'm well, thanks.
   kala ef**ha**risto Καλά ευχαριστώ.

Essentials

Do you speak English?
   mi**la**te an**gli**ka? Μιλάτε Αγγλικά;
I understand.
   katala**ve**no   Καταλαβαίνω.
I don't understand.
   dhen katala**ve**no Δεν καταλαβαίνω.
Where is ...?
   pou **i**ne ...?   Πού είναι ...;
How much?
   poso **ka**ni?   Πόσο κάνει;
When?
   pote?   Πότε;

The Greek Alphabet & Pronunciation

Greek	Pronunciation Guide		Example		
Α α	a	as in 'father'	αγάπη	*agha*pi	love
Β β	v	as in 'vine'	βήμα	*vi*ma	step
Γ γ	gh	like a rough 'g'	γάτα	*gha*ta	cat
	y	as in 'yes'	για	*ya*	for
Δ δ	dh	as in 'there'	δέμα	*dhe*ma	parcel
Ε ε	e	as in 'egg'	ένας	*e*nas	one (m)
Ζ ζ	z	as in 'zoo'	ζώο	*zoo*	animal
Η η	i	as in 'feet'	ήταν	*i*tan	was
Θ θ	th	as in 'throw'	θέμα	*the*ma	theme
Ι ι	i	as in 'feet'	ίδιος	*i*dhyos	same
Κ κ	k	as in 'kite'	καλά	ka*la*	well
Λ λ	l	as in 'leg'	λάθος	*la*thos	mistake
Μ μ	m	as in 'man'	μαμά	ma*ma*	mother
Ν ν	n	as in 'net'	νερό	ne*ro*	water
Ξ ξ	x	as in 'ox'	ξύδι	*ksi*dhi	vinegar
Ο ο	o	as in 'hot'	όλα	*o*la	all
Π π	p	as in 'pup'	πάω	*pao*	I go
Ρ ρ	r	as in 'road'	ρέμα	*re*ma	stream
		a slightly trilled *r*	ρόδα	*ro*dha	tyre
Σ σ, ς	s	as in 'sand'	σημάδι	si*ma*dhi	mark
Τ τ	t	as in 'tap'	τόπι	*to*pi	ball
Υ υ	i	as in 'feet'	ύστερα	*i*stera	after
Φ φ	f	as in 'find'	φύλλο	*fi*lo	leaf
Χ χ	h	as the *ch* in Scottish *loch*, or	χάνω	*ha*no	I lose
		like a rough *h*	χέρι	*he*ri	hand
Ψ ψ	ps	as in 'lapse'	ψωμί	pso*mi*	bread
Ω ω	o	as in 'hot'	ώρα	*o*ra	time

Combinations of Letters

The combinations of letters shown here are pronounced as follows:

Greek	Pronunciation Guide		Example		
ει	i	as in 'feet'	είδα	*i*dha	I saw
οι	i	as in 'feet'	οικόπεδο	i*ko*pedho	land
αι	e	as in 'bet'	αίμα	*e*ma	blood
ου	u	as in 'mood'	πού	*pou*	who/what
μπ	b	as in 'beer'	μπάλα	*ba*la	ball
	mb	as in 'amber'	κάμπος	*kam*bos	forest
ντ	d	as in 'dot'	ντουλάπα	dou*la*pa	wardrobe
	nd	as in 'bend'	πέντε	*pen*de	five
γκ	g	as in 'God'	γκάζι	*ga*zi	gas
γγ	ng	as in 'angle'	αγγελία	ange*li*a	classified
γξ	ks	as in 'minks'	σφιγξ	*sfinks*	sphynx
τζ	dz	as in 'hands'	τζάκι	*dza*ki	fireplace

The pairs of vowels shown above are pronounced separately if the first has an acute accent, or the second a dieresis, as in the examples below:

γαϊδουράκι	gaidhou*ra*ki	little donkey
Κάιρο	*kai*ro	Cairo

Some Greek consonant sounds have no English equivalent. The υ of the groups αυ, ευ and ηυ is generally pronounced 'v'. The Greek question mark is represented with the English equivalent of a semicolon ';'.

Small Talk

What's your name?
pos sas lene?   Πώς σας λένε;
My name is ...
me lene ...   Με λένε ...
Where are you from?
apo pou iste?   Από πού είστε;

I'm from ...
ime apo ...   Είμαι από ...
America
tin ameriki   την Αμερική
Australia
tin afstralia   την Αυστραλία
England
tin anglia   την Αγγλία
Ireland
tin irlandhia   την Ιρλανδία
New Zealand
ti nea zilandhia   τη Νέα Ζηλανδία
Scotland
ti skotia   τη Σκωτία

How old are you?
poson hronon iste?   Πόσων χρονών είστε;
I'm ... years old.
ime ... hronon   Είμαι ... χρονών.

Getting Around

What time does the ... leave/arrive?
ti ora fevyi/ ftani to ...?   Τι ώρα φεύγει/ φτάνει το ...;

plane	*aeroplano*	αεροπλάνο
boat	*karavi*	καράβι
bus (city)	*astiko*	αστικό
bus (intercity)	*leoforio*	λεωφορείο
train	*treno*	τραίνο

I'd like ...
tha ithela ...   Θα ήθελα ...
a return ticket
isitirio me epistrofi   εισιτήριο με επιστροφή
two tickets
dhio isitiria   δυο εισιτήρια
a student's fare
fititiko isitirio   φοιτητικό εισιτήριο

Signs

ΕΙΣΟΔΟΣ	ENTRY
ΕΞΟΔΟΣ	EXIT
ΩΘΗΣΑΤΕ	PUSH
ΣΥΡΑΤΕ	PULL
ΓΥΝΑΙΚΩΝ	WOMEN (toilets)
ΑΝΔΡΩΝ	MEN (toilets)
ΝΟΣΟΚΟΜΕΙΟ	HOSPITAL
ΑΣΤΥΝΟΜΙΑ	POLICE
ΑΠΑΓΟΡΕΥΕΤΑΙ	PROHIBITED
ΕΙΣΙΤΗΡΙΑ	TICKETS

first class
proti thesi   πρώτη θέση
economy
touristiki thesi   τουριστική θέση

train station
sidhirodhro- mikos stathmos   σιδηροδρομικός σταθμός
timetable
dhromologio   δρομολόγιο
taxi
taxi   ταξί

Where can I hire a car?
pou boro na nikyaso ena aftokinito?   Πού μπορώ να νοικιάσω ένα αυτοκίνητο;

Directions

How do I get to ...?
pos tha pao sto/ sti ...?   Πώς θα πάω στο/ στη ...;
Where is ...?
pou ine ...?   Πού είναι...;
Is it near?
ine konda?   Είναι κοντά;
Is it far?
ine makria?   Είναι μακριά;

straight ahead	*efthia*	ευθεία
left	*aristera*	αριστερά
right	*dexia*	δεξιά
behind	*piso*	πίσω
far	*makria*	μακριά
near	*konda*	κοντά
opposite	*apenandi*	απέναντι

Can you show me on the map?
borite na mou to dhixete sto harti?
Μπορείτε να μου το δείξετε
στο χάρτη;

Around Town

I'm looking for (the) ...
psahno ya ...
Ψάχνω για ...

bank	*trapeza*	τράπεζα
beach	*paralia*	παραλία
castle	*kastro*	κάστρο
church	*ekklisia*	εκκλησία
... embassy	*tin ... presvia*	την ... πρεσβεία
market	*aghora*	αγορά
museum	*musio*	μουσείο
police	*astynomia*	αστυνομία
post office	*tahydromio*	ταχυδρομείο
ruins	*arhea*	αρχαία

I want to exchange some money.
thelo na exaryiroso lefta
Θέλω να εξαργυρώσω λεφτά.

Accommodation

Where is ...?
pou ine ...? Πού είναι ...;
I'd like ...
thelo ena ... Θέλω ένα ...

a cheap hotel
ftino xenodohio φτηνό ξενοδοχείο
a clean room
katharo dhomatio καθαρό δωμάτιο
a good hotel
kalo xenodohio καλό ξενοδοχείο
a camp site
kamping κάμπιγκ

single	*mono*	μονό
double	*dhiplo*	διπλό
room	*dhomatio*	δωμάτιο
with bathroom	*me banio*	με μπάνιο
key	*klidhi*	κλειδί

How much is it ...?
poso kani ...? Πόσο κάνει ...;
per night
ti vradhya τη βραδυά

Emergencies

Help!
voithya! Βοήθεια!
Police!
astynomia! Αστυνομία!
There's been an
accident.
eyine atihima Εγινε ατύχημα.
Call a doctor!
fonaxte ena yatro! Φωνάξτε ένα ιατρό!
Call an ambulance!
tilefoniste ya asthenoforo! Τηλεφωνήστε για ασθενοφόρο!
I'm ill.
ime arostos (m) Είμαι άρρωστος
ime arosti (f) Είμαι άρρωστη
I'm lost.
eho hathi Εχω χαθεί
Thief!
klefti! Κλέφτη!
Go away!
fiye! Φύγε!
I've been raped.
me viase kapyos Με βίασε κάποιος.
I've been robbed.
meklepse kapyos Μ'έκλεψε κάποιος.
Where are the toilets?
pou ine i toualetez? Πού είναι οι τουαλέτες;

for ... nights
ya ... vradhyez για ... βραδυές
Is breakfast included?
symberilamvani ke pro-ino? Συμπεριλαμβάνει και πρωϊνό;
May I see it?
boro na to dho? Μπορώ να το δω;
Where is the bathroom?
pou ine tobanio? Πού είναι το μπάνιο;
It's expensive.
ine akrivo Είναι ακριβό.
I'm leaving today.
fevgho simera Φεύγω σήμερα.

Food

breakfast	pro-ino	πρωϊνό
lunch	mesimvrino	μεσημβρινό
dinner	vradhyno	βραδυνό
beef	vodhino	βοδινό
bread	psomi	ψωμί
beer	byra	μπύρα
cheese	tyri	τυρί
chicken	kotopoulo	κοτόπουλο
Greek coffee	ellinikos kafes	ελληνικός καφές
iced coffee	frappe	φραππέ
lamb	arni	αρνί
milk	ghala	γάλα
mineral water	metalliko nero	μεταλλικό νερό
tea	tsai	τσάι
wine	krasi	κρασί

I'm a vegetarian.
ime hortofaghos   Είμαι χορτοφάγος.

Shopping

How much is it?
poso kani?
Πόσο κάνει;
I'm just looking.
aplos kitazo
Απλώς κοιτάζω.
I'd like to buy ...
thelo n'aghoraso ...
Θέλω ν΄αγοράσω ...
Do you accept credit cards?
pernete pistotikez kartez?
Παίρνετε πιστωτικές κάρτες;
Could you lower the price?
borite na mou kanete mya kaliteri timi?
Μπορείτε να μου κάνετε μια καλύτερη τιμή;

Time & Dates

What time is it?
ti ora ine?   Τι ώρα είναι;

It's ...	ine ...	είναι ...
1 o'clock	mia i ora	μία η ώρα
2 o'clock	dhio i ora	δύο η ώρα
7.30	efta ke misi	εφτά και μισή
am	to pro-i	το πρωί
pm	to apoyevma	το απόγευμα
today	simera	σήμερα

tonight	apopse	απόψε
now	tora	τώρα
yesterday	hthes	χθες
tomorrow	avrio	αύριο

Sunday	kyriaki	Κυριακή
Monday	dheftera	Δευτέρα
Tuesday	triti	Τρίτη
Wednesday	tetarti	Τετάρτη
Thursday	pempti	Πέμπτη
Friday	paraskevi	Παρασκευή
Saturday	savato	Σάββατο

January	ianouarios	Ιανουάριος
February	fevrouarios	Φεβρουάριος
March	martios	Μάρτιος
April	aprilios	Απρίλιος
May	maïos	Μάιος
June	iounios	Ιούνιος
July	ioulios	Ιούλιος
August	avghoustos	Αύγουστος
September	septemvrios	Σεπτέμβριος
October	oktovrios	Οκτώβριος
November	noemvrios	Νοέμβριος
December	dhekemvrios	Δεκέμβριος

Health

I need a doctor.
hriazome yatro   Χρειάζομαι ιατρό.
Can you take me to hospital?
borite na me pate sto nosokomio?   Μπορείτε να με πάτε στο νοσοκομείο;
I want something for ...
thelo kati ya ...   Θέλω κάτι για ...
diarrhoea
dhiaria   διάρροια
insect bites
tsimbimata apo endoma   τσιμπήματα από έντομα
travel sickness
naftia taxidhiou   ναυτία ταξιδιού

aspirin
aspirini   ασπιρίνη
condoms
profylaktika (kapotez)   προφυλακτικά (καπότες)
contact lenses
faki epafis   φακοί επαφής
medical insurance
yatriki asfalya   ιατρική ασφάλεια

Numbers

0	*midhen*	μηδέν
1	*enas*	ένας (m)
	mia	μία (f)
	ena	ένα (n)
2	*dhio*	δύο
3	*tris*	τρεις (m & f)
	tria	τρία (n)
4	*teseris*	τέσσερεις (m & f)
	tesera	τέσσερα (n)
5	*pende*	πέντε
6	*exi*	έξη
7	*epta*	επτά
8	*ohto*	οχτώ
9	*enea*	εννέα
10	*dheka*	δέκα

20	*ikosi*	είκοσι
30	*trianda*	τριάντα
40	*saranda*	σαράντα
50	*peninda*	πενήντα
60	*exinda*	εξήντα
70	*evdhominda*	εβδομήντα
80	*oghdhonda*	ογδόντα
90	*eneninda*	ενενήντα
100	*ekato*	εκατό
1000	*hilii*	χίλιοι (m)
	hiliez	χίλιες (f)
	hilia	χίλια (n)

one million
    ena ekatomyrio   ένα εκατομμύριο

Transliteration & Variant Spellings: An Explanation

The issue of correctly transliterating Greek into the Latin alphabet is a vexed one, fraught with inconsistencies and pitfalls. The Greeks themselves are not very consistent when it comes to providing transliterated names on their signs, though things are gradually improving. The word 'Piraeus', for example, has been variously represented by the following transliterations: Pireas, Piraievs and Pireefs; and when appearing as a street name (eg Piraeus Street) you will also find Pireos!

This is compounded by the linguistic minefield of diglossy, or the two forms of the Greek language. The purist form is called Katharevousa and the popular form is Dimotiki (Demotic). The Katharevousa form was never more than an artificiality and Dimotiki has always been spoken as the mainstream language, but this linguistic schizophrenia means there are often two Greek words for each English word. Thus, the word for 'baker' in everyday language is *fournos*, but the shop sign will more often than not say *artopoieion*. The baker's product will be known in the street as *psomi*, but in church as *artos*.

As if all that wasn't enough, there is also the issue of anglicised vs hellenised forms of place names: Athina vs Athens, Patra vs Patras, Thiva vs Thebes, Evia vs Euboia – the list goes on and on! Toponymic diglossy (the existence of both an official and everyday name for a place) is responsible for Kerkyra/Corfu, Zante/Zakynthos, and Santorini/Thira. In this guide we have usually provided modern Greek equivalents for town names, with one or two well known exceptions, eg Athens and Patras. For ancient sites, settlements or people from antiquity, we have attempted to stick to the more familiar classical names; so we have Thucydides instead of Thoukididis, Mycenae instead of Mykines.

Problems in transliteration have particular implications for vowels, especially given that Greek has six ways of rendering the vowel sound *ee*, two ways of rendering the *o* sound and two ways of rendering the *e* sound. In most instances in this book, *y* has been used for the *ee* sound when a Greek *upsilon* (υ, Y) has been used, and *i* for Greek *ita* (η, Η) and *iota* (ι, Ι). In the case of the Greek vowel combinations that make the *ee* sound, that is οι, ει and υι, an *i* has been used. For the two Greek *e* sounds, αι and ε, an *e* has been employed.

As far as the transliteration of consonants is concerned, the Greek letter *gamma* (γ, Γ) appears as *g* rather than *y* throughout this book. This means that *agios* (Greek for male saint) is used rather than *ayios*, and *agia* (female saint) rather than *ayia*. The letter *delta* (δ, Δ) appears as *d* rather than *dh* throughout this book, so *domatia* (rooms), rather than *dhomatia*, is used. The letter *fi* (φ, Φ) can be transliterated as either *f* or *ph*. Here, a general rule of thumb is that classical names are spelt with a *ph* and modern names with an *f*. So Phaistos is used rather than Festos, and Folegandros is used rather than Pholegandros. The Greek *chi* (ξ, Ξ) has usually been repres-ented as *h* in order to approximate the Greek pronunciation as closely as possible. Thus, we have 'Haralambos' instead of 'Charalambos' and 'Polytehniou' instead of 'Polytechniou'. Bear in mind that the *h* is to be pronounced as an aspirated *h*, much like the *ch* in loch. The letter *kapa* (κ, Κ) has been used to represent that sound, except where well known names from antiquity have adopted by convention the letter *c*, eg Polycrates, Acropolis.

Wherever reference to a street name is made, we have omitted the Greek word *'odos'*, but words for avenue *(leoforos)* and square *(plateia)* have been included.

For a more detailed guide to the Greek language, check out Lonely Planet's comprehensive *Greek phrasebook*.

Glossary

Achaean civilisation – see *Mycenaean civilisation*

acropolis – highest point of an ancient city

AEK – Athens football club

agia (f), agios (m) – saint

agora – commercial area of an ancient city; shopping precinct in modern Greece

amphora – large two-handled vase in which wine or oil was kept

ANEK – Anonymi Naftiliaki Eteria Kritis; main shipping line to Crete

Archaic period (800-480 BC) – also known as the Middle Age; period in which the city-states emerged from the 'dark age' and traded their way to wealth and power; the city-states were unified by a Greek alphabet and common cultural pursuits, engendering a sense of national identity

architrave – part of the *entablature* which rests on the columns of a temple

arhontika – 17th and 18th century AD mansions which belonged to arhons, the leading citizens of a town

Arvanites – Albanian-speakers of north-western Greece

Asia Minor – the Aegean littoral of Turkey centred around İzmir but also including İstanbul; formerly populated by Greeks

askitiria – mini-chapels; places of solitary worship

baglamas – miniature *bouzouki* with a tinny sound

basilica – early Christian church

bouleuterion – council house

bouzouki – stringed lute-like instrument associated with rembetika music

bouzoukia – 'bouzoukis'; used to mean any nightclub where the bouzouki is played and low-grade blues songs are sung; see *skyladika*

buttress – support built against the outside of a wall

Byzantine Empire – characterised by the merging of Hellenistic culture and Christianity and named after Byzantium, the city on the Bosphorus which became the capital of the Roman Empire in 324 AD; when the Roman Empire was formally divided in 395 AD, Rome went into decline and the eastern capital, renamed Constantinople after Emperor Constantine I, flourished; the Byzantine Empire dissolved after the fall of Constantinople to the Turks in 1453

caïque – small, sturdy fishing boat often used to carry passengers

capital – top of a column

cella – room in a temple where the cult statue stood

choregos – wealthy citizen who financed choral and dramatic performances

city-states – states comprising a sovereign city and its dependencies; the city-states of Athens and Sparta were famous rivals

classical Greece – period in which the city-states reached the height of their wealth and power after the defeat of the Persians in the 5th century BC; ended with the decline of the city-states as a result of the Peloponnesian Wars, and the expansionist aspirations of Philip II, King of Macedon (ruled 359-336 BC), and his son, Alexander the Great (ruled 336-323 BC)

Corinthian – order of Greek architecture recognisable by columns with bell-shaped *capitals* with sculpted elaborate ornaments based on acanthus leaves

cornice – the upper part of the *entablature*, extending beyond the frieze

crypt – lowest part of a church, often a burial chamber

Cycladic civilisation (3000-1100 BC) – civilisation which emerged following the settlement of Phoenician colonists on the Cycladic islands

cyclopes – mythical one-eyed giants

dark age (1200-800 BC) – period in which Greece was under *Dorian* rule

delfini – dolphin; common name for hydrofoil

diglossy – the existence of two forms of one language within a country; has existed in Greece for most of its modern history

dimarhio – town hall

Dimotiki – Demotic Greek language; the official spoken language of Greece

domatio (s), domatia (pl) – room; a cheap accommodation option available in most tourist areas

Dorians – Hellenic warriors who invaded Greece around 1200 BC, demolishing the city-states and destroying the Mycenaean civilisation; heralded Greece's 'dark age', when the artistic and cultural advancements of the Mycenaeans and Minoans were abandoned; the Dorians later developed into land-holding aristocrats which encouraged the resurgence of independent city-states led by wealthy aristocrats

Doric – order of Greek architecture characterised by a column which has no base, a *fluted* shaft and a relatively plain capital, when compared with the flourishes evident on *Ionic* and *Corinthian* capitals

ELPA – Elliniki Leshi Periigiseon & Aftokinitou; Greek motoring and touring club

ELTA – Ellinika Tahydromia; Greek post office

entablature – part of a temple between the tops of the columns and the roof

EOS – Ellinikos Orivatikos Syllogos; Greek alpine club

EOT – Ellinikos Organismos Tourismou; national tourism organisation which has offices in most major towns

Epitaphios – picture on cloth of Christ on his bier

estiatorio – restaurant serving ready-made food as well as a la carte dishes

ET – Elliniki Tileorasi; state television company

evzones – famous border guards from the northern Greek village of Evzoni; they also guard the Parliament building

Filiki Eteria – friendly society; a group of Greeks in exile; formed during Ottoman rule to organise an uprising against the Turks

fluted – (of a column) having vertical indentations on the shaft

frappé – iced coffee

frieze – part of the *entablature* which is above the *architrave*

galaktopoleio (s), galaktopoleia (pl) – a shop which sells dairy products

Geometric period (1200-800 BC) – period characterised by pottery decorated with geometric designs; sometimes referred to as Greece's 'dark age'

GESEE – Greek trade union association

giouvetsi – casserole of meat and pasta

Hellas, Ellas or Ellada – the Greek name for Greece

Hellenistic period – prosperous, influential period of Greek civilisation ushered in by Alexander the Great's empire-building and lasting until the Roman sacking of Corinth in 146 BC

Helots – original inhabitants of Lakonia whom the Spartans used as slaves

hora – main town (usually on an island)

iconostasis – altar screen embellished with icons

Ionic – order of Greek architecture characterised by a column with truncated flutes and capitals with ornaments resembling scrolls

kafeneio (s), kafeneia (pl) – traditionally a male-only coffee house where cards and backgammon are played

kafeteria – upmarket *kafeneio*, mainly for younger people

kalderimi – cobbled footpath

kasseri – mild, slightly rubbery sheep's-milk cheese

kastro – walled-in town

Katharevousa – purist Greek language; very rarely used these days

katholikon – principal church of a monastic complex

kefi – an undefinable feeling of good spirit, without which no Greek can have a good time

KKE – Kommounistiko Komma Elladas; Greek communist party

Koine – Greek language used in pre-Byzantine times; the language of the church liturgy

kore – female statue of the Archaic period; see *kouros*

kouros – male statue of the Archaic period, characterised by a stiff body posture and enigmatic smile

KTEL – Kino Tamio Ispraxeon Leoforion; national bus cooperative; runs all long-distance bus services

Kypriako – the 'Cyprus issue'; politically sensitive and never forgotten by Greeks and Greek Cypriots

libation – in ancient Greece, wine or food which was offered to the gods

Linear A – Minoan script; so far undeciphered

Linear B – Mycenaean script; has been deciphered

lyra – small violin-like instrument, played on the knee; common in Cretan and Pontian music

malakas – literally 'wanker'; used as a familiar term of address, or as an insult, depending on context

mangas – 'wide boy' or 'dude'; originally a person of the underworld, now any street-wise person

mayiria – cook houses

megaron – central room of a Mycenaean palace

meltemi – north-easterly wind which blows throughout much of Greece during the summer

metope – the sculpted section of a *Doric frieze*

meze (s), mezedes (pl) – appetiser

Middle Age – see *Archaic period*

Minoan civilisation (3000-1100 BC) – Bronze Age culture of Crete named after the mythical king Minos and characterised by pottery and metalwork of great beauty and artisanship

moni – monastery or convent

Mycenaean civilisation (1900-1100 BC) – first great civilisation of the Greek mainland, characterised by powerful independent city-states ruled by kings; also known as the Achaean civilisation

myzithra – soft sheep's-milk cheese

narthex – porch of a church

nave – aisle of a church

Nea Dimokratia – New Democracy; conservative political party

necropolis – literally 'city of the dead'; ancient cemetery

nefos – cloud; usually used to refer to pollution in Athens

NEL – Naftiliaki Eteria Lesvou; Lesvos shipping company

neo kyma – 'new wave'; left-wing music of the boîtes and clubs of 1960s Athens

nomarhia – prefecture building

nomos – prefectures into which the regions and island groups of Greece are divided

nymphaeum – in ancient Greece, building containing a fountain and often dedicated to nymphs

OA – Olympiaki Aeroporia or Olympic Airways; Greece's national airline and major domestic air carrier

odeion – ancient Greek indoor theatre

odos – street

ohi – 'no'; what the Greeks said to Mussolini's ultimatum when he said surrender or be invaded; the Italians were subsequently repelled and the event is celebrated on October 28

omphalos – sacred stone at Delphi which the ancient Greeks believed marked the centre of the world

OSE – Organismos Sidirodromon Ellados; Greek railways organisation

OTE – Organismos Tilepikinonion Ellados; Greece's major telecommunications carrier

oud – a bulbous, stringed instrument with a sharply raked-back head

ouzeri (s), ouzeria (pl) – place which serves *ouzo* and light snacks

ouzo – a distilled spirit made from grapes and flavoured with aniseed

Panagia – Mother of God; name frequently used for churches

Pantokrator – painting or mosaic of Christ in the centre of the dome of a Byzantine church

pantopoleio – general store

PAO – Panathinaïkos football club

PAOK – main Thessaloniki football club

paralia – waterfront

PASOK – Panellinio Sosialistiko Komma; Greek socialist party

pediment – triangular section (often filled with sculpture) above the columns, found at the front and back of a classical Greek temple

periptero (s), periptera (pl) – street kiosk

peristyle – columns surrounding a building (usually a temple) or courtyard

pinakotheke – picture gallery

pithos (s), pithoi (pl) – large Minoan storage jar

plateia – square

Politiki Anixi – Political Spring; centrist political party

Pomaks – minority, non-Turkic Muslim people from northern Greece

Pontians – Greeks whose ancestral home was on the Black Sea coast of Turkey

PRO-PO – Prognostiko Podosferou; Greek football pools

propylon (s), propylaia (pl) – elaborately built main entrance to an ancient city or sanctuary; a propylon had one gateway and a propylaia more than one

psarotaverna – taverna specialising in seafood

psistaria – restaurant serving grilled food

rembetika – blues songs commonly associated with the underworld of the 1920s

retsina – resinated white wine

rhyton – another name for a libation vessel

rizitika – traditional, patriotic songs of Crete

sacristy – room attached to a church where sacred vessels etc are kept

sandouri – hammered dulcimer from Asia Minor

Sarakatsani – Greek-speaking nomadic shepherd community from northern Greece

SEO – Syllogos Ellinon Orivaton; Greek mountaineers' association

skites (s), skiti (pl) – hermit's dwelling

Skopia – what the Greeks call the Former Yugoslav Republic of Macedonia (FYROM)

skyladika – literally 'dog songs'; popular, but not lyrically challenging, blues songs often sung in *bouzoukia* nightclubs

spilia – cave

stele (s), stelae (pl) – grave stone which stands upright

stoa – long colonnaded building, usually in an *agora*; used as a meeting place and shelter in ancient Greece

taverna – traditional restaurant which serves food and wine

temblon – votive screen

tholos – Mycenaean tomb shaped like a beehive

toumberleki – small lap drum played with the fingers

triglyph – sections of a *Doric frieze* between the *metopes*

trireme – ancient Greek galley with three rows of oars on each side

tsikoudia – Cretan version of *tsipouro*

Tsingani – Gypsies or Roma

tsipouro – distilled spirit made from grapes

vaulted – having an arched roof, normally of brick or stone

velenza – flokati rug

Vlach – traditional, semi-nomadic shepherds from northern Greece who speak a Latin-based dialect

volta – promenade; evening stroll

volute – spiral decoration on *Ionic* capitals

xythomyzithra – soft sheep's-milk cheese

zaharoplasteio (s), zaharoplasteia (pl) – patisserie; shop selling cakes, chocolates, sweets and, sometimes, alcoholic drinks

Lonely Planet Journeys

Journeys is a unique collection of travel writing – published by the company that understands travel better than anyone else. It is a series for anyone who has ever experienced – or dreamed of – the magical moment when they encountered a strange culture or saw a place for the first time. They are tales to read while you're planning a trip, while you're on the road or while you're in an armchair in front of a fire.

These outstanding titles explore our planet through the eyes of a diverse group of international writers. JOURNEYS books catch the spirit of a place, illuminate a culture, recount a crazy adventure or introduce a fascinating way of life. They always entertain, and always enrich the experience of travel.

MALI BLUES
Traveling to an African Beat
Lieve Joris (translated by Sam Garrett)

Drought, rebel uprisings, ethnic conflict: these are the predominant images of West Africa. But as Lieve Joris travels in Senegal, Mauritania and Mali, she meets survivors, fascinating individuals charting new ways of living between tradition and modernity. With her remarkable gift for drawing out people's stories, Joris brilliantly captures the rhythms of a world that refuses to give in.

THE GATES OF DAMASCUS
Lieve Joris (translated by Sam Garrett)

This best-selling book is a beautifully drawn portrait of day-to-day life in modern Syria. Through her intimate contact with local people, Lieve Joris draws us into the fascinating world that lies behind the gates of Damascus. Hala's husband is a political prisoner, jailed for his opposition to the Assad regime; through the author's friendship with Hala we see how Syrian politics impacts on the lives of ordinary people.

THE OLIVE GROVE
Travels in Greece
Katherine Kizilos

Katherine Kizilos travels to fabled islands, troubled border zones and her family's village deep in the mountains. She vividly evokes breathtaking landscapes, generous people and passionate politics, capturing the complexities of a country she loves.

'beautifully captures the real tensions of Greece' – *Sunday Times*

KINGDOM OF THE FILM STARS
Journey into Jordan
Annie Caulfield

Kingdom of the Film Stars is a travel book and a love story. With honesty and humour, Annie Caulfield writes of travelling in Jordan and falling in love with a Bedouin with film-star looks.

She offers fascinating insights into the country – from the tent life of traditional women to the hustle of downtown Amman – and unpicks tight-woven western myths about the Arab world.

Lonely Planet Travel Atlases

L onely Planet has long been famous for the number and quality of its guidebook maps. Now we've gone one step further and produced a handy companion series: Lonely Planet travel atlases – maps of a country produced in book form.

Unlike other maps, which look good but lead travellers astray, our travel atlases have been researched on the road by Lonely Planet's experienced team of writers. All details are carefully checked to ensure the atlas corresponds with the equivalent Lonely Planet guidebook.

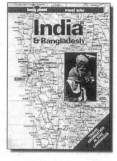

- full-colour throughout
- maps researched and checked by Lonely Planet authors
- place names correspond with Lonely Planet guidebooks
- no confusing spelling differences
- legend and travelling information in English, French, German, Japanese and Spanish
- size: 230 x 160 mm

Available now: Chile & Easter Island • Egypt • India & Bangladesh • Israel & the Palestinian Territories • Jordan, Syria & Lebanon • Kenya • Laos • Portugal • South Africa, Lesotho & Swaziland • Thailand • Turkey • Vietnam • Zimbabwe, Botswana & Namibia

Lonely Planet TV Series & Videos

L onely Planet travel guides have been brought to life on television screens around the world. Like our guides, the programs are based on the joy of independent travel and look honestly at some of the most exciting, picturesque and frustrating places in the world. Each show is presented by one of three travellers from Australia, England or the USA and combines an innovative mixture of video, Super-8 film, atmospheric soundscapes and original music.

Videos of each episode – containing additional footage not shown on television – are available from good book and video shops, but the availability of individual videos varies with regional screening schedules.

Video destinations include: Alaska • American Rockies • Argentina • Australia – The South-East • Baja California & the Copper Canyon • Brazil • Central Asia • Chile & Easter Island • Corsica, Sicily & Sardinia – The Mediterranean Islands • East Africa (Tanzania & Zanzibar) • Cuba • Ecuador & the Galapagos Islands • Ethiopia • Greenland & Iceland • Hungary & Romania • Indonesia • Israel & the Sinai Desert • Jamaica • Japan • La Ruta Maya • London • The Middle East (Syria, Jordan & Lebanon • Morocco • New York City • Northern Spain • North India • Outback Australia • Pacific Islands (Fiji, Solomon Islands & Vanuatu) • Pakistan • Peru • The Philippines • South Africa & Lesotho • South India • South West China • South West USA • Trekking in Uganda & Congo • Turkey • Vietnam • West Africa • Zimbabwe, Botswana & Namibia

The Lonely Planet TV series is produced by: Pilot Productions
The Old Studio
18 Middle Row
London W10 5AT, UK

Lonely Planet Online

W hether you've just begun planning your next trip, or you're chasing down specific info on currency regulations or visa requirements, check out Lonely Planet Online for up-to-the-minute travel information.

As well as miniguides to more than 250 destinations, you'll find maps, photos, travel news, health and visa updates, travel advisories and discussion of the ecological and political issues you need to be aware of as you travel. You'll also find timely upgrades to popular guidebooks that you can print out and stick in the back of your book.

There's an online travellers' forum (The Thorn Tree) where you can share your experience of life on the road, meet travel companions and ask other travellers for their recommendations and advice.

There's also a complete and up-to-date list of all Lonely Planet travel products including travel guides, diving and snorkeling guides, phrasebooks, atlases, travel literature and videos, and a simple online ordering facility if you can't find the book you want elsewhere.

Lonely Planet Diving & Snorkeling Guides

B eautifully illustrated with full-colour photos throughout, Lonely Planet s Pisces books explore the world s best diving and snorkeling areas and prepare divers for what to expect when they get there, both topside and underwater.

Dive sites are described in detail with specifics on depths, visibility, level of difficulty, special conditions, underwater photography tips and common and unusual marine life present. You ll also find practical logistical information and coverage on topside activities and attractions, sections on diving health and safety, plus listings for diving services, live-aboards, dive resorts and tourist offices.

LONELY PLANET

Guides by Region

onely Planet is known worldwide for publishing practical, reliable and no-nonsense travel information in our guides and on our Web site. The Lonely Planet list covers just about every accessible part of the world. Currently there are thirteen series: travel guides, shoestring guides, walking guides, city guides, phrasebooks, audio packs, city maps, travel atlases, diving & snorkeling guides, restaurant guides, first-time travel guides, healthy travel and travel literature.

AFRICA Africa on a shoestring ● Africa – the South ● Arabic (Egyptian) phrasebook ● Arabic (Moroccan) phrasebook ● Cairo ● Cape Town ● Cape Town city map● Central Africa ● East Africa ● Egypt ● Egypt travel atlas ● Ethiopian (Amharic) phrasebook ● The Gambia & Senegal ● Healthy Travel Africa ● Kenya ● Kenya travel atlas ● Malawi, Mozambique & Zambia ● Morocco ● North Africa ● South Africa, Lesotho & Swaziland ● South Africa, Lesotho & Swaziland travel atlas ● Swahili phrasebook ● Tanzania, Zanzibar & Pemba ● Trekking in East Africa ● Tunisia ● West Africa ● Zimbabwe, Botswana & Namibia ● Zimbabwe, Botswana & Namibia travel atlas
Travel Literature: The Rainbird: A Central African Journey ● Songs to an African Sunset: A Zimbabwean Story ● Mali Blues: Traveling to an African Beat

AUSTRALIA & THE PACIFIC Auckland ● Australia ● Australian phrasebook ● Bushwalking in Australia ● Bushwalking in Papua New Guinea ● Fiji ● Fijian phrasebook ● Islands of Australia's Great Barrier Reef ● Melbourne ● Melbourne city map ● Micronesia ● New Caledonia ● New South Wales & the ACT ● New Zealand ● Northern Territory ● Outback Australia ● Out To Eat – Melbourne ● Papua New Guinea ● Pidgin phrasebook ● Queensland ● Rarotonga & the Cook Islands ● Samoa ● Solomon Islands ● South Australia ● South Pacific Languages phrasebook ● Sydney ● Sydney city map ● Tahiti & French Polynesia ● Tasmania ● Tonga ● Tramping in New Zealand ● Vanuatu ● Victoria ● Western Australia
Travel Literature: Islands in the Clouds ● Kiwi Tracks: A New Zealand Journey ● Sean & David's Long Drive

CENTRAL AMERICA & THE CARIBBEAN Bahamas, Turks & Caicos ● Bermuda ● Central America on a shoestring ● Costa Rica ● Cuba ● Dominican Republic & Haiti ● Eastern Caribbean ● Guatemala, Belize & Yucatán: La Ruta Maya ● Jamaica ● Mexico ● Mexico City ● Panama ● Puerto Rico
Travel Literature: Green Dreams: Travels in Central America

EUROPE Amsterdam ● Amsterdam city map ● Andalucía ● Austria ● Baltic States phrasebook ● Barcelona ● Berlin ● Berlin city map ● Britain ● British phrasebook ● Brussels, Bruges & Antwerp ● Budapest city map ● Canary Islands ● Central Europe ● Central Europe phrasebook ● Corsica ● Croatia ● Czech & Slovak Republics ● Denmark ● Dublin ● Eastern Europe ● Eastern Europe phrasebook ● Edinburgh ● Estonia, Latvia & Lithuania ● Europe on a shoestring ● Finland ● France ● French phrasebook ● Germany ● German phrasebook ● Greece ● Greek phrasebook ● Hungary ● Iceland, Greenland & the Faroe Islands ● Ireland ● Italian phrasebook ● Italy ● Lisbon ● London ● London city map ● Mediterranean Europe ● Mediterranean Europe phrasebook ● Norway ● Paris ● Paris city map ● Poland ● Portugal ● Portugal travel atlas ● Prague ● Prague city map ● Provence & the Côte d'Azur ● Romania & Moldova ● Rome ● Russia, Ukraine & Belarus ● Russian phrasebook ● Scandinavian & Baltic Europe ● Scandinavian Europe phrasebook ● Scotland ● Slovenia ● Spain ● Spanish phrasebook ● St Petersburg ● Switzerland ● Trekking in Spain ● Ukrainian phrasebook ● Vienna ● Walking in Britain ● Walking in Ireland ● Walking in Italy ● Walking in Spain ● Walking in Switzerland ● Western Europe ● Western Europe phrasebook
Travel Literature: The Olive Grove: Travels in Greece

INDIAN SUBCONTINENT Bangladesh ● Bengali phrasebook ● Bhutan ● Delhi ● Goa ● Hindi & Urdu phrasebook ● India ● India & Bangladesh travel atlas ● Indian Himalaya ● Karakoram Highway ● Kerala ● Mumbai (Bombay) ● Nepal ● Nepali phrasebook ● Pakistan ● Rajasthan ● Read This First: Asia & India ● South India ● Sri Lanka ● Sri Lanka phrasebook ● Trekking in the Indian Himalaya ● Trekking in the Karakoram & Hindukush ● Trekking in the Nepal Himalaya
Travel Literature: In Rajasthan ● Shopping for Buddhas

LONELY PLANET

Mail Order

Lonely Planet products are distributed worldwide. They are also available by mail order from Lonely Planet, so if you have difficulty finding a title please write to us. North and South American residents should write to 150 Linden St, Oakland, CA 94607, USA; European and African residents should write to 10a Spring Place, London NW5 3BH, UK; and residents of other countries to PO Box 617, Hawthorn, Victoria 3122, Australia.

ISLANDS OF THE INDIAN OCEAN Madagascar & Comoros • Maldives • Mauritius, Réunion & Seychelles

MIDDLE EAST & CENTRAL ASIA Arab Gulf States • Central Asia • Central Asia phrasebook • Hebrew phrasebook • Iran • Israel & the Palestinian Territories • Israel & the Palestinian Territories travel atlas • Istanbul • Istanbul to Cairo • Jerusalem • Jordan & Syria • Jordan, Syria & Lebanon travel atlas • Lebanon • Middle East on a shoestring • Syria • Turkey • Turkey travel atlas • Turkish phrasebook • Yemen
Travel Literature: The Gates of Damascus • Kingdom of the Film Stars: Journey into Jordan

NORTH AMERICA Alaska • Backpacking in Alaska • Baja California • California & Nevada • Canada • Chicago • Chicago city map • Deep South • Florida • Hawaii • Honolulu • Las Vegas • Los Angeles • Miami • New England • New Orleans • New York City • New York city map • New York, New Jersey & Pennsylvania • Pacific Northwest USA • Puerto Rico • Rocky Mountain • San Francisco • San Francisco city map • Seattle • Southwest USA • Texas • USA • USA phrasebook • Vancouver • Washington, DC & the Capital Region • Washington DC city map
Travel Literature: Drive Thru America

NORTH-EAST ASIA Beijing • Cantonese phrasebook • China • Hong Kong • Hong Kong city map • Hong Kong, Macau & Guangzhou • Japan • Japanese phrasebook • Japanese audio pack • Korea • Korean phrasebook • Kyoto • Mandarin phrasebook • Mongolia • Mongolian phrasebook • North-East Asia on a shoestring • Seoul • South-West China • Taiwan • Tibet • Tibetan phrasebook • Tokyo
Travel Literature: Lost Japan

SOUTH AMERICA Argentina, Uruguay & Paraguay • Bolivia • Brazil • Brazilian phrasebook • Buenos Aires • Chile & Easter Island • Chile & Easter Island travel atlas • Colombia • Ecuador & the Galapagos Islands • Latin American Spanish phrasebook • Peru • Quechua phrasebook • Rio de Janeiro • Rio de Janeiro city map • South America on a shoestring • Trekking in the Patagonian Andes • Venezuela
Travel Literature: Full Circle: A South American Journey

SOUTH-EAST ASIA Bali & Lombok • Bangkok • Bangkok city map • Burmese phrasebook • Cambodia • Hanoi • Healthy Travel Asia & India • Hill Tribes phrasebook • Ho Chi Minh City • Indonesia • Indonesia's Eastern Islands • Indonesian phrasebook • Indonesian audio pack • Jakarta • Java • Laos • Lao phrasebook • Laos travel atlas • Malay phrasebook • Malaysia, Singapore & Brunei • Myanmar (Burma) • Philippines • Pilipino (Tagalog) phrasebook • Singapore • South-East Asia on a shoestring • South-East Asia phrasebook • Thailand • Thailand's Islands & Beaches • Thailand travel atlas • Thai phrasebook • Thai audio pack • Vietnam • Vietnamese phrasebook • Vietnam travel atlas

ALSO AVAILABLE: Antarctica • The Arctic • Brief Encounters: Stories of Love, Sex & Travel • Chasing Rickshaws • Lonely Planet Unpacked • Not the Only Planet: Travel Stories from Science Fiction • Sacred India • Travel with Children • Traveller's Tales

LONELY PLANET

FREE Lonely Planet Newsletters

We love hearing from you and think you'd like to hear from us.

Planet Talk

Our FREE quarterly printed newsletter is full of tips from travellers and anecdotes from Lonely Planet guidebook authors. Every issue is packed with up-to-date travel news and advice, and includes:

- a postcard from Lonely Planet co-founder Tony Wheeler
- a swag of mail from travellers
- a look at life on the road through the eyes of a Lonely Planet author
- topical health advice
- prizes for the best travel yarn
- news about forthcoming Lonely Planet events
- a complete list of Lonely Planet books and other titles

To join our mailing list, residents of the UK, Europe and Africa can email us at go@lonelyplanet.co.uk; residents of North and South America can email us at info@lonelyplanet.com; the rest of the world can email us at talk2us@lonelyplanet.com.au, or contact any Lonely Planet office.

Comet

Our FREE monthly email newsletter brings you all the latest travel news, features, interviews, competitions, destination ideas, travellers' tips & tales, Q&As, raging debates and related links. Find out what's new on the Lonely Planet Web site and which books are about to hit the shelves.

Subscribe from your desktop: www.lonelyplanet.com/comet

Index

Bold indicates maps.

528

Bold indicates maps.

Boxed Text

MAP LEGEND

HYDROGRAPHY

...............Coastline
...............River, Creek
...............Lake
...............Canal
...............Spring, Rapids
...............Waterfalls

AREA FEATURES

...............Building
...............Park, Gardens
...............Cemetery
...............Market
...............Pedestrian Mall
...............Urban Area

ROUTES & LAND TRANSPORT

...............Freeway
...............Highway
...............Major Road
...............Minor Road
...............Unsealed Road
...............City Highway
...............Road
...............City Street

...............Lane
...............Pedestrian Mall
...............Tunnel
...............Train Route & Station
...............Metro & Station
...............Tramway
...............Cable Car or Chairlift
...............Walking Track

WATER TRANSPORT

...............Daily Ferries
...............Low Frequency Ferries
...............Hydrofoil
...............Excursion Boats

BOUNDARIES

...............International
...............State

MAP SYMBOLS

✈ ....Airport
...............Ancient or City Wall
∴ ....Archaeological Site
Θ ....Bank
🏖 ....Beach, Surf Beach
...............Border Crossing
☗ ....Castle or Fort
🏛 ....Church
...............Cliff or Escarpment
◷ ....Embassy
✛ ....Hospital
✳ ....Lookout
◖ ....Mosque
🛆 ....Monument

- ○ **CAPITAL** ....National Capital
- ◉ **CAPITAL** ....State Capital
- ● **CITY** ....City
- ● **Town** ....Town
- ● **Village** ....Village

- ■ ....Place to Stay
- ⚑ ....Camping Ground
- 🚐 ....Caravan Park
- ⌂ ....Hut or Chalet
- ▼ ....Place to Eat
- ☕ ....Pub or Bar

▲ ....Mountain or Hill
🏛 ....Museum
)(...............Pass
★ ....Police Station
✉ ....Post Office
❖ ....Shopping Centre
⛷ ....Ski field
🏛 ....Building of Interest
🏊 ....Swimming Pool
✡ ....Synagogue
☎ ....Telephone
▣ ....Tomb
❶ ....Tourist Information
⊖ ....Transport

Note: not all symbols displayed above appear in this book

LONELY PLANET OFFICES

Australia
PO Box 617, Hawthorn, Victoria 3122
☎ 03 9819 1877 fax 03 9819 6459
email: talk2us@lonelyplanet.com.au

USA
150 Linden St, Oakland, CA 94607
☎ 510 893 8555 TOLL FREE: 800 275 8555
fax 510 893 8572
email: info@lonelyplanet.com

UK
10a Spring Place, London NW5 3BH
☎ 020 7428 4800 fax 020 7428 4828
email: go@lonelyplanet.co.uk

France
1 rue du Dahomey, 75011 Paris
☎ 01 55 25 33 00 fax 01 55 25 33 01
email: bip@lonelyplanet.fr
www.lonelyplanet.fr

World Wide Web: www.lonelyplanet.com *or* AOL keyword: lp
Lonely Planet Images: lpi@lonelyplanet.com.au